D1266249

A Zinfandel ODYSSEY

A Tale of California's Most Captivating Wine Grape

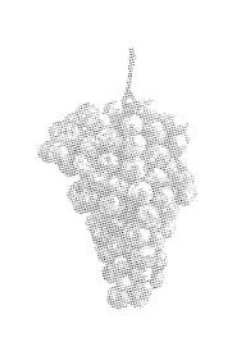

By Rhoda Stewart

First published in North America in 2001 by PWV Inc.,
58-D Paul Drive, San Rafael, CA 94903
415/479-5819; practicalwinery.com

ISBN: 0-9715820-0-9

Commissioning Editor: Don Neel
Executive Art Director: Terry Lockman, Lumina Designworks
Editor: Andrew Hidas
Photography: Rhoda Stewart
Cover concept: Peter Byck
Typeset in Bembo and Dorchester Script

Printed and bound by McNaughton & Gunn, Inc.
in the United States of America

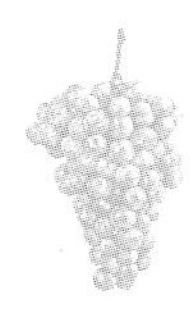

Dedication

To Christina Biale (1896–1999), Louis Martini (1918–1999), Louis Pagani (1902–2000), Valle Rossi (1910–1999), and George Zeni (1923–1999): Without their pioneering spirits, hard work, and passion for Zinfandel, there could not have been a story. May their souls rest in peace.

And to Dr. Kirk Reid, Dr. Richard Bien, Dr. Alan Katz, Dr. Christian Anderson, Dr. Paul Dugan, and the Breast Center and the Radiologists and Radiation Therapists of Queen of the Valley Hospital, Napa, California — without whom this book might not have been possible.

A portion of my proceeds from this book will be donated to breast cancer research.

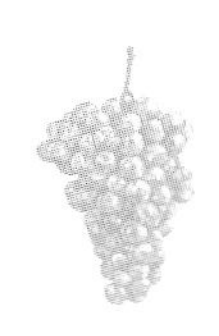

Acknowledgements

Napa Valley College Faculty Senate, for approving my 1996–97 sabbatical leave request, and the Board of Trustees for granting it. One needs both time and funding for a project like this.

Dr. Steve Krebs, Professor of Viticulture and Winery Technology, Napa Valley College, for providing a thoughtful and meticulous early reading of the manuscript, and overall invaluable suggestions on style and clarity.

Richard Bremer, Professor of English, Napa Valley College, for generously providing technical support and sharing his computer expertise.

Andrew Hidas, Bridge Communications and Consulting, for his perceptive and expert editing. A good editor is worth his weight in gold, someone said. Andrew is worth his weight in gold — and Zinfandel.

Peter Byck, artist and filmmaker, for an inspired conceptual cover-design sketch, made one July evening as we sat over Wine Country Film Festival conversation and glasses of Zinfandel.

Jeff Nicholas, Sierra Press, for his pragmatic advice as to what the novice wine drinker needs to have included in a book like this.

My cousins Ken Kjellander and Carol Baker, Victoria, Canada, for their suggestions on what enthusiastic Canadian Zinfandel wine drinkers would like to see included in a book like this.

Arnaud LeBihan and Guillaume Cornu-Thènard, international business students from Paris on internships with Napa Valley wineries, for providing a delightful French perspective on Zinfandel — and life.

Susan and Tom Ridley, for allowing me unlimited access to their beautiful Brookside B&B swimming pool.

Everyone whose name appears in this book, for your patient and enthusiastic support for and belief in my book and me. Your cooperation went above and beyond my greatest expectations, and did much to make this book happen.

All others who in any way helped me to complete this book. Thank you!

Table of Contents

Foreword

by Susan Goss,
Chef/Owner of Zinfandel Restaurant, Chicago

I was attending Culinary School in New York when I tasted my first Zinfandel. It was a revelation. This *tasted good!* Here was a wine to drink, not analyze!

Since I am mostly interested in eating, I want wines made to drink with food. I don't want a wine just to keep in the basement as a trophy and talk about. When I get home from work at 10:30 p.m., I want to be able to pull out a bottle and have a glass with my late supper. And I have to be able to feel good about corking that bottle again and saving it for the next day. While Zinfandels are now being recognized as world-class wines, they are still more like a warm comfortable sweater than a trendy dress.

"Here was a wine to drink, not analyze!"

Susan Goss

For my first 10 years as a chef, I was doing "fusion cuisine" — that uncertain blending of flavors from hither and yon created to dazzle, but not to nourish. The plates were pretty, the food tasty, and the guests were happy. I was the only one not satisfied. There was something missing. Why didn't I feel nourished by our restaurant's food? Why, on our few days off from the restaurant, did I fall back to childhood favorites and feel so satisfied? When I stopped one day to think about my passion for food, I realized that it was the comforting American food that I loved — those home-grown specialties that nourished me spiritually as well as physically. Fortunately, at that time American farmstead cheeses were beginning to pop up, and the newest vintages of Zinfandel were appearing at wine stores. My background in anthropology made me curious about our nation's culinary heritage.

As I began my exploration of things American, I soon uncovered culinary secrets that were destined to disappear unless someone excavated them, dusted them off, and reintroduced them to the public. I discovered what I call Ethnic American Cooking

New American Cuisine — a type of fusion cuisine — embraces influences from around the globe, reflecting America's cultural melting pot. What I call Ethnic American Cooking also reflects that melting pot, but it looks to discover what exactly melted into the pot. What happened to Italian food when the Italian immigrants settled along the eastern seaboard? What made Italian-American food different from the food the Italians left in Italy? How did Pennsylvania Dutch cuisine evolve from its German and Swiss roots? How is Creole cooking different from the food you might eat in France?

Zinfandel restaurant grew from my passion for my culinary past, and also from the availability of American-grown products: Wisconsin's cheeses, Florida's Tupelo honey, Vermont's maple sugar, and, of course, California's Zinfandels. Just like our American food, Zinfandel is uniquely American.

Sure, the grape is a European transplant (as is our food), but it has evolved (as has the food) to a uniquely American flavor. While you can compare a California Chardonnay to White Burgundy, or Oregon Pinot Noir to Red Burgundy, or a Washington State Riesling to an Alsatian wine, it is hard to compare a Zinfandel to any other wine because there is no world-class European counterpart.

At *Zinfandel,* we search out traditional ethnic flavors of American cooking, and in our exploration we find that no matter what the flavors of the region are, there is a style of Zinfandel that complements them. The roasty brown spice of Paso Robles Zinfandels or the exotic Middle Eastern flavors of Napa Carneros are right at home with the "Seven Sweet and Seven Sour" tastes so important to the Pennsylvania Dutch. Sonoma Old Vine Zinfandels, with their intense, blackberry jam fruit, cut the deep spiciness of a traditional Kentucky Burgoo, while the sturdy, Bordeaux-style Zinfandels of Napa come alive with the richly-flavored lamb stews from Basque kitchens in Idaho. Amador County's dry, brambly fruit, so reminiscent of France's Côte Rôtie, complements the chiles, cilantro, and lime flavors found in the dry, hot desert Southwest. A braised pheasant breast, cooked in a Low Country style with salty Smithfield ham and thick cream, practically begs for a glass of a supple, sexy-sweet late-picked Zinfandel from one of Napa Valley's 75- to 100-year-old vineyards.

A glass of wine is the perfect accompaniment to food; the two create a wonderful synergy that is one of the greatest pleasures you will ever experience.

Zinfandel is the quintessential food wine: it can be aggressive, restrained, subtle, or bursting with fruit. It can accompany bratwursts, grilled venison, braised mushrooms, and falafel sandwiches. You can drink it at 11 a.m. or at 11 p.m. It even makes delicious sangria for afternoon fiestas.

So whether you like to keep your Zinfandels in the cellar for a few years, or enjoy the fresh fruit character that is so appealing in young Zinfandels, the point is to enjoy them — and enjoy them often and with many kinds of food. It's a wine you really cannot get tired of.

Every wine needs an advocate and Rhoda Stewart is Zinfandel's advocate. She is also its cheerleader. Rhoda loves not only Zinfandel wine; she loves the grape, the leaves, the briars and brambles. Her photographs capture the beauty of the vines and the faces of the vineyards as the seasons change. Rhoda writes not just of the romance of the grape and its curious travels from the Old World to the new, she also explains the science of its clonal variations and DNA structure. *A Zinfandel Odyssey* is a wonderful blend of scientific fact and romantic lore. Rhoda's passion for Zinfandel, the plant, the vine, the grape, and the wine fills each page and leaves the reader thirsty for a glass of the quintessential American wine.

Susan Goss

Introduction

Arriving in California as an obscure and mysterious table grape nearly 150 years ago, the Zinfandel grape's potential for producing a red table wine "good enough for anyone" was discovered soon thereafter by knowledgeable winemakers. Its ultimate rise to veneration, however, has been a long and uncertain — but nonetheless inevitable — journey. California's Zinfandel grape is greeting the new millennium as perhaps the most venerated wine grape variety in the world.

Although the Zinfandel grape has long had an ardent following among its constituents — growers, producers, wine store personnel, and consumers — it was the phenomenal red Zinfandel wines of the 1990s from California's best Zinfandel grapegrowing regions that dramatically increased this following. The increase has been especially noticeable in an organization called Zinfandel Advocates and Producers (ZAP).

Founded in 1991 by a few California Zinfandel producers who believed that Zinfandel wine could rival the best red wines that the world has to offer, ZAP's first-year membership consisted of about 20 producers and 50 advocates. By January 2000, producer membership had reached 227, and advocate membership had reached 5,500. At the 9th annual ZAP barrel tasting of Zinfandel wines at Fort Mason in San Francisco, 210 of these producer members poured their most recent vintages. Over 6,000 tradespeople and aficionados of Zinfandel as a red table wine attended from all over the U.S. and from several foreign countries.

Recently entered into the *Guinness Book of World Records,* ZAP's annual Zinfandel-only barrel-tasting event is like no other wine-tasting event in the world. It is just one more indication that Zinfandel has become America's most fascinating and captivating red wine grape.

That California's Zinfandel grape has triumphed in its epic struggle to take its rightful place as one of the four or five noble red wine grape varieties of the world can be attributed to four distinguishing characteristics of the grape:

- The unmistakable varietal character of the wine it produces (it's the fruit!).
- Its stylistic versatility.
- The distinct differences in wine character that different soil, climate, and location, often referred to as *terroir,* bring to the wines, even as they retain their varietal character.
- The historical significance of the grape. Zinfandel vines have longevity of well over 100 years, making the grape America's connection to viticultural antiquity.

Today, winemakers are competing with each other for the fruit of all the remaining, and in some cases nearly forgotten, old Zinfandel vineyards up and down the state. In addition, many California growers and winemakers are cautiously planting new Zinfandel vines on suitable acres that they either own or lease. This despite the high costs of planting grapes and the fact that even young Zinfandel vines usually must be restricted to about five tons per acre for premium quality grapes. Varieties such as Cabernet Sauvignon or Merlot easily produce up to ten or more tons of high quality fruit, thus providing much higher return on investment in new plantings.

It is the wine made from the historic Zinfandel vines, however, that established Zinfandel as a world-class red wine. Nonetheless, well made wine from the fruit of carefully tended younger Zinfandel vines planted in well-suited vineyards show the same luscious fruit character expressed by the wines from ancient vines. Zinfandel-loving consumers also eagerly seek out such wines, sometimes even preferring them to those made from old vines.

A Zinfandel Odyssey is an account of my search for clues to Zinfandel's enigmatic history and persistent appeal. The clues, I soon discovered, lie in the vineyards, so my search became a 14-year odyssey to the regions where the treasured Zinfandel vines are grown. In each of these regions, I walked Zinfandel vineyards both new and historic, and got to know the origins and the different look of each. Especially awe-inspiring is the appearance of a staunch and gnarly 100-year old vine. Once you've sat with your camera under such an historic specimen, and thought of all the generations of hands that have touched and cared for it, you remember that old vine as if it were an old and beloved family member.

Of the thousands of acres planted with Zinfandel in California today, less than 1 percent is more than a century old. Only a few hundred acres are over 50 years old. Most of the producing Zinfandel vineyards today were planted in the 1970s and 1980s.

How many of these young Zinfandel vineyards will see the year 2100? These young vines are the next century's connection to California's viticultural antiquity. Zinfandel vines at 30 or 40 years of age are barely out of their teens, while vines of many other varieties are often ready for replacement at that age.

During my odyssey, I sought out growers, some of whom are as old as the vines they grew up with. From them, I learned the story of their vineyards and the particular practices they feel are necessary to keep the vines healthy and in balance for their regions, vineyards, and winemakers' styles.

I also met many winemakers who have produced wine from the fruit of these vineyards. I listened to explanations of their practices and stylistic choices — and wherein lay the magic of Zinfandel for them. It has been for love, not money! Zinfandel wine may make a winemaker famous, but seldom rich. With these talented and enthusiastic winemakers, I tasted many of their luscious medium- to full-bodied red table wines produced from the best vineyards.

By the end of my odyssey, I came home with a deepened appreciation for how *terroir* contributes to the great variations in the fruit character and style so unique to Zinfandel wines in the bottle. Zinfandel is a red table wine that comes in many styles and with many regional characteristics. I came home with a better understanding of the historical, economic, and cultural significance of the Zinfandel grape to the California wine industry.

And I came home with a deepened appreciation for the growers and producers who have been so captivated by this grape that they have let it shape their lives — and in some cases their fortunes. They are the reasons why this most Californian of wine grapes is now attracting wine lovers the world over.

As a red wine lover myself, and one who appreciates the health benefits of including it in my diet, I also came home much better informed to choose the Zinfandel wine that best suits my dining preferences — and my budget. Although a small core of producers tends to dominate the winepress, there is a red Zinfandel table wine for just about everyone's style and taste preference and pocketbook. Zinfandel is the red wine for people who don't think they like red wine. Zinfandel is a red wine for all people.

Rhoda Stewart
Napa, California
June 2, 2001

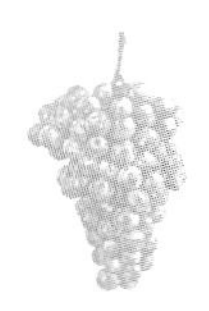

Part 1

The Zinfandel Grape: An Historical Overview

What is a "Fine Wine" Focus? Winemaking Practices Described

Characteristics of a Great Vineyard

Zinfandel Table Wine: a Definition

My Romance with Zinfandel

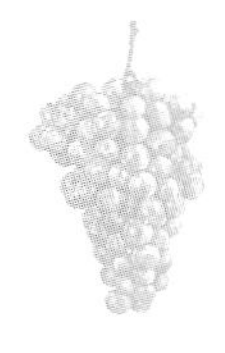

The Zinfandel Grape: An Historical Overview

The Zinfandel grape originated in Europe, but only in California, where the first Zinfandel vineyards were established nearly 150 years ago, is it being perfected as a premium wine grape. Its development takes on a quality of high drama when we consider the mystery of its origins and how it came to California.

Zinfandel is clearly a member of the *Vitis vinifera (Vitis* = vine; *vinifera* = wine-producing species), yet no vine by the name of Zinfandel exists in Europe. *Vitis vinifera* is the species that gives us all our world-class wine grapes, table grapes, and raisin grapes. An example of an American species is *Vitis Labrusca,* which gives us Concord grapes.

Wine historian Thomas Pinney states that *Vitis vinifera* is the "vine of European winemaking, the vine that Noah planted after the Flood.... *Vitis vinifera* is the vine whose history is identical with the history of wine itself: the leaves of *vinifera* bind the brows of Dionysus in his triumph; the seeds of *vinifera* are found with the mummies of the pharaohs in the pyramids. It was the juice of *vinifera,* mysteriously alive with the powers of fermentation, which led the ancients to connect wine with the spiritual realm, and to make it an intimate part of religious ceremony. *No such grape is native to North America."* [1]

In what European region did Zinfandel thrive, and under what name was it known by there? Under what name, or names, did it arrive in

[1] Thomas Pinney, *A History of Wine in America. From Beginnings to Prohibition* (Berkeley: University of California Press, 1989), 5

America? How did it acquire its name? These are some of the questions that we will explore through the rest of this section.

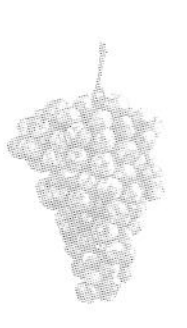

Three Mysteries of Zinfandel

Red table wine, dessert wine, sparkling wine, white wine, pink (or rosé) wine — the Zinfandel grape can produce them all. As versatile a grape as ever existed, it even makes for good eating. In fact, that is how Zinfandel got its start in the United States: as a table grape.

In his report, "Zinfandel: A True Vinifera," Charles Sullivan identifies three mysteries surrounding the Zinfandel grape's origins: "The first concerns its ancestral roots in the Old World.... The second involves the grape's transit to North America from Europe.... The third ... is how the Zinfandel came to California and how it developed into a wine grape that was to become basic in the production of California's dry red table wines."[2]

Since the **third mystery** is the focus of Sullivan's report, and is the only one that we can solve with confidence, let us begin there. We will then work backwards to confront a vast number of still unresolved questions in our attempt to set Zinfandel's mysterious pilgrimage to the new world in the proper context.

When and how Zinfandel arrived in California should have never become a mystery, Sullivan claims. Zinfandel "had long been used in New England as a popular table grape before its introduction into California's graperies and vineyards" in the 1850s.[3] Part of the profitable fruit culture that had developed in New England in the decades after 1830, particularly the growing of grapes under glass, Zinfandel "had a lesser reputation than the Black Hamburg or the Golden Chasselas as a table grape, [but] was well liked and successful. First exhibited as a table grape in 1834 by Samuel J. Perkins of Boston, it won its first premium in 1839...."[4]

That the historical record should have become muddied is the fault of Arpad Harazthy, son of Agoston Harazthy, Sullivan argues. According to Sullivan, Arpad concocted a rather preposterous account in 1886 of how his father brought the first Zinfandel cuttings to California in 1852, from his native Hungary, then part of the Austro-Hungarian Empire. Not a shred of evidence exists to support Arpad's claim, declares Sullivan.[5]

Rather, Zinfandel most likely came to California in the 1850s as part of the standard New England collection of grape varieties, imported by men who were familiar with the grape, but knew not of its winemaking

---

2 *The Vinifera Wine Growers Journal,* Summer 1982, Vol. 9., No. 2, 71-2.
3 *Ibid.*, 71
4 *Ibid.*, 76
5 *Ibid.*

potential. It was apparently imported under two names: Zinfandel, usually spelled "Zinfindal," but also as "Zeinfindall" and "Zenfenthal"; and Black St. Peters. It wasn't many years before both Zinfandel and Black St. Peters vineyards were known as "Zinfandel." But how or from where the name "Zinfandel" originated is still a complete mystery.[6]

Sullivan's argument is compelling. The mystery concerning the manner in which Zinfandel arrived in California is, he writes, "persistently troublesome to writers of the state's wine history precisely because the introduction of the grape was no mystery at all. It arrived almost unnoticed and ... was selected out of the chaos of foreign varieties by intelligent and experienced winemakers ... it spread throughout the state with few taking note of it at the time. In the confusion of early nursery propagation, it was confounded with other grapes. That it arrived from New England as a table grape grown under glass added to the later confusion [as did] the miscellaneous spellings in early publications."[7]

Add to this the "disingenuous attempt [of Arpad Harazthy] to impose upon the documentary evidence a theory of origin that cannot be reconciled with the evidence available today," [8] and you have a popular but false myth that dies hard, indeed.

Nor has it died to this day. At every turn, it seems, I encounter Zinfandel enthusiasts who still believe that Agoston Harazthy brought the vine to California from his mother's vineyard in Hungary. Yet, Sullivan states, there is no evidence to suggest that such a vineyard ever existed. Nonetheless, by Sullivan's own account of Zinfandel's journey from the nurseries of New England to California, there exists plenty of room for mischievous speculation! [9]

The **second mystery** has yet to be probed in depth by researchers. Currently, there are no published theories as to who brought Zinfandel to America, nor from where it was taken, nor under what names it traveled by.

The **first mystery** is the subject of an ongoing investigation by Dr. Carole Meredith, Professor of Viticulture and Enology, and plant geneticist at the UC Davis. Since Dr. Meredith has spent considerable time and effort in recent years exploring Zinfandel's ancestral origins in the Old World, I conclude this section with an almost verbatim transcript of an interview I conducted with her one November 1997 afternoon. Dr. Meredith, who lives in Napa, came by my house after leaving the Davis campus.

An attractive, outgoing silver-haired woman of medium height and slender build, she was wearing an olive-colored cotton turtleneck sweater, matching corded trousers, soft boots. Professional, friendly, and gracious, she said she had only about an hour to discuss with me my interest in Zinfandel's European origins.

---

6 *Ibid.*, 80
7 *Ibid.*, 82
8 *Ibid*
9 *Ibid*

We sat down at my kitchen table, which was illuminated by the soft golden light of the late November afternoon, and over a glass of a Sierra Foothill Zinfandel, she told me the story of her research, her discoveries — and her non-discoveries.

"First of all," said Dr. Meredith, "California's Zinfandel and Italy's Primitivo *are* proven to be genetically indistinguishable. Dr. Austin Goheen made that connection at Davis in the late 1960s. We've since shown by DNA analysis that Zinfandel and Primitivo are the same variety."

"Is this true for all clones of Zinfandel and Primitivo?" I asked.

"Yes, and it's been done in several countries, too. So the Zinfandel in Australia and Italy are all the same as Primitivo. But Primitivo has not been in Italy for very long. In fact, the earliest records of Primitivo being in Italy are not as early as the earliest records of Zinfandel being in California. And the official Italian ampelography says that it is not an indigenous variety, that Primitivo is a variety that came from somewhere else — and that it came quite recently — the late 1800s. That suggests that both California and Italy got the grape from a third place. The question now is 'from where?'

"California's Zinfandel and Italy's Primitivo are proven to be genetically indistinguishable."

Dr. Carole Meredith

"If you look at a map of the area of Italy where Primitivo is grown, which is Bari, in Puglia, in the heel of the country, you'll see that it is directly across the narrow Adriatic Sea from Croatia. There has been trade between Puglia and Croatia for centuries. It's a very short distance, so it is easy for people to move back and forth daily. So it is quite logical that a grape introduced into Puglia might have come from Croatia. Furthermore, there is a grape in Croatia that tastes a lot like Zinfandel — the Plavaç Mali, the grape that Mike Grgich has been touting, and that the *Wine Enthusiast* made a big case for.[10] (In this article, Grgich claims that for decades the Croatians have believed the Plavaç Mali to be identical to Zinfandel. The two varieties look and taste like each other, and the wines have similar character.)

"But that's not new," pointed out Dr. Meredith. "The idea that Plavaç Mali might somehow be connected to Zinfandel has been around for a long time. It's just that there has been no real way to test that idea until recently. We have had some Plavaç Mali in our National Grape Germplasm Repository at Davis since 1977. Grown side by side with Zinfandel, they

[10] Terry Robards , "Zinfandel: The Mystery Solved," *The Wine Enthusiast,* August 1996, Vol. 9, No. 7, 44-48

looked similar, but not identical in the way Primitivo and Zinfandel did when they were first grown side by side.

"With the development of DNA typing technology, we recently did a comparative DNA test on the samples we have with Zinfandel. Ours was not the same as Zinfandel.

"We thought that maybe we have the wrong thing. We have two Plavaç Malis: one from a collection in Zagreb in Croatia, which is nowhere near where Plavaç Mali is grown, which is on the coast — Zagreb is inland; our other came to us from a collection in Italy. These two Plavaç Malis were shown to be the same as each other, but they were not the same variety as Zinfandel. So we thought, maybe these collections were wrongly named.

"We thought we should try to get some more Plavaç Mali directly from the region where it is grown. So I got in touch with the Institute of Adriatic Studies in Split, Croatia, an ancient city on the Adriatic coast and right in the heart of the Plavaç Mali region. Dr. Peter Males, who has made a detailed study of Plavaç Mali, and has identified at least four types, has felt for quite some time that Plavaç Mali was Zinfandel. He has even stated that it is. He doesn't have much evidence; but he is convinced.

"So I asked Dr. Males if he could provide us with several accessions [samples from different vineyards] of Plavaç Mali from several locations. Plavaç Mali is an ancient variety. When you have an ancient variety, there is a greater chance for diversity within the variety — just as with Pinot Noir. Also, the coastline of Croatia where the variety is grown is full of islands — they call themselves 'The Land of 1,000 Islands' — and Plavaç Mali is grown on many of these islands. When you combine the age of the variety with the geographically isolated areas, those are additional reasons to believe that there might be more than one thing grown as Plavaç Mali. That is why we asked Dr. Males to send us several accessions of Plavaç Mali from different places."

"What he sent us were cuttings from three separate vineyards, but all on one island. It wasn't what we were hoping for, but it was a start. That was February 1997. When we tested them, we found that of the three accessions that he sent us, two were identical to the Plavaç Mali we already had at Davis, which indicated that our original samples were indeed Plavaç Mali. The third accession was heterogeneous. He sent us several cuttings from each vineyard, and they were not uniform. While most of the cuttings were the same as the other two, a couple were different. They still weren't Zinfandel, but they were different from the other Plavaç Mali as well.

"But all of them — the two Plavaç Mali types and the Zinfandel — were close enough in their DNA patterns to indicate clearly that they were all close relatives of each other," emphasized Dr. Meredith. "And that's where we stand now — that the Plavaç Mali that we have done DNA tests on is not Zinfandel, but it is very close to Zinfandel — much closer than we would expect just by random sampling. Both Plavaç Mali types are close enough to be a parent, a sibling, or a seedling of Zinfandel. Without more data, though, we cannot say which of these relationships is the true one."

Although Dr. Meredith did not wish to speculate further, she did voice her own pet hypothesis: that Plavaç Mali is a family of highly similar grapes, and because it is such an old variety, and because it is grown on islands, Plavaç Mali is not a uniform grape like Cabernet Sauvignon or Chardonnay, in which all clones within these two varieties have the same DNA patterns.

"We have detected two Plavaç Mali types," she explained. "I expect that if we test more Plavaç Mali accessions from vineyards on more islands, we will find more types. We've found two types so far from just looking at three vineyards on one island. I predict that we are going to find more types, more vines that people call Plavaç Mali. And even though they may say that there is one main type, I think they will accept that, in practice, there are some variants that we can show are genetically different, but that are close enough in their appearance and fruit character to be called Plavaç Mali in commerce. I believe that if we keep looking, we have a reasonable chance of finding one that is Zinfandel.

"So my hypothesis is that there is a Plavaç Mali type that is Zinfandel. Of course, we can't know this for sure until we look at more Plavaç Mali accessions. I do believe that, unlike most mainstream Western European varieties which are genetically uniform, this one being an ancient variety from an area that has not been in the global mainstream, that it is a complex of very similar grapes. Who knows how many? Maybe there are just three, and we have already seen two. And maybe the third one is identical to our Zinfandel. Or maybe there are 15, or even an infinite number. Maybe we will never find a type that is genetically identical to Zinfandel.

"You see, the grape plant does not breed true from seed. If you plant a grape seed, you will not get the grape variety. That is why grapevines are propagated from cuttings [a cane pruned from an existing vine]. Still, many of the seedlings will be quite similar to the parent grape, although they won't have the same DNA pattern as the parent. However, the fruit character might be similar enough, and the flavor might be similar enough that, if a few hundred years ago a seedling had popped up in an old Plavaç Mali vineyard, it would be absorbed into the vineyard. You can understand that before they had rootstock, and where vines died all the time because of disease, if the seedling ended up looking like the rest of the vines, and if the fruit looked and tasted pretty similar, then it would be considered part of the variety. In old varieties, it isn't uncommon that a genetically dissimilar type could be included in the variety, because there was no way to distinguish it.

"Over time, since vineyards are propagated by cuttings from preexisting vineyards, a slightly different type could end up getting propagated on a larger scale. That would account for having multiple genetic types all going by Plavaç Mali.

"That's the notion I have," she concluded, "but I don't have the evidence yet to support it. The only evidence I have is that we have looked at three Plavaç Mali vineyards, and found two types, neither of which are genetically identical to Zinfandel.

"So while we don't have any evidence against this notion, we do need to look at many more Plavaç Mali accessions, to see if my idea has any validity or not."

The golden light of the November afternoon had faded into darkness. As she rose to leave, Dr. Meredith told me of her plans for visiting Croatia in spring, 1998, to have a look around for herself.

* * * * *

I spoke with Dr. Meredith again in October of 1998, and she gave me the following account of her Croatian sojourn in search of the elusive Zinfandel:

"I went to Croatia in May 1998. Mike Grgich provided me with a place to stay, and several colleagues at the University of Zagreb (Ivan Pejic, Edi Maletic, and Nicola Mirosevic) helped me to locate Plavaç Mali vineyards and obtain leaf samples. I obtained about 150 samples, each from a different vine, from all over the main Plavaç Mali growing regions along the Dalmatian coast of Croatia. Some of the vines looked very much like Zinfandel, while others did not.

"I brought the samples back to UC Davis, and we extracted the DNA from them and analyzed it. We finished most of this analysis in September 1998, and concluded that *none* of the samples was the same as Zinfandel. Most had exactly the same DNA pattern as the two Plavaç Mali examples that we already had growing at UC Davis.

'We conclude from these results that most Plavaç Mali is of a single type, which is not the same as Zinfandel, although it seems closely related to Zinfandel. We have observed a few rare variants of Plavaç Mali that are a little different, but they are also not the same as Zinfandel.

"We cannot conclude from our study that Zinfandel did not originate in Croatia, only that it is not the same as the main Plavaç Mali type growing there today. There may have been more diversity in Plavaç Mali before 1900, before the spread of phylloxera forced growers in Croatia and throughout Europe to graft their winegrapes to rootstocks. There may well have been a Plavaç Mali type at that time that was the same as Zinfandel. It may even exist today in some remote Croatian location, but we did not obtain samples from everywhere, only from the main growing regions.

"So that's the up-to-the-minute news. Sorry I can't tell you that we've finally found it — yet, but some people would probably prefer that it remain a mystery."

Cultivation of Zinfandel in California

Although Zinfandel's origins in Europe are still a mystery, as is the means by which it traveled to America, there is no mystery about its early success establishing itself in California. Soon after its introduction into the state in the 1850s, Zinfandel's potential for making a red wine superior to that from the ubiquitous Mission grape was widely recognized. By 1880, the Zinfandel vine had supplanted the Mission in every region best suited to it — and even in some regions not so well suited. The impetus for the growers came from the fact that as early as 1869, Zinfandel wine was fetching $.75 a gallon, while Sonoma Mission wine was getting only $.40 a gallon.[11]

But given that the Mission grape was well established and still profitable, it did not disappear. Far from it. Today, there are still a few blocks of ancient Mission vines scattered throughout the state. For some Portuguese and Italian families, it is still the only wine worth drinking. "They will tell you in no uncertain terms, 'Any other wine is dishwater,'" said Paul Hofer III, fifth generation Cucamonga Valley Zinfandel grower and owner of a fine stand of huge old Mission vines beside Ontario airport. Hofer was speaking of his longtime Portuguese customers.

Then came Prohibition. From 1920 until its repeal in 1933, the 18th Constitutional Amendment known as the Volstead Act declared the commercial production and sale of alcoholic beverages illegal. Zinfandel was then the most widely planted red wine grape in California. Among home winemakers, many of whom were European émigrés, coast to coast it was the grape of choice. The head of a household could produce 200 gallons per year. By then, these winemakers knew that Zinfandel grapes from the premier regions were the best red wine grapes American soil was producing. Indeed, they likely realized that they were tending some of the best red wine grapes in the world. After all, many of these home winemakers had grown up in some of the finest grapegrowing regions of Europe.

Peter Mondavi Sr., brother of Robert Mondavi and owner with his sons of Charles Krug Winery, St. Helena, recounted how his Italian-born parents, Caesaré and Rosa, came to Lodi from Minnesota in 1916, where

[11] Charles Sullivan, "Zinfandel: A True Vinifera, *Vinifera Wine Growers Journal*, Summer 1982, Vol 9, No. 2, 82.

they had been grocers, to ship wine grapes to Minnesota and points east for home winemakers.

"Did your father come with the intention of shipping Zinfandel?" I asked Peter during our first conversation in February 1998.

"I don't know about that," replied Peter. "I am sure he knew of Zinfandel, and coming from Italy, he very quickly caught on to which red grapes were the best. Of course, that meant Zinfandel. He became a grape shipper out of Lodi in 1918, and remained a shipper even after he and my mother bought the Charles Krug Winery in 1943. He was a shipper until he died at age 73. He also shipped Muscat, another grape popular in Lodi."

Zinfandel grapes from non-irrigated vines were the preferred, even revered, "juice" grapes for home winemakers across the nation. Cucamonga Valley had the most plentiful source, along with the preferred blending varieties, which were also important. According to Cucamonga Valley shipper Don Galleano, home producers found that Zinfandel shipped best when picked at about 23° Brix. So they preferred Zinfandel in the following blending ratio to other varieties:

- 50 boxes of Zinfandel
- 15 boxes of Muscat of Alexandria for sugar and flavor
- 5 boxes Alicante Bouschet to bump up the color.

This was the typical blend for shipping to the old-timers back east, according to Galleano.

The acceptance of the distinctive and mysterious Zinfandel grape as one of the noble red grapes of the world, however, would take until the end of the 20th century. As early as 1884, the distinctive character of its wine had been noted, evoking ambivalent responses that would be echoed by wine writers a century later. In an October 1924 article entitled "The Zinfandel," Frederic T. Bioletti quotes Professor Hilgard's 1884 writings: "It is estimated that the Zinfandel constitutes two-fifths of all the vines planted in the State. The cause of this preference ... is the rapid growth, hardiness, and high production of the Zinfandel vine, together with its adaptation ... to a great variety of soils; while the red wines yielded by it, though not rising to the highest quality, form thus far the bulk of 'California clarets,' and when sound are pleasant table wines, endowned [sic], however, with a flavor peculiar to the grape, not easily mistaken, and too pronounced for the taste of many who are accustomed to the Bordeaux type of table clarets."[12] About 80,000 acres were planted to Zinfandel in the 1880s.

In contrast, George Husmann, a professor of agriculture at the University of Missouri and an expert on American viticulture, felt no such ambivalence. In 1888, he was praising the Zinfandel grape for its ability to produce a superior red table wine: "I have yet to see the red wine of any

[12] "The Zinfandel," *California's Most Important Juice Grape Varieties*, ed. E.M. Sheehan (San Francisco: California Grape Grower, Oct. 1, 1924), 16.

variety, which I would prefer to the best samples of Zinfandel produced in this State.... A Zinfandel claret from locations best adapted to it, carefully made, is good enough for anyone." [13]

Husmann's main complaint was that such achievements were rare, and difficult to accomplish. He attributed this to the character of the grape:

"Zinfandel needs a soil rich in minerals, iron especially, to produce its best fruit. Then, it must be well ripened, and many cannot wait for this, but pick it when fully colored. As, with a fair percentage of sugar, it also contains abundance of tartaric acid, it will make a wine that is greenish, harsh, and sour, if picked too early. Then it ripens unevenly, often having a large quantity of shriveled berries together with un-ripe ones, on the same bunch. This is apt to deceive the winemaker, as the sugar contained in the over-ripe berries does not appear fully in the must [the fermenting juice, seeds, and grape skins], when testing with the saccharometer. When this is the case, and there many of these dried berries, the juice will really come to 25° Brix [pronounced "Bricks," it is a measurement of sugar content], when it shows but 22° or 23° Brix. Moreover, these dried berries are a troublesome element in fermentation, and need careful watching and frequent stirring to bring it through safe. But for all this, it is a noble grape, and deserves all the care we can give it.[14]

"The worst consequence of Prohibition was 'the way in which it had warped American attitudes toward drinking... If they were older Americans, they had forgotten what the civilized use of wine was; if they were younger, they had never known.'

Thomas Pinney

Bioletti also defended the worth of the grape while acknowledging its imperfections: "The grapes are rather thin skinned and must be very carefully handled if shipped for any considerable distance. They are easily injured by rain in the coast districts and by black mold in the interior. They are also subject to premature drying on the vine in hot weather.... In spite of these defects, it has been one of our best grapes. Most of its defects are due to improper care, overbearing, or planting in unsuitable localities. It is so prolific under nearly all conditions that it invites neglect from the careless or unskillful...." [15]

---

13 George Hussman, *Grape Culture and Wine Making in California* (San Francisco: Payot, Upham, & Co., 1988), 152

14 *Ibid.*, 151-2

15 *California's Most Important Juice Grape Varieties*, 16.

Such ambivalence toward the Zinfandel grape endured for decades. Always popular with home winemakers and for generic red table wines, Zinfandel's worth as a grape capable of producing a red table wine good enough for anyone was nearly lost to memory in the years following repeal of Prohibition. The worst consequence of Prohibition, writes Pinney, was "the way in which it had warped American attitudes towards drinking.... If they were older Americans, they had forgotten what the civilized use of wine was; if they were younger, they had never known."[16]

When California's wine industry resumed production in 1934, the focus had shifted from high quality table wines to fortified wines and generic jug wines. The grape varieties most in demand were not the best wine varieties: "Table grapes, raisin grapes, and inferior, but productive, varieties of wine grapes were the overwhelming basis for California winemaking for years after Prohibition," Pinney points out. "Even as late as 1961, a whole generation after Repeal, there were only about 800 acres of Cabernet Sauvignon to supply the entire American wine industry. The same sorry figures held for the other distinguished varieties: 600 acres of Pinot Noir, 450 of Riesling, 300 of Chardonnay ... appalling numbers at a time when California already had 424,000 acres of vines. And no adage is truer in winemaking than the one that says the wine can be no better than its source. The degradation of the California source was a direct and lasting effect of Prohibition." [17]

For the most part, Zinfandel became numbered among the inferior, but productive, varieties that Pinney speaks of above, or as a home winemaker's grape. Prices dropped, and the only growers who prospered were those with irrigated vineyards — primarily in the Central Valley — which were capable of producing eight to ten tons per acre and more of fruit for these generic red wines. Although the quality of many of these wines was excellent, Zinfandel remained associated for many years with jug wine and fortified wine production, and as a rough homemade wine. As a varietally identified and valued premium red wine grape that had been so praised by Husmann and Biolotti, its reputation was nearly sunk forever.

Following repeal of Prohibition in 1933, owners of the best remaining non-irrigated, or dry-farmed, Zinfandel vineyards had a mighty 60-year struggle: first, just to pay the costs of keeping their vines cared for; and second, to see the quality of their Zinfandel grapes recognized.

Ninety-seven year-old Louis Pagani's experiences were typical. With his 94-year-old sister, Olive, he owned a 40-acre Zinfandel vineyard near Kenwood in the Sonoma Valley. The vines were planted in 1903, the year he was born. There are also a couple of small blocks of Alicante Bouschet and Mataro. Only in 1991 was his Zinfandel separated out and given vineyard recognition. It was Paul Draper of Ridge Vineyards who took this historic step. In 1995, when Ridge's 1992 vintage Pagani Vineyard Zinfandel made it

---

[16] Pinney, 441
[17] Pinney, 438

to the *Wine Spectator's* list of the world's top 10 wines, Louis felt justice had at last been achieved, and he was enjoying the belated attention.

"Even five years ago, people were calling my grapes 'junk grapes,' and saying they were hardly worth the picking," Louis recalled. "Now," he told me, chuckling, "those same folks are knocking on my door for these grapes — at any price!"

Some of the other wonderful vineyards, of course, were not so fortunate. The vines did not stay in the ground long enough to get their deserved recognition. The owners of those that survived give considerable credit to the unbroken support of enthusiastic home wine producers who stayed loyal to their favorite vineyards. Many growers still hold back a few tons of grapes for their long-time home winemakers, who are now into third- and even fourth-generation families. Mostly, however, during the 30 to 40 years of hard times that followed repeal, these growers maintained a few acres of their finest Zinfandel vines because of their love of the grape and the wine made from it, not for the money. Maintaining a supplementary source of income also was a factor. The loyal, even fierce, attachment of these growers and amateur producers to this dusky and succulent *Vitis vinifera* is inspirational and awe-inspiring.

Fortunately, California's wine industry began to prosper and grow by the 1960s. The old-style Zinfandel producers such as D'Agostini, Seghesio, Pedroncelli, Sebastiani, Louis M. Martini, E & J Gallo, Galleano, and Pesenti, were joined by some notable newcomers. Lee Stewart purchased the 1887 Rossini Winery on Howell Mountain in Napa in 1943, renaming it Souverain. Caesaré and Rosa Mondavi purchased the Charles Krug Winery in Napa, also in 1943. Bob Trinchero purchased Sutter Home winery in 1946. Other producers from the 1940s and 1950s remembered for their Zinfandels are Larkmead and Fountain Grove. In 1962, Dave Bennion established Ridge Vineyards. Joe Swan established Swan Vineyards in 1969.

Lee Stewart, when he was winemaker for Souverain, was among the first to champion Zinfandel as a premium red wine varietal. "Souverain Mountain Zinfandel produced from Stewart's source in the Atlas Peak area helped break down the post-Repeal low-quality stereotype that had plagued that variety prior to the sixties," wrote Charles Sullivan in 1994.[18] According to Peter Mondavi Sr., Charles Krug Winery was among the first to age its red wines, including Zinfandel, in small French oak barrels, starting in 1963.

These newcomers, of course, owed much to the historic wineries.

In the 1970s, Ridge's Paul Draper, Edmeades' Jed Steele, Monteviña's Cary Gott, and Ravenswood founder Joel Peterson joined these names. Since the esteemed European varieties were in short supply, these young winemakers had to cast about for quality red wine grapes to supplement their beginning inventories of Cabernet Sauvignon, Chardonnay, and Pinot Noir. Their search, of course, led them straight to the many fine old Zinfandel vineyards, whose owners were thrilled to see their fruit finally receiving attention from winemakers willing to

---

18 Charles Sullivan, *Napa Wine, A History from Mission Days to Present* (San Francisco: The Wine Appreciation Guild, 1994), 243.

treat it as a world-class varietal. In fact, a few winemakers like Joel Peterson chose Zinfandel because the old vineyards were the only historically proven vineyards in California, and because of the creative opportunity it provided him. Since these winemakers were among the first to take notice of the finest of the old Zinfandel vineyards, they had the privilege of choosing as they pleased among the ones still in production, and establishing long-term relationships with their favorites. They also were the ones who set the style for premium red Zinfandel.

Also in the 1970s, new Zinfandel vineyards were being planted in the regions historically proven to be well suited to it.

In El Dorado County, Lloyd Walker established eight acres on his sheep and walnut ranch above Placerville in 1972. A year later on the other side of Placerville, Greg and Susan Boeger established their winery and vineyard on Carson Road just below Apple Hill. A few miles above Apple Hill, on High Hill Road, Dick and Leslie Bush established and planted about eight acres of Zinfandel on their 3,000-foot elevation site, making it the highest elevation Zinfandel vineyard in the world.

In Napa Valley, Bernard Portet, Clos du Val's founding president/winemaker, even planted 10 acres of Zinfandel in his newly established Stags Leap District Clos du Val Vineyards, next to the historic Grigsby Winery (now Regusci Vineyards). "You couldn't call yourself a winemaker in the Napa Valley in 1972 and not make Zinfandel," the Bordeaux-born Bernard told me in our December 1996 interview. I had asked him why a vineyard and winery established on the Bordeaux model produced an estate Zinfandel. Zinfandel and Cabernet Sauvignon were his flagship wines. Clos du Val is today the only Stags Leap District estate Zinfandel producer, and one of few Napa Valley producers with a continuous 25-year history of making Zinfandel from Napa Valley grapes.

By the late-1970s, the potential of Zinfandel from the best vineyards to produce premium dry red table wine was again becoming known among select producers and consumers. Yet the longstanding and widely held perception of Zinfandel as an inferior wine grape would prevail for many more years. Joel Peterson recalls trying to sell his Ravenswood Zinfandel wines in 1978. "Zinfandel?" the store owners would respond. "That's a nothing grape."

By 1982, the responses were improving, Peterson recalls, but they were still far from enthusiastic. It would take another flattening of Zinfandel prices, the loss of a few more fine vineyards in the late 1970s and early 1980s, and additional producers dedicated to understanding the Zinfandel grape's potential, before unqualified recognition of Zinfandel as a noble red wine grape occurred.

Still, the improving returns for their grapes, in many cases because of the highly popular white Zinfandel, kept most of the best vineyards not only in the ground but well cared for. Growing Zinfandel grapes for the production of white Zinfandel wine was profitable because the grapes needed to reach only about 20° Brix, rather than the 24° Brix required for red wine production. At such an early stage of ripening, it is much easier to pick a harvest date. Also, vines can ripen a much bigger crop to 20° Brix than they can to 24° without the clusters becoming in danger of bunch rot, or the vines becoming excessively stressed. In addition, grape flavors between Zinfandel grown in the best locations and in the inferior locations are pretty much indistinguishable at this stage of ripeness.

The prestige of a Zinfandel vineyard, however, rests in its ability to produce premium *red* wine.

By the late 1980s and continuing into the 1990s, good-to-great red Zinfandel table wines produced by winemakers more interested in the quality of their Zinfandel wines than in profit were coming to market with increasing consistency from all regions.

"Zinfandel is the lowest profit wine I make, but I intend to keep making it, since I like it, and the grape source is excellent," said Gary Farrell, winemaker for Davis Bynum Winery in Russian River Valley. In 1982, Gary established his own Gary Farrell label. The Gary Farrell 1990 Zinfandel from the Collins Vineyard, priced at just $14, won the 1993 Sonoma County Harvest Fair Sweepstakes Award, beating out wines two and three times the retail price. "Producing the highest quality wine is my first consideration. There has always been the potential to make this [world-class] style of Zinfandel. But it's been a matter of economics for most people. The shelf price isn't there. I don't consider profit when I make a wine. I feel that if I get a reputation for quality, the rest will come," Gary told me in 1993. By 1997, Gary's Zinfandels were still modestly priced for the quality, and still stealing the spotlight from more expensive competitors. At the California State Fair, the Gary Farrell 1995 Russian River viticultural area Zinfandel took "Best of Show."

When the 1990 vintage was released in 1992, the "rest" indeed began to come — not only for Gary but also for many other producers who had stuck with the grape through its years of obscurity. Consumers attracted by the affordable prices and the favorable wine publication reviews began trying the wines anew — and liking them. Their enjoyment was helped along by newly published reports of red wine's health benefits. They have been lining up for the red stuff in increasing numbers ever since.

What was it about the 1990 vintage that had wine writers waxing eloquent about vintages throughout the state? Why were winemakers jumping for joy at wine tasting festivals, and consumers snatching up every drop produced in every region?

It was a combination of factors. The winemakers who, because of their consistently well-made wines, survived the collapse of the red Zinfandel wine market in the late 1970s and early 1980s were joined by others equally dedicated to searching out the best Zinfandel grapes and making the best red wine they could — cost notwithstanding. As winemakers found vineyards they liked, they began to pay growers better prices. In some cases, they mentioned growers on labels to encourage them to keep up the quality. With better grapes bringing better prices, more growers got interested.

Such increasingly well made, delicious, and affordable wines attracted favorable reviews from wine writers, which in turn attracted more consumers. Then Mother Nature handed down the 1990 vintage: the summer cool and long, the fall warm and dry without being excessively hot. Yield was smaller than usual; the grapes hung long on the vine, taking their time in coming to full maturity. Growers had little to do except watch their grapes slowly achieve optimal maturity and ripeness. Chock full of rich, intense flavors at harvest, with acid and sugar contents well-balanced, they required little of their winemakers besides crushing, fermenting them to dryness, racking the wine into barrels, and sitting back to watch the wine mellow into near perfection over the next 12 to 14 months. The wines that resulted were succulent, luscious, fruity, and balanced, with both incredible appeal upon release in 1992 and fantastic potential for ageing.

I don't think many bottles of the 1990 vintage Zinfandel, though, got put into cellars for ageing. It was just too good when it was released.

I met Michael Collins, partner in Limerick Lane Vineyards, in the fall of 1990. Upon discovering our mutual passion for Zinfandel, he gave me a bottle of his 1988, his first vintage and current release. When I called him a few days later to tell him what a smashing wine I thought it was, he said, "Wait until you taste the 1989. You'll want to pour the 1988 down the sink."

I didn't think so, but I eagerly anticipated the 1989. When it was released, Michael said as I exclaimed over it, "Wait until you try our 1990. You'll want to pour it…"

Michael even sold me — at his cost or very near it — a few cases for the Napa Valley College Faculty Association's 1991 year-end dinner. The wine was a perfect match-up with the entrees catered by Andrews Market of Napa. Once the wines were opened, the group of mostly casual wine drinkers was soon emptying the bottles faster than I could pull their corks. It was surely the best retirement dinner the Faculty Association ever sponsored.

When the 1990 came out, however, I didn't hear Michael say anything about wanting to pour it down the sink. Limerick Lane's 1990 Zinfandel took the 1993 Vintners Club Zinfandel tasting by storm, scoring 15 firsts to the three that the second placed wine received. (The Vintners Club is a San Francisco wine tasting club established in 1972.)

Other 1990 wines statewide were similarly well received by consumers and wine writers alike. By 1992, Zinfandel was causing a buzz even in the popular *Wine Spectator,* which finally ran a cover story on Zinfandel in its October 15 issue, inspired in good part by the fabulous 1990 vintage.[19] By 1996, it seemed that new labels were turning up on wine store shelves daily. I was getting phone calls more often about developments in new regions (new to me, that is), like El Dorado, Paso Robles, Lodi, and others.

These delicious, sensuous, blockbuster, world-class red table wines of the 1990s brought to the Zinfandel grape, once and for all, international recognition as one of the noble red wine grapes of the world. They also brought to the dedicated growers and patient producers the necessary economic rewards for their years of loyalty to the grape, ensuring that its future is safe — at least for now.

19 James Laube, "Zinfandel's New Look," *Wine Spectator,* Vol. XVIII, No. 12, Oct. 15, 1992, 25-28

What is "Fine Wine"?

Winemaking Practices Described

Three practices are fundamental to fine winemaking:

- Leaving the fermented wine on the skins for a long period of time (known as "extended maceration");
- Taking the wine through full malolactic fermentation (MLF) to reduce acidity, by converting the malic acid to lactic acid;
- Ageing the wine in small oak barrels for several months before bottling.

Leaving the wine on the skins after dryness has been achieved requires additional tank space, which adds to the cost of production. Since Zinfandel traditionally was not regarded as a fine wine, it was seldom given such priority treatment. Today, this is still something of a style choice, but more producers are giving it a try with their Zinfandels. See the Lucas Winery section in Part II for an in-depth discussion of the benefits of extended maceration.

According to such venerable winemakers as Louis P. Martini and Peter Mondavi Sr., red wines probably were going through malolactic fermentation long before the process was recognized for what it was. The malolactic bacteria were pretty much indigenous to wineries in the 30 years following Prohibition repeal. Once the process was recognized, winemakers made an effort to use the best strains of malolactic starters, and to control how and when it happened. This has added to quality control.

Ageing Zinfandel in small oak barrels did not become standard practice until well into the 1990s. Traditional producers felt that large redwood tanks preserved the fruit. That was the style their generations of customers had come to expect. Many new producers used oak ovals or tanks, believing that the oak character imparted by small barrels, unless the barrels were well seasoned, masked the delicate fruit. However, as California's wine industry expanded, more Zinfandel producers realized that new customers had come to expect a layer of oak wood flavor in their red wines — Zinfandel included.

"Putting Zinfandel in small oak barrels doesn't necessarily make it better, just different," said Louis P. Martini. "The oak adds a layer of flavor that customers have come to expect." (See Appendix I, "Time Out for Quercus.")

Martini, however, had no need to apologize for his decades of ageing Zinfandel in large redwood tanks. The Zinfandels most often mentioned to me by winemakers throughout California as the ones that got them thinking about becoming a Zinfandel producer are the Martini Zinfandels of the 1960s. Balanced and with alcohol content ranging between 12.5 percent to 13.5 percent, the wines aged exceedingly well, acquiring a delightful bottle bouquet over the years while maintaining their fruit. "The fact that they were stored in redwood tanks might even have contributed to their long bottle ageing potential," said Martini. "Wines don't oxidize very much while stored in redwood tanks."

Fine winemaking begins with selection of the harvest date. It is the winemaker's first critical decision. Most winemakers harvest their grapes according to their sugar content (measured in degrees of Brix), titratable acidity (T.A., which consists of tartaric and malic acids), and pH. Ideal harvest numbers are about 24° Brix sugar content, 6.0–8.8 g/L acid (with most of that being tartaric), and a pH of 3.35 to 3.6. Wines made from grapes with such numbers are balanced when made, and they stay balanced. No acid adjustments are necessary because there is little change in either titratable acid or pH after malolactic fermentation. If much of the T.A. is malic, then there will be a significant rise in pH; if most of the T.A. is tartaric, then there will be little rise in pH.

A finished wine pH of 3.6 or less is desired for three reasons:

- the spoilage yeast brettanomyces does not thrive in a pH environment under 3.6;
- lower sulfite levels are required at bottling;
- wines of 3.6 pH or less have greater ageing potential.

For these reasons, pH is becoming increasingly important to winemakers. It is also an important indicator of when the integrity of the fruit is breaking down, with a pH of 3.7 signifying that the fruit has gotten as ripe as it is going to get.

Some winemakers, however, ignore the numbers, picking when about 90 percent of the grapes in a Zinfandel cluster taste ripe. Ripe flavors are not necessarily indicated by degrees of Brix, since grapes can taste sweet and ripe at 23°, or lack flavor at 26° Brix. Since about 1990, the trend for most winemakers has been to pick by taste of the grapes and the color and flavors in the seeds. This requires much practice.

Sonoma County's Seghesio family decided in 1992 to downsize its winery and produce only premium quality estate wines, (most of which is Zinfandel). General manager Peter Seghesio later reflected: "We had a lot to learn. We discovered that it doesn't matter what the numbers and chemistry of the grapes are at harvest; it's how the grapes taste. I learned how to chew and taste not only the grapes but also the seeds. We want nice brown seeds, and grapes that taste good. We want brown tannins, not green ones."

Deciding upon the optimum harvest date for Zinfandel continues to be an inexact science — making it much closer to art. (Some would say it is more like a roll of the dice.) Zinfandel grapes typically ripen unevenly, with mature clusters running the gamut from shriveled and even raisined berries to a few green ones. These shriveled berries are loaded with sugar, which soak out during the first hours of fermentation. This can significantly raise the sugar content of the juice. Sugar converts to alcohol during fermentation. Sugar content is ultimately important to everyone, since it determines the percentage of alcohol in the finished wine. To get the fully ripe flavors so bewitching to consumers, alcohol percentages typically range from 13.5 percent to 15.5 percent. Maintaining ripe, rich flavors — without raisiny or pruny qualities — while staying within this alcohol content window is a primary challenge for Zinfandel winemakers and grape growers. Most winemakers have a few tricks they resort to from time to time — depending on the vintage.

Once the winemaker has harvested the crop, the next step is to crush and destem the berries. This entails use of a machine to do the job with the least detriment to wine quality. The process is affected both by winemaking style and budget. The trend today is to do little more than gently destem the berries so that the skin is just split; the berries are either not crushed, or just slightly crushed. Bitter, hard tannins from heavily crushed skins and seeds that consumers got so tired of in the early 1980s are avoided. The Delta destemmer-crusher is one machine winning approval by Zinfandel producers worried about harsh tannins in their wines.

With the grapes destemmed and crushed, choices have to be made regarding what size fermentation tank to use, and whether it should be open top or closed top. If a winemaker wants to hand-punch the wine, then a small open top fermentor is necessary. Some winemakers also prefer open top fermentors because they allow some alcohol to evaporate during fermentation. This may be desirable with Zinfandel, whose alcohol content is usually over 14 percent. Closed top fermentors accommodate larger volume of must, and provide for automated or mechanical pumpover. They also inhibit evaporation of volatile elements in the fermenting must.

Those choices being made, the wine is pumped, gently, into fermentation tanks, where another choice is made: to add commercially prepared yeast, or to let the indigenous yeast do the job. Sometimes, the wine is allowed to cold-soak for a few days before yeast is added. These decisions being made, the wine begins to ferment, forming a thick cap of skins and seeds at the top of the tank. This cap must be mixed in with the fermenting wine several times daily. And here, another choice is made: to hand-punch down the cap; or to mechanically pump wine from the bottom of the tank over the cap.

Some winemakers use other methods such as submerged cap, or a new approach called "drain and return." The latter basically means just what it says: the wine is drained from the bottom of the tank, allowing the cap to sink to the bottom. The wine is then pumped back into the tank, and as the cap rises, extraction occurs.

Once these choices are made, there is little more to do until the wine reaches dryness. Dryness means that all the sugar is converted to alcohol, so that fermentation stops — since there is no more sugar to feed the yeast cells.

Once dryness is achieved, another decision: to leave the wine on the skins for a couple or three weeks ("extended maceration") before putting it into barrels; or to rack it into barrels immediately.

The next choice is selection of oak barrels. Premium wines have historically been aged in small oak barrels. The use of these barrels for ageing of their finest red wines became the practice of California's top wine producers by the mid-1960s — at least for their very best Cabernet Sauvignons. Zinfandel was another story.

Since Zinfandel had no history as a premium red wine, ageing it in small oak barrels was revolutionary, not to mention financially risky. Barrels are expensive, while Zinfandel was cheap. Nonetheless, barrel ageing was what many of the earliest producers did with their best Zinfandel, cost aside, simply because they knew what they had. Now, it is standard practice.

Then, of course, the question became whether American or French oak barrels were better for Zinfandel. Controversy continues over this issue.

After ageing questions are settled, all that is left to do over the winter and spring months is the really subtle part of winemaking: tasting and smelling the wine as it matures in the barrels. This has to be done frequently, with every barrel sampled. Wine matures in barrels differently vintage to vintage, vineyard to vineyard — even block to block in the same vineyard. Many changes occur in barrels, with the taste and smell of the wine indicating what the winemaker needs to do next. This is where the winemaker's skill is really put to the test.

After barrel ageing, more decisions are made: whether to fine or filter. Both practices are applied before the wine is bottled. Fining involves adding a substance such as raw egg whites to the holding tank to precipitate out bitter tannins. Filtering is done prior to bottling to remove various particles that might cause cloudiness or spoilage in the bottle. Ultimately, quality depends upon whether the wines needed one or both of the above steps, and if they did, whether it was done right. The only test that matters is how the finished wine tastes.

Bottling takes place anywhere from 10 to 20 months following harvest. Since the wine may need some time to get over the shock of bottling, it is held by the winery for a few weeks or months of bottle ageing before being released.

Such winemaking practices are expensive. Nonetheless, as a fine wine, Zinfandel still comes to the market for much less than Cabernet Sauvignon or Pinot Noir of comparable value for several reasons:

- Lower costs of grapes;
- Earlier maturing of the wine in the barrel and bottle, which means lower labor, topping, and case-storage costs associated with the shorter cellar time and earlier showing in the bottle;
- Increasing consumer demand, which means premium Zinfandel sells out within a few months of release, providing early cash return on investment;
- More juice per ton of Zinfandel grapes than from the other popular varieties. Zinfandel grapes are larger than Cabernet Sauvignon and Pinot Noir grapes, so juice-to-skins ratio is greater. According to Bill Gage, production manager for Rosenblum Cellars, Zinfandel grapes can yield up to one-third more juice per ton than the other leading red grape varieties.

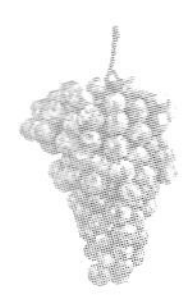

Characteristics of a Great Vineyard

Great wines begin in great vineyards. A great vineyard is one that meets three basic criteria:

- It has been established in a *terroir* best suited to the varietal. A well-situated red grape vineyard has the *terroir* necessary to develop grapes with intense flavors, deep color, and acid, pH, and sugar content appropriate to the style of wine being made. Such grapes require little winemaker intervention in order to produce a flavorful and balanced wine.
- It has been propagated from suitable clonal selections.
- The grower's viticultural practices have contributed to the quality of the grapes.

The question remains regarding what viticultural practices, or human intervention by the grower, are necessary to keep vines in balance with their soil, climate, and site. A balanced vine is one whose crop size is matched to the vine's ability to ripen it.

Two viticultural practices have the greatest effect on keeping the vines in balance:

- how the vines are planted and trained;
- how much water the vines receive.

Viticultural Practices

Effect of "Terroir"

All winemakers know that *terroir* has an effect on wine character, no matter the source of budwood. A consumer cannot simply buy a Zinfandel by one producer and expect it will be just like the one he or she bought the day before made by a different producer — or even by the same producer from a different vineyard. The flavors and character can be so dramatically different from one *terroir* to another that you may wonder if the wine you just drank was made from the same grape as the wine you had the day before. Zinfandel is one of the few red wine grapes that presents a broad range of flavors and aromas and overall wine character reflective of the *terroir* the vines are grown in, even as it maintains its distinctly juicy, fruity, spicy varietal Zinfandel character.

Clonal Research: Interview with Dr. Amand Kasimatis

A clone is a group of genetically identical plants descended from a single common ancestor. A vine propagated from a cutting becomes a clone of the vine the cutting was taken from. Individual vines propagated from each cutting off the parent vine are known as "clonal selections," and all have the same DNA pattern. There is still uncertainty as to whether the differences in grape and wine quality among vineyards are due to clones or to *terroir* and viticultural practices.

Dr. Amand Kasimatis is a UC Davis, emeritus extension viticulturist. Actively involved in UC Davis's clonal research in the 1980s, he has been working since 1990 with his successor, Dr. James Wolpert, in developing a "heritage" collection of Zinfandel clones.

On a July, 1997 afternoon, I arrived at his house on a quiet, tree-lined street in Davis, and was cordially greeted at the door by a tall, distinguished-looking gentleman wearing a cotton shirt and knee-length khaki shorts against the heat of the afternoon. Graciously ushered in toward a spacious, cool, comfortable living room, I was invited to sit on a commodious sofa. Kas, as he is known by his friends, began at once to sort out my confusion regarding the meaning of field selection cuttings, clones and clonal selection, and rootstock — and the relevance of all this to Zinfandel.

"Research done in the 1920s," Kas began, "showed that there was no difference among a group of vines. At that point, there wasn't much interest in what we today call clones.

"Since then, interest in clones has increased in France and Germany. The goals are usually to improve quality and yield. If you can find one vine that seems to bear superior fruit, then it may be worth it to try and propagate an entire vineyard from that parent vine.

"In California, this renewed interest came to a head through UC Davis's Foundation Plant Material Service (FPMS), a unit of the university that is involved in a state-wide program identifying clean stock, maintaining it, then supplying it to nurseries under a certification program through FPMS. The State Department of Agriculture administers the certification program. The program was proposed by UC Davis's Dr. Harold Omo in the mid-1950s, and carried forth by Dr. Bill Hewlitt in plant pathology. Although it wasn't in Dr. Omo's original plan, it worked out that the university's role was to develop the clean material and make it available. The certification part, which meant maintaining it in commercial supply and build-up by nurseries, was to be handled under the Department of Agriculture.

"The motivation at the time for propagating clonal selection vines in California was to get rid of virus diseases. Grafting readily transmits virus diseases. The most insidious way is by grafting onto virused rootstock. Many of the rootstocks do not show symptoms, whereas the scion varieties do show some symptoms, which are sometimes very distinctive and recognizable. Under this [FPMS] program, scientists in the university would look for clones — that is, single vines — out in the field that appeared to be virus-free. It is very important to keep in mind that a clone is a single vine. They brought this material back to Davis to be tested for disease.

"From the type of clonal selections propagated, they were looking for productive as well as healthy vines. In broad terms, I don't know that they had anything else in mind, or had reason to have anything else in mind. Emphasis at that time was on the economics, not red Zinfandel wine quality. Growers were paid by the ton, no matter the region. More tons meant more money.

"Nonetheless, this idea that UC Davis clones were the result of seeking big crops is simply false. Nobody was talking about crop size back then. Here was this material being offered out of FPMS, but there was no published history of its performance as a wine grape. When growers ordered it, they were ordering Zinfandel. There was no thought of clones then at all. Growers bought it because it was available, certified clean, with the intention of planting it, then finding out what kind of fruit it yielded in their vineyards, and how to make a good wine from it. It's only in retrospect that people can talk about size of yield in relation to wine quality."

Most of the new plantings of the early 1970s and into the 1980s came from FPMS material. In fact, because of the likelihood of acquiring virally infected budwood from field selection cuttings, many growers (even into the 1990s) purchased UC Davis's certified, virus-tested clonal selection material. There is still some question whether size of yield results from a combination of *terroir* and the fact that vines propagated from the UC Davis virus-tested clones almost always have been trellised and irrigated rather than being head trained and non-irrigated, in the old style.

"Interest in Zinfandel clones as relevant to wine quality didn't develop until the early 1980s," Kas continued. "Sure, Sutter Home (with the Deaver Zinfandels) and Ridge were making headlines with their big, alcoholic Zinfandels of the 1970s. Admittedly, they started something, but it didn't last very long. The wine writers raved about those wines, but the consumers didn't like them. They were little more than an anomaly. So Zinfandel as a varietally identified red table wine didn't do much for several years — and then white Zinfandel came along."

Although they did not produce premium quality grapes for red Zinfandel wine, clonal selection Zinfandel vines developed by UC Davis were just wonderful for white Zinfandel. With trellises and irrigation, the vines could easily ripen from 10–20 tons of fruit per acre to the 18°–20° Brix required for this style of wine.

"By the 1980s," continued Kas, "interest in Zinfandel as a red table wine was increasing. That is when the second big planting took place (the first was a decade earlier). Much of the early crops still went into the white Zinfandel program. When growers attempted to switch to the premium red Zinfandel program in the late 1980s and early 1990s, they found that the white Zinfandel program of the 1970s and 1980s had spoiled them. They got much higher tonnage, since they didn't have to get high sugar, and also high prices — as much as $1,200 per ton.

"But growing for white Zinfandel is a different approach. So when they switched to the red Zinfandel program, the growers wanted the quality, but they still wanted that higher tonnage, since prices weren't always proportionately higher for the red Zinfandel program. It usually took them a couple of years to come to terms with the fact that quality and yield are intimately related."

With the renewed interest in premium red Zinfandel wine, growers began paying more attention not only to crop size but also to clones, to find out whether they had any connection to wine quality.

For today's high quality red Zinfandel wines, acknowledged Kas, there is general agreement that it starts with the basic plant material. "You can obviously do much towards improving wine quality with viticultural practices," he said, "but there's a limit."

Many winemakers believe that clones from vines showing no symptoms of virus disease, which produce smaller bunches of fruit with smaller berries, tend to produce the most balanced and intensely flavored red table wine. That is why Kas and his successor at UC Davis Extension, Dr. James Wolpert, beginning about 1992, have been roaming the oldest Zinfandel vineyards throughout the state searching for such clonal material. Some 60 selections have been made; that is, wood from 60 individual vines has been propagated.

From these clonal selections taken from vineyards 60 years old and older, a small "heritage" Zinfandel vineyard has been propagated on clean St. George rootstock at UC Davis's Oakville Station in Napa Valley.

Clean rootstock is the other half of the virus-free equation. The phylloxera-resistant St. George, which was developed in France in the 1890s, seemed made for Zinfandel, which does well as a non-irrigated varietal on hillsides. The St. George is a vigorous vine with an extensive and deep root system. When farmed without irrigation, the vine sets loosely formed bunches, which is desirable in the bunch-rot prone Zinfandel grape.

Since 1970, UC Davis's St. George rootstock is entirely developed from Australia's St. George #15, because it is free of known virus disease. The rootstock that originated in France was not clean, and could not be certified.

The idea behind the heritage Zinfandel vineyard, explained Kas, is to plant all the heritage clonal selections side by side, and to use identical vineyard practices on them in an attempt to determine if, in fact, there are clonal differences, or only differences of *terroir*.

"Is it your feeling at this time that the wine made from these clones will be better balanced and more intensely flavored than the wine from the earlier UC Davis clones?" I asked.

"Yeah, sure. At least, I hope so!" replied Kas. "But only because we had more specific goals in mind than did the scientists collecting material in the 1950s — who had only general goals of collecting disease-free productive material. Which was what the farmers then wanted, to meet the demand then. Yet there always were old growers who kept growing Zinfandel, like up in Dry Creek, who always had selected vines out of their own vineyard for propagation. They didn't fool around with the new stuff at all. They stayed with their own field selections. I know of several growers who did that. They propagated new plantings from the vines they knew, budded to clean St. George rootstock."

While Kas believes that the heritage collection of budwood should more reliably produce high quality red Zinfandel wine, it will be some time before researchers will be able to draw any such scientific conclusions. "Since the budwood all came from different locations, we don't as yet know if smaller berries and bunches are the result of the clone or the conditions (*terroir*). Bringing the vines into balance is the key for premium red wine production, whatever the source of budwood. Balance for individual vineyards can range from two tons per acre to five or seven tons — even 10 tons per acre on a divided canopy system, depending on the area. For a region like Lodi, climate is an important contributor, permitting much higher yields per acre while maintaining top quality for the area.

"Until you get the clones propagated all under the same conditions, you can't draw any conclusions about the character of their fruit. It just takes a long time. We have eight vines of each clone now. Nineteen ninety-eight will be the first year we can make them separately as wine."

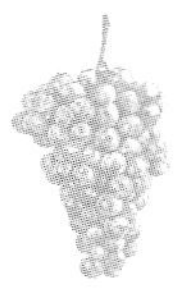

How Are Zinfandel Vines Trained?

On the question of how Zinfandel vines are best trained, it has been historically proven that Zinfandel vines are well suited to head training and spur pruning. A head-trained vine is one with a freestanding trunk that supports a circle of fruit-bearing arms. The shape is usually referred to as a "goblet," or occasionally "wagon wheel." Today, it is preferred because it lends itself well to balancing crop level with the vines.

In the 1970s and 1980s, however, some growers planting new vineyards chose to give new technology a try. So they set up with trellises and cordon-trained vines — that is, a trunk with one fruit-bearing branch strung along the wire in each direction from the trunk. Each cordon was pruned to about five spurs, each spur with two buds. This was a popular style of training in the 1970s and 1980s, because trellised vines could carry a larger crop, which at that time was as important as varietal quality.

Bringing trellised Zinfandel vines into balance for premium red wine production is labor-intensive and costly; but it can be done.

Old head-trained vine, Moore (Earthquake) Vineyard

I remember vividly my first look, in mid-August of 1996, at Lava Cap's Zinfandel vineyard, planted in 1980 high up in El Dorado County. Like many people who planted Zinfandel vineyards in the 1970s and 1980s, Lava Cap's owner, David Jones, chose a UC Davis, certified virus disease-free clone. He liked the complex spicy flavors in the grapes that he felt went beyond the usual black pepper, black cherry of the old clones. It was also what was available.

Originally, the fruit was sold for white Zinfandel. Bringing the vines into balance for the intensely flavored red wines that Jones had begun to make in the 1990s was a battle. Although there were already dried-up, bunch-thinned clusters lying under the cordon-trained, trellised rows, the clusters on the vines were big enough to fill my two arms.

"Good heavens!" I gasped to Jones upon seeing the vineyard. "What are you growing up here — table grapes?"

"Come back next month," replied Jones, with a smile. "See all those unevenly ripened clusters? They'll all be down there with the ones we've already thinned. In fact, we'll be cluster thinning for the second time in the next week or so."

I took him at his word, and returned in September, a few days before the grapes were to be harvested. All that remained on the vines were some of the most luscious, blue-black, evenly ripened clusters of Zinfandel I'd ever seen. And their taste was irresistible.

"Well, I am simply amazed," I admitted to Jones, as he proudly held a beautiful cluster in his two hands. Yes, the cluster was still enormous; but given the severe crop thinning he and his vineyard manager son, Charlie, had done, the remaining clusters had ripened beautifully.

"Until we implemented these practices," said Jones, "we were despairing of our Zinfandel. Now, we're winning gold medals!

"You have to be brutal in multiple pruning and thinning," he emphasized. "We green prune [that is, crown sucker to remove weak, straggly shoots] and cluster thin. Yes, it's expensive for two reasons: the labor costs; and the loss of crop. But if you want quality from these vines, there's no alternative."

How is Water Delivered?

Water delivery historically has been strictly from Mother Nature's cloud-laden skies. Reliance on such heaven-sent annual rainfall is known as dry farming. Such naturally occurring water usually has been adequate, if not abundant, in most regions, and Zinfandel vines are good at extracting water from the ground during the dry summer months. The stress of doing so tends to develop more intensely flavored grapes. Zinfandel vines living in luxury do not produce well-flavored grapes.

However, in regions like Lodi and the Cucamonga Valley, where soil is sandy and the climate is warm, irrigation has been necessary to keep the vines productive and the growers in business. According to Craig Rous, director of research for Mondavi-Woodbridge from 1979 to 1998, and one of that company's top growers for its red Zinfandel program, "The tool that growers here still use that has the largest impact on quality of Zinfandel is irrigation."

Although some Zinfandel producers look with a jaundiced eye upon irrigated Zinfandel vines, the question to be asked is not whether the vines have been irrigated, argues Rous. Rather, three questions should be asked: How is the water delivered — by furrows or by drip lines; how much water is delivered; and when is the water delivered. These are the irrigation questions that affect grape quality — not whether the vines have been irrigated.

Mark Shimazaki

Mark Shimozaki, another of Mondavi-Woodbridge's top red Zinfandel growers, corroborated Rous' argument. "There's nothing wrong with irrigation," he said. Shimozaki owns 15 acres of 10-foot by 8-foot spaced, head trained Zinfandel vines in Victor, just east of Lodi. Eight acres are 60 years old, and to the best of Shimozaki's knowledge, are on St. George rootstock; in 1989, he propagated seven additional acres with cuttings from the older vines budded onto Harmony rootstock.

"The dry farming mystique is false," Shimozaki believes. "Many regions, including the Bordeaux, have abundant annual rainfall. To say that such vineyards are 'dry farmed' is little more than a romantic misnomer. Non-irrigated, yes, because irrigation would be superfluous. But 'dry farmed?' Hardly. If we get past this false mystique, the question isn't whether or not a grower irrigates. The question is whether or not the vines are in balance, and do the grapes have the quality. For growers in regions like Lodi, where the soil is sandy, you can't be a serious grower if you don't supplement your seasonal rains with some kind of irrigation in the summer months. You can be a 'fun-farmer,' and get along on two or maybe three tons per acre, but you can't be a full-time farmer with yields like that. You'd have to have another source of income."

Furrow irrigation was the early method of water delivery used by Lodi and Cucamonga Valley grapegrowers in the years following repeal of Prohibition. These two regions are home to most of the state's oldest

Zinfandel vineyards, many of them pre-Prohibition. The problem, however, is that it is difficult to control the amount of water each vine receives with furrow irrigation; they get either too much or too little. Skilled furrow-irrigators, who, some owners were convinced, could make water run uphill, were valued employees at the time. But no matter the skill of the irrigators, it was a difficult and labor intensive task to keep the vines in balance. However, given the generic nature of the wines in demand then, it didn't much matter that the flavor and color of the grapes were inconsistent. The price per ton was the same, whether the grapes were from furrow irrigated vineyards in Lodi, or from non-irrigated hillside vineyards in Sonoma. They all went towards the production of fortified and inexpensive jug wines.

For today's premium wine production, most growers have found furrow irrigation to be unsatisfactory. When interest in premium red Zinfandel table wine picked up in the mid-1980s and 1990s, the higher grape prices gave Zinfandel growers the incentive and means to improve the quality of their grapes. Top growers such as Mark Shimozaki have converted to drip lines for their water delivery, as have many Cucamonga Valley growers.

Craig Rous also has equipped his non-irrigated vineyard with drip lines. By changing the delivery system from furrows to drip lines, learning the best time to water, and determining how much water is optimum, growers can bring their vines into balance for premium winegrape production. With such careful application of irrigation, crop size is balanced to the vines throughout the vineyard, and overall grape flavor and color are dramatically improved. Wine quality follows.

Growers in traditionally non-irrigated regions are also examining the benefits of supplementary water delivery. "Irrigation can never do the harm to a vine that excessive stress can," points out Amador County grower Frank Alviso.

With the 8-foot by 10-foot spacing of his head trained and drip irrigated Zinfandel vines, Mark Shimozaki's annual average yield is between six and eight tons per acre of premium quality fruit — enough to afford him a living.

Other Viticultural Practices

Other methods of bringing the vines into balance and improving grape quality, whether the vines are head trained or trellised, irrigated or non-irrigated, are to crown sucker the vines, to cluster thin as necessary; to remove leaves to expose clusters to filtered sunlight; and to do all of the above in keeping with the season Mother Nature gives you.

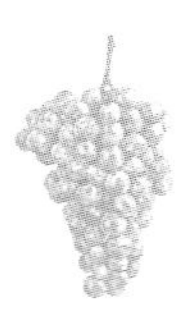

In Summary

Whether farming older head trained, non-irrigated, and, to some extent, virused Zinfandel vines, or younger, trellised and irrigated, and certified, virus-tested vines propagated from UC Davis budwood, considerable work is required of the grower to consistently produce high quality grapes vintage after vintage. Few growers are allowed the luxury of becoming complacent about their Zinfandel vineyards, no matter how old or famous they have become. There's still too much to be learned.

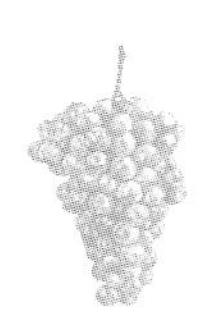

Zinfandel Table Wine: A Definition

Table wines are wines that are served at table with food. To match well with food, wines should meet certain criteria of alcohol content.

According to the Bureau of Alcohol, Tobacco, and Firearms (ATF), wines with 14 percent or less alcohol may simply be called "Table Wine." They are not required to have their alcohol content displayed on their labels. Wines with alcohol content *over* 14 percent must have the alcohol percentage declared on the label. Table wines are usually, but not always, dry wines (wines having less than 0.5 percent residual sugar — not perceptible as a sweet taste to the consumer) that may be served daily with meals. Wines other than table wines are referred to as Aperitifs (before-dinner wines) and dessert and port wines (after-dinner wines).

However, Zinfandel as a red table wine is a fully extracted, fruity, intensely flavored, sensuous, full-textured dry red wine with alcohol content usually, but not always, *over* 14.1 percent alcohol. It is delicious when released, about two years after crush, and gains in interest, flavor, and complexity if left in the bottle for a few years longer.

Zinfandels over 14.1 percent alcohol content mostly result from the characteristic uneven ripening patterns in the Zinfandel clusters, which almost always contain a small percentage of shriveled and even raisined berries. During fermentation, these overly mature berries soak out, with their higher sugar increasing the overall sugar content, and thus the alcohol content, of the fermenting must.

It is therefore the industry-wide standard — rather than the exception — that Zinfandel as red table wine approaches, and sometimes exceeds, 15 percent alcohol before fermenting to dryness. The challenge for the winemaker, therefore, is to keep the wines in balance with the alcohol content, rather than worrying about how high the alcohol content is.

Red Zinfandel table wines made in a style that exceed 15 percent alcohol before fermenting to dryness, or near dryness, are widely considered specialty table wines — that is, wines served with food specially prepared to complement their high alcohol, rich, highly extracted style. Wines containing over 15 percent alcohol sometimes carry perceptible residual sugar, and usually require special food considerations.

Daryl Groom, Australian-born winemaker for Geyser Peak Winery, recalled his first taste of Zinfandel, when he arrived in California in 1989: "People were raving about Williams Selyem Zinfandel. I remember being introduced to a 1984 Zinfandel in a half-bottle. It was high in alcohol, and sweet. As an Australian winemaker, I found that quite awkward that someone could put out a red wine that was sweet and high in alcohol. It wasn't Port; it wasn't Late Harvest. It was just a sweetish red wine, one that didn't ferment out, and that was the way the red wine was, and people raved about it.

"While I appreciated the wine for the qualities that were there, I found it hard to drink. Wines are for drinking with food — and for many people, it's hard to pair food with such an alcoholic, sweetish, extracted wine as the Williams Selyem was."

Learning as much as possible about the stylistic practices of the producer, as well as reading the label for percentage of alcohol, is important to determine the style of Zinfandel wine the bottle contains.

As Groom indicated above, the question to ask isn't, "Which Zinfandel is the best one?" Rather, the question to ask is, "Which style of Zinfandel will best complement the food I am going to eat?" The question of "best" wines as presented in wine journals is purely subjective and personal (that is, best according to whom — or what?). Apart from defects in wine, which are objective issues, there are a great many "best" wines on the market — best, that is, to complement the food you are going to have with it.

Still valued for its incredible versatility, Zinfandel continues to be marketed in several styles besides red table wine:

Late Harvest Zinfandel — Traditionally a non-fortified dessert wine with perceptible residual sugar and an alcohol content ranging from 15 percent to nearly 18 percent, made from very ripe grapes, many of which are raisined. Zinfandel wines labeled "Late Harvest" should declare both the sugar content (degrees of Brix) at harvest and percent of residual sugar at bottling.

Some "Late Harvest"-labeled Zinfandels, however, are dry Zinfandel wines with over 15 percent alcohol (for example, Davis Bynum, 1990). Others such as Pesenti, although labeled "Late Harvest," are both dry and contain less than 15 percent alcohol.

Again, learning as much as possible about production styles and reading labels will tell you about the stylistic practices of the producer, and the percentage of alcohol. These facts are important if you are to know just what kind of wine is in that "Late Harvest" bottle.

Zinfandel Port — A sweet, fortified dessert wine of 18 percent or 19 percent alcohol made from very ripe grapes.

Beaujolais-style Zinfandel — An under-14 percent alcohol, fruity, dry table wine made from whole berry fermentation, meant to be drunk when young (for example, Gallo's "Zinfandel Cafe").

Zinfandel Rosé — Also under-14 percent alcohol, slightly sweet pink wine made from leaving the juice on the red skins of the grapes just long enough to extract a deep rose color.

White Zinfandel — Under-14 percent alcohol, slightly sweet, nearly white wine made from red Zinfandel grapes by taking the juice off the skins immediately after crushing, to minimize extraction of color from the skins

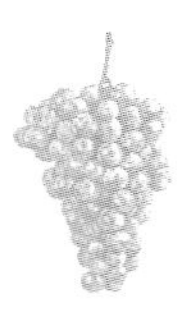

My Romance with Zinfandel

California's Zinfandel country is a world unto itself. It is inhabited by growers and winemakers who became so bewitched by the beauty of this mysterious grape, and the many distinctly different yet luscious wines it is capable of producing, that they have allowed it to shape their lives and sometimes even their fortunes. All of us within this country have a story to tell about how this marvelous grape has touched our lives.

My story begins in the fall of 1977 — and it is linked to a brief romance with a certain man. I was living in the Sunset District of San Francisco, and had just been hired by Napa Valley College as an English teacher. On almost the same day, I hung my very first photography show at University of California, San Francisco. My daily 50-mile commute to Napa Valley College took me over the fabled Golden Gate Bridge, past Black Point in Marin and Sears Point in Sonoma, then meandered through the Carneros region wine country of the world-famous Sonoma and Napa valleys.

On my very first trip, the beauty of the fall vineyards inspired me to keep my vintage 35mm camera loaded and at hand. By the time the September vineyards had turned into a blaze of fall colors, I found myself roaming though Napa Valley on my first photographic and wine-tasting adventure, a sojourn that led me to make my first Zinfandel photo image — and to taste Zinfandel for the first time.

It was at the V. Sattui Winery, the first one I visited. Darryl Sattui, owner and winemaker, was at the side of what was then a one-building winery. He was pressing Amador County Zinfandel. Garnet-colored teardrops of Zinfandel juice spilled like delicate chains from the fermentation tank. I had my camera ready. In an instant the image was framed, the film exposed. It was my very first Zinfandel photograph.

Inside the tasting room, I toasted what I hoped would be my first successful wine country image with a fragrant glass of Zinfandel. My romance with the grape had just begun, although it took a few more years for me to realize it.

I knew about Zinfandel before I arrived in Napa Valley. A fellow graduate student had brought a bottle to a party once, and had proudly declared it California's very own variety. I had just arrived from Canada, and knew little about wines. Then, my favorite drink was single malt Scotch over ice. That was in the late 1960s. I wonder now whose Zinfandel it was, since few were produced back then under the variety name, and I regret that I declined the invitation to try it.

By the early 1980s, when I had become a tenured member of Napa Valley College's English Department and a Napa resident, I found myself roaming the vineyards of Napa and Sonoma valleys, photographing their beauty in all seasons. Still, I was seeing the grapes only as white wine grapes and red wine grapes. Beyond that, I did not know one from the other. I just loved being in the vineyards photographing the wonderful configurations of vines and grapes. When people asked me what grapes were shown in my photo prints, I couldn't tell them. It seemed important enough to the people interested in my work, though, that I began to inquire. Pretty soon, I could tell a few of them apart. It didn't take me long to realize that the vineyards I was most attracted to were Zinfandel.

Inspired by the beauty of the vineyards, I began to sample many wines. More and more often, I would ask for Zinfandel (the red stuff) in tasting rooms. A few, like Sutter Home Winery's Amador Zinfandels, were already legendary wines. My San Francisco roommate had had a couple of this winery's early Amador vintages that she was holding back for just the right occasion. (Unfortunately, such an occasion had not occurred before I moved to Napa.) Yet the more Zinfandels I sampled and Zinfandel winemakers I talked to, the more aware I became of symptoms that a deep ambivalence toward Zinfandel had developed in the marketplace.

On one hand, it seemed Zinfandel had a small but steadfast following among consumers. Many growers were standing by their old vineyards (some even planting new vines), and winemakers were speaking lovingly of particularly favorite vineyards and vintages. And in specialty wine stores, Zinfandel was given a good chunk of coveted shelf space.

Yet paradoxically, the list was long — and getting longer — of wineries that had found their inventory of bottled Zinfandel stacking up in warehouses, and their salespeople threatening mutiny if asked to spend even one more day on the road trying to sell it.

Growers tired of casting about for buyers for their grapes at any price were budding over their historic Zinfandel vines to the more profitable and less confusing Bordeaux varieties — Cabernet Sauvignon, Merlot, Cabernet Franc — or were even bulldozing them. One grower in Paso Robles whose Prohibition-era vineyard was considered among the best opted to plant barley. I'd even heard of a grower or two who found it more profitable to leave their land bare than to keep their Zinfandel vines in the ground.

Newly graduated winemakers were matching their winemaking expertise, and their wineries' reputations, against the best from France by giving their best to the newly planted French varieties. Yet in the back of the winery, they often had a barrel or two of some old vine Zinfandel perking along. "Just for kicks," they told me. "Had one last chance to get the grapes cheap, before the vines got 'dozed out or budded over, just a winemaker's fun sort of thing for the staff."

This uncertainty about the worth of Zinfandel came about in good part because wine writers had begun to give the commercial bottlings ambivalent reviews in their articles and columns. They admittedly liked many of the wines, and it was rumored that they all knew exactly which barrels contained those private batches of their favorite Zinfandel, and when the cellar crew planned to bottle them. But when evaluated by the same standards used on classic European varieties, Zinfandel often didn't measure up. Sometimes, its fruitiness was almost too good — it tasted too much like Zinfandel and not enough like fine French claret. Other times, it was an out-of-balance tannic, alcoholic monster. There were at least a dozen style variations; it was unpredictable in its ageing potential, and so on.

The ambivalence expressed by these wine writers spread to consumers, who felt they could no longer be sure of what they were getting when they bought a bottle of Zinfandel. And if they found one they liked, they were afraid of being seen as country bumpkins for saying so. Their ambivalence led to depressed sales. Shelf space for Zinfandel in the stores shrank dramatically.

This ambivalence towards Zinfandel during the early 1980s mystified me, and before I knew I had begun, I was engaged in a quest to trace its source. Soon, I learned that as early as 1869, Zinfandel was sufficiently respected to be varietally identified on wine bottle labels. Although it wasn't widely named on labels, it was the grape identified more often than any other varietal until well after Repeal. Whether or not its presence was proclaimed by name on the label, to many growers and producers in those pre-Prohibition days, it was a revered grape.

I wondered why it now seemed to be such a pariah.

It wasn't until August of 1984, when I made my first fateful journey to Amador County, that some additional light was shed upon my question. I had traveled up to meet Daniel D'Agostini, a contributing photographer, as I was, for *Wine Country* Magazine. Daniel's family had owned D'Agostini Winery from 1911 to 1984. In fact, they had just sold the winery that spring. (D'Agostini Winery is now Sobon Estate, and is a State Historical Site.) Little did I realize that I was journeying to Zinfandel Country itself when I turned onto Shenandoah Road out of Plymouth that gorgeous late

August morning. My heart was soon to be shot through by one of Cupid's double-tipped arrows.

Less than one-half mile out of Plymouth, I took the left fork, as instructed, and soon found myself climbing between vineyards of gnarly head trained vines, their gold- and bronze-tinged leaves unable to conceal the luscious clusters of blue-black Zinfandel dropping among them. Lines from D.H. Lawrence's poem "Grapes" came to mind:

See how black, how blue-black
Globed in Egyptian darkness
Dropping among his leaves
Hangs the dark grape. [20]

I was enraptured.

The road climbed, and as I passed by the eastern intersection of Steiner Road and Shenandoah Road, in the rear-view mirror I could see Sacramento Valley under a dismal bluish haze, falling away from reality. I felt as if I were entering an enchanted land.

I met the slender, brown-eyed, soft-spoken Daniel in his partly finished, hand-built two-story studio that stood at the edge of the walnut grove behind the family house. The early afternoon was still and warm. Just the hum of bees among the flowers, and squawks of a few Stellar's Jays broke the silence. Daniel showed me his personally designed darkroom, and pulled out portfolios of his lovely black and white photography. We sat on the steps of the unfinished studio and talked in the company of his cat, drinking old-fashioned D'Agostini Zinfandel and Reserve Burgundy from the family cellar. The Zinfandel was delicious, and I didn't feel like a country bumpkin for thinking so.

Sometime later, he gave me a walking tour of the D'Agostini vineyards, among vines he hand-hoed as a teenager, and the historic winery (the third bonded winery in California). He took me to meet his then-living 84-year-old grandmother, Carlota, who lived in the house built on the hillside over the wine storage "caves" below. He showed me rows of 20,000-gallon redwood fermentation and storage tanks that he cleaned regularly when he was a teenager. A note of sadness underlay his voice as he recounted those delightful days; he had found it difficult to reconcile the family's sale of the winery.

On one of my next visits, Daniel gave me a grand tour of Shenandoah Valley. Soon after turning off Shenandoah Road onto Schoolhouse Road, which loops through vineyards and walnut groves and little fields of fluffy sheep, past Monteviña Winery, and back to Shenandoah Road, he indicated a small vineyard of Zinfandel, and remarked, "That's the home of the Deavers, and some of the vineyards that made Sutter Home Winery famous. The historic Davis Vineyard, which was planted in the late 1800s by Ken Deaver's stepfather, is up on that hill behind us."

---

[20] D.H. Lawrence, *The Complete Poems of D.H. Lawrence*, Eds. Vivian de Sola Pinto and Warren Roberts (New York: Viking Press, 1964, 1971), 286

I was speechless. These little vineyards hidden away in this little valley way up here! Could that old Davis Vineyard really be the vineyard that my San Francisco roommate's Zinfandel was made from? Indeed it was.

Now, I had to find out more about this mysterious grape whose ability to cast a magical spell seemed undiminished despite years of obscurity, neglect, and modern-day ambivalence. "You need to talk to Leon Sobon of Shenandoah Vineyards, just over on Steiner Road," Daniel suggested. "He left a successful ceramics engineering career in Silicon Valley in 1977 — he even has a couple of break-through patents to his name — to move his six kids (all in school), and his wife up here to make Zinfandel. He and his wife, Shirley, probably can give you lots of answers. Next time you come up, I'll take you over to meet them."

A few weeks later, Daniel and I sat down with the Sobons to a lunch of scallops in a wine sauce over fettuccini that Leon had prepared. A couple of their friends and the children who were still at home joined us. With a view out of the dining room window over the golden rolling hills to the north, I began to hear of how Zinfandel, and Amador County, had woven its magic on Leon as a home winemaker. He told us how long it took him to convince his wife and family to join him in this monumental lifestyle change. Shenandoah Vineyards, established in 1977, became the third bonded full-time winery in Amador County — after D'Agostini, Monteviña Wines, and three tiny "weekend" wineries: Story, 1973; Stoneridge, 1975; and Argonaut, 1976.

From Leon, I learned that Amador Zinfandels were at least part of the cause for the ambivalence I had discovered. It had started with Sutter Home's famous 1968 Deaver Ranch Zinfandel. A "monster" by any definition, it has been described to me as high alcohol (over 15 percent), tannic, and with the rich flavors of moist raisins and prunes that came from the super-ripe state of the grapes at harvest — which traditionally back then occurred after deer-hunting season. Unlike anything that had ever appeared at wine tasting competitions, this Sutter Home Zinfandel simply blew away the competition at a Berkeley wine festival in 1971 — which was exactly what owner Bob Trinchero intended.

I later learned that in 1970, Ridge's founding winemaker, Dave Bennion, was also looking to produce a big, rich, late harvest Zinfandel. In Occidental Vineyard, Sonoma County, owned by Robert von Weidlich, he found what he wanted.

"Occidental Vineyard Zinfandel was exactly what Bennion was looking for to make a late harvest benchmark Zinfandel," recalled Robert when I talked to him a few years later about his vineyard. Robert had bought the vineyard in 1968. Situated on Harrison Grade Road just outside the village of Occidental, it occupies land that used to be forested with coastal redwood trees. The soil, called Gold Ridge Loam, produces fruit with high acids (13 g/L). This means that the fruit needs to be 26° Brix or more at harvest in order to produce balanced and flavorful wines. Grapes like these can produce big wines with a bottle life of up to 20 years.

Exactly what Bennion was looking for. Such was Bennion's enthusiasm for the grapes, said Robert, that Bennion offered him a contract that paid his mortgage for two years. Although the going price for Zinfandel grapes then was only $175 per ton, Bennion offered Weidlich $650 per ton, plus $100 per ton for each degree over 24° Brix, plus $100 per ton for shrinkage. The grapes, about 15 tons, were harvested at 29° Brix.

By all reports, the wine was phenomenal. According to Paul Draper, winemaker since 1970 for Ridge Vineyards, it was still a beautiful wine 20 plus years later — just as von Weidlich and Bennion had predicted. Bennion bought Occidental Vineyard Zinfandel grapes through 1973.

With successes like these, it was inevitable that a "bigger must be better" philosophy would take hold of producers hoping to cash in on a monster Zinfandel phenomenon.

Leon himself admitted to holding that philosophy when he began.

"Between 1974 and 1978, the big, rich, tannic wines of Ridge and Sutter Home had acquired cult status. Many winemakers had come to believe that overripe was better than ripe. I was one of them. In fact, those were the kind of wines I came up here in 1977 to make," he recalled. "However, it was a belief that somewhat spoiled Zinfandel's reputation in the late 1970s and early 1980s, since few wines could carry such high alcohol levels and stay in balance."

By the time I met Leon in 1985, he had long since come to his senses, and was working diligently, and with increasing success, to produce a balanced, under 15 percent alcohol Amador Zinfandel wine from its legendary old vines. His 1982, 1983, and 1984 Zinfandels were my first Amador Zinfandels, besides the V. Sattui, made with a fine wine focus. These wines became benchmarks for me of what Zinfandel as a red table wine could be. I have since learned that they became benchmarks for a few winemakers as well.

Admittedly, it was quite a romantic beginning for me, made even more so by the sweetness of memory. Yet it could not have happened otherwise. Zinfandel is a mysterious and irresistible grape. Its origins are uncertain, and it has thrived for decades in all regions throughout the State. It has withstood innumerable winemaking and viticultural impositions. It has often been described as a peasant grape, because of its unabashed fruitiness and sensuously delicious flavors and textures.

Perhaps it took a peasant hardiness and unbridled lustiness for Zinfandel to have survived its many trials over so many decades. Perhaps it took peasant roots not only to have gone deeply into the ground in search of water and nutrients, but also to have gone deeply into the hearts of growers, many of whom could never quite part with their last few acres of old vines — no matter how cheap the price offered for their grapes became.

Within the year, the talented and charming Daniel and I had gone our separate ways; my romance with the mysterious Zinfandel, however, was just beginning. In my search for the source of the ambivalent feelings that Zinfandel was causing throughout the wine community, I, too, became its captive. Its deep and ancient roots had found their way into my heart as well.

In winter of 1986, I approached Don Neel, editor and publisher of *Practical Winery & Vineyard* (***PWV***), about my enchantment with the Sobons and their Shenandoah Vineyards. "If you want to write a report on Zinfandel for *Practical Winery & Vineyard*," Neel responded to my proposal, "you can't just stop at Amador County. There are other 'best' locations for Zinfandel, you know. You'll have to talk to producers from Mendocino, Sonoma, and Napa counties as well. And there are some good Zinfandel plantings in El Dorado County, the Lodi-Woodbridge region, and the Central Coast region of Paso Robles," he added. "What interests me about Zinfandel is what, if any, distinct regional character have winemakers found in the Zinfandel fruit they work with, what challenge does this regional character present to them, and how do they work with it. Do you think you can handle that?"

Although a little taken aback by Neel's characteristic bluntness, I readily seized the opportunity to do the story — especially when I saw the list of names he wanted me to start with. It turned out to be a list that grew as word got out that ***PWV*** was researching an in-depth report on Zinfandel. Neel never insisted, however, that I go beyond Amador, Mendocino, Sonoma, and Napa counties. For my part, given my limited time, the growing list of producers I already had to interview in the Amador and North Coast regions, and the need to stay within ***PWV's*** editorial guidelines, I never managed to investigate these other plantings and producers until recently.

Perhaps just as well, since in the intervening 10 years, El Dorado County and the South Central Coast region of Paso Robles have experienced an explosion of newly bonded wineries dedicated to producing premium Zinfandel wine. Zinfandel plantings intelligently matched to soil, microclimates, and location have also dramatically increased.

In the Lodi-Woodbridge region, long-established growers have begun producing small lots of estate Zinfandel under their own labels. Zinfandel plantings are steadily increasing. The Lodi-Woodbridge region also is the most important source of Zinfandel grapes for the large case production of value-priced Zinfandel table wine by such producers as Sebastiani under its Talus and Vendange labels, Ravenswood for its Vintners Blend, and Gallo, Mondavi-Woodbridge, Sutter Home, and Fetzer.

In Riverside County, the Zinfandel vineyards are all at least 50 years old. Small lot bottlings of premium Zinfandel from these few remaining, mostly pre-Prohibition Zinfandel vineyards in the Cucamonga Valley made by regional producers are winning acclaim at affordable prices. Premium producers from other regions are also now looking at both the Lodi-Woodbridge and Cucamonga Valley regions as still-available sources of old-vine Zinfandel vineyards for their high-end red table wines.

Also, viticultural and winemaking practices in these regions have benefited significantly from the mistakes and subsequent improved understanding of Zinfandel growing and production in the regions better known for premium dry red table wines.

My first ***PWV*** report, "The Challenge of Zinfandel," was published in May-June and July-August, 1987.

This led to my second two-part report, "Zinfandel: The Affordable Luxury," published by ***PWV*** in fall of 1993. It analyzed the economics of growing and producing Zinfandel.

Beginning with my initial assignment for ***PWV*** and ending with my 1996-97 sabbatical leave year from Napa Valley College, my exploration of Zinfandel has taken me to all the regions in California best suited to growing Zinfandel grapes. It has even taken me to northern Baja California to visit a 65-year old, non-irrigated, head-trained Zinfandel vineyard called Rancho Escondido. Rancho Escondido is located between Tijuana and Tecate, and is owned by Don Luis A. Cetto. Cetto also owns Vinícola L.A. Cetto (founded 1926) in Valle de Guadalupe, 25 kilometers inland from Ensenada.

In each of these regions, I have tasted many vintages of Zinfandel at various stages of their development. I have followed vintages from fermentation bin or tank to barrel to bottle. Producers from every region have provided me with vertical tastings, and I have learned to recognize the distinctive regional and stylistic accents in these wines — whether from south of the border or north of Ukiah.

It is to all these regions we now journey. Each region and its Zinfandel grapegrowing and winemaking inhabitants are unique, as was my experience among them. So hold onto your corks, and prepare to discover the many faces of the captivating Zinfandel, and of the people who grow the grapes and produce the wines.

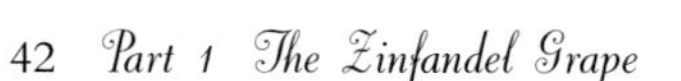

Part 11
The Regions

Sierra Foothills

Lodi

Contra Costa County

San Luis Obispo County

Southern California and South-of-the-Border

Lake County

Mendocino County

Sonoma County

Napa County

Within Sight of San Francisco

The Sierra Foothills

Amador County

Cowan Vineyard

There are four distinct growing areas within Amador County. Two of them are generally recognized as having different aroma and flavor profiles — Shenandoah Valley and Fiddletown. It was the Zinfandel of Amador County that first drew me to this enchanting wine nearly 15 years ago.

My favorite approach to Amador County is via Highway 16, the Jackson Road, which exits Highway 50 in Sacramento. In the spring, the sides of Highway 16 from Sacramento to Rancho Murietta are covered with a thick and dazzling array of multi-hued wildflowers. Upon entering Amador County just east of Rancho Murietta, the highway becomes an even wider two-lane road that gently climbs through meadows populated by sheep and cows, or by just a few rocks and oaks, until it joins Highway 49 about two miles out of Plymouth. In the spring, the meadows are a resplendent expanse of Tidy Tips and Buttercups; in the summer and fall, they are like gleaming antique gold.

Highway 49 climbs dramatically in a sweeping curve onto the plateau that the little village of Plymouth (population 750) is built upon, offering vistas of deep canyons and purple hills to the east. When you crest the plateau and enter the rustic village of Plymouth, you are at 1,100 feet elevation.

At the northern end of Plymouth, you make a right turn onto Shenandoah Road, and will soon find yourself climbing higher still into Shenandoah Valley.

Shenandoah Valley is the principal wine grape region of Amador County, and it seems to be one of those regions especially intended by Mother Nature for Zinfandel. A tiny paradisal valley of rolling hills studded with oak trees and rocks, it is just three miles wide by six miles long. The valley's elevation rises from 1,200 feet to 2,000 feet, which puts it above the daytime fog line and gives it an extraordinary number of sunny days.

The soil is designated "Shenandoah Loam," which consists of non-compacted decomposed granite. It is unique to Shenandoah Valley. Many aficionados claim that the reddish-brown soil gives the Zinfandel wines their distinctive earthy blackberry fruit character. The chief supply of nutrients lies well below the topsoil, which varies vineyard to vineyard from two to 20 feet deep. Annual rainfall averages 36 inches, which means the vineyards can be non-irrigated without putting undue stress on the vines. Some drip-line irrigation was installed during the drought years of 1976 and 1977, but mostly to start new vines. Mature vines are not irrigated. Dry farming combined with the dry, warm summers results in little threat of mildew. Growers seldom need to sulfur their vines more often than once or twice per season.

The first vineyards were planted about 1854, the same year the county was formed and named, and five years after the Gold Rush. The agricultural potential of the region had attracted settlers wishing to farm, not mine, in this "garden spot" of the Mother Lode. The region's first winery, and the state's third, was bonded in 1856 by Adam Ulhinger. It had a storage capacity of 10,000 gallons, and between 15 and 20 acres of vineyards.

Uhlinger was among the first Amador growers to supplant Mission grapes with Zinfandel.[21] In 1911, he sold the winery to Enrico D'Agostini. The D'Agostini family operated the winery for more than 70 years. During the family's ownership, the winery became designated a State Historical Site. In 1984, the D'Agostinis sold the winery and vineyards to Armagan Ozdiker, a wine merchant from Sacramento. In 1989, Leon and Shirley Sobon purchased the D'Agostini Winery, renaming it Sobon Estate. They restored the old buildings and remaining remnants of early equipment to their historic splendor. The facility today is a tasting room and historical museum. The community has donated much of the equipment on display.

Between 1880 and Prohibition, Shenandoah Valley's producing vineyards had grown to nearly 500 acres, mostly Zinfandel. The primary market for these grapes was immigrant home winemakers — Italian, Swiss, Basque, Serbian — who early discovered that Zinfandel grown in Shenandoah Valley consistently yielded the high sugar, high acid, and intense flavors they sought for their robust, old-country style wines.

---

21 Eric Costa, *A History of Winegrapegrowing in Amador County* (Jackson, CA: Cenetto Publication, 1994), 26

It was this same home winemaker style of mouth-filling, high-alcohol wine produced by Napa's Sutter Home Winery in 1968 from the Deaver Vineyard that stole the show when released in 1971 — and established Sutter Home as a Zinfandel winery.

Only about 200 acres in Shenandoah Valley survived Prohibition, among them, Teri Harvey's "Grandpère," the Eschen Vineyard (Fiddletown AVA), the Sadie Upton vineyard, the Fox Creek Vineyard, and Ken Deaver Vineyard.

By 1965, nearly 600 acres were planted to wine grapes, with 400 of those Zinfandel. By 1994, there were over 2,000 acres in wine grapes. Zinfandel is still by far the most widely planted variety, but it is being supplemented by a few select northern Italian and Rhône varieties.[22]

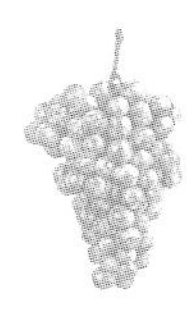

The Deavers

I met Ken Deaver Sr. very early one September morning in 1986. I had journeyed up from Napa to meet him and his son, Ken, Jr. The elder Deaver was a rugged six-foot seven-inch giant of a man. (He died in 1989.) Ken Jr. was a younger, but equally imposing version of his father.

Arriving at Ken Jr.'s brand new house set amidst one of the family's newer vineyards just off Shenandoah School Road at an elevation of about 1,600 feet, I joined Ken and his father at the long oak kitchen table. By 1986, the Deaver Ranch consisted of 200 acres of Zinfandel (14 acres being the original John J. Davis Vineyard planted by Ken Sr.'s step-grandfather at age 16), and six acres of historic Mission vines — "old keepsakes," Ken called them, as they are reportedly the oldest Mission vines in the state. Ken Sr.'s mother had married a man named Davis following the death of her first husband. That is how the J.J. Davis vineyard came to be in the hands of the Deavers. The Davises homesteaded 160 acres when they arrived in the 1860s, planting apples and walnuts as well as grapevines. Some apple trees on the property are easily 80 years old.

"Zinfandel grown in Shenandoah Valley," began the elder Ken, "is unmatched by Zinfandel grown in any other region. Shenandoah Valley Zinfandel consistently, year after year, produces the same high sugars, high acids, and intensity of flavors, while in other regions, the crop may approach Amador-like intensity only occasionally."

In the early 1960s, said the elder Ken, Zinfandel was the preferred grape for home winemakers of the region, who paid double the going rate paid by large commercial producers. "They knew their grapes," he continued. "You couldn't substitute new grapes for the old ones. They'd catch you every time. They could even tell the difference on sight between my grapes and my neighbor's grapes." Between 1940 and 1965, Deaver's home winemaking customers were primar-

22 *Ibid.* 72, 76

ily the workers at the Susanville Mills. Fruit from the younger vines, which Deaver had planted in the mid-1950s, he sold to Gallo beginning in 1962.

Deaver's remarks corroborated some discoveries that I had made in my earlier research on the region. I had been investigating why Shenandoah Valley Zinfandel grapes were so appealing, and had come across a clipping from a January, 1913, issue of *The Great West* magazine, eloquently praising Amador County's fruits:

"The beauty and quality of Amador County fruits are proverbial. The three great advantages of the climate there — abundant heat, continuous sunshine in summer, a dry air — taken in connection with the fitness of the soil and the great length of the growing season, insure the characteristic excellence of the fruit, and of the early maturity, great growth and abundant fruitage of the trees and vines. Heat, sunshine, dry air, and a rainless summer also minister directly to the curing of fruits in the open air.... All that a man needs to get a start in Amador County is sufficient money to buy a few acres of land, and the rest will come easy, provided only that he is not afraid of work and has average judgement for the direction of his affairs."

Ken Deaver

The wonders of Amador County's Shenandoah Valley Zinfandel could not remain a secret known only to foothill-dwelling home winemakers forever. The "flatland" commercial wineries, as folks in the foothills call the producers in the coastal valleys dedicated to making premium table wines, were bound to find out. And find out they did — through a flatland home winemaker, Charlie Myers.

Myers, whom Cary Gott, founding winemaker for Monteviña Wines, regards as "the father of Amador Zinfandel," is the owner of Harbor Winery. He is also a retired Sacramento City College English professor. He began home winemaking about 1950, while at University of California, Berkeley. Myers was one of the first flatlanders to go into home winemaking, he told me when I met him at his winery one spring day in 1987, while he was still a professor. His discovery of Shenandoah Valley Zinfandel occurred by chance in late October 1963 through his friendship with Dr. Gene Story, who had already founded tiny Story Winery. Charlie was looking for some Muscat to round out his cellar. His inquiry revealed that the Muscat of the Lodi area was all picked. Through his friendship with Dr. Story, he found himself directed to the Deaver ranch.

Finding his way one misty Saturday morning (after much assistance with directions from neighbors along the way) to the home of Ken Deaver, Charlie found his Muscat. He bought 132 pounds for $6.60. While there, he noticed some other grapes.

"What are these?" he asked.

"Zinfandel," was Deaver's reply.

"Zinfandel !" exclaimed Myers. "They don't look like any Zinfandel I've ever seen."

Zinfandel nonetheless they were. I asked Charlie why this discovery so amazed him.

"Well," he said, "they were looser in the bunch than flatland grapes, and darker, and cleaner, much cleaner. They were free of mildew and bunch rot."

Two years later, Charlie got back to Deaver and bought some Zinfandel at $75 per ton. When he tested them out, the sugar content was 25° Brix; the acid, 8.2 grams per liter (g/L).

"The acid-sugar balance was just beautiful," recalled Charlie. "That is the one truly exceptional quality of Shenandoah Valley Zinfandel — their high sugar *and* high acid."

The early home winemakers, of course, prized these qualities. For one thing, high alcohol wines keep — an important factor to winemakers who added neither chemicals nor preservatives of any kind. As Charlie put it, "Nothing is going to happen to wines with 16 percent or 17 percent alcohol."

Charlie gave some of his 1965 vintage to Darrel Corti, a Sacramento wine merchant, and through Corti, it became the wine that introduced Bob Trinchero, proprietor of Sutter Home Winery in Napa Valley, to Amador Zinfandel.

Trinchero shared with me his oft-told story of how he was in Sacramento having dinner with Corti one spring evening in 1968. Prices for Napa Valley grapes had risen to $200 per ton, and Bob, who until 1984 owned no vineyards, was expressing to Darrel his need to find cheaper grapes, and also his desire to make a wine that would give him an edge in what was becoming a competitive marketplace. Darrel recommended Shenandoah Valley Zinfandel. To back up his recommendation, he gave Bob a taste of Myers' 1965 vintage. Duly impressed, Bob, accompanied by Myers and Corti, soon after went to Shenandoah Valley to meet Ken Deaver.

"I signed a contract that day for 20 tons," said Bob. "That was spring of 1968. The next year, I bought 30 tons, and by 1971, I was buying Deaver's entire crop, and have been doing so ever since."

When the Deaver grapes were delivered to Sutter Home Winery that fall of 1968, they came in at a sugar level of 32° Brix. Trinchero had not thought to specify what sugar level he wanted (around 24° Brix). Therefore, Deaver picked for Sutter Home at the same time he picked for his home wine market: after deer-hunting season. So Sutter Home's 1968 vintage was a robust, tannic wine with a distinctive port quality, and alcohol over 15 percent.

Said Bob, "It was the best wine I'd ever made. It was unbelievable. So was its reception."

Sutter Home's 1968 Amador Zinfandel took first place at a Berkeley Wine and Food Society Zinfandel tasting upon its release in January of 1971, and sold out before the year's end. The big, mouth-filling, intensely flavored, alcoholic

Deaver Ranch Shenandoah Valley Zinfandel had indeed given Sutter Home Winery the competitive edge Trinchero was looking for — so much so that from then on, Sutter Home, which had been a multi-varietal winery, became almost exclusively devoted to Zinfandel.

It wasn't until October 1997 that I got back to see Ken Jr. at his beautiful lakeside bed and breakfast facility and tasting room on Steiner Road. Ken's mother runs the bed and breakfast. Still an imposing figure in his floppy felt hat and thick rimless eyeglasses, Ken Jr. welcomed me with a jovial greeting and cordial handshake.

Having only a small winery, Ken has most of his 2,000-case production vinified and bottled at Granite Springs Winery just up the road in El Dorado County. The Deaver label was established in 1986. About 500 cases of his production are Zinfandel. Considering the varieties in his production, the 500 cases of Zinfandel is one of his more significant lines. In 1994, Ken selected for the first time grapes only from the historic (J.J. Davis) vineyard for his Zinfandel production.

"Do you like the 1994 better than the wine you made from your younger vines [which are in fact 40–50 years old]?" I asked Ken, as he offered me a tasting of both vintages.

"No," he replied. "It's different, but I don't think it's any better. And maybe the difference is the result of vine age, but maybe it isn't. It could be the vineyard location, and the vintage. What we need to do is vinify wine from both the old and the younger vineyard, side-by-side, for a few years, to see if there is any difference we can attribute to age of vines. We haven't done that yet; that probably should be our next step."

I agreed with him that the wines were different, and both very nice. If anything, I preferred the 1994 made from the old vineyard. But I can't say it was better than the 1993, only different — perhaps fuller bodied and a little more intensely flavored.

Then it was into Ken's pick-up for a tour of the historic 14-acre Zinfandel and Mission vineyard off Shenandoah School Road. As we rolled slowly through the vineyards, we carried on a rather desultory conversation interrupted by my requests for photo-ops.

"The vineyard that was planted by your step-great grandfather (J.J. Davis) consists of about 14 acres, and all the vines are own-rooted, non-irrigated, and they date to about 1880?" I verified.

"That is almost correct," replied Ken. "The old Mission vines date to about 1850; the Zinfandel dates to about 1860. The problem is that we have to count backwards based on what history has told us, and look a little at records in the *Amador Dispatch*."

In the early November afternoon light, the vines looked healthy, sturdy, and reposed. It seemed a good place for a couple of photographs, so I coaxed Ken out of the truck and placed him among the colorful vines.

As we stood among the vines in the peaceful autumn afternoon, I asked, "What kind of yield do you get from them?" They looked capable of a respectable crop load.

"Same as from the younger vines — three to four tons per acre. Last year, we got only two tons from some blocks. But three is average, which is what we got this year."

"That's pretty good yield for 137-year-old, dry-farmed vines, isn't it?" I remarked. "Do you get four tons per acre very often?"

"In years when everything goes well, it isn't uncommon," he replied.

Although Ken had no idea where his step-great-grandfather got the cuttings for the vineyard in 1860, he does know that most of the still-standing old Amador vineyards planted later got their budwood from UC Davis.

In 1963, the Deavers began planting additional Zinfandel vineyards to meet the demand of their well-established California-based home winemaking market. Following their first contract with Sutter Home in 1968, they continued increasing their Zinfandel vineyards, a few acres at a time, to a total of about 200 by the mid-1980s. In the mid-1990s, Ken planted an additional 100 acres, bringing his total Zinfandel acreage to 300 — "small by industry standards, but for us up here, it's a pretty good size," he said. Deaver and Frank Alviso are now the two largest Zinfandel growers in Amador County.

"Are you the winemaker as well as the grower for your label?" I asked.

"No," Ken replied. "I made wine once." There was a pause. "Now I hire someone to make the wine for me," he added, laughing. "That someone is Craig Boyd at Granite Springs. Before that, it was Les Russel [founder and former owner of Granite Springs]. Craig makes our Zinfandel and our Barbera." Ken has his white and dessert wines vinified at Windwalker, also in El Dorado County.

When it comes to winemaking style, Ken is not a fan of a lot of oak, so his Zinfandel typically has been aged in mostly neutral barrels (three-, four-, and five-year-old barrels). For his 1997 vintage, he experimented with some brand new American oak barrels, and he also played with a tiny batch of wine aged in French oak, just to compare. "A couple of years ago," he explained, "I played around with ageing a little of the vintage in new oak, and it seemed to give the wine an added layer of complexity without overpowering the fruit. It made a really interesting wine *extremely* interesting. Whether it should be new French oak or new American oak seems to be mostly a taste preference," observed Ken, "rather than a quality thing. Some customers like American oak, others French."

The shadows were stretching across the beautiful valley by the time we got back to the tasting room. I felt a sense of completeness, that I had at last experienced a missing piece of the history of this paradisal little valley. Leaving Deaver Vineyards, I cruised down Shenadoah Road to Plymouth and beyond, returning to my flatland home in Napa.

With vintage 2000, Ken has increased his Zinfandel production to 1,500 cases, 1/3 of which is Zinfandel Port. He is also producing small lots of estate Sangiovese, as well as a red table wine.

Ferrero Vineyard

A few years ago, I was asking Bill Cadman, owner and winemaker of Tulocay Winery in Napa, about his secret for consistently making award winning wines.

"Start with great grapes," was his reply. One of Tulocay's greatest wines, according to Bill, was its first — an Amador County Zinfandel made from grapes from the John Ferrero vineyard, Shenandoah Valley. Crushed in 1975 and released in 1978, the wine was an inky-purple, full-bodied Zinfandel, and was simply outstanding. Recalled Bill, "It sold out immediately. I could have sold 10 times as much as I had made."

Although we had spoken on the phone from time to time, it wasn't until October 1996 that I met John Ferrero in person. The 40-acre Ferrero Vineyard lies at about 1,300 feet elevation in the corner formed by Shenandoah Road and the eastern end of Schoolhouse Road. The 80-year-old John met me in front of his white two-story house, which stands at the end of the long lane leading in from Shenandoah Road. He has lived in this house his entire life. A short, thin, slightly bent yet vigorous and charismatic farmer with a self-deprecating sense of humor, he was still doing most of the vineyard work himself despite a hip replacement that would have to be redone a year later. The view to the west was of colorful Zinfandel vines. Every aspect of the ranch looked neat, well tended, and healthy, including John's garden and the remnants of fall flowers about his house and along the drive. Even the sheep in the meadow at the foot of the vineyard looked carefully tended.

There was a decided nip in the air, so John invited me into his neatly kept but well-lived in kitchen to talk. He began by assuring me that apart from a "dust-break" of Mission vines that he planted in 1961, his vineyard is entirely Zinfandel. "I'm prejudiced," he explained. "Zinfandel is all we've ever grown on this ranch." His father, who came from Turin, Italy, at age 15, bought the property in 1910, and planted the first Zinfandel vines in 1915. John has long since removed these because they were on a low-lying piece of land and frequently suffered frost damage. He replaced the vines with walnuts, which are doing fine. "I could afford a wind machine today," he said. "But back then, no way."

About two acres of Zinfandel vines planted along the lane in 1920 still survive. The rest of the vineyard was planted in blocks between the years 1947 and 1982. Vines are head trained and pruned to two buds per spur, six spurs per vine. Although John dug a well some years ago and supplemented the rainfall with moveable pipe irrigation as needed, the vines are for the most part non-irrigated. The only other care the vines need is occasional spraying for mites and mildew. Average yield is 3½ to four tons per acre.

John makes a comfortable living off his Zinfandel grapes, but his father had to work off the ranch from time to time in the years between 1915 and 1950. "It was tough to make a living in those days," he said. "Price per ton of grapes reached a low of $25 in the 1920s and was only between $50 and $60 until well into the 1950s, when it began to inch up a bit." It took John until 1975, though, to break the $100 per ton mark.

John still sells to a few home winemakers who have stayed with him through rising prices ($1,000 per ton in 1997). Some of them represent the third generation of their families. "They really must like your grapes," I remarked.

"They do," he replied. "Some of them remember coming up here with their grandfathers, who bought grapes back then from my father."

John Ferrero

John's first commercial customer was Gallo. "Their buyers came out in business suits and ties, would take a walk through the vineyard, then come back and make an offer. I usually made a counter offer, and so they would go out and take another turn through the vineyard, then we would settle on a price — always higher than their first offer. I never saw anything like those Gallo buyers," John recalled.

Then Sutter Home became his primary customer between 1970 and 1974. Between 1975 and 1989, Ferrero again sold to Gallo. In 1987, he began selling to Amador Foothill Winery, as well as to buyers all over the state. In 1989, Sutter Home again became his principal buyer. His grapes were used mostly for white Zinfandel wine in the 1970s and 1980s. Contracts, however, were never part of the deal. "I never signed a contract in my life. Oh, it looks good on one side, but on the other side, it is all in the winery's favor. Forget it!" he exclaimed.

"What's the biggest change you've seen in your years as an Amador Zinfandel grape grower?" I asked him, our conversation nearing an end.

"In the early years, I would pick in October, with sugar content at 30° Brix, the grapes fully ripe to raisined. Now, I pick in August, at a Brix of 23° to 24°, and fewer raisins in the clusters. Sutter Home was the first to ask for less ripe fruit when they first bought from me in the early 1970s. Now, everyone wants them less ripe. But me, for my own home wine, I still like them at 30° and the berries ripe to raisined. I still make 100 gallons a year whenever I have a good second crop. I don't much care for these new styles of Zinfandel wine and all that new oak flavor," he said. "I even like to make a little Mission wine. Would you like to try some?"

Of course, I replied, at which point John disappeared into his cellar, to reappear with two dusty and unlabeled bottles of wine. Pouring out a little from each bottle into a couple of glasses, we sat for a few more minutes as

I sipped these robust old-world-style wines, while John quizzically watched me. What did I think of them? he wondered. Though the style was not to my taste, I recognized its intrinsic quality. I thought the wines were delightful, and I told him so.

Soon after, with the flavors of John's old style Zinfandel and Mission wines on my lips, I bade adieu to this cheerful Zinfandel farmer.

Bill Cadman never did make another Ferrero Vineyard Zinfandel. In 1976, a drought year, Ferrero had no grapes to spare. By 1977, Bill had established a connection with the Phillips Vineyard on Hagen Road in Napa, which he maintained until 1983, the year the owner died. Bill Moore ultimately bought Phillips Vineyard, and the Zinfandel grapes are now contracted to Turley Wines.

Tulocay, however, is again making an Amador Zinfandel from Tim Pemberton's vineyard just above the Ferrero Vineyard, as well as a Zinfandel from Chiles Valley, and one from the tiny Casanova Vineyard, Napa.

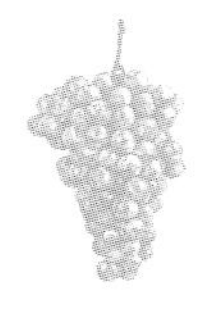

Shenandoah Vineyards

By 1980, Amador Zinfandel wines, which Terry Robards of the *New York Times* had described as the "biggest, richest, spiciest, most intensely flavored... produced in the nation" had lost much of their appeal.

For those winemakers still loyal to Amador Zinfandel, the challenge became how to make a Zinfandel table wine that kept all its wonderful fruitiness, intensity, spiciness, and berry-like flavor without it turning into an overpowering, food-hostile monster. The first to rise to the challenge was Leon Sobon, of the newly established Shenandoah Vineyards.

Since meeting the Sobons for the first time in 1984, I have visited Shenandoah Vineyards many times. It has never ceased to be a pleasure to turn off Steiner Road onto the lane up to Shenandoah Vineyards, which is flanked on one side by the ancient Grandpère Vineyard and on the other by sheep and a new vineyard.

My most recent visit was in February 1997. Leon began the conversation by reminiscing over his earliest Zinfandels — the 1977, 1978, and 1979. He had opened a couple of bottles just a few days before my visit. Those vintages were the tannic, full-bodied wines made from fully ripe to overripe fruit — in the style of Ridge and Sutter Home Amador Zinfandels.

"How were they?" I asked him.

"Fan-TAS-tic!" he replied. "Every last drop was savory! The 1977, 1978, and 1979s are all still beautiful."

Perhaps they were not as out of balance as the novice commercial winemaker Sobon thought they were in 1977, I suggested.

"Perhaps not," agreed Leon. "In 1977, 1978, and 1979, drought years, there was a lot of raisining, and tannins were heavily extracted," he recalled. "To make matter worse, I was drawing off juice for white Zinfandel, increasing the already high tannin concentration. Those vintages were out of control, unbalanced. Nonetheless, they were popular then; there was still some good press for big Amador Zinfandels. And they've all aged very, very well, but I don't believe they would be accepted in today's market."

Perhaps they wouldn't. Yet I recalled being at Shenandoah Vineyard's 10th anniversary celebration on the riverboat *Matthew McKinley* on the Sacramento River in April, 1987, where Leon provided his guests a 10-year vertical of his Zinfandels. At that time, I had found that even his first three tannic monsters had aged into lovely, chocolatey, earthy wines with a bouquet of spice, dried apricot, and prunes.

Wisely, nonetheless, by 1980 Leon had determined to change course and work towards producing balanced fruity Zinfandels with alcohol between 13 percent and 14 percent, and moderate tannin extraction. Back then, he was buying from the Eschen Vineyard in Fiddletown, and the Dal Porto, Fox Creek (the original Monteviña Vineyard), the Hoffman, and occasionally the Ferrero vineyards in Shenandoah Valley. All the vineyards are non-irrigated with an average age of 60 years. Elevations range from 1,200 to 1,800 feet. Leon's goal was to pick with only about 10 percent shriveled fruit, and with a Brix that soaked out to about 23.5° in the fermentor.

But getting the fruit in before it became raisined and overripe was always a challenge. "Small crops from old, dry-farmed hillside vineyards ripen fast up here," said Leon. "You have to be in your vineyards daily, sometimes twice daily, in order not to lose track of the sugar. Amador Zinfandel has an especially good balance of fruit (black cherry, cassis, blackberry) and spice (cinnamon). It can be overpowered by tannin and alcohol if you're not careful. Acid levels vary among old vineyards up here. Cool years produce high acid levels — a requirement if wines are to keep at all well]. Especially good was 1982, as were 1984 and 1985. Well balanced Amador Zinfandel will gain in complexity in the bottle for several years. It seems to progress in spurts, then hold, then progress. It perhaps loses a little of its berry fruit, but it will made up for in complexity."

Sobon's improved method of winemaking beginning in 1980 included fermenting his Zinfandel warm, pumping over twice daily, and pressing the wine before dryness to lessen tannin extraction. Press wine (the wine extracted out of the wine after the free run has been drawn off) was added back. Then the wine was transferred into 1,000 gallon French and American oak tanks to complete fermentation off the skins, and to go through malolactic fermentation. Following a year in the tanks, the wine was racked into small barrels for another year.

After barrel ageing, Leon gave the wine a gelatin fining, a rough polish filtration, then sterile filtration at bottling — a practice he adopted after a conversation with Cary Gott, who was winemaker for Monteviña at that time. "Cary Gott was my mentor, and showed me some data a long time ago where he'd compared his Zinfandel wines a year later — or maybe two years later, I'm not sure — unfiltered versus sterile filtered," Leon said. "I'd tasted some of those wines, and the sterile filtered wines were better. But they may have been better for a different reason. Maybe something else was going on in the wines not sterile filtered. That's how I got to sterile filter all my Zinfandels up until I don't even know how long — at least to the middle 1980s."

Perhaps, I suggested, the sterile filtering had something to do with their long-lived health. "Well, it's hard to say," was Leon's only comment.

Leon continues to be very much a man of his times. His Zinfandels are a product of his unceasing endeavor, shared since 1990 by son Paul, to better understand both his vineyards and his winemaking practices. There have been several significant changes in Sobon's Zinfandel program since those 1977–1979 Zinfandels — both in viticultural and winemaking practices. Much has changed, in fact, since about 1993, and most of it is in the vineyard.

One of the most important differences, emphasized Leon, is that he now owns his Zinfandel vineyards. Two, which he has named Rocky Top and Cougar Hill, are separate blocks in the original D'Agostini Vineyard — now known as Sobon Estate, which Leon and Shirley purchased in 1989. Planted on St. George rootstock in the 1950s by the D'Agostinis, these were the two most promising remaining blocks when Sobon bought the winery and property. Although the vineyard under D'Agostini ownership dated to 1911 (and before that to 1856 under its founder, Adam Uhlingher), it originally was own-rooted, as was (and still are) many Amador vineyards. Much of it succumbed to Phylloxera.

Between 1989 and 1992, Sobon produced a single Sobon Estate Zinfandel from a blend of these two blocks. "Before I bought it," explained Leon, "the vineyard had been leased for a couple of years by someone selling the fruit for white Zinfandel. The vines had been cropped for seven to eight tons, and had never been suckered. They were severely stressed, so it took my son Paul and I three years to restore them to vigor. But when we did, we noticed distinctive flavors from each block, and so we separated them, and named them 'Rocky Top' and 'Cougar Hill.' Rocky Top has about four acres, the Cougar Hill about three. The vineyards are adjacent, separated only by a tiny stream, but are on two distinctly different soil types — a splendid example of *terroir* at work."

The third Sobon Estate Zinfandel vineyard is the Lubenko, in Fiddletown viticultural area. It dates to 1910. The vineyard thrives, yielding flavors vintage after vintage unlike any of those Leon has experienced in Amador County Zinfandel.

"Owning your own Zinfandel vineyards makes all the difference," said Leon, clearly thrilled with the quality of fruit he has discovered in these well-situated blocks. "There isn't a grower alive who doesn't want more crop than the producer wants. In order to balance out the underripe fruit that can come with even a slight overcropping, growers may let the whole vineyard go to overripe. But overripe grapes are the source of a distinct and mostly undesirable raisiny, pruny flavor so often in the past associated with Amador Zinfandel. When we were buying grapes, we always sorted like crazy. And you always miss 90 percent of what you sort. You're just throwing bunches away as fast as you can. The fact that we are growing all our own grapes is one of the primary reasons for why our wines are better now than they have ever been. We have 100 percent control of our grapes. All we buy is 15 to 20 tons of Eschen for our Shenandoah Reserve. We now have no bunch rot, no mildew.

"Owning your own Zinfandel vineyards makes all the difference when you want that little edge in wine quality," Leon emphasized. "Now, we try everything we can to *not* get overripe. We prune our vines so there is air moving through them all the time, and the bunches are exposed to the sun. We also thin heavily in the spring. There are no hidden grapes down inside the foliage. Later in the season, usually after verasion, we usually bunch thin if we think there's too much crop for the vines to ripen, or if there's bunches that are distinctly pink. That way, the fruit ripens evenly.

Leon Sobon, Shenandoah Vineyards (photo by Larry Angier)

"But you also have to be careful not to *undercrop* your vines. If you have a vineyard too lightly cropped, it will ripen too early. The grapes won't hang on the vine very long. You have to balance your crop; you can have undercropped vines as well as overcropped — which will give you a relatively simple wine. Hang-time is important. That's how you can sometimes get full flavors with less sugar content, so your wines come in at lower alcohol levels.

"Our 1995s were picked almost into November; in 1996 we picked our last grapes November 8. Not a single one of our 1996s is over 14 percent. Some are under 13 percent, and will be some of our best wines. We're also 100 percent organic, and we do not irrigate. We only sulfur as necessary, and if there's a mite problem, we introduce predator mites. It's a lot more labor intensive, since you have to walk every single row. Yet it is all these factors that really make the difference. A good share of our quality improvement has to do with acquiring control over our vineyards.

"We can avoid pruniness now. The fruit has to be ripe, but I think another big difference is that we don't determine ripeness by measuring sugar content anymore. We determine by flavor, just by walking the vineyards."

"Is picking by flavor difficult?" I asked.

"No. It's relatively easy to do, once you know your vineyards and the flavor profiles that you're looking for. That takes years of experience. Every vineyard is different; every vineyard ripens differently. Sometimes the bunches ripen differently on individual vines in different vineyards. But we have finally got it. Rocky Top, for instance, is a very well drained rocky knoll. It drains quickly; the flavors there are easy to recognize because the bunches ripen evenly. It's not like some of the lower areas that have deeper soils, where there is uneven ripening, and you can have shriveled berries and almost green berries in the same bunch. Rocky Top is not like that. It is relatively easy. But the point is that there's a certain flavor that happens. You just notice it. You learn to recognize it, that the fruit is ready. And that flavor is really the flavor of *ripe* Zinfandel.

"You can always find that flavor in a couple of grapes in the vineyard, but what I've learned is to be able to walk the vineyard and judge when 80 percent to 90 percent of the grapes are of that flavor. That's what you have to do if you want the very best wines your vineyards are capable of producing. It's too easy, as you're walking along... your eyes are always attracted to the ripest grapes, and it's always easy to pick the ripest one and say, 'Oh! That's delicious. The grapes are ready. Let's go!' But you have to double-check, and be sure most of the grapes taste that way.

"We also constantly monitor vineyards for sugar content, acid, and pH as harvest approaches."

"What have you found the numbers to be over the past three years, that accompanied the flavors you wanted in the grapes?" I asked.

"It depends on the growing season, but usually between 23.5° and 24.5° Brix.... We've seen a correlation of the pH changing with ripeness. At harvest time, we usually check every vineyard once a week for the numbers until the grapes get close to ripeness, based on flavor. Then we check every three days. There's a definite pH increase as the flavor changes. We'll see the pH going along at 3.0, 3.1, 3.2 — and all of a sudden the flavor will start changing, we'll start getting that ripe Zinfandel flavor, and we'll double-check it just to be sure. And we'll say 'YES! Look at the pH. It is going up!'

"The pH does go up; it will go up a couple of tenths, to 3.5 or 3.6 — although sometimes it won't go above 3.4. So you can't go by pH alone to pick harvest date. The grapes still have to have that ripe flavor. In 1996, we had some pHs at 3.7 and 3.8, which is getting a little high. But it is controllable, and the flavors were excellent because of it. If we think the pH is too high, we add tartaric acid, to get a safer fermentation.

"What we look for in the grapes as ripeness nears is a *change* in pH, a relatively quick rise in pH. What's important to remember, though, is that we don't choose harvest date by numbers anymore." Yet Leon also pointed out that the Lubenko consistently has the best overall numbers: Brix is 25° or 26°; total acid is 8 or 9 grams per liter; and pH is 3.2. Couldn't ask for better!

Another significant change for Leon and Paul is how they barrel-age their Zinfandels. The wines spend much less time in barrels these days — one year at the most. The wines used to spend 18 to 24 months in wood — 12 months in oak tanks and eight to 12 months in small barrels. "I even used to write that up as part of my press release," laughed Leon, "that I aged in a wood tank for a year and in barrels for a year. Not anymore. Now, it's half that time, or less, and a higher percentage of new wood, too, all for the better. We use American oak on the Rocky Top and Cougar Hill, and our Shenandoah Reserve.

"For our new Vintners Selection, we chose French oak — because it seemed to fit. It suited the grapes. This is a very different style from the Cougar Hill and Rocky Top, or Lubenko. It's a lighter, silky, elegant wine, so full of fruit and delicious flavors you can't stop drinking it. The Lubenko goes into Slovenian oak — to go with the Slovenian name. All our Zinfandels get different kinds of new oak. We have found that different oaks seem to fit different vineyards. This is not widely written about. It just seems to fit.

"The Zinfandel all sees new oak, but only for a month or two — two months in new oak, and nine months in older oak — which means about 20 percent new oak. The Vintners Select gets about three months new French oak, or about 30 percent. The entire batch is exposed to the new oak, as there is a certain amount of new flush of flavors when a new barrel is used. We want that in the whole batch.

"Our style of Zinfandel today doesn't benefit from long barrel-ageing. Of course, part of our style change is a marketing strategy. Although we're market-driven, to a point, by bringing out these younger wines and making them just so delicious-tasting that no one can resist them, we've also helped to manipulate the market. That's why Zinfandel is selling so well. We're making something the consumers cannot get enough of."

Another significant change for Sobon Family Wines is that Leon no longer filters any of the Sobon Estate Zinfandels nor the Shenandoah Vineyards Vintner's Select. The only Zinfandel now sterile filtered at bottling is Shenandoah Vineyards Special Reserve — the "$9 bottling that goes to supermarkets and other big accounts." He hasn't fined in three years. "Zero fining. I don't think we need to anymore. We've developed our viticultural and fermentation techniques so we don't get the [hard] tannins. And the wines always clarify easily because they are all barrel-aged. The tannin in the barrels helps to clarify them. We don't need to fine anymore for clarification, or filter."

"What is it about your wines that you like better now?" I asked.

"I personally like these younger Zinfandels. What I am doing now, along with many other producers, is taking advantage of the fruitiness of Zinfandel, this beautiful fruit that Zinfandel has when it is young. In the old days, we would ferment very hot and very long, to get all this extraction, because we were trying to mimic some perceived ideal. But we would get the hard tannins, and you would have to age the wines for two or three years to get rid of the tannins. But by then, you would have lost the fruit. Those were wines you got tired of pretty soon.

"Of course, then we had the turn-around where everyone was trying to make table wine or easy-drinking food wine, as they were called for a while. Those were the stripped out wines, wines that were stripped of flavors and aromas as well as the tannins — to make them easy to drink. I was a part of that trend, too. I was still fermenting hot and long, then fining with gelatin or egg whites, and I would filter, filter, filter. I even filtered before ageing, when the wine was only six months old. Those are techniques popular in Europe and Australia. It was common practice even among UC Davis graduates. So we would D.E. (diatomaceous earth) filter our Zinfandel before barrel ageing, which strips quite a bit of flavor out of them. But you do have nice clean wines in your barrels. You don't have to worry about sediment, and can keep it in barrels longer without racking. Those wines were always good wines, but never great wines. Now, Zinfandel is luscious and fruity and sensuous yet without being simplistic from having all the tannins stripped out."

What I am doing now is taking advantage of the fruitiness of Zinfandel, this beautiful fruit that Zinfandel has when it is young."

Leon Sobon

Quite an achievement, I had to agree. But a nagging question still remains: Will these lovely, fruity, sensuous Zinfandels age as well as the earlier, more tannic ones — and if they don't, does it matter?

Leon responded, "Well, look at the Zinfandels that are selling. It's all these delicious young current releases. Anything older is suspect, and is a difficult sell."

Okay, so does that mean he no longer cares whether his Zinfandels age?

"Yes! I care about whether my wines will age," he hastily explained, "because ultimately, if they aren't still good in five years, my customers are going to be back at us asking,'What's happened? Why don't these wines age?' So, yes, how well they age is still an important consideration. They can't *just* be delicious at release. I do have a lot of hope for the ageability of our new styles, the Sobon Estate Zinfandels especially. The wines we've tried now — and we've used the same technique since 1992 — are all ageing beautifully — except for the 1993 Lubenko. It is throwing sediment, which means its fruit is also falling out, like it is ageing prematurely. It was perhaps too heavily extracted. Perhaps it should have been fined and filtered. But who knows — it may be marvelous in five years. All the others, though, are ageing beautifully.

"However, I don't know if our new style of winemaking is producing Zinfandels that will age well. I think the jury is still out. There's still a lot to say about how Zinfandel ages. There is this old myth that Zinfandel wines had to be monster wines to age well. And people still come here and say,'Oh, God! Such a big wine! It will probably age beautifully.' Well, that may not be true. Lighter wines age beautifully, too. There's always that comparison with Louis Martini wines from years ago. They were made light and nice and drinkable and there's hardly a wine in California that aged better than Martini wines. Those old Louis Martini Barberas, Zinfandels, and Cabernet Sauvignons were all relatively light, were drinkable when they were released. But 15 or more years later, they are still lovely wines."

For his part, Leon would rather drink younger Zinfandels. "But it might be a matter of availability. We don't have as many older wines to open and try as we do younger ones," he explained. When he does open one of his few remaining 20-year Zinfandels, he says, "I savor it to the very last drop."

Well, it was time for lunch, and Leon, like so many winemakers, is an excellent cook. Soon, we were in Shenandoah Vineyards' large, bright kitchen, with views over the rolling hills of Shenandoah Valley even to the snow-capped Sierra. Offering to be *sous chef*, I mostly watched as Leon with the speed of a short-order cook whipped together risotto with turkey and vegetables — a perfect accompaniment to the remainder of the Vintners Selection brought back from the tasting room. By the time lunch was on the table, we were joined by Leon's wife, Shirley, a daughter and daughter-in-law, and a few grandchildren who also came skipping into the kitchen for lunch after a morning's hike. This is how it should be, I thought. Wine, after all, was always made first and foremost for the family, and to complement food.

Grandpère

It's always a thrill to walk through Teri Harvey's 10-acre Grandpère vineyard. Head-trained and non-irrigated, the vineyard is located on a north-facing slope directly below Shenandoah Vineyards. Teri Harvey and her former husband, Scott Harvey, signed a lease/buy contract for it in 1984, when it was called Downing Vineyard. Upon its purchase in 1988, they renamed it Grandpère. When Teri and Scott divorced in 1997, Teri acquired full ownership. Teri, her three daughters, and her fiancé, Gordon Binz, do all vineyard care.

I met Scott and Teri Harvey in the mid-1980s. Soon after, Scott gave me an overview of Grandpère, which included its history and his viticultural practices. Grandpère was one of the first Zinfandel vineyards (and longest surviving) to be planted in Shenandoah Valley, circa 1870. All but one acre of its original 10 acres of vines are productive today. Ownership documents held by Teri were originally thought to pertain to this vineyard. But further research by Eric Costa suggests that Teri's documents pertain to a vineyard a few hundred yards to the west, long since pulled out. There is little doubt, however, that Grandpère is the oldest surviving vineyard in Amador County, and was probably planted in the late 1860s or early 1870s. Still healthy and balanced, the vines require little care in order to produce three tons per acre. But the vines weren't always so well off.

Upon signing the lease/buy agreement in 1984, Scott's first improvements consisted of removing the poison oak and severely pruning the vineyard in order to reduce the crop from over five tons per acre to about three. "This vineyard had a reputation for producing moldy grapes," recalled Scott. "In fact, when my mentor, Cary Gott, heard that I was buying the Downing Vineyard, his first remark was, 'Don't those grapes get moldy?' They did, but only because the vines were overcropped. Downing tried to get six tons per acre; usually he got five, which was still far too many. There were too many bunches for the vines to ripen properly, the vines weren't opened up for light and air penetration, so powdery mildew was a big problem. Properly cropped vineyards have healthy, disease- and pest-resistant vines that require less chemical intervention. Integrated pest management can work on healthy vines."

Scott Harvey

Terri and her father took the next steps toward reducing the crop and restoring vine vigor by further pruning back all the arms to one spur, so that the vines were like big bowls, with the spurs forming the rim, leaving the center of the vines open. Once Teri and her father had finished the final pruning, Scott removed with a chain saw any arms that would impede the tractor during cultivation and other vineyard work. "I removed three cords of wood that year," he said.

Scott and Teri farmed Grandpère with the fewest chemicals possible, which, said Scott, is actually better than organic. "For control of powdery mildew, which was our main problem, I used Bayleton, which is classified as non-organic. But it doesn't kill predator mites and other friendly insects, and does not change the pH of the soil. Sulfur does all of this, yet it is classified as organic. Further, I needed only one application of Bayleton per season, so I ran the tractor fewer times over the soil, thus compacting it less, and used less diesel fuel. The vines that I had to replace in this vineyard died from soil compaction around their roots, not from any disease or pest damage."

Scott's approach to producing Amador Zinfandel from Grandpère's grapes was to pick the fruit when fully ripe, but not shriveled, when the grapes taste good. He took me on a walk through the vineyard one September, when the grapes were within a day or two of picking, to show me what he meant. I was looking for a typical cluster of ripe Grandpère to photograph. After walking through several rows, I saw a cluster I wanted to make an image of. It was a good choice, he said.

"See these berries. They are the ones that need to taste good." He pointed to plump, blue-purple berries that promised a burst of juice and flavor. (I could understand why Zinfandel was first treasured as a table grape in the U.S.) Most of the cluster consisted of these plump, juicy sweet berries. But they weren't Scott's only criterion. He also counted the shriveled berries, as well as the green ones. "This is a perfect cluster. It has about 10 percent to 15 percent shriveled, and a few green berries. That's what an Amador Zinfandel cluster should look like at harvest. The ripe berries give the blackberry/spice character; the green berries, the citrus flavor; and the shriveled berries, the pruniness. You need some pruniness as part of the regional flavor. As for the numbers for acid, pH, and sugar, I probably won't even look at them — at least not until the juice is in the tank.

"You cannot go by the numbers when you work with Amador Zinfandel," insisted Scott. "The taste has to be in the fruit at harvest, if it's going to be in the bottle." Scott (like Leon Sobon) described the challenge of Amador Zinfandel grapes as a tannin problem rather than a high sugar/high alcohol problem. However, since tannin extraction is increased by high alcohol, these two characteristics of Amador Zinfandel go hand in hand. Scott was outspoken about what he feels is the mistake winemakers most frequently commit when working with Amador Zinfandel: which is to try to develop a recipe for it, UC Davis style. "There is *no* recipe," he said emphatically. "Recipes consider only the chemistry; they don't consider the organisms or the flavor. You cannot make a first-class Zinfandel by considering just sugar, acid, and pH.

"Amador fruit always comes in with numbers that lower elevation growers consider overripe. But that's when they taste good. I've never even thought about harvesting Grandpère, when I was selling part of the fruit, until I saw my buyers out checking the numbers. Then I knew that I had about two weeks after they picked until I needed to start tasting the fruit," Scott said, his face and voice lighting up with amusement. "Zinfandel is indigenous to Shenandoah Valley, and Amador Zinfandel is an authentic red wine, almost in the Old World style of a Chianti. Amador Zinfandels are now being recognized for the distinctive wines they are. For those who never stopped believing in the distinctiveness of Amador Zinfandel, and didn't try to make it into something it couldn't be, like Dry Creek [Sonoma] Zinfandel, the rewards are coming through."

To control tannin extraction, Scott said, "I liked to push as many whole berries through the crusher/destemmer as possible, as less tannin is extracted from whole berries than from crushed berries. The ideal berry is one that, when cut in half, is firm on both sides. You have to choose your crusher carefully when working with Amador Zinfandel, because of the high tannins."

Scott also used closed-top fermentors and pressed the wine off the skins before dryness —between 5° and 12° Brix, depending on when the fermenting must tasted right. "You need a trained palate to taste the fermenting wine because it will always taste sweet. You have to be able to distinguish flavor and tannin extraction over and above sweetness." By pressing before dryness, Scott explained, and allowing the wine to finish fermenting in small neutral oak barrels, he lessened tannin extraction, and retained more of the fruit components.

Scott gave his Zinfandels only a rough polish filtration before bottling. He rarely fined, since he believed that his winemaking practices had kept the tannins in balance, and he did not want to lose any of the delicate fruit flavors that would inevitably be fined out with some tannin.

Born in Germany to American parents who returned to California when he was 6, Scott spent one more year in Germany in 1973 to study winemaking. Upon completion of that study, he came back to Amador and began making wines.

Scott was winemaker for Santino Wines from its founding in 1979 until 1995. In 1993, he co-founded Renwood, for which he also served as winemaker until 1995. In 1994, Scott and his Renwood partners purchased Santino Wines. In 1995, Santino Wines became an asset of Renwood.

"I built Santino Wines, and with its label I won worldwide recognition for Amador wines," he said. "I've always had a dream, and that dream has been to become a leader, to be the best — from the soil. With Renwood Grandpère Zinfandel, I achieved that dream. I proved that by working with the fruit of the region, by working with what the soil produces, not against it, I can produce an ultra-premium world class red wine from Amador Zinfandel."

In 1996, Scott became winemaker for Folie A'Deux in Napa Valley.

Fifty percent of Grandpère's fruit is contracted to Scott Harvey and Folie A' Deux until 2009. The remaining 50 percent is contracted to Renwood through 2001.

After the legacy of Cary Gott's Monteviña Zinfandels, which many aficionados still consider the benchmark Zinfandels from Amador, both Scott Harvey and Leon Sobon were to establish benchmarks of their own for world-class dry red Zinfandel table wines from Amador County.

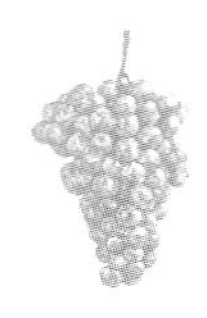

Cary Gott: A Retrospective Interview (December 1996)

Cary Gott's name comes up frequently as the winemaker whose style influenced almost all those who came to Amador County after him to make Zinfandel. Who is he, and why did he have such an immense and lasting impact on the winemakers who followed him to the region?

In 1973, Cary Gott, his wife, Vicki, and his father-in-law, W.H. Field, founded Monteviña Vineyards. Field purchased about 150 acres of land in Amador County, which included the Massoni Ranch — 60 acres of own-rooted, non-irrigated Zinfandel vineyard that had been planted between 1900 and 1910. Cary and Vicki moved onto the Massoni Ranch, which is known today as Fox Creek Vineyards. They planted new vineyards as well. Monteviña Wines was the first new winery to be established in Amador County in the 20th century and the second winery in Amador County — after D'Agostini.

As founding winemaker for Monteviña Wines, Cary set the style and tone for Amador Zinfandels for the next decade.

In 1980, Mr. Field, as he is still referred to by Amador winemakers, built a handsome mansion on a piece of the property overlooking the current location of Monteviña Winery, and moved to Amador. Just two years later, in August 1982, the relationship between him and Cary fell apart. Until then, the two men got along well enough, it seems, despite markedly different personalities and lifestyles. The fact that there was a distance of 150 miles or so between them no doubt helped. But once Mr. Field established himself in the region and was at the winery every day, sparks flew.

Cary's charismatic personality included love of fast red sports cars and generous expense accounts, which outraged his father-in-law. Mr. Field took a far more conservative and utilitarian approach to the wine business. Despite the attention that Cary's personal and winemaking style was bringing to the business, Mr. Field, according to observers on the scene at the time, felt a need to tone down Cary's showy image. Cary, however, was never one to be fenced in. In August 1982, just as harvest approached, he gathered up his family and left Monteviña Wines for good.

In 1987, five years after Cary's departure, Mr. Field sold the winery and 75 acres, 20 of which was in vineyard, to Sutter Home Winery's Trinchero family in Napa Valley. He then left the area. Jim Fox purchased the other 75 acres, which included the Massoni Ranch Zinfandel vineyard and Cary and Vicki Gott's homesite. He renamed the vineyard Fox Creek. Fox Creek's Zinfandel blocks are today known as Jack Rabbit Flat, Rocky Ridge, and Sea of Grapes. Customers for these grapes include Gordon Binz, winemaker for the newly established Villa Toscano, Scott Harvey, Buck Cobb (for his Warrior Fires), and Renwood.

When I met Cary for the first time in December 1986, he was executive winemaker for Sterling Vineyards in Napa Valley. Blond, pale-complexioned, lean and spirited, he was everything I had expected him to be from the many stories I had heard and read about him, down to the slender white hands which had long ago lost their red grape stains. As we sat in his comfortable office, he provided additional background on what I had already learned indirectly about his nine years with Monteviña Wines, and on his feelings about Amador County Zinfandel.

"We purchased a great property that had some great old Zinfandel vines on it. The Massoni Ranch Zinfandel went back to the turn of the century," he began. "We also pulled out some young vines that had been planted in the 1960s, just before we bought the property, and planted more vineyard, and planted new varieties. I was young and full of energy, and had been taught by David P. Massoni to farm the grapes in an old Amador style. Mr. Massoni, whose father had planted the vineyard around 1900 then lost it during Prohibition, had been manager since the 1920s of the vineyard Vicki and I built our house on. In fact, it was his house that we moved into in 1973 before we built our own. The original Monteviña Winery was in the basement. I had the connections with local and California viticulture people who could bring a sense of modern farming to what I was doing; from Mr. Massoni, I got a sense of how to dry farm up in Amador County."

"What was the old Amador style of farming?" I asked.

"Cross-cultivated head-pruned vines that really rolled with the amount of rainfall we got each year. If it had been light rainfall or if we had had a 'viticultural streak,' whatever that was — it could have been an early frost — the size of crop could definitely be altered, as it was in 1972. We had a small crop that year; the next two years we had huge crops. So we made very different styles of wines those two years.

"The viticulture was relatively simple. It's warm during the days, and the relatively cool air at night has low humidity because it's coming out of the Sierra. We're right at the point where the warm air rises out of the Central Valley in the daytime, and the cool air sinks out of the Sierra at night. It is a good combination for developing good sugars, good acids, and well-balanced grapes. So it was very easy to make very sweet grapes into very huge wine. We had some Zinfandels that had from 14.5 percent to 15 percent alcohol content. They were big, dark, inky black wines with a lot of flavor and texture. That was a popular style in the California wine industry at that time. You didn't normally see wines like that here in Napa Valley. People weren't making big, heavy, thick Zinfandel wines here. I use the word 'thick' to mean a lot of texture and flavor and style.

Fox Creek Vineyard

"When I went up there, I wanted to make big wines with lots of flavor and lots of texture, and I had many friends in the business to give me guidance. Maybe the guidance was different from what it is now, but I was young, and had friends who were older, and they said to me, 'Do this or do that,' or 'You should focus on this,' or 'Have you thought about this,' or 'Here's a style,' or whatever. Remember that there weren't very many people in the business in the early 1970s, at least small wineries. We crushed only 40 tons in 1973 for 2,000 cases — all Zinfandel.

"We also used the Zinfandel grapes to make many different wines. We were making a carbonic maceration Zin, and a carbonic maceration and regular fermented Zinfandel blend — which was an early-ageing sort of normal red wine — and also a full-bodied Zinfandel. If the year gave us the grapes, we would do a Late Harvest or 'thick extract' wine, which sometimes ended up being sweet enough to be considered dessert wine. We also used the variety Mission to make Mission del Sol, a technique I learned from Charles Myers, owner of Harbor Winery. That was a unique style.

"You know, Charlie Myers really has to be called 'The Father of Amador County.' The wine bug bit Charlie when he was an English professor at

Sacramento City College. Amador was the closest grape-growing region, and he discovered the Deavers in the late 1960s. It was Charlie Myers to Darryl Corti to me to Bob Trinchero that really set the style. I would have to call Charlie the 'Old Spiritual Leader' of Amador Zinfandels. I was a student at UC Davis then, in enology and viticulture, and knew Darryl because he had an interest in wine and I had an interest in wine, and our family wanted to do something in the wine business."

Cary left UC Davis in his senior year to go to work for Sterling Winery, becoming its second employee in 1969. "I had already worked in Inglenook, where my father was running the show. I am fourth generation in the California wine industry," he continued. "This painting," pointing to a large work hanging above the small table at which I was sitting, "was done by my great-grandmother, Daisy Cary, in 1894. Those are the varieties that the family grew in Lodi. My grandparents were also in the grape business. Then my father, after World War II, became general manager and head of production for United Vintners. He ran Inglenook until the end of his career. I started working there in 1969 for Al del Bondio, and came here [Sterling] in 1969-1970. Then we moved up to Amador County in 1971, and had the winery from 1973 to 1982, when we had the big family battle, and things blew up."

"I Think Amador Zinfandels have to show their regional style, which are big, fruity, spicy, fully extracted wines, but they should not be high-alcohol monster wines."

Cary Gott

As Cary spoke, I was thinking about how he had described his early Zinfandel wines as big, thick, full-bodied, full-textured wines of 14.5 percent to over 15 percent alcohol — wines that no one else was making at the time. I asked him what he thought about the fact that many red Zinfandel wines today are in that alcohol range.

"I wonder if those huge wines that are 14.5 percent to 15.7 percent alcohol content are really commercial style wines anymore. I think it is very different, the age we are in now. If I were in Amador today, I wouldn't strive to make those wines. I think Amador Zinfandels have to show their regional style, which are big, fruity, spicy, fully extracted wines, but they should not be high-alcohol monster wines. I think any wine at 15.7 percent alcohol appeals only to a limited consumer base in today's market. And, yes, I think most of the producers up there are into the proper style," he added, anticipating my next question.

"What do you think has changed in viticultural and winemaking practices that allows for the fully ripe flavors at the lower sugars, so you don't get these huge Zinfandels so much anymore?"

"Viticultural practices make a huge difference," responded Cary. "Many of the old head trained vines are going to be gone in the next few years. So now the decision has to be whether or not to continue to plant in the dry-farmed, head-trained style. If I were to put in a new vineyard up there, I would not head-train the vines. I would plant cordon-trained vines, so that I could use drip irrigation. I would want to experiment with drip irrigation and the right clones for Amador, and really see if dry-farmed and head-pruned, or trellised and drip irrigated vines, was the way to go. The value of drip lines would be to deliver precise amounts of water in a heat wave in August or September, so that the grapes don't bake into ripeness, but rather keep their moisture, and continue with their ripening pattern.

"One of the things that also has to be settled for the area is the level of oak in the wine. Here in Napa Valley, the style of Cabernet Sauvignon that we produce has a pretty strong oak influence. Does Amador Zinfandel need much oak? I don't think it needs so much. It's a piece of the picture, but I would moreso tend towards a collection of barrels. At the beginning would be a heavy toast, so that you got sweetness out of the oak, but not a sawdusty, dill flavor. I would want the sweetness to add some continual mid-depth to the wine, which means that you don't need to have grapes so ripe, so you're not dealing with 14.7 percent alcohol wines. That way, you get some sweetness and depth from the barrels, but you haven't hung a real woody note in the wine. I think that the contribution of heavy toast in barrels is an oak influence we need to learn more about."

In the past, Cary preferred Yugoslavian oak. He also used American oak from whiskey barrels.

Cary also reflected on some of the old style practices, which, when combined with the newest tools, would, he felt, yield big, fully flavored Amador Zinfandels under 14 percent alcohol. "One of the great Amador wines — and it's too bad it's gone — was the half-gallon jugs of D'Agostini Reserve Burgundy — a blend of Zinfandel and Mission and other varieties. There was a lot of brettanomyces spoilage bacteria, there was a lot of cellar smell to the wine, but it was good, sturdy wine from not overripe grapes. The Mission knocked the sugar down, and there were other flavors and textures in there; there was not a big oak influence. It was a great wine, and I know I drank more than a few bottles of that stuff! It was sold in half-gallons for $2.79.

"But it was a style of wine that came from a different age and time. We will probably never see those wines again. Yet we can still use some of those old-style practices."

Cary also enjoyed the wines he made that had a small amount of carbonic maceration in them. "It elevated top fruit in the wine," he said. "The key up there [in Amador] now is understanding all the tools you have as a winemaker."

Cary would like to return to Amador. "It's been a long time," he said, holding up his hands, "since these hands have been near grapes." He would like to experiment with the wine barrels used today in Napa Valley and throughout California — American oak made in the French tradition — as well as levels of toast, the different forests, and the best French oak for the "Opus I" of Amador County Zinfandel. "Why not use the most expensive French oak that has a much more subtle impact for those few outstanding sites in Amador County, like the area around our house? [Cary and Vicki's — today Fox Creek Vineyards] I consider that site some of the finest Zinfandel ground in Amador County. This is not the only site; there are a lot of them. For the grapes from those vineyards, why not use the best oak available?

"If I were to go back up there, I would want to work with all the tools available. I would use drip irrigation only as the last line of defense. You can see wild swings up there in moisture from year to year, which make a difference in your wines. My intention would be to give it a vintage variation more spoken for by the weather at harvest than by the total rainfall that occurs four or six months before the vines are giving up their grapes. If you look at an area like the Bordeaux, they have rains all summer long. In California, we don't get rain in the summer.

"Here in Napa, we've switched to drip irrigated vines, to give ourselves finer control. So I would look to going back to Amador to practice finer control of the vineyards in terms of clones, rootstocks, and drip irrigated vines on trellises. It would be interesting to see what kinds of rootstocks would work best in that droughty soil, and how trellising would work in Amador, with its warm to hot days and cool nights."

I was also interested in Cary's thoughts on the age-worthiness of Amador County Zinfandel wines.

"To me, the wines that have great ageability are the wines that have great balance when they are young. These are wines that have come from a vintage having a relatively cool summer and beautiful fall weather. The 1974s up in Amador County tasted great when they were young, and they were big, beautiful, balanced wines. They also aged well.

"Yet these are often the vintages that collectors have rejected. The 1973 and 1983 Amador County Zinfandels, for example, were relatively big vintages, with moderately big crops, and got maybe a bit of rain in September. Those grapes were a bit pumped up, and took longer on the vine to get ripe. So they had longer hang time, and the fruit was sound when it came in. As I recall, they probably got into the winery at about 23.5° Brix. But the wines were not 'firecracker' wines when they were young. They were just good, stable, mid-intensity wines upon release, so few people thought to buy them for cellaring.

"Real hard vintages, vintages for which you had extremely high heat and the grapes were forced to ripeness by dehydration, and which turned into high alcohol wines — those are more likely to be 'dumb' vintages. They taste sweet and good when they are young, but they won't age. Also, vintages that have a lot of tannin are usually too puckery and astringent to drink when young, and while some of that tannin will fall out during ageing, most people today agree that high tannins are not the key to fine winemaking."

In Cary's view, the challenge for Amador County Zinfandel producers today is to develop a regional style. "I am not saying there isn't already one; nor am I saying there is one. There is a small area with a huge number of new vineyards coming in, relative to the size of the area. Obviously rootstocks are going in, and different clonal selections. With all those things in the new vineyards, I wonder if there is going to be a consistent style. Are we going to have some people making Zinfandel from grapes picked at 24.9° Brix — big extracted wine with 0.3 percent residual sugar? And they may want to, and have a great market for them. Or is it going to be more of a table wine style? I think the challenge now for Amador's future, as those old head-trained vines die out and the vineyards get replanted, is to have most people making the same style of wine. That isn't to say that they are not now. Yet it is a challenge."

"Do you have a style in mind?" I asked, wondering just where Cary was trying to take me with these equivocations.

"Scott Harvey really set a very strong and very likeable style of Zinfandel with the wines he made at Renwood. Those wines showed a lot of class, texture, and style. To me, that would be an ideal style for Amador County," Cary replied without hesitation.

He continued: "If we still owned Monteviña, I would probably have a line of Zinfandel that sold for $9.99. It would be partially tank-aged and partially barrel-aged. It would not have a lot of young oak, but it would have some new oak, and probably have 10 percent carbonic maceration in the blend. It would be a very stylish wine, and would be quite profitable at $9.99, because I would strive to grow most of those grapes. For that style of wines, I would have the vines trellised and drip irrigated, and I wouldn't strive for a huge crop — maybe about 5 1/2 tons per acre. I would strive to see through the winemaking from a long-term perspective."

It was nearing time for Cary's next appointment. Did he have any parting words?

"To be successful in Amador County, you have to totally immerse yourself in viticulture and winemaking, and develop some new styles of winemaking — to be sure you're contemporary in making wines that somehow speak to the *terroir* of the area. Although I think that *terroir* is such an inappropriate term, since it is French, nonetheless the area does have its soil and climate, and you have to be well attached to it. When I was young, I probably didn't do a very good job. I just happened to be fortunate enough to have good vineyards and good guidance from a lot of reliable people. It's too bad I'm not still there," he concluded, "since I believe I would be very, very good at it."

I took my leave from Cary feeling his edge of sadness for the unfortunate circumstances that so many years ago sent him from the region and its Zinfandel that he obviously still feels passionately connected to. I couldn't help but feel as he did that if he were still there, he would be very good at producing Zinfandel from Amador fruit.

★ ★ ★ ★ ★

In 1999, Cary Gott became consultant winemaker to Renwood Wines in Amador County.

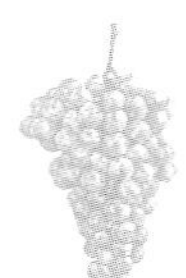

Monteviña Wines

Jeff Runquist and Jeff Meyers became co-winemakers at Monteviña when Cary Gott left. In 1986, Jeff Runquist departed, leaving Jeff Meyers as sole winemaker. Jeff Meyers has stayed in that position through the purchase of Monteviña by Sutter Home winery in 1987.

It was a misty, mild late October morning in 1996 when I arrived at Monteviña Vineyards to renew my acquaintance with this somewhat philosophical, somewhat laid back, and entirely engaging Jeff Meyers. Happy to see me, he remarked on how refreshing it was to have a wine-journalist come by to spend an unhurried couple of hours with him to talk about Amador Zinfandel. "No matter what kind of packages we offer the wine critics and writers, it's really difficult to get them up here," he lamented. We both were puzzled by such neglect. Certainly, I needed no enticement beyond the unparalleled beauty of the region, the warmth and friendliness of its people, and the appeal of its legendary Zinfandels to find my way thither as often as possible. Consumers, it seemed, needed no further enticement, either. Twenty thousand visitors came through Monteviña Vineyards in just 1996 — representing a 200 percent increase over 1995, reported Jeff.

It took Jeff a few years to get the wine quality back to what it was when Cary Gott left. "Cary's sudden departure really did leave us in a bit of a muddle," said Jeff. "Neither Jeff Runquist nor I knew which growers he had contracted with, or for what grapes. So when the grapes began arriving a few weeks later, our situation was about as close to chaotic as I ever hope to be."

After Runquist left in 1986, both Mr. Field and later Sutter Home stuck with Jeff Meyers, and supported as best they could his continuing efforts to regain Monteviña's reputation for outstanding wines. By 1996, Jeff had determined his approach to Zinfandel production from Amador fruit. He likes to maximize extraction to create full-bodied, full-flavored wines that do not have excessive astringency and bitterness.

"Up here, 23.5° to 24.5° Brix is really ripe fruit, which produces a wine between 13.5 percent and 14 percent alcohol content," he said.

"These are wines with lushness but without hotness. I think I pick riper than most of my neighbors, but I pick at less ripeness than Cary Gott did. He loved 15 percent alcohol wines, and established such wines as benchmark Zinfandels for Amador County, which is a killer reputation to shake off. If Amador Zinfandels are over 15 percent alcohol, I find they have a rubbing alcohol, medicinal character to them that I don't like. Also, overly ripe Zinfandel grapes impart a pruny flavor to the wines, and such wines don't age very well. Some of Cary's, though, aged very well — and some didn't. I still have a few of his. Some are still good; some aren't. His 1974 is holding up nicely, but the 1977 and 1979 are gone, tired, dead.

"One of the practices of the early Italian growers that we've been trying since 1995 is to double-pick the vineyard. The first pick is for the less ripe fruit, which goes into our white Zinfandel program. The second pick is for the fully ripe fruit. We are striving for the best possible fruit for our red Zinfandel program. We want the fruit as evenly ripened as possible, in order to diminish the pruny character. You cannot eliminate it — nor would we want to. But we can tame it with improved viticultural practices.

"Some of our changes over the past five years have been to convert entirely to head training and spur pruning. None of our Zinfandel is cordon-trained. The trend generally has been to forego production for improved quality, although most growers need four tons per acre to survive. So there's been some experimentation with rootstocks. Although St. George is well suited to non-irrigation, it also tends to set a lighter crop. Growers have been happier with the newer rootstocks such as 110R and 1103 Paulson."

Monteviña owns 10.6 acres of the old D'Agostini vineyard, a hillside vineyard planted on St. George in the 1950s, and 20 acres near the winery. An additional 80 acres has been added in 20- to 30-acre blocks since 1990, for a total of 115 estate-owned acres — most of which is Zinfandel. The budwood is either from the Deaver Ranch or from the Fox Creek vineyard. "Of course," said Jeff, "it is widely believed that the Fox Creek budwood originally came from the Deaver vineyard."

Monteviña has also made a few significant improvements in winemaking practices. Most notable has been the conversion to the tank press. A gentle press, it has enabled Jeff to add press wine to his free run, which adds a bigger middle palate to the wine without adding astringency and bitterness. Storage is in mostly neutral oak, with 30 percent new Seguin Moreau French oak and Canton Cooperage American oak. Wine is kept in the new wood for only four months. "I don't like a lot of oak flavors in Zinfandel," explained Jeff. "But a little adds flavor, aroma, and ageability."

For Terra D'Oro, he still uses only free run from the two best vineyards: the D'Agostini (1954) and the Crane (1968). Both vineyards are on St. George rootstock.

In 1997, a more dramatic change occurred: Sutter Home decided to separate the Deaver Ranch's Davis Vineyard Zinfandel for estate bottling by Monteviña. Jeff Meyers was clearly thrilled. "The 1997 vintage is just outstanding," he exclaimed, as he led me to the barrel room for a sneak preview of this first crush in March 1998. "It's just what I had always imagined it could be — full-bodied, dark-colored, full ripeness with little pruniness, perfect numbers. It could be our best Zinfandel ever." As I savored my sample, I could only enthusiastically agree. The wine was gorgeous — aromatic, deeply colored, and richly flavored with cassis, ripe sweet black berries and cherries, and balanced with a lingering spiciness. Jeff released it under the Terra D'Oro program, as the first vineyard-designated Zinfandel, in fall 1999.

As additional support for this program, Sutter Home has also provided Monteviña with a state-of-the-art facility. "Now, I can start making wine the way I've always wanted to — with no compromises," Jeff said. The huge new facility received its first grapes in 1999.

Karly Wines

Buck Cobb, a former Air Force jet fighter pilot and Berkeley-trained nuclear engineer, came to Shenandoah Valley with his wife, Karly, in 1976 more or less to retire. But once there, the lure of Zinfandel, together with Buck's love of fine wines, worked its magic. Soon, he was hanging out with his winemaking neighbors learning all he could about Amador Zinfandel and winemaking. Buck was especially impressed with the matchup of soil, climate, and Zinfandel in Shenandoah Valley. By 1980, he and Karly had established Karly Wines on Bell Road, and were beginning to establish a legend of their own.

On my first visit in spring of 1986 to their charming, secluded winery and tasting room off Bell Road, I was nearly as impressed with Karly's enticing wood-stove-baked crusty breads and platters of Brie cheese as I was with the wines Buck provided for me, both from bottle and later from barrel. Of course, there was method to this enticing madness: the wines and bread and cheese were beautifully matched!

Buck's enthusiasm for Amador Zinfandel was unabashed. "Even in bad years, you can make a good Zinfandel from Amador fruit," he told me then, once he was able to tear me away from the tasting room's samples of wine and bread and cheese. "Take 1983: the summer was too hot; it rained during early harvest; then it got extremely hot again after the rain. The vines went into shock. The fruit hung up around 20° Brix, and ripened, finally, by burning, by drying out. Yet the 1983 Zinfandel was a good Zinfandel."

Although he admitted to being "very biased towards old vines," Buck had found one "knock-out young vineyard" that produced wines with "the fruitiness, lightness, and elegance of a Burgundy." This discovery led him to acknowledge that, "Age of vines might not make as much difference in Zinfandel character as I had formerly thought. Today, I feel that the vineyard itself might be more important than age. The key is balance between open leaf areas and fruit. Old vines get it right automatically; with young vines, one must intervene and make it happen. The Eschen Vineyard is especially fine as much for its location as for its age. Although dry farmed, it is never water stressed. That vineyard functions photosynthetically better than any other in Amador."

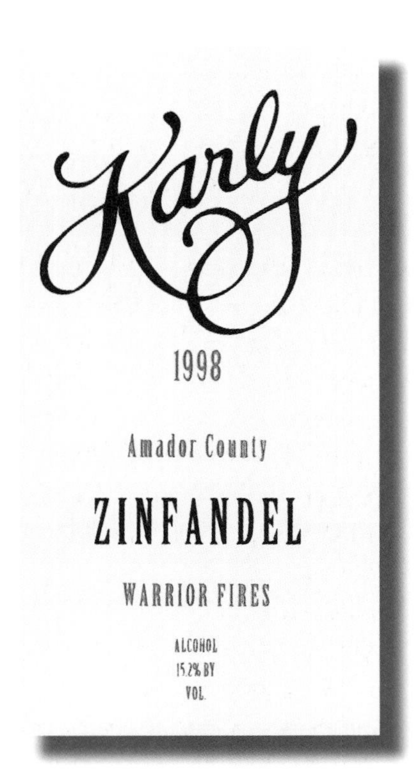

His favorite vineyard is the one planted by Sadie Upton in 1922. Buck, who had no previous winemaking experience, was also learning how difficult it was to pick the best harvest date for Amador Zinfandel. "It takes years to develop a palate to determine harvest date by taste," he said, "but I am convinced that for those who can do it, it's the best way."

Working hard back then to get a handle on it, Buck began harvest countdown by closely watching the Sadie Upton vineyard after verasion. About two weeks before anticipated harvest date, he daily monitored the appearance of the grapes, along with pH, sugar level, and taste. "The taste of the grapes will tell you when they should be picked. I'm starting to get the hang of it. For example, the Eschen Vineyard is almost always picked slightly green — 22° Brix, because that is when those grapes taste ripe. The clusters in another vineyard need to have about 10 percent raisined clusters before the grapes taste good."

In his early days, Cobb preferred the big, tannic Amador wines; he was not concerned if his wines went over 14 percent alcohol. "To get the body, flavor, and spice that Amador Zinfandel is famous for, in certain years one has to let the alcohol go that high. I am not overly concerned with the possibility of excessive grape tannin extraction, either, for two reasons: Amador Zinfandel juice has tannins that soften early; and I have a high tannin tolerance, and I have consumers with the same tolerance. There is a market niche for these big wines left by wineries who followed the trend to lighter Zinfandels."

Buck's approach has modified a little since then. In a January, 1997 phone call, just a few days before the ZAP 1997 tasting in San Francisco, he explained his evolution. Like Leon Sobon, he is moving towards ownership of his vineyards. In addition to his own three acres planted in 1981, he manages another five acres, and was increasing his own acreage by another five in 1997.

Buck also has made some stylistic changes in winemaking. It began almost by accident in 1987, when he picked at a less ripe Brix than usual. The wine developed into a Napa Valley style, which he liked. In 1988, he deliberately picked early again, to duplicate the style. Although Buck also liked his 1988, by now his customers, used to the big tannic wines he had established his reputation upon, backed off. "It took nearly four years to sell out that 1988," said

Buck, "and even longer to gain back my customers. Yet those wines have now developed into two of the loveliest wines I've ever made.

"But the winery is a business, and I have to be able to please my customers to sell my wines, and stay in business. So I've developed a three-tier system. The first tier is Pokerville Zinfandel, a soft, fruity wine made from a blend of vineyards, which sells for under $10. The second tier is Buck's 10-point Zinfandel, an Amador Zinfandel retailing for $16.

"My third tier, priced $20 to $22, has three wines: there's a vineyard designated bottling from the Sadie Upton Vineyard; there's 'Warrior Fire,' which is a blend of the best lots of the best vineyards in best years. The wine got its name from evidence that the valley's Native American population once used the sites of some of the vineyards for ceremonial fires. The Zinfandel vineyards used for Warrior Fire may vary vintage to vintage, but the 10 percent to 15 percent Petite Sirah I add to the blend is always from my home vineyard. And there's a Late Harvest called 'Deer Hunter.' With these tiers, 95 percent of our Zinfandel is made to please our customers; 5 percent I make to please me — and those few customers who like to put their Zinfandel away for a few years. So far, it's working."

Buck's winemaking practices have changed little. Fruit is crushed in five-ton lots and is inoculated with Montrachet yeast. The temperature is encouraged to reach at least 85°F and stay there for 24 hours. "I have found that the flavors I like are extracted at higher temperatures," Buck explained. "The cap is punched four or five times daily for about 15 minutes."

After six to 10 days in the fermentor, the wine, which is then between 2° and 6° Brix, is gravity-emptied into a mobile tank press, a gentle method of transportation that minimizes exposure to air. After pressing, the wine is moved into stainless steel tanks for a few days before being put into French oak barrels. It finishes primary fermentation and goes through malolactic fermentation in barrels.

When all fermentation is complete, usually in about 10 months, the wine is racked, the lots blended, and the blended wine put back into barrels for another year. At the end of barrel ageing, the wine is coarse-filtered into bottles, and held from 30 to 60 days before release. Buck does not fine his Zinfandels.

Karly has a reputation for age-worthy Zinfandels, and they do gain complexity in the bottle, but Buck does not believe that potential for bottle ageing is necessarily the mark of a great Zinfandel. "It was, after all, the British who made ageing an issue. They bought bulk Bordeaux and bottled it in Bristol. They found that it developed character and complexity over the years. Ageing was probably a necessity for these bulk clarets. The French, however, never used to age them."

I have tasted the 1995 Warrior Fire, and found it to be a wonderfully aromatic, flavorful, full-bodied, balanced Zinfandel — among the prettiest of the 1995 Amador Zinfandels that I tasted.

In 1998, Garth, Buck and Karly's son, who was assistant winemaker for three years, stepped into the role of winemaker.

Success with wine, however, has not kept Buck on the ground. Hearkening back to his younger days as a fighter pilot, Buck today enjoys aerobatics — an international competitive sport participated in by about 500 pilots worldwide. He flies a custom-built bi-plane with a "souped up" engine. The Eastern Block aviators (male and female) are particularly good at the sport, said Buck, their superior skill in part the enduring residual benefit of state-sponsored athletic competition in Cold War days. Buck holds his own, but the top pilots are usually Russian, and to compound the affront, most of them today have moved with their training system to the United States.

"Not to worry, though," said Buck. "Their wines are still terrible!"

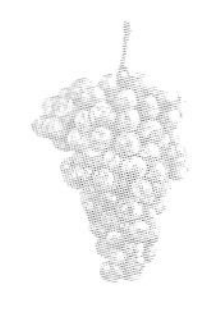

Clockspring Vineyard

Another grower who chose to plant Zinfandel in Amador County as a viable way to establish a lifestyle and earn a living is Frank Alviso. Frank and his business partner began looking about the north coast for vineyard property in 1972. They looked in Napa, Sonoma, Mendocino, and San Luis Obispo counties, and even in the San Joaquin Valley. Alviso, who grew up in Turlock in the Central Valley, remembers the vineyard owners in that region.

"They grew small blocks of some horribly obsolescent varieties such as Thompson, Tokay, Alicante Bouschet, and Palomino — good heavens — and a bunch of other varieties that probably should never have been there in the first place and had no useful purpose. These people did not live a prosperous life," he began, showing great energy on the subject. "These varieties all tended to end up in bulk programs, primarily the Gallo's. The people seemed to lead the same life as dairy owners, which was to die off or go to work somewhere for hourly wages, or to live in poverty if they stayed. Some people did come in and establish huge vineyards of primarily Chenin Blanc and French Colombard. They argued that while their grapes weren't worth much, they could get 10 to 12 tons per acre as opposed to the four or five tons of higher-priced varieties in other regions, equaling out the profits. I didn't want to be involved in that end of the grapegrowing business. As it turns out, the fashionable fad for the cheap, clean white wine those grapes were used for was a short-lived one, and left a lot of growers of these varieties ruined.

"Then, through a social accident, I met Cary Gott when he was winemaker for the newly established Monteviña Wines. Gott was the first of the truly new wave of winemakers in Amador County, and Monteviña was a truly impressive operation as a start-up. Of course, Cary was a magnetic and fascinating person, and we were quite taken by all that."

Frank's decision was also influenced by the Sutter Home 1968 and 1969 Deaver Vineyard Zinfandels. "Good God!" he had exclaimed upon tasting these wines. "They can do that there!"

With a partner, Frank established his 400-acre Clockspring Vineyard in Amador County in 1973. There are 260 acres of Zinfandel. In the end, Alviso chose Amador County because he not only wanted to grow the best, he wanted to grow "on scale" as a way to make a living. "As a long term investment, there's no point in growing second best," he said. "With the limited resources we had, we could start a real business here, rather than just being hobby farmers in Napa or Sonoma."

The property that came available early in 1973 was formerly owned by the Dal Porto family, consisting, Frank recalled, of "113 acres and change." Frank pitched a tent in March 1973, and lived there about 90 days, when he was able to replace the tent with a small mobile home. Those months in a tent cured him, he said, "of any taste for camping ever again. It was a great luxury to move that first mobile home in there, have a roof and showers — things one grows accustomed to; things not necessary, but things one grows accustomed to.

"About 65 acres is what we planted in 1973 and 1974. It had been farmed to small grains in alternate years for well over 100 years, as was most of this area. There was great demand for fodder to feed the draft animals in the woods and in the mines around the turn of the century. Some of the property also had been used for pasture, so we had to clear the scrub and poison oak.

"In 1978, the adjoining property, the Bell ranch, came on the market. A very desirable ranch, it had perhaps the most desirable soil and water of any property in Shenandoah Valley — something we couldn't pass up. Although purchased under a different partnership arrangement, it is all managed and marketed by Clockspring Vineyard.

"Clockspring was all Zinfandel in the early years," said Frank, even though Dal Porto had warned him of an impending fall in the market for Zinfandel grapes. "In 1973, Zinfandel was fetching $400 per ton, and Mr. Dal Porto told me,' This is a bad thing; this will lead to overplanting and low prices.' He was right; prices fell to $250 in 1978-79. In 1980, there was a pick-up in the top red wine scale. Tom Peterson, executive winemaker in those days for Monterey Vineyard [MV], was a friend, and bought all our crop until about 1984, when there was a change of ownership, and he left, and MV got out of the red Zinfandel business."

Frank's main customers today are Sutter Home, Fetzer, and several small Sierra foothills producers.

The block beside the driveway is trellised because, explained Frank, "I was uncertain in 1973 which was the proper way to train vines. It was also in part because I thought that since head training was the way the old guys did it, and trellising was the modern way, it would lead to better production and to some other desirable results. I was a little afraid in the long term of labor problems, and I didn't want to lock myself out of machine harvest. Since then, I found that machines don't work terribly well here, particularly on Zinfandel — and that the way it had been done up here for 120 years had a lot of merit. From 1974 on, all the red wine grapes were head trained."

"Did you find that trellising diminished quality of the grapes, or was it simply a matter of trellises being an unnecessary expense?" I asked.

"You get winemakers saying how you can't irrigate. Well, you cannot cause as much harm to the fruit with water as you can with stress."

Frank Alviso

"Some people believe that Zinfandel grapes grown on trellises are of lesser quality than grapes grown on head trained vines," Frank replied. "I believe that they sometimes are, because it is easier to overcrop the vines trained to trellises. It's more difficult to maintain control of crop level. But if you pay attention, do proper pruning and a little crown suckering, you can grow every bit as fine a quality of red Zinfandel on wires as you can by head training. Fetzer takes the Zinfandel grown on trellis because they are not prejudiced against wires [trellis]. If fruit tastes good, they buy it. They are not stuck-up about head training. But there are many superstitions about many things," he remarked, looking off at the distant horizon.

"Another of those superstitions," continued Frank, "concerns the judicious addition of water. You get winemakers saying how you can't irrigate. Well, you cannot cause as much harm to the fruit with water as you can with stress. The wages of non-irrigation are often stress on the vines. A stressed vine is like a stressed chicken or any other organism: it is more subject to disease and death. The wages of stress on a vine are often high pH in the grapes and flaccid, unstable wines. The judicious application of water at the right time maintains the health of the vine, and therefore grape quality. Depending on your soil and climate, you may need to add water early on, and then after verasion, if the vines begin to show stress in the afternoon. If your vines lose their leaves, you will not get mature, flavorful fruit. That's what water is for, if you have it. Otherwise, you are at the mercy of the seasons. If you have a great vineyard in Bordeaux, God knows you get great wines when it happens, which might be every seven or eight years or 12 years. Which is fine if you can get *that* kind of money every seven or eight or 12 years. You don't stay in business that way in California.

"Historically, the economics of farming up here in those early days were pretty marginal. 'Capital intensive' simply didn't apply. The price of grapes wasn't very high. Grapes were primarily for the growers' own winemaking, or to sell to home winemakers. So the old guys used short stakes, not for cultural reasons but because they were cheaper. There was no irrigation put in because it didn't make any sense. They brought the vine up the stake one bud at a time. This way, the vine developed a massive root system that could extract the native soil moisture before it had set any real canopy. So there are ways to deal with dry-farming viticulturally. One bud a year was how the old guys trained the vine. Of course, it was low to the ground when it began forming a canopy. And it took time to reach some height — three to four years. But they had plenty of time back then; there was no rush."

"Have you any idea where your cuttings came from?" I asked. "Were they from some of the historical old vineyards?"

"Except for a few cuttings from one of the Deaver vineyards, I have little idea what were the parent vines or vineyards to these cuttings. My best guess is that they might have come from the Mirasou Vineyard near San Jose," recalled Frank. "Clockspring Zinfandel does not taste like Deaver Zinfandel.

"Budwood, stakes, and vineyard material were extremely scarce in the early 1970s, when we were setting up. If the UC Davis clone had been available, I think I probably would have gone with that clone, when we were making those decisions in 1973 and 1974. Now, I am just as glad there wasn't any. Whatever I have in this vineyard, it is definitely a field selection, after the style of the oldest vineyards. There's some feeling today that field selection budwood, as opposed to a single parent vineyard, make for more interesting wines."

Clockspring Vineyard's average yield in 1997 for red wine was less than four tons per acre. Frank controls crop size by pruning and some crown-suckering. "I am not a fan of bunch-thinning," he remarked.

Since about 1987, Zinfandel grapes from Clockspring Vineyard have been used mostly for red Zinfandel wine. Notable producers are Black Sheep Vineyards, Calaveras County; Amador Foothill; Fetzer; and Sutter Home. Some acreage, however, has gone back to white Zinfandel production because Monteviña Wines, owned by Sutter Home Winery, is committed to producing its white Zinfandel entirely from Amador fruit. Of course, Frank would rather his vineyard go entirely for red wine production, but since Sutter Home is his biggest customer, "What they want, they get," he said. "And they like my fruit for their white Zinfandel."

Today, as Frank enjoys the sweeping views of the rolling Amador hillsides and his thriving vineyards from the comfort of the spacious, cheerful, almost finished new craftsman-style home that he shares with his wife and two young sons, he says with quiet satisfaction, "One need not live any better than this."

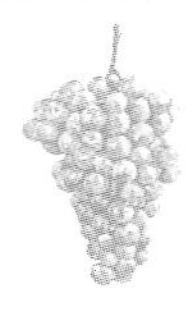

Domaine de la Terre Rouge/ Easton

Bill Easton's earliest memories of Amador County and its memorable wines go back to 1960. He was 8 years old, accompanying his parents on their trips to the D'Agostini Winery for its 100 percent varietal Zinfandel and Reserve Burgundy, the family's two favorite everyday table wines. As he grew up, he, too became a supporter and fan of Amador wines, finding the viticultural area to be one of the most European in California because of its expressive *terroir.* Among his favorites were his family's preferred wines from the old D'Agostini Zinfandels, as well as Cary Gott's Monteviña Zinfandels, Scott Harvey's early wines at Santino, and Leon and Paul Sobon's Sobon Estate and Shenandoah Vineyards Zinfandels.

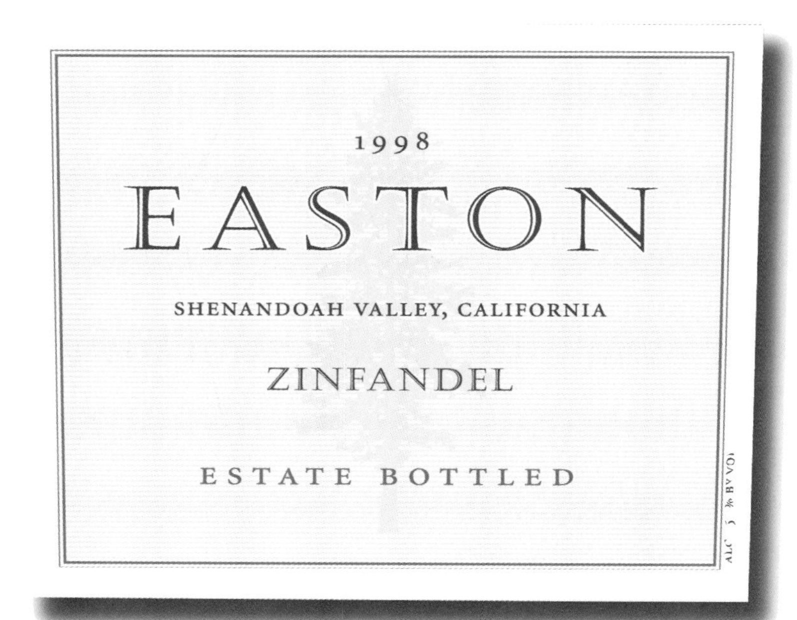

In 1983, Bill and his wife, Jane, began living part-time in Amador County while Bill ran a wine/restaurant business in the Bay Area. In 1985, they established Domaine de la Terre Rouge. Five years later, they began living full-time in Amador County. In 1994, Bill sold his business of 17 years and moved his operation into the defunct and empty Baldinelli Winery facility. Domaine de la Terre Rouge today produces two brands: Terre Rouge for Rhône varieties; and Easton for traditional varieties including old vine Zinfandel, Barbera, Criolla, and Cabernet Sauvignon.

On a beautiful, sunny and cool, late October morning in 1996, I visited Bill for the first time at his Domaine de la Terre Rouge facility. A tall, well-built man with a flowing mane of hair and full beard greeted me. He ushered me into the small, neat building filled with the pungent, heady aroma of freshly fermented wine. I asked Bill to elaborate upon some points he had made on the phone a few days earlier, when I called to make the appointment. He had very clear ideas about what a Zinfandel wine should be.

"I want my Amador Zinfandels to be wines to enjoy with food," he began. "So I want to have both power and finesse. By 'power,' I mean deep color, moderate extraction, balanced phenolics, and ripe and flavorful fruit that will yield 14 percent or higher alcohol. This kind of power comes only from fully ripe grapes. By 'finesse,' I mean not ponderous on the palate; the first glass should invite a second. The tannins should be 'unperceived,' that is, not noticeable; the acids should be crisp, the fruit complex and full-bodied in the mouth; the wood should support the wine character, but not be rough or intrusive."

To achieve these qualities, Bill insists upon French rather than American oak barrels. He also goes to great lengths to see that the fruit is not excessively ripe. "Different vineyards achieve ripeness at different degrees of Brix," he explained.

"I insist that the wine ferments to dryness. Excessively raisined clusters can make this difficult." To minimize extraction of the harsher tannins, he applies gentle techniques from destemming to bottling.

After destemming, which leaves most of the berries whole, he pumps the wine into five- and 10-ton stainless steel tanks, and lets the temperature go into the 90°F range in order to extract aroma and fruit. "High temperatures do not bring out harsh tannins," explained Bill. "It's beating up the wine during pump-over that does it. I punch down, and use some cap irrigation, then gently shovel the wine into the press when dryness is achieved. I generally even add back my press wine."

The wine is stored in French oak, which is replaced every five years.

"Wine appreciation grows through experimentation, and it takes a certain vocabulary and some experience to appreciate refinement and subtlety."

Bill Easton

"The popularity among the critics and many consumers — at least in 1997 — it may change in the future — of a heavy layer of American oak in Zinfandels, and the deliberate touch of 0.5 percent or more residual sugar, are simply a reflection of the unrefined nature of the American wine consumer's palate," said Bill. "We're a soda-pop culture, which likes sweet drinks and heavy flavors. Wine appreciation grows through experimentation, and it takes a certain vocabulary and some experience to appreciate refinement and subtlety. It takes a long time to develop a refined palate and taste buds. American oak on a certain level can be somewhat appealing in young Zinfandel wine. As the wine ages, this quality can become bitter and drying on the palate."

Bill produces three Zinfandels under his Easton label: old vine Shenandoah Valley AVA, old vine Fiddletown AVA "Eschen Vineyard," and a wine from the general Amador County viticultural area. His decision to use the Easton label for Zinfandels and Terre Rouge for other wines was made partly in tribute to his father, who is a Zinfandel aficionado, and partly for marketing purposes.

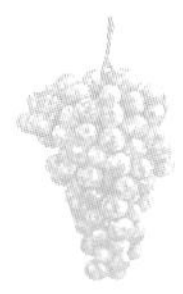

At the Caffè Via d'Oro

My leisurely wine-scented week that late October 1996 allowed me to renew old acquaintances and establish new ones among Amador's growers and producers. The week culminated in a winemakers' lunch at Sutter Creek's Caffè Via d'Oro. Organized by Leon Sobon, he and I were joined by Jeff Meyers, Ben Zeitman (owner with his wife, Katie Quinn, of Amador Foothill Winery), Bill Easton and Leon's son, Paul. Jerry Budrick, owner of Caffè Via d'Oro, provides a menu well suited to the region's Zinfandels.

The fruity, spicy elegance of Easton's Shenandoah Valley Zinfandel, which was mostly from old Story Vineyards fruit, nicely complemented my polenta appetizer. The "power" and "finesse" Bill Easton had spoken of were definitely apparent.

In the past, Amador Foothill's oldest Zinfandel source was the Eschen Vineyard, Fiddletown. Regrettably, said Ben, Chester Eschen had to pull out the section going to Amador Foothill because of low yields caused by the slow but relentless progress of phylloxera. Eschen fruit quality was always reliable, since the vineyard is among the best-situated in Amador County. But picking was always a challenge because the rows ran right up the hill. There was always an array of grapes ranging from under-ripe to nearly raisined; nor was it uncommon for the pickers to include grass and tar weeds as well.

"Yes, Chester gave you everything," Ben remarked with a bit of a wry laugh, "which has meant a lot of hand-sorting on the crush pad. We always wished for the fruit to come in a little cleaner, but that's the way Chester has been farming for years. So we have put up with him because the quality of the fruit gave us some very age-worthy wines."

Ben, who founded Amador Foothill Winery in 1980, first bought Ferrero Zinfandel in 1987. The age of the vines and the consistent farming practices of John Ferrero ("Every day is a grape day for me," John once said) seem to be producing better fruit each year, observed Ben. "Either that, or my wife and I are learning how better to read the vineyard for optimum maturity. Of the older vintages, the 1989 and 1991 are drinking very well, and the 1994 and 1995 are the recent standouts thus far. Now I often wonder why it took me so long to discover Ferrero Vineyard Zinfandel," Ben added, as we savored his still-holding-up 1989 vintage over lunch. "Not only do we get incredible fruit each year, but also John spoils us. We rarely need to sort out a leaf at the crusher."

Amador Foothill also added a Clockspring Vineyard vineyard-designated Zinfandel to its collection in 1994, making it among the first producers to give that vineyard a well-deserved vineyard designation on the label.

Amador Foothill's most recent addition is the Murrill Vineyard on Sutter Ridge (first vintage, 1996; 300 cases). Respected worldwide as a professor of dairy science, Frank Murrill retired in the early 1980s to Amador County to rejuvenate the abandoned 80-year-old Carignane and Zinfandel vineyard. Some of the vines had survived 40 years of abandonment. After restoring to health as many of these old vines as possible, Murrill cleared the remaining vineyard site and replanted with about 1,000 vines each year, to bring the vineyard back to its original 10 acres. The 1996 barrel sample of Murrill Vineyard Zinfandel that Ben brought to lunch was showing bright fresh fruit with soft tannins, and no pruniness. Well-situated, the vineyard holds great promise.

Speaking of his 20-year love affair with Amador Zinfandels, Ben remarked, "Not only are there a multitude of vineyard-designated Zinfandel wines on the market, the fruit lends itself to a multitude of stylistic choices by the winemaker. With style preferences layered onto the site-specific characteristics of the vineyards, you get a multitude of flavors and wines to choose among. There's hardly another wine grape varietal like it. Amador Zinfandel's distinctive character that comes from its unique soil and climate is still among the most esteemed by consumers."

"So you regard the 'site-specific characteristics' of Amador Zinfandel as a plus, not a minus?" I queried of Ben. After all, I have sat beside a wine critic or two who have scored down Amador Zinfandels just because of their detectable regional character.

"Absolutely!" he cried. "It's the soil and climate that make these wines so very special."

Bill Easton echoed Zeitman's sentiments: "*Terroir* is a plus, not a minus!" he exclaimed. "*Terroir* makes the difference in all the world's great wine regions, including Amador. Our *terroir* is similar to the hilltops of Napa and Sonoma counties with rocky soils, cool nights, and high average winter rainfall. Such naturally devigorated mountain soils force the vines to struggle. Four tons per acre of Zinfandel is a big crop, with two or three tons from many of the old dry-farmed vineyards in this *terroir* being the norm.

"You see, our soils here in Amador are largely granitic, slate/quartz, or volcanic rubble," Bill emphasized. "Such soil in conjunction with two other factors — our afternoon maritime influence from the San Francisco Bay through the Delta that pushes up from our river canyons, and our dramatic nighttime cooling that originates at 10,000-foot peaks of the Sierra Nevada just due east from our wineries — makes a perfect *terroir* and climate for Zinfandel.

"In Dry Creek Valley, the uniqueness of *terroir* is in its old river bed soil and its proximity to maritime influence. How warm or cool the summer is inland influences how much fog or sun the grapes get during the growing season. I think in Dry Creek, it is the climate that is a more of an integral part of the *terroir* than the soil. In Amador, I'd have to give the edge to the soil aspect of the *terroir* and the signature that it offers. But obviously *both* soil and climate are important in each region."

I was gratified by such clear, passionate, and unequivocal advocacy on behalf of Amador's unique location and the distinctive and beloved Zinfandel wines it produces.

Since all events must end, we finally disbanded. My dining companions returned to their wineries for the afternoon's work awaiting them, and I headed out once again from this enchanting valley and its legendary Zinfandels, reassured that for the time being, their future is secure.

The Sierra Foothills

El Dorado County

The Mountain Vineyards of Sierra Foothills

Lloyd Walker Vineyard

El Dorado County sits at a higher elevation than its neighboring Amador County. Though it was an important Zinfandel grape-growing region in the early days, only remnants of the old plantings survived Prohibition — most notably the 1908 Higgins vineyard. So its emergence as a modern force in Zinfandel grapegrowing is of relatively recent history.

El Dorado County wine grapegrowing resumed in 1968 with a UC Davis test plot on the 2,100-foot-elevation Lloyd Walker ranch. Walker, a native of the region, had bought his grandfather's place, and wanted to grow something besides apples, pears, or walnuts. With help from UC Davis, which also wanted to restore grapegrowing to the region, a test plot of several varieties was planted, Zinfandel being one of them. Walker now has an eight-acre, own-rooted Zinfandel vineyard, planted in 1972 with UC Davis certified virus-tested clonal selection budwood. The vines are head trained, and the natural moisture that falls on the six- to seven-foot deep Auberry series soil is supplemented as needed with drip irrigation. Walker's yield is consistently about four tons per acre. The fruit from the vineyard produces award-winning Zinfandel wine for Greg Boeger, owner of Boeger Winery, Placerville.

Other Zinfandel plantings soon followed Walker's. In 1972–1973, Greg and Susan Boeger established their winery, planting four acres of Zinfandel in their V-shaped vineyard on Carson Road just to the north of Placerville. They also used UC Davis certified virus-tested clonal selection budwood, but theirs was grafted onto St. George rootstock. The vines are planted on two sites, are head trained, and are supplemented by some overhead irrigation.

In 1973–1974, Dick and Leslie Bush planted Madroña Vineyards to Zinfandel (eight acres) and other varieties at the 3,000-foot level just above the town of Camino. The Zinfandel vines were propagated on their own roots from a certified, virus-tested clone from a Soledad nursery. In 1980, the Bushes established their winery.

On the south side of Placerville, at the end of Leisure Lane in the vicinity of the Lloyd Walker vineyard, John and Barbara MacCready had purchased 40 acres of land in 1972 that would become Sierra Vista Winery and Vineyard in 1977. Soon after, John's sister, Enid, and brother-in-law, Doug Reeves, joined in the Sierra Vista effort by planting five acres of Zinfandel for John to lease. The budwood was a clonal selection from UC Davis's mother block; the vines were established on their own roots.

In 1981, several more new growers established Zinfandel vineyards. Les and Lyn Russel planted their 20-acre Granite Springs Vineyard in the Consumnes River Valley near Fairplay. Cuttings came from Madroña Vineyards and from a Stockton nursery, and were propagated on their own roots. The same year and just across the road from Granite Springs, what is now the seven-acre Single Leaf Zinfandel Vineyard was established on its own roots with cuttings from an obscure old El Dorado field selection. In the same valley, but on Omo Ranch Road, Frank Latcham budded over Sauvignon Blanc to Zinfandel. Budwood came partly from a UC Davis certified, virus-tested clone, and partly from non-certified field selection budwood propagated by Kunde nursery from the old Weiss Vineyard on Nun's Canyon Road, Sonoma. In 1981, Lava Cap was founded, and an eight-acre Zinfandel vineyard propagated from certified, virus-tested UC Davis Clone #4, obtained from a Sacramento-area nursery.

By 1997, El Dorado County had 186 acres of bearing and 17 acres of non-bearing Zinfandel vines.[23]

There are over 20 wineries in El Dorado County. Nineteen of these are members of El Dorado Winery Association.

---

23 Agricultural Commissioner of El Dorado, June 10, 1998.

At the invitation of the Association, I paid my first visit to the Zinfandel vineyards and wineries of El Dorado County one smoke-hazy August 1996 morning. Organized by the association's executive director, "Pooch" Pucilowski, my two-day visit began with a brief vineyard tour and a soils type lecture at Lava Cap Winery. Lava Cap is situated on Fruit Ridge Road above Placerville at about 2,650 feet. David Jones, professor of geology at the University of California, Berkeley, and his wife, Jeanne, are its owners. Also present were guests from Madroña, Venezio, and Sierra Vista.

An outspoken and unabashed advocate for El Dorado grapegrowing, Jones began the tour with an admonishment: "One of the first things you need to know," he said when he greeted me on the deck of his beautiful winery, "is that El Dorado County wine producers are known for more than Zinfandel. Zinfandel is just one of the red grape varieties that does well up here."

As I was adjusting my perspective and my expectations to accommodate this blunt directive, Jones presented a brief lecture on the region's soils types. "All soils here are residual; none are alluvial. There are three main types: decomposed granite, found mostly in the lower elevations (2,100–2,400 feet) of south county, near Somerset; volcanic, known as eroded mehrten (a cobbly, coarse, gravelly loam), found on the high ridges where Lava Cap and Sierra Vista wineries lie; and sedimentary (a residual slate), which makes up most of Boeger Vineyards. Zinfandel does well in these soils, but so do many of the North Italian varieties as well as the Bordeaux and Rhône varieties."

Boulders large and small of the cobbly mehrten type bordered Lava Cap's vineyard. They provided a good visual sense of what Jones was describing.

Then we moved on to a stroll through Lava Cap's trellised Zinfandel vineyard. I could not help but notice the large clusters of Zinfandel grapes hanging from the vines. Some clusters looked big enough to fill my two arms. Beneath the vines lay dried-up clusters that had been "thinned" some weeks earlier. Well exposed to the sun by extensive leaf removal, some of the remaining clusters still contained large, watery, pinkish-colored grapes.

When I remarked to Jones about the clusters, he laughed. "In a month, all those clusters with the pink berries, or big water berries — they will all be gone, down on the ground with the others you see there. Come back in a month — you'll see for yourself."

Before verasion, Jones explained, clusters are thinned to two per shoot; and after verasion, all under-ripened clusters, or clusters showing reddish grapes, are dropped. So all the big clusters of pink-tinged fruit would soon be on the ground, limiting the final crop to about three tons per acre. It sounded like a rather labor-intensive undertaking for a variety that was just one of several the region was cultivating. Could Zinfandel perhaps occupy a more special place in Jones's heart than he was willing to let on?

From the vineyard, we returned to the winery's deck overlooking the vineyards and surrounding mountains for a delicious lunch prepared by Jeanne and accompanied by a crisp, fragrant Lava Cap Sauvignon Blanc. Following lunch, we all trooped upstairs to a small conference room featuring beautiful views from two large windows. Our El Dorado Zinfandel tasting of mostly the 1994 vintage was about to begin. This was a much-anticipated wine tasting for me. I was about to discover the true status of Zinfandel among El Dorado County growers and producers. Was it going to be just one of several red grape varieties that do well? Or would it turn out to be a regional specialty?

The impressions I was to get from this tasting would reveal that Zinfandel was right at the crossroads — just beginning to be regarded as the red wine grape *best* suited to the region, and worthy of more focused attention — especially in the vineyards.

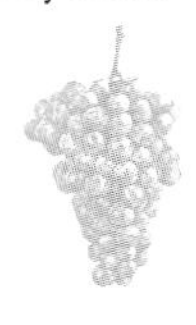

El Dorado Zinfandel Tasting

First were two 1994s from Boeger Winery: a Walker Vineyard and an estate Zinfandel. Both were lovely wines full of spice, earthy chocolate, and delicate raspberries, with the Walker being the more elegant, and having more delicate new oak aromas than the estate. I knew that Greg Boeger, founder and owner, was a grandson of Napa's Anton Nichelini, so his Zinfandels had a long family history to live up to — which they did. (I later found out that his 1993 Walker Zinfandel took a double gold at the 1995 California State Fair — out of 170 Zinfandels.)

The 1994 Granite Springs was next. I had high expectations, given that Granite Springs Zinfandel was possibly the first El Dorado Zinfandel I had ever tasted. For several years they were among the first I sought out whenever I put together a Sierra Foothills wine tasting. Under the winery's founder and previous owner, Les Russell, Granite Springs Zinfandels always brought with them a healthy dose of robust, old-style Zinfandel magic. One knew by the taste and character of the wines that this luscious grape had bewitched people at Granite Springs.

This 1994 vintage, crushed and fermented by Les Russell before he left the area, and finished by Craig Boyd, winemaker for the newly founded Granite Springs/Latcham Vineyards, fulfilled expectations. It was full-bodied, fruity, and layered with medium-toast Demptos oak — a monster Zinfandel that could probably benefit from a kiss of "finesse." Still, it was a true-blue Zinfandel, and I liked it. Give Craig Boyd another year or two and these will be wines to watch out for. The magic was still there.

Then came the big, lush, earthy, chocolatey, blackberry fruit 1994 Lava Cap Zinfandel with about 0.5 percent residual sugar — just enough to take the edge off the tannin. At $20 per bottle, it was the most expensive wine in the tasting — the others mostly in the $10 to $12 range. It was a knock-your-socks-off Zinfandel, and never mind what the fruit looks like on the vines before the final cluster thinning! It was also the wine that took a double gold, plus Best of State, in the 1995 State Fair.

"It was the first Sierra Foothills wine to ever win Best of State," recalled Jones. "With this wine, we went from no medals for our Zinfandel to Best of State. It all had to do with improved practices both viticultural and in vinification. Until this vintage, we were despairing of our Zinfandel."

The next Zinfandel came from the 3,000-foot elevation Madroña Vineyards, made by winemaker Hugh Chappelle. A medium-bodied 1994 wine with hints of strawberries and a slightly tannic finish, it was a pleasant Zinfandel from Madroña's 20-year old trellised mountaintop vines. In that vineyard, three to four tons per acre is the norm, and some uneven ripening is tolerated. Chappelle worked to bring out more of the fruit character of this high elevation vineyard by harvesting the fruit in two pickings — the first at 24.5° Brix, the second at 25.5°. The double picking creates a better balance of acid, pH, and sugar content, as well as preserving the complex fruit character. The 1993 was the first vintage produced from two pickings. The lovely fruit and spice in this Zinfandel created anticipation for the 1995, as Chappelle was more successful each vintage at expressing the fruit character potential of this marvelous vineyard.

The 1993 Perry Creek, another medium-bodied, fruity, slightly tannic Zinfandel with distinct vanilla-oak flavors, was next. Produced from three-year old trellised vines, credit Nancy Steele, winemaker, for her skillful use of new French oak barrels to fill out the bright berry fruit, and to create such an elegant wine from very young vines.

The next two wines were both from Sierra Vista: a 1994 El Dorado Zinfandel, and a 1993 Five Star Estate. I had tasted Sierra Vista Zinfandels from time to time, most notably at the Vintners Club in San Francisco. They had always been well received by this group, and they scored well that day with me — especially the Five Star Reserve, with its full-bodied lush flavors, and plentiful oak flavors, tannins, and acids. I wondered what it would be like in about five years.

The El Dorado County Zinfandel tasting so far was supporting Jones' claim that Zinfandel was indeed well suited to these mountain vineyards with their residual soils.

Then I came to the two 1993 Single Leaf Vineyards and Winery Zinfandels. After a quick sniff and one sip from each — an El Dorado estate, and an estate Reserve — I felt a shiver run through me. "These are both really nice wines," I exclaimed, laying down my pen and savoring this rare and magical moment that I had come upon so unexpectedly. This was my first encounter with Single Leaf wines. "Yes, Single Leaf is pretty focused on Zinfandel," was the consensus statement of my fellow wine tasters, whose attention was caught by my response.

They hardly needed to tell me. Single Leaf Vineyards too had been touched by the magic of Zinfandel. I could taste it in the wines; I could feel in my blood. Like the Granite Springs Zinfandel, this was an old-style country Zinfandel — big, robust, tannic, and loaded with fruit and spice.

The impact the Single Leaf Zinfandels had upon me led me to ponder: Why was it that while most of the Zinfandels in this tasting were indeed lovely, even exceptional, two from the same producer clearly thrilled me? What brought about this feeling? What was its source? Was it because for most of the El Dorado producers, as Jones had pointed out, Zinfandel is just one of several red varieties that does well up there, while for Single Leaf's Scott and Pam Miller, it is their *raison d'être*?

I hardly knew what it was that caught my attention. Perhaps it was simply because I tasted the wines in a wine tasting. Wines are made to be consumed with food, but I tasted the wines in the company of each other, not in the company of the food I would normally serve them with. It was also a hurried tasting — we had only a half-hour.

Next day I would find out more, when I met Single Leaf's owner, Scott Miller, at the Latcham Vineyards luncheon, and later get to walk with him through his vineyard. I would also find out more when I returned on follow-up visits to several of the vineyards.

Sierra Vista Vineyards and Winery

After our El Dorado Zinfandel wine tasting, Pooch and I loaded ourselves into his Honda Civic. Destination: Sierra Vista Winery and Vineyards. John MacCready, formerly a Sacramento State University engineering professor, owns the winery with his wife, Barbara. He led the way across Placerville to Pleasant Valley Road and up Leisure Lane to his winery on Cabernet Way. Although Zinfandel is John's special love, this tiny family-owned winery is probably as well known for its Syrah and other Rhône-style wines as it is for Zinfandel. At its altitude of 2,850 feet, the soil is the volcanic mehrten formation. On a clear day, the view of the Sierra Nevada from the winery's picnic area is spectacular — one of the best in the region.

The five-acre estate Zinfandel vineyard is on land owned by John's sister (Enid Reeves), and leased to John. The budwood came from the UC Davis mother block, and is own-rooted, trellised, and drip irrigated. Like David Jones, MacCready has had problems with pink water berries in some of the clusters of this UC Davis clonal selection. But with diligent vineyard management, he too has been able to produce intensely flavored and balanced Zinfandels of consistent quality. "The key to success is to sacrifice yield," said John.

"What do you keep it at?" I asked. "About three tons per acre?"

"Or less," said John, wincing slightly at the thought. No grower enjoys the sight of his grapes lying on the ground. "You have to thin the crop severely to get the quality. Of course, such sacrifice diminishes the profitability of the variety, since our bottle price cannot quite compensate for the loss of crop. But for the quality of wines we want, and have become known for, there is no alternative. Even with our most intense vineyard management practices, we can't totally eliminate the water berry problem — only control it."

In 1985, Sierra Vista produced a Special Reserve Reeves Vineyard Zinfandel from this vineyard. After 1987, John began combining the Reeves Vineyard fruit with fruit from his second vineyard.

Sierra Vista's second Zinfandel vineyard is the six-acre Herbert Vineyard. The Herberts planted it in 1976 from an older field selection budwood — source unknown. Since Mr. Herbert's death in 1992, John has leased the Herbert Vineyard from his widow. The vineyard is own-rooted, head trained, and drip irrigated.

"I know it's an older clonal selection," said John, "because both the bunches and the berries are smaller and more intensely flavored than in the Reeves Vineyard, and we have less problem with water berries. The soil is decomposed granite, and the elevation is lower than the Reeves, giving the vineyards two distinctly different *terroirs*."

Until 1996, Sierra Vista produced two Zinfandels: an estate El Dorado (900 cases), which was a blend of the Herbert and Reeves vineyards; and in certain years a Five Star Reserve (250 cases) from the best lots of both vineyards, for a total annual production of almost 1,200 cases.

On a mild and rainy December 1996 evening, I returned to Sierra Vista for one of the winery's rare vertical tastings of its Zinfandels (1989 to 1994), including two of the Five Star Reserves. I was really curious to discover the difference between the El Dorado and the Five Star Reserve, and to find out what made the difference. Sierra Vista's fan club also seemed curious to find out more about the winery's Zinfandels, since the small number of tickets was sold out.

John, a tall man with rather time-worn rugged looks and an engaging professorial manner, set about in high good humor to explain the difference to the festive crowd. The difference begins in the vineyard, he said, where the bunches on the vines selected for the reserve have been hand-thinned. At the crusher, any bunches showing signs of bunch rot, green berries, or water berries are discarded. Only uniformly ripened bunches are used. Once the fruit has been gently crushed, the wine is put into small fermentors, and the cap is hand-punched. When dryness is reached, the wine is put into 100 percent new French and American oak barrels for six to eight months. The Five Star Reserve is bottled unfiltered and held for a few months to acquire a little bottle age before release.

In 1994, John began adding a little more new oak to his El Dorado blend because, he said, of "pressure from wine critics and my customers. Customers have come to expect that little layer of flavor that new oak barrels impart."

With its intense cassis, blackberry, and black cherry fruit character, and the substantial backbone of tannins, Sierra Vista Zinfandel seems well able to carry the extra new oak. These wines benefit from a few years cellaring, but the wait is worth it.

By the end of his presentation, John's face was glowing with enthusiasm for the challenges and joys his Zinfandels present him with. The effects that time had etched upon his craggy visage were greatly softened.

In 1996, John bottled the Herbert Vineyard Zinfandel separately for the first time. Upon its release it won several gold medals, followed later by the Best of Show award at the 1998 El Dorado County tasting. In 1997, he planned to once again bottle the Reeves Vineyard Zinfandel separately, giving him two vineyard-designated bottlings. He also planned to continue with his Five Star Reserve program in years when the fruit from both vineyards is exceptional, for a total of three Zinfandel wines.

Perhaps Zinfandel is not Sierra Vista's most profitable wine; however, the variety definitely seems to be earning its keep. In fact, with John's diligent attention in the vineyard and winery, I shouldn't be surprised before long to see it occupying a place of honor at the Sierra Vista table.

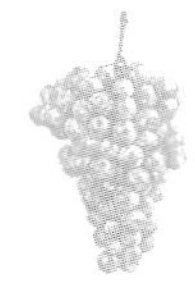

Boeger Winery

Relentlessly holding us to our itinerary, Pooch was soon hustling me back into his Honda Civic for our short journey back across Placerville to Boeger Winery, which is situated on Carson Road just below Lava Cap, with vineyards at elevations of 2,100–2,300 feet. Its soils are primarily sedimentary. It was Greg and Susan Boeger, along with Lloyd Walker, who re-established winegrape-growing in El Dorado County in the early 1970s. The bespectacled and fair-skinned Greg greeted us at the winery with a robust handshake and a radiant smile that made me think of sunshine on a rainy day. Greg is Swiss on his mother's side and German on his father's side. Within minutes, we were being bounced up through terraced rows of Zinfandel in Greg's vintage doorless, roofless jeep for a hasty but up-close look at his vineyards.

Established in 1972, Boeger Vineyards has about seven acres of Zinfandel. Four acres of an old UC Davis clone were planted in 1972 on St. George rootstock. In 1991, three acres of French Colombard on St. George rootstock (7 x 12 spacing) were budded over to Zinfandel. Budwood was taken from a few virus-free 100-year-old vines on the ranch property, which so far show no signs of virus.

Getting the best wine possible from his fruit has become Greg's primary concern. In order to do this, he has established viticultural practices intended to coax the Davis clone into the most intensely flavored, balanced fruit possible. The vines are head trained, leaves are pulled, crop is thinned for best spacing, shoulder clusters are removed, and a cover crop is grown between the vines. Greg does use an overhead sprinkler system to help the vines survive in their shallow sedimentary soil. Crop size is limited to three tons. Fruit is fermented in 1,000- and 2,000-gallon fermentors, the wine punched down twice daily. Juice is left on the skins for about eight days, and the new wines are stored in used French oak barrels. The Estate El Dorado sees no new wood; the Walker, only new innerstaves (from Innerstave) for about two months.

Greg Boeger

It was in part Lloyd Walker's success with winegrape-growing that drew Greg and Susan to the area. Greg, however, did not come to El Dorado County in 1972 particularly to grow and produce Zinfandel. "This was a new area," explained Greg, "and while I definitely wanted to plant Zinfandel, because I knew it would probably do well, I was interested in discovering what else would do well."

Greg's first Zinfandel vintage came from his home ranch in 1976. The Walker Vineyard Zinfandel came a bit later. Since that early beginning, Greg has used Lloyd's Zinfandel fruit for his Walker Vineyard Zinfandel, a mutually beneficial winemaker/grower relationship that has only grown stronger with time.

I returned to Boeger Winery in February 1997 to learn a little more about Greg's newly focused attention on his Zinfandel. "Zinfandel was big in the late 1960s and mid 1970s. Then it sort of fell out of favor; everyone was going to white Zinfandel," he began. Maybe I just kind of went along with the trend. Now, there's a strong resurgence of interest in red Zinfandel wine, so I decided to renew my efforts, and give my vineyards another chance, and see just what I could do."

In 1990, Greg began leaf removal on his own home ranch Zinfandel vineyards, a fairly new practice in California vineyards. He also began cluster thinning. He gives most credit to these two practices for his dramatically improved wine quality. "The very first years we harvested — 1976, 1977, and 1978 — were dry years anyway, so there wasn't a lot of foliage and the crop wasn't particularly heavy. Therefore, those vintages, as I recall, even though the vines were only a few years old, were very intense wines with deep color, much like I am finding now, after I leaf- and crop-thin. I don't think it is the age of vines that makes the difference so much as it is crop load and exposure of the fruit to the sun. Older vines tend to self-regulate, but if you limit crop size on young vines, you can certainly improve the color and intensity of flavor. With our first vintages, the weather regulated crop size and exposure to sun — so the fruit produced really intensely flavored, well-colored wines.

"What I've learned over the years is that reducing quantity and improving exposure of the fruit to the sun improves the quality of the finished wine so much that you can get a higher bottle price — which makes up for the loss of some of the crop. At least, that is what I've learned about working with the UC Davis clones. The fruit can be luscious and well-flavored and colored if you manage the vines right. The old clone vines tend to have a thinner canopy, but I still go through and make sure no vines are too heavily shaded."

Pre-prohibition view of Boeger winery.

"Have there been any lessons learned up at the Walker Vineyard?" I asked.

"Lloyd has been implementing some of the same practices, most notably leaf removal. He hasn't gotten too much into crop thinning, yet. But he's looking at it. We both agree that in the years when the season and weather limited crop size closer to three tons per acre, the wine was more intensely flavored and had more complexity. So we're discussing crop thinning up there as well."

"What kind of flavor changes have you been able to bring about?" I asked.

"Instead of the lighter, fruitier characteristics, we're getting more intensity, more pepper, an inkier, thicker wine — not pruny, but certainly like ripe plums, with some berries in it. I'm not very good at these descriptors," Greg said, apologetically.

"Have you changed anything significant in your winemaking practices to help bring about these improvements?"

"No, no. The winemaking is pretty much the same. Maybe I've changed yeast selection, but that isn't a major change. I never had a problem with harsh or excessive tannins, which I attribute both to our location (altitude and soil) and to punch-down rather than pump-over. I have all old equipment, but it's gentle equipment. I have an old crusher/destemmer, which does little more than pull the stems off the grapes, and an old must pump that works like one of the modern positive displacement pumps.

"Also, we're labor intensive here. Once the grapes are destemmed and in the fermentors, we punch down. When fermentation is complete, we shovel the pomace into a gentle bladder press. Nothing goes through pumps until after the wine is pressed out and into the tank. There's no opportunity for excessive tannin extraction. The only additional tannin the Zinfandels might pick up in the future would be from our small addition of Petite Sirah. I still use mostly neutral oak barrels, except for the Walker, which gets a couple of months of new French oak innerstaves from the Innerstave Company."

Greg rarely fines his Zinfandels; he almost always puts them through a moderately tight filter. "For the long haul, I've found that filtration cleans up the wines just a little, so that they are clean and stable and have excellent ageing potential. No one has ever complained of the taste; our wines are doing really well. In fact, Robert Parker declared that our 1990 Walker Vineyard Zinfandel, which he scored a '90,' was a good example of a *non-filtered* wine. The wine, however, had been sterile filtered. If you can't taste the difference, why not take that step to safeguard the stability of your wines? I know I sleep better and keep my mind clear when I filter my wines. If I am worried about my wines, I just don't function well. One of my first Zinfandels fermented out to 15 percent alcohol and had a touch of residual sugar, and hadn't finished malolactic by the time I was ready to bottle it. I thought, 'It will be okay without filtration.' The minute it got in the bottle, despite the 15 percent alcohol — Boom! It took off.

"That was my only experience with selling 'sparkling Burgundy,'" Greg recalled with a wry laugh, "It taught me to either leave stuck wine alone until it finishes all fermentation, or if you're going to chance bottling it, then do it right. Our 1990 Walker Vineyard had a little residual sugar, and was sterile filtered. Yet it won a gold medal at the State Fair.

"So the improved wine quality is more directly connected to what I've begun doing in the vineyard. Leaf removal has given us more even ripening, so it's easier to pick the harvest date — which is pretty much based on sugar content. I have been picking at about 25° Brix, which I can do now, because the crop is more evenly ripened. Pre-1990, before I began leaf removal and crop thinning, I had a heavier crop and less evenly ripened fruit. While I threw out most of the pinkish clusters, that didn't compensate for the heavier crop, which in turn affected flavor, even if the sugar content of the Brix was the same. I have found through experimentation in 1996 that a harvest Brix of 25° is best for our vineyards. That is when the fruit tastes best."

Even though Boeger Winery was founded in 1972, Greg feels that the potential not only for Zinfandel but also for all El Dorado varieties is still being discovered.

"In 1990, I was at the point of pulling out my home ranch Zinfandel vineyard," he admitted. "It wasn't on the best soil, and the wines were a little weak. But I decided to give leaf removal and crop thinning a chance. Sure enough; it seemed to make a world of difference, and has made it worthwhile to hang onto the vineyard a little longer.

"It's taken a good many years to get this all sorted out. Back in the 1980s, we weren't thinking too much about the effect of viticultural practices on Zinfandel wine quality. Who knows why. For my part, I was growing 25 other varieties, and I more or less let the Zinfandel just do its own thing. As I have become more mature, and have tasted other Zinfandel wines, I have begun to recognize differences. If you can manage your vineyard so as to bring about desirable changes, it's worth doing."

"Have you not always liked Zinfandel?" I asked, thinking of the fact that Greg is grandson to Anton Nichelini, founder of Napa's Nichelini Winery.

"Oh, sure, I've always liked Zinfandel," he replied.

There's no question that Greg's renewed interest in his home ranch Zinfandel is also tied to the Nichelini cousins' reorganization of the Nichelini Winery in Napa in 1990. "Once I got involved with the family winery, that renewed my interest in Zinfandel, got me thinking more about it, and what I could do with my vineyard up here. It's one of those personal things."

Greg's estate 1994 vintage, which included the first crop from his old ranch clone block, showed the effects both of the addition of the old clone fruit and the leaf- and crop-thinning practices on his UC Davis clonal selection vineyards. He feels that the quality of his estate Zinfandel since 1994 is now pretty much on a level with the Walker Vineyard Zinfandel. But his 1996 estate vintage was the one Greg was especially excited about. "I have three separate Zinfandels off our home ranch this year [1996]," he said. "One is from the old clone block planted in the late 1800s, and two are from the older plantings of the UC Davis clone: one from the upper vineyard and one from the lower vineyard. They are all different; they are all good; and there is an intensity to the old clone lot that makes it just an enormous wine. The other two also have a lot of complexity, too. Would you like to taste them?"

We first tasted the two lots made from the 26-year-old UC Davis clonal selection blocks, and they were indeed distinctive — medium-bodied, with spicy fruit and good balance. The old ranch selection, which Greg offered me last, was a big, full-bodied, dark and intense wine, loaded with blackberry fruit, pepper and spice — incredible, even though the fruiting Zinfandel vines were only a few years old. How could Greg possibly not keep this lot as a separate bottling, I asked him. It seemed a shame, almost a sacrilege, to blend it in.

"Well, yes, I could keep it separate," Greg agreed, "and sure, with such a beautiful and intense wine, I'm tempted. But what happens to my estate blend, if I keep this wine separate? It would be like taking the heart out of it. Also, I would have less than 300 cases, so few of my customers would be able to get it. I'm not sure I want to get into that kind of game. I am not yet sure that that any of these wines are as good by themselves as they will be together. I'll just have to wait and see. Come back in a year and see what you think of them then."

I did just that in February 1998 — while on a Foothills Zinfandel-buying mission for a Napa Valley College tasting. "I think I've got a blend worked out," Greg said. "Come, and tell me what you think."

With a barrel sample of each lot, I tasted them to see how much they had changed over the year. They were all still lovely, with the old clone lot still a knockout. Then Greg explained the proportions for his blend, which included about six percent estate Petite Sirah. With the blend put together in a fourth glass, I tasted it. To my own surprise, the blend was indeed superior to any of the separate lots — including the old lot. "Well, Greg, a lesson learned," I exclaimed. "This blend is truly a gorgeous wine with loads of complexity. I'll be back when it's in the bottle."

"Reducing quantity and improving exposure of the fruit to the sun improves the quality of the finished wine so much that you can get a higher bottle price— which makes up for the loss of some of the crop."

Greg Boeger

Greg's renewed enthusiasm for his estate Zinfandel has inspired him to lease some property adjacent to his own. In fall 1998, he began planting additional acreage with his old ranch selection budwood, as well as some Primitivo — which is simply another clone of Zinfandel.

Annual case production of the El Dorado Zinfandel is 1,000; of the Walker, 2,000. Prices for the 1996 vintage were about $14. Greg's showcase wines are Boeger Winery's El Dorado estate Zinfandel, its Walker Vineyard Zinfandel, and its Barbera from the Ritchie Vineyard.

That summer, as I was perusing the "Release Dates" section of my July 1998 "Zinfandel Express," the 1996 Zinfandel wines listed under Boeger Winery arrested my attention. There were three, not two. Were my eyes playing tricks? There were the Estate and the Walker, and — what's this? An Old Clone Zinfandel! I called Greg, and sure enough, he had decided to bottle his Old Clone lot separately after all. "I had a couple more wine writers, and a restaurant and wine store owner or two, who shared your opinion that this was just too good to lose into the blend," he explained.

Winemakers! Can't trust them for a minute. Nonetheless, I was thrilled. And wouldn't you know it — Boeger Winery's Old Clone 1996 Zinfandel took a double gold at the July 1998 San Francisco Fair. Greg was also clearly thrilled. His radiant smile seemed to be illuminating the very sound waves as he conveyed to me this exciting, happy news. His joy was contagious; I was ready to jump in my car and head for Placerville that very moment to get some. "Don't worry, I'll save you a few bottles," he assured me.

Like the Walker Vineyard Zinfandel, the Old Clone Zinfandel was given about six weeks of new French oak innerstaves before bottling. "I just don't like a lot of oak obscuring the flavors of my Zinfandel," Greg emphasized. "Six weeks to two months of new French oak innerstaves is plenty."

The Old Clone Zinfandel was released at between $18 and $20 per bottle, closing at last the large gap between his top Zinfandel and the benchmark Lava Cap.

What about his Estate Zinfandel, which Greg had convinced me, needed the old clone lot to round it out? "It's probably a little less intense without the old clone," admitted Greg, "although I did round out its structure a little with about 15 percent estate Petite Sirah. It's still a very nice wine," he assured me, and would remain at a $12 bottle price — a good deal.

Greg also agreed that perhaps the Old Clone Zinfandel by itself was not as complex as the blend he had contemplated. "What it lost in complexity, though, it made up for in its intensity," was how he summed up his decision. Of course, with only 285 cases of the Old Clone Zinfandel, availability to customers is limited, as are all such intensely flavored benchmark Zinfandels. Production of these wonderful wines is necessarily limited to a few hundred cases per vineyard, because most of these vineyards are small — as are their yields.

But that's the deal: there can be a few hundred cases of intensely flavored, exceptional Zinfandels available from time to time — so grab them when you can. Or winemakers can blend all the lots all the time to create a few thousand cases of consistently good-to-excellent Zinfandels — no surprises; no standouts. For Greg, his last-minute decision to keep this marvelous wine separate was necessary if for no other reason than to make a statement, to claim his well-deserved place among the best of the best Zinfandel producers. "I'm not saying I will have an Old Clone Zinfandel every year," he said. "It will depend on the year and the crop — and other factors."

For my part, I am glad he decided to bottle his Old Clone Zinfandel separately, if only once. Yes, availability of the wine is limited. Still, to get just a bottle of such a memorable wine makes it all worth doing.

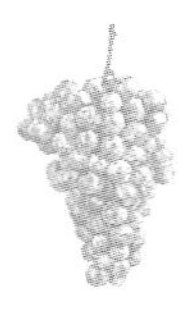

Madroña Vineyards

My last stop for Day One of my El Dorado vineyard tour was the 3,000-foot-high Madroña Vineyards on High Hill Road, owned by Dick and Leslie Bush. Dick holds a Ph.D. in metallurgical science; Leslie is a concert-trained pianist. Tall cedar and pine trees delightfully shade the tiny rustic winery, the Bushes' retirement haven. The vineyard takes its name from a huge madrone tree standing in the Zinfandel vineyard. The eight-acre vineyard is on volcanic soil. It was established in 1973–1974 on own-rooted, certified, virus-tested UC Davis clonal selection cuttings obtained from a Soledad nursery. "I definitely wanted certified virus-tested material," said Dick, a tall, slender, soft-spoken, and decidedly intellectual man. Zinfandel is one of several red varieties successfully grown at Madroña Vineyards.

The vines are trellised, and consistently yield between four and five tons per acre of small, loose, and evenly ripened clusters. Some cluster thinning and leaf removal is done to maintain the best balance of crop to vine. The vineyard is farmed with a cover crop that is mowed, and it is equipped with neutron probes to determine moisture content of the soil. An overhead sprinkler system has been installed. Irrigation is used only as necessary; otherwise, the sprinklers are turned on for frost control in the spring — or perhaps occasionally to give the vines a good wash.

Dick and Paul Bush

A few weeks later, I returned for an afternoon with son Paul Bush, the vineyard manager, and winemaker Hugh Chappelle, who came on board in 1992. Awaiting me was a vertical tasting that Paul had assembled of Madroña's Zinfandel wines from 1981 through a barrel sample of Hugh's benchmark 1995 vintage, to a tank sample of the still fermenting 1996.

Madroña's winery was bonded in 1980, which was also the year that Dick Bush made his second vintage. In the beginning, Dick had taken it upon himself to be winemaker, with the assistance of a consultant until 1985. That year, he brought Mark Foster on as winemaker. In 1992, Mark left to become winemaker at Nevada City Winery. Hugh Chappelle replaced him.

While Paul agreed with me that Hugh's 1995 vintage is "spectacular," he also pointed out that the 1993 and 1994 vintages, as well as the 1995, all won gold medals at the Orange County Fair. Furthermore, he said, "Dad and I feel that our breakthrough vintage of Zinfandel was the 1980, the second vintage Dad produced."

Although there was none of the 1980 left, the 1981 Zinfandel that Paul presented to me that fall of 1996 had retained its fruit, along with a cedary note. The tannins, however, were the most dominant note, which is characteristic of the region. The 15-year-old Zinfandel was holding its own, and I only wished there had been a 1980 to try also. The 1981 had been harvested at 22.6° Brix.

Hugh's goal was to develop a riper style of Zinfandel. To that end, he worked closely with Paul to fine-tune viticultural practices. In 1993, he began double-picking the vineyard — to get a tank Brix of between 24° and 25° for the 1995 — up from 23° in 1992. The higher sugar content of course meant that the alcohol content went over 14 percent — something Dick had been resisting for many years. Convinced, however, by the quality of the 1995 vintage that the wine is more intensely flavored and balanced when the grapes are picked at over 24.5° Brix, it looks like Hugh made his point. Dick concurred. "The goal is to produce a balanced wine that gives full expression to the vineyard. The higher alcohol in Zinfandel wine is merely an incidental quality."

"The goal is to produce a balanced wine that gives full expression to the vineyard."

Dick Bush

Although the grapes tend to have a higher pH and lower acids than one might expect for the elevation, the finished wines retain their bright fruit character as well as their fully ripe flavors. The wonderful 1995, however, came in with a lower pH, and required no acid adjustment.

The fruit character of Madroña Zinfandel is rich and intense, tending towards red berries and a blend of spices. The spice character is accented by 15 percent to 20 percent new American oak for between 11 and 14 months. Because of the balance of fruit, alcohol content, acids, and tannins, these wines all have great ageing potential.

Characteristic of Zinfandel wine from this vineyard, and also of Boeger and Lava Cap Zinfandels, is a quality called bright fruit character. This means that the fruit is a fresh crisp flavor, brought about by the higher, cooler region and the soils.

On the subject of Zinfandel wines and their regional and stylistic differences, Dick Bush strongly believes that the wines should not be compared. Rather, he said, "The proper question for a consumer to ask is, 'What style of Zinfandel would I like for dinner tonight?'" In other words, don't go by published buying guides and their rating systems to determine which wine will be best for *your* food and style preferences.

In 1995, Madroña Vineyards and Winery produced about 1,000 cases of Zinfandel table wine and about 300 cases of a Late Harvest Zinfandel. In 1996, Hugh added a limited production Reserve bottling. The fruit from select blocks was allowed to ripen to between 25° and 26° Brix. Although riper than the fruit used for the El Dorado bottling, the pH in the wine was somewhat lower (3.6) because of the higher acid content in the raisined fruit. The Reserve Zinfandel is aged in small American oak barrels, 20 percent new, for about 11 months, then bottled, and held for a few months before release. Price for the Reserve was $16 per bottle.

Zinfandel production will increase a little when the vineyard owned by Paul Bush and his brother near Sierra Vista Vineyards comes into production. The new seven-and-a-half-acre vineyard was established on 12-inch long hardened bench grafts on devigorating rootstock.

Madroña Vineyards is the highest elevation Zinfandel vineyard in California. The view from the vineyard west over the El Dorado foothills is awesome.

In a phone conversation with Hugh in August 1998, he offered these additional comments on Madroña Zinfandel:

"The improved quality of Madroña Zinfandel can be attributed to five factors. First is canopy management. That means leaf removal so the grapes get better sunlight exposure. Second is crop thinning — don't be afraid to get out there and drop some poorly ripened clusters, or clusters with red berries. Third is water delivery — an additional irrigation each season. Fourth is picking for riper style, including multiple pickings for fully ripe grapes. And fifth is in new plantings, best match-up of budwood and rootstock."

Also, Hugh used less than 20 percent new American oak with the 1997 vintage. The El Dorado blend gets about 10 months; the Reserve gets 13-14 months.

"All these factors result in a more intense and balanced wine — fruit to acid to alcohol. The 1996 Reserve was released at $16," Hugh said.

Pricing is always a delicate issue among winemakers, but Hugh indicated an improving picture for El Dorado Zinfandels.

"Until the 1996 or 1997 vintages, most El Dorado Zinfandels were underpriced — Lava Cap was the exception at $20. Now, Boeger's old clone is at $18 to $20 and Madroña's Reserve at $16, and the prices are becoming more equitable with quality. They were not making much money at our former prices. But with the region's participation in such organizations as ZAP and the Rhône Rangers, they have been able to compare styles and prices, and become a little less provincial. The regional character will always be there, but we're learning how to make the wine better. We'll always be known for good value for our popular El Dorado blends, but we are also becoming known for a few select *terroirs* that will command the higher prices for a few small lot releases — such as Boeger's Old Clone and Madroña's Reserve. Also Latcham Reserve.

"Overall, they're maturing as a region," concluded Hugh. "While Zinfandel wines from El Dorado have been acquiring a following since the early 1980s, the 1995 vintage seems to be the one that has demonstrated to a broad base of consumers and wine writers the high quality of wines that this region is capable of producing."

Madroña's 1997 Reserve won "Best Zinfandel of the Sierra Foothills" at the 1999 California State Fair. An elegant, spicy wine loaded with blackberry fruit, it has an alcohol content of 14.4 percent. It is a classic style from that high-elevation vineyard.

In summer of 2000, Hugh Chappelle left Madroña Vineyards to become winemaker for Flowers Vineyards, located in the coastal region of Sonoma County just north of Jenner. Heather Nenow joined Madroña as Hugh's replacement.

Lava Cap

I returned to Lava Cap in early October. Zinfandel grapes were still on the vines. Beneath the rows now lay a second layer of thinned clusters. The remaining clusters were big enough to fill two hands, but the grapes were evenly ripened to a deep velvety purple-black, and they were luscious tasting — just like David Jones had predicted when I left him the previous month. To emphasize his point, David broke open a few grapes randomly selected to show me the ripe brown seeds. "You'll find brown seeds throughout the clusters," he said, "not green ones."

It took David and his sons, Tom, the winemaker, and Charlie, the vineyard manager, a long time to get the Zinfandel vineyard to this point. "We built the winery in 1986 — the year when El Dorado County grapes could hardly be given away," recalled David. "Our early red wines were overly tannic. This is tannin country up here, and believe me, it's a myth created only by wine writers that excessively tannic Zinfandel wines are long ageing wines. In the years 1986 to 1992, we were getting five tons per acre, and getting some critical recognition from some wine publications. But I was not happy with the wines. I didn't like these stripped-down restrained food-style wines that everyone seemed to be trying to make then."

Despairing of their Zinfandel, but not ready to give up, by 1993, the Jones team had gotten organized. Their inspiration to change their approach to Zinfandel was sparked by the excitement at the early ZAP tastings at Fort Mason in San Francisco, and by the "renaissance of the big rich lush monster Zinfandels wines," said David. "These big rich wines created a level of excitement I had never before experienced. The people coming to these tastings seemed to be longing for those rich trend-setting wines reminiscent of the Zinfandels of the late 1960s and early 1970s that had made Ridge, Sutter Home, and Monteviña famous.

"Further, the concept of restrained wines is French. But it's a phony comparison," he said with undisguised vexation. "The French climate precludes the kind of exuberance we can get in our Zinfandel, because of our warm dry summers. We can produce beautifully balanced wines that are nonetheless big and rich and luscious. These styles of Zinfandels were the wines generating the excitement at the ZAP tastings. The wines have elegance, because they are balanced. But they are not restrained. Zinfandel is not meant to be restrained, and any attempts to do so simply strip the flavor out of it. Let's leave the restrained style to the French — since that is what their climate is best suited to."

The Jones team, however, had its work cut out for it to become a part of the renaissance of the monster Zinfandels. Beginning in the vineyard, Charlie implemented his regimen of severely thinning the crop and removing leaves for improved sun exposure of the fruit. Limiting the yield to three tons per acre seemed a radical move, but to produce award-winning Zinfandel wine, he had no other choice. "You have to be brutal in multiple prunings and thinnings," said David. "Zinfandel has a natural tendency to overcrop; no other vine requires such intensive management, and carries such high costs of labor and crop loss. But to avoid bunch rot and mildew, the vine has to be opened up to the sun and air. If you do this, even with the UC Davis clonal selection, you can produce an intensely flavored, full-bodied Zinfandel wine."

In the winery, to control the tannins, Tom bought in a Delta destemmer/crusher, and a positive displacement pump — one among many pumps. (Tom does not believe that a winemaker can have too many pumps — at least so said his father!) The Delta destemmer just knocks the berries off the stems, leaving some berries whole, some with split skins. None is crushed or macerated, so that no bitterness is imparted to the wine from crushed seeds. The pump simply moves the wine to the fermentation tank without any further damage to the seeds and skins. Tom also increased hose diameter from two to four inches.

In the tank, the cap is irrigated with a gentle sprinkler-type pumpover controlled by a timer, to keep the cap moist but not to break it up. This is a major step towards controlling the harshness of the tannins.

The wines are cellared for about a year in a mixture of French and American oak barrels, 30 percent of which is new.

Their hard work paid off. The 1993 vintage won a double gold and Best of State — the first Sierra Foothill wine to win such an accolade. Three days after it was released, the 500-case production was sold out —

a bargain to many at $20 per bottle. At the ZAP event, the Lava Cap table was one of the centers of excitement, drawing not only consumers but also personnel from other wineries.

Before I left that October morning, David offered me a barrel sample of his 1995 vintage. Another luscious rich wine with its signature ripe jammy blackberry fruit and spice, its tannins mellowed with just a hint of residual sugar. It was beginning to work its magic on me. Sooner or later, I knew I would be adding a bottle or two of Lava Cap Zinfandel to my collection, for special occasions and specially prepared meals.

Outside, David pointed out a new vineyard being prepared for Zinfandel vines propagated from old field selection clones. "I was happy to get UC Davis clonal selection for our first vineyard," explained David, "because I like the spicy character it gave to the wine. Now I'm wondering how much difference the old clones will make — if any. So we're giving them a try."

It looks like Zinfandel may become something more to this low-key, talented, and dedicated Lava Cap quartet than just one of the red grape varieties that do well in El Dorado County. In fact, in David's closing words to me upon my most recent visit, he declared that Zinfandel would be Lava Cap's most prestigious variety going into the 21st century — closely followed by Syrah. Hardly a surprise. Despite his crusty exterior and his disclaimer that Zinfandel is just one red grape variety that does well in El Dorado, it was obvious to me from the day I met him that David Jones is about as passionate a Zinfandel enthusiast as I have met. I look forward to the effect the fruit from his vineyard — established with old field selection budwood — will have on his already dramatic Zinfandel wines.

Day one of my El Dorado vineyard tour ended with dinner in the company of several growers and producers. We dined at Zachary Jacques, a lovely French restaurant on Pleasant Valley Road on the outskirts of Placerville. Following dinner, Pooch escorted me to The Seasons Bed and Breakfast in Placerville, our innkeepers for the night. Given my choice of the room on the second floor of the house or the cottage at the back of the garden, I choose the luxurious quiet of the cottage. Soon I was gratefully snuggled into the scented sheets, and heard not another sound until the first birds began chirping outside my windows, signaling the arrival of the dawn light.

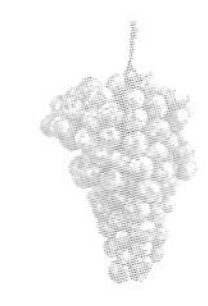

Latcham/ Granite Springs Vineyards

What a thrill it was at 9:00 in the morning to turn off Omo Ranch Road onto the oak-shaded lane that leads up to Latcham Vineyards — a vineyard I had long wished to visit. Waiting for us was owner Frank Latcham, a white-haired, semi-retired attorney from San Francisco, and his vineyard manager, Bill Naylor, gamely and cheerfully coping with crutches and a leg in a walking cast from a vineyard mishap.

Established in 1981, Latcham Vineyards did not start out being a Zinfandel winery. "I didn't come up here to grow Zinfandel," said Frank. "Sauvignon Blanc was making a resurgence then, and was well suited to this region. But by 1988, Zinfandel was proving to be a better choice for our vineyard. We budded over four acres with budwood taken from the Weiss Vineyard in Sonoma, which had been prepared by Kunde nursery that year, and two more in 1989 using a UC Davis clonal selection. Yes, it's all on AxR-1, carefully chosen to prevent 'you know what,'" said Frank with a wry laugh. The best of the four acres budded from the Weiss selection is used for Latcham's Special Reserve Zinfandel. Yield is 3½ to four tons per acre. The 1996 vintage Latcham Reserve won Best of Show at the Amador County Fair. It was released at $16.

The two acres budded from UC Davis clonal selection Zinfandel have since been budded to Cabernet Franc, a variety also especially well suited to the location.

An hour later, we left Frank to oversee the lunch he was hosting for the south El Dorado County group, and wended our way over to Granite Springs Winery located just off Fairplay Road at an elevation of 2,300 feet. Wineries in this south El Dorado County region have formed their own local association that goes by the slogan, "Fair Play Wineries: Wines with an Attitude."

Les and Lynne Russell planted Granite Springs' seven-acre Zinfandel vineyard in 1981. Cuttings were collected from Madroña Vineyards and from a nursery in Madera. The Russells, who had been living in Marin County, bought the property in 1979, the year Lynne was diagnosed with breast cancer. They moved up to plant a Zinfandel vineyard and fight Lynne's cancer.

GRANITE SPRINGS
1999 SIERRA FOOTHILLS
Zinfandel
La Falda de la Sierra
ALCOHOL 14.4% BY VOLUME

"I didn't know much about growing grapes," Les told me in a phone interview in fall of 1996. "I just liked Zinfandel, and figured it would do well up there — and it did. I didn't know much about rootstock, so stayed with the common stock [rooted cuttings] for economic reasons. And I didn't worry much about clones, either. Clones were not so much of a big deal in the early 1970s as they are now."

The vineyard is dry farmed, head trained, and yields three to 3½ tons per acre. The soil is a coarse sandy loam known as Josephine soil. The vineyard is situated on a knoll that gives it both north and west exposure. Such dual exposure provides the winemaker opportunity to give the wine "a different look," said Craig Boyd, "since each exposure has a different ripening curve.

If the fruit is picked with different hang times, the resulting wines will reflect this complexity." Whether it was just plain good luck or good common sense (or both) on Les's part, Granite Springs is one of El Dorado's most promising Zinfandel vineyards.

Les's style of winemaking was to pick the grapes at 23.5° Brix to 24° Brix. He fermented the wine in 1,000-gallon tanks, and punched down several times daily. When the wine reached dryness, it was racked into neutral oak barrels for the first few months. Then Les would rotate 10 to 15 percent new American oak into the barrel regimen for the last few months. Simple winemaking, but given how well suited the grapes were to their location, Granite Springs Zinfandel has been among my favorites from the first time I discovered it on the shelves of Pokerville Market in Plymouth.

In March 1994, Lynne lost her battle with cancer. Les sold Granite Springs Winery and Vineyard to Frank Latcham in fall 1994, and moved to Nevada County, where he is farming 80 acres of vineyard planted to various varieties. Craig Boyd, a tall and exceedingly amiable young man with long dark curly hair, had begun working with Les as assistant winemaker in 1991-1992, then returned in early 1995 to take over winemaking for Frank Latcham. Les had crushed and fermented the 1994 vintages for both Granite Springs and Latcham before leaving. Craig finished them. Since 1995, he has been the winemaker for Latcham/Granite Springs.

Craig has enjoyed the opportunity of working with both the Latcham and Granite Springs vineyards, and discovering the potential of each. He has continued with many of Les's practices — most notably picking at the same ripeness and fermenting in small tanks, and ageing the wine in a mixture of new and neutral American oak barrels. He has also added some of his own touches.

Most notably, Craig likes to cold soak the wine for three days. Then he adds Assmanshausen yeast to the Granite Springs must and LSSS6 yeast to the Latcham Vineyards must. Once the wine begins to ferment, he pumps over twice each day for one hour. Fermentation usually lasts 14 days. When the wine reaches dryness, Craig puts it into American oak barrels, 15 percent to 20 percent new, for about 16 months. He is developing a five-year program for his barrels, seeking to add 20 percent new each year for five years.

Following my first visit to Granite Springs in August 1996, I returned several times. One notable visit was for the El Dorado Winery Association's 1997 Passport Weekend. What especially drew me to the event was Granite Springs' one-time offering of a 10-year vertical tasting of Zinfandel — 1985 through a barrel sample of the still-unbottled 1995 — Craig's first solo production. The wines were all holding up; some were exceptional. Then there was the 1995 barrel sample — redolent with cassis, blackberries, spice and chocolate, yet balanced and almost elegant despite its huge style.

In June 1998, the 1996 vintage was in the tasting room — just released. A dramatic, intense, huge yet elegant Zinfandel, the promise in the tank sample was fulfilled. Price per bottle of the 1996 was $12.

Zinfandel production for Latcham/Granite Springs was about 3,000 cases in 1998 — 1, 000 cases each of Latcham Special Reserve, Latcham El Dorado, and Granite Springs Estate.

Total winery production for all varieties was 10,000 cases for Granite Springs and 6,000 cases for Latcham. The family's goal was to bring both labels to 11,000 cases for year 2000. The expansion was to come from purchased fruit.

The 1996 Latcham Special Reserve Zinfandel was awarded Best of Show at the 1998 Amador County Fair. Release price was $16.

★ ★ ★ ★ ★

In April 2000, Craig Boyd left Latcham/Granite Springs to become winemaker at Oakstone Winery. He was replaced by Italian-born Ruggiero Mastroserio.

Perry Creek Vineyards

Following an introduction to Perry Creek Vineyards winemaker Nancy Steele and a wonderful truck ride through the vineyards with vineyard manager Skip Lovin, we headed back to Latcham Vineyards for a delicious lunch graciously hosted by Frank Latcham.

Since that visit, Skip Lovin has left Perry Creek to return to Mendocino County as vineyard manager for Parducci. Bill Bertram, formerly with Karly Wines, has replaced him at Perry Creek. Keep your eye on the Zinfandels coming from this producer.

Lunch at Latcham Vineyards

Back at Latcham Vineyards, my attention was drawn to the playful talk and infectious laughter of a fair-haired man of medium height whose slightly graying beard could not conceal the laugh lines setting off eyes as blue as a warm summer morning. This was Scott Miller, owner of Single Leaf Vineyards and Winery. Lunch was ready, and it included Craig Boyd, Bill Naylor, and the handsome, burly, and bearded Brian Fitzpatrick, owner of Fitzpatrick Winery, which is perhaps as well-known for Brian's massive hand-made log hospitality lodge as for his organically grown wines. Seated beside Scott, I asked him what brought him to El Dorado County to buy a Zinfandel vineyard, build a winery, and make wines. His and his wife's original interest, he said, was to buy in Mendocino and grow

Pinot Noir, or somewhere in the Foothills and grow Zinfandel, their two favorite red winegrapes. After looking at some property in Mendocino's Anderson Valley and finding it beyond their working-class means, they came upon the seven-acre Zinfandel vineyard that is now Single Leaf Vineyards. "This will work," Scott recalled saying when he first set eyes upon the property in 1988.

Situated across the road from Granite Springs, the vineyard was planted in 1981. Upon receiving assurance from Granite Springs' Les Russell that the vineyard was indeed worth buying, Scott and his wife, Pam, set about attracting 100 percent discouragement from loan institutions to which they went for capital. "We never expected to be turned down by every institution we applied to — 13 all told," said Scott. In the end, the Millers financed it themselves. In 1993, they opened their winery, also self-financed, and had their first on-site crush.

Commenting on those early years, Scott said, "Never underestimate what has to be done to run a vineyard/winery business. I know it's supposed to be cool and romantic, and it is. But it's also a hellacious amount of hard work. But we've never minded hard work, and we like the lifestyle that it brings us. It's also shown us who our friends are; they're the ones without whom we couldn't have survived, who came to help whenever help was needed, never mind what had to be done."

Pam and Scott live in Carson City, Nevada, with their teenage son. Scott holds the position of administrator for the Division of Museums and History for the State of Nevada. Pam works for a contractor's association. They also have two daughters in college. Their winery/vineyard is a weekend commute, with longer stays during crush. Scott was expecting to be at Single Leaf Winery and Vineyards full time by 1999.

As lunch was ending, I asked what this South El Dorado County group of growers and producers thought about Zinfandel. What was its importance to them? Their answers reflected a growing attachment to this versatile, hardy grape.

"In five years," said Brian, "Zinfandel will be one of five wines the county is known for."

"Zinfandel is our bread and butter," said Scott. "We like Zinfandel."

"It's a peculiar grape, with its different maturation curve on each vine. We haven't quite got it figured out yet here in our vineyard," said Frank Latcham, "but we're working on it."

"I'd like to plant Frank's entire 40 acres in Zinfandel, given the demand today, and how well suited this gravelly loam, known as Josephine soil, is to Zinfandel. I think it's the easiest grape to grow up here," said Bill Naylor.

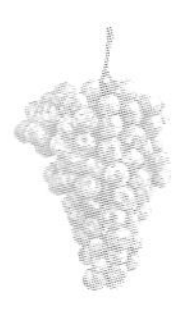

Single Leaf Vineyards

Lunch was now over, and Pooch was signaling that it was time to follow Scott over to his Single Leaf Vineyards and Winery. In five minutes we were there, standing at the edge of his crush pad overlooking the seven-acre, dry-farmed, head-trained vineyard planted in 1981. "The best I recall the previous owner telling me," said Scott, "was that the cuttings came from a Sacramento Valley nursery."

Scott tries to keep to the basics in his approach to winemaking. "Pay attention to the simplest details: clean vineyards, clean barrels, and try not to add anything or take anything out — unless absolutely necessary. Zinfandel producers seem to be struggling mightily to produce a pedigreed Zinfandel — but maybe we shouldn't be. I know that a pedigreed Zin isn't what I want to make. There's magic about Zinfandel that historically has touched people in the industry. I don't want to lose that magic."

Like Greg Boeger, Scott uses old equipment and lots of hands-on labor. He ages his reserve Zinfandel in a mixture of well-seasoned American and French oak, and about 5 percent new American oak. His El Dorado Zinfandel sees about 15 percent new American oak. Both styles are kept in barrels for one year.

Scott Miller

As we stood on the crush pad overlooking the vineyard, Scott pointed out which blocks of the vineyard provided fruit for his regular Zinfandel, his reserve, and the port. "It takes a long time to get to know a Zinfandel vineyard," he said. Crop size for Single Leaf's Reserve is 2½ to three tons per acre; for its El Dorado Zinfandel, about three tons.

Following Scott down into the vineyard, I found that here, as in Granite Springs, the Zinfandel clusters and berries were smaller than those I saw at Lava Cap and Sierra Vista, and the clusters were rather loosely formed. The berries were of a dark purplish-black color. I watched Scott gently push aside the canes and leaves to reveal the blue-black clusters hanging among the leaves, or to point out a little bird damage. When he explained why bird damage wasn't a big concern, and why, yes, sure, he'd like to have five tons per acre, too (from an economic perspective), but how for the best Zinfandel wine, he keeps it to three tons and less, I saw how his blue eyes got that dreamy, far-away look. I was beginning to understand where the magic in his two Zinfandel wines at the tasting the day before came from. I could feel the same thrill running through me again as we stood there in his quiet vineyard drenched in the afternoon foothill sun. I told Scott I could feel that Zinfandel was pretty special to him. "Yes, we like Zinfandel; we make other red wines as well, but let's put it like this: If Pooch had told me you were writing a story about Cabernet, I would have stayed in Carson City."

In a conversation some weeks later, I remarked to Scott that someone familiar with the UC Davis clone #2 wondered if his vineyard might have been planted to that clone. Scott replied, "No idea on UC Davis #2. At this point, I don't ask a lot of questions — just happy they keep putting out *these* grapes."

In 1997, the Millers built a charming little tasting room at the end of the winery. In 1999, Scott left his job with the Division of Museums and History and moved his family to El Dorado to become a full-time winemaker.

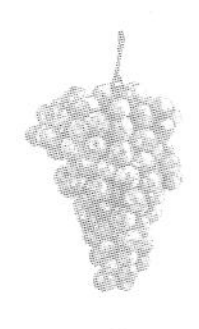

Closing thoughts on El Dorado

After my many visits to the wineries and vineyards of El Dorado County from August 1996 through summer 1998, I discovered through vertical tastings offered by Boeger, Madroña, Granite Springs, and Sierra Vista that Zinfandel has long shown the potential to be a signature wine for El Dorado County.

However, there is no question that since the 1994 vintage, many of the El Dorado producers have been focusing more attention on their Zinfandel wines. This attention has been most notably reflected (to date) in the 1995, 1996, and 1997 vintages, which all show increasingly distinctive and well-developed expressions of their vineyards and winemaker styles.

Most of El Dorado County's 21 wineries produce a red Zinfandel table wine. Several also produce a Late Harvest or Zinfandel Port. Besides the fact that El Dorado Zinfandel wines are wonderful in their varied styles, they are also affordable. Although the bottle price of a few top medal-winning Zinfandels have edged upward since the 1994 vintage, Zinfandels from El Dorado County remain a great value. As Dick Bush suggested, to be properly appreciated, wines should be tasted on their own, and with food, not in terms of other wines. They should not be compared to one another. That is certainly the best way to approach these distinctive wines from El Dorado County, a place I will return to again and again. My expectation is that increasing numbers of Zinfandel lovers will be following me in the years ahead.

Lodi
Beyond Jug Wine

Mission Vineyard

In September 1996, a call from Mark Chandler, executive director of the Lodi-Woodbridge Winegrape Growers Association, became the catalyst for another long overdue and exciting visit to Zinfandel Country — this time to the Lodi viticultural area situated in the northwest corner of San Joaquin County. The Lodi-Woodbridge winegrape-growing region borders the Sierra Foothill County of Amador to the east, the Consumnes River to the north, the San Joaquin and Sacramento deltas to the west, and the Calaveras River to the south. It is an alluvial fan that washed down from the foothills in these watersheds. What makes it unique are its warm days that are cooled at night by delta breezes coming in through the Golden Gate and upriver to the Lodi-Woodbridge vineyards — creating a Mediterranean-like climate with excellent ripening conditions.

In 1996, there were about 18,000 acres of Zinfandel in Lodi-Woodbridge, supplying 125,000 tons of grapes, or 38 percent of California's total Zinfandel production. Zinfandel has increased from 15 percent of the region's total winegrape acreage in 1985 to 35 percent (of 46,000 total acres) in 1996. An additional 3,800 acres were just coming into production. As of January 2001, this acreage remains pretty much unchanged. The region rightly lays claim to having the largest Zinfandel acreage of any county or region in California.

By comparison, there are about 9,000 acres of Zinfandel in the Merced/Modesto region; 4,600 in Sonoma County; 2,400 in the Sierra Foothills; 2,200 in Napa County; 2,000 in Mendocino County; 1,800 in Paso Robles; and 600 in Cucamonga Valley.

Considered primarily as a source for generic jug wines in the decades following Repeal, Zinfandel's image began to change in 1977, when David Lucas, owner of The Lucas Winery and Vineyard, began producing an estate Zinfandel, Lodi viticultural area, from the best three acres of his 40-acre, 70-year-old vineyard. A few more owners of the finest of the old vineyards have joined Lucas in the 1990s, notably Lance Randolph, owner of Peirano Estate Vineyard, and Charles and Betty Ann Spenker, owners of Spenker Vineyards. The 300-acre Peirano Estate Vineyards includes 75 acres of 100-year-old Zinfandel, which makes it the largest block of 100-year-old, own-rooted Zinfandel in the world. Peirano Estate Vineyards label was established in 1992. The Spenkers built their winery in 1994.

In 1990, Robert Mondavi Winery, Woodbridge, began bottling a varietal Zinfandel produced from 60 percent to 80 percent Lodi-Woodbridge grapes. Before this, its Zinfandel went into its "Bob Red" table wine blend. Production in 1996 was 150,000 cases of California Zinfandel, making it the second largest production of single label, varietally identified Zinfandel in the world. The largest is Sutter Home, which has produced over 200,000 cases of California Zinfandel since 1994. E&J Gallo bottles more varietally labeled Zinfandel than either Woodbridge or Sutter Home, but not under one label.

Sebastiani also has three brands that produce Lodi-based Zinfandel: Talus, Vendange, and August Sebastiani Heritage — for a *combined* total brand production of about 180,000 cases. Of the Talus brand, which is the next to highest end (after Sebastiani's Sonoma Cask wines), Doug Davis, production manager, commented: "Even though less Sonoma County Zinfandel is used in the 1994 and vintages following, we feel the quality that we achieved in our first Talus vintage, which came from the mostly Sonoma County fruit, has been retained in the subsequent vintages because of the improved viticultural practices of our Lodi-Woodbridge growers."

In March, 2001, Sebastiani Vineyards and Canandaigua Wine (a division of Constellation Brands), entered into an agreement in which Canandaigua would purchase the assets of Turner Road Vintners from Sebastiani which includes the Vendange, Talus, and Heritage brands.

As of 1996, Ravenswood's Vintner's Blend is made from over 40 percent Lodi viticultural area Zinfandel. In fact, it would be safe to assume that any California viticultural area Zinfandel contains a fair percentage of Lodi fruit. Most of those with a Coastal viticultural area have made up the 15 percent allowable non-AVA fruit from Lodi.

Ravenswood has also released a 1996 Lodi viticultural area Zinfandel; in 1999, Turley Wines released a 1997 vineyard-designated Lodi Zinfandel. By January 2001, according to Mark Chandler, about 35 producers show Lodi viticultural area on their labels.

Mark Chandler organized my introductory tour of this impressive region, and served as my guide. We were to visit Peirano Estate Vineyard, the Lucas Winery and Vineyard, and Craig Rous's vineyard.

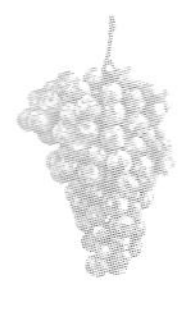

Peirano Estate — Lodi Viticultural Area

Our first stop was at Peirano Estate Vineyard, which consists of 300 acres lying just a few miles north of Lodi beside Highway 99 on Acampo Road. In addition to 75 acres of Zinfandel, it grows Cabernet Sauvignon, Sauvignon Blanc, and Chardonnay.

Lance Randolph, fourth generation owner of Peirano Estate, met us at his historic vineyard wearing his *de rigueur* summer outfit of hiking boots, red shorts, "Stuck-in-Lodi-and-Loving-it" T-shirt, and wide-brimmed straw hat. His mother, Charlotte Peirano Randolph, has passed down the Peirano heritage and name.

Being out among his 75-acre block of 100-year-old Zinfandel vines is one of Lance's greatest pleasures. The vines were planted on their own roots in 1895 by his Genoa-born great-grandfather, Giacomo Peirano. "I've always been a farmer at heart," said the tall, deeply tanned and charismatic Lance. "I was driving a tractor when I was 5 years old, and wanted to work on he ranch when I finished high school. But my father said that education came first, so off to college I went, for a business degree. Then I spent 10 'suit and tie' years in Vancouver, Canada, as a salesman — from 1973–1983. I came back here in 1983 and bought the ranch from my family.

"My first decision was whether to keep the Zinfandel, which is perhaps the largest single block of 100-year-old natural-rooted, head trained Zinfandel left in California — or the world. At 2¼ to 2½ tons per acre for the past 30 years, from an economic standpoint keeping these old vines didn't make much sense, when I could plant other varieties that get 10 to 12 tons per acre, for five times the income. But I knew the Zinfandel was good. Besides, these old vines have been in my family too long, and working among them is the most enjoyable part of my job.

"I like walking among my vines, not just at harvest but all year, to see how each one is doing. I wouldn't want anyone else doing that. I personally cultivate them, because it takes an owner's love to spare those arms that often extend into the path of the tractor. I don't hesitate to stop the tractor, and maneuver it to work around the parts of the vines that are in the way. And often, in the spring, a quail will build her nest inside the hollow part of an old trunk. I'm happy to wait until she has hatched her eggs, and taken her brood out, before I work around that particular vine.

"Nonetheless, economics cannot be ignored. I needed to know if the grapes could generate additional income by being vinified into premium Lodi viticultural area Zinfandel table wine. So in 1992, I made 540 cases at Roche, Sonoma — only as much as I could drink if it came to that. The fruit came in at 25° Brix, with pH at 3.57, and T.A. of 6 g/L. I bought six new French oak barrels, which cost more than the grapes were worth — $4,000 compared to $3,600 for the nine tons of grapes at 1992 prices of $400 per ton." (Prices for Lodi Zinfandel in 1996 were $800 per ton.)

"The wine sold out quickly, so in 1993, I made 1,500 cases, which sold out in nine months — at $9.95 a bottle. My case production is up to

3,500 since 1994. Not only have I been able to increase production each year, I have also been able to raise my price a little, to where I am getting back at least a small profit. As long as I can make a modest profit, and continue to sell out my wine, it's worth it in economic terms to keep the old vines in the ground.

"It's been the fourth generation Zinfandel growers like me who have taken the economic beating from Zinfandel's roller-coaster road to its current success. It's been a tough call to stay with these old vines, when Zinfandel grape prices, whether for white or red Zinfandel, were less than $400 per ton until just the last couple of years." Lance could say this now with a certain matter-of-factness — his vineyard is no longer in danger of falling to the bulldozer. The 75 acres of Zinfandel vines make up one quarter of Peirano Estate vines.

Lance Randolph

Although essentially dry farmed, the vines are supplemented with both drip and furrow irrigation. His first drip system was installed around 1980, making him just about the first grower in Lodi viticultural area to convert. "It's definitely the best system, since I can deliver precise amounts of water during the last few weeks of grape maturity, keeping the grapes hanging longer without being dehydrated," he said. "You can't do that with furrow irrigation."

Lance would never consider putting Zinfandel on wires. "For premium red table wine production, Zinfandel vines are best when head trained," he firmly believes.

Lance is equally attentive to the details of how to vinify his grapes into the best Lodi viticultural area Zinfandel table wine possible. The grapes are hand-harvested into one-half ton bins, which minimizes pressure on the fruit, then sent directly to the winery. At the winery, the grapes are lightly crushed into the fermentation tank. The juice is fermented to dryness and left on the skins just long enough to produce a rich, darkly colored wine with bright aromas and flavors. After pressing, the wines are aged in oak for nine months. His cellaring program consisted of 20 percent new Seguin Moreau French oak, and one-, two-, and three-year-old French barrels. Lance wants only enough oak to round out the nose and palate with a hint of toast, yet not so much as to overpower the luscious fruit aromas and flavors of cranberries, currants, black cherry, and plums.

"I went into Zinfandel production with the belief that Lodi could produce a premium Zinfandel at a reasonable price," he continued. "I personally believe that premium estate-produced wines should be available for good value. If Peirano Estate Zinfandel, Lodi viticultural area, can be that wine, then it's worth it to me to keep these old vines going. So far, it seems to be happening."

At this point, Lance asked me if I would like to try his 1992 vintage, or was it "too early in the day?"

"It's never too early for a taste of Zinfandel," I assured him. Mark Chandler agreed. Lance then disappeared into the old ranch house that he grew up in, which is being renovated into offices and a hospitality center, to reappear shortly with three glasses and a bottle of his flagship vintage. At that time, his tasting room consisted of a wagon parked under a walnut tree beside his historic vineyard. Given the warmth and beauty of the day, and with the old Zinfandel vines as a backdrop, it couldn't have been a better set-up.

Extracting the cork, which made its trademark soft 'pop' as it exited the neck of the bottle, Lance poured out the rich-looking, purple-black wine into glasses dappled with sunlight filtering through the tree. He handed them to Mark and me. As we perched along the edges of the wagon, enjoying the view over the drowsy vineyard, I savored the distinctive and unusual aromas of black tea, allspice, nutmeg, and ripe purple plums. With such exotic aromas, I wondered what would it taste like. It was full-bodied and richly flavored with black currants and ripe purple plums, and perhaps a hint of dried apricots and prunes, along with the black tea and spices. The exotic aromas and flavors of black tea and nutmeg especially struck me, which, combined with the plums and currants, provided a completely new Zinfandel experience. With four years' age, it was a lovely wine.

A few weeks later, I met Lance at Kunde Estate Winery in Kenwood, where Peirano Estate's 1996 vintage was being processed. We were to taste his 1996 vintage from a selection of barrels: new French, older French; new American, older American. As we walked down the long tunnels of Kunde Estate's barrel-lined wine caves towards the section that housed his wines, I asked him what he had been doing since we last talked. "Riding around in cars with salesmen," he replied. "And the more time I spend out with my salesmen, learning about the headaches of marketing Lodi viticultural area wines, the more I like being a farmer." It's not the fault of the salesmen that he would rather be riding his tractor, he added. However, he felt that it was important to help get his Zinfandel and the Lodi region the recognition they both deserve.

"I'm a man with a mission — which is to make the best wine to ever come out of the Lodi viticultural area, and market it at a fair price," he said. When he is on that mission, he finds a certain joy in getting people to try his wine, and an even greater joy when they call him a few days later asking for a case. Sometimes, he told me, he'll mill about in a regional wine store that carries his Zinfandel, waiting for a customer to pick up one of his bottles. Once, he said, he heard a person exclaim, "Nine dollars for a Lodi Zinfandel!" and then set it back on the shelf. At that point, he approached the customer, saying, "I'll buy this wine for you. Just call me and let me know what you think of it." It's a special thrill for Lance when the customer is from Lodi, and through Peirano Estate wine discovers for the first time the quality that Lodi viticultural area Zinfandel grapes can produce. "They often call me," said Lance, "and tell me, '*We* make pretty good wine here in Lodi, don't *we*?' They're suddenly taking pride in the quality of their community's product. And that makes me happy, too."

But Lance is equally happy to hear from out-of-state customers — such as the woman who called him from Vermont asking for a case. She had sampled it at a wine store in Missouri.

Back at the Kunde caves, we were now standing by Lance's barrels of 1996 Zinfandel. We started with the one-year-old French oak, followed by the one-year-old American oak — both by Seguin Moreau. Both samples had a spicy black tea aroma and flavor, which is becoming almost a signature character of Lodi viticultural area premium Zinfandel, I'm discovering. In addition, the wine from the American oak barrel had accents of medium toasted oak, notably a chocolate/roasted coffee bean/molasses aroma. Both had a rich creamy texture and black fruit and purple plums flavor — exotic and delicious.

"The more time I spend out with my salesmen, learning about the headaches of marketing Lodi viticultural area wines, the more I like being a farmer."

Lance Randolph

Samples from the new French and American oak barrels had most of the same aromas and flavors as from the one-year-old barrels, but with more pronounced sweet vanilla, coffee bean, and unsweetened chocolate accents. A truly distinctive Zinfandel — and positively bewitching in its exotic combination of flavors and aromas.

As a new producer, Lance has been experimenting with harvesting choices. His first vintage, the 1992, got away from him, he felt, coming in a little overripe, with a Brix of 25°, and 15.3 percent alcohol — although balanced and fruity. Both his 1993 and 1994 were pretty much right on, he said, with a harvest Brix of between 23° and 23.5°, and finished alcohol of 14.5 percent. "That's also the style of the 1996, and that's the style I'm going to stay with," he said. The 1996 was harvested at 24.8° Brix, and finished with an alcohol of 14 percent or higher.

"But remember," said Lance, "the harvest Brix is only a part of the picture. Peirano Estate wines begin in the vineyard. Our philosophy is to let the grapes speak for themselves through their flavor. Therefore, prior to each harvest, we walk the fields daily and taste the grapes until they have reached their peak ripeness. That intense ripe flavor is what you will taste in our wines."

Having now tasted the 1992, 1994, and 1996 vintages, I could agree, even though I hadn't at that time tried the 1993. Especially, the 1996 in barrels promised to be irresistible. Sometime later, I had opportunity to try both the 1993 and the newly released 1995, and found no reason to change my opinion. However, I wouldn't have objected to another vintage like the 1995 — a lovely, balanced, elegant wine showing notes of fruit and berries, especially raspberries, mingled in with that exotic spicy black tea character.

The 1995 and 1996, according to Lance, experienced ideal growing conditions. In response to Mother Nature's blessing, the old vines yielded a small crop of intensely flavored, luscious, and healthy fruit in both years.

Lance's production has stabilized at 3,500 cases annually of Zinfandel, and about 1,500 cases each of Chardonnay, Merlot, and Cabernet Sauvignon for a total of 8,000 cases. Having given me these numbers, he then said, "That makes me the biggest winery in the world." When I turned my eyes on him in amazement, wondering if I had heard right, or had missed something I should have known, I caught a mischievous twinkle in his brown eyes. Before I could gather up my shocked wits to close my mouth, he continued, "... within the Lodi viticultural area!"

Yes, Lance Randolph is indeed a man with a mission — and a sense of humor — about his Lodi viticultural area wines.

From 1997 to 1999, Pierano Estate grapes were crushed by Associated Vintners Group (AVG) in Gratton. In 2000, the grapes were crushed by Codera Group, which purchased AVG. Lance hopes to be in his own "cut and cover" winery for the 2002 crush.

Lucas Winery and Vineyard

From Peirano Estate Vineyard, Mark and I drove across town to Lucas Winery and Vineyards on Davis Road just west of Lodi. When we arrived that afternoon, David Lucas, wearing a debonair Panama hat, was waiting for us on the porch of his lovely old country house that was surrounded by lush green lawn and shady trees. Nearby were rustic wooden winery buildings and a tasting room, all beside an old, small-statured, head trained and healthy-looking Zinfandel vineyard.

As David came down the porch steps to greet us, a playful half-grown orange tabby kitten frolicked beside him — a present from his daughter, Mitra. First on our agenda was a walk into the vineyard to examine the 77-year-old vines. The kitten followed us.

David purchased his 20 acres of Zinfandel planted in Hanford "sandy-sandy" soil in 1977. Seven acres are 77 years old, and are planted on their own roots. It is from this block that he has selected out three acres for his own Zinfandel production. Ten acres are 45 years old, and are on St. George rootstock. The average yield is 1½ to 2½ tons per acre from his special three-acre block. His numbers are usually excellent at harvest: 3.43 pH; 0.72 total acid; and a Brix of 24.5° to 25°.

Convinced that he could make a dry red Zinfandel wine worthy of his time and expense from the grapes off the best of his oldest acreage, David produced his first Zinfandel in 1977 (barely 500 cases), and marketed it as Lodi viticultural area — the first winery to do so and a courageous step given the widespread belief among Zinfandel consumers that Lodi Zinfandel was fit only for mass production of inexpensive generic jug red wine.

"This sandy soil is why the vines do so well on their own roots," he explained. "Phylloxera does not thrive in sandy soil, especially such deep sandy soil. It's 24 feet down to water here."

Despite his success with own-rooted vines, in 1994 David interplanted his three acres of 10-foot by 10-foot-spaced vines with vines propagated on 1104 Paulson. Vines are now spaced 5 feet by 10 feet. Budwood for each vine came from the "mom" beside it, said David. It took three years for the new vines to yield a meager crop. "I wanted low vigor," he said, "but not that low." The young vines began coming into production with the 1997 vintage.

David Lucas

After seeing David's vineyard, watching him punch down his 1996 vintage with his trusty garden hoe, and tasting just about every vintage he has made, I could appreciate the appeal not only of his distinctive wines but also his winery and his personal style. I knew I'd be back for a longer talk — and for some of his small-production, handcrafted Zins.

A few weeks later, I sat down with David on a chintz-covered sofa in his rustic and homey tasting room to discuss in depth his views on Lodi viticultural area Zinfandel. I also wanted to discuss his viticultural and winemaking practices that led him to successfully defy popular wisdom on the production and marketability of a Lodi viticultural area Zinfandel.

First, in addition to being a Zinfandel grower and winery owner, David had been vice president of winegrape grower relations for Mondavi-Woodbridge since 1982. Before then, he was involved in grower relations in India two years, in Persia for three years, and in Nepal for six months — when he was in the foreign service and the Peace Corps. He learned, he said, that getting growers to change their practices is something of an art. "You look for the catalyst within the village structure, and you look for demonstrations or quick snappy wins — to establish credibility for changing."

So when it came to his own vineyard, through his years of experience in grower relations worldwide, Lucas had come to understand the relationship between modern viticultural practices and improved wine quality. By 1992, when he determined to make the best Zinfandel he could from his vineyard, he knew how to get immediate quality enhancement.

In the spring, he removes all weak shoots, and at verasion he thins bunches for uniform placement as well as for removing less ripe fruit. He also leaf-thins as necessary, teaching his workers to judge the need for leaf-pulling by the density of each vine's shadow. A dense, black shadow on the ground indicates the need for leaf-pulling; a filtered shadow shows that adequate light is getting into the vine and onto the grapes.

Other important improvements in viticultural practices include reduction to nearly zero the use of fertilizer, changing from furrow irrigation to drip irrigation, and managing carefully the amount and timing of water delivered to the vines. "These old vines have a root profile that goes down 14 or 15 feet. Our average annual rainfall is 16 to 18 inches, and that's exactly the total amount the old vines need for a two to 2½ ton yield. With drip irrigation, I can dial in exactly how much each vine needs. With furrow irrigation, given that some parts of the vineyard are as sandy as a beach, consistent delivery of water to each vine was impossible. I still haven't figured out how to bring a vine into balance in a wet year (more than 16 inches of rainfall). Cover crops help — and maybe I should try sponges."

David also considers himself part of a modern group of farmers who are aware that they can grow in an environmentally sensitive way. "It's truly an integrated approach, an art," he explained. "It doesn't mean that we don't still have lots of problems in agriculture to solve. But vineyards are on the front edge of sustainable agriculture, because they require low input in the first place, so viticultural practices can easily and efficiently be integrated into the environment. The Lodi viticultural area has a highly successful Integrated Pest Management program that includes owl and hawk nesting boxes in the vineyards, and other environmentally harmonious pest management practices. Also, I have seeded my vineyard with a cover crop that I just mow; I disk every other row, since I have young vines, and it's easier for the viticulturist to do the necessary work around them if there is some loose dirt to get their shovels into. Besides, it makes the ride while applying sulfur easier on the old bones.

"The benefits are easy to see. Every morning, when I go out into the rows that have been mowed, not disked, there are dew-covered spiderwebs everywhere, and you know that something is going on, something is living out there. And mowing is a lot easier than disking: you use a smaller tractor, hence less fuel, and it is easier on the ground and the vines. Cover crops also benefit wine quality, especially in wet years. Cover crops reduce the amount of available water, and therefore keep the berry size down for improved berry flavor and concentration in the wine."

The use of cover crops is a radical departure from an earlier generation of farmers. He used his father as an example; "My father values a spotless, immaculate, weed- and grass-free orchard. So when he now visits, he takes one look at my cover-cropped vineyard, goes into the house, opens a Guinness, and watches TV. My farming practices are incomprehensible to him."

David believes that making Zinfandel is a process of discovery. "It's always a challenge to discover the vineyard's true character, and then to express that in the wine. But I start in the vineyard. I like to think that I am growing wine, not growing grapes."

Yet it took him a long time to place quality of wine above crop yield. When he started out in 1977, he was getting five tons per acre — considered light in the district. Since 1992, he's confronted his grower persona in the vineyard head-on, and even though there's still a struggle between the two "hats," he said, "As a winemaker, I just grab that 'grower hat,' and whip it back each time it tries to take over. And you can just taste it in the vintages."

David's average crop yield since 1992 has been between two and 2½ tons per acre.

David cannot emphasize strongly enough the importance of understanding how to balance crop size to vines. The best wine comes from grapes that need little intervention in the fermentation tank. And the best grapes are those that taste good at harvest. However, determining harvest date by flavor is a relatively new concept in California.

"Growers are contracted by wineries to harvest their grapes by sugar content [degrees of Brix]. The problem with such an approach is that the grapes may have achieved the desired sugar content, but are they ripe? How is the ripening curve influenced? What factors enhance flavor? All this takes experience to understand — that is, to recognize the highest potential of a great *terroir*. When you harvest just by Brix, if the grapes don't have the right acid and pH, you add tartaric acid — which is a by-product of grapes. You add tartaric to get to the magical numbers. Yet every time I did that, when I got through my tank or barrels, I found the tartaric acid at the bottom. It had precipitated out. Now, I believe that to make these soft, round wines that the consumer has come to like so much, you don't get there by adding acid. If the viticultural practices are in balance, if your vines are uniform and properly tended, there's rarely any need to adjust acid. Great wine begins with great grapes. My challenge (the fun stuff) is to define my style, and to assist in developing the vineyard and vintage's greatest potential."

Even David's crushing begins in the vineyard. He uses an Italian-made crusher-destemmer that he modified to connect to his tractor. An advantage of this set-up, he pointed out, is that by taking the crusher-destemmer into the vineyard, he both reduces the workload, and he can evaluate on the spot the ripeness of the crushed grapes by looking at the free run juice. "As the juice is being pumped in, you can see the little color ripples and wave effects slowly spreading out. If I suddenly see that the wine doesn't have much color, then I'll just get out in front of the pickers, and start walking and squeezing and tasting, until I come to the fully mature grapes. Then I'll move the tractor maybe 15 vine rows up, and come back for the other grapes a week or so later."

Once the grapes are crushed, he allows fermentation to begin with wild yeast. At the end of fermentation, he adds cultured yeast to make sure fermentation goes to dryness. "Sometimes wild yeast doesn't have enough vigor to go to dryness, and residual sugar is the perfect nutrient for all kinds of bacterial spoilage," he explained. Fermentation usually takes 10 days at 83° F or 84° F, a temperature he maintains by running well water through the jacketed milk tanks. He punches the cap three times each day.

When fermentation is completed, David puts the wine into a holding tank for extended skin contact. "It's a European technique that we in California have shied away from for a long time," he said. "What this extended skin contact does for the wine is to soften the tannins, so that they go from a kind of prickly harsh character to a longer, softer character — sort of the way whiskers feel when they grow from stubble to a fully-grown beard. Another analogy," said David, rubbing his unshaven stubble (it was Saturday), "would be the difference between skim milk and whole milk. The extended skin contact adds a lovely middle body, and gives the wine a silky, creamy texture. It also helps to stabilize the wine, so that it requires less winemaking intervention later on. It's an expensive process, but it really adds wonderful, wonderful characters, and a suppleness to the wine — provided you start with splendid healthy grapes." At the end of skin contact, David moves the wine to a holding tank where it is allowed to settle for several weeks, usually into January or February. Then he racks it into the oak barrels, where it is allowed to age anywhere from 10 to 16 months, depending on the vintage.

My father values a spotless, weed-and-grass free orchard. When he visits, he takes one look at my cover-cropped vineyard, goes into the house, opens a Guinness, and watches TV."

David Lucas

At the end of its barrel time, David may fine with egg whites, "an inexpensive technology I can handle on my small scale," he explained. "What fining does — sometimes I fine in barrels, sometimes in the tank after blending the barrel lots — is to take the coarseness out — what I call the 'nickel and dime effect.' It feels like you have a mouthful of nickels and dimes. It's a coarseness, a dryness, or puckeriness. The egg whites go for just that coarse edge. They don't remove any of the color or the beautiful bouquet. You separate out the whites, and froth them up with a little wine, then stir them in by hand in the barrels. At the end of about three weeks, it has all settled to the bottom of the tank, where it is practically invisible. It forms a thin layer that stays behind when the wine is racked off."

When it comes to barrels, François Freres is David's favorite cooper. But he has recently begun to look at some American barrels coopered by the French. "Years ago," he said, "when I tried American oak, it was just too piney, too lumbery; it had a real lumber yard character that dominated the varietal and the *terroir* of the vineyard. All I was getting in the wine was the oak. I want to protect the character of the grapes that those old vines give me. But now we have French coopers here in America producing barrels using American oak, and air-drying it for two years rather than kiln-drying it. These American oak barrels made in this way are getting to be pretty darned nice. And there's a cost factor. French barrels are about

$650 apiece; the American barrels are $300 to $350. I'm now looking at it from the perspective of my ability to travel the endless summer and 'catch waves.' If I save the cost of two French oak barrels, that's 12 days' surfing in Hawaii! May not be the best way to make wine," he added with a laugh, "but it works! As I've said earlier, when I started out, I chose all French oak to stylistically set myself apart from the crowd of Zinfandel producers who were using American oak. Today, though, both are really wonderful oaks. The American oak coopered in the traditional European way is really very nice. In any case, I use only 10 percent of any one cooper, to add complexity.

David's style has brought him an enthusiastic and distinctive band of customers.

"The people who come out to my winery are a different sort of Zinfandel personality," he remarked. "They're the fun wine people. They're likely to be driving 1959 Buicks with 'Zin Geek' license plates, and often they've driven up and down Davis Road for a half hour looking for me, since I don't have a winery sign out. But they persist, and come in, and leave with smiles and as much Zinfandel as they can afford."

It was time to taste the wines. The first sample was the 1996 Zinfandel from a five-year-old François Freres barrel. The age of the barrel led to commentary on barrels and putting together the final blend. "You don't get any oak flavors from them when they're this old. But they're still good for ageing wine. These two here," he said, tapping a couple of barrels at the end of the row, "didn't make it into the 1995 blend. They were a little off. When I'm putting the blend together, I'll sample every single barrel, taste them, have a couple of friends come up and taste together — I don't like to do it alone. I'll do that three times when I'm getting ready to put the blend together. I'll pull out any barrels I don't think should go in."

The wine we were sampling had been put into barrels in mid-January. The 1996 crop gave Lucas barely two tons per acre, so from his three acres, he got under 400 cases. The sample from the 12-year-old François Freres was rich in red cherries aroma combined with a spiciness of black tea and cloves. "This is really a footprint of that vineyard," said David. "It's got such nice bright fruit my Dad says, 'Why don't you just bottle it like this?'"

Part of the reason for the bright red cherry fruit, according to David, was the rain during the 1996 vintage bloom. The crop was reduced, and extraction was less intense. "The 1996 is one of my more elegant vintages," David said. "The 1997 crop size appears to be bigger, and that's a blessing, because of the over-average rainfall we've had. When your normal rainfall is 18 inches, and you get 25 inches, where is that excess water going to go, if it doesn't go into more grapes? Partly, into the cover crops. Also, in a wet year like this one, I'm the last person to prune in Lodi; I want the amount of rainfall as information to make pruning decisions. If the vines develop too much crop, I can cluster thin, and still get a good yield with lots of intensity."

Our second sample came from a new American oak barrel. "In this one," said David, "we'll pick up the oak expression both in the nose and in the finish — definitely in the finish. But there's no piney character in this. They are doing a very nice job. But in the finish, I can't taste any fruit — only oak."

This was a signal for one of David's entertaining digressions. "I used to be a short order cook, on the graveyard shift," he said, "and our menu featured what I called "Java and Pancakes to Burn." Every once in a while during my shift, I'd burn one side of a pancake, and I'd slip it out burned-side down. Most of my regular night-owl customers didn't care. But even they would notice by the second or third bite, 'Hey, there's some burn here.' That's what all this new American oak is like for me. You cannot taste the vineyard," he emphasized. "It's totally dominated by the oak. Now, we'll go to a newer François Freres [only five years old], for comparison. With this sample, there's a nice long finish that's mostly fruit, which lasts maybe half a minute, and just a hint of oak. The footprint of the vineyard is what's dominant."

David then led me into a blending demonstration, where I saw how the new oak recedes when the three samples were mixed to become just a component in the wine, allowing the juiciness and ripe fruit characters to dominate. "That juiciness is what I've always loved about Zinfandel," he said. "That almost-sweetness that Zins have."

Our tasting ended with the 1995 — "an astounding vintage, just astounding," said David. "This could be my next 'Reserve.' "

Perhaps it will also be the wine he will use to toast a ride on one of those last big waves he has yet to surf, or a run down one of those last big mountains he has yet to snowboard. Break a leg, David!

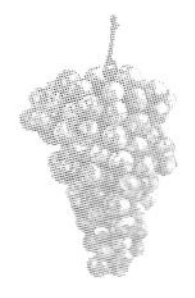

Robert Mondavi Winery, Woodbridge

In January 1997, I returned to Lodi to meet with three people who are centrally concerned with the production of Mondavi-Woodbridge barrel-aged red Zinfandel.

Brad Alderson, general manager, was waiting for me in the lab, which was ringed with barrel samples of Chardonnay. David Akiyoshi, director of winemaking, and Craig Rous, director of research and one of Mondavi's top Zinfandel growers, joined us soon after. On the table stood one seven-glass flight of Zinfandel for each of us. The first three were the 1993, 1994, and 1995 vintages. The 1994 and 1995 were in current release. The other four were barrel samples from individual 1996 grower lots. Each grower's vineyard is fermented and barrel-aged separately at Mondavi-Woodbridge, so that vineyard quality can continually be assessed.

"David Akiyoshi," said Brad as we were introduced, "is the newcomer. He's been here only 16 years [1981], and took over complete winemaking about seven years ago. Craig [who started in 1979] focuses on quality enhancement, which basically consists of teaching growers how to produce the right grapes for winemaking. He helps our 500 growers to see that what they decide to do in the vineyard affects wine quality. This is critical to the quality of our wine. If you don't have the right material, you're never going to have good wine."

"I think what else that group has done is to make the growers into winegrowers," added David. "They used to think that when they brought their grapes to the winery and got their checks, that was the end of their involvement. Now, they understand that it goes beyond that. They are now judging themselves on the quality of grapes they are bringing in, and the quality of wine those grapes produce."

David Akiyoshi

Brad then briefly described Lodi-Woodbridge's soil makeup. "You're standing on 30 feet of top soil," he began. "When that fan washed down out of the hills over hundreds of years, it brought with it at least 30 feet of sandy loam."

"What does that amount of top soil do for the grapes?" I asked.

"That's the question," replied Brad. "Answering that question is part of what Craig's quality enhancement group of growers struggles with."

Our conversation moved on to how Mondavi-Woodbridge could afford to invest in such quality enhancement practices in a wine whose suggested retail price was only $5.99 for its 1995 vintage — and usually available in retail markets for less.

"Our goal was to get people to try Zinfandel as a varietal, so it is a little bit subsidized. We're taking a hit on the [profit] margin right now just to get the appeal out there, to get people to try it," said Brad.

I was astonished to hear that people needed to be *enticed* to try Zinfandel.

"Well, you have to remember," Brad continued, "that outside of California, Zinfandel is pretty unknown. Believe it or not. Sounds crazy, I know," he laughed. "Among casual wine drinkers, to try a wine as an everyday wine, Merlot is now pretty well-known, Cabernet Sauvignon has always been well-known, and also Pinot Noir. Beyond those few, casual wine drinkers aren't very adventuresome."

"When you say 'outside California,' are you talking nationally or internationally — or both?" I asked.

"Both. Certainly internationally, Zinfandel is not at all well-known," replied David.

"It's only the experienced wine drinker who has a passion for Zinfandel," explained Brad. "To wine drinkers outside the wine community, Zinfandel is white Zinfandel."

Of course! Brad's point reminded me of some conversations I had had with a few of my Napa Valley College students who told me that Zinfandel was their favorite wine.

"Which Zinfandel do you like?" I would ask them doubtfully.

"Sutter Home, Beringer, Napa Ridge," were some of the most common replies.

"And what color is the wine?" I followed up.

"Kind of a pale rose," they replied, "or white."

"That's not Zinfandel!" I would bark at them, but in a nice way. "Zinfandel is a *red* wine."

"A red wine?" some of them stammered, incredulous. "Are you sure? I've *always* thought it was a white wine," others replied with maddening certainty. "The label says the wine is Zinfandel."

"Yes, I am sure," I would patiently reply. "Those wines are white Zinfandel, which is a white wine made from red grapes. True Zinfandel wine is a red wine."

"You have to remember that Mondavi-Woodbridge deals with the public, not just the people who know something about wines," Brad was continuing, bringing me out of my reverie. "We make wines for people who know something about wines, but when you're selling 150,000 cases of Zinfandel, you go well beyond the serious wine drinker. If we're not the largest single brand producer of Zinfandel, I know we're one of the three or four biggest.

"Our strategy in the beginning," he explained, "was to subsidize it, to go out at a price to get people to pick it up on price alone, and try it. Only 18 percent of the domestic population drinks wine, and 5 percent of that 18 won't pay dear money for it. We wanted to expand that wine drinking population by appealing to them on price. Now we have good reception, and now we're starting to get the price back up to where the profit margin matches what we pay to the growers, and what we need to pay them."

"What would you like the price per 750 ml bottle to be?" I asked.

"We think it should be the same price as our Cabernet Sauvignon," replied Brad, "which is between $7 and $8. Our 1996 will be released at the higher price."

"That is still a heck of a buy," interjected Craig.

"Yes, and at that price, we can afford to pay the growers a reasonable return," agreed Brad.

At that point, I turned to Craig, whose Zinfandel grapes are among the most highly prized by Mondavi-Woodbridge's winemaking team, to ask him if he felt his return was reasonable.

"At the 1996 price of $800 per ton for Lodi Zinfandel, we're no longer just trading dollars," he replied. "But we're not making much money, either. We're getting enough to keep these old vines in the ground, and that's about it. If the grower I bought the vineyard from had been in it to make money, the vines would have been pushed out — probably long ago. You have to have a love for these old vines, and the wine they produce, and the lifestyle, to stay with them. They produce between two and 2½ tons per acre. Other varieties can produce as much as six to eight tons."

"The newer vineyards such as the Sowles, which is planted on 110R, is cordon-trained, and is in its fourth crop," said Brad. "It can yield four or five tons while maintaining quality. For such new Zinfandel growers, it's an economic venture. Remember, whether you get 2½ tons or five tons, the farming costs are pretty much the same. That extra two or more tons per acre is pure profit — although new growers are repaying their investment costs with their first few years of crop. So at first, the profit isn't all profit either.

"Also, Mark Shimozaki gets six to eight tons per acre on his 15 acres. But he's one of the most efficient farmers I know of. His vines are all head trained and spur-pruned, but he trains them in such a way as to take maximum advantage of our climate in order to get optimum crop quantity and quality from each vine. When you taste his wine, I think you'll agree."

"It's still pretty amazing to me that you can sell a million and a half cases of Cabernet Sauvignon at $8 a bottle, but have to coax people to try Zinfandel at under $6," I protested. "For my $8, I would take your Zinfandel any day over your Cabernet Sauvignon at the same price. And at $6 for Zinfandel, Cabernet Sauvignon doesn't have a chance with me — unless, of course, the Zinfandel is sold out! Do you think part of the consumer's resistance to your Zinfandel is that it is from Lodi ?"

"It's put out as a California viticultural area. No, it's because there's a huge public out there for whom $6 or $7 a bottle is its top price," responded Brad. "Anything more, and they stop buying wine. The volume of wine sales has grown, and we've managed to trade up people to better wines. But they've traded up to where the $6 or $7 they are now spending on a fifth [a 750-ml bottle] they used to spend on a gallon jug. That's where most of them stop. You see it as well in other countries. In England, the price point is five pounds, which is about $7.50. That is the absolute price point you have to get in at. At five pounds, you'll do great. Even at that price, if you drink two glasses each day, that's a bottle of wine every three days. That's a fair chunk out of the income of most wine consumers."

I was starting to get it. If $8 for a familiar and esteemed varietal like Cabernet Sauvignon was the price point for the vast population of casual wine drinkers, then a strange bird like *red* Zinfandel surely would have to compete for attention by having not only an attention-getting price but also superior quality for that price.

And that has been Brad's exact marketing strategy.

"Eventually, we need to get to the point where the growers make money, the winery makes money, and the consumer isn't spending *too* much money. It's finding that magic point. So initially, we wanted to have a head-turning quality at an attractive cost. We were sure the customers would go along with a few modest price increases once they tried the wine. But first, we had to get them interested in Zinfandel as a varietal, and then as a wine that has style. And we have. We probably could have sold twice what we had of our last couple of vintages. Some markets have already taken it to the same price as our Cabernet and Chardonnay — to see if it could survive on its own, unsubsidized. It has to if it's going to grow. And it has."

"So are you going to expand production, then?" I asked.

"Yes," responded Brad. "We already expanded our 1996 to 200,000 cases. We think we can grow 50,000 cases of Zinfandel each year, to where we've doubled our current production. It means we have to find an additional 1,000 tons of top-notch Zinfandel each year. In today's climate, to find between 500 and 1,000 additional tons per year is very doable. I see some opportunities coming up. But we had to look for those opportunities."

"In many people's minds, to come out with 150,000 cases of Zinfandel was bordering on madness."

Brad Alderson

"You have to be much more selective in choosing sources of Zinfandel when trying to increase production," said David, keeping before us the winemaker's perspective. "There are finite, limited regions where Zinfandel grows well."

"Is it difficult to get people to grow Zinfandel specifically for red wine production?" I asked.

"If you ask a grower which he'd rather grow, Cabernet or Zinfandel, he'll say Cabernet every time," replied Brad. "It's easier to grow high quality Cabernet than high quality Zinfandel, and you'll get more tons per acre. You don't have to worry about it. The grapes all ripen at the same time; they don't rot; they don't crack."

"On the other hand," pointed out Craig, "it isn't hard to get people to plant Zinfandel for red wine. They have that same love as we do. They just don't want to put all their land into red Zinfandel. If they find a 100-acre plot out there to buy, and put into vineyard, they might plant 20 acres into Zinfandel, 40 acres of Cabernet, and 40 acres of Chardonnay."

"So it's still a grape people grow for the love of it?" I persisted.

"Yeah," said Craig. "I was just going to say that they do it because there's still a kind of mystique about growing Zinfandel that there's not about growing Cabernet or Chardonnay. Cabernet and Chardonnay will pay the bills. Zinfandel is a risk, but one they will take as part of their planting, because they want to be a part of that mystique."

"So people are planting Zinfandel specifically for red wine production?"

"Sure. The Sowles, one of the grower lots in front of you, was planted specifically for our red Zinfandel program," Brad replied.

It was time to taste that tempting bank of Zinfandel in front of us, and talk about the style as we went along. David Akiyoshi led the discussion.

"What we try to do at Woodbridge — as you said, we're a large facility — we try and do our wine at a scale that reflects the size of the vineyards that we receive here. One of the most important programs we have is to keep vineyard lots separate. This selection in front of you will, we hope, tell you a little bit about Lodi. If you look around the room, you'll see that we're now tasting our Chardonnay. All those bottles of white wine you see are Chardonnay grower lots — also on the other table — that Brad needs to taste today," he added with a distinctly devilish laugh.

"What's important about grower lots," he continued, "is our quality enhancement teams, which Craig also can talk a little about. What we do is go back to those teams and tell them what was good and what wasn't so good about the wine from each vineyard, and maybe things they can do differently. It's a continual learning process. We tell them what we're looking for, and that gives them opportunity to help us achieve quality enhancement."

"They also tell us what they are looking for, too," Craig added. "It really goes back and forth."

"What would the growers be looking for?" I asked. This was a new twist.

"The question becomes how can David get across to the growers what is important to him in grape quality?" said Brad. "How can he let them know what it is that makes these wines consistently high quality every year? We teach that to our growers. We teach them how to taste, and they learn the important things that David knows about what makes quality Zinfandel."

"Now, how do we do that in the vineyard?" Craig continued. "Nobody knows the answers to all those questions. But these groups investigate all these factors: How do we make better color? How do we make better pH, better flavor? How do we develop these in the vineyard?"

"What are the signals in vineyard?" Brad interjected. "In grapegrowing, a lot depends upon observation, just wandering the vineyard, taking in visual clues, and trying to compute where you are in growth, in quality. As harvest date nears, you look at berry size and leaf color, how's the light penetration — all those clues are an accumulated set of symptoms. It's like being a doctor, doing all your diagnosing of the health of the patient by relying just on hands and eyes, and only very few instruments. We know it takes years and years to become a good doctor, years of poking and prodding and asking questions. What we as producers haven't done for growers is to give them that residency, that post-doctorate study. Nor have we accumulated the information as winemakers. So that's what we're doing now."

"So you help your growers understand the importance of paying attention to their vineyards," I observed.

"We help them understand the importance of being *in* their vineyards," David replied. "The best thing a farmer can put into his vineyard is his footprints," he added. "That's one of the few remarks from one of my UC Davis professors that I've never forgotten. Much of our success is because we're so close to our growers."

"It all hinges on keeping these grower lots separate — as David pointed out earlier," emphasized Craig. "If we don't do that, we don't have feedback for either ourselves or our growers from which to learn and improve."

"This all sounds like an incredibly expensive approach to making a $6 to $8 bottle of wine," I remarked.

"It's tremendously expensive," Brad said. "Further, it's not just expensive in dollars, it's expensive in complication — in life in general. It's a layer of complication to someone who wants just to crush everything into one tank, then put the press to the bottom."

David agreed. "That's both easier and more economical."

"So you've traded off some of your profit margins for quality enhancement and control?" I queried.

"Yes, it's the price you're willing to pay to be able to do that," acknowledged Brad, with a laugh. "This is expensive information we collect, very expensive. But we have the results to prove its value. Before we started quality enhancement with our Cabernet growers in 1992, the wine was pale, thin, and insipid. Once we started working with the growers and improving viticultural practices, the wines became dark, inky colored, intensely flavored, lush. You would have hardly believed it was from the same vines."

We were at last ready to sample the Zinfandels. We started with the 1993, 1994, and 1995.

"There are a couple of key note characteristics to Lodi viticultural area Zinfandel that we get consistently," said David. "One of them is tea, or black tea. And another is dried herbs, or herbal."

"It reminds me of a sort of brush, or sage brush," said Brad.

I, too, noticed the herbal or sagebrush character in the nose, which was less pronounced as we progressed from the 1993 to the 1995. The black tea character was a new aroma and taste to discover in a Zinfandel. As I've mentioned in my descriptions of both the Peirano Estate and Lucas Winery and Vineyard Zinfandels, it's there, too, which gave the wines an exotic and intriguing character. In the 1994, I picked up hints of black pepper and spiciness. "That's from the small percentage of Barbera that we include," said David.

The wines also were holding up nicely. They had a lovely soft feel in the mouth, thick and velvety, yet also had a lingering finish from the balance of acid and tannins. Had they found that their Zinfandel would hold up for a few years in the bottle?

"As far as we know," replied Brad.

"This is still a relatively new program, and we're learning more and more with each vintage about how to make our wines and our vineyard selections," continued David. "With respect to the 1995, we're making a more vibrant wine. That's an interesting comment you made about the structure of the Zinfandel. One of the things we're most cognizant of in making our Woodbridge wines is the mouth-feel. We put a lot of wine-making and wine processing into the mouth feel. We put a lot of money into trying to attain that type of a wine. We ferment in small lots — small for us — 25 tons, which is a truckload. Especially, we are dedicated to extended maceration on our Zinfandel, which means we have a large number of small tanks for holding the wine and skin and seeds for extended contact — 21 to 28 days."

"What are you seeking in the wine from extended maceration?" I asked.

"As the maceration progresses, you get what we call a super-saturated wine where the skins and seeds are contributing tannins to the wines. As you taste the wines as they are ageing in this extended maceration mode, you'll find that the tannins will polymerize. This polymerization gives you more stable color, and it gives you wine with structure but softness because the single tannin molecules that don't polymerize fall out. These are the harsher tannins and also the ones subject to bleaching. Polymerized tannins will not bleach out readily."

"Generally, do you have a problem in Lodi Zinfandel with the hard, puckery tannins?"

"No, our tannins are soft, naturally — yet the wine retains its rich, bright reddish-purple color," said Craig, with a grower's pride. "The extended skin maceration David described makes them even softer. We don't have the hard tannins some regions struggle with."

"True, Craig," said Brad. "But think back a little. We've also changed our winemaking. The pressing we're doing, the maceration, how we're handling the fruit, how we're crushing it, we're not breaking seeds — if you break seeds you extract those bitter seed tannins — we're handling the fruit gently at every stage. Each year, we're finding that the wine needs less and less intervention. Our 1995, David neither fined nor filtered."

"When we did fine," said David, "it was only with egg whites, and few at that. In fact, we were using so few, we began questioning whether it was necessary, or whether to let it go unfined, and let the small amount of excess sediment precipitate out in the bottle, or in the bottom of a consumer's glass."

"Also, in the years 1993, 1994, and 1995, you're seeing the effects of the teamwork kicking in," said Craig, coming back to the winery's basic premise that great wines begin in the vineyard. "Although we had a Cabernet Sauvignon quality enhancement group for several years earlier, we started our Zinfandel quality enhancement group in 1992. In 1993, the growers wouldn't have had much time to implement some of the recommendations. But as you go through these vintages, you're seeing a step-by-step improvement in quality. Certainly, much of the credit has to go to improved winemaking practices and gentle handling of the fruit; but you also have to give credit to the growers who are learning how to produce better quality wine grapes."

Our discussion of the three vintages continued. "One of the things you find in these wines is their finish," said Brad. "That finish is one of the things that really grabs people. It's a nice, long, lingering sweetness. As you taste through from the 1993, you'll notice in the 1995 that the herbal character is less pronounced. That's the result of viticultural practices. You can tone that quality down, although you can't get rid of it completely. It's a characteristic of Lodi Zinfandel. It's also in our Cabernet and Merlot. Remember, we're a Region III, which is one of the warmer regions, and that character comes with warmer regions. It's part of our *terroir*."

"That and the raspberry/black tea," added David. "It's an intriguing note, and most un-Cabernet Sauvignon-like. When Zinfandel is allowed to express its *terroir* or regional character, it's a distinctive wine; it's never just another nice red wine. That's one of the reasons we find it so interesting. It has its own style, structure, and flavors."

"When Zinfandel is allowed to express its terroir or regional character, it's a distinctive wine; it's never just another nice red wine."

David Akiyoshi

This was an interesting and original point from David, I thought — and one that only a true 'Zin' believer could make.

We now moved on to the 1996 grower lot barrel samples. The wine is kept in barrels for only six months, for a "Burgundian influence," said Brad. Wood is two- three-, and four-year old and older French oak and 20 percent new American oak from four or five cooperages. "We like how American oak works with our Zinfandel," said David. "Our choice isn't just an issue of barrel cost. It gives a warmth to the wine."

The samples were drawn only from neutral oak, however. "The new wood dominates the wine," said David, "until it's blended. Then it becomes just a part of the total effect. For that reason, we rarely look at the wood as part of a tasting. What we're interested in is how does the wine taste."

"One of the things to notice in these wines," said Brad, "is the depth of color. The 1996 vintage is going to be a dynamite year. The other thing to think about is that although these are young wines — only about two and a half months — they've all gone through extended skin contact, and they are all through malolactic, so taste the finish."

There were four vineyards:

The first was the Sowles, planted in 1991 to UC Davis clone #3 on 110R rootstock and cordon-trained to produce grapes for Woodbridge's red Zinfandel. Yield is about five tons per acre.

The second was the 15-acre, 75-year old own-rooted Mission Vineyard, purchased by Charlie Lewis in the 1950s. His 1996 crop was the first to go to Woodbridge's red Zinfandel program. Still furrow-irrigated, and cropped for five tons per acre, Lewis changed the vineyard to drip irrigation in 1997. Lewis was also in the midst of planting another 10 acres of Zinfandel for Woodbridge's red Zinfandel program from old vine cuttings grafted onto Freedom rootstock.

The third was the 100-year-old Craig Rous Vineyard, dry farmed and on St. George rootstock, at two and a half tons per acre.

The last was the 15-acre Mark Shimozaki vineyard, seven acres of which was 17 years old and eight acres 60 years old. Average yield: six to eight per acre. All of Shimozaki's vines are own-rooted, head trained, and spur pruned in a spiral shape, and drip irrigated since 1991. Since 1996, all his fruit has gone into Woodbridge's red Zinfandel program.

Each wine had distinctive color, aroma, and flavor. Black cherries stood out in the Sowles. The Mission was more distinctively cinnamon and nutmeg spicy, but had none of the black tea character. The Rous had exotic raspberries, cassis, and only faint black tea and spices in combination. The Shimozaki had a dramatic dark cherry, black pepper, spice character. Three of these vineyards (the Mission, Shimozaki, and Rous) are in the Victor part of the viticultural area, and quite near each other. "You could throw a rock from one to each of the other two," said Craig. They perhaps even shared the same clone or budwood. Yet each had a distinctive micro-*terroir* character.

"The Victor area is just about the best micro-region for Zinfandel in this viticultural area," said Craig, a tall, fair-haired man who graduated from Fresno State University in 1979 and signed on with Robert Mondavi Winery, Woodbridge, immediately thereafter. "The soil is 'Tokay Series Fine Loamy Sand,' and is unique to the Victor area. To the west of Lodi, the soil is sandy loam. It has to do with how much organic material is in the soil."

"The 1996 year was exceptional," said David. "The fruit all came in so healthy — no bunch rot, the fruit was loose in the bunches, the berries smaller than usual — we did no hand-sorting."

Each of these wines was so exceptionally good that I asked Brad if Woodbridge has considered bottling these as vineyard-designated Zinfandel.

"What we're thinking of doing is having a small lot bottling, maybe 2,000 cases, of what we call 'on-premise' Lodi viticultural area Zinfandel, from the best lots of the best of these vineyards, for smaller restaurants. Other than that, given that our production is heading for 300,000 cases over the next few years, to have 2,000 or 3,000 case bottlings of special vineyard-designated Zinfandel, it's not the road we've chosen to go down."

Brad continued to describe the wine's character, and Woodbridge's approach to its Zinfandel. "Our style is more Burgundian," he emphasized. "You can see how soft these wines are already. They are already quite approachable, and delicious. I could go on tasting, there's no palate fatigue.

They are already attracting me, even though I know they will get better over a few more months in the barrels."

"There's even that perception of sweetness, adding to the lusciousness," remarked Craig. "Yet the wines are bone dry — or maybe carry a 0.02 percent or 0.03 percent residual sugar."

With such delicious Zinfandel as I had just tasted through, I really wondered why it had taken so long for the quality of Lodi fruit to be uncovered. The reasons, according to Brad, David, and Craig, had everything to do with California's slow evolution to a fine wine focus over the 50 years following Repeal. Widely accessible, inexpensive wines were what the consumers wanted in those earlier years. So the large producers who opened wineries in the 1930s and 1940s, and contracted Lodi Zinfandel, wanted tonnage more than high quality fruit.

Craig Rous

Irrigation was perhaps the single most significant viticultural practice. Farmers furrow-irrigated their vines, even fertilized them, to encourage big, vigorous, strong vines with lots of fruit on them. That was their idea of successful grapegrowing for years. "The tool that growers use, still, that has the largest impact on quality of Zinfandel is irrigation," said Craig. "Reducing the amount of irrigation, and learning timing, are equally important to improved grape quality. Also, how the water is delivered — whether by furrows or by drip lines."

"Why is irrigation necessary at all?" I asked, "Aren't the old vines dry farmed?"

"It takes between 17 inches and 20 inches of water to mature a grape crop. Lodi's average annual rainfall is 17 inches, compared to Sonoma's, whose average is 40 inches. Napa's is 24 inches. Also, because of our sandy soil and deep top-soil, the vines don't have a chance of reaching underground water tables," explained Brad.

"Nor does the sandy soil hold water very well," said Craig. "But all you want to add is the difference between what the year's rainfall has been and what the grapes need. All I added this year was about three inches — which isn't very much. I also use drip irrigation."

Improvements in reasonably priced wines like Woodbridge have resulted partly from consumer willingness to pay more — but not too much more — for wine, even as those wines have educated consumers' palates and made them more willing to pay more than jug wine prices.

"When I came here in 1974," said Brad, "two-thirds of the wine grape crop was going to Gallo, the other one-third to cooperatives, who blended the wine from here into wines from all over the state. Then we started keeping grower lots separate, and we could see the potential, which also created a problem. You don't want to change the dynamics of the market too much. Yet the grower has to get financial rewards for growing quality grapes, because he's going to take a hit on tonnage. Before the emphasis on quality, tonnage was the only way growers could make money. Now, they make money on quality. So you've got to change their perception of profitable grapegrowing, and that's a slow procedure. Improved quality doesn't happen in one year. You might have a grower who does great one year, then bombs next year, because he doesn't have control over his farming practices. He just lucked out one year. You've got to get him to where you both have confidence that he has control over his farming practices, that he understands the consequences of what he does, in order to consistently get quality year after year. Nor is this a phenomenon exclusive to Lodi. Growers all over the state have had to improve their viticultural practices as more and more producers joined the move to a fine wine focus."

"The best thing a farmer can put into his vineyard is his footprints. Much of our success is because we are so close to our growers."

David Akiyoshi

Yet organizing the growers into quality enhancement groups is a potentially risky business.

"This is dangerous, keeping grower lots separate like we do," said Brad. "Hey, Craig can decide to build a little 2,000-case winery, and keep all his fruit to himself. That could happen."

"Or," added Craig, "I can decide I want to sell to another producer who has just offered me twice the price per ton for my grapes. Why should I stay with Woodbridge? That's the other argument against involving growers in quality enhancement programs."

"Once you show people how good their product is, you're potentially asking for trouble," said Brad. "For the grower, there's not a quantum leap in prices year to year, as quality enhancement programs develop. Then someone comes in and says, 'Hey, I can take you to the big leagues,' and they may be gone. On the other hand, that's a risk we have to take. Not every wine in the United States can be sold for $20 a bottle. The market for $20 bottles of Zinfandel (and not just Zinfandel) is pretty much saturated. So we all have to be willing to help these wines make it at $9 or $10 a bottle."

I was interested in what led Mondavi-Woodbridge to begin producing a varietal Zinfandel in 1990 — two years before Mondavi-Oakville added Zinfandel to its varietal line of red wines.

"We've always had it in the backs of our minds that Zinfandel would make a nice wine by itself," said Brad, "So it became one of those ideas that we decided to try out on a few people — like a chef who has created a new dish in the back, and needs to know how his customers will receive it. Zinfandel was a wine we'd been playing with for at least a decade, since we always kept it separate before we made our final red wine Cabernet Sauvignon-based blend. We knew it was pretty good. When we decided to push to add a wine to the Woodbridge lineup, some people actually thought it should be Merlot. But we had Zinfandel in mind. We said to ourselves, 'We can make a gorgeous Zinfandel, and we'd rather make a gorgeous Zinfandel than a mediocre Merlot.' So we got the support, even though — in many people's minds, to come out with 150,000 cases of Zinfandel was bordering on madness. Until then, a large case production of good value Zinfandel was 40,000. That was a huge amount — and we were about to come out with 150,000 cases! Yes, it was a big step, and we faced a challenge just to get shelf space in stores for that much of a new varietal. Remember, it wasn't until about 1992 that Zinfandel really caught fire.

"Another reason we decided to go with it, is we saw a lot of old vineyards around here that produced four tons per acre for white Zinfandel, and if it was for red Zinfandel, it was four tons per acre. From an economic standpoint, these growers needed an additional incentive to keep those old vines in the ground. They needed some kind of value added. So the growers were excited about our interest in producing a high quality varietal Zinfandel from these old vines. In this region, red Zinfandel never did lose its cachet. The growers always knew what it could produce; they had tasted it."

"Many of our growers make wine — and it's always Zinfandel," added Craig.

"Also," said Brad, "red Zinfandel fell from grace in the 1970s particularly because of the glut of high alcohol monsters that were popular for a while. Now take our wines: can you taste the alcohol in them?"

I couldn't, of course. In fact, the alcohol percentage hadn't even crossed my mind until then. There was a reason for it.

"What we prefer, what we strive for in our Woodbridge Zinfandel," said David, "was said best by an 82-year-old retired Italian gentleman, Samuel Sebastiani. His test of wines is one we've followed carefully: *Quando un bicchiere porta un altro, il vino è buono.* In English, that roughly translates to 'One glass leads to another.' The glass that goes down easy, that complements foods, those are the wines that invite you back for a second glass. Those are the wines we strive to make."

"There are some wines," said Brad, "you'll drink a glass and say, 'Yeah, that's big and brash, but I don't think I want another glass.' Those are not the wines we strive to make. Our goal is to make wines that the consumer both wants to drink every day, and can afford to drink every day. You have to set your own style, and make your own wines. You have to decide whether you're making wines to win awards, or to please your customers. That's one of the things our Quality Enhancement Team is working on — getting those mature flavors, that depth of flavor, without getting high alcohol. Our alcohol runs about 13.5 percent.

"Our last goal has been to convince people that our Zinfandel is a better wine. There are some other low-end Zinfandels out there that aren't as well made. They run a little sweet, and don't have the extraction ours has. We seemed to have met that goal as well, since we could have sold twice what we made in 1994. That's why we're able to both increase production in 1996 and our price a little."

"I'm still somewhat bewildered by the fact that people will pay $8 or $9 for your Cabernet Sauvignon, and your Zinfandel has been a bit of a step-child even at $5.99," I reiterated. "To my taste, your Zinfandel is a nicer wine."

"We think so too," David chimed in. "It's our favorite wine, as well. In fact, it's the favorite, hands down, among Mondavi's 800 staff members, company-wide. It's preferred three or four to one over Cabernet, among sales staff.

"Yet it's a wine people still don't know much about," he continued. "It's down there with Pinot Noir. Zinfandel is still just a small blip in California wine production. Even for large case producers such as Mondavi-Woodbridge, who make nearly two million cases each of Cabernet Sauvignon and Chardonnay, 150,000 cases of Zinfandel is tiny by comparison. While we'd love to make 2,000,000 cases [this accompanied by laughter], for now, we are happy to be making 150,000 cases. It's still a specialty wine, even for large producers. And it always will be."

"Yet at some point along the way, Zinfandel will have to be more highly valued in economic return than Cabernet for the world to be in order," said Brad, at last showing in all their glory his true Zinfandel colors. "If you look at what it takes in investment and struggle and everything else, Zinfandel requires a lot more work and attention than Cabernet Sauvignon ever does. If all were right with the world, that work and worry and struggle would be more highly valued. That's how it should be. But it may never happen. Right now, if a person sets $20 as maximum for a bottle of Cabernet, then it will be $15 for a Zinfandel."

With those parting words, Brad slipped out the door to his next appointment, leaving Dave, Craig, and me to linger a few more minutes over the savory barrel samples before us.

I returned to Mondavi-Woodbridge twice more for barrel samples of those same four vineyards. The last time was during Lodi viticultural area's first Passport Weekend on June 1, 1997. Five wineries participated. At Woodbridge, I followed Brad Alderson as he led an eager group back to the barrel room. Pulling out a sample of the Mark Shimozaki, he filled our waiting glasses, then sampled his. A look of blissful joy crossed his face. "Now that wine," he said with a happy sigh, "if I were bottling a vineyard-designated wine, that would have to be one of them. That's an incredible Zinfandel!"

I concurred — as did the group. Not bad for a 6 to 8 tons per acre irrigated vineyard!

In January 1998, Brad Alderson confirmed that Mondavi-Woodbridge would be releasing a 1996 On Premises Reserve Zinfandel, Lodi viticultural area. Discussion was on going as to what its label would be. Twin Oaks was being considered. Production was 5,000 cases. The Rous, Shimozaki, and Mission vineyards dominate the blend. "We didn't want to just call it Woodbridge Reserve," explained David, "because 'reserve' is overused, and we wanted to show our restaurant customers something that indicated a selection of wines. We wanted a distinctive label for our on-premises restaurant accounts that would distinguish this Zinfandel from our Woodbridge label."

After one of my tours of the Victor area vineyards with Craig Rous, we ended up at Sherri Smith's Wine and Roses Country Inn for lunch. An historic-looking structure set at the back of a park-like setting, the establishment is also a bed and breakfast.

Serving only wines made with a preponderance of Lodi viticultural area fruit, Sherri's Zinfandel list was impressive. When Craig let it slip that I was on a Zinfandel mission, she provided a bank of Zinfandels for us to sample with our lunch of vegetables and cheese served in a croissant. I found my favorite two to complement the lunch. Sufficient to say that the wines and the menu were exceptionally well suited. Now I knew why people were wearing those "Stuck in Lodi and Loving It" T-shirts.

The challenge of Zinfandel.

Zinfandel (yellow leaves) and Alicante Bouschet (red leaves) on Pagani Ranch—a typical "mixed black" vineyard.

Harvest ready Zinfandel cluster in Grandpere Vineyard, Amador.

Trellised Zinfandel vine in Henry Vineyard, Napa.

Clockspring Vineyard (260 acres), Amador County. (Bottom middle)

Zinfandel in bloom.

Fire heating (for bending) and fire toasting oak barrels at Demptos, Napa, CA. ➤

Pagani Vineyard filled with mustard in full bloom ▼

Rancho Escondido, Northern Baja — an 80 hectare (200 acre) non-irrigated Zinfandel vineyard planted in 1928-30.

L.A. Cetto Vineyards, Valle de Guadalupe, Baja, CA (fed by the Guadalupe River).

V. Sattui Winery.

Benny Dusi Vineyard, Paso Robles (bottom middle).

"Cowboy Buck," grandson of Russ Oles with Rick Schuetz in Korte Vineyard.

Cucamonga Zinfandel 1920's shipping box label. (bottom)

100 year old Zinfandel vines in Pagani Vineyard

Contra Costa County

Richard Pato Vineyard

Fifty miles west of the Lodi viticultural area is the wine-grape-growing region of eastern Contra Costa County. The cities of Oakley and Brentwood are in this region, which forms the bottom of the Sacramento River delta and the apex of San Francisco Bay. Climatically, it is considered Region III. When Prohibition ended, Zinfandel was thought to be about 2,000 acres. Today, it is less than 1,000, although the increasing demand and respectable prices being paid for Contra Costa Zinfandel grapes are inspiring young people interested in staying in the region and becoming farmers to establish new vineyards.

The regional climate is similar to that of Lodi — warm days with the cooling influence of afternoon breezes from the delta. The soil is also similar, especially in the Oakley area near the river, but finer. While Lodi has sandy loam and loamy sand, the soil in the Oakley area is Delhi Sand Series, which is decomposed granite that is the finest classification of sand. Walking through an Oakley area Zinfandel vineyard is akin to walking on a sandy beach. Your feet slip and you cannot go very fast. In the early days, the residents of Oakley were even called "sand lappers," according to Matt Cline, owner with his brother, Fred, of Cline Cellars, because the fine sand picked up by the afternoon breezes off the bay would get into everything. Phylloxera does not thrive in this soil, and so the vines, including many new plantings, have been propagated on their own roots.

A few hundred yards inland, closer to Brentwood, the soil changes to adobe, and here the vineyards are propagated on St. George rootstock, or even on native roots.

According to second and third generation Contra Costa County growers, the first Zinfandel vines were planted as early as 1880, along with a few acres of Carignane and Mourvedre. By the time of Prohibition, there were 20 to 30 little wineries in the Oakley region. Although the wineries did not survive this period, because of the demand for grapes by home winemakers the vineyards did — which saved Oakley. In fact, planting during Prohibition increased. Because the region is warm, the grapes easily ripened to 27° to 28° Brix by August, and were shipped out early. The home winemakers liked the high sugar content. They could add water and increase the quantity of their wine without losing quality. And they also liked the touch of sweetness that usually remained at the end of fermentation.

Few Contra Costa Zinfandel vineyards are irrigated, although with the increasing demand and rising prices today, some growers are investigating the viability of digging wells. Drip irrigation would improve yield and overall quality considerably, said Matt Cline. Judicious delivery of water would improve canopy and thus offer the grapes protection from scorching, not only by the direct rays of the sun but also from reflection off the sand. It would also protect the vines from excessive stress during the heat of the late summer, and could increase yield slightly in years with less than average rainfall, such as 1997.

The third smallest of the Zinfandel grape regions in California included in this book (after Lake County and Cucamonga Valley), it was mostly overlooked as a source for premium Zinfandel production except by Cline Cellars. In 1987, through the wines produced by Cline Cellars, Zinfandel from this region came to the attention of Rosenblum Cellars. Today, Rosenblum Cellars and Cline Cellars are the two largest producers of Zinfandel from Contra Costa grapes. In addition, several other producers — such as Carmenet Vineyards, Turley Wine Cellars, and Franus Wines — now buy Zinfandel grapes from one or two Contra Costa sources.

To learn a little more about the historic Zinfandel vineyards of Contra Costa and why Kent Rosenblum, founder and winemaker for Rosenblum Cellars, was attracted, if belatedly, to this region's Zinfandel, I joined Kent and his staff in June 1998 for their second annual "Growers Day," which was set in Contra Costa. It included a tour of the vineyards that supply Zinfandel grapes to Rosenblum Cellars.

Especially impressive among Kent's sources are the pre-Prohibition vineyards owned by John Continente, Stan and Gerti Planchon, and Richard Pato.

Continente Vineyards

The oldest blocks of the 24-acre Continente Vineyard, Blocks C and D, were planted in 1879 and 1898 as rooted cuttings or grafted onto native roots, according to owner John Continente (who refers to native roots as wild roots). Some Carignane and Mataro are interplanted with the Zinfandel. During Prohibition and into the 1930s, the Continente family shipped the grapes to New York. Between 1960 and 1990, they shipped to Canadian home winemakers. In 1990, John began selling to Rosenblum Cellars, which meant a change in his picking arrangements.

"Home winemakers liked the old style vineyards, with everything picked together," explained John. "Kent, however, doesn't like the Carignane and Mataro mixed in with the Zinfandel, so we pick them separately."

Carole Meredith, Richard Pato and John Continente

The region has been zoned for light industrial development since 1918, which has enabled the Continentes to develop other sources of income, such as their walnut business. "The old vineyards pay for themselves, but they would not provide a living for a family," said John. "Because of the zoning, I can hang onto my old vineyards, and still earn a living."

In fact, Zinfandel is doing so well for John that in 1978, he added two new Zinfandel blocks. Block A is Zinfandel and Carignane; Block B is Zinfandel and Mourvedre.

Pato Vineyard

According to Richard Pato, his Zinfandel vines were planted in 1896 on St. George rootstock. They are head trained and irrigated once after harvest. Historically, the vineyard has been disked three times each spring, and sulfured twice. It yields an average of 3½ tons per acre.

The vineyard is located on a slope that provides a beautiful unobstructed view across the hills of Mount Diablo.

Planchon Vineyard

Just across the road from the Pato Vineyard is the Planchon Vineyard, which was planted about 1902. Stan Planchon's father originally had 40 acres of vineyard; now there are six. The vineyard is head trained and yields about three tons per acre. Rosenblum Cellars and Franus share the fruit.

Rosenblum Cellars has been working with growers Dwight Meadows and Tony Cutino to plant new vineyards propagated from budwood taken from the Hendry Vineyard, Costa Magna, St. Peters Church, Brandlin

Ranch, and Samsel Vineyard. The Meadows Vineyard is new, has 1,200 vines per acre, and is trellised and trained to unilateral cordons. In the Cutino Vineyard, a few rows of Zinfandel vines originally propagated from a large berry clone were T-budded to the Samsel field selection.

Rosenblum Cellars in conjunction with Meadows and Cutino is eager to discover if the budwood taken from north coast vineyards will produce grapes of similar character in the warmer region of Contra Costa. That is, they are tackling the unsettled question of which is more important for wine character: *terroir* or clonal selection.

As of April 2000, said Kent Rosenblum, only the St. Peters Church selection is showing promise of bringing distinctive character to the *terroir.*

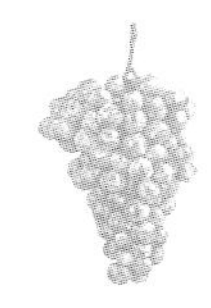

Cline Cellars

Cline Cellars, Sonoma, got its start in Contra Costa County in 1982. Brothers Matt and Fred Cline credit their maternal grandfather, Valeriano Jacuzzi, for igniting their passion for winemaking and for Contra Costa old vine Zinfandel and Mourvedre. "We grew up in Los Angeles, but we spent our summers with our grandparents Jacuzzi on the family farm near Oakley, very near to the present day Pato and Planchon Vineyards," explained Matt during a telephone conversation in November 1996. "The beautiful view across the rolling hills towards Mount Diablo that you see from the road beside these vineyards was the view that we had from our grandparents' place. The family owned some land near Brentwood, which has adobe soil rather than the Delhi Sand series soil. My grandfather planted 30 acres of vines on their own roots, but lost them because of Phylloxera. He also leased some vineyards and planted vines, earning at least subsistence in the 1920s, 1930s, and 1940s. And he always made wine for the table. He would put a few drops of wine in our water glasses when we were children — just enough to impart the flavor of the wine.

"It was Fred who got bitten by the winemaking bug first," Matt continued. "After our grandfather died, Fred came in 1978 to live with our grandmother for his last two years of high school. He ran the family farm, and continued the tradition of making wine for the table. When he graduated from high school, he studied agriculture at UC Davis. In 1982, he established Cline Cellars on the family property. He leased the 220-acre Dupont Chemical Company property, which had some ancient Zinfandel vines, and planted more vines. When Dupont bought the property, the company pulled out an old orchard, but not the old vines, and sectioned off 50 acres for their chemical processing plant. Fred farmed the vineyard, and planted new vines. He also purchased grapes, mostly Zinfandel, from many of the same old-time growers our grandfather had bought from. I joined him as winemaker in 1986.

"In 1991, Fred and his wife, Angie, purchased 350 acres here in Sonoma, and have increased that acreage to 700. In keeping with our preservation philosophy, they have 400 acres in vines, and have left 300 acres of natural oak forest intact."

Cline Cellars Zinfandel, however, is produced primarily from Contra Costa County fruit. "We think that Zinfandel grapes from Contra Costa's old vineyards are some of the best available in the state," Matt explained. "It has been an undervalued source, and the fact that we had opportunity to lease some of these vineyards early on enabled us to establish ourselves as a Zinfandel producer, and to increase production. In 1982, Contra Costa Zinfandel from 75- to 80-year-old vines was selling for $280 to $350 per ton, mostly to shippers. We offered $450 per ton. Soon, other growers were offering us their grapes.

"As a result of our success with this fruit, other producers, notably Rosenblum Cellars, began to seek out these old vineyards, which has driven up the price. In 1999, Contra Costa old vine Zinfandel grapes were bringing $1,400 per ton," said Matt.

"We think that Zinfandel grapes from Contra Costa's old vineyards are some of the best available in the state. It has been an undervalued source."

Matt Cline

"Zinfandel vineyards in Contra Costa County are either pre-Prohibition or have been planted in the 1980s. The old vines are scattered throughout the county in blocks of from two acres to 20 acres, and all are in danger of losing out to urban encroachment in the next 10 to 20 years. I remember as a child looking out the window at the town of Oakley at night, and seeing just a couple of street lamps and a few lights of houses. Now, you look out at night and see the lights of a city."

While Matt agrees that the higher prices now being paid for Contra Costa grapes will help to forestall the demise of these wonderful old vineyards, he believes it is inevitable that some of them will be lost over the next few years.

It was the Cline brothers' desire to preserve their two favorite 90-year-old vineyards — the 20-acre Bridgehead and 14-acre Big Break — and to secure their sources of grapes that inspired them to "break the bank" in 1999 by purchasing the 220-acre Dupont property. "Dupont decided to close down their Oakley operation and demolish their plant, although the plant was not included in the sale. The key to our continued success with Contra Costa Zinfandel is to own our vineyards. We will keep the Dupont for as long as we are in the wine business," Matt assured me.

The Clines have also purchased a few smaller vineyards, among them Live Oak, for a total of 300 acres of vineyard property in Contra Costa. They also have long-term leases on a few others.

Yield from the old non-irrigated vineyards is one to 1½ tons per acre, but Fred and Matt are consulting with their vineyard managers about ways to improve the vineyards and their yields. "Dry farming does not necessarily produce the best quality grapes," said Matt. "Stressed vines sometimes produce grapes with too much intensity and concentration. In 1997, we got more rain than usual, and our yield went to three tons per acre. This still is not a high yield, but it was twice what we get in a normal rainfall year. Nonetheless, the grapes had as much color and flavor as we usually got, and even better balance in acid, sugar content, and pH. The 1997 wine is one of our best ever. The 1999 vintage also is going to be outstanding. With drip irrigation, we think we might be able to get more vintages like those two."

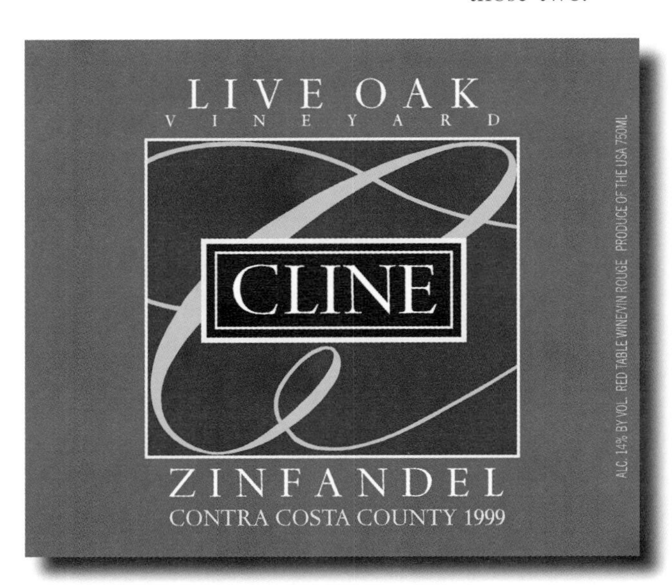

The Clines' interest in Contra Costa vineyards does not stop with ownership of a few of the oldest vineyards. They have planted some new acres from cuttings taken from the original vines. In addition, they are encouraging their growers to lease other old vineyards, and are providing them with the capital and information necessary to do so. "We are working with other growers interested in preserving Contra Costa's old vineyards and also in establishing new ones," said Matt. "As a result, some children from the old families have been inspired by our help to plant more Zinfandel, and also Mourvedre. For many of these families, farming Zinfandel is an ideal way to make a living. They grew up in the area, and like the lifestyle. With the fair prices now being paid for Contra Costa Zinfandel, and also for the Mourvedre and Carignane, becoming a grape grower is again a viable choice as a way of life."

Matt then offered an enthusiastic closing thought that seemed to come straight from a Cline Cellars publicity brochure. "We are happy to be a part of this resurgence, and we will continue to do as much as we can to encourage the preservation of Contra Costa's remaining old Zinfandel vineyards and the continuation of its viticultural industry."

Cline Cellars produces four Contra Costa Zinfandel wines: Live Oak, Bridgehead, Big Break, and Jacuzzi (a blend of best lots from the first three). I tasted all four of the 1997 vintages on a quiet December 1999 afternoon as an interlude from the Millennium 2000 hype. I found all these wines to be big, luscious, and dark colored, with varying aromas of red and black currants, minty eucalyptus, and earthy spices. I thought that the Jacuzzi, Bridgehead, and Live Oak were exceptional. These wines will all keep well into the first decade of the new century.

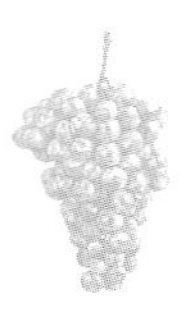

San Luis Obispo County

Pesenti Vineyard

Most of the producers and growers of San Luis Obispo County are located in the Paso Robles/Templeton area. By the time that I had visited there in November 1996, it had become clear to me that the irresistible appeal of Zinfandel lay in its rich ripe fruit character. Certainly, other factors are important: the romance surrounding the grape, the sentimental attachment to old plantings, the grape's versatility, the affordability of the wine, and the fact that Zinfandel was the wine many of the growers and producers had grown up with. But throughout my notes over the years, there was one recurring theme: People love Zinfandel for its fruit.

Yet it seems Zinfandel producers must rediscover this central character of Zinfandel again and again. Perhaps it is easy to miss this subtle appeal of Zinfandel amidst the vast weight of the more popular varieties. The fruit character of Paso Robles Zinfandels, however, was not to be missed.

On my drive from Napa to "Paso," as its residents affectionately call Paso Robles, I became caught up in the romance that awaits visitors to the region. The first romantic hints come from the vistas of row crops and vineyards stretching on both sides of Highway 101 to the looming purple mountains from Salinas south. The fragrant aromas of celery, cabbage, cilantro, basil, broccoli (and more) that emanate from the vast and immaculately cultivated fields as soon as you break free of Salinas always give me a feeling of being in a limitless open-air Italian or Mexican kitchen. The best air freshener in the world, these earthy fragrant aromas. They are especially appealing on a cool November morning. I rolled down the windows, put back the sunroof, and breathed deeply of the crisp air.

Further south, vast colorful vineyards that seem to roll like golden-orange oceans right up to the towering blue mountains replace the row crops. How could all this not put one in an expansive frame of mind? And to arrive at the wineries, many of which are newly built and of elegant architecture in pastel tones — it is almost too much to bear.

Yet it is also the wines that attract the visitors, and help to keep them coming back. And what Zinfandel wines these "Paso" producers have!

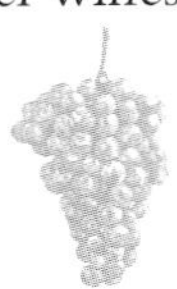

Eberle Winery

My first stop was at Eberle Winery, on Highway 46 East. Eberle Winery established its label in 1982, opened in 1984, and made its first Zinfandel in 1989. A native of Pittsburgh, Pennsylvania, Gary Eberle went to Penn State University on a football scholarship; he was a defensive lineman. When he came out of his office to greet me that lovely November day, I realized I had never before been face-to-face with a football lineman. With legs the size of ancient Sequoia tree trunks and arms like their branches, the tall, fair-haired, and cordial man filling the doorway looked as if he could take his place at the drop of a football on the scrimmage line of any contemporary professional team. Yet here he was, owner, with his wife, of one of Paso Robles' first premium wineries, and getting a reputation far and wide for his Sauret Vineyard Zinfandel.

It happened like this, he told me. While at Penn State, he balanced his studies in biology with his football duties so well that he earned admission to graduate studies in cellular genetics at Louisiana State University (LSU). Befriended there by a professor who was also a connoisseur of fine wine and food, Eberle discovered in the course of this friendship the subtleties and pleasures of wines from Bordeaux. Fascinated with the nuances of fine winemaking, Gary switched graduate programs — trading cellular genetics at LSU for enology and viticulture at UC Davis. Upon graduation from UC Davis, he moved to Paso Robles in 1973 with the intention of planting and producing Cabernet Sauvignon that would rival the best wines of the great Bordeaux houses. After establishing the Estrella River Winery and Vineyards, Eberle and his wife, Jeanie, achieved the next stage of their dream by producing their own Eberle Cabernet Sauvignon.

Gary produced Zinfandel under the Estrella label in the 1970s and 1980s from 47 acres he had planted as part of the winery's eastside vineyard. "It was one of the first eastside Zinfandel plantings," said Gary, "and it made a nice Zinfandel — not the jammy ripe fruit Zinfandels you get from westside fruit, but lighter, with delicate, red raspberry character. The 1978 and 1979 were especially nice." Yet it took Toby Shumrick, now owner of Tobin James Cellars just a few miles east of Eberle on Highway 46, to reveal to him the magic of Zinfandel's fruit.

The year was 1987. A vineyard manager who had more than he could sell to existing contracts brought a load of Zinfandel grapes to the winery. Gary refused these few tons of nearly free grapes. But Toby (Tobin James) Shumrick, his young assistant winemaker, asked if he could have the grapes and process them into his own wine. Gary agreed, and so the first Tobin James Zinfandel was produced. For payment, Gary took a pallet of the wine. Toby struck the same deal with Gary in 1988. In 1989, Toby left Eberle.

Now on his own, Gary realized that Paso Robles Zinfandel was worth adding to his list of wines, so in 1990, he secured the Belli Acres parcel of Richard Sauret's Zinfandel acreage. He now produces between 1,500 and 2,000 cases of Sauret Vineyard Zinfandel. It has become one of his best known and well-regarded wines, even rivaling his Cabernet Sauvignon for popularity. The key to Gary's success?

"The fruit," he said. "Sugars are completely irrelevant. It really doesn't matter to me if they soak out to 27° or 28° Brix, as long as the fully ripe fruit taste is there, and the acid and pH are within acceptable ranges. A dry red wine with alcohol of 14 percent to 14.9 percent is becoming the normal range for my Sauret Zinfandel." His 1995 Sauret, in fact, is even higher — 15.8 percent. His usual vinification consists of pumping the destemmed and lightly crushed fruit into 6,000-gallon tanks, and inoculating with Prise de Mousse yeast. The wine is allowed to reach a "spike" high temperature of 90°+, then is cooled to 80° to 85°F. Pumpover, in order to rupture the skins of the whole berries, is done three times daily. This procedure gets the fermentation off to a good start, which Gary feels is important with such high sugar content. The cooler temperature for the duration of fermentation (usually about 12 days), holds the fruit while softening the tannins. "I've had no problem with the wine fermenting to dryness with this regimen," he said.

Because of his appreciation for Zinfandel's characteristic fruitiness, Gary has modified his oak barrel program to fit. He has found that American oak matches best with the Sauret fruit, and needs only 10 percent new wood (Demptos) with the balance of two- to four-year-old barrels.

To convince me of his point, Gary led the way to his newly constructed (1995) wine caves, where he took me on a barrel-tasting tour of his benchmark 1995 Sauret that I'll long remember. Drawing samples of this soon-to-be bottled wine from two-year- and one-year-old French oak, and also from a five-year-old American oak barrel, we could not miss the vivid differences in the fruit and accompanying flavors associated with each barrel.

Our first sample was from a two-year-old French oak barrel. Along with the luscious fruit were overtones of vanilla and caramel. The next sample was from a one-year-old French oak barrel. This sample had distinct aromas and flavors of green stems and something else, which Gary identified as gunpowder. The last sample came from a five-year-old American oak barrel. This sample was loaded with luscious blackberry fruit, black currants, and raspberries. A rich, succulent wine, it was Gary's preferred sample.

"With such beautiful fruit as this wine has, why cover it up with oak?" he asked.

Why, indeed, I agreed. Perhaps, as Jed Steele has pointed out (see Steele Wines) we aren't prepared for a dry red table wine to taste so good. We aren't prepared for its almost sweet taste from the rich fruit flavors that fully ripe, properly farmed and cropped Zinfandel grapes produce. When it does, we think it too good to be true, that a dry red table wine shouldn't be so delicious and fruity and sensuous. But why shouldn't it be?

"The red Zinfandel boom reached Paso Robles in 1990 and 1991, and got really fired up in 1992," said Gary. "We have potentially some of the best Zinfandel in the state in the Pesenti, the Sauret, and Benny Dusi vineyards. These three old vineyards are among the last of the truly old style dry-farmed vineyards. Today, unless a producer is willing to pay $2,000 per ton for the fruit, few growers can afford to dry farm their vineyards. I feel very privileged to have Sauret's Belli Acres grapes. Richard [Sauret] is certainly one of the best grape growers in the area. That's why I put his name on the label."

Yet Gary believes that Zinfandel extracts a cost from its growers and producers. "No grape is harder to work with," he commented. "Every bad thing that a grape can do, Zinfandel does it. It's the Bad Boy of California varieties." Even so, Gary is planting about 10 acres near his eastside winery) that he is planning to trellis and drip-irrigate. "No way I'm taking a chance on dry farming out here," he said. "The soil is too thin, and the average rainfall is only 12 to 14 inches — less than half of what the westside gets."

I didn't ask Gary to explain his reasons for adding Zinfandel to his own plantings, given his feelings about its "bad boy" behavior. I felt the reason was obvious: He, too, had been bewitched by the magic of the Zinfandel fruit. Besides, the afternoon was getting late, and I had Fratelli Perata to visit.

As I left, I could not help but think about the beautiful fruit I'd tasted in his 1995 Sauret, and found myself wondering if fruit really is enough for a wine to have going for it. What about that layer of new oak flavor I'd been hearing so much about? Was it really unnecessary, just an individual flavor preference? Something to catch the attention of tasting panels, who tend to award their highest scores to the well-oaked Zinfandels? Or was it a matter of *terroir* and vintage — some benefiting from new oak, some not? What about the question of age-worthiness? Do these luscious, fruity Zinfandels age well, taking on a beautiful mature character and bottle bouquet in eight or 10 years that rival the appeal of the sensuous, up-front fresh fruit character of the young wines? These were questions to continue pondering as I made my way to Fratelli Perata — a tiny, family-operated estate vineyard and winery across town on Paso's west side.

Fratelli Perata (Brothers Perata)

Early November shadows were stretching across the vineyards when my car rolled onto the gravel drive in front of Carol and Gene Perata's hilltop home on Arbor Road, which stands beside the small winery. After preliminary greetings, Carol walked me across the lawn to their white barn-like winery, where Gene joined us. My visit began with a vertical tasting of their Zinfandel from 1989 through 1994 (minus the 1992; the vintage did not meet their standards for bottling under their label). The 1990 through 1994 all showed a rather delicate, yet fully ripe fruit, moderately soft tannins, and exquisite balance — the kind of Zinfandels you'd want to reach for again and again. The 1995 I tasted at the March 1997 Paso Robles Zinfandel Festival was much like the 1994, with perhaps slightly more intense fruit. I had been told that I would be sorely remiss if my visit to Paso Robles did not include a visit to this small-production, small-budget, family-owned, hands-on premium winery. The recommendation was sound.

Gene and Carol chose the property in 1977 for its cooler climate and limestone-clay soil. "You know you won't be able to get a phone line in here!" their real estate agent warned them at the time. Their research had shown them that this westside region of Paso Robles was well suited to Zinfandel and northern Italian varieties. "We saw how well the Dusi, Sauret, and Pesenti vineyards had done for years on this westside soil and climate," said Gene. With a long history of winemaking in his family, Gene abandoned graduate school at Washington State University (just shy of a Ph.D. in sociology), to return with his Washington state-born wife to the south-central coast of California to plant Zinfandel and make wine. His goal, with the help of his brother, was to hand-craft the best wines he could from grapes he grew himself. When I asked him, "Why Zinfandel?" his answer was no surprise. Zinfandel was always the beloved grape for his Italian-born family's home winemaking production. And for Gene's family, who lived in the south-coast city of Ventura, Paso Robles was the preferred region to get their Zinfandel grapes from. Fratelli Perata's 25 acres of vineyards are now planted to Zinfandel, Cabernet Sauvignon, Sangiovese, Merlot, and Nebbiolo.

But it took Gene a while to reach this point. Advised against planting Zinfandel in 1978 by just about everybody in the business (price per ton then was between $75 and $150), he nonetheless did — five acres all planted to Dusi Vineyard cuttings on their own roots. "Chenin Blanc was the big thing then, supposedly getting five to seven tons per acre. So against my better judgement, I planted more Chenin Blanc than Zinfandel — and was lucky to coax three tons per acre from them on this soil and climate," said Gene, with a wry laugh. The Chenin Blanc has long since been budded over to Cabernet Sauvignon and Merlot.

Of the five acres of head-trained, dry-farmed Zinfandel, three remain. "Those top two acres caught the full force of the wind," said Gene, as they walked me through the terraced vineyard. The setting sun was lighting up the late fall sky, casting purple shadows over the rugged hills beyond. "It wreaked havoc on those head trained vines. I guess we could have trellised them, but that wasn't our style with Zinfandel. So in 1990, we budded them over to Sangiovese — which we have trellised, and it is doing just great." Sangiovese was the second northern Italian varietal to be added to their collection. In 1983, a few acres of Nebbiolo were planted, since Gene knew from his grandfather that Nebbiolo did well in northern Italy, and the conditions were similar.

Not in the business to generate a big income, Gene and Carol do not see themselves ever becoming a much larger operation. "I couldn't do 300 acres; 40 would be about right," said Gene. They are content with the fact that their Zinfandel produces the ripe red berry/ black currant and spice flavors that they prefer for their style of wine at less than two tons per acre. "Two and a half tons is too much for these vines," Carol said.

With such an outlook, they set themselves distinctly apart from the region's many new growers of the 1990s. "Now that the cattle business has gone bust here," said Gene, "many former cattle ranchers are planting grapes. But for us, it's always been a love. We do everything ourselves: vineyard care, harvesting, crushing, and the cellar work. From start to finish, we make our wines by tasting them."

Fratelli Perata grapes are picked when flavors are ripe, which usually occurs at a Brix between 23° and 24°, and with pH of 3.3 to 3.4. Acid adjustment is rarely required. Once picked, the grapes and wine are handled gently in order to preserve the delicate fruit flavors and prevent excessive extraction of the harder, bitter tannins. The grapes are just destemmed, not crushed; the wine is inoculated with yeast, and fermented in small bins for easy hand punching. When dry, the wine is pressed out, and the wine is put into neutral American oak barrels, where it completes malolactic fermentation, ageing for about 19 months. It is bottled unfined and unfiltered. Between 350 and 500 cases are produced annually.

Although Fratelli Perata is a small winery, Gene and Carol try to keep their prices affordable. Their 1995 Zinfandel was released at $12 a bottle; they envision only modest price increases. "Our other wines carry higher bottle prices," Carol said, "because they are much more labor-intensive and expensive to make. Our Cabernet Sauvignon, for example, is aged in 100 percent new French Chateau barrels, and takes 30 months from vineyard to bottle. All that extra time and new barrels add substantially to the cost of the finished wine."

With so much hard work for modest returns on such beautifully crafted wines," I wondered aloud, "Where's the magic for you, since it's obviously not in counting your dollars?"

"When we were just growing grapes, before we had the winery, the magic was seeing the truck loads of grapes going down the road each fall," said Carol without hesitation. "Now, it's the moments just after we've finished pressing off the new wine from the skins, and are putting it into barrels. All the beautiful aromas are coming back at you, and you can just smell all the wonderful possibilities. You almost know where the wine is going — but maybe not. That's the magical moment for me," she said. "But until then, while the wine is fermenting, there are too many variables to really know what you've got. But once it's pressed off, that's when the joy begins."

Gene was nodding his agreement to Carol's words.

I left Fratelli Perata in the glow of their modest pride and clear satisfaction in the quality of their wines. I was deeply impressed by the love, the dedication, the *heart* for this business that had placed them among the most esteemed producers of this region; I was even more impressed by the fact that neither Carol or Gene dwelled upon their years of struggle for their modest returns. The magic and romance of the lifestyle that is a partner to the struggle prevailed.

With these thoughts, I wended my way back to Highway 46 and across town to begin my journey up the now pitch-black Peachy Canyon Road. Doug and Nancy Beckett of Peachy Canyon Winery awaited me — and my visit to the Paso Robles area was still in its first day!

Peachy Canyon Winery: The Romance Continues

Although only six winding miles from downtown Paso Robles, it seemed like 10 before I came upon the white railing fence that borders Peachy Canyon Winery's walnut orchard. Then, my headlights lit up the Peachy Canyon sign, and the next instant I was climbing what seemed like a driveway straight up to the stars. However, I remained earth-bound, and the driveway led me to the parking area in front of the big white two-story house replicated on the Peachy Canyon Winery label. Escorted across the porch to the door by the winery's four rag-tag woofers, I rang the bell, which summoned Doug Beckett. Reserved, soft-spoken, shaggy-haired, lightly bearded, and dressed in ancient Levis and Peachy Canyon

T-shirt, Doug welcomed me in, and then showed me up the stairs to a room furnished in the country style of the house. Two bedrooms with adjoining bathroom were previously occupied by Doug and Nancy's two sons, now college students. Nancy was at her dancing class (she's the teacher).

By the time I had showered off the day's road dust and found my way down to the kitchen, Nancy, petite, blond, and vivacious, was home. A bowl of guacamole and tortilla chips were on the table, and an open bottle of Peachy Canyon Zinfandel stood nearby. Had I arrived in heaven after all? Shortly thereafter, we regrouped in the dining room for dinner, the Peachy Canyon Zinfandel supplemented with a bottle of 1993 Limerick Lane that I had brought along. The quiet reserve with which we all greeted each other for the first time only minutes before dissolved in the ambience of delicious food, great Zinfandels, and spirited conversation. "Quiet reserve" hasn't a chance in the presence of such wondrous Zinfandel wines — and the people touched by them.

Nancy and Doug Beckett

But my investigation into the particular appeal of Peachy Canyon's several Zinfandels would have to wait for a day or two. The next day I was scheduled to meet with Arroyo Grande's Bill and Nancy Greenough, at their Saucelito Canyon Winery and Vineyard, the most southern San Luis Obispo County Zinfandel vineyard. My journey took me south on Highway 101 into San Luis Obispo, out past the airport and onto Biddle Road, which presented me with more oceanic, fall-hued vineyards. My first stop was the Greenoughs' residence.

Saucelito Canyon Vineyard and Winery

"Wine, Pure Zinfandel. Saucelito Vineyard, five gallons a mere 50¢ a gallon, plus container." Thus read an agricultural advertisement in a 1935 Arroyo Grande newspaper that Bill and Nancy Greenough had awaiting me at their Biddle Ranch Road home, just past Edna Valley Vineyards, when I arrived that sunny, cool November morning. Bill, looking almost scholarly with his sandy hair and wire-rimmed glasses, and Nancy, blond and blooming, welcomed me with tea and biscuits. Their dining room table was covered with old newspaper clippings, photographs, and other such fascinating bits of history on their 1880 Zinfandel vineyard. In 1997, a bottle of Saucelito Canyon Zinfandel was selling for $17. That the old Saucelito Vineyard should have survived to see such a price for its wine is another Zinfandel miracle — a miracle brought about by Bill Greenough. Bill, a Santa Barbara native and Dunn School, Santa Ynez, alumnus, purchased the property from the granddaughters of the original homesteader-owners in 1974. Shortly thereafter, Bill and his first wife moved into an old ranch house that sat on an 80-acre parcel further up the valley that the granddaughters still owned. The land on the parcel was rented to ranchers for grazing.

For two years, Bill and his wife lived in the nearby ranch house while he set about restoring the vineyard, which had been untended for the 40 years since the granddaughters had moved off the property. The soil, Bill explained, is formed of an ancient uplifted sea terrace about 100 feet deep. Average rainfall is 22 inches. Along with several fossilized sea creatures, Bill found the surviving vines — about a quarter of the original planting (or about three acres) and all on their own roots — overgrown with poison oak and chaparral. He cleared away the overgrowth and suckered the old vines, then trained up one new shoot from each living root crown to create a new trunk. "Sure," he said, "I could have torn out the old Zinfandel and gone high-tech in replanting to more profitable varieties. But I found it challenging to restore the old vines and the vineyard. Also, part of the reason the Ditmas granddaughters sold the property to me in the first place was that they could tell I was dedicated to restoring the old place. That was important to them."

At the vineyard site, Bill set up a generator-powered refrigerator and a bathtub. Each morning, he said, he would put two martinis in the freezer. At the end of the day, he retrieved his frozen martinis, filled a tub set under a giant oak tree from water heated by an old army immersion heater in a 55-gallon drum of water, and sat back in the hot water to enjoy the sunset. The "two martini sunset" became the inspiration for Saucelito Canyon's label.

"Quite an undertaking," I commented later in the afternoon, as we sat upon the spacious deck of the "functionally obsolete" ranch house built a few years later. The deck overlooks the immaculately tended vineyard and the mountain ranges beyond.

"They may not have been the best two years of my life," Bill replied, "but they are close to it." Bill and his second wife, Nancy, were married in 1980. Since then, the ranch house has been enlarged to accommodate the growing family. Today, it also serves as a country retreat for various family members. A little 2,500 case winery was opened in 1982.

Soon after looking at more of the early photographs and old newspapers came the moment that I had been holding my breath for: "If you'd like to see the vineyard," Nancy said, "Bill will take you out now." Well, it took me less than a split second to gather my camera equipment from my car and join Bill in his Jeep for the 15-mile ride to Saucelito Canyon, and his restored 116-year-old Zinfandel vineyard hidden away at the end of it.

I thought that our conversation, the photographs both early and recent, and the awesome vistas provided by the winding 15-mile drive had prepared me. Yet nothing could have prepared me for the unutterable beauty of the little vineyard and winery nearly lost among the surrounding ridges and mountain ranges. A stainless steel "Time For Milk" truck gleamed incongruously near the winery door. "Sluggish fermentation," said Bill, in answer to my astonished look. "I've had sluggish fermentation every year since our first vintage in 1980. Everything gets cold (50°F) out here by November. Usually the wine just sits in barrels over the year. Then with the warm weather in spring, it all starts up again — both primary and malolactic. But this year, we had unseasonably early cold weather, and one batch slowed prematurely. I always like to ferment and barrel age each lot separately, to bring complexity to the finished wine. But I had to blend some of the lots together this time. The milk truck, rented for two days, was the perfect vessel to get it going in — which it did. Now I'll find out if blending some lots before barrel ageing brings as much complexity as blending after."

Bill Greenough

Then it was on to a walk through the vineyard to see and touch the vines trained up from the 1880 root crowns. At one point, Bill crouched under one of the restored vines to scoop up a handful of sea-terrace dirt for my examination, and to show me how he went about clearing off the original root crowns. A certain remembered joy illuminated his face beyond the light of the sun's rays.

Two and a half acres worth of the cleared vineyard were planted in 1977-78 to nursery-rooted cuttings. In 1980, Bill added another 1½ acres, this from rooted cuttings off the original 1880 vines. Another acre from the old wood followed in 1996, for a total of eight acres of Zinfandel. Bill is looking to replant back to old clone Zinfandel one acre of 12-year-old Cabernet Sauvignon, Merlot, and Cabernet Franc on clay soil. "The soil and climate," he said, "are unsuited to the Bordeaux varieties. But the Zinfandel does well." Although some of his newer Zinfandel plantings are trellised to help combat bunch rot from the frequent thick morning fogs that roll in all summer, he is going back to head trained for this replanting. "We make such a big deal out of old vineyards, and that they were all head trained and dry farmed, that I am going to keep the tradition from now on with this old budwood."

Back in the winery, Bill explained his approach to winemaking. "We pick the vineyard blocks at different times. We pay our workers by the hour, and ask them not to pick second crop. We used to ask them to leave any excessively raisined bunches, but that became too difficult, so now we hire four guys just to hand-sort out raisins on the conveyor belt. Although we would like to have our wine under 14 percent, we've found that for best flavor, the grapes come in at between 25° and 26° Brix, for an average alcohol in our wine of 14.5 percent. Vigorous sorting out of raisined clusters keeps the wine under 15 percent. Raisins, we've found, add alcohol without adding flavor. We usually begin harvesting the third week in September, and it lasts from one to two and a half weeks.

"Fermentation is fairly warm, for maximum extraction and intensity of fruit, in some three-quarter ton containers, some 2,000-gallon open-top tanks, for easy punch-down and pump-over. Average maceration is six to eight days, the wine is pressed before dryness, and it finishes both primary and secondary fermentation in barrels. Our barrels are from 10 years old to new Demptos American oak. We bottle our wine, sterile filtered, the following August, before the next harvest — which gives it about 10 months in barrels. Our consultant, Lane Tanner (of Lane Tanner Wines), feels that the wine keeps its fruit best after only 10 months. Also, sterile filtering really tears up the wine, so it needs the additional bottle age to recover before release the following spring."

"I thought sterile filtering was anathema to fine winemaking — unless desperate," I remarked.

"I've been sterile filtering since the 1986 vintage, and that was the Zinfandel that won us our first gold medal," said Bill. "Our wine doesn't always ferment completely dry, it doesn't always complete malolactic, because, as I've explained, it gets cold out here. So sterile filtering ensures that the bottled wines will not restart fermentation. Perhaps if we had our own lab, and could do cultures, we wouldn't always need to sterile filter. But we don't, and there's no convenient lab nearby. I know I've been sleeping better since we started sterile filtering. Our wines are very well-received by our customers and judges alike."

"Will they be as likely to age as well as non-sterile filtered?" I asked.

"Probably," he replied, "But to my taste, any Zinfandel that is older than 10 years is just another old wine; it's no longer Zinfandel."

The early November afternoon light in that remote canyon was changing by the minute. Bill offered to take me up the ridge behind the winery in the two-cylinder open-topped "mule." From this vantage point, we could see mountain ranges one after another, each a different shade of mauve or purple. Directly below us lay the colorful, immaculately tended little vineyard accented by four yellow aspens off to one corner. Each row of vines looked like a colorful thread in a tapestry. The vista inspired reverential silence. After a few moments, I remarked to Bill, "That little vineyard cannot possibly pay for its keep, can it? It and the wine it produces exist only out of your love for them, am I not right?"

"No, you're wrong, it does pay for itself. However, if I had been restoring the vineyard strictly for the money, I would have ripped them out, and replanted to more profitable varieties. But this is one of the pockets of old Zinfandel that survived to the early 1970s. It deserved to be restored, and it took someone like me to do it — who isn't doing it strictly for money."

We returned to the winery for a tasting of the 1996 — both from barrels and from the blended tank. First sample was from a two-year-old French barrel. The wine was rich in flavors of chocolate, espresso coffee, dark molasses, and cassis. The next sample came from a four-year-old neutral oak barrel, which displayed brighter acids and less of the rich fruit. The third barrel sample was from new Demptos American oak. Along with the lush blackberry fruit was that smoky toasty oak layer so discernible from fresh newly toasted oak. Then Bill drew me a blended sample from the fermentation tank. This presented lovely, rich, luscious fruit character along with the molasses espresso coffee flavors I had until then associated with new oak. But this wine hadn't yet seen an oak barrel! Those wonderful complex flavors came entirely from the grapes. It was a stunning wine. "There's that fruit again," I thought, remembering a similar taste experience from Eberle's 1995 Sauret Zinfandel.

After looking into some stainless steel barrels filled with whole clusters of raisined berries that were slowly fermenting into a rich 15 percent residual sugar, 15 percent alcohol, Late Harvest dessert wine (about 200 one-half bottle cases worth), I wandered back to the Jeep while Bill made some phone calls.

It was now 2:45 in the afternoon. I sat back in the Jeep, and for a few minutes just took in the incredibly quiet, beautiful scene. Gradually, a few sounds became apparent: acorns falling onto the Jeep's roof, sounding like little rocks; some birds whistling; bugs buzzing nearby; the gentle trickling of the nearby stream. At the edge of the vineyard stood pepper trees, huge, beautiful, one with red berries. In the distance was the deepening blue sky, the golden leaves of trees, and purple mountains forming a backdrop to it all. I felt the Jeep rock gently, and realized that Bill had come back from the winery and was sitting on the tailgate, in a similar state of reverie. California mystique; Zinfandel mystique. It was time to go — but which of us should speak first? I can't remember who made the move, but the next moment, we were wending our way back down the canyon past grazing cattle to the entrance gates — and on back to Biddle Road. A special afternoon never to be forgotten.

Return to Peachy Canyon

Twilight was settling as I made my way back up to Peachy Canyon Winery, where I found Doug and Nancy Beckett and their winemaker, Tom Westberg, in the winery tasting some barrel samples of their 1996 Zinfandels. The first was from the six-year-old westside Richardson Vineyard in a two-year-old French oak barrel. The wine demonstrated the importance of grapegrowing practices and location. Although made from young vines, the wine had lovely blackberry fruit and zesty spice character that needed little oak flavor for complexity.

The next sample came from Leona's Vineyard, a 30-year-old westside vineyard on Willow Creek Road. The second crop fruit from this vineyard is so good that Doug identifies it as such on the label. Some of the Leona's, along with the Richardson and Dusi, form the basis for Doug's Westside Zinfandel. Leona's and Dusi also are bottled with vineyard designations.

From the winery we went to the tasting room where Doug opened bottles of each of Peachy Canyon's 1994 Zinfandels — a total of six

(Incredible Red, Eastside, Westside, Dusi, Leona's 2nd crop, and Estate). The Incredible Red, a soft spicy wine with red raspberry fruit, is made from 90 percent Zinfandel and 10 percent Cabernet Sauvignon. "It brings people into the Peachy Canyon camp, gets them to drink red wine," said Doug. The Eastside is primarily from the Cromwell vineyard, a 10-year-old, own-rooted planting (source of cuttings unknown), trellised, irrigated, that used to provide fruit for white Zinfandel. The wine is well rounded with lots of bright fresh red raspberry fruit.

"Zinfandel is such a beautiful grape," said Doug. "Here in Paso Robles, you get different degrees of intensity and flavors from each micro-climate and *terroir*. The fruit flavors, acid, and pH are different between eastside and westside fruit. That is why I coined, first, westside, and then eastside, because the flavors and intensity differ on each side of the Salinas River. The land on the eastside is flatter, the soil is sandy loam, and the micro-climate hotter. The westside is benchland and hills, the soil is lime-stone clay, which encourages the vines to put down deep roots. And the climate cools off at night because of breezes coming in from the ocean."

The third 1994 was the Westside — a blend mostly of the Benny Dusi and the Richardson vineyards. A big wine of subtle fruit and hints of spice and black pepper, it was a Zinfandel that could either be enjoyed now with a range of foods or stored away for the long haul.

Then came the Benny Dusi vineyard-designated Zinfandel — the one I had been most anticipating. Peachy Canyon and Ridge have been Benny Dusi's only customers for many years, and they both produce a vineyard-designated Zinfandel from this ranch. Doug had begun producing a Benny Dusi Zinfandel in 1981, under the Tobias label — a move, he said, that had probably more to do with Peachy Canyon Winery's success today than anything else that he did.

"In 1981, Zinfandel was an affordable grape. Benny had called us, since he had 40 acres of old vines, and Ridge [who began its long-term contract with Benny Dusi in 1976] was not taking the entire crop. Had I not started making Zinfandel in 1981, when only two other Paso Robles wineries were making Zinfandel [Pesenti and York Mountain], we would not be where we are today. Had we not made beautiful, saleable Zinfandel under our Tobias label, had we not continued to work with Benny, our reputation would not be close to what it is now. We wouldn't be making six Zinfandels. Our success did not happen overnight. It's a long process of hard work. It takes a long time to achieve success in the wine business — and a lot of imagination. I think Peachy Canyon's success has done much towards gaining recognition for Paso Robles Zinfandel. Even sec-ond crop, which used to be free, is now being sold commercially. And everyone wants Benny Dusi's fruit!

"The bottom line," he continued, "is we have to sell our wine. For us, it is a business first, and a love affair second. It is a vocation and livelihood for the owner and a profession for the employee."

As he poured a tasting of his Dusi Ranch, Doug explained in some detail his winemaking approach to this Zinfandel. It is fermented cool and slow to dryness in one-half ton bins, with punch-down three times each day, then pressed, and put into mostly neutral (three-year-old) French barrels and 20 percent new American for about 12 months. "When the wine is lovely and fruity as this is, you can only screw it up. Why mask these flavors with a lot of new oak? Oak's role is to soften tannins. Wine needs slow oxidation, so putting it into barrels is simply part of the finishing." A fuller-bodied, darker, spicier Zinfandel than the previous three, it had a modest 13.6 percent alcohol.

The next Zinfandel was the Estate, the third vintage from Doug and Nancy's own dry-farmed vineyard planted on 110R rootstock budded to the Dusi ranch clone. An elegant wine with bright red raspberry fruit, it was the one I enjoyed most with that evening's dinner of grilled salmon. The last was Leona's Vineyard 2nd crop — with luscious black currant, blackberry fruit flavors. The second crop fruit was picked at 29° Brix, and at a pH of 3.26, such numbers being possible, some old time local observers say, because the vineyard's Willow Creek Road location falls within the westside's "enchanted kingdom of vineyards." The finished wine has an alcohol of 15.2 percent, and is a favorite with Peachy Canyon's customers.

"I have two keys to my success," said Doug, "a willingness to blend, and a recognition of good vineyards on my labels. I have to give credit to Toby Shumrick [owner of Tobin James Winery since 1994] for introducing me to the art and merit of blending. Toby was cellar worker and winemaker for two years — 1990 and 1991. Both our 1989 and 1990 "Reserve Special," which was mostly Dusi fruit, achieved critical awards. The 1989 won a double gold medal from the San Francisco Wine Tasting, and the 1990 Westside made it into the *Wine Spectator*'s top 100 wines of the world. It was a fairy tale of two wines and two wineries — Peachy Canyon and Tobin James.

"My vineyard designations are for those vineyards, or blocks of vineyards, that cannot be improved upon by blending. I'm adding two more vineyard-designated Zinfandels: the Old Bailey (1995); and the Richardson (1997). They are getting that good." When I tasted the 1995 Old Bailey at the ZAP 1997 tasting in San Francisco, I agreed with his decision. In fact, I felt this vineyard might be his best yet.

A few months later, at the March 1997, Paso Robles Zinfandel Festival, I had an opportunity to taste a vertical of Peachy Canyon Dusi Ranch Zinfandels from 1989 to 1994. Notably, the 1989 Reserve Special had reached its peak; the 1990 was holding together beautifully. The 1992 Dusi Ranch was the first to show the influence of the explosion of fine Zinfandels of the 1990s. It had softer tannins, lovely up-front fruit, elegance, spiciness, and just enough new oak to add an additional layer of complexity. The 1994, under the hand of Robert Nadeau, was bigger than the 1993. As described above, it was a dark, full-bodied wine that should be good for the long haul.

In May 2001, Tom Westberg became winemaker for the Eschelon Vineyard in Edna Valley. He was replaced by Florence Sarrazin, a graduate of the University of Bordeaux. The Beckett's son Josh became assistant winemaker and son Jake, vineyard manager.

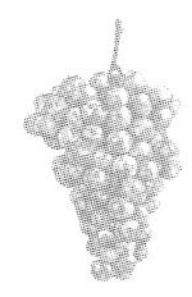

Benito (Benny) Dusi

The Dusi vineyard lies between the Salinas River and Highway 101 just south of Paso Robles. To get there, I followed Doug Beckett south from Paso Robles on Highway 101 to Ramada Drive, and then down the gravel lane leading between rows of Zinfandel to Benny Dusi's neatly kept white house surrounded by shady trees and a multitude of bright flowers. The nearby garage, sheds, and tiny wine cellar were also neatly kept. Benny, who has lived here all his life, was standing in the driveway awaiting us.

After a quick introduction, Doug took off, leaving Benny and me to get to know each other. Benny, a bachelor in his early 60s, is a soft-spoken and observant man whose love for trains, trucks, and tractors is second only to his love for his vineyard. He's also an avid reader, and his first offering following our introduction was to show me an armful of books and magazines that had photos, stories, or some other mention of Dusi Ranch Zinfandel. Well-read, he knew every word of what had been written about his ranch, where every photograph was, and what kind of ratings his Zinfandels had been getting over the years. "Very close to the top all the time," he said with a touch of pride.

Benny Dusi's father bought 20 acres of one-year-old vineyard on the western benchland of the Salinas River in 1924. He planted an additional 20 acres in 1931, also with Zinfandel. All the original vines were own rooted and dry farmed with 12 x 12 spacing.

"The key to successful dry farming," said Benny, "is to till the soil good, to get it nice and fluffy. That's when it holds the moisture best." In recent years, some of the vines have succumbed to phylloxera, and Benny has been replanting them with budwood grafted onto both St. George and 110R rootstock. In dry years, he supplements the low rainfall with some drip irrigation. Although he now has a portable irrigation system, he pointed out a bunch of white five-gallon pails lying in a heap in his shed. "Those buckets make the best drip irrigation system," he said. "What you do is punch a tiny hole in the bottom of each bucket, and set them under the vines. Then all you need to do is service each bucket with a tractor and water tank. The water seeps slowly through the little hole in the bottom, making a perfect drip irrigation device. With these head trained vines, it's the easiest way to water them."

We were walking through the vineyard now, and I was listening to the way he talked about his vines, and also about the oak trees shading the house, and cherry trees down by the river. When he wanted to tell me why he preferred 110R rootstock over St. George, he did so by reverting to a typical expression: "Those guys," he said, indicating a block of healthy-looking vines, "don't make many grapes."

"Which guys?" I asked, since in their November dormancy, all the "guys" looked alike to me.

"Those guys on St. George," he said, pointing out a nearby block. "They produce too many leaves and vines. St. George has a great root system, but it has taken six years for them to produce a decent crop. Over there," he said, pointing further, "is 110R. Now those guys I like because they give more crop and produce less leaves and vines early on."

As we walked along, I asked him, "Have you ever thought of taking out your Zinfandel ?"

"No! Absolutely not," he exclaimed, stopping dead in his tracks, and looking sharply at me. "I grew up with it. I like it. Zinfandel has been in Paso Robles for 100 years." A few steps further on, he said, "Do you know what's interesting about Zinfandel? It's a beautiful grape, but it was a lost grape for many, many years. Now, it's been coming back these past 20 years."

"Who did you sell your grapes to all these years before Ridge and Peachy Canyon began buying them?" I asked.

"In 1968, Ridge bought from me for the first time. From 1970 to 1976, Paul Masson bought my grapes, and paid $200 per ton at first. Every year, the price increased, until Masson was paying me $400 per ton. I was living in luxury then. Masson was always a fair player, always paid good prices. I also sold to Roy Thomas of Monterey Peninsula Winery for several years, in the late 1970s and early 1980s. In 1976, Ridge came back, and has been buying from me ever since. I also have always sold to home winemakers." (In spring of 1997, I spent a morning with Roy Thomas in his Monterey home, and tasted his 1978 Dusi Zinfandel. Still holding up, still with some of its fruit and spice, it was a distinctly respectable 19-year-old wine.)

"How much of your crop does Ridge buy?" I asked.

"About 60 percent," said Benny. "Beckett [Peachy Canyon] gets between 15 percent and 20 percent, and I still sell to some long time home-winemaker customers."

"So what kind of work does a vineyard like this require? Do you do some of it yourself?"

"There's work every month," Benny replied. "I hire one person year-round, and a picking crew at harvest — it's crazy then. In the winter, there's always pruning. My hired man does that. The cultivating I do. That's what I like best. I've even bought a new tractor," he said, pointing to a bright blue tracklayer tractor parked between rows nearby.

"Do your winemakers visit the vineyard?" I asked. "Do they ever try to tell you how to farm your vines?"

"Beckett likes to come out to the vineyard from time to time," Benny replied. "David Gates [vineyard manager for Ridge] used to come two or three times as harvest neared. But then he stopped. He said,'Benny, you know the grapes best.' When Dave Bennion was alive, he would come down often."

When talking about Dave Bennion, Benny's eyes took on a faraway look. I could tell he held Dave in high esteem. I had long heard about the barbeques that had become traditional for the two men whenever Dave visited. Benny no doubt missed the fellowship. No one, though — not even Dave — has ever tried to tell Benny how to farm his vineyard.

"It's a beautiful grape, but it was a lost grape for many, many years."

Benito (Benny) Dusi

"What's the hardest part about growing grapes for two such producers as Ridge and Peachy Canyon?" was my next question.

"It's hardest to get the sugar content where the producers want it," he replied without hesitation. "Sugar's critical. If it comes in these days at 23° Brix, they're unhappy. Between 24° and 25° Brix, they won't bark at you. If it comes in at 26° Brix, they're jumping for joy. But if it's 27°, you're looking for trouble.

"I used to pick samples twice each day, while I was learning how they ripened. Now, it's more like once a week. As harvest date gets closer, it's probably twice per week, and even once each day at the end."

"What kind of yield do you get now?"

"Usually two tons per acre. That's what I like to keep them to. But this year (1996), the crop is way down — only one ton per acre — 49 tons instead of my usual 100 tons."

How did this low yield affect the price per ton of grapes? I wondered. Did his contract provide for such a short fall? "I've never signed a contract in my life," said Ben. "Everything's a handshake, and we always settle on a price after the grapes are picked. I've never had a problem. I've always found that wineries are considerate with their price in times like these."

"What is the secret to the quality of your grapes?" I asked.

"Good grapes go back to the soil. The soil here is lean, extremely lean. It's a gravelly loam; it's hard, dry, and shallow. The moisture goes straight down, and the roots go down with it," he explained.

Before I parted from Benny Dusi a couple of hours after having met him, I asked if he would mind posing for a couple of photographs beside the little shed that held his collection of Dusi Ranch Zinfandel bottles. Perhaps he would get a couple of his favorites — for the record?

Graciously accommodating my request, he stepped into the shed and emerged holding a gallon wine bottle of estate-produced Dusi Ranch Zinfandel under one arm and a Ridge Dusi Ranch under the other. "Did you produce your own Zinfandel at one time?" I asked in some surprise, as I examined the gallon jug label.

"Yes, from 1955 to 1968. This little shed was my tasting room," he replied. But he gave up winemaking, he said, up when he realized he had managed only a 10¢ per gallon price increase in 13 years. It had become more profitable for him just to sell his grapes. Now, of course, Dusi Ranch Zinfandel sells for over $20 per 750ml bottle, or over $100 per gallon! And the price for his grapes was about $1,600 per ton in 1996.

After our photo session, I shook hands and said farewell. As I drove down the lane towards Highway 101, I thought about how different a man Benny was from what I had been expecting. I had expected a rather shrewd businessman who knew the value of his vineyard. What I found was a man who, yes, knows the value of his vineyard, but who also knows the value of a handshake relationship with his buyers. A fair price for his grapes is important to him, but equally important is an honorable relationship with the people who use his grapes for premium Zinfandel. For Benny, the two inevitably go together.

I realized how few people like Benny Dusi I had met in my life. While pleased with the financial returns his Zinfandel vineyard had brought him, he also seemed to feel an artisan's gratification for the recognition his wines had been receiving. Far from being just a shrewd businessman, Benny is representative of many second generation Zinfandel winegrape growers — a shy, well-informed, and courteous Old World farmer living in solitary but modern comfort in the midst of a growing, bustling agriculture community. It is a community whose economy he has contributed much to. As Doug Beckett said, without Benny Dusi's enduring patience and love for his Zinfandel, Peachy Canyon Winery probably would not be where it is today. It might not even "be" at all.

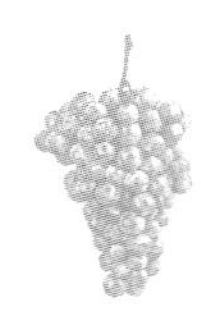

Pesenti Vineyards and Winery

After leaving Benny Dusi, I made the short drive across Highway 101 to Vineyard Drive and Pesenti Vineyards. I found Frank Nerelli, grandson to founder Frank Pesenti, and his father, Aldo, in the historic winery's little tasting room when I arrived there at high noon that lovely gold and blue November day. The entrance to the tasting room is just past the fermentation room containing the winery's six original 10-ton open-top concrete fermentors, and is across the wide breezeway from the barrel room and bottling line. The breezeway leads up a ramp to the warehouse. The winery on tree-lined Vineyard Drive is nestled at the base of a 50-

acre rolling vineyard. The vineyard, located at the eastern end of the Templeton Gap, is, according to the opinion of many of the region's winemakers, the best situated in the area. Under the tasting room sign was a plain door cut into the aluminum-sided wall. I threw it open to come upon Aldo and Frank standing in the middle of the cozy old-fashioned tasting room, whose walls were lined with items of food, drink, and a colorful selection of gifts. I almost felt as if I had burst in upon them in their private parlor. But their warm and cordial greeting left no doubt as to my being in the right place — at the expected time.

Aldo, slender, pale-complexioned, and quiet, had been engaged in stocking food items. Frank, olive-complexioned, black-haired, intense, enthusiastic, joyous even, is the winemaker. He made up for his father's quietness with energy to spare. He was working the tasting room. After our introductions, Aldo went quietly back to his work and Frank went behind the small bar, whose rich warm wood tones gleamed from years of polishing and use. He poured a taste of his 1994 Zinfandel into one of the winery's trademark ancient shot glasses. I took my glass, which showed a deep-garnet colored wine with aromas of spice and blackberries, opened my notebook, and claimed a space at the end of the bar, ready for all that this articulate, knowledgeable, and engaging winemaker, supplemented occasionally by Aldo, had to tell me.

Frank Nerelli, Aldo Nerelli and Vic Pesenti

Thirteen acres of own-rooted Zinfandel, they told me, were first planted in 1923. Another 40 acres were planted, this time on St. George rootstock, in 1942; and in 1949, three more acres on St. George were put in. The soil is limestone-clay, the location rolling hillside at the eastern end of the Templeton Gap — the breezeway from the ocean that Highway 46 West follows. The grapes during Prohibition were sold to home winemakers. The winery was built in 1934. "Until 1970," said Aldo, "we were one of only three wineries in Paso Robles producing Zinfandel. But we always felt we were better off sticking with something that we knew than switching to the newest thing."

The nearly 50-acre vineyard is dry farmed and head trained, with 10 x 10 spacing. Frank likes the 1½ to two tons per acre of fruit that the dry-farmed Zinfandel produces on St. George rootstock, which in a rare year like 1997 may reach three tons. "It's all been dry farmed from the get-go, and without pesticides or herbicides — only an occasional light sulfuring." said Frank. "It is possibly the largest dry-farmed vineyard in California."

"Did your grandparents not even water the vines when they were planted?"

"Never gave them a drop," Frank replied. "It's all a matter of knowing when to plant — which is usually in February, in the middle of the rainy season. Although when my grandparents planted their first vines, they didn't get to it until April, and all the neighbors said the cuttings would surely die. But that night, my grandmother said her rosary and went to bed. Five inches of rain fell over the next couple of days, and every single cutting grew."

Frank's educational preparation for winemaker consisted mostly of some tutorials by "a couple of University of California, Davis, guys — Bob Pike and Mark Caparelli. I finished high school, but never did go to college," he told me, without apology. "They taught me lab stuff — how to use sulfur dioxide, what pH means, malolactic fermentation — stuff like that. The rest, they told me, would have to come from within myself, from the heart."

Since 1994, Frank's goal for Pesenti Zinfandel has been to produce one of the best Zinfandels in California for a reasonable price. "But we've been a jug wine producer since we built the winery in 1934," he said. "All we've ever had is Zinfandel grapes, and the demand after Repeal was mostly for sweet wines and jug wines. We even used to sell our Zinfandel by the 50-gallon barrels to dairies and sheep ranches from Fresno to Lancaster in the Central Valley. The workers were all given a gallon a day ration; if the wine ran out, they wouldn't work until they their got their rations. It's been hard to get away from that image, since we have such a long-established customer base. Nor do we want to lose them, either. We need our oldest customers."

The move away from jug wine production, nonetheless, was inevitable. When his father experienced a heart attack in early fall 1982, Frank's attention was taken up by his father's illness. The grapes hung longer than usual before they were harvested. But in those fully ripe grapes, Frank was alerted to their potential to become something other than jug wine with plastic corks or screw tops. A 1982 nine-litre salmanazar — a beautiful bottle with an etched blue label — now sits on the tasting room shelf in honor of both his father's survival of his heart attack and of the year the turnaround in Zinfandel production began for Frank.

In the 1970s, before his father's illness, Frank said that it had been agonizing for him to watch Ridge bottling Paso Robles Zinfandel in cork-sealed fifths while he was still putting his in jugs with screw tops and plastic stoppers. "We were among the first in the region to build a winery and produce Zinfandel, and now the newcomers were passing us by." However, the mortification he felt prepared him to seize the opportunity given him by the nearly tragic circumstances of his father's heart attack. In that vintage, Frank saw that his vineyard was every bit as capable of producing high-end Zinfandel as the Dusi and York Mountain vineyards. Frank also credits the award-winning westside Paso Robles Zinfandels by newcomers Toby Shumrick (now owner of Tobin James Winery) and Peachy Canyon's Doug and Nancy Beckett in the late 1980s as being the final "kick in the butt" he needed to get out of his rut. "Some people were even making gorgeous wines out of *our second* crop — that we were just giving away!" he exclaimed.

"Although Zinfandel was not a prestigious wine for many years following Repeal in 1933, it was what we had, and what we founded our winery on," said Vic Pesenti, Frank's uncle, who had joined us in the tasting room. "In the 1950s, it hit a real low point, when so many of the new wineries coming on, and their newly developing wine consumers, got enamored with the Bordeaux varieties. But much has changed since then. With each successive year, Zinfandel's popularity has been increasing, especially over these past 15 years. And now that the quality of our old vines down here has been newly discovered, our Zinfandel is getting some of the recognition it deserves."

"Zinfandel is a captivating grape — Zinfandel draws you in, if you let it. Or maybe it just gets its hooks into you, and gets ahold of you."

Frank Nerellli

It was not until 10 years after his father's heart attack that Frank was able to get his family and customers to support him in his fine wine focus for Pesenti Zinfandel. When he had bottled in cork-closed fifths some of the best barrels during those years, his customers had been unimpressed. "Oh, look, you've put a cork in your bottles!" they would exclaim. And then they would buy the still-available three-liter jugs for $5.50.

But Frank stubbornly held onto his dream. "I was born under a vine," he said ardently. The vine, of course, was Zinfandel, which perhaps explains why, when asked by a visitor if he liked Zinfandel, he replied, "Like it? I'm *passionate* about Zinfandel!" It also perhaps explains why his dream had little to do with increasing profits with higher priced bottlings. "Money has been the farthest thing from my mind since I embarked on this dream," he stated. "This is a beautiful country. If you don't get greedy, you can make a good product *and* a good living.

"Zinfandel is a captivating grape. I saw an opportunity to create something beautiful out of love, by creating a synergy with the vineyards and the wines. I walk the vineyards practically every day; I go down to the winery at night, and walk among the barrels, even talk to the wines. It also means hands-on winemaking, punching the cap, not using a machine. Zinfandel draws you in, if you let it. Or maybe it just gets its hooks into you, and gets ahold of you. Either way, I feel fortunate to be a part of all this, to have this opportunity to make the best Zinfandel in California, and package it in a beautiful bottle, at a fair price for the consumer. I think the consumer deserves the best, and that it be affordable."

In 1992, Frank made his move. He examined patches within his vineyard for grapes favorable to the style of Zinfandel he wanted to make, crushed them separately, and aged the wine in neutral oak barrels for several months. When he released the wine in 1994, it caught the attention of Gerald Asher, who was in the region preparing his Paso Robles Wine Journal for *Gourmet* magazine. Any last doubts Frank might have had about the wisdom of this move to cork-closed fine wine were erased when Asher's report came out in the September 1994 issue. In it, Asher describes Frank's 1992 Zinfandel as "a truly exquisite wine." [24] Asher also believed that Frank had no need to apologize for his screw top Zinfandel jugs. "The standard Pesenti Zinfandel, on sale at the winery for $5.50 for a three-liter jug, is excellent — robust, fruity, well-made. It's the best value in red wine anywhere in the world." [25]

As good a value and wine as Asher found Pesenti's jug Zinfandel, its days were numbered. Each year following 1992, Frank augmented his original block of superior grapes with fruit from additional superior patches, going for both increased production and a bolder, bigger, fruitier style, which is shaped somewhat, he said, by women's palates. "When women's palates take over a style, you know it's here to stay." His 1993 production was also about 350 cases; the 1994, 1,000 cases; 1995 was back to about 750 cases; his 1996 was nearly 1,200 cases — which is about as much as he ever intends to make. By 1996, the wine that formerly went into the Pesenti jug Zinfandel was being sold as bulk wine to a high-end North Coast producer, subsidizing Frank's premium Zinfandel production. Pesenti's traditionally made, high quality, affordable Zinfandel had joined the growing number of extinct jug wines.

The wine now being sold as bulk was receiving accolades anew. "This producer told me it's just about the best bulk Zin he's ever tasted. The wine is used in their $16 to $18 dollar a bottle Zinfandel," said Frank. When I asked him who his happy North Coast producer was, he replied, 'My lips are sealed — at least until your book is published! Our return on our bulk wine is the equivalent of over $2,500 per ton of grapes. So by crushing the fruit and selling it at a respectable per-gallon price, I can afford the beautiful Italian bottles for my premium Zin and still sell it at $12 a bottle."

"If your North Coast producer gets $18 a bottle for wine made from your bulk lots, why do you not charge more for your 'blue label' Zinfandel?" I asked.

"I'm just not interested," he replied. "Although people tell me I should be charging $25 a bottle for my 1995 Zinfandel, I want people who can't

---

24 "Paso Robles California, Country Style," *Gourmet*, September 1994, 82.

25 *Ibid.*

afford the $25 a bottle price to still be able to have the best Zinfandel California has to offer. Perhaps that's a bewildering philosophy to many folks, but that's the kind of guy I am. Also, for years we were the butt of jokes about our screw-top jug wines. Now, all the new producers here want Pesenti grapes because they've seen just how good the wine can be. But given the low-end price for Paso grapes, I'm not about to cut my own throat by giving up my profitable bulk contract for less than half the returns that we'd get on the grapes. Besides," he added with a subtle smile, "in some ways I feel as if I'm getting a little of my own back."

"What about your long-time jug wine customers? Have you just let them go?"

"No," he replied. "In addition to my high-end dry table wine, I also make a 13.5 percent alcohol dry late harvest, so called because it is made from the last-picked grapes. I make this wine as a lower priced Zinfandel for our oldest customers who still miss our jug wines." For his customers with a sweet tooth, there's a ruby Zinfandel, a medium-sweet wine with 13.6 percent alcohol.

In fact, for many years after Frank had established his blue label Zinfandel, these were still the wines customers were traditionally served when they visited the tasting room, especially if Aldo or Vic were pouring. At least this was the experience of many of my friends and acquaintances whom I told should visit Pesenti for a taste of the new style wine.

"Either we didn't taste the wine you described, or we have a much different idea from you as to what is a good Zinfandel," they would tell me later. On subsequent visits to the tasting room with friends, Aldo and Vic also first offered me either the dry late harvest Zinfandel or the ruby Zinfandel, served in their trademark thick-walled shot glasses. Sometimes, the blue label Zinfandel was not available for tasting.

But this was the tradition of Pesenti Winery and Vineyard, the tradition Aldo and Vic had grown up with. The blue label Zinfandel was Frank's dream, and visitors interested in this wine soon learned to make an appointment with Frank for a private tasting in the barrel room.

In 1996, Frank also produced a small amount of Zinfandel Port, and bottled it in exquisite tenths with a gold silk-screened label. "I fell in love with the shape and size of the bottles," he told me, a smile threatening to undermine the seriousness of his look and tone. "I just knew I had to make something to put in it." Delighted with his 1996 Port, which took a silver medal shortly after being bottled, he plans to keep this succulent dessert wine in his lineup.

His focus, though, is on his ultra-premium dry table style Zinfandel.

At that point, Aldo took over in the tasting room, and Frank invited me to follow him across the breezeway to the barrel room. There, uninterrupted by tasting room visitors, he explained his Zinfandel style, which begins with harvest. "We hire pickers we can rely on to sort out any excessively raisined or bunch-rotted clusters, we pay them well, and treat them well. But we're not fanatical about a little M.O.G. [material other than grapes]. Nor do we mind if a few grapes come in botrytised — we seem to always get some botrytis in one small patch. It usually takes us six to eight weeks to complete harvesting our 50 acres because we manipulate harvest Brix to get a reasonable alcohol level in the finished wines. Some blocks are picked at 28°; some at 21°. We've found that our customers like our Zinfandel best at less than 15 percent alcohol. They enjoy it for its wonderful array of flavors, not for the alcohol. And they want to be able to enjoy more than one glass with a meal. This means it has to stay below 15 percent. Alcohol is simply an obstacle to overcome."

His 1995 wine was left on the skins for 21 days, until it had fermented to 5° Brix. After pressing, it was transferred to stainless steel tanks, and re-inoculated with KI yeast. It fermented to dryness and went through MLF in the tanks in about two months. When all fermentation was complete, the lots were blended, then put into mostly well seasoned French oak barrels in April for 12 to 14 months. Frank had enhanced the wood flavors only with the addition of oak nuggets in "tea bags." "Zinfandel doesn't need a lot of new wood, since it doesn't have the harsh tannins that Cabernet Sauvignon has," said Frank.

Then Frank drew a sample of the 1995 from the barrels, and I wrote these notes about it: "14.7 percent alcohol; aroma has hints of blackberry fruit, black pepper, allspice, and nutmeg. Full-bodied, nicely textured feel in the mouth; lovely center palate of black cherry, blackberry fruit; balanced edges; lingering finish." Like so many 1995 Zinfandels throughout the state, the Pesenti 1995 was showing the results of perhaps a little riper style, and gentle handling throughout the vinification.

The wine was bottled unfined in March of 1997, and given only a rough diatomaceous earth (D.E.) filtration out of barrels — a "different twist to my previous practices," Frank said. "I also stepped up the sulfur dioxide to microbial stability — still under 20 ppm. I'm highly sensitive to free sulfur dioxide. Anything over 25 ppm I can detect in a heartbeat. But at 20 ppm — what a difference to the wine that has made!" he exclaimed.

For his 1996, Frank evolved to a somewhat more elaborate fermentation program. Using three open-top concrete tanks, he fermented in three lots. The first tank contained 90 percent crushed and 10 percent whole-berry. It was fermented at 85°F, and was pressed off in 12 days. The tank maxed out to 27.5° Brix.

In the second tank, he mounded a pyramid of whole berries, and surrounded it with must showing a Brix of 25°. This tank was also fermented at 85°F, and pressed off at 14 days. "I only punched the wine," he said. In the third tank, he used 50 percent whole berries, and added back 1,000 pounds of stems, then fermented at 90°F for nine days. "Everything was punched three to four times daily for two weeks. The intention was to get lots of skin contact and extra fruitiness from the whole berries, and spiciness from the stems."

By November, when I was there, the 1996 lots had been blended into one stainless steel tank, and the cuvée just pressed out of the fermentor. Frank drew me a sample, about which I wrote these notes: "Peppery, chocolate, espresso coffee, center of black cherries and cassis fruit cream!" It was filled with promise. How would it develop?

"Because of all the whole berries, it's just finishing primary fermentation," said Frank in a phone conversation March 26, 1997. "I pressed the wine at about 2° Brix. But the whole berries still had sugar, and when pressed, the sugar was released, which raised the Brix to between 6° and 8°. The fermentation then finished in barrels, which now includes about 8 percent new American oak barrels, to soften tannins while retaining all that gorgeous fruit. It's still going through MLF."

A couple of weeks later, I called him to ask how the MLF was coming along. "It's just finishing MLF," he said. "The alcohol now is only 13.8 percent, but you'd think it was 15 percent by the mouth-feel — it's so rich in fruit and texture. You've got to get back down here and try it soon," he said enthusiastically.

"I'm on my way," I said. In reality, it would be a month or so before I could actually accept his invitation.

However, I did taste the pre-release bottled 1995, along with the 1994, when I was at the Paso Robles Vintners Zinfandel Festival in March 1997. The 1994 was a lovely wine when I first tasted it, and was simply getting better. The 1995 was gorgeous, both as a result of the vintage and Frank's handling of the fruit and vinification. With each successive vintage, he said, he is that much closer to achieving his ideal style. The 1995 Pesenti Zinfandel was released in June 1997. In May, when I was down for the Paso Robles Wine Festival, I tasted the developing 1996. If I thought the 1995 a stunning wine, the 1996 surpassed it — if that is possible. It seemed as if Frank had indeed hit his stride.

As for bottling more than his 1,200 cases annually, Frank isn't interested. "More cases would mean more work and worry. To get out from under some of the work is why I downsized in the first place. I have only one full-time employee, Kevin Healy, who has been with me since 1982. He and I do all the routine work in the vineyard and winery. The only extra help I hire is our picking crew, and a couple of people to help out with bottling. This is the size of operation I like. Life is good now. There's a lot of things I want to do besides make wine.

"Building an estate winery and vineyard over the years, through thick and thin, is a lot of hard work," continued Frank, with both pride and a little weariness in his voice. "The industry overall deserves a lot of credit for what we in California have achieved in such a relatively short period of time. I haven't tasted a bad wine produced in California in 10 years. Yet few people appreciate the hard work that goes into a product that most of them see only in glamorous or festive settings. But I'm not complaining," he assured me, a bright smile lighting his face. "Life is good. And if I had it all to do over again, and could choose who and where I wanted to be, I'd be right here. I'd choose the same grandparents — my hardworking grandmother is my heroine." He showed me the one-room cabin his grandparents lived in and in which his mother was born. It still sits at the side of the vineyard. "I'd choose the same parents, I'd be living the same life. I have a beautiful wife and two kids — a son in college, and a graduated daughter 'enjoying life at home for a while.' And there's still a lot I want to do."

The November afternoon sun was beginning to cast golden light across the historic vineyard that covered the undulating hills above the winery. It was time to pack up camera and tripod, and spend an hour among the vines glowing dark-trunked and golden-leafed on the pale limestone-clay hillsides. A few minutes on the highest knoll, with the vine-covered hills setting off like a frame the white roof of the winery below, reminded me once again of the partnership between romance and hard work that is the hallmark of such a family operation. In the midst of these lovely, ancient, silent vines, and the panoramic view around me, I found it easy to forget about the difficult and relentless effort that brought this setting into existence.

In March 1997, Frank established a three-acre block of Zinfandel beside his house. The budwood was taken from the family vineyard, then was heat treated and certified virus-tested, then bench-grafted onto St. George rootstock. Although the block was established as a non-irrigated vineyard, Frank admitted to delivering a couple of gallons of water a week from a tractor-drawn tank to each of the new vines as the spring weather heated up. In 1997, no rain had fallen on Paso Robles after the end of January, and it was then end of May — a weather rarity.

Frank's decision to continue with the practice of dry farming puzzled a county farm adviser, who had remarked to him, "You don't get much grapes by dry farming." To which Frank apparently replied, "I don't *want* much grapes!" Frank is one of a tiny group of California Zinfandel grape-growers who continues to practice what has become the nearly lost art of dry-farming. His expects that his first vintage from his newly planted Zinfandel vines will be in year 2001. "When you taste that first vintage," Frank said confidently, "you'll see the difference dry- farming makes to the fruit from even very young vines."

In October 1998, I visited Frank at his house just off Highway 41 to see how his 18-month-old vineyard was doing. As we walked among the thriving, waist-high young vines in their second leaf, Frank remarked upon their vigor. "No one who sees the vineyard can believe it is entirely dry farmed. They just shake their heads in amazement," he said.

But that is Frank's genius. "You have to think every day like a grapevine to be a successful grower," he said. "This vineyard is a museum piece, an historical reminder of the origins of Zinfandel's greatness, since all the finest remaining old Zinfandel vineyards were always dry farmed, and yet today, true dry farming is becoming a lost art. My little dry-farmed vineyard will remind people what it was that established Zinfandel as a world class grape."

In 1999, two years ahead of schedule, Frank made three barrels of Zinfandel from his vineyard. "The vines were in their third leaf," said Frank. "Yet my wife and I dropped about seven tons of fruit, and harvested 1½ tons, which will make 67 cases. When the vineyard is fully mature, I will limit the crop to 1½ tons per acre, or about 4½ tons for the vineyard, for about 300 cases of wine. I have aged the wine in neutral oak barrels — none new. As far as I am concerned, people who age their wines in new oak barrels, whether the barrels are French or American oak, are amateurs. People who put their Zinfandel in new oak don't know how to make wine. I will be releasing this wine in year 2001 for $400 per case, and I have already sold half of it based on the barrel samples. That is how good it is already. By the time the vineyard is mature, it will produce the best Zinfandel in the world."

Frank has plans to build his own Nerelli Winery next to his vineyard. "When you have the goals and the passion, anything is possible," he said.

Frank Nerelli definitely has both.

★ ★ ★ ★ ★

On May 15, 2000, Larry Turley, owner of Turley Wine Cellars in Napa Valley, purchased Pesenti Vineyards and Winery from the Pesenti and Nerelli families. The winery will remain Pesenti Vineyards and Winery, and Frank Nerelli stays on as winemaker. Both Larry Turley and his winemaker, Ehren Jordan, are excited about the purchase. "The clincher for us," said Ehren, "was that Frank agreed to stay on as winemaker and vineyard manager. When you look at the quality of wines he has been making within the family tradition and with little in the way of budget for innovations, as far as we are concerned, he is a genius winemaker. The only changes we are going to make will be to improve the existing facility. We will install a deer fence around the vineyard, insulate the fermentation and barrel rooms, add cooling systems, rewire the buildings, and give Frank a budget for new oak barrels. Oak pellets in mesh bags have a place in winemaking, but not in the ultra-premium wines the grapes in that magnificent vineyard are capable of producing."

"I have taken the winery as far as I can on my own," said Frank when he told me about the deal. "And I'm tired of being stuck in the mud. Most Zinfandel producers were born with their corks. I've had to earn mine. With this partnership, I won't be working harder, just smarter. Pesenti is about to enter the realm of super-premium Zinfandel."

Thus an old era ends, and a new one begins.

★ ★ ★ ★ ★

And I am left wondering: What are the jug wine customers to do now? As my odyssey continued, I discovered that there is still at least one die-hard traditional Zinfandel jug wine producer left in California — although who knows for how much longer.

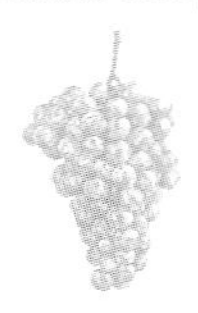

Norman Vineyards

From Pesenti, my next and last stop for the day was to be Norman Vineyards, reached by following Vineyard Drive across Highway 46 and along the oak-shaded, secluded pastoral valley west of the city of Paso Robles to Jensen Road. At that intersection was Norman Vineyards — owned by Art Norman, a retired mechanical engineer, and his wife, Lei. The winemaker is Robert Nadeau.

"I've been a Zinfandel lover for many years, ever since my first good one in the 1950s, which was a Louis M. Martini," said the laid-back Art Norman, when I asked him what led to his planting six acres of own-rooted Zinfandel in 1971. Nor did he think twice about planting Zinfandel as his flagship varietal. The Adelaide soil — limestone mixed with clay — is well suited to the varietal. Norman's Zinfandel acreage is now nearly 10. The vines are propagated from UC Davis certified, virus-tested cuttings, and are trellised and drip irrigated.

"We use just enough irrigation to get the vines through the driest months. The worth of the old, dry-farmed vines," Art feels, "lies in the fact of their age, not that they are dry farmed. We keep our crop to about four tons, although in 1996, we got less than three. Three tons is probably ideal, given our location, and the fact that some of the vines are infected with leaf-roll virus — which delays ripening. We don't have a lot of degree-days [a system used to determine the sun/heat exposure] here," he said, "which makes it difficult for the diseased vines to get ripe by the time we need to pick — even though we cluster thin before verasion, and harvest in multiple pickings."

When the winery was built in 1992, Art began supplementing his own Zinfandel with fruit from two small Jensen Road Zinfandel vineyards planted to cuttings from the Old Casteel Vineyard. Since 1995, Norman Vineyards has produced three Zinfandel wines: the Monster — from one Jensen Road Vineyard; the Classic; and the Jensen Road — the latter two a combination of Norman's own, plus fruit from the two Jensen Road vineyards.

Winemaker Robert Nadeau has been on board with Norman Vineyards since the beginning. He uses one procedure for all the red wines. The fruit is crushed in a Demoisey crusher/destemmer, the wine is put into small closed-top tanks left open, then inoculated with "good old laboratory-developed, prepared Pasteur Red yeast," he said. "Also known as 'Bordeaux Red,' it has strong, vigorous cells that ferment all the way through, which is important when our grapes have such high sugar." The wine is pumped over twice daily until the cap sinks, then pressed off and pumped into variable capacity stainless steel tanks where the wine finishes secondary fermentation and "settles out" by gravity for one to three months. The now clear wine is moved to barrel for about 12 months of ageing.

There is some variation in the oak program for the three Zinfandels. The Monster and Classic are given about 12 months in three-year-old and older French oak. For the Jensen Road, a lighter style, about 20 percent of the blend is aged for 4 to 6 weeks in 100 percent new American oak. "It's just enough," said Nadeau, "to deepen the color, add oak tones and a touch of vanilla, and give the wine a nice soft middle palate with a little more middle weight while adding a layer of complexity. This small percentage of new wood helps push the wine into becoming something special, rather than something just nice.

"It's also how we break in the barrels for our Cabernet Sauvignon," said Art, still the practical mechanical engineer of his pre-winery life.

Philosophically, Robert believes that when Zinfandel is from good vineyards, "it's best to go light on the lumber. It is best when used as just another tool to make the wine better. Vineyard Drive, Willow Creek Road, and Peachy Canyon form an enchanted kingdom of vineyards. Zinfandel from such vineyards is all fruitiness. It's a brash, spirited, in-your-face wine whose fruit should be preserved. New oak can get in the way. However, since we produce no less than a half a dozen lots of Zinfandel in any vintage, inevitably one of those lots will be deficient in color and/or depth. The new oak treatment can push a reasonably nice lot of wine, like our Jensen Road blend, over the edge into something special. Our virus-infected vines are the source of the lot which usually sees the new lumber."

Art agreed. With his first vines now 25 years old, he has had time to reflect on what it means to be a vineyard and winery owner. The engineer in him has learned to live with an essential fact: "Mother Nature is in charge here. And if you're lucky enough to get good grapes at harvest from good vineyards, the best you can do with them is leave them alone."

The first Norman Zinfandel was the 1992 Monster. We made it first," recalled Art, "because that was the kind of fruit we had."

The wine consisted mostly of fruit from one of the Jensen Road vineyards, which, according to Robert, is traditionally huge, intense, inky-purple, and with acid high enough, and pH low enough, to easily carry a sugar content of 26° Brix — or higher. It also contained about 200 gallons of Pesenti Vineyards wine, a one-time deal, and "some of the best wine we've ever been able to purchase," he said.

A 14.7 percent alcohol wine, released in April 1994, sold out by June.

Art offered me a tasting of the Monster. We were sitting on a sofa in the spacious living quarters of the beautiful apricot/beige-colored mission-style structure that is also the winery. A dog and cat lolled by the fireplace set between French doors that opened upon a deck overlooking the vineyard. When Art went behind bar near which I was sitting to get the wine, I realized with some astonishment that their living room was also the winery's tasting room. Or was it the other way around? I knew I had followed the signs up the stairway to the tasting room, but once there, and settled into my conversation with Art, I felt as if I had traversed through to their living quarters. One and the same, I realized, as Lei came into the kitchen behind the bar to begin preparing the family dinner. The winery itself, which we later visited, was on the ground level, and accessed through a door near the kitchen. As it turns out, a house separate and secluded from the winery is on the drawing boards.

Astonishment aside, I had a lovely Zinfandel to taste, and a question about the label.

"What's with the cougar?" I asked Art concerning its symbolic meaning.

"It's a tribute to our resident big cat. We call him (or her) our organic deer control. It can hang out in our vineyard anytime it wants to," Art explained.

With the label question settled, I could concentrate on the Monster in my glass. It lived up to its name — a big, fruity wine with flavors of plums and black cherries. "How well do you think it will age?" I asked.

"From a winemaker's point of view, all our Zinfandels are made to taste good upon their release. We leave the decision of whether or not to age them up to the customer. How well Zinfandel ages depends upon its condition at bottling. If it is clean, and without volatile acidity, it will age 10 years, and will still have great fruit. After 10 years, it will become more and more like an old Bordeaux."

Art's preference is for the Classic Zin, which has alcohol at 13.5 percent. It's a popular wine, too, but not as poplar as the Monster. "However," he added with a laugh, "my preference in Zinfandel has nothing to do with what I make."

In keeping with his increasing appreciation for Zinfandel, Art is assisting Barbara Wyatt, owner of the Old Casteel Vineyard, with its restoration. Using cuttings from the Beckwith vineyard, which was propagated from Old Casteel Vineyard cuttings some years ago, Art is replanting the old vineyard with offspring from its long-gone vines. The vineyard will be trellised and drip irrigated, a break from its original tradition, but in keeping with the practices Norman has established on his own Zinfandel vineyard.

"Dry farming is nearly a lost art," said Robert, who, inspired by Frank Nerelli, sees more benefit from dry farming than Art, and is establishing his own new five and a half-acre Zinfandel vineyard to head training and dry farming. Robert's's vineyard is one of a tiny number of newly established dry-farmed vineyards in California. "They don't even teach the art of dry farming at UC Davis anymore," he added.

Prized in its day by Ridge and Monterey Peninsula Winery, Old Casteel Vineyard will be a new addition to Norman's Zinfandel lineup once it comes back into production in a few years.

After a walk down the inside stairs to the snug little winery and a stroll around the tanks and barrels, I gathered up my notes and camera, got back in my car, and found my way down Vineyard Drive to the western end of Peachy Canyon Road. Again, it seemed like an hour of twisting narrow road before I spotted high on a hilltop — like a beckoning angel against the dark sky — the big, brightly-lit white house that is home to Peachy Canyon Winery.

Arriving safely, I found the Becketts as tired as I was from a busy, intense day; yet we were all eager to talk over our day's events. But with the help of another of Nancy's delicious dinners and some Peachy Canyon Zinfandel, it wasn't long before talk trailed off into drowsy monosyllables. Tomorrow, my last day, was too soon coming. I had Tobin James Cellars and grower Richard Sauret on my calendar; Doug and Nancy were to pour at a tasting in San Diego.

Tobin James Cellars: The Wild Child Winery

"It's pretty much been me and Peachy Canyon that got Paso Robles rockin 'n rollin' Zinfandel-wise," were Toby Shumrick's first words to me when I spoke to him on the phone about my planned visit to San Luis Obispo County's Zinfandel country. I never met anyone who contradicted him in the several visits and interviews I've had with Paso Robles Zinfandel growers and producers since then.

My appointment with Toby, as his friends know him, was at 10:30 Saturday morning. It was a sleepy-eyed Toby who came down the stairs from the apartment above the winery where he lived then with his twin 1-year-old daughters and their mother, Ermie Morones. Wearing below-the-knee navy-colored shorts and matching shirt, and rubbing his short, thick black hair straight up, he offered me a cordial handshake, and an invitation into the barrel room where we could talk in relative quiet and taste some wines.

Toby is an original personality if ever I've met one. Upon our meeting, despite his sleepy eyes, he began sizing me up, trying to determine what I was about as a wine writer. What were my intentions, my background? How much did I know? Could he trust me? I think in the end that he got in as many questions as I did. But I managed the one I was always the most curious about: Why Zinfandel ?

"If you were to put a Zinfandel down beside a Cabernet Sauvignon, Merlot, or Cabernet Franc, I'd take Zinfandel any day — for its fruit." So declared Tobin James. "What's the point of drinking a wine if you can't taste the fruit? Zinfandel is just filled with raspberry flavors and aromas. Now tell me, who doesn't like raspberries?"

It was those gorgeous raspberry aromas that hooked Toby on Zinfandel in the first place. It happened in 1987 while he was assistant winemaker (1984–1989) for Gary Eberle. A vineyard manager, Laz Morones (that's right: he's now grandfather to Toby's daughters!) had come in with some Westside Zinfandel grapes rejected by another winery. Eberle, whose focus then was on Cabernet Sauvignon, also didn't want them. But Toby took one look at the quality of the fruit, tasted a couple of grapes, and asked if he might take them and vinify them at Eberle's Winery. Gary agreed. The grapes were crushed that day, and when Toby came in next morning, the raspberry aromas filled the winery. That was Toby's first wine, and it was a winner — bringing in a string of medals from Zinfandel competitions when it was released.

"I'm not a wine drinker," said Toby. Can he be serious? I thought, looking at him in disbelief. Catching my quizzical look, he explained, "My job is to make wine, not to drink it. I'm a winemaker, not a wine drinker. I know an animal when I see it; I also know what people like."

In 1990, Toby left Eberle and approached Peachy Canyon's Doug Beckett, whose winery then was known as Tobias, and which was becoming famous for its Zinfandel. Proposing to work for free if he could produce his own Tobin James wines in Beckett's facility, he found Doug receptive to the idea.

By February 1994, Toby's success with his Zinfandels enabled him to open his own winery — Tobin James Cellars — on Highway 46 East, about eight miles out of Paso Robles.

Zinfandel remains his flagship wine. "I pay more per ton for Zinfandel than I do for Cabernet Sauvignon," he said. "I buy from a few small, older westside vineyards, as well as from Dante Dusi.* No, I'm not telling you where my vineyards are. It's getting just too competitive out there.

"Here's my 1995 James Gang Reserve." He drew a sample from a nearby barrel with the wine thief (a glass tube used to extract wine samples from barrels). "It's from a 25-year-old trellised, dry-farmed westside vineyard whose average yield is 2½ tons per acre. The vineyard is equipped with drip irrigation, but it is used only sparingly." I tasted the wine as Toby watched.

"I just brushed my teeth," he said, explaining why he didn't taste with me.

***Note:** Dante is Benny Dusi's brother. When Zinfandel prices dropped out of sight in the 1970s, Dante tore out some old vineyards. His son has since replanted the vineyard with Zinfandel.

The wine was luscious and full-bodied, with flavors of chocolate, blackberries, blackcurrants, and black pepper; alcohol was over 14 percent. Toby seemed to like what I said about the wine, as he went on to get me a sample of the 1995 Wild Child — flagship wine — first produced in 1994. Wild Child has 70 percent Dante Dusi fruit and 30 percent from two other westside vineyards. The resulting wine is a little lighter bodied than his Reserve, with distinctly bright acids and hints of black pepper, along with black cherry and a touch of caramel-vanilla. Alcohol was right around 14 percent.

Next, Toby wanted me to taste his 1993 Zinfandel Port, as yet unfortified, but already at18 percent alcohol and 5 percent residual sugar. It was a dusky, spicy wine with flavors of plump raisins and dried black currants. He followed the Port with his 1994 Late Harvest, alcohol at a mere 15.5 percent. It had similar flavors to the Port, but also some of those red raspberries. "My customers just love these wines," he said.

Toby's production is about 1,200 cases of Wild Child; 125 cases of James Gang Reserve; and 1,000 cases (375-ml bottles) of Late Harvest. Case production of the Port was at that time undetermined.

For both the Wild Child and the James Gang Reserve, he likes the grapes to come in at full ripeness, even with some raisins. Best sugar content is between 25° and 27° Brix. The wines are aged in a mixture of French and American oak, all two years old and older, for about 14 months, and are given a light filtration at bottling. Toby still feels that blended Zinfandel is usually more exciting than single vineyard Zinfandel. It is only the exceptional vineyards, he believes, that can produce a Zinfandel as tasty and exciting as a blend.

Toby also was in the process of planting five acres beside his eastside winery to Zinfandel using local cuttings. "I pay five cents a cutting. Budded rootstock is $4.50 each," he answered in response to my question, "Why own-rooted cuttings?" As for the suitability of the soil to Zinfandel, he gave me a typical "Tobin James" response: "It's dirt so it seems logical to plant grapes — Zinfandel. As to what kind of dirt, I'm no mud doctor. It's just good old dirt."

With the critical accolades and customer response that his Zinfandel has garnered, Toby has been able to fulfil a dream he's had since age 18. "Having my own winery was the only thing I've ever really wanted to do," he said. His success with his winery has much to do with his personal style. When the subject of favorite wines and best vintages came up, Toby returned to his bantering, half-playful, half-serious tone. "I've never received a bad load of grapes. The ones I get are always just what I wanted. The wines they produce are always my best ever. Light or heavy, it's just a state of mind. My best grapes are always the ones I just got in, and my best wine is always the one I'm about to release — or perhaps it's the one I have the most of. I make wine to pay the mortgage; but I'm also in the business to make a good product and have fun doing it. That's why I play country music, and have a 'jail' for the kids to play in — so people will feel comfortable coming in to taste wine — not intimidated. Wine's intimidating enough for most people, without making them feel uncomfortable when they do finally come by to try some."

Given the throngs of people enjoying the wines, the country music, and the barbecue during the Paso Robles Vintners Association March Zinfandel weekend, folks definitely seem to feel pretty comfortable at Tobin James Cellars.

I was beginning to get used to Toby's style — keeping me at a slight distance, but revealing just enough to show me how he makes it all work for himself. Even without his engaging style though, his wines would have been enough to get me back time and again.

Nor does Toby seem to lose sight of the grape he's hung his winemaking hat on. As I was about to depart, he offered me these words of appreciation: "If there is a wine god, it has to be Zinfandel. The Zinfandel god has made my dream come true."

It was now approaching 1:00 p.m. — time to rendezvous with Richard Sauret, who was to take me out to San Marcos Road a few miles north and west of Paso Robles for an examination of his Zinfandel vineyards.

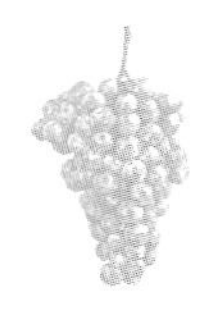

Richard Sauret, Sauret Vineyards

When the big pick-up truck with the tall, black-haired man behind the wheel came in a bee-line to my car in the parking lot of Payless Drugs at the north end of Paso Robles just after 1:30 that afternoon, I figured it had to be Richard Sauret. I had described my car to him, complete with the vanity plates lettering. And it was Richard.

After our greetings and self-introductions, I bundled up my camera bag and notebook and climbed into Richard's truck for our short journey to his vineyards. When we reached the San Marcos Road exit, we saw before us a vast scene of rolling hills covered with autumnal grasses. Feeding in the corner of one field nearby was a group of snowy white cows, the pale light gleaming off their spotless hides. They added yet another exotic, romantic touch to the vast countryside. Before long, we were climbing the lane past Zinfandel vines up to Richard's residence, which commands a peaceful and idyllic panoramic view over the vineyards falling away from the house, and to the hills beyond in every direction.

In the vicinity of his house and on neighboring parcels that he manages, Richard has over 30 acres of Zinfandel (five of them newly planted) and a few acres of Petite Sirah and Barbera. The Zinfandel and Petite Sirah are contracted to Rosenblum Cellars, who has been his customer since 1990. The Barbera is contracted to Eberle. The Zinfandel is on its own roots and was propagated both from the old Rotta Vineyard cuttings, and uncertified, but clean, nursery budwood; the Petite Sirah and Barbera are on 110R rootstock. All are head trained and dry farmed, but the vineyards also are equipped with drip irrigation. "The 12 to 15 inches of rain that we normally get is sufficient, once the vines are established. Timing of irrigation is important," he explained. Richard also occasionally uses irrigation to add nutrients to the limestone-rich soil.

Across the little valley from his vineyards is the Belli Acres ranch, which Richard used to own but now leases. Belli Acres Zinfandel is contracted to Eberle Winery, who also became a customer in 1990. Ten acres are in production, eight more are being planted.

A welcoming party of a red Abyssinian cat and a Maltese dog met us on the lane up to the attractive ranch house set amidst the vineyard and surrounded by fruit and nut trees. The animals belonged to Patti, the woman who lives in the ranch house.

Richard Sauret

In an extraordinarily picturesque vineyard, Belli Acres Zinfandel vines resemble miniature trees. Six and a half acres were propagated on their own roots in 1969; Richard himself lovingly trained up the vines. "Each vine is an individual, a personality, telling you a story," he said. "Just by looking at it, you can tell what its needs are. They're like little soldiers. Each one has its own personality, and I care about what each individual vine is going to do."

The Rotta Vineyard, along with the Dusi, Pesenti, and York Mountain vineyards, all date from the early 1920s. Richard remembers the Rotta Winery in the 1950s. The wine was fermented in concrete fermentors, and then aged in 11,000-gallon redwood tanks for three to four years, after which time it was bottled into one-gallon screw-top bottles and delivered weekly to a distributor in Santa Barbara. Only the Benny Dusi and Pesenti Vineyards have survived to modern times. The old Rotta vines were taken out in the 1970s, and acreage replanted.

A grape grower all his life, pruning and picking Zinfandel even as a child, Richard remembers a conversation in 1978 with the late André Tschelistcheff, who was a consultant then for Hoffman Mountain Ranch (HMR). "Keep growing grapes like these," André had told him, "and you'll never have to worry about a thing."

Richard agreed. "Paso Robles is red wine grape country," he told me. His particular region north and west of the city is one of the best, he believes. "The climate is 15° warmer here in the summer than the Templeton gap region south of Paso, and the vineyards all have southern exposure. It's easy for the grapes to ripen to 24° or 24.5° Brix, which produces a super wine just loaded with fruit, since Zinfandel likes a warm climate, but the quality of the fruit also depends upon a combination of weather, soil, and proper vineyard management."

Proper pruning is essential. "I prune to eight two-bud spurs per vine, which in good years will produce up to four tons per acre. In a good year, the bunches are bigger and heavier — they have more juice. For the quality I like to produce, though, you should keep the crop level low — more like two or three tons per acre — 3½ tops. Sometimes, like 1996, the yield was only one ton."

Such low yields usually mean an intense, richly flavored wine. But it also means an economic shortfall for the grower. Sauret, however, doesn't complain. "If you're a farmer, you have to be prepared for whatever Mother Nature gives you. It's only an ill-prepared grower of any crop who would be financially devastated by such occasional low production."

"Each vine is an individual, a personality, telling you a story. Just by looking at it, you can tell what its needs are. They're like little soldiers."

Richard Sauret

He also knows that less crop means better wine. "There's an old saying," he told me. "Put three calves on a cow, none will be any good. It's the same with grapes. And the vintner and consumer always come back if the quality is there. Quality has to come before quantity for the best red wine."

Richard is also a fan of head training and dry farming. "Quantity, or high tonnage per acre, in the short run can seem to bring higher returns than lower production. But in the long run, quality always wins out. Head training requires no cost outlay in trellises or in their maintenance, so there is more profit per ton. Furthermore," he emphasized, sounding a bit like a Ford Motor Company ad, "quality is my number one priority because the consumer deserves it."

A Zinfandel lover for as long as he can remember, Sauret, now 61, said he came to enjoy the wine by eating the ripe grapes when a child. He said he would sit under the trees where the filled boxes were stacked, and feast to his heart's content on the rich, ripe grapes. But it wasn't until 15 years ago that he became a serious wine drinker. "Being a Zinfandel grower has made me a better wine drinker," he said. "I like Zinfandel. If I have a choice of Zinfandel or other wines, my choice is always Zinfandel. It's my favorite wine, not just my favorite red wine." With such good grapes, and a fondness for wines produced from them, does he want to get into the winemaking business? I asked him. "If you're going to grow grapes, you can't be involved in too many other things," he answered. "Being in the winemaking business is another business altogether."

By the time I had walked through the vineyards and photographed the Abyssinian cat named Ramses perched up in an old vine (the closest I'll ever get to photographing a cougar in the vineyard), the afternoon light was beginning to cast a lavender glow over the golden hills surrounding us. Richard and I joined Patti on the steps of her house, to watch the breathtakingly beautiful light show that was unfolding around us as the sun waned. Beneath the huge almond tree, the Maltese dog was searching the ground and driveway for fallen almonds — and finding plenty. I decided to join him, and soon Patti, Richard, and I were all scavenging for almonds with the little dog. Talk trailed off into silence as we found ourselves wrapped up in the changing late afternoon light. "I suppose I should be getting back," I said at one point to Richard.

"Sure, anytime you're ready," he replied. Neither of us moved toward the truck. The stillness over the hills was mesmerizing. No one spoke. The only sounds were of the dog crunching almonds.

At last, however, the light over the hills went dim; it really was time to be getting back to my car, and to Peachy Canyon. Another special Zinfandel day had come to its close — a perfect finish to both my day and to my first sojourn to San Luis Obispo County's Zinfandel country.

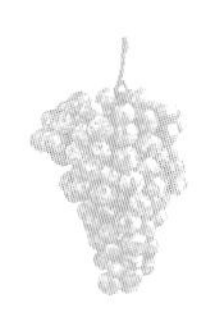

South Coast and South-of-the-Border

José Lopez Vineyard

When I met Jerry Mead, whose syndicated column "Mead On Wine" is familiar to many wine enthusiasts, at Sutter Home Winery's Zinfandel Symposium in May 1989, we talked a little of his long-time obsession with Zinfandel, and of my ***PWV*** reports and on-going research on the subject. I must have mentioned my vision of a book, because I've held a memory ever since of him giving me his card, and saying to me as we parted, "Well, keep me posted."

It wasn't until spring of 1997 that I felt I had something to "post" him about. Although his card was long out of date, Scott Miller of Single Leaf Vineyard in El Dorado County had mentioned that Jerry was his neighbor in Carson City, Nevada, and that he would be happy to give Jerry my phone number. A few days later, I received a call. The conversation went something like this:

"Hello, this is Jerry Mead. Scott Miller said I should call you. Could you remind me of where I know you from, and why I should be calling you?"

"Oh, sure," I replied, "We met at the Zinfandel Symposium at Sutter Home Winery eight or nine years ago. You told me I should keep you posted on my Zinfandel book, if it ever materialized. It is now materializing."

"Ah, yes. I remember the Symposium," replied Jerry. "But I am afraid I don't remember a conversation with you. However, Scott did say something about your book. How can I help you?"

"Well, I just wondered if you might have any suggestions for me?"

"Whom have you talked to down south?" he asked without hesitation. I caught a suspicious edge in his voice.

"Oh, nearly all the important growers and producers in the Paso Robles/Arroyo Grande region," I replied, yet with a distinct feeling that that region wasn't what he meant when he said "down south." I was right.

"No, I mean down **south**!" he repeated, more emphatically.

"Well, how far south are you talking about?" I responded a little nervously.

"I'm talking Cucamonga Valley, Riverside, Temecula," he answered. "Have you talked to Don Galleano in Riverside?"

"No. I've just this very minute heard of Don Galleano," I answered. "Is he someone I should talk to?" I could tell he was, and that my visit to the Cucamonga Valley of Riverside and San Bernadino counties was long overdue. This region in bygone days was home to 35,000 to 40,000 acres, one-third of which was Zinfandel. Now, maybe 600 acres of the old non-irrigated Zinfandel vines remain, they having escaped the developers' bulldozers (barely) because their fruit was treasured by those who made Zinfandel wine from them. Jerry's reply echoed my thoughts.

"Definitely! You cannot write a book on Zinfandel and not include Don Galleano and the Cucamonga Valley," he barked at me, but in a nice way. "Let me give you his number. You have to call him immediately. He's the main reason why there's even 600 acres of old Zinfandel vines still in the ground there."

With that unequivocal recommendation, I called Don Galleano at his office at Galleano Winery in Mira Loma in Riverside County. He enthusiastically granted my request for a visit to his winery, a tour of the Zinfandel vineyards under his management, and an interview. Soon, we had a schedule for a three-day visit in May that would include wineries in Temecula that used Cucamonga Valley Zinfandel grapes. Don also offered to make arrangements for me to stay at Riverside's historic Mission Inn Hotel — a must-see, he said, for my first ever visit to the region.

Before our conversation had ended, Don made one more recommendation: that I cross the border into Baja California, and visit Vinícola L.A. Cetto in Valle de Guadalupe, and its historic Zinfandel vineyard known as Rancho Escondido, and discover Mexican Zinfandel — since I would be so near the border anyway.

Needless to say, if there was an important old Zinfandel vineyard in Baja California, I was going to have to see it, and taste the wine that came

---

***Note:** Jerry Mead died in April 2000, after a lengthy illness. The last judging that he participated in was the New World International in February 2000. He was publisher of the *Wine Trader* newsletter. May his Zin-loving soul rest in peace.

from its fruit. My three-day trip south was growing into a five-day trip. I made a few more phone calls, which ultimately put me in touch with Javier Flores, the production winemaker at Thornton Winery, Temecula. Javier was born in Tijuana, and had worked for Vinícola L.A. Cetto for ten years before immigrating to the U.S., and becoming assistant to Thornton's winemaker, Jon MacPherson. Once I explained to Javier what I wanted, he took over the arrangements, and when the time came, escorted me to my destination: Valle de Guadalupe and Vinícola L.A. Cetto.

But first, Cucamonga Valley and Galleano Winery.

Cucamonga Valley

Cucamonga Valley, a 109,400-acre valley straddling Riverside and San Bernadino counties 50 miles east of Los Angeles, became an American Viticultural Area (AVA) May 1, 1995. The soil is sandy loam, and has been almost entirely delivered over centuries by the winds from the desert to the east of the mountains. The climate is warm to hot, and is classified as Region IV. Wine grape vines, probably Mission, were first planted in Cucamonga Valley around 1840. Zinfandel followed, possibly as early as 1867, but didn't became a significant variety in the region until 1900, the year Secondo Guasti planted between 5,000 and 6,000 acres of wine grapes in one block, perhaps as much as half of it Zinfandel. The Guasti vineyard was the largest contiguous dry-farmed vineyard in the world. The vines were planted on their own roots, head trained, and, despite the low annual rainfall (12 to 14 inches), non-irrigated. The water table at that time, however, was high. You could strike water at 26 feet back then, I was to learn.

In the 1940s and 1950s, there were over 35,000 acres of vineyard in Cucamonga Valley. About one-third of that was Zinfandel. By 1995, there were less than 2,000 acres, with about 600 in Zinfandel, most of it planted before Prohibition. The remaining acreage was in Mission, Grenache, Mourvedre, Chardonnay, Palomino, Carignane, Pedro Jimenez, and others. Since the trend in Cucamonga Valley has been to urban development, not vineyard expansion, few vines have been planted since the end of World War II. Rather, thousands of acres of vines have gone down to the blade of the bulldozer, including those in the 100-acre Captain Paul Garrett Zinfandel vineyard.

The remaining acreage is in the hands of a half-dozen owners, only a few of whom are committed to keeping their historic vines in the ground. Don Galleano is one of them.

Galleano Winery

Monday morning, May 19, 1997, I called Don Galleano from the spacious suite of rooms the beautiful and historic Mission Inn had reserved for me. I had found it the evening before without difficulty (little smog that day). Arriving in Riverside after a five-hour drive from Paso Robles and its annual May wine festival, I had reached the hotel in time to check in, have a refreshing shower, and a light and delicious dinner in the balmy patio restaurant. I had also been wondering where the Zinfandel vineyards could possibly be. The view from freeways 15 south and 60 east did not offer many clues. Yet I was feeling cheerful.

When Don told me that I needed to backtrack on Highway 60 west to get to Wineville Road, Mira Loma, the location of his winery, I felt a shudder of apprehension. I had not seen anything along Highway 60 that remotely suggested an historic winery and vineyards.

Nonetheless, I gathered up my tape recorder, notebook, and camera, along with a still cheerful attitude, and headed out into the warm, hazy morning. It was a short drive west on highway 60 to my exit at Etiwanda Avenue. The directions then put me onto Riverside Drive, which runs along side the freeway I had just departed. I drove past various dismally unadorned industrial warehouses to Wineville Road, were I saw a big sign announcing Galleano Winery. Turning onto this road lined with Eucalyptus trees, I found the scene a little more uplifting — but only a little. On my right was a huge compost field, and behind it a stream of traffic flying along Highway 15. On my left was an enormous Home Depot/Costco warehouse. There also had to be a dairy or two nearby; I could smell them! Napa Valley this wasn't!

Before my apprehension had turn into despair, I arrived at the Galleano compound. The historic winery, the oldest in Riverside County, and, as of 1993, a County Historical Landmark and State of California Point of Historical Interest, was on my right; behind it, Galleano's 100-acre vineyard stretched to the freeway. The offices and the Galleanos' historic residence were on my left. In the midst of the noise, air pollution, and hostile industrial development that had decimated the vineyards and wineries in this fertile valley, it stood as a startling and remarkable oasis. What I was about to find was an impressive and beautiful working wine museum, a few remarkable old Zinfandel vineyards, and Donald Galleano — who is as deeply rooted to his birthplace and his region as are the historic old vines. Of the 600 acres of pre-Prohibition era, non-irrigated Zinfandel remaining in Cucamonga Valley, Donald farms most of them.

My cheerfulness restored by the beautiful old buildings, the flowers and trees, and the sounds of activity in the winery, I entered the office in search of the person responsible for the phenomenon of this fully operational working winery-museum.

"He'll be right out," said Debbie Kreinbring, the friendly office manager.

From our phone conversations, I was prepared to meet an energetic, dynamic man with a commanding presence, and a passion for Cucamonga Valley wine grapes and his wonderful winery. He was all of that. Tall, with strong, well-defined features and short thick black hair showing streaks of silver, he looked as if he would have been as comfortable on a magnificent Spanish steed saddled in black and silver as driving about in his shiny deep green Jeep parked by the gate.

His greeting was cordial, bordering on the irreverent, as he invited me into his rustic office furnished with antiques, and offered me a coffee — "unless, of course, you'd rather have a whiskey," he quipped.

Although I felt that I could do with a whiskey, I accepted the coffee. My three-day visit to Galleano Winery and Cucamonga Valley, after all, was just beginning!

Don Galleano

Joining in the conversation was Bob de Berard, another of the few remaining long-established winegrape growers of Cucamonga Valley. Bob de Berard's eight acres of "Home Ranch" Zinfandel vines were planted in "1902 — or 1903 or 1904," said Bob. "That's all that is left of that original planting." Bob also has 10 acres left of the Mission vines that his father planted in the years following Repeal, and that he is grafting, 10 rows at a time, to Zinfandel. "These days, I get four times as much for Zinfandel as I do for Mission," he said. He is also getting name recognition from Jon MacPherson, at Thornton Winery, who is proud of the historic Cucamonga Valley vineyards he is buying from, and the fact that all his wines are from South Coast and Cucamonga Valley viticultural areas.

It hasn't always been like this. The recent demand for Cucamonga Valley Zinfandel, as a varietal, is a phenomenon new to current growers, and not experienced in the valley since the last days of Prohibition.

"Why would anyone have planted Mission following Repeal, when it seemed there had been such a demand for the non-irrigated Zinfandel grapes during Prohibition years?" I queried.

"That's where the money was — in tonnage. At that time, we weren't after varietal fruit," replied Bob.

"The deal was," chimed in Don, in response to my bewildered look, "that with Zinfandel, here locally, you can get only a couple of tons to the acre. With Mission, if you had access to water, you could generate eight to ten tons to the acre. Although the price per ton was the same — whether for Zinfandel or Mission — you got much more tonnage off the Mission for the same cost of production. Also, remember that 80 percent of the wine that was being produced in this valley, and most of the wine that was being consumed in America after Repeal and through the 1950s, was fortified wine. Mission was the basis for that wine.

"In 1928, when they planted that vineyard here in the Cantu Ranch, it was right at the tail-end of Prohibition. There was a huge demand in the east for non-irrigated Zinfandel grapes. That's why they planted those grapes — to satisfy that huge demand, for non-irrigated wine grapes for homemade table wine. The reason there is so much Zinfandel in Cucamonga today is that it shipped well, during Prohibition. The home winemakers, many of whom were Italian, found that when picked at 20° Brix, it shipped better than at higher Brix. To bump up the color, they liked a little Alicante Bouschet; for flavor and spice, Muscat Alexandria. Today, growers who were shippers then still have vineyards in good condition."

Donald's point brought Craig Rous's words back to me: "When Mondavi-Woodbridge decided to produce a Zinfandel wine in 1990, we went looking for growers whose families had been shippers during Prohibition," he had told me.

"But that all changed with Repeal," continued Don. "The commercial demand after Repeal was for fortified Sherries and Ports. Since you could convert the Zinfandel into Port, that was primarily what Zinfandel was used for. The Mission vine was planted in the 1930s and 1940s because with irrigation it produced four to five times the tonnage over Zinfandel. That fruit could go into 'Angelica,' Port, or into generic red or white table wines. Producers like Gallo, who bought the old Pio Winery on Arrow Highway, liked Mission because it was cheap, and they could make a lot of different wines from it. It is a remarkably versatile grape. Through Phil Modica, their buyer for the Pio Winery, the Gallos told the local growers what varieties they wanted — and Mission was a big favorite. That's why growers like the de Berards and the Hofers planted Mission in the 1940s."

I was starting to get it! Irrigation became viable in Cucamonga Valley with the advent of electricity, which came to the area about the time of Repeal. With electrically powered pumps, water could easily be delivered by furrow to 10- or 20- or 30-acre blocks of Mission vines, since you didn't need much land to grow a lot of Mission grapes. From 10 acres of irrigated Mission vines, one could get up to 100 tons. The flavor of the grapes didn't matter that much, especially for fortified wines.

Zinfandel, of course, was rarely irrigated because the quality of the non-irrigated fruit was treasured both by home winemakers and as a flavor base for the generic and fortified wines. Also, irrigation was costly. Since Zinfandel plantings in the Post-Repeal years ran to the hundreds, even thousands, of acres into the 1960s, irrigation of Zinfandel on such a scale was unthinkable. Further, contrary to a popular but misguided belief, a grower can increase the size of his Zinfandel crop only minimally with irrigation. With too much water, Zinfandel berries swell up, the clusters become tight, and the thin-skinned fruit splits, inviting sour bunch rot. The tree-sized Mission vine, with its big bunches of tough, thick-skinned fruit was another story.

"So when did the focus on Zinfandel as a variety begin again here in the Cucamonga Valley?" I asked Don.

"When I got involved in this business in 1968 and 1969, my dad had custom-crushed Zinfandel for a big grower by the name of Nick Devito. Nick wanted to custom-crush Zinfandel because wineries weren't paying much for Zinfandel in 1968. His idea was to custom-crush his grapes, then sell the wine on the bulk market."

"He had a *lot* of Zinfandel!" said Bob.

"Yes," agreed Don. "He had a lot of Zinfandel — about 2,000 acres, all non-irrigated. So it was really lovely Zinfandel! That's my first recollection of becoming aware specifically of Zinfandel as a varietal. My dad made some really nice Zinfandel wine from those old non-irrigated grapes."

"Did your father bottle any of the Zinfandel under the Galleano label?"

"Yeah, and sold it from the store here. But Devito never did. He sold it all on the bulk market."

"Also, the largest winery in the valley after Repeal was Regina Grape Products,"* said Don. "When Regina was at its peak of producing cooking wine and wine vinegars in the 1960s, we sold grapes to them. I used to sit up there and watch these perfectly lovely Zinfandel grapes coming in, to be made into vinegar. Price paid for Zinfandel then was about $135 a ton. I couldn't help feeling that the grapes would be better used to make Zinfandel table wine. It made me think about a date I had with a girl when I was still working in Bakersfield, after graduating from San Jose State. I took her to a Basque restaurant, and the wine on the table was Zinfandel. That was my first memory of really enjoying a red table wine."

"So you're saying that interest in Zinfandel as a variety revived in Cucamonga Valley in the late 1970s?" I asked Don.

"About then," he confirmed.

However, although Don had some interest in bottling Zinfandel and other varietals under its own label for sale from its retail tasting room and store, Galleano Winery was primarily a bulk wine operation. With its redwood tanks ranging in size from 2,000 gallons to 15,000 gallons and its five closed-top 10,460-gallon concrete fermentors, it was not suited to premium table wine production. Whatever the winery bottled and sold in the retail store was the same blend that was sold as bulk. Don continues to

---

***Note:** Regina Grape Products was established in 1906 as Regina Winery by Claudio and Caterina Ellena. It was renamed Regina Grape Products in 1934 by sons John and Louis. By 1949, John and Louis had added fine wine vinegars to their list of wine products. And by 1968, it was the nation's leading producer of wine vinegars, made principally from Zinfandel. The facility was sold to wine giant Heublein in 1971, and sold twice more after that. The last grapes crushed and wine produced at the facility was in 1991. The winery stood empty and neglected for the next few years, until the city of Rancho Cucamonga purchased it. J. Fillippi Winery now leases part of it for use as a winery, tasting room, and vineyard education. Community interest in preserving the entire facility as an historical site is keen.

have a large customer base for his traditionally made redwood tank fermented Zinfandel.

"I am not set up to keep vineyard lots of wine separate and bottle them as vineyard designations. I don't keep any small oak cooperage here," he said. "Nor am I a great fan of oak barrels, although neutral oak is fine. But most of the wine that goes through here does not see a barrel. It's turned around quickly because I like the freshness. I have grown accustomed to it, because this is the way I've grown up here at this winery. I like to drink wines that are fresh, that have been stored in California redwood. The redwood may instill some character or flavor, I don't know, but I do know that I like the fruitiness and freshness of new wines, especially of Zinfandel, that have not been in oak. That's my palate. That's the palate of most of my customers."

Annual retail sales of Zinfandel under the Galleano label total about 4,000 cases.

"Have you any plans on getting out of the jug wine business, or converting just to oak- aged premium Zinfandel," I asked Donald. "I know of several long-established family producers who have stopped using redwood tanks for storage, and have stopped bottling Zinfandel table wine in screw-top jugs. Now that premium oak-aged Zinfandel is winning acclaim as a world-class red table wine, they felt they wanted to shed the stigma of being a jug Zinfandel producer."

"I haven't stopped," said Don sharply, with a defiant toss of his head. "I don't give a damn about what anyone might say about my producing screw-top jug wines. It's traditional. We had a guy in here yesterday who has been buying jugs of wine here for his father-in-law and for himself for 50 years. These are the kind of guys, they're Italian-American for the most part, who buy their wine in jugs. I think it's a bit pretentious, a bit snobby, to just say to these long-time customers, 'Okay, we're not going to deal with that anymore.' Let me tell you something: I'm a southern California winemaker. I drink a bottle of wine — just like that." He snapped his fingers at me. Sparks flew from their tips. "I'm not going to pay $15 for a bottle of wine; I'm not going to pay even $6. When I go over to the house, I grab a 4-liter jug of Zinfandel. That's what we drink. And that's what all my friends drink. It's a damn good wine, price aside. There's no correlation between price and quality."

"So you leave the oak ageing of Cucamonga Valley Zinfandel to producers like Thornton?" I asked, although it was more of a rhetorical question. Could I have any doubts by now of where Donald stood with regard to his tradition of Zinfandel production? Also, I liked how he had dug his heels in on this issue.

"Yes, let the other guys do the oak," Donald reiterated. "Jon MacPherson [winemaker for Thornton Winery, Temecula] does vineyard designations from Cucamonga Valley Zinfandel vineyards: de Berard

Home Ranch; Hofer Ranch; Clark Ranch; Lopez Ranch. This guy has got the kind of operation whereby he can do that and age them in French oak, some of it new. It's a pretty small operation. Also, Joe Hart."

"I've tasted every one of them," said Bob de Berard, "and they are all different."

"I'm not surprised," I commented. "Vineyards even when they are side by side seem to have micro-*terroirs* that impart distinctive characters to the wines."

"There's also different clones here in the valley, there's no question," said Don. "You need to come down when the grapes are ripe, and take a look at the different clones."

Thinking the subject was closed, I was about to ask another question when Don suddenly added, with a hint of a chuckle, "Although I'll tell you what we've done this year [1996], we produced some wine here, and sent it down to Thornton Winery for oak storage — about 600 cases worth. It was some of the first Zinfandel we had harvested from the Lopez Ranch, Gateway, and Filpi — not Fillippi, *Filpi* — before that extreme August 1996 heat wave, which drove the Brix from 22° to 27° in seven days. The first harvest was early for Zinfandel, and was some of the best Zinfandel of the 1996 vintage.

"In a hot region here," Don explained. "When you get caught in a heat wave that drives sugars, then you need to add water to the must to reduce your sugars so you don't get stuck fermentation, and you need to add tartaric acid to correct acid imbalance. I always have believed that the grapes that have the proper pH are always better than the stuff that you have to do some adjustments on. The grapes that came in after the heat wave, during our second and third week of Zinfandel harvest, weren't of the quality of the fruit that came in before the heat wave, when the sugars weren't hammered.

"So the first part of the 1996 vintage was the best. Some of it I shipped off to Fetzer: and some of it I kept — about 1,300 gallons, and shipped down to Thornton Winery for barrel ageing. I had 'Jonny Mac' order in 25–30 new American oak barrels for us when he was ordering his own. So now we are barrel-ageing Zinfandel in brand new American oak barrels at Thornton Winery, which is something I've always belly-ached about — that the guys who do this are creating wine that tastes more like baseball bats than wine. So now I'm guilty of doing the same thing for the first time in my life!"

Both Bob de Berard and I stared at Donald in silence, astonished by this unexpected revelation.

Bob was the first to recover his voice. "You've got a Zinfandel in new oak barrels down at Thornton?"

'Yeah. It will go into a Reserve package, a higher end package," said Donald, chuckling, seeming to enjoy our amazement.

"How much will you sell this Reserve Zinfandel for?" I asked. Was this going to be his show piece Zinfandel — the one out to garner the critics' attention with its oak-aged character and its high price?

"I don't know. We sell our non-oak-aged blend over here right now for $6 a bottle. We sell our 4-liter jugs of Zinfandel, right straight out of redwood, for $8.50. I do know the $15 per bottle the other guys are getting is way out of range for my customers, although I think the quality of that Reserve lot is excellent. When you go down there tomorrow," Donald said, looking at me, "you'll get to taste it from the barrel. You can tell me what you think of it.

"I'm thinking right now that I'll probably release it for $8 or $9 a bottle," he continued. "Frankly, I think people are nuts to be pricing Zinfandel wines at $15 and up. There are some really nice wines coming out of South Africa, Argentina, and Europe for $5 or $6. When you start charging $15 for a bottle of wine, you are really restricting the amount of wine that you can sell; you're restricting people's ability to buy it. Who's going to pay $15 for a bottle of wine, when there are nice wines available for $5? As I just told you, what I drink in the house is my 4-liter jug."

(Galleano Winery's 1996-reserve style Zinfandel has been named "Pioneer Legendary Zinfandel," and was released in winter 1998 for $12/bottle.)

"So now your Zinfandel production is both in your traditional redwood tank aged style and a Reserve style?" I asked, wondering if his jug wine days were numbered.

"Yeah," he replied.

"And people are lucky that he still does this," added de Berard.

"It also looks like you have come to believe that when an exceptional block or vintage of Cucamonga Valley Zinfandel comes in, it is worthy of the expense of world-class treatment?" I asked.

"Yes, we believe in Zinfandel," he assured me, side-stepping my question a little. "In fact, you'll be glad to know that I just bought an old 40-acre Zinfandel vineyard in Fontana that was destined to fall to the developer's bulldozer." After waiting a moment for this news to sink in, he continued, "I'm on a mission to buy up as many of the remaining old vineyards as I can. I'm a Zinfandel preservationist," he stated firmly, but with good humor."

At this point, Don walked me to the winery, for a taste of his non-vintage dated 1996 Zinfandel. As we tasted our samples of the 1996, Donald remarked, "It has a nice cheesy character, don't you think?"

"It's soft, yet spicy, with a nice clean, slightly bitter, finish," I replied. "I'm not sure what you mean by 'cheesy.'" Alcohol was right at 14 percent.

Donald looked at me quizzically, shrugged, but offered no further comment.

Galleano Winery's 4-liter jugs of Zinfandel are the best buy around, if you want to drink wine every day. It's a lot of wine, but all you need to do is decant it into fifths, one of the cellar workers told me, and shove an old cork down into it, and it will keep for as long as you need it to.

"Our wines spend up to six months in redwood tank," explained Don. "The wines are full-bodied, but we don't like to have a lot of tannin in the jugs. Our customers like fairly big wines, but they don't want them to bite their heads off."

Despite Don's adamant and passionate fondness for traditionally made wines, Galleano Winery is gearing up for the 21st century.

In summer of 1997, shortly after my visit, Don hired 25-year old Jason Bushong, a Riverside native and passionate Zinfandel advocate, as Director of Wine Production. By late fall, Jason had ordered in a few dozen new American oak barrels, and was working to change the focus of Galleano Winery from production of mostly bulk wine to small lot bottlings of Zinfandel table wine, Zinfandel port, and other wines from the vineyards under the control and management of Don.

When I paid a second visit to the winery in January 1998, the sherry room was filled with oak barrels, as was the old concrete fermentor that had been used as a hospitality room. "It's cool, dark, damp, and quiet," said Jason, "a perfect environment for ageing red wines.

"Don Galleano farms most of the remaining pre-Prohibition vineyards in Cucamonga Valley," explained Jason. "He has under his control more old-vine Zinfandel acreage than any other grower in the state — nearly 600 acres," he said. "If anyone should be a 'Zinfandel house,' it is Galleano Winery. While our ports and other dessert wines have always been highly regarded, we are also capable of producing world-class Zinfandel table wine from these fabulous old vineyards. Just try our 1996 American oak-aged Pioneer's Legendary Zinfandel."

Other changes are also taking place at Galleano Winery.

There are a couple of 15,000 gallon jacketed stainless steel tanks at the back of the building — for the Chardonnay. A relatively new press is installed, and all the electrical wiring in the historic building has being upgraded.

Even with these additions, Galleano Winery is not planning on phasing out production of its redwood tank aged 4-liter jugs of screw top Zinfandel. Rather, the winery will simply downsize its bulk wine operation as it adds on premium wine production capacity.

It is the historic vineyards that make all this possible. It is time now to venture back out onto the streets and freeways in search of these old vineyards that seemed to have acquired a sacred status by virtue of their having survived to see the day when once again their fruit would be esteemed. As quiet as its been kept, Galleano's well made, value priced Cucamonga Valley Zinfandel wine is being sought out by such central and north coast wineries as Bernardo, Delicato, Burgess, Fetzer, Firestone, R.H. Phillips, and Geyser

Peak wineries. Some of these producers are even bottling some vineyard lots under vineyard designations, for higher priced releases.

"Cara, Debbie's sister, is going to take you up to Paul Hofer's ranch. It's a neat drive, and you're not going to believe what we're doing here in a very urban setting," Don said, by way of preparing me. "Hofer is right beside Ontario International Airport, so you will see the old vineyard, and right across the road, the international airport, with the big jets coming and going. Keep going up Haven to the D'Ambrogio Ranch, which is probably the classiest old Zinfandel ranch in the Valley. Those vines go back to the late 1800s. Mary D'Ambrogio just recently told me that when she was married 50 years ago, the vines were already 80 years old. So they must have been planted in 1867."

"That makes that vineyard as old as the famous 'Grandpère' in Amador County," I exclaimed. Bob de Berard was equally surprised.

"Really!" he exclaimed. "So D'Ambrogio bought a vineyard already planted? That's before ours."

"Yeah, his dad did," answered Donald. "That vineyard always got well taken care of because Frank D'Ambrogio was a shipper; that vineyard's grapes always got shipped. So it's a real classic Zinfandel vineyard. Daryl Groom likes these grapes so much he's hoping to make a D'Ambrogio Vineyard-designated Zinfandel from the 1997 vintage."

As I struggled to reconcile these seemingly irreconcilable images of tradition and modernization, Cara arrived, ready to take me on my eye-popping tour of historic Zinfandel vineyards thriving among the urban landmarks of international airports, high-tension power lines, and multi-laned freeways. Was I ready for this?

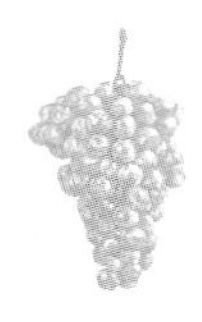

Hofer Ranch: Paul Hofer

Our first stop on my Cucamonga Valley urban Zinfandel vineyard tour was the Hofer Ranch, whose home buildings are right beside the Ontario International Airport. The City of Ontario acquired its airport property — 300 acres — from the Hofer family by the law of eminent domain. Once you enter the residential compound itself, however, you momentarily forget that you are next door to an international airport. Surrounded with a tall fence and dense, protective trees, the compound is not visible from the road. Upon our entering between cut stone gateposts, we found ourselves on a long driveway lined with tall palm and eucalyptus trees. Inside stood many of the original buildings in excellent repair. Along the fence near the ancient Mission vineyard stood a row of classic old farm machinery. Towering trees cast plentiful shade; flowering shrubs and plants abounded. It was another oasis in the middle of brutal industrial encroachment, the sounds of which are never long absent.

Cara and I had no sooner gotten out of Don's jeep when the 20th century roar of a Boeing 737 taking off blasted me back into reality. At the same instant, Paul, representing the fifth generation of family on the ranch, approached us. His family came here in 1882. Moderately tall, black-haired, blue-eyed, quiet, good-looking, and dressed neatly in plaid shirt and jeans, he greeted us with a warm smile, then invited us into the relative quiet of his small office.

Inside, my attention was drawn to the walls, which were covered with framed fruit and grape box art, and a huge black-and-white photo print of the Cucamonga Valley, taken in the 1940s when it was covered with 40,000 acres of vines. All you could see for miles was row upon row of head trained freestanding vines, with the impressive San Gabriel Mountains forming a fabulous backdrop. Cucamonga Valley at that time was home to the biggest planting of vineyard in California.

One of the grape box pieces caught my eye, as it proudly proclaimed to hold only non-irrigated Cucamonga Valley juice grapes, which the customers understood to be Zinfandel.

"Non-irrigated Cucamonga Valley Zinfandel grapes were greatly prized by home winemakers back east during and after Prohibition," Paul explained, as I admired the print. "Zinfandel was one of the predominant grapes in this valley then. It obviously grows well here, and we are crazy enough to still believe that this is one of the best places to grow Zinfandel. Secondo Guasti, who came here about 1900 from Piedmont, Italy, and was quite the innovator, had a lot to do with Zinfandel being planted here. He had 5,000 acres in a single block of Pedro Jimenez, Mission, Zinfandel, and other varieties — a big deal then. And his winery was on a scale beyond what anyone else was doing at that time.

"This valley did so well in Prohibition because the Volstead Act provided for a head of household to make 200 gallons for personal consumption. It was also a time of great Italian immigration into the U.S., and they weren't about to give up drinking wine just because of our silly law. There was this incredible demand for grapes. Non-irrigated Zinfandel from the Cucamonga Valley was the grape of choice for many. The home winemakers didn't want any hint of bunch rot, and so the demand for our grapes was incredible."

"Have you never irrigated your Zinfandel? I asked, a little incredulous. It didn't seem possible for vineyards to thrive in that hot dry climate without irrigation.

"Before 1920, only citrus was irrigated, because that was where the money was," recalled Paul. "California's south coast supplied all the citrus for the entire country then. I have heard it said that a family of four could live comfortably and send their children through college on 10 acres of oranges back then — without ever setting foot in the orchard. The contracting company took care of everything. They brought the water down from the foothills in a system of weirs [dams] and pipes, maintained the trees, and brought in the picking crews. All the family did was cash the check that came a few weeks later.

"But there was no system of irrigation for vineyards here until the 1920s, when the advent of electricity made electrically-powered high volume pumps possible. Then wells were drilled, and furrow and concrete pipe irrigation became feasible because electricity was cheap and got cheaper the more you used. A good furrow irrigator could just about make water run uphill. So most of the growers took advantage of its availability. Mission grapes were big producers and in demand both for home wine and fortified wines. The more water they received the bigger crops they produced. Mission could handle as much as 18 inches of water in addition to our annual rainfall.

Paul Hofer Jr. & Paul Hofer III

"But not Zinfandel. Any water added during the growing season tends to create tightly packed bunches with pumped up berries. All you need is one ruptured berry to cause bunch rot. So we have rarely irrigated our Zinfandel. It is a deep-rooting vine, and because of the sandy soil, the vines have thrived on their own roots, and go extremely deep in search of water. Even though our average annual rainfall is only 12 to 14 inches, non-irrigated Zinfandel year after year produces 2½ to three tons of disease- and pest-free intensely flavored fruit — which isn't much, compared to the Mission. But the fruit quality is superb."

"Nonetheless, 12 inches isn't much rainfall for vines to get along on," I remarked.

"It isn't," Paul agreed. "But early on in this valley, there was a lot of ground water. The windmill you see across from the office here was put up in 1917, and reached water at 27 feet. These buildings are on the high piece of ground in this area. When my great-great grandparents came here in 1882, the water table was so high in wet years that my great-grandmother remembered seeing bears coming out of the foothills in the summer and taking mud baths just a couple of hundred yards down from where we are sitting. There was a low spot there that was muddy year-round. Our neighbors had artesian wells for many years. Zinfandel did well without irrigation then, and no one would spend money just to be spending money.

"But since people and industry started thronging out here at the end of World War II, the water table over the years has dropped so much that now you have to go down 185 feet to reach it. I remember my mother saying after the war that whenever the family got a little money ahead, it all went into a new well.

"Today, most of us have installed overhead moveable aluminum pipes. However, despite the low water table, we still rarely irrigate Zinfandel. Their roots are deep, so we find that only when we have two dry years back to back do we need to supplement the annual rainfall. We still find it best to deliver water between February 1 and May 1, when the vines are dormant. Irrigating then is like naturally occurring rain, since we deliver only enough water to supplement whatever Nature doesn't give us by April — up to the equivalent of 14 inches.

"I try not to deliver water after May 1 because we don't want tight bunches that are more likely to develop bunch rot. Also, we are convinced that irrigation after May 1 diminishes grape quality and intensity of flavors. Therefore, our Zinfandel crop remains at between 2½ to three tons of fruit per acre."

"When were your Zinfandel vineyards planted?" I asked.

"The best we can figure is that our first Zinfandel was planted in the 1890s," replied Paul. "What Zinfandel we have left, about 40 acres, is across the street. According to my dad's memory, it was planted about 1910, which makes it about 85 years old."

"So you're not about to give up on your old Zinfandel vines, even though they now require more work to keep alive and to produce top quality grapes?"

"Not at all!" Paul replied unhesitatingly. "Zinfandel is still my favorite grape, and a favorite for those of us who grew up here. I love Cucamonga Zinfandel, and I find myself comparing all other red wines to Zinfandel, especially to Cucamonga Zinfandel. I think the best here can be as good as the best from the north coast. Since we converted to sub-soil tillage with the "noble blade," we have mulch in the vineyards, and far fewer pests like the leafhopper that plagues some of the north coast vineyards. Mildew and bunch rot are also uncommon. We have always been partial to Zinfandel, especially Zinfandel stored in redwood tanks."

"You really are partial to redwood-aged Zinfandel ?" I asked him. "Or is it sentimental attachment?" I am not sure why I thought that, since I had found Don Galleano's traditionally made redwood tank-aged Zinfandel a very lovely wine.

"Well, it's like anything you learn on. You come to think that this is how Zinfandel is supposed to taste. In fact, at our [still standing Pioneer] winery, which we haven't operated for 17 or 18 years now, even our fermentors were redwood. The wine was fermented in redwood, and stored in redwood. We produced mostly bulk wine. We fermented, and stored in redwood for maybe a couple of months. Then it would go out in rail cars to other wineries. We didn't do a lot of our own bottling. Just enough for ourselves. Using redwood makes a heavy wine, since redwood contributes a lot of tannin. We all still like that flavor, although pretty much everybody is going to oak."

The subject of ageing Zinfandel in small oak barrels led Paul to a point that rankles him — high-priced wines and pricey wine lists in restaurants.

"Nothing upsets me more than to have a waitperson in a restaurant look down his or her nose at the beginning wine drinker. It's snobby, and it hurts both the beginning wine drinker and the industry. In the first interview he ever gave, Ernest Gallo told the *Wine Spectator* a few years ago that the American wine industry had made a big mistake in targeting the wine connoisseurs and wine aficionados. In doing so, Mr. Gallo pointed out, it had bypassed the everyday wine drinker."

"I love Cucamonga Zinfandel, and I find myself comparing all other red wines to Zinfandel, especially to Cucamonga Zinfandel."

Paul Hofer

At this point, Paul opened a copy of the *Wine Spectator* that was lying on his desk, so that I could read the relevant passage: "I think it's a challenge for wineries to develop not only wines that are more appreciated by the general public, but to create new wines. You're not going to like to hear this," Mr. Gallo said to Marvin Shanken, the *Wine Spectator*'s editor and publisher, "but I think that too many in the wine industry have been producing wines to please self-appointed wine writers. And that particular style may not be what the public out there is enjoying to the point where they'll repeat-purchase."[26]

"I agree with Mr. Gallo," Paul stated. "Cucamonga Valley Zinfandel has traditionally been an everyday wine consumer's wine. Restaurants should make it a point to carry traditionally made, but inexpensive, wines like Galleano's redwood tank-aged Zinfandel. That way, beginners don't feel intimidated by the prices to try a wine with their meals."

However, the traditional redwood tank-aged style of jug wine is an endangered species, and a rare find in a winery, let alone on a restaurant's wine list.

Despite the popularity of Cucamonga Valley non-irrigated Zinfandel at the end of Prohibition, the Mission soon became the preferred grape for the sweet and fortified wines so popular in America in those years following Repeal.

"The problem was that after Repeal, Zinfandel became just another grape for making fortified and sweet wines, which it lent itself well to,"

26 Marvin R. Shanken, "Gallo's Dramatic Shift to Fine Varities," *Wine Spectator*, Sept. 15, 1991, Vol. XVI, No. 10, 25.

said Paul, corroborating what Don Galleano had explained to me earlier. "Prices dropped from $50 per ton to $32, and stayed there right up to the early 1970s, when they went up to $135.

"Since most of the Zinfandel vineyards were dry farmed, yield was low. If we ever got three tons, we were standing in tall cotton. But the demand for land in the Cucamonga Valley after World War II was for urban development, not vineyards. Most of the vineyards were sold off at that time for houses and industry. By 1965, acreage had fallen to 30,000, and has been in decline ever since. Mission did well because it was irrigated, and produced five times the tonnage for the same cost of production. New plantings immediately after Repeal were mostly the Mission grape.

"Now, of course, in 1997, our dry-farmed Zinfandel is once again worth five times the Mission grape. But there isn't much of it left. Two thousand acres total of remaining vineyard in Cucamonga Valley is a generous estimate today," Paul said, "with about a third of that Zinfandel — nearly all of it pre-Prohibition. But those of us still here have dug in, and are trying to hold onto what we still have in the ground, and take care of them, and maintain quality. Six to eight growers own all the remaining vineyards, but many of them are farmed by Galleano."

It was time for Paul to move on to his next appointment and for Cara and me to continue with our vineyard tour. After walking with Paul to his historic redwood barn for a peek at the collection of small home wine presses his father had bought up in the 1960s, when the home wine boom was going bust, I shook hands with this charming and fervent Cucamonga Valley Zinfandel grower. I left feeling both inspired and depressed by all that he had told me.

The José Lopez Ranch

Since Don Galleano had piqued my interest in the José Lopez Ranch from our first phone conversation, I opted to visit it next. Located on a rocky slope above the town of Rancho Cucamonga, the Lopez Ranch is generally considered to be one of the best Zinfandel vineyards in the region for premium wine production. Because of the age of the vines, the thin rocky alluvial soil, the absence of irrigation, and the hot dry climate, yield is normally low. Add in the fact that the vineyard had suffered years of neglect; by 1996 yield had dropped to barely three-quarters of per ton per acre. The vineyard ripens early, usually before the onset of hot August days. It is picked at peak ripeness, with excellent numbers for acid, pH, and Brix.

Now that it is under Galleano's care, there is hope for improved yield in years to come. In 1997, he began vineyard practices to help restore the vines to vigor. He cleared accumulated dirt and rocks from the crowns of all the vines and reactivated a couple of wells on the property to supplement seasonal rainfall with drip irrigation during the late spring months.

"It is in such deteriorated condition that the workers are demoralized by the sight," Donald had told me. "So we have to work to keep ourselves motivated to restore the vineyard to health. But with the recent intense interest in it, not just by R.H. Phillips, but also by Joe Hart, Jon MacPherson, and myself, we'll make it," he assured me. "We also have to try and keep owner Joe Lopez from selling any more acreage for houses."

After driving ten minutes along Highway 15 north, Cara and I came to the Rancho Cucamonga exit. Within a few minutes, she had parked the Jeep at the edge of the vineyard, and the vision that greeted my eyes left me thunderstruck. Before me was a vast, dry, stony vineyard of tiny, struggling midget vines that seemed to be cowering under the magnificence of the lofty power line towers set amongst the vines themselves. As with Don Galleano's vineyard, a freeway formed the backdrop at the end of the vineyard, the traffic zooming along like remote-controlled toys. Barely visible in the sunny haze was Cucamonga Peak, a towering mountain that on a clear day would make a breathtaking sight.

I stepped out of the air-conditioned Jeep, and found the afternoon had become suffocatingly hot. Lingering just long enough to make a few photo images before retreating to the Jeep, Cara and I then took time out for a greatly welcomed late lunch at a cool nearby restaurant.

I remained haunted by the image of that parched vineyard of struggling little vines, and when a few weeks later Ric Tracy, Zinfandel winemaker at R.H. Phillips, asked me whether I happened to see any grapes on the vines, I had to say no. But I hadn't looked closely, either. His question left me wondering: Could those little baked vines on that stony, thin alluvial soil possibly produce any grapes? The answer, I have since learned, is yes, indeed — about 150 tons off the 250 or so acres. Simply amazing. A miracle.

By the time that we had finished lunch, the afternoon was nearly over. Since I was to spend the next day with Gino Filippi and his winemaker, Nick Karavittas, at J. Filippi Winery, the other vineyards on my list — the Captain Paul Garrett, the D'Ambrogio and the Gateway — would have to await my return visit.

★ ★ ★ ★ ★

At the ZAP 2000 tasting at Fort Mason, San Francisco, Don Galleano presented me with a tasting of Galleano Winery 1999 José Lopez Ranch Zinfandel. A deep burgundy-colored wine with aromas of black currants, spices, chocolate, and rich ripe blackberries, it was a beauty. "I'll probably release it for under $15," said Don, standing by his tradition of producing a top quality yet affordable wine from Cucamonga's finest grapes.

Given the age of the vines, their tiny yield, and the superb quality of this wine, it seemed to me that it would be a bargain at three times the price.

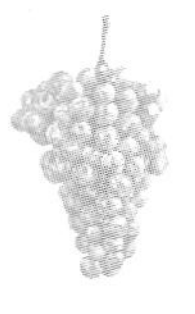

Joseph Filippi Winery

The Filippi family has been winegrape growing since 1922. Giovanni Filippi settled in Cucamonga Valley from the Veneto region of Northern Italy in 1920. Two years later, with his son Joesph, he planted 22 acres at what would become the Joseph Filippi Winery in Mira Loma. The winery was established in 1934. The family's name became synonymous with the region, which was widely recognized as "California's oldest wine district." In 1967, the family purchased California's oldest winery, Thomas Winery and Vineyards, located in Rancho Cucamonga — California Historical Landmark No. 490. The property was sold in 1985; the building still stands. By 1969, under the direction of Joesph's oldest son, Joseph A. Filippi, enologist and viticulture graduate of UC Davis, the vineyards had grown to 400 acres. By 1974, J. Filippi Winery storage and fermentation capacity exceeded one million gallons.

In 1992, Joseph A. Filippi's middle son, Gino, took it upon himself to get Cucamonga Valley recognized as an AVA. Gino's commitment to getting AVA recognition for Cucamonga Valley has helped to reawaken community pride in the valley's worth as a winegrape region, a region that Dan Berger in his *Los Angeles Times* article of May 19, 1994, called California's "lost wine country." The AVA was approved in May 1995.

In 1993, Joseph A. Filippi's sons Jamie, Gino L., and Joseph Paul (J.P.), fourth generation Filippis, were forced to relocate the winery from its original site of 70 years to the historic Ellena Bros./Regina Grape Products facility in the city of Rancho Cucamonga. Some of the family had taken it upon themselves to sell the property out from under the winery just one day before the suicide death of Joseph A. Filippi, president and third-generation winemaker. Gino and Joseph Paul, who is now president, have overcome great adversity to revitalize the family winery.

Nick Karavidas, Joseph Paul (J.P.) Filippi & Gino Filippi (photo by Rachael Weill)

As I set out from the beautiful Mission Inn that hazy May morning and maneuvered onto the freeways that would take me to Rancho Cucamonga, I was looking forward to my visit to the Joseph Filippi Winery at its new home, and to seeing the historic Regina Grape Products facility and its veritable forest of still-standing giant redwood tanks. There, I was to meet Gino and winemaker, Nick Karavidas.

"The history and significance of Cucamonga Valley is mostly forgotten to many modern wine writers," said Gino when I met him in his gleaming office just off the tasting room and gift shop. "But having been here for 75 years as a family, it is what we know best. Fortunately, there seems to be a resurgence of interest in the history of the old Cucamonga Valley, and its significance as a winegrape region. Who would ever have thought there would be a buzz about Cucamonga Valley Zinfandel in 1997?" he asked, referring to my research visit.

"Every square inch of vineyard here is vulnerable to urban encroachment, unless dedicated as valuable vineyard land for the future," said Nick, upon joining us. "Yet despite high land value, Zinfandel was planted as late as the mid-1960s, partly to supply the Regina Grape Products demand for Zinfandel grapes for its gourmet wine vinegars."

To do his part in saving land for vineyard, Nick has acquired a 12-year lease on 10 acres inside Rancho Cucamonga city limits, which he planted with Zinfandel in summer of 1997. "At the end of the 12 years, we'll know whether the vineyard is valued for its grapes, or should be turned into urban development. At least it's an opportunity to generate some interest and support for the land for more local vineyards."

Still getting established in their new location, Joseph Filippi Winery has not limited itself to producing wines from their grapes of the Cucamonga Valley or South Coast viticultural area. However, Cucamonga Valley Zinfandel still has a special claim on the family, which has taken control of the historic Johnston-Clark Zinfandel Vineyard in Rancho Cucamonga. Joseph Filippi Winery crushed its first "Clark Ranch" vintage in 1997. "We still have a lot of work remaining as we retrain the vineyard back into balance and production," said Nick, when he showed me his extensive plans for the old vines.

Like Donald Galleano, the J. Filippi family has dug in, and is making every effort to continue the tradition of wine production in Cucamonga Valley. Before I parted from Gino, he showed me around their restored facility. The tasting bar and wine library are both made from restored staves of old giant redwood casks. There are also a beautiful gift shop, meeting rooms, and museum and art gallery. Guided winery tours were soon to be in operation as well.

And, yes, I got to walk through the forest of giant redwood tanks in the old vinegar facility. An awesome sight! The now empty tanks, however, were in need of attention, since they had become very dry and their bands were slipping. How much longer could they stand in their current condition? Gino informed me that in February of 1995, the City of Rancho Cucamonga declared the old winery and its large collection of tanks as historic landmarks. "Restoration will continue!" he said.

From Joseph Filippi Winery, I went with Nick Karavidas to view the Johnston-Clark Vineyard. The 17-acre vineyard dates back to the early 1900s and was re-planted in the late 1950s. "This property currently earns about $40,000 each year as vineyard. It would probably bring $5 million for housing development," said Nick.

Pride in its winegrape heritage does seem to have some influence over its Rancho Cucamonga owners, though, as Nick pointed out when he showed me the extensive improvements the winery had made to the vineyard. For the present, the vineyard is not in danger of being sold for housing. Yet for how long is it safe? He also showed me the 10-acre piece that he had leased for his Zinfandel vineyard. The owners of the property, he said, are willing to give Zinfandel a chance.

Amidst the ruins of once magnificent Zinfandel acreage, there are indeed welcome and hopeful signs of vineyard renewal.

Leaving the Clark Vineyard, Nick took me to see the old Guasti Winery and former home of the late Brookside Vineyard Co., now a State Historic Landmark. Built in 1904, it is a remarkable place with an appealing ambience. All we had time for was a drive through the grounds and a brief visit to the Joseph Filippi Tasting Room, which is occupying the cooper shop for the former Italian Vineyard Company founded by Mr. Guasti. Then it was time to seek refuge in a cool dining room, this time in the Double Tree Hotel, Ontario.

In January 2001, I tasted the Joseph Filippi 1998 Zinfandel, Cucamonga Valley, Winemaker's Reserve Limited Release. It was a lovely, nicely balanced wine, spicy and full of luscious dark berry fruit, with pleasant but not predominate oak tones.

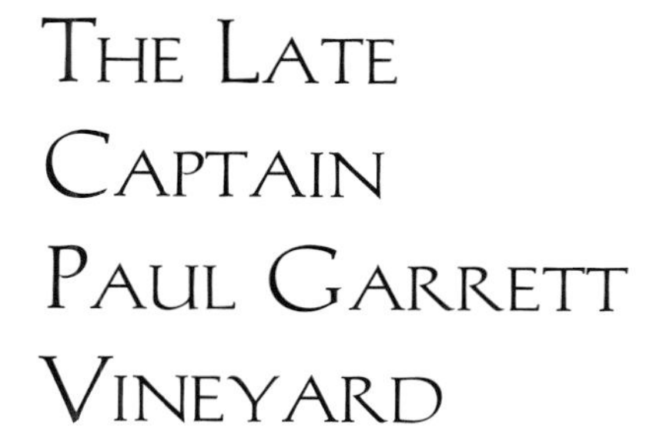

The Late Captain Paul Garrett Vineyard

"If you want some pictures of an historic Zinfandel vineyard being bulldozed out, here's your chance," said Don Galleano when he picked me up at Ontario Airport in January 1998 for my return visit. So the 100-acre Captain Paul Garrett Vineyard was my first stop when Galleano's winemaker, Jason, and I took off in the winery's brand new pickup truck for part two of my "Urban Zinfandel" tour.

Located between a busy street and the City of Ontario's dump, it was a fine looking old vineyard. Trained low to the ground and alive with rabbits bounding through them, the vines were healthy and vigorous.

All but a few acres on city property, and closest to the dump, were in the process of being bulldozed out even as we watched. Rows of dead vines formed brown lines across the now cleared land. I didn't have the heart to approach them. Rather, I focused on those that would survive a little longer; then Jason and I bid a final farewell to this historic vineyard, soon to be the site of more urban development.

Gateway Vineyard

So named because it sits beside Rancho Cucamonga's Gateway business complex, the 50-acre Gateway Vineyard is beautiful and old, low to the ground, non-irrigated, and healthy. Owned by the Mormon Church, Don Galleano farms it under a renewable one-year lease. For now, it is safe from development.

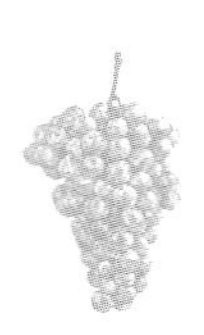

D'Ambrogio Ranch

The moment I laid my eyes upon the D'Ambrogio Vineyard in downtown Rancho Cucamonga, I understood why Daryl Groom had fallen in love with it at first sight. Fifty acres of head trained, non-irrigated vines ran the length of a couple of city blocks straight back to the original Virginia Dare Winery. Behind it all gleamed the towering Cucamonga Peak in the afternoon haze, a dusting of snow adding to its enchantment. Bordering one side of the vineyard were condominiums; bordering the other was a busy four-lane street.

Could this historic, well-cared-for vineyard, which perhaps shares the claim with Teri Harvey's Grandpère of being oldest in the state, survive urban encroachment for many more vintages?

"I don't know how much longer we'll have it," said Don Galleano when I asked him later that day. "We're hoping that maybe the City of Rancho Cucamonga will declare it a State Historical Site, and buy it — since it is for sale."

Temecula Winemakers

Hart Winery: Joe Hart, Winemaker

Early morning of the third day of my first visit to Cucamonga Valley, I was back on Highway 15 south. An hour's drive brought me to the picturesque little mountain town of Temecula, sitting at about 1,200 feet elevation on the east side of the San Margarita Mountains just 20 miles from the ocean. Taking the Rancho California Road exit, I followed it east for four miles, where I found Joe Hart's cozy little hilltop winery and Thornton Winery across the road from each other. Joe was my first call.

Founded in 1980, Hart Winery is committed to using only local grapes. Joe's first commercially released Zinfandel was the 1994 vintage, made from 100 percent Old Clark Ranch Zinfandel, now leased by J. Filippi. Hart's 1995, 1996, and 1997 vintages are Cucamonga Valley Zinfandels, which are a blend of three or four vineyards farmed by Don Galleano.

"We're just establishing ourselves as a Zinfandel producer," said slender, tanned, and strikingly white-haired Joe. He grew up in Southern California, but had no wine background as a child. His father was a flight instructor during World War II. Joe tasted wine for the first time as a young man visiting Europe, and "fell in love with it, and my interest grew from there. But Zinfandel has always been a favorite of mine. The very first bottle of California wine I ever bought was a Charles Krug Zinfandel. It was back in the 1960s, probably a 1962 or 1963 vintage, and was the most widely available red wine at that time. Zinfandel then came in all kinds of configurations, from gallon jugs to premium 375-ml bottles. It was an interesting time for wine. Prices were good; selection was good."

As we stood at the intimate little bar in Hart Winery's tiny tasting room, which is really just the end of the winery's barrel room, Joe offered me a tasting of the 1994 Clark Ranch. Picked at 22.8° Brix, 0.6 TA, and 3.45 pH, it needed a little acid adjustment, but not much. The resulting wine was on the light side, with distinctive, nearly overpowering aromas of eucalyptus and mint. Nonetheless, it was an appealing, bright, fresh, and fruity wine.

Then he got a tank sample of 1995 Cucamonga Valley, where it was being held for bottling. Primarily a blend of Lopez, Captain Paul Garrett, and Hofer vineyards, it was picked at higher Brix, and smelled of lush, rich, spicy, plummy, fully ripe fruit — no eucalyptus or mint. "One lot came in at just under 23° Brix, and the other lot at 25° Brix," said Joe.

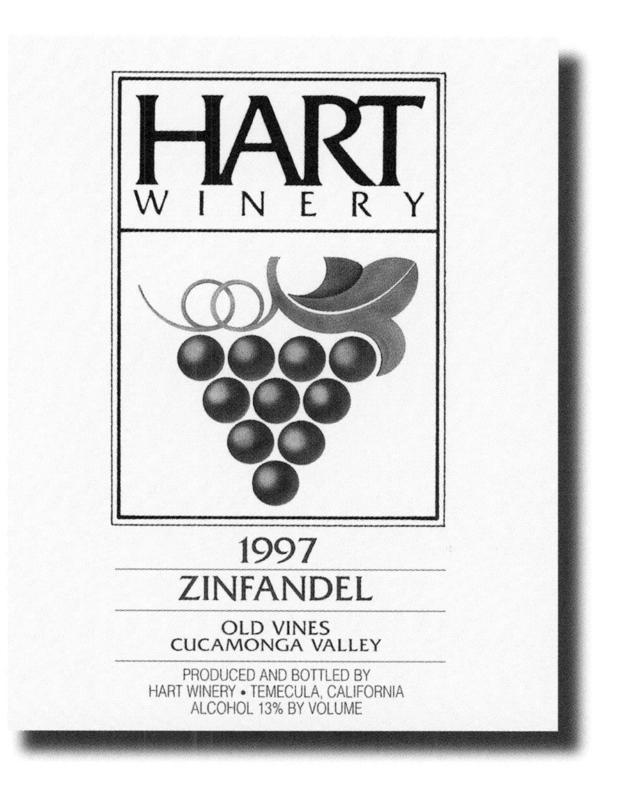

"It's a gorgeous wine," I remarked, draining my glass, and looking about for more. There wasn't any, since it had been drawn from the tank.

"It just goes to show you what Cucamonga Valley Zinfandel can be," Joe replied, smiling.

Joe presses his Zinfandel soon after dryness, not giving it the extended skin contact he gives to his Bordeaux varieties. The small lots are punched down, the larger lots pumped over. The wine is aged in some new American oak, and one-year old French oak.

At this point, son Bill arrived with a barrel sample of the 1996, which is a blend of the same vineyards as the 1995.

"If this is anything like the 1995, you can fill my glass," I told him.

"It's similar. It has a little higher percentage of the Lopez, which Jon [McPherson] and I are really hot on. The vines grow in that gravelly, rocky alluvial soil, and are small and old, and extremely low yielding. I think those Lopez Ranch vines are about as stressed as vines can be, and still live," said Joe. I couldn't agree more, haunted as I still was by the vision of that huge field of struggling little vines under the baking sun.

"Jon and I would like to lock that vineyard up," said Joe. "But I guess R.H. Phillips since 1996 is taking most of it. It's a fair-sized vineyard, but the yield is so low. We hope to continue getting a few tons each year."

With his 1994 priced at $12 per bottle, Joe is "comfortable with these prices for now. I think $12–$14 a bottle for our Zinfandel is a fair price. Our wine is good, but we don't have the reputation of some of the central and north coast wineries."

Ah, yes, once again the point that bottle price reflects not only the overall cost of wine production and quality, but also the producer's reputation. Price is rarely a reliable indicator of wine quality. This is especially true of Zinfandels such as these from Cucamonga Valley.

Although Hart Winery's first wines were Bordeaux-style reds, and its reputation has been established on the Rhône varietal wines and blends from Temecula and Cucamonga grapes, Zinfandel will be a part of its lineup for some time to come. Fortunately for southern California Zinfandel lovers, the wines are delicious, and the price is right. But there isn't much of it.

Leaving Joe, a pilot like his father, to finish preparations for his plane trip to Baja, I went across the road to Thornton Winery, looking forward to lunch at its elegant Cafe Champagne, where I was to meet Jon MacPherson, and sample more of these tasty Cucamonga Valley Zinfandels.

Thornton Winery: Jon MacPherson, winemaker

"Joe Hart and I both started doing Zinfandel out of Cucamonga in 1994," said the young Texas-born Jon MacPherson when he joined me over lunch. His melodic and mesmerizing Texas drawl gave Zinfandel a new dimension. "Don [Galleano] was always on us, 'You guys need to do a Cucamonga Valley Zinfandel. If anybody can do it, you guys can. These are some great old vineyards.'

"Me, I was strictly trying to be a Mediterranean Rhône, Italian kind of winemaker then. But one day I said to Don, 'You know what? You're right. This area is incredible when you're dealing with vineyards as old as these. I'm a *foo-ul* not to make Zinfandel,'" he said, his drawl adding emphasis to the word "fool."

"Don's take was that Joe Hart and I had the capability to do more with the grapes than he did. He was right, and we were foolish not to take advantage of those wonderful vineyards. Then Don told me, 'I got this one vineyard. It's great. You gotta try it — the Clark Ranch. It's one of the oldest and best vineyards up here in the San Gabriel foothills — it and the Lopez.' Don at that time was farming Clark Ranch.

"So I said, 'Okay.' I did my first Zinfandel in 1994 from the Clark Ranch. But I also ended up pulling some fruit out of Temecula Valley. I figured I have two different areas, two different Zinfandels to blend. It was 100 percent Zinfandel, but I didn't necessarily want to rely on one vineyard. I wanted to create something that depended upon my skills as a winemaker, as well as upon the vineyards and regions. My 1994 has about 75 percent Clark Ranch, which Don was farming then. Joe Hart's 1994 was 100 percent Clark. Of course, wouldn't you know it — the next year [1995], the Filippis take over the Clark Ranch."

I was drinking Thornton's 1994 with my lunch, which my waitperson had selected to complement the wine. It retailed for $16 in the tasting room. Not only was the wine minty, with aromas of eucalyptus, it was also distinctly chocolate-flavored. It was like having your chocolate brownie and your raspberries together in the glass.

"One of the things that at first made me uneasy about the Clark was its distinctive eucalyptus and mint character. One of my first responses was, 'I don't want anything more to do with this vineyard.' Then, as the wine came along, I found myself saying, 'I want everything this vineyard puts out.' My brother, a winemaker in Texas, pointed out that the Clark Ranch's distinctive character was what made it special and charming. It was another of those one-of-a-kind Zinfandels that comes with a special and unique vineyard. Now, I really like that layer of distinct mint and eucalyptus aromas and flavors it brings to my blend."

Jon also has a distinctive winemaking style. He conveys whole clusters right into the fermentation tank. "This way, I have all whole berries, that is, the berries were not destemmed off the cluster. The whole time I'm loading the tank, I'm inoculating with yeast and a little bit of $S0_2$. Within 12 to 24 hours, I have fermentation going well. Then we start our twice-daily pump-overs with a little Carlson cap irrigator. I know I am walking a tightrope as far as stemmy flavor problems, V.A. problems, odd flavors, or stuck fermentation. I have yet to have a problem, but the potential is always there. I take the risks because I like the result," explained Jon.

"What are the benefits of such risks?" I asked.

"Richer, more intense varietal flavors, certain complexities that can come only from lignified portions of the grape stems, which means that the stems must be ripe as well as the grapes," Jon explained.

"The wine ferments out to dryness in about two weeks. So it's a long fermentation. I always start out the process cold — 45°F to 50°F, so the fermentation starts slowly. Once fermentation takes over, I just let it go, always making certain that I get my pump-overs done. By the time it heats up, the wine is already down to 8° or 10° Brix after about the first week, since I chill it down so much at the start. Once it really gets going, it gets up to 95°F, and peaks generally at 95°F to 100°F."

After pressing, Jon puts his Zinfandel into one-year-old French and American oak for six to eight months. It is bottled 12 months after crush and held for about six months before releasing.

After lunch, Jon took me into the barrel room to sample both his and Don Galleano's reserve 1996 Zinfandel. Don's was ready to be racked and bottled then — at the end of May. It tasted delicious. Jon's, more recently put into barrels, was also delicious but showing a different style and vineyard blend. It would stay in the barrels until January of 1998.

Beginning in 1998, Jon has been making a José Lopez Ranch Zinfandel. "It had about 10 percent new French oak, less than I would like to use, but that is the economic reality for us," Jon told me in January 2001. "In a way, we are caught in a vicious circle. Economics are driven by sales, and sales are driven by the perception the consumers have of the area. As long as the perception of Cucamonga Zinfandel is that it is not worth higher prices, we are limited in buying the equipment and barrels that we need to make wine better. Nonetheless, our customers love our Lopez Ranch Zinfandel. So while we haven't been getting the rave reviews in the *Wine Spectator*, nor winning the accolades that Geyser Peak has gotten for its D'Ambrogio Zinfandel, we are happy that we are pleasing our customers. The 680 cases that we made in 1998 are long sold out. So our 1999 is going to be released probably a little sooner than I would like, because of customer demand." Thornton Winery's 1999 José Lopez Ranch Zinfandel retails for $18 per bottle.

"This area is incredible when you're dealing with vineyards as old as these..."

Jon MacPherson

However, Jon hopes that with the success that Geyser Peak had with its 1997 D'Ambrogio Zinfandel, and continued success of the Temecula producers, consumer perception of Cucamonga Zinfandel will change. Yet he couldn't resist offering some frank remarks on Geyser Peak's California State Fair award for its 1997 Cucamonga Zinfandel.

"It was nice for Daryl Groom to have won Best of Southcoast Region with a Cucamonga Zinfandel. But it's kind of tough to lose an award that is typically given to a winery in the region to a Sonoma County winery that is using local fruit. Beaten with our own grapes, so to speak. Hart, Mount Palomar, and myself were the first Temecula producers to make a Cucamonga Zinfandel. It was our Zinfandels (helped along by Don Galleano twisting our arms) that helped to bring the attention of Daryl to this region.

"When consumers begin to support higher prices for Cucamonga Zinfandel, Temecula producers will be able to afford the technology and barrels that they need for better-made wine. I would love to have had a spinning cone for my 1999 Lopez Ranch Zinfandel. It has an alcohol content of 14.8 percent; I would have preferred it to be under 14 percent."

When I tasted the 1999 Thornton Winery José Lopez Ranch Zinfandel, I was struck by the rich aromas of blackberries and cassis. It had a deep purple-black color, indicative of its very young age — just 18 months, with only a few days in the bottle. When I tasted it, my mouth was filled with the wonderful blackberry, black fruit flavors, which were followed by a distinctive tannin component. The wine definitely needs another year or two in the bottle, for my taste, although it nicely complemented the tasty entrée of ravioli I had picked up to serve with the wine.

Baja California

As Thornton Winery winemaker Jon MacPherson and I were enjoying the barrel samples, Tijuana-born Javier Flores, Jon's production winemaker and my companion and guide for my next day's journey to Vinìcola L.A. Cetto in Valle de Guadalupe, Baja, California, joined us. Greeting me with a bright smile and soft Spanish-accented English, he was a tall, well-built, serious fellow of 37 years. His seriousness gave way to warmth and friendliness as we confirmed our arrangements.

At eight o'clock next morning, I picked up Javier at Thornton Winery. Barely an hour and a half later, we had gotten Mexican auto insurance, crossed the border into Tijuana, and were heading down the Avenida de la Revolución to Vinìcola L.A. Cetto's visitor's center at 2108 Cañon Johnson. This center also held the winery's elegant and spacious barrel and bottle ageing caves, completed in 1994.

Welcomed by hospitality manager Oscar Acevedo, we were taken to the beautifully designed and light-filled tasting room for a sampling of the non vintage-dated 1995 Zinfandel. It was a pleasant, soft, fruity, tank-aged, and light-bodied wine — typical, I would later learn, of the year. Then it was on to a tour of the caves, where the reserve red wines are stored both in barrels and bottles. Since he holds his reserve lots of red wines for several years in bottles, Don Luis Cetto had niches tunneled into the walls of the caves sufficient to hold thousands of bottles for up to six years before release. The bottling line was also housed within the caves.

Greatly impressed by the facility, I was ready for the second stage of our journey. We were to drive down the scenic Ensenada Cuota highway, which runs along, and in places high above, the Pacific Ocean, to Ensenada, then onto Highway 3, the Tecate road, for about 25 kilometers into the mountains to Valle de Guadalupe.

My anticipation mounted as we passed through some vineyards just outside the tiny village of Guadalupe. "This is part of Valle de Guadalupe," said Javier, "but not the main valley." Passing through the village, the road climbed slightly through a cut in the ridge. Gaining the top of this cut, we were greeted by a spectacular view of the 3,000-acre (1,200 hectares) Valle de Guadalupe, covered by rows and rows of immaculately tended, healthy vines. Surrounded by dry, rocky, lavender-tinted mountains, the valley with its rows of green vineyard was a breathtaking sight.

Descending into the valley, we immediately found on our left the gigantic Vides del Guadalupe-Domecq Winery. On our right was the entrance to the sandy/loamy lane that led through vineyards lined with olive trees to Vinìcola L.A. Cetto, which stands far back from the road at the edge of its vineyards near the valley's wall.

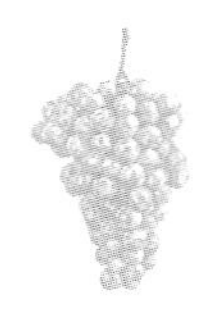

Vides del Guadalupe-Domecq

Our first stop was at Vides del Guadalupe-Domecq, to meet its American-born winemaker, Ron McClendon, who joined the winery in the mid-1990s. Formerly with San Pascal Vineyards, R.H. Phillips, and Thornton Winery, Ron had taken over Vides del Guadalupe-Domecq Winery with the intention of increasing the facility's output of fine wines. A Spanish house known for centuries for its wonderful brandies, it was recently sold. Under its new ownership, the Mexican facility is attempting to gain recognition for its table wines and for its brandies. Ten acres of trellised and irrigated Zinfandel vines propagated on their own roots from cuttings taken from L.A. Cetto's beautiful old Rancho Escondido vineyard grow beside the winery. Yield is about five tons per acre.

"I'm working to help the company develop a stronger fine wine focus," said Ron, as he showed us around the enormous facility, which included some caves that housed both barrels and bottles, and a newly-purchased large-capacity Delta destemmer/crusher. I asked him about his Zinfandels. "We're just now releasing our 1989 reserve red wines," he said. "But our Zinfandel is still treated more as an everyday wine, or a white wine, rather than one of our top-priority reds," he explained. "I'm working on them, though," he said with a laugh. "I'm a fan of Zinfandel, and our Zinfandel here can make a pretty nice wine — as you'll see when you go over to L.A. Cetto and taste Camillo Magoni's Zinfandels from the old vineyard."

Sometime later, when I was back home, I dug out the bottle of 1994 Zinfandel Ron had sent home with me. When I read the label, I discovered that "Valle de Calafia" was the source for the grapes. More curious now, I poured a little out into a glass; it looked inky dark. Swirling it, I brought it to my nose and picked up a slightly burnt, dried fruit aroma, blended with lush black cherry aromas. Tasting it, it had that distinctive Zinfandel black fruit character, although with a hint of a bitter after-taste. For a price of less than $3 U.S., it was a terrific bargain.

I'll be watching Ron McClendon and his Vides del Guadalupe-Domecq for further Zinfandel developments — especially if he follows Camillo Magoni's advice to convert his best situated five acres (two hectares) to head training and dry farming. "That part of Ron's Zinfandel vineyard could make excellent Zinfandel," Camillo told me later that day. "And I know, because I put in that vineyard, when L.A. Cetto and I used to manage the winery and vineyards — before it was sold."

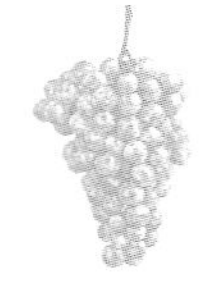

Vinìcola L.A. Cetto

Bidding farewell to Ron McClendon, Javier and I drove across the highway and down the long, dusty olive-tree-and-vineyard-lined lane to the L.A. Cetto winery, which was set in the midst of vineyards near the base of the ancient stone-strewn mountains. Although it was just a dusty road running through a vineyard encircled by old mountains and lined with olive trees, the setting had an exotic feel. I could barely keep my eyes on the road, I was so bedazzled by the sights all around me. Here I would taste world-famous wines made under the gifted hand of Italian-born winemaker Camillo Magoni. Camillo has been with Don Luis Cetto for 32 years.

"It's Camillo who has proven the potential of this region to produce world-class table wines," said Javier as we made our way towards the huge facility. He had worked under Camillo for 10 years. Arriving at the winery, I parked beside the thick lawn that surrounded the office buildings. Colorful bougainvillea climbed over a vintage wooden cart, while palm trees, white picnic tables and chairs under a canopy accented the lawn and view over the vineyards. It was a gorgeous and peaceful sight. A flagstone walkway led to a tiny tasting room, then continued across the grass to a modest one-story building which housed a small lab and some sparsely furnished offices. Behind us stood the huge tan-colored winery buildings, dwarfing a tanker truck that was being filled with wine for transport to Tijuana. Camillo told me later that his reserve wines are transported to Tijuana in their barrels. Surrounding us were vineyards and mountains.

Camillo Magoni

We were greeted on the lawn by Camillo and Don Luis, who had just arrived by private plane from business in Hermasillo, in the province of Sonora. Hugs all around for Javier, who hadn't seen his former employers for some years. Then Camillo, a cheerful and outgoing man of middle height, short dark hair mixed with a little gray, and pale blue eyes, welcomed me with a warm and disarming smile, and a cordial handshake. The glint of a couple of gold crowns gave his smile additional brilliance. After an introduction to the more reserved but exceedingly gracious Don Luis Cetto, Camillo led the way across the flagstones to the office building. There, his assistant, Joaquin, was preparing a tasting of a few of his best red wines: the 1995 vintage-dated Zinfandel ; the 1990 Cabernet Sauvignon Reserva Limitada; and the 1993 Nebbiolo Reserva Limitada.

Before our tasting, Camillo sat down with me at a long table in the bright conference room, and told me how he met Don Luis Cetto's father in Italy nearly 35 years before.

"I worked in the Valtellina region of Italy for over two years, and then I decided to go somewhere else," Camillo explained in English, his third language after Italian and Spanish. "I met 'Mr. Cetto father,' and he said to me, 'You want to come and work for me? I wait for you there.' I thought, why not? So I came, and saw, and stayed," he explained, laughing. "So I have participated in all the development of all the vineyards, the wineries, and it has been very, very interesting. For Mexico, this is the more important area, and the best area for making quality wines. Winemaking in this area began in Tijuana and Tecate during the Prohibition era in the U.S. The Cetto family came from Italy in the 1920s, and established the winery in Tecate in 1926. This facility here in Valle de Guadalupe we built in 1973."

The windows were open, allowing the refreshing breeze from the vineyard and the ocean beyond to blow gently over us. A huge tree just outside the window shaded the room from the warm May sun. The weather and temperature of this day were typical of the entire summer, Camillo told me. Extreme heat is a rarity.

"So tell me about your Zinfandel," I began, as we got ourselves settled.

"The Zinfandel vineyard, which we call "Rancho Escondido," is located just south of the U.S.-Mexico border, and on the east side of Tijuana, not too far from Tecate. It is a small and very beautiful valley of around 80 hectares (200 acres), all Zinfandel. The first vines were planted in the early 1930s, from cuttings from the Escondido region of California, or from Cucamonga Valley. At that time, there were close relationships between Escondido, Cucamonga, their wineries, and the viticulture here. As far as I know, it is the only piece of vineyard in Mexico fully Zinfandel, only Zinfandel. Some more, four hectares, was planted here, in Valle de Guadalupe, what we call Rancho El Tigre, about 30 years ago — in the 1960s.

"The Rancho Escondido vineyard was established and owned by Señor Reynoso until the Cetto family bought it 30 years ago. We have improved it a little bit, and planted a little more. The production is not so high, between two and three tons per *hectare* depending on the rains. [Author's note: That's barely one ton per *acre*. One hectare equals 2.47 acres.] It is very small production. We preserve the vineyard as it was. It is head trained, the old style, and all own-rooted; it's beautiful because the area is a small valley shaped like a cup. The soil is light, and very fine — like talcum powder. All the soil came from winds, so it is very light and very deep. It's all fine sand — and beautiful."

"Do you have any problem in your Zinfandel with mildew or bunch rot?" I asked.

"Minimal — minimal," replied Camillo, "because of the dry farming. There is practically no humidity. Usually we dust once with sulfur each spring. Usually that's enough. At ripening time, sometimes we have some vines ripe before others. But that's the particular problem with Zinfandel."

"Do you have any other pest problems, like mites?"

"No, nothing. All we need to do is we put only one sulfur dusting on the grapes each year. And we cultivate two or three times, depending upon the rains."

"What is the elevation of Rancho Escondido ?" I asked.

"About 300 meters, around 800 feet — just a little less than Valle of Guadalupe. It's about 400 meters here, or 1,100 feet."

"What kind of numbers do you like to have when you harvest the Zinfandel?" was my next question.

"We start picking at 23°or 24° Brix. The acidity is usually around 7 g/L; the pH is 3.5 or 3.6. Those are excellent numbers. Our process of fermentation is traditional. We crush and destem, and ferment around 26°C or 28°C — not too high. We put the wine in tanks, about 20 tons in each tank, and pump over. Fermentation is about 10 days, and then we rack it off, and let the wine go through malolactic in tanks. Then we maybe age it a few months in 3,000-gallon upright neutral Yugoslavian oak tanks, and bottle in June — about 10 months after crush — and give the wine a little bottle age before release."

"Why don't you vintage-date all your wines?" I wanted to know.

"Why don't we vintage-date? That's a story for L.A. Cetto," replied Camillo, laughing. "In all our traditional *reserva* labels, the wines are vintage-dated. We vintage-date the wines we export to Europe. Only wines for Mexico, for our domestic market, are not vintage-dated, although the wines are all the same. We don't vintage-date for the domestic market because our Mexican consumers will say, 'The first vintage is good, the second not so good, the next, even less good.' So if we don't vintage-date, they can't compare the vintages," he explained, laughing at the idea.

"You don't keep lots of Zinfandel separate, when you ferment, and bottle the best under the vintage-dated label?" I queried.

"No, no," replied Camillo. "Because the valley is cup-shaped, the exposures are different, so I keep the different exposures separate. When it comes time for selecting the blend, I keep only the best, and sell the rest in bulk. The domestic wine, although in a different label, is the same blend. But now we think we will start vintage-dating all our wines. It's the direction, world-wide, everyone is going in."

"How many cases of Zinfandel do you produce, usually?"

"15,000 cases, 12,000 cases — it depends on the rainfall. In 1996, we got only about 6,500 cases. This year [1997] I think we produce only about 4,500 cases, since we've had only four inches of rain. The vines have only three or four small bunches each," Camillo explained. "Our normal rainfall is 10, 12, even 14 inches. Would you like to try the 1996 as well as the 1995?" he asked.

"I would love to," I replied.

After a few words in Spanish to Joaquin, who was setting up our special tasting, two tank samples of the 1996 Rancho Escondido Zinfandel appeared, each sample from a different exposure on the cup-shaped valley.

I asked Camillo how he felt about Zinfandel as a red table wine.

"My personal opinion?"

"Yes."

"In my opinion, Zinfandel is the only California wine, no? Zinfandel is California; maybe not in the origin of the grape, but the name, yes. One of the best red wines that I tasted in northern California was Zinfandel from the Martini Winery more than 40 years ago. If I remember right, it was 1958. I think the market needs more varieties for the consumer. In my opinion, the Zinfandel is a variety that, if you want a yield of six or eight tons per acre, you don't plant Zinfandel. Zinfandel needs small production, stressed vines, small bunches, small berries, and then you get another opportunity for the consumer to taste something different. We want always to present wine with different styles. Some, we want the fresh fruit character, like the Zinfandel. Others, we want them to be aged in barrels; others, we age in bottles for three or four years, so that they are an aged wine when we release them, like our 'Reservas' sitting before you. We like to have different styles of wines for the consumer to choose from.

"I personally like Zinfandel wines," Camillo continued. "Especially, I like to make the style of the wine without wood, because I like the taste and flavor of the natural grape. We made several experiments some years ago, with Zinfandel. We put it in some newer oak barrels, and we lost the fruit character. It lost its personality. If you lose the fruit character of Zinfandel, I think it is like a guy without a last name."

Pausing momentarily to let me digest this colorful simile, Camillo continued: "I think Zinfandel's fruit character offers a good opportunity for winemakers and for the consumer to have other varieties than Cabernet Sauvignon and Chardonnay. Especially Zinfandel — because it is the California grape. I also think it is the perfect grape for this climate, because we have dry summers. If you have a few rains during the ripening time, forget it. Everything will rot."

"Are you never troubled by tropical rainstorms in August?" I asked, remembering something Joe Hart had told me about such storms wreaking havoc with Temecula Valley Zinfandel.

"Maybe once in every 10 years, we have some small rains coming from the south Pacific, in August. These storms, though, usually enter through La Paz, at the end of the peninsula, then to Sonora, Hermosillo, and then they go to Chihuahua, and on to Texas. Usually, it's completely dry from the end of March to the end of September. We don't start having our first rains until October. So it's a perfect climate for Zinfandel. We have the blooming the second week of May. We start harvesting about August 20."

"Do you get much morning fog?"

"Yes, especially in May and June, and then again in September. It's gone by 9:00 or 10:00 in the morning."

"Do you like working with Zinfandel ?" I asked, "Or would you agree with Paso Robles' Gary Eberle, who calls Zinfandel 'the bad boy of wine grapes,' because everything that can go wrong, will go wrong with it?'"

"Because," said Camillo, laughing, "it's a wine you have to manage differently. The other varieties, you manage all the same way. With Zinfandel, you have to know the vines, the vineyard. Zinfandel is a vine for stressing, not irrigating."

"How do your Mexican consumers feel about Zinfandel ?" I asked.

"There are many who like it because they know about it. The older consumers know about it, and they appreciate it. But the new consumers, no, because they don't hear about the Zinfandel. They just hear about the Chardonnays, the Cabernet Sauvignons, and now, the Merlots. And that's all. The wine world consists of just three wines for most wine consumers," said Camillo, with a laugh that contained an edge of frustration.

"Where do you sell most of your Zinfandel ?"

"Mexico City, and here in Baja, in Tijuana, Ensenada. They are coming to know about it, and they appreciate it, and like it. We also export a little to England — but in England we sell more Petite Sirah — and Europe. Ninety percent of our Zinfandel is sold in Mexico — in Mexico City, and here in Baja."

Joaquin was now pouring the wines for our tasting, and the banks of wineglasses filled with their deep purple libations were tempting us with their fragrances.

"If you lose the fruit character of Zinfandel, I think it is like a guy without a last name."

Camillo Magoni

The first wine we tried was the vintage-dated 1995 Zinfandel. "The spring of 1995 was much more humid that usual. We had rains until June. Almost every other day we had one-tenth of an inch. Then, the summer was very hot, so it speeded up the maturation. In 1995, the yield was 180 tons," said Camillo. I now understood why the 1995 was a lighter wine, and although pleasant, was unexceptional. It tasted like the some of the flavor had been burned out of the grapes. In fact, it had been.

"The 1996 was more normal. The summer was not so hot, and we had less production, just 130 tons," resumed Camillo. We tasted the 1996 tank samples from the two different exposures in Rancho Escondido. The flavor, color, and aroma in both were noticeably more intense than the 1995. The samples were rich tasting, dark, succulent, somewhat reminiscent of Galleano Winery's redwood tank-aged Zinfandel. Given that the Rancho Escondido was likely propagated from cuttings taken from Cucamonga Valley, that the climate and soil are somewhat similar, and that neither wine was oak-aged, it was not surprising that they should be reminiscent of each other.

It was quite a treat to taste such a simply made Zinfandel wine. Although stainless steel fermentation tanks are a modern addition to winemaking, I nonetheless felt that the purity of the fruit character of Camillo's Zinfandel was probably close to the flavors that historically captured the attention and imagination of California's earliest winemakers.

The pleasant afternoon was coming to a close. But before sending us on our way back to Tijuana for dinner and home to Temecula, Joaquin offered to take us up to the fiesta pavilion at the eastern end of the valley, just above the winery. The setting sun was casting a soft glow over the hazy clouds at the western end of the valley, highlighting the brilliantly colored bougainvillea that was in profuse bloom along the edges of the pavilion. The air was still, clean, quiet. Peace and beauty at that moment were united. Fortunately, I had my camera. Then it was time to go. Reluctantly, Javier and I bid everyone "*Adios*" and "*Hasta la vista*." I would return at the end of August for the Fiesta Colores de Vendemia, and to visit Rancho Escondido.

Rancho Escondido

It was Sunday morning, August 31, the morning after the food, wine, and music-filled Fiesta de Colores Vendimia. Guillermo, an architect with L.A. Cetto at the Tijuana facility, called for me at the beautiful new Hotel Camino Real, in downtown Tijuana, and off we went along the starkly lovely Tecate 'Cuota' highway through the mountains. Destination: Rancho Escondido.

Fifteen or so kilometers out of Tijuana, and through two toll-booths guarded by armed soldiers in army camouflage, we exited the freeway through a primitive clover-leaf system that returned us to the west-bound lane where we would find our exit to the vineyard.

We proceeded a few kilometers in the westerly direction, where we exited onto an unmarked sandy lane running between two rows of barbed-wire fence. The lip of the valley where Rancho Escondido awaited was a few kilometers in the distance. The morning was warm, dry, and very, very still. Just a couple of roadrunners observed our passage along the trail. Then the road climbed a little, and suddenly there was Rancho Escondido lying before us.

My heart nearly skipped a beat, I am sure, so quiet and remote-seeming was this lovely, cup-shaped, old-style Zinfandel vineyard of 200 acres surrounded by towering, ancient mountains. I stopped the car, and we stepped out into the soft, warm and dry air of the utterly still morning. I was silenced, awestruck even, by the stark beauty surrounding me. I felt as if I were in the presence of a profoundly spiritual element. Everything Camillo had said about Rancho Escondido's remote and lovely setting was true.

Returning to the car, we followed the lane down to the side of the cup to the home of the vineyard manager *(el gerente de las viñeda)* named Julio. From there, we drove a short ways along one of the roads through the vineyard, stopping here and there to pick a grape or two from vines yet unharvested and savoring their warm ripe flavors. The talcum-powder-like soil was soft and deep, the bite of the sun tempered by a gentle, cool breeze. Harvest would be finished next day. After Julio led us on a short hike to a small hill above his house for a panoramic view of the valley, Guillermo and I made our way back to Tijuana, a little quieter than when we drove out. I was under the influence of the incredible silence and spirituality of this magnificent old vineyard. That the 65-year-old vines not only survived, but were able to produce as much as 100 tons of Zinfandel grapes on as little as five inches of annual rainfall defied belief. But it was so.

In Tijuana, Guillermo saw me safely to the border crossing, then left me with a kiss on my cheek, and a wish of "*Buena suerte*!"

I remained under the spell of the fiesta and Rancho Escondido all the way to the San Diego airport, and my journey back to Napa.

In 1998, the northern Baja California region received 75 centimeters (30 inches) of rain, which replenished the nearly depleted reserves of ground water caused by the exceedingly dry 1997. The spring was dry, sunny, and warm, providing a good set — that is, the blossoms all turned into grape berries.

For the 1998 crush, Vinícola L.A. Cetto provided Camillo with a small-production facility in Valle de Guadalupe for his *Reserva Limitada* and *Reserva Primera* red wines. The reserve Cabernet Sauvignon, Nebbiolo, Barbera, and Petite Sirah wine was processed in this small state-of-the-art facility. Only the grapes from the best blocks in the vineyards were used for these wines. Beginning with the viticultural practices and continuing through harvest and into the winery, the grapes from these special blocks were given special treatment. The fruit was picked into small tubs or boxes in the cool of the morning and early evening, gently destemmed by the Amos destemmer/crusher, and fermented in small stainless steel tanks. The cap was hand-punched, and the wine aged in a combination of new and used French and American small oak barrels, depending upon the variety and vintage.

I asked Camillo if he might produce a few cases of oak-aged Zinfandel. "Yes, I think so," he replied, since he personally enjoys barrel-aged Zinfandel as well as non-barrel aged. "Perhaps just 100 cases of a reserve Zinfandel. Then, if it doesn't sell, I drink it!" he laughed. I promised him that I would be glad to help him out in that unlikely event.

In 1996, Valle de Guadalupe's newest winery, the tiny family-operated Chateau Camou, crushed its first grapes, Zinfandel being among its varieties.

Cucamonga Valley Zinfandel: a Northern California Perspective

As I drove past Cucamonga Valley on my way back to Napa from Baja California, many thoughts were on my mind. Definitely, this region was not Napa Valley and its lush, beautiful, wall-to-wall vineyards. Yet there was something inspirational, even fierce, in the passionate attachment of the few remaining growers to their historic vineyards amid the industrial desertification. And now that Cucamonga Valley Zinfandel is again creating a buzz for the first time since Prohibition days, this connection to the vineyards has been revitalized. The roots of the remaining families have dug in a little deeper.

The buzz is not simply about lower cost grapes for the value-priced Zinfandels, either. Don Galleano's commitment to promoting Cucamonga Valley's old vines Zinfandel is also leading to increased interest in the region as a source for premium wines. Not only have Temecula producers Thornton and Hart begun awarding vineyard designation and viticultural area recognition to the historic old Zinfandel vineyards, but also, up north, the Giguierre brothers of R.H. Phillips and Geyser Peak's Daryl Groom have become excited about a couple of Cucamonga's old, low-yielding Zinfandel vineyards. Almost overnight, it seems, producers have awakened to the potential of these historic vineyards. The grapes are no longer to be had for the asking. Decades of neglect and complacency have given way to aggressive solicitation of Cucamonga Valley's Zinfandel grapes.

The increasing demand for the grapes is providing incentive and means to install drip irrigation and to take better care of these fine old vineyards.

Nonetheless, trucking Cucamonga Valley Zinfandel 12 to 16 hours up to Northern California wineries, for limited bottling high-end winemaking, seems an extreme measure, even for old vine Zinfandel. Could these nearly forgotten old Zinfandel vineyards be that special? I would have to find out from the producers buying them.

DARYL GROOM — "WRAPPED" IN CUCAMONGA VALLEY ZINFANDEL

Daryl Groom, executive vice-president/winemaker for Peak Wines International, Geyserville, came to Geyser Peak Winery in 1989 from Penfolds of Australia. It was October 1997 when I finally got my chance to ask him if it were true that he was considering a 1997 vineyard-designated D'Ambrogio Vineyard Cucamonga Valley Zinfandel.

"Yes," he admitted. "Under our Venezia label, which is our specialty and experimental wines label."

"How did you ever come across Cucamonga Valley Zinfandel?" I asked this engaging, exceedingly fit-looking, and somewhat small-statured Australian. His short, tightly curled, black frosted-with-silver hair exactly complemented his sparkling personality, which seemed to have preceded him into the room where I awaited him at his new Geyser Peak office.

"I met Don Galleano in the Southern California judging circles in 1994," Daryl explained, as we seated ourselves. "We were judging the 'New World Wine' and the 'Pacific Rim' competitions in Los Angeles and Riverside, and I gradually got to appreciate his palate for fine wines. Then I got to talk to him from a historical perspective about the region he was involved in. 'Cucamonga' was a foreign and unfamiliar name to me. Don had talked about some of the old vine material there. Particularly, I was interested in Shiraz, which he didn't have any of. Then we talked about some of the other old vines — Mourvedre, Grenache, and, of course, Zinfandel.

Daryl Groom

"As it happened, we were wanting to get into a Zinfandel program, and realized that in Dry Creek, or Sonoma County generally, all the old vine Zin was already spoken for. We were looking for some old vine material; then it became a perfect match, that perhaps we should try some of the material Don had in Cucamonga Valley. Don was very gracious to allow us to have a peek at some of his ranches.

"It was very unusual for me as a winemaker in California to find myself sitting on a 737 flying down to southern California to inspect a vineyard. That was just wee-ird!" commented Daryl, laughing, his Aussie accent catching my attention, "not to be sitting in my car to go and inspect a vineyard, but to be sitting in an airplane. So it seemed to be foreign, because it was so far away.

"But from the first sight of the vineyards, we fell in love with them. We see a lot of reasonably old vine Shiraz in Australia. The things that are very characteristic of old vine Shiraz are the low head trained, or cordon-pruned vines, the rolling hills, and the dry, sandy soils. Those were things that we noticed when we first stepped out of Don's car and walked through the vineyards. Especially, it was the sandiness and the dryness of the soil.

"I had been luckily involved in making a product in Australia called 'Penfolds Grange Hermitage' from old vine Shiraz. It's a very famous

Australian wine. As soon as I walked into Galleano's vineyards, I was reminded exactly of those old vine Australian Shiraz vineyards. So the love was automatically there, and the belief that this would work. From a winemaking perspective, seeing these relatively small bunches of Zinfandel, the low vigor vines with a yield of one-half to three-quarters ton per acre, you just knew it was going to make great wine.

"We first purchased Cucacmonga Valley Zinfandel in 1996," continued Daryl, "a couple of truck-loads (one being 20-25 tons), from the 130-year-old D'Ambrogio ranch, the Gateway Vineyard, and from a number of other old vineyards. Our intention was to produce 'a big, fat, trendy' old vines Zinfandel wine. But we missed the boat a little bit on our first vintage [1996]. By the time we got down there to look and make the decision to pick, the sugar level had skyrocketed, because of the heat wave the week before.

"When you get into an area like Cucamonga, which gets less than 14 inches annual rainfall, when you get a heat wave, things concentrate quickly. The wines we brought in from that first harvest, while they were great blending wines, had lost their individuality because of their overripeness. The sugar level was 29°–30° Brix, which fermented out to 17 percent alcohol, and the pH was fairly high. So the wine became part of our Geyser Peak Sonoma County 1996 blend, which was a little bit weaker from the more productive younger vines we buy from in this area of Sonoma County. The Cucamonga wines enrichened it.

"In 1997," continued Daryl, "we spoke for three truck-loads, and we made a concerted effort to get it right. In early August, I contacted Don Galleano about coming down there. Again, we missed the boat slightly. By the time we got there, the sugar levels had shot up, because it was an early harvest. The grapes came in a little less ripe than the year before — at 26.5° Brix. But with the new wave of Zinfandel drinkers enjoying these richer, raisiny, slightly jammy, a little-on-the-alcoholic side, maybe even a touch sweet, Zinfandels, we think it has produced exactly that type of wine. So we are just as pleased as we can be with it — particularly with the D'Ambrogio Ranch grapes.

"I had a group of eye doctors here this morning, and I showed them all the wines out of barrels. The entire group was really 'wrapped' in the Cabernets we produce, and the Merlots, and Shiraz — all from expensive grapes grown on hillside vineyards," said Daryl, in his enthusiasm resorting to an Aussie expression. "The last one I showed them was the Cucamonga Zinfandel. It just stood out as Zinfandel like you would not believe! And they were just wrapped! Out of all the wines I showed them on this particular day, that was the one they were the most wrapped with, the one they asked, 'When is this going to be ready? When can we buy this wine? How long until this wine is going to be on the market?'"

"'Wrapped,' were they?" I repeated Daryl's Aussie word, trying it out on my own tongue. Hmm. "So when will you be releasing this dramatic Zinfandel?" I asked.

"Fall, 1999."

"Have you any idea of its age-worthiness, or have you thought about it yet?"

"We haven't yet quite worked out the age-worthiness of Cucamonga Valley Zinfandel. The wine we had this year has all the hallmarks to age particularly well. The numbers are just unbelievable: the pH was 3.4, the T.A. was 7 g/L — absolutely superb numbers, numbers most people think you could never get out of a hot, relatively dry region. It also has the richness there of the Zinfandel fruit, and the tannins, although not overly tannic; it has everything — the numbers and the fruit — to make it a long-lived wine. I have every reason to believe that it will age as well as a Dry Creek Zinfandel, or Zinfandel from any other region — hitting its peak somewhere between five and seven years. It's just exactly the kind of wine I expected from the vineyard, when I first saw it. And it's what I would expect out of a $20 bottle of Zinfandel — one that could last even 15 years, and still have its Zinfandel fruit character.

"We've had to wake up to these old vineyards. We've become a bit complacent about them, believing that they've always been there, and that no one else is going to become interested."

Daryl Groom

"That's how Zinfandel should be, since it is such a unique variety. Some of us can drink a big, rich Merlot, and think it is Cabernet; but Zinfandel is unique in that the Zinfandel character should always be there — that briary, peppery, luscious, succulent fruit character that you would never confuse for a Cabernet or Merlot. It's hard to describe; it's just what I call that 'Zin character.'"

"What winemaking practices do you give your Zinfandel?"

"Our normal procedure with our red wine is put it through a Healdsburg crusher that will destem the berries. From the crusher, we put the wine into a rotary fermentor, which is a static fermentor turned on its side, and operates like a cement mixer. We find this wonderful for all grape varieties, including Zinfandel. We work the rotary fermentor to extract color and flavor quite early. We get highly colored red wine within three days. Then we run the juice off the skins a lot earlier than you would normally, before we start getting bitter tannin extraction. It's three-to-four day maceration. We run off at about 10° Brix, and then complete primary, and also malolactic fermentation in the barrel. We did that with our Zinfandel this year also. All fermentation is usually finished by December."

"Do you give your Zinfandel any new oak?"

"Our oak program is a combination of new and used oak. We don't think Zinfandel handles 100 percent new oak, and we don't want to over-oak the wine. Zinfandel has such distinctive fruit character on its own that we don't want to mask that fruit character with full-strength oak. We want to complement the fruit; we want to enhance it; but we don't want to mask it. So we're a combination of both new and used oak.

"When all fermentation is complete, we rack the wine out of the barrels, wash them and add a little sulfur, then put the wine back in the barrels for another 10 months — which gives the wine 12–14 months' maturation in barrel."

But even with his big, jammy Cucamonga Valley Zinfandel, Daryl wants to keep the alcohol under 15 percent.

"We're trying to create a big, rich, trendy Zinfandel, but we don't want it to be too alcoholic. So apart from consciously not using a lot of new oak, the other decision we have made is to use modern-day technology, the spinning cone, to reduce alcohol without diluting the flavor, or concentration, of the particular wine. Without alcohol reduction, the 1997 Cucamonga wine had 17 percent. We're trying to get it down to between 14 percent and 14.5 percent.

"To me, alcohol is fine in Zinfandel, if it's balanced. But we've seen some Zinfandels that we think are just too hot, too alcoholic. Our ideal is not to produce a wine to a certain alcohol level. If the richness of a wine could carry a 19 percent alcohol wine, and you couldn't pick up that it was alcoholic, then we would produce that. However, in the Cucamonga Zinfandel, the alcohol stands through it. The extraction isn't there. I don't think too many wines have the extraction to carry those real high [16, 17, or 18 percent] alcohols. The hotness stands through most of them."

"The spinning cone doesn't affect the flavor or concentration of the wine?" I asked.

"Not at all. In fact, in certain situations, we think it might enhance or concentrate the flavor. If you take, say, 10 percent of your blend, and take the alcohol out of it, you are taking clear liquid, which concentrates the remaining components. You end up with a slightly increased concentration of flavor and color, which at the same time is lower in alcohol. We've got some wine that I'll show you that is still in barrel, that is still a little bit sweet, and is about 16.5 percent alcohol. Then there's one other portion that we take some of the alcohol out of. You can see how unaffected the flavor is in the de-alcoholized one, and that it is less hot. So why don't we go out there, and have a look?"

I was ready.

The barrel tasting of the D'Ambrogio and the Cucamonga Valley blend showed both to be lovely, rich, mouth-filling and fragrant wines. When we returned to Daryl's office, I carried my last sample with me. My question now was if he had any long-term plans for the D'Ambrogio and other Cucamonga Valley vineyards.

"Our tack now is to produce two Zinfandels. One is our Sonoma County viticultural area Zinfandel, which we first produced commercially in 1995 under the Geyser Peak label. This is our elegant, food-friendly, easy-to-drink Zinfandel. It is a soft, lower 13.9 percent alcohol wine with some nice Zin fruit — more in the Alexander Valley style. We produce up to 7,000 cases (1996), and sell it under $10 a bottle. We also now have our Venezia label Cucamonga Zinfandel, a limited release big, jammy, trendy wine with over 14 percent alcohol.

"I remember when I first came here in 1989. People were raving about Williams Selyem Zinfandel. I remember being introduced to a 1984 Zinfandel in a half-bottle. It was high in alcohol, and sweet. As an Australian winemaker, I found that quite awkward that someone could put out a red wine that was sweet and high in alcohol. It wasn't Port; it wasn't Late Harvest. It was just a sweetish red wine, one that didn't ferment out, and that was the way the red wine was, and people raved about it.

"While I appreciated the wine for the qualities that were there, I found it hard to drink. So we certainly have to be conscious that our wines are not just for smelling and lining up against others for comparing. Wines are for drinking with food. Geyser Peak has a reputation of good value for the money. It has a reputation for drinkable wine, so our Zinfandel that we produce under that line of wines has to be in that mold.

"Our Venezia label allows us some room to open up new avenues, and have some fun, and try some things that we couldn't try under the Geyser Peak line. It gives us opportunity to explore richer, higher alcohol wines such as the D'Ambrogio Zinfandel from vines more than 100 years old."

"There's always going to be a place for specialty wines, to pair with that specialty dinner," I remarked.

"Sure, there are some foods that will pair with these richer wines, but it's hard to drink such wines very often."

"Well, I am just thrilled that you have taken an interest in those old Cucamonga Valley Zinfandel vineyards," I found myself saying. "Those are truly heritage vineyards, and given the demand for the land there, and that these old vineyards are so low-yielding, it's truly remarkable that they still exist. In my opinion, the quality of those grapes until very recently has been greatly undervalued by just about everyone but their growers. You are lucky to have come along when you did."

"I think so," agreed Daryl. "Even today, when we say to a few other winemakers up here that we bought some great Zinfandel from Cucamonga Valley, everyone snickers. It must be the name, or the reputation or tradition of what Cucamonga means or is, that they are snickering about. They obviously haven't seen the vines, or tried wine made from the grapes. So I say, 'God, you ought to go down and have a look at these vines. If you saw these vines in Dry Creek, or any other traditionally known area, you would pay $3,000 or $4,000 per ton for the grapes; you would die to get the fruit from those old vines."

"How much did you pay?" I asked.

"We paid about a quarter less than that," Daryl laughed. "The trucking costs added a little more. I have to admit that some people looked at us a little weirdly when we told them we were trucking Zinfandel from Southern California. But in Australia, we were used to trucking grapes 10 hours; it isn't unusual for us to do. It doesn't hurt the grapes, and they were definitely worth getting. We are glad to have come across them."

"That's part of the magic of Zinfandel, as I have seen it," I remarked. "Would you be hauling three truck-loads of grapes 12 to 15 hours from Southern California if they weren't Zinfandel?"

"Probably not," replied Daryl. "It's the Zinfandel we're doing it for. We've had to wake up to these old vineyards. We've become a bit complacent about them, believing that they've always been there, and that no one else is going to become interested. We think we can play our cards, and just take them when we want. We are at that stage with the D'Ambrogio Ranch, now that we've seen its potential this year. We know we had better think about locking it up before it's gone, or before some other winemakers realize how good it is."

When I left Daryl that afternoon, I had learned that for him Cucamonga Valley Zinfandel was more than an old vine Zinfandel vineyard. It was a lucky match made in heaven.

Although Zinfandel is only one of several red wines he enjoys, he is definitely "wrapped" in Cucamonga Valley Zinfandel. Thanks to Jerry Mead, I, think that I, too, am now "wrapped!" As will be many wine drinkers, I am sure, when they have the opportunity to taste these lovely Zinfandels from the historic Cucamonga Valley of Riverside and San Bernardino counties.

★ ★ ★ ★ ★

In summer 1998, the bourbon company Jim Beam purchased Geyser Peak (Peak Wines International), as that company's first venture into the wine production business. So when it came time to release the Cucamonga Valley D'Ambrogio Ranch Zinfandel, Geyser Peak adjusted its marketing strategy for this wine. Instead of being released under the Venezia label, it was released under Geyser Peak "Winemaker's Selection" label. Seven hundred cases made up the lot, selling at $25 per bottle, "which is too cheap for a Zinfandel from such beautiful old vines," exclaimed Daryl.

A huge wine with 15.4 percent alcohol, it had all the spiciness and lovely fruit necessary for immediate enjoyment, but it also had the sturdy tannins and structure necessary to carry it for several years. The wine had done well in competitions, too, winning gold medals and four-star awards in Orange County, California, and in London. Jerry Mead awarded it 96 points. Perhaps its ultimate achievement was winning the "Best of Region — South Coast" gold medal at the 1999 California State Fair. "I can tell you that I was extremely proud to accept the award for our D'Ambrogio Vineyard Cucamonga Valley Zinfandel. It was also the wine that we ran out of before the evening was over. People just loved it," said Daryl the day after the fair award. I was not surprised.

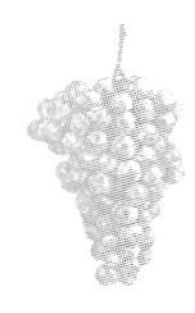

Lake County

Catfish Vineyard

Lake County has only a couple of surviving pre-Prohibition Zinfandel Vineyards: the Duncan Vineyard and the Catfish Vineyard. The Duncan Vineyard fruit is sold for white Zinfandel. The Catfish Vineyard fruit has been sold to Jed Steele since 1992 as one of his three vineyard-designated Zinfandel wines. The Staehli family in Lakeport originally owned the Catfish Vineyard. The late Rose Genevieve Strickler (1926–1992) purchased it in 1959.

Since Lake County Zinfandel is closely connected to the story of Jed Steele, my narrative here begins with my first meeting Jed in April 1986, when he was winemaker for Kendall-Jackson located in Kelseyville, Lake County, and I was on my first assignment for *Practical Winery & Vineyard.*

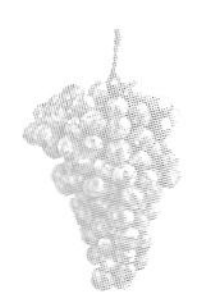

Jed Steele, Winemaker

When I met Jed Steele in preparing for my "The Challenge of Zinfandel" report for *Practical Winery & Vineyard,* I learned about the old Southwest Mendocino ridge-top vineyards and their regional characteristics and challenges. These vineyards had been his sources since he made his first Zinfandel from the 70-year-old DuPratt Vineyard in 1974 as founding winemaker at Edmeades. It was with these vineyards that he had learned of Zinfandel's potential for producing exquisite red wines. They also established his benchmark for what he appreciated in Zinfandel vineyards and wines. The California State Fair Board had twice named Steele "Winemaker of the Year." As I climbed the narrow steel stairs to his office in Kendall-Jackson Winery, I felt apprehensive.

My apprehension was well founded, since Jed, a tall burly fellow, quiet and rather soft-spoken, didn't go out of his way to put me at ease. He greeted me with the words, "I have an hour. What can I tell you?" I got the feeling that he would not have given me even that if I hadn't been on magazine assignment. It was obvious, after all, that whatever success I may have enjoyed in my career as an English professor, I was a rank novice on the subject of red winemaking. It didn't take him long, though, to realize that I was clearly smitten with Zinfandel. That seemed to be enough for him to forgive my requests for some rather basic explanations. His reserve melted, and he began imparting as fast as I could take down notes all the essential information about what he liked about his sources — four southwest Mendocino County ridge-top Zinfandel vineyards — and his winemaking style.

Jed Steele

"I like those three old southwest Mendocino County ridge-top vineyards — the Zeni, Ciapucci, and the DuPratt-DePatie [today known as the DuPratt], as well as the recently established Mariah," Jed told me then, "because the cool climate and mountain soils produce grapes that are more evenly ripened than in lower, warmer regions. And the acids are usually very high, the pH low. The acids can range from 8 g/L in ripe years to nearly 20 g/L in cold years. The pH is consistently below 3.40 at harvest; in cold years, it can be as low as 2.85."

Jed had come to appreciate Zinfandel from these coastal ridges, roughly between the points where the Navarro and Gualala rivers empty into the ocean, during his years in the mid-to-late 1970s as the founding winemaker for Edmeades Winery, Philo, in the Anderson Valley. He crushed his first Zinfandel in 1974 from the 75-year-old DuPratt Vineyard just off Greenwood Ridge Road about six miles out of Anderson Valley. The vineyard belonged to one of the winery partners' mother and father-in-law. By 1979, Jed had also secured as a source the two-acre, 80-year-old Zeni Vineyard; and in 1980, the nine-acre, 90-year-old Ciapusci Vineyard, both on Fish Rock Road. These three ridge-top vineyards contain the last old vines of Zinfandel plantings in southwest Mendocino County. At the time of Prohibition, vineyard acreage totaled about 350. As of 1997, it totaled about 40 — up about 10 acres over the past decade.

When he left Edmeades to go to Kendall-Jackson, Jed continued to source grapes from Mendocino. The region, he said, is "a classic match of grape variety with a particular climate, one that leads to the ultimate in winemaking fruit."

Jed also carried the imprint of the winemaking style he acquired at Edmeades with him to Kendall-Jackson. When it came to fermenting Zinfandel grapes and cellaring the wine, he continued to give Zinfandel the same red wine "priority treatment" that he developed at Edmeades. I had no idea what "priority treatment" consisted of. So I asked.

It meant that the wines were treated exactly as if they were a fine Cabernet Sauvignon, Jed told me. Among other things, this meant they were aged in Nevers French oak barrels, from 35 percent to 50 percent new, for 6-16 months — a bold treatment then for Zinfandel." I began using French oak when I was at Edmeades," explained Jed, "because that was the winery's policy — to use only French oak. When we crushed our first Zinfandel grapes from the DuPratt, I made the wine the way we made our other red wines, which was to age it in Nevers French oak barrels. I didn't realize how good a wine we had until I tried a barrel sample that winter (1975). At that point I was hooked on Zinfandel, those old southwest Mendocino County ridge-top Zinfandel vineyards, and French oak. The wine was a consistent award-winner, so I've stayed with the French oak."

At the end of our interview that day, Jed recommended that I find some time to journey over to those historic and spectacular vineyards and see them for myself — which I did in spring of 1987, and several times since. (See "Mendocino County.") He also took me to the tasting room for a sampling of the available Zins, and he left me with the words, "Call if you have any more questions."

At the end of that day, I felt I had passed one of the most important tests of my life: my entrance exam to the complex and challenging world of Zinfandel production.

In 1991, Jed terminated his position as winemaker for Kendall-Jackson, and founded his own label: Steele Wines.

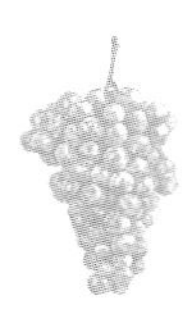

Steele Wines: Where Zinfandel Gives Pleasure at Every Stage

Following my first meeting with Jed Steele in 1986, I had many more fascinating interviews with him, by telephone and in person, over the next 10 years. Although better known (he says) for his Pinot Noir and Chardonnay, Jed continues to regard Zinfandel as an important grape in his production line-up. In fact, he can wax positively eloquent about this intriguing all-American *Vitis vinifera*.

"Zinfandel is the only California varietal that carries with it a sense of our very own viticultural antiquity. Speaking generally, it is the focal point of our winemaking culture. It may be 'the prince that will never be king.' However, in a winemaking democracy such as ours, having served its constituency so faithfully for all these years, it perennially occupies the highest elected varietal office in the land," he offered as his quotable quote over lunch at Calistoga's All Seasons Cafe one late June 1992 day.

"Everyone likes Zinfandel because it gives pleasure at every stage," he continued. "You can savor it in the cellar as it matures, you can savor it at release, and you can lay it down for several years. Zinfandel represents a constant string of enjoyable moments. It's the most hedonistic wine I know.

"Many people, though, still treat it much like a friend or relative whom you know intimately, so it's hard to be objective about their qualities. It's hard to admit the greatness of someone you've grown up with and know intimately."

Jed's sources for Zinfandel under his own label still include his favorite southwest Mendocino County vineyard, the DuPratt. The Zeni and Ciapusci vineyards stayed under contract to Kendall-Jackson after Jed left there; Mariah went on contract to Fetzer. In addition to the DuPratt, he acquired a portion of the crop of another Mendocino County Zinfandel source, the 30-acre, 50-year-old Pacini Vineyard, above Talmage and on the Talmage Bench.

Jed's search for additional new sources led him to discover Lake County's oldest Zinfandel vineyard, the seven-acre Catfish Vineyard planted in 1901 on its own roots as part of the pre-Prohibition Staehli Winery. Located on the slopes above Kelseyville, which has a climate that is warm and dry (very unlike the Mendocino County ridge-top vineyards), the soil in Catfish Vineyard is shallow and sparse. This combination of soil and climate restricts the crop to about three-quarters to one ton per acre of tiny clusters of evenly ripened and intensely flavored small-berried fruit. Under Jed's hand, these little clusters and berries have consistently produced an elegant, fruity, flavorful Zinfandel table wine. A typically late-ripening vineyard, the fruit consistently comes in between 23.5° and 24.5° Brix, 0.70 T.A., and 3.45 pH — "very good numbers for a Lake County red; it's a wine with a lot of flavor, but it isn't weighty," is how he described it. Jed has been producing a Catfish Vineyard Zinfandel since 1989 from this own-rooted, dry-farmed, head-trained vineyard.

"Zinfandel is the only California varietal that carries with it a sense of our very own viticultural antiquity."

Jed Steele

In fall 1996, Jed and his wife, Marie, purchased the Konocti Winery in Kelseyville, and renamed it Steele Wines. It was their first winery.

In January 1997, just a few months after they had moved into the facility, I caught up with Jed in his office for a much-interrupted conversation about the state of Zinfandel in the Steele Wines varietal lineup. Dressed in a colorful red plaid shirt and jeans, and wearing his signature tinted glasses, he welcomed me into his office. I was struck by how he was still very much the same tall burly, no-nonsense, gruff fellow whom I had met 10 years earlier. However, I was by now used to his direct and frank style of answering my questions. "Is Zinfandel still a revered grape for you, now that you own your own winery?" I asked.

"Oh, sure," he replied, "It's a minor grape in my production, because I rely on just a few specific small vineyards, but one I enjoy. I produce between 3,000 and 4,000 cases annually, which is about 20 percent of my total production. I still buy all the 5½-acre DuPratt, and some of the 28-

acre Pacini Vineyard near Talmage. I would buy more of that fruit if I could, but the owner's philosophy is to not lock himself up with just one winery. Any expansion of my Zinfandel production can happen only through the Pacini Vineyard. And I buy all the fruit from the Catfish Vineyard, a small and ancient vineyard. However, I wouldn't want Zinfandel to become any more than 20 percent of my production. Chardonnay makes up 60 percent. People usually think of me more as a Chardonnay winemaker than a Zinfandel winemaker. Anywhere I have been, Zinfandel never has been the primary grape in my production."

"That's a startling revelation to me," I replied. "I've always had the impression that you were a kind of 'Mr. Zinfandel.'"

"Well," replied Jed, "I've been doing it a long time, and I've been fortunate to have had some really good vineyards, and to have consistently turned out some fantastic wines. But in terms of total production, my goodness, when I was at Kendall-Jackson, I don't believe that our Zinfandel production was ever over 5 percent of what we did. I probably made more at Edmeades. Zinfandel production peaked out there, in the early 1980s, to maybe 30 to 35 percent. Still, Zinfandel was never the major grape that I worked with."

"George Zeni told me, with great energy, that even though Zinfandel from his and Ciapusci's vineyards made up just a tiny part of K-J's production, it was their vineyard-designated ridge-top Zinfandels made under your hand that won the gold medals, and made Kendall-Jackson famous," I remarked.

"Yes, I brought a number of very good vineyards with me when I went over there, and, yes, we were able to get a degree of notoriety for the Zinfandel, though they were tiny production lots. The Zinfandels also helped position Kendall-Jackson in the marketplace. The winery was seen by some as this 'mass producer' of millions of gallons of Chardonnay. To have these vineyard-designated, small-lot productions of Zinfandel gave the winery a degree of validity, not that it needed it, but in the eyes of some who might be critical — the fact that we would make small lots of Zinfandel gave these critics pause in characterizing the winery simply as a 'mass producer.'"

I also asked Jed if he still gave his Zinfandel "priority treatment," and if so, has it changed any?

"Yes, our approach is still to treat it like a Cabernet Sauvignon. We used to make it exactly the same as our Cabernet. Now, it is slightly different in that we bottle Cabernet in April, 14 to18 months after harvest. We bottle some Zinfandels at 14 months and others after only 9 to 10 months in barrel. There is a fruity element in Zinfandel that you want to preserve, and there is not a disagreeable aroma early on, that you get in Cabernet Sauvignon, that you have to work out of the wine.

"We've found that especially with some of these old Zinfandel vineyards, if you leave the wine in barrels too long, as I am sure you have experienced, there is a sensation of less than supple tannins, a drying, harsh tannin. We try to get away from that by bottling earlier. The Catfish Vineyard Zinfandel is normally bottled in late August. The same for the Pacini. So we're talking about a little less than a year, or a little over a year, in barrel. The DuPratt, which is the richest of the three, will be bottled at the earliest at 14 months — maybe 16. So you can see that we tend not to leave any of our Zinfandels in oak as long as we leave our Cabernet Sauvignon."

Jed also has refined his oak program. He never uses more than 50 percent new oak. The Pacini gets much less. Its fruit naturally provides a tannic structure, he explained, that you have to be careful of. It gets only 25 percent new oak, for about nine months. The Catfish Vineyard still gets 50 percent new, for 9-12 months, and the DuPratt, 50 percent new for 12–14 months.

"Do you still believe that French oak is better to use for Zinfandel than American oak?" I asked.

"In 1974, I made my first Zinfandel from the DuPratt Vineyard while I was with Edmeades. I was fortunate in getting such a great vineyard for my first Zinfandel vineyard, and that winery's policy was to use French oak — 20 percent to 25 percent new. It was a great match with that vineyard."

It also turned out to the wine he sent to the Four Seasons Hotel in New York in 1980 for its annual Barrel Tasting of California wines. Perhaps in some people's eyes, sending off a Zinfandel from a newly established winery in 1980 to a prestigious New York barrel tasting was a pretty bold thing to do — although Ridge Vineyards had done it in previous years. Jed, however, recalled: "I sent it because I thought it was the best wine we had to show." Also, he said, it was the wine Gerald Asher, the event's organizer, had requested, since he had been a big fan of this vineyard. The wine was a hands-down favorite at the tasting.

"Didn't you tell me once that someone made the remark that it was 'almost too good to be real?'"

"Yeah, something like that. You have to remember that in the first place, with few exceptions, the wineries that championed Zinfandel were not wineries that — in the 1960s — were of the old school. That is to say, Inglenook in the period 1930-1970 did not champion it; BV [Beaulieu Vineyards] did not champion it; Beringer really did not champion it; Mondavi really did not champion it; nor Charles Krug. So the old school of that era really was not that closely identified with Zinfandel. A lot of the problem was perhaps because of the post-Prohibition prejudice against it. So when these wineries went into making finer varietal wines, they went with Cabernet Sauvignon, Pinot Noir, Chardonnay, things like that. It wasn't until Ridge made a thing out of Zinfandel — and of course, Lee Stewart when he was at Souverain in the 1960s made excellent Zinfandel — that people started taking Zinfandel seriously. It was the generation of winemakers who came on the scene in the mid-1960s to mid-1970s and later who revived interest in Zinfandel.

"To this day, BV is not a Zinfandel producer; Robert Mondavi made one initially when they started, but discontinued it for over 20 years before starting up again [1991]. Martini was a consistent Zinfandel producer, but even then it was not a specialty wine for him. He was probably just as well known for Barbera as for Zinfandel."

"You were one of the earliest producers, then, to treat Zinfandel as a world-class red wine, when you were at Edmeades ?"

"Well, yes, and when I started out there, Cabernet Sauvignon was to be the winery's focus. I soon learned that Cabernet Sauvignon-making in the Anderson Valley was a risky venture. The quality goes up and down dramatically according to the vintage [year]. Whereas the old Zinfandel vineyards like the DuPratt, which at that time [1974] was close to 60 years old, consistently made a more substantial wine. Cabernet Sauvignon in Anderson Valley occasionally made a dramatic wine — and still does; but it's two years out of five compared to five years out of six for the DuPratt coming out as a truly spectacular wine.

"So anyway, we had French oak, we got into the style," Jed continued. "I liked it. Again, if I had been making a Zinfandel from another vineyard, I don't know but what I might have tried American oak. However, the [DuPratt Zinfandel] wine was well received early on. The 1975, our second vintage, got tremendous accolades. It created demand for the wine. The 1978 and 1979 vintages were great. So we were able to charge a fairly good price that made it economical to use French oak — $10 to $12 a bottle, when others were getting between $5 to $7.

"To this day, I don't make Zinfandel from many vineyards. For the Catfish, I use French oak; for the Pacini, we use French and some American, but of my three vineyards, the Pacini is the least intense. I still think that with good Zinfandel vineyards, French oak is a wonderful match. You have wineries like Ridge that have set a style with American oak and understand it very well. And I love those wines, and order them when I go out to eat; I have a couple in my cellar. But stylistically, I like French oak better — as long as the Zinfandel vineyard is an excellent vineyard.

"Again, there was a mind-set in the late 1960s through the 1970s, cut and dried, that if you made Cabernet Sauvignon or Pinot Noir, you used French oak; if you made Zinfandel or Sauvignon Blanc, you used American oak," Jed pointed out. "This practice was in good part based on economics — what you could get for a bottle of wine. There are exceptions, of course: BV was using American oak for its Cabernet Sauvignon, also Ridge. Jordan and Silver Oak were probably the most prominent wineries after BV to incorporate American oak into their Cabernet Sauvignon programs. But back then, Jordan leached out its new American oak barrels with soda ash, essentially turning them into one-year-old barrels in terms of flavor effect. So there were a few exceptions.

"Today, of course, American oak is much better coopered; the somewhat raw flavors of American oak have been, if you will, somewhat tamed. There's no need to worry about using a brand new American oak barrel. The American oak we're talking about in the late 1960s and into the 1970s was far removed from what we're seeing today. Back then, you bought a whiskey barrel, which had either no char or toast at all, or a heavy char like a bourbon barrel. They were 53 gallons. It was a totally different American cooperage world then."

I had a couple of questions remaining for Jed. Both had to do with what the more expensive bottles of Zinfandel offered for the money. First, did ageability contribute to the cost of a bottle of Zinfandel?

"The reality is," he replied, "that most of us are making wines for people to enjoy. All this other gobbledygook doesn't really mean much to anyone. But as a winemaker, as a professional (and I am in the vast *minority* in terms of people who open a bottle of wine), I like to recognize, or have a feel for what the wine is. When red wines age past a certain point, they become varietally indistinguishable. I like wines both young, and with some bottle age on them. But from an intellectual and professional point of view — because this is what I do for a living and this is my mind-set, for better or for worse — I like to be able to identify them varietally. After 10 or 12 years, it is difficult to distinguish most red wines varietally."

"Apart from your insistence that wines be varietally distinct, you don't believe that they should be able to age for six or eight years to be worth, say, $20 a bottle?" I asked him.

"No. But that's a good question — that is, should ageability, *per se*, be one of the factors that contributes to the high price of a bottle of wine? While I have heard people present this as a logical rationale for their higher prices, and I can concur with some of their reasoning, there are wonderful wines that are wonderful at two to five years. With red wines, though, yes, usually the assumption is that the wines will age if you pay a lot of money for them. That's the assumption. The reality is that regardless of how much people pay for a bottle of wine, they generally will still end up drinking it soon after purchasing it.

"Probably the perfect wine — and I think this is why Zinfandel has the appeal it does — is one that gives a tremendous amount of enjoyment soon after bottling, with that enjoyment continuing over two or three years; and is also enjoyable in eight to 10 years."

"That's the 'string of enjoyable moments' you described to me over lunch one day in Calistoga some years back," I noted.

"Right, sure," he agreed, "and that's of value."

My other question had to do with whether such factors as extraction, percent of alcohol, etc., had anything to do with the cost of a bottle of wine.

"Well, in theory," replied Jed, "you're buying a lot of things when you buy a higher-priced bottle of Zinfandel. Let's assume that a group of wine drinkers say that this tastes good; therefore, it is a good, sound wine. Then you get into all kinds of different realms. Obviously, concentration of flavor is important — Zinfandel has to have a certain degree of concentration to work; I think people have come to expect that. I don't think percent of alcohol should in itself influence the cost of the wine.

"Typically, good Zinfandels can have between 13.5 percent and low 15 percent alcohol. I normally try for 14 percent to 14.5 percent. But as you well know, with Zinfandel, it's easy to err on the side of ripeness, because you wait and wait for that fully ripe flavor. So sometimes we get them at 13.8 percent, sometimes at 15.2 percent. You know, it's common practice for winemakers to add water to Zinfandel when the sugars are high. I just do not like to do that at all. I like to work with what we've got. If the sugars are way up there, we use stronger yeast, to ensure that the wine ferments dry.

"But in terms of an expensive bottle of wine," getting back to my question, "the reality is that we are in a trendy business, and factors such as scarcity and hoopla can have a great effect on the price of a bottle of wine. I think it's great that some people are charging $45 a bottle for Zinfandel. It makes it easier for me to charge $20, even though some people may believe that mine are on the same qualitative level as the ones at $45. It also has to do with styles of wine. Just as in music or painting, at any given time, certain styles come into popularity for a time. Frankly, I am not at all surprised that Zinfandel has become popular, and that there's a certain market for high-priced, scarce lots of particular styles. People have always liked Zinfandel as a wine to drink."

A knock on Jed's office door announced that his daughter, Benecia, had arrived, and was calling a staff meeting to order. On that note, Jed and I parted company, with me wishing him well with his winery, and he assuring me that it was perfectly safe to take a short cut over Cobb Mountain back to Highway 29 into Calistoga.

I did just that in the misty twilight of that January afternoon, feeling somehow — was it because of the 10-year retrospective? — that I was returning from a sojourn much farther afield from Napa than 75 miles.

In 1998, just three years after the untimely death of Larry Pacini in 1995, Jed and Marie purchased the Pacini vineyard.

In 2000, Jed, now divorced from Marie, purchased Catfish Vineyard.

Mendocino County

Islands in the Sky (Mariah Vineyard)
Photo by George Rose

Mendocino County is part of California's North Coast wine region. Directly north of Sonoma County, it is bounded by California's coastal mountain range, the Pacific Ocean, and the great northern redwood forests. Its vineyards are located among several small Mayacamas and Coastal Range valleys that follow the drainages of the Russian and Navarro rivers, and on the southwest Mendocino County ridge tops. Of its nine viticultural areas, three are especially well suited to Zinfandel: Redwood Valley; Ukiah Valley; and Mendocino Ridge. There are about 2,000 acres of Zinfandel in Mendocino County, with most of that acreage located in Redwood and Ukiah valleys.

Redwood Valley runs 10 to 12 miles along the Russian River, beginning a few miles north of Ukiah. It covers 35 square miles, and is home to about 2,400 acres of grapes, one-third of which are white and two-thirds of which are red. The soil is Redvine Series and Pinole Gravelly Loam, unique to the region. The county's first vineyards were planted here in the 1850s and were mostly Zinfandel.[27] Redwood Valley is home to the Annette's Vineyard (fruit purchased by Rosenblum Cellars), the Ricetti Vineyard, and such Zinfandel producers as Lolonis Winery and Vineyards, and Fife. Altogether, there are 66 vineyard owners and seven wineries.

Fife winemaker, John Buechsenstein, likes this region. "It is high Region Two or low Region Three," he explained, "which means that we have a cool/warm alternation in our climate, and 20 percent more rain

27 Mendocino Winegrowers Alliance

than the Ukiah Valley. The climate leads to later-maturing grapes, which allows for maximum flavor development, good acid/sugar balance, and overall sound structure. However, because of the climate, growers must be attentive to their viticultural practices."

Ukiah Valley extends south from the Redwood Valley along the Russian River for 20 miles. The benchlands on the east side of the Russian River Valley in the Hopland-Talmage area have always been a favorable location for Zinfandel, according to Jed Steele, owner of Steele Wines (Konocti). The Scharfenberger Vineyard is in this viticultural area, and also the Pacini Vineyard, which was purchased by Jed Steele in 1998. Although Russ and Ann Nyborg, owners of Whaler Vineyard on Eastside Road, Hopland, did not buy their property in 1972 with the intention of growing Zinfandel, they soon discovered that it was the premium varietal recommended for their location and soil. In 1973, they planted 24 acres with Zinfandel, trellised and cordon-trained.

Fetzer Vineyards has produced Zinfandel from Redwood and Ukiah valleys since its founding in 1968.

Fetzer Vineyards

Fetzer Vineyards was the first winery *Practical Winery & Vineyard* publisher Don Neel sent me to for my "Challenge of Zinfandel" report in 1986.

It was a gorgeous early May morning drive through Napa and Alexander valleys and up Highway 101 to what was then the family winery just north of Ukiah. Paul Dolan, winemaker from 1977 to 1992, was long-haired and mustachioed in those days. He welcomed me when I arrived after my two-hour drive, then invited me into a conference room, where we sat down to talk about Zinfandel's place in Fetzer Winery.

In 1986, Fetzer was producing a Ricetti Vineyards vineyard-designated Zinfandel, a Mendocino County Zinfandel, and a Lake County Zinfandel. Paul explained that the location of his Mendocino and Lake Zinfandel vineyards made as much difference to the flavor and intensity of the wines as the age of vines. The Mendocino County Zinfandel was produced from three dry-farmed and head-trained vineyards located in Redwood and Ukiah valleys. These were Fetzer's Home Ranch, the Lolonis, and the Sharffenberger. The vineyards were planted in the 1940s and 1950s and are on St. George rootstock. All grow on well-drained benchlands and hillsides whose soils are friable gravelly red clay that contain some shale. Younger plantings in these vineyards were propagated from budwood from the older plantings. These factors contribute to smaller, more intensely flavored berries with a good balance of tannins and acids, which produce a fuller-bodied wine, Paul explained.

The Lake County vineyards Fetzer was using for its lighter-style dry Zinfandels were propagated from a bigger berry UC Davis clonal selection. The soil in the Lake County region is thinner, the climate hotter, so tannins and acids are lighter, the fruit less intense, the pH higher. "All these factors combined to yield a lighter-bodied, lighter-alcohol, yet fruity wine that was best consumed upon release," continued Paul.

Paul also provided one of my first perspectives on the significance of harvest Brix as well as the acid and pH of the grapes, and how region affects it all. Few of his Mendocino County Zinfandels were picked above 23° Brix because, said Paul, higher ripeness usually carried some raisining, which he didn't like. "There are years," he said, "when you get full ripeness without a lot of raisining. Such 'reserve-quality' wines usually end up over 14 percent alcohol, and can go as high as 15 percent without a raisiny quality. You have the fruit along with the acids, tannins, and extract necessary for the wine to gain in the bottle several years. In less exceptional years, Mendocino's Redwood Valley Zinfandel is best when harvested for under 14 percent alcohol, and with only two to four years in the bottle." His favorite vineyard for a Reserve Zinfandel, in addition to the Ricetti, was the Lolonis.

In 1987, a Red Zinfandel and white Zinfandel program replaced Fetzer's Mendocino and Lake County viticultural area Zinfandels. The Mendocino vineyards made up the Red Zinfandel, the Lake County fruit went to the white Zinfandel. "We were sitting on all this Mendocino and Lake County [red] Zinfandel, but the white Zinfandel was booming, so we hoped this way we'd get some crossover business from the white Zinfandel crowd," Paul reminisced.

It didn't work; in fact, it mostly just confused consumers. So in 1988, Fetzer scrapped its Red Zinfandel brand, and created in its place the Barrel Select Program — also a blend of all four Mendocino County Zinfandel vineyards — about 28,000 cases retailing for under $9 per bottle. The Lake County fruit continued to go to the white Zinfandel program. In exceptional years, Paul continued his practice of keeping separate a few small lots of Reserve Zinfandel from the best Mendocino County blocks. This approach met with consumer approval.

In 1992, Brown-Forman Corporation purchased Fetzer. Paul Dolan was named president, and Dennis Martin, assistant winemaker since 1985, moved up to winemaker. In 1996, Dennis was named vice president/winemaker for all Fetzer wines. Bill Leair is now the assistant winemaker, red wine production. In January 1997, I spent an afternoon with Dennis and Bill at the winery's new Hopland location, catching up on the changes Fetzer has made in its Zinfandel program since about 1992, and the challenges it is currently facing.

I found Dennis in his office located in the collection of portable buildings beside the winery. Busy with the demands of his new position, yet cheerful, gracious, and forthcoming, Dennis set out explaining to me Zinfandel's continuing importance to Fetzer's wine production, and the changes that had been occurring in the product line.

"Beginning with the 1995 vintage, we will stop marketing our Barrel Select brand domestically," said Dennis. "To replace it, we created a Home Ranch Zinfandel in our proprietary line, to match up with our Valley Oaks Cabernet Sauvignon, Eagle Peak Merlot, Sundial Chardonnay, and Echo Ridge Fumé Blanc. The proprietary line and the Barrel Select line were coming into conflict with each other, so we took our Barrel Select Zinfandel out of the domestic market and have replaced it with a proprietary brand at the same retail price because our customers know us so much for our proprietary brands. Until the 1995 vintage, we've had a California Zinfandel that we've exported. Now, I've taken that California Zinfandel blend and expanded it, to make one big proprietary brand blend. Export will continue to get their cases, in addition to the Barrel Select cases they want. We'll also have an inventory for domestic markets — of a popularly priced Zinfandel. We will continue to source as much North Coast Zinfandel as we can to support the Barrel Select business. Some will also be for the new proprietary line.

"In addition to our Amador sources [Clockspring and Arnese], we have begun to look at Lodi Zinfandel as well as a source for our proprietary brand. We think we can make a very high quality product at this price, given some of the vineyards we've seen in Lodi, because Zinfandel in Lodi can do very well if you get it ripe, and farm it properly. We're even taking a few hundred tons from Galleano Vineyards in Riverside County. Traditionally, we've been a Mendocino County winery. But with North Coast grapes being so darned expensive now, we saw an opportunity to create a quality product at a popular price by opening ourselves up to sources outside Mendocino."

"Are you going to work with the growers?" I asked.

"Oh, yes, absolutely! It is critical. You have to. And we have to identify growers who are responsible farmers. Focus on quality, focus on fewer brands, and reposition some of our inventory to a more opportune program. That's the direction we're going with Zinfandel. We see a real opportunity to get more people interested in Zinfandel as a red table wine. Zinfandel is highly popular and interesting to countries outside the U.S. — more so than Cabernet Sauvignon, Chardonnay, and Merlot, which are grown in countries all over the world. Zinfandel is unique to California, and hasn't been associated with any other variety in Europe.

"In addition, we will continue to make small quantities of Reserve Zinfandel in years when we're blessed with a great harvest, and we get the kind of character and extraction and sugar and alcohol that we need for that kind of special lot wine." For example, one lot of the 1994 Arnese Zinfandel was so good that Fetzer made a Reserve that got very good reviews. According to Bill Leair, one block of the 1996 Mariah Vineyard has every appearance of being Reserve quality.

"We're also revisiting how we make Zinfandel. My goal now on making these [Barrel Select and proprietary Zinfandel] wines is to try and capture the fruit, to feature the fruit through 20 percent to 30 percent whole berry fermentation. We can do that now with the destemmer we have, and how we position the oak in the blend so that it becomes an integral, but not dominant, component of the wine. With Zinfandel, I really want to feature the fruit, and the oak should be just a complexing companion to that fruit. If I'm self-critical about the Zinfandels we've made in the past, I think it is that we've featured the oak maybe a little too much, at least for this style of wine. When it comes to the Reserve wines, that's a whole different animal.

"We make wines to drink. Not to say some of our wines are not cellar-worthy. But I think most people buy wine to drink, and that's how we have to make our wines — for people to drink and to enjoy.

"Our consumers do appreciate our efforts to provide quality at a popular price. Our Zinfandel does very well. People are always looking for a quality product at good value. Fetzer started out [in 1968] with Zinfandel and Petite Sirah, so our customers know us for these wines. They are important parts of our business. Fetzer has a heritage with our customers in Zinfandel and Petite Sirah of providing quality at a good price."

Dennis's point raised a question I had been agonizing over for months: What additional quality does one get in a bottle of Zinfandel at the higher prices? Is it age-worthiness? And if so, what is in the more expensive wine that enables it to age, if the customer chooses to lay it away for a few years, that the more "value priced" wines do not have? So I asked him, "What's twice as good about the $18 bottle of Zinfandel over the $9 bottle? What is twice as good about a bottle of Fetzer Wines Reserve Ricetti or Mariah or El Dorado over the proprietary?"

"I think what you get," responded Dennis, "is more extract in the fruit; you get more flavor-richness and character from the grapes, assuming you can get them ripe and get the right alcohol. The challenge there is to get the fruit ripe with a certain amount of shrivel without having the shrivel go to raisins.

"My criticism of big, full-bodied Zinfandels is they are sometimes too ripe, and have raisiny, pruny characters that I personally don't care for in a Zinfandel — or in any red wine for that matter. The fruit should be mature, it should be fully ripe, but not over-ripe. Then you get all the flavors, all the fruit, and all the extract of the flavor without those over-ripe raisin and prune characters. Then you have all the good numbers — good acid, good pH, and good alcohol. I think if you buy a higher priced Zinfandel, you should expect some alcohol — probably over 14 percent. I'm not opposed to it being over 14 percent. Case quantities are generally smaller; the tax issues are probably not as big an issue at the higher prices." (Wines with over 14 percent alcohol pay higher taxes than those 14 percent and under.)

But over 15 percent, "you're pushing it — as a table wine, anyway," said Dennis. "That was part of the problem Zinfandel ran into in the late 1960s and early 1970s, when there was so much confusion about what Zinfandel was. Everybody was making it differently; the consumer didn't know what to expect in the bottle. Then, when white Zinfandel came along, at least people knew what they were getting. Out of that phenomenon came the opportunity for serious Zinfandel producers to create something interesting — and relatively consistent. Of course, the rest is now history. Now, the consumer seems to realize that if you buy those higher-priced Zinfandels, you're probably going to have alcohol over 14 percent. But over 15 percent is getting out of the realm of table wine, I think."

"In addition to higher alcohol and more extract, is ageability part of what the consumer also gets in the more expensive Zinfandel?" I persisted. "That is, should people be able to expect that such wines will, if they decided to put them away for a while, age into something more complex and interesting?"

"That's a tough call," Dennis responded. "That whole ageing thing is a really difficult conversation. Our core business [here at Fetzer Vineyards] is to appeal to people who want to enjoy a bottle of wine every day. Even our occasional small case production of Reserve wines I like to drink young. They are drinkable when we release them. But they are certainly age-worthy as well, and do appeal to collectors. We certainly see that in some of our older Zinfandels. Ten, even 15 years, are not a problem. Those older, higher alcohol, very extracted wines generally from older vines and dry-farmed vineyards from Redwood Valley and benches in Ukiah, we've gone back and tasted those of the inventory we still have available of our late 1970s and early 1980s vintages, and they are really still quite good."

My afternoon at Fetzer ended with Bill Leair taking me through a tank tasting of some of the best samples of 1996 grower lots, and a 1995 barrel tasting of a few of the finest Mendocino County vineyards. One block of the 1996 Mariah, as mentioned above, is being considered for a Reserve bottling; all the others that I sampled, both 1995 and 1996 vintages — and there were some lovely wines among them — were destined for the Barrel Select blend. Before I left, Bill took me to the hospitality mezzanine overlooking the winery's 48,000 barrels — it looked like at least an acre of barrels stacked six high! Despite its large production, the wines are all barrel-aged, with vineyards being aged separately and blended at the end of their barrel time — not before.

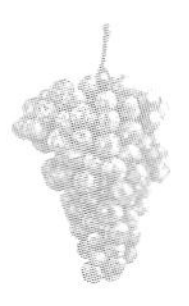

Mendocino Ridge: "Islands in the Sky"

Long recognized for its mountain-grown Zinfandel, Mendocino Ridge was awarded American viticultural area (AVA) status in October 1997, making it the world's first non-contiguous viticultural area — that is, the vineyards making up this viticultural area are not adjacent to each other. The vineyards, all six of them totaling 75 acres, are located above 1,200 feet elevation on three coastal ridges in the southwest corner of Mendocino County. They are scattered across the ridge tops "like islands in the sky," says Dan Dooling, owner of the 2,600-foot elevation Mariah Vineyard located on Mountain View Road above Point Arena. Dan was one of the driving forces behind the AVA application.

Because of this unusual aspect of the AVA, the Bureau of ATF was skeptical that the region was deserving of its own viticultural area. But Dan knew that these ridge tops shared common elements that distinguished them from elevations below 1,200 feet. The vineyards sit above the coastal fog line. When the valleys below are cold and damp throughout the day, the mountain vineyards often bask in sunlight. However, the fog that nightly curls about the lower elevations keeps the nighttime temperatures in the vineyards above cool. This combination of sun above and fog below creates ideal conditions for the Zinfandel grapes to achieve full ripeness without raisining. The wines made from these grapes are indeed distinctive.

Dan and his fellow growers provided bundles of weather, soil, topographical, and historical data to ATF to support their claim to AVA status. It took over three years for the ATF to be convinced that the unconnected vineyards formed a uniform area.

The first settlers to the Mendocino ridges were Italian immigrants who came to the area to peel tan bark, and in some cases to carve out Zinfandel vineyards in the midst of dense redwood and Douglas fir forests above the coastal fog line. Remnants of three of the original vineyards planted between 1880 and 1900 have survived: Zeni and Ciapusci Vineyards on Fish Rock Road, and DuPratt Vineyard on Greenwood Ridge. These three vineyards contain the last old vines Zinfandel plantings in the region. At the time of Prohibition, acreage totaled about 350. In 1987, it totaled about 30.

These were the three old vineyards that captured the imagination of Jed Steele during his years in the mid-to-late 1970s as the founding winemaker for Edmeades Winery in Philo. These coastal ridge vineyards, roughly between the points where the Navarro and Gualala rivers empty into the ocean, provided, according to Jed, "a classic match of grape variety with a particular climate, one that leads to the ultimate in winemaking fruit." [28] (See also "Steele Wines.")

Inspired by the quality of fruit from these three historic vineyards, Dan and Vicki Dooling established Mariah Vineyard in 1978. In 1994, Steve Alden established Alden Ranch Vineyards on Fish Rock Road. During the 1990s, George Zeni increased his Zinfandel vineyard from two to 12 acres, so by January 2000, Mendocino Ridge vineyard acreage was back up to 80, and rapidly increasing.

Mariah Vineyards and Zeni Ranch are two examples of Mendocino Ridge Zinfandel vineyards.

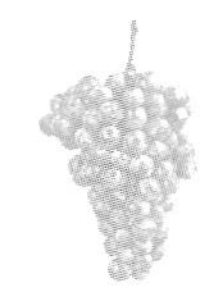

A Vineyard Called Mariah

Acting upon Jed Steele's recommendation, in mid-April 1987 I was on my way to Boonville in the pastoral Anderson Valley to meet with DuPratt Vineyard manager, Steve Tylicki. After a brief tour of the beautiful six-acre DuPratt on Greenwood Road, Steve took me to Mariah Vineyards, which is two ridges south of DuPratt, and the vineyard that Jed Steele had said I had to see to believe.

The day was bright and sunny. When Steve and I turned onto Mountain View Road out of Anderson Valley for the steep and twisting 15-mile journey up to Mariah Vineyards, I let my imagination run free with the changing views. What would Mariah be like, I wondered? Why does Jed Steele think it so special? When we turned onto the lane that leads from Mountain View Road to the Dooling home, I was awestruck by the vista. The lane is bordered on one side by towering, ancient Douglas firs and on the other by the immaculately tended 20-acre Zinfandel vineyard. At the end of the lane was the hand-built redwood house. What a special place indeed, I thought.

Dan and Vickie Dooling and their two small children met Steve and me on the deck of their sturdy rustic house that stood under an enormous bay tree at the edge of the lovely vineyard. Vicki was pregnant with their third child. I was later to learn that even paradise has its limits when a couple is trying to raise two (soon to be four) small children in such a remote location. Since the generator that produced their electricity was turned off at night, it was a great surprise to their children that when they went to San Francisco for the first time, the city lights stayed on all night. "They must have a lot of generators," Vicki recalled one of them saying.

The day being so lovely, we all sat around a table on the deck overlooking the vineyard, and Dan told us about the creation of Mariah Vineyards. It was Zinfandel that Dan and Vicki had selected as their grape.

28 "Coastal Ridge Zinfandel," Ridge Review, Vol. 5, No. 1, 1985, 7.

Their award-winning 20-acre vineyard had been a labor of love. "When we planted it in 1980, Zinfandel was only $250 per ton," he recalled.

However, even before buying the 90-acre property (purchased out of a 1,200-acre ranch), Dan knew that the fruit from the DuPratt, Zeni, and Ciapucci Zinfandel Vineyards was greatly treasured, especially by Jed Steele, then winemaker for Kendall-Jackson. In fact, Jed had much to do with Dan's decision to plant Zinfandel. He promised he would buy the fruit if Dan planted Zinfandel. Jed felt strongly that the Mariah Vineyard had a nearly perfect trilogy of climate, *terroir,* and varietal matchup to grow Zinfandel.

Given the location, the establishment of Mariah Vineyards was a true pioneering venture. Before laying out the vineyard on the flat-to-rolling mountain top terrain that includes the highest point of the property, Dan had to log off Douglas fir and clear away madrone, tan oak, thickets of intense manzanita, and brush. He sold the good timber to help finance the grapegrowing effort.

Dan and Vicky Dooling (photo by George Rose)

Once the land was cleared, Dan and Vicki set about fencing their vineyard (that's another story), and then planting it using UC Davis clone #6 budded to AxR-1 and St. George rootstock. They admit to making some early mistakes, although using AxR-1 was not one of them. Their location is too remote for phylloxera concerns. The most notable mistake was to establish the vineyard to the head-trained, dry-farmed style. Dan planted 12 acres in 1980 spaced 10 x 10 and another eight in 1982. The first crop was harvested in 1983, and yielded only three tons of hand selected clusters. Dan recalled the day he delivered the crop to Jed.

"This looks great," said Jed. "When are you bringing in the rest of it?"

"This is the rest of it," replied Dan.

Because of the acid-rich loam-type forest soil (today known as Josephine and Hugo loams) and heavy rainfall — from 75 to 135 inches annually — the grapes on head trained vines were exposed to extreme mildew and bunch rot conditions. "The young head trained vines formed little humidity traps," said Dan. "I was lucky to have saved even three tons that year."

After the 1983 harvest, Dan installed trellises and a drip irrigation system of his own design for the entire 20 acres. By training the vines to cordons, Dan was able to spread the canopy along the wires and up to the top two wires, for air and light penetration. For irrigation, he created a lovely spring-fed 175-foot x 600-foot pond that is 22 feet deep. To run the irrigation pump on his mountaintop, Dan uses a Volkswagen engine hooked up to a Berkeley PTO pump to lift water from the pond to the top of the vineyard.

As a result of this change, in 1984 the yield was three to 3½ tons.

This system of trellises and drip irrigation allowed Dan to work better with the natural conditions of the vineyard and reduce costs.

First, trellises allowed him to spread out cordons, space spurs, and position shoots, so the constant winds that blow across his mountain top can dry the heavy moisture efficiently.

Second, the trellises allowed Dan to develop natural farming practices that in return have lowered his costs overall. By drilling a cover crop mix into two tons per acre of compost spread over the vineyard, he has controlled erosion, fixed and retained atmospheric nitrogen, and created a biomass that he lets grow for 18 months. He controls the crop with an average of three mowings, using a flail mower. These practices have helped to reduce costs by reducing the equipment running time and draft power/fuel ratio.

But the real savings, Dan said, are in "the hidden cost benefits of the cover — beneficial insect habitat, reduction of compaction by running machinery on a mowed cover, and on and on." As the cover crop became established, he found that he needed to disk only every other row, cutting his tractor time in half. Also, when he sulfured and tended his vines in other ways, he ran his machinery over the mowed cover crop, which kept dust to a minimum — thereby reducing spider-mite infestation. "It is hard to put a dollar figure on these savings, but I know they are significant," he noted.

More recently, Dan has converted to a permanent clover crop over the entire vineyard.

Dan expressed a long-term commitment to growing world class Zinfandel on Mariah Vineyards. "I'm past the pioneering stage," he told us that afternoon in 1987. "Now I am fine tuning farming methods. I'm becoming a serious grapegrower. I've outgrown my five to seven years of ignorance and the mistakes that went with that ignorance. It takes time and mistakes to become a viticulturist."

In order to protect the quality he has wrested from his mountaintop, Dan acquired a Mariah trademark in 1985, which carried with it a responsibility for quality assurance. The trademark gave Dan and Vicki legal leverage to deny vineyard designation or the use of the name on any wines that are not 100 percent Mariah Vineyards fruit, or do not meet premium wine standards.

By now, the afternoon sun was waning, and my first visit to the ridgetop vineyards of southwest Mendocino County was coming to a close. It had been wonderful to bask in the warm mountain sunshine, listening to Dan's account of how he and Vicki worked side by side to establish the immaculate vineyard that lay before us. They even brought out their photo album of the step-by-step transformation. Now, it was time for a walk to the vineyard's highest blocks, which overlooked the ocean six miles to the west, to watch the late afternoon light gleaming off the ruffled water that lay at our feet. Dan and Steve went ahead, to talk about technical matters. My more leisurely pace soon brought me a companion in the form of 6-year-old Nicole, who took me by the hand and began telling me about what life was like for her on the mountaintop.

The memory of that visit had left a deep and vivid impression in my mind, so it was with great pleasure that I revisited Mariah Vineyards in June 1991, and again in spring 1993. I was investigating the economics of Zinfandel at that time, and wondered how the Doolings were getting along. Was their venture an economic success? Although they had sold their grapes to Edmeades and then Kendall-Jackson from 1983 until 1990, they were now selling to Fetzer for its reserve vineyard-designate program.

Their vineyard was thriving, and their contract with Fetzer Winery provided a fair return on their grapes, they told me. But the location made it difficult to improve their economics by increasing yield. From their 20 acres, they were averaging 2½ to 3½ tons per acre, which was about all the crop that the vines could bring to ripeness in that climate and soil while retaining the quality that had earned Mariah Vineyard its wall of gold medals. "I have to ripen my fruit evenly to 23° to 24.5° Brix before the fall rains come," said Dan. "Since bud-break and blossoming are on an average four weeks later than at lower elevations and inland locations, I have to maintain tight control of production to bring the crop to desired ripeness."

Dan prunes to four to five spurs per cordon, and later bunch thins any weak or over-cropped vines. He has dropped up to 30 percent of the crop in some years.

But no matter how many steps Dan takes to maintain grape quality, Mother Nature has remained an unpredictable and daunting force. In September 1989, a storm (with a wind called Mariah) blew in at 85 mph, downing 30 rows — completely disregarding the steel stakes. Only some of the downed crop was salvageable. Then in May 1990, a storm dumped 17 inches of rain in four days. The vines were in bloom, and over half the primary crop was shattered. Primary crop yield in September was just 18 tons. The vines did, however, throw a 20-ton second crop that ripened to 20° Brix. In appreciation for Dan's commitment to quality, Fetzer Winery, who had contracted Mariah Vineyard's entire 1990 crop, took both the 18-ton primary crop and the 20-ton second crop, at a fair price for both.

"Fetzer Winery," said Dooling, "is in the forefront of sustainable agriculture. They understand that their primary assets are their growers and their grapes. They understand both the investment required and the risks faced by premium grape growers, an understanding that has benefited both Fetzer and us."

Dan and Vicki's only option for improving their economics was to establish their own Mariah Vineyards label, which they did in 1991. Their 1991 estate-bottled Mariah Vineyards Zinfandel consisted of just 300 cases, and was made by Jed Steele. In 1992, they produced 400 cases, but in 1993, they felt the quality was not up to their standards for their estate bottling, so they sold the wine on the bulk market. Their last Mariah Vineyards Zinfandel was the 1995 vintage.

These four Mariah Vineyards vintages, however, were enough to catch the attention of Brown-Forman, the parent company of Fetzer. In 1996, Brown-Forman proposed an alliance with Mariah, whereby it would acquire the "Mariah" trademark as part of its artisan series, and take all Mariah Vineyards grapes to be bottled under the Mariah label. It took two years of negotiations to complete the 15-year alliance agreement.

Under terms of the alliance, which was signed in 1998, Brown-Forman pays the Doolings a premium price for their grapes. As part of the deal, Dan travels for Brown-Forman and the Mariah label 30 days each year, and continues to have a say on quality issues of Mariah wine. The wine is currently vinified at the Fetzer facility by winemaker Nancy Walker. "Nancy makes the wine in small open-top fermentors, hand-punches the wine, and ages it in 100 percent French oak barrels, about 25 percent new. Brown-Forman is dedicated to the highest quality production," Dan explained.

A nice deal for what was a 400-case production brand! This new-age pioneer farmer has come a long way from the days when he hand-watered his new vines from a tank truck.

"We had taken our small brand, Mariah Vineyards, as far as we could," said Dan. "I am amazed that Brown-Forman should have been interested in acquiring the trademark, because we were such a small operation. But obviously they saw the potential. Now, production is 3,000 cases. The 1996 vintage, the first under Brown-Forman's Mariah label, won a double gold at the 1998 San Francisco competition, and *Bon Apetit* placed it among the year's 10 best wines. The retail price per bottle has gone from $18 to $34. It is also on some of the best wine lists in New York. So the potential was obviously there."

In 1997, production under the Mariah label consisted of 2,700 cases of Zinfandel and 300 cases of Syrah from Dan's newly established 11-acre Syrah vineyard. Wine bottled under the Mariah label must be made from 100 percent Mariah Vineyards fruit.

Dan, however, did not sign away the store when he signed the alliance agreement with Brown-Forman. Besides the trademark Mariah, he retained three additional registered trademarks for future winemaking ventures: Mariah Vineyards; Syriah Vineyards; and Islands in the Sky. "I don't have any Mariah Vineyards fruit to use for these trademarks," admitted Dan. "But there is always a little Mendocino Ridge fruit available. I do not have to use my own fruit to use these trademarks."

In February 2000, I asked Dan about his thoughts on the pioneering venture that he had undertaken 21 years earlier. Had the economics finally improved sufficiently so that he and Vicki and their four children can get off the mountain when they need to? If he were doing it again, would he? Would he still plant Zinfandel?

"Yes, I would do it all over again," said Dan, "but I hesitated for a second or two. Ten years ago, I would not have hesitated at all. The difference between then and now is, perhaps, because I am older, I can see the toll it has taken on us, particularly on Vicki, who has had to get four children to schools in Point Arena and Mendocino every day. It's been hard on her. It's been hard work for me, too, but I have kept my 'Peterbuilt.' People sometimes forget that I had a job before we bought this property and moved up here to become grapegrowers. I was a long-distance trucker, and I loved it. I still miss it, and love to go on a run. But I drive only about 15,000 miles each year now, compared to 150,000 before we moved up here. Between trips, my truck just sits in the shed resting and waiting for its next run off the mountain. Some people think I am nuts to keep that big 'Peterbuilt' truck for 15,000 miles of work, but it is my diesel magic carpet ride out of here, when I really need a break."

"Now, when I do go on a run, I am glad to get back home. Even though our electricity is still produced by a generator, we have added onto our house as the children got older, and it is very comfortable. It's home. Vicki can get away more now, too, especially to ski in the winter, and to a resort with a swimming pool in the summer. She looks forward to the day when she can spend six months in Italy, though.

"Would I plant Zinfandel again? Yes, even though it is a pain in the ass to grow. It has red grapes, ripe grapes, and raisined grapes all at the same time, and it is a bitch to pick. But there is something about the soil here and its variety: when it is a good year, it is wonderful. That makes it worthwhile. Also, I was a blue-collar kind of guy when I planted this vineyard, and Zinfandel was a blue-collar kind of grape. We have both come a long way. I now wear an expensive suit, tie, and shoes when I go on the road, and my wine sells for $80 a bottle in a New York restaurant. So Zinfandel was a good match-up with Mariah."

In addition, Dan and Vicki have always pointed out that hopes of great economic rewards were not what led them to search out their mountaintop location. "You won't get rich farming a mountain top vineyard," he said. "It is the indescribable satisfaction that comes from overcoming the obstacles — including the wind 'Mariah' — associated with pioneering a piece of land, that are the biggest rewards. You clear the land, you prepare it, and plant your vines, and watch them grow. You see wines made from your grapes win gold medals. And then, when you are working the higher ground on a sunny day, you have the ocean sparkling right at your feet — it's that, too — the ocean, the trees, the lifestyle that makes it worthwhile. It's part of the reason why I trucked 2 million miles over the road in a big rig those earlier 12 years — to finance this dream.

"Maybe the only thing I would change, if I were to do it over," continued Dan, almost as an afterthought, "I would not have come up here so young. Vicki and I had just gotten married; I had been trucking every day until we came up here, and we really never had any time to enjoy just being young-marrieds, partying, staying out late, going skiing on the weekends. Brown-Forman held one of their big meetings up here last summer, and had come in by helicopter. Nicole, my eldest child, now16, asked if she could go for a ride, and Vicki went with her. When they came back, Vicki said to me, 'Well, that was counterproductive.'"

"What do you mean?" I asked her.

"'I always thought we lived in the middle of nowhere; now I *know* we do,'" she replied. "That is when I realized that she had never been up in a helicopter before, although I had been several times. So it's been tough on both of us, but more particularly on Vicki, to live up here and raise four children.

"But we did it, all the children are doing well, and now the economics are better. Our Zinfandel is gaining national and even international recognition, and this is definitely home. I really would not have wanted it any other way."

George Zeni — Au Naturel

In June 1991, four years after my visit to DuPratt and Mariah Vineyards, it was another fresh and sunny morning, and I was at last on my way to the Zeni Ranch. The ranch sits at 1,800-foot elevation on Fish Rock Road above Yorkville in Anderson Valley. I got to Yorkville, little more than a road sign and a post office on Highway 128, about 10:00 a.m. A few miles further on, I made the left turn onto Fish Rock Road, and soon found myself climbing a narrow road lined by a thick forest of tall redwood trees. The air was crisp and exhilarating as up, up I went. Then brightness, a clearing — no, a lovely small mountain meadow. I stopped the car, got out, and when I slammed the door in the brilliant quietness, I startled doe and twin fawns feeding along the meadow's edge nearest the road.

I watched them a few minutes as they pranced off, indulging my senses with the quiet, clean, tangible beauty. Then I resumed my journey.

Shortly after passing through the Maillard Redwood Preserve, I ran out of paved road. Considerably slowed, I bumped along over the graveled surface until I found myself approaching a ridge upon which I could see a couple of horses, an old barn, and above them, vineyards. Just as I was about to follow the road's curve to the left, I saw a driveway angling to my right. Over this drive was an oak banner with "Zeni Ranch" carved into it.

I had arrived at yet another generator-powered Zinfandel paradise!

Upon parking my car in front of the historic ranch house, which enfolded the original cabin George's father had built before 1900, I saw approaching me a weathered but vigorous-looking man wearing a red baseball cap, old plaid shirt, and old jeans. He was walking with a slight limp (from a broken leg he received in World War II. The leg was later rebroken when his tractor fell over on him when he was working the ranch.) It was George Zeni himself.

As I got out of my car, he greeted me with a smile, warm brown eyes, and a work-roughened handshake. "So you found us okay?" he queried. "Well, let me call up Shirley [his wife], then we can all talk."

Shirley was found in the lush garden that spills down the slope across Fish Rock Road. When she joined us, we retreated to the cool kitchen, where the stove is propane and the electricity is produced by ranch generator. After cups of coffee were placed on the table, George began to tell the story of how his family came to this place and planted their first Zinfandel vines just about a century ago.

In 1892, George's father Eduino Zeni came to America from his native village of Cavedago, in the Lombardy province, which was then part of Austria. Just 24 years old, he worked his way to the west, and by 1897, found 160 acres he liked on Signal Ridge between Gualala and Yorkville. It was government land, and he decided to homestead it. Once he had cleared the land and built a cabin, he sent for his mother and asked her to bring him a bride-to-be. His father had died when Eduino was a child. In 1901, mother and bride-to-be arrived, and within two days, Eduino and his bride were married. In 1923, George Zeni was born, the eleventh of 12 children.

Today George lives on the original homestead on Fish Rock Road with his second wife, Shirley, his son Ray, and Ray's family. He also has an older son, John, and daughter, Linda, both of whom help George with ranch operations

Eduino planted 25 to 30 acres of vineyard between 1900 and 1925, mostly with Zinfandel but with some Carignane, Palomino, Grey Reisling, and Muscat mixed in.

The winery was bonded in 1910. The earliest plantings provided only enough grapes to produce wine for Eduino's family. By the time of Prohibition, said George, the family had enough grapes to make wine for sale to Swedish, Finnish, and Italian tie-makers living in Gualala. "They had to go to the Italians because that's the only ones who grew grapes. They all used to walk from Gualala clear up here on weekends, and pack eight to 10 gallons of wine clear down there so they could drink wine during the week while they were making ties. Yeah!"

All vines were propagated from cuttings. "We just took a cane, about this long, [spacing his hands about two feet apart] and just leave one bud on top and just dig a hole, and put it in the ground, throw a little water on it, stomp on it, cuss it a little.... Back in the early days, you never threw any canes away.... I've had people tell me, 'Aw, if you use common stock they won't live that long.' [Common-stock vines are propagated from cuttings, as opposed to being budded to phylloxera-resistant rootstock.] Well, hell, these vines here's 100 years old, and hell, they're livin' just fine. So how much longer you want the damn things to live?" exclaimed George.

Both grapegrowing and winemaking in the early years were what George calls crude. "Everything was natural. I never knew what a herbicide was in them days. They never knew anything about any chemicals in those days. About the only thing we used was sulfur for mildew.... And we never *heard* of waterin' down a grape. We used to get maybe three to four, two to three tons per acre, three to four tons when it was new vines.... Today, it's coming out with organic, but we didn't call it that in the old days. Zeni's didn't call it [organic]. It's just the way they did it in Italy.

"When they first come out with stainless steel tanks, we all thought they were crazy. Hell, you can't make wine out of a stainless steel tank or glass-lined tank. If you want to make good wine, you got to have good barrels and good grapes, and don't take nothin' out, and don't put nothin' in. If you got good grapes, leave them alone."

However authentic it might have been, Zeni's crude winemaking lost ground to technology, commercialism, and state regulations after Repeal. Following World War II, the Zeni family began to sell their grapes to commercial wineries. The reputation of their mountain grapes, dry farmed and grown without chemicals, was established by the home winemaking trade, and also by the local wine barter trade that had grown up during and following Prohibition. Commercial wineries such as Italian Swiss Colony and Pedroncelli "come out here, because they wanted our grapes. Later, Ridge, too, came over here for a couple of years. They wanted the mountain grapes, 'cause there was more sugar and it'd make a better wine. In fact, it's still doing that right now. Why do you think Kendall-Jackson comes over here and buys Ciapusci's grapes and my grapes? That's where they get all their gold medals. Hell, I must have a dozen gold medals over there, Kendall-Jackson has over there at Lower Lake. So does Ciapusci."

Today, only 2½ acres of the 30-acre vineyard remain. They produce between five and seven tons of grapes — total. In 1992, Zeni Zinfandel commanded a price per ton in the $1,000 range. "At those prices, I can afford to cut back on Christmas trees a little, and expand my Zinfandel vineyard," said George, who has been growing about 80,000 Christmas trees. "Christmas trees are too much work now that my Zinfandel is getting the recognition and prices it deserves. I can afford to increase my vineyard about two acres per year over the next five years. I can make a dollar now, on Zinfandel at these prices."

George credits Jed Steele, who began his winemaking career with Edmeades in 1972 and bought Zeni Ranch grapes for the first time in 1979, with saving his vineyard. Upon recognizing the quality of the ridge top Zinfandel vineyards of southwest Mendocino with his Du Pratt/DePatie vintage in 1974, Steele treated these grapes to the same vinification practices accorded to the winery's other premium reds, including storage in French oak cooperage. In addition, the wines from each vineyard were kept separate, and each bottled under vineyard designation. When Steele went to Kendall-Jackson in 1981, he took the Dupratt, the Zeni, and the Ciapusci vineyards with him. (For additional discussion of Jed Steele and Zeni Zinfandel, see Lake County section.)

In 1988, Kendall-Jackson purchased Edmeades, and began vinifying the Zeni Zinfandel at that facility. Since then, the price per ton for Zeni grapes has risen considerably higher than $1,000, and the wine now retails for over $30 a bottle. It's a price that still dazes George.

"Did you ever think you'd live to see the day when Zinfandel from your grapes would bring such a price?" I asked him in a January 1998 telephone conversation.

"No, I never did," he replied, "not in my wildest dreams! Hell, I remember when it was two bits a gallon."

In 1991, Jed Steele left Kendall-Jackson to establish his own Steele Wines label. Zeni Ranch Zinfandel remains under contract to Kendall-Jackson through 2001.

The fair price now paid for his grapes, which have become famous among Zinfandel consumers and producers alike, has enabled George to embark upon his five-year expansion program.

In February 1999, I journeyed for a second time to the Zeni Ranch. I wanted to see the new plantings, and also to spend a day with George, who was in frail health.

This time, the day was overcast and threatening rain. Fragments of white mist clung to the walls of the valleys, and across the tips of the mountains. The 15-mile drive from Yorkville up through the redwood trees, past meadows, through more redwoods, and finally along the gravel road that provided glimpses of the rugged coastal mountains and thickly forested canyons, was breathtakingly beautiful. Just at the end of the gravel road, I once again found myself turning into the driveway that led to the historic ranch house identified by the hand-carved Zeni Ranch banner. I was again struck by the remoteness of the ranch, and by the incredible achievement of George's father, who came to the site on foot over 100 years ago. Here, he planted the vineyard and orchards and built his house by hand.

When I entered the house, George, who had been resting on a couch, sat up and greeted me with a robust handshake. His health may have been fragile, but his upright and well-muscled frame belied this fragility. True, his hair was now white, his eyesight was failing because of medications, and he had lost his summer tan. But he had not lost his enthusiasm for his beloved Zinfandel, his thriving vineyard, nor his sense of humor and colorful speech. Since raindrops had begun to fall and lunch was still simmering on the wood burning stove in the kitchen, we decided to take a turn through the vineyards before the weather got worse.

Leading the way to his big, well-used ranch truck, he invited me to climb in, and that is just what I did — climb in. As the truck gently chugged up through the vineyard, which was partly pruned already, George commented on the vines as he drove. From time to time, I asked him to stop for a photograph.

"Now this old vineyard is between 90 and 100 years old," he said, indicating the well tended, head-trained and pruned vineyard we were driving past. "Now this one," he said, indicating a newly established vineyard on his left, "I planted just last March. It isn't even a year old. I've pruned it back to just two buds per shoot. These vines were T-budded onto St. George rootstock, but all the ones in the milk cartons are the ones that didn't work," he explained. "So I replanted them with just rooted cuttings, common stock," he said, chuckling a little.

We drove on. "Now this here vineyard [indicating a new vineyard on the right] is four years old. Look at how it has grown. This is all non-irrigated, you know, so you have to give the roots some time to establish themselves before you start encouraging too much crop. 'Give up a year's crop now, and you gain two years' worth later on,' is how I see it," he said.

George Zeni

A little farther along, we came to a T-budded vineyard. "Remember that block of Grey Riesling I used to have?" he asked. "Well, this is it. I had it T-budded to Zinfandel, and they all grew. Only five or six didn't make it. I'll tell you, them son-of-a-guns really grew! They are just three years old now, but look at the canes. I had to come up here the last two years and cut off grapes. There were just too many for the vines to ripen. The root system is 100 years old, and the vines just took off."

A little further along, we came to another new vineyard, about two acres, established on rooted cuttings. "I've tied them all up," explained George, "but I really have to go back and cut them off to two buds. When you grow without water, you have to let the root system build up. Instead of losing a year, you gain a year in the end. When you dry farm, you have to do things just a little bit different than you would when you are watering. (This despite his region receiving as much as 75 inches of rain annually.) All that your vine is doing when you water is living off the nutrients and the water that you give it. Its roots don't go down into the ground. Then, after 30 to 35 years, they die, because they have been over-cropped and they never had a chance to establish their root system. For me, I believe in quality, not quantity." George still limits his production to four tons or less per acre — depending on the season and condition of the vines.

"Dry farming is nearly a lost art, isn't it?" I asked. "I know of only a few other growers besides yourself who have established new vineyards without water."

"Yes," agreed George, "because it doesn't provide you with quantity to make a living and pay for the god-darn high costs of buying the land and putting in a new vineyard. So you've got to have 10 to 15 tons per acre."

With his recent planting of new vines and T-budding the Grey Reisling with Zinfandel, George now has about nine to 10 acres, which was his goal when I visited him in 1991. He had about 500 more vines to plant in 1999, and was hoping to plant one pretty little flat area still in

Christmas trees the following year. "It depends," he said. "I'm getting old, you know. I've put a lot of hard work into this vineyard, too. Why, I remember how we had to wrestle with a redwood tree stump sometimes for three weeks to get the darned thing out. My dad put a lot of work into establishing this vineyard, but we put a lot of work into it, too." (George is 76 at this writing).

We were now back at the house and ready for lunch. But before we got out of the truck, George had a few more things to say about Zinfandel.

"Zinfandel producers have lost the Zinfandel flavor in the last 40 years. They are making Zinfandel too sweet. Zinfandel, the way we used to make it years and years ago, never was sweet. You picked the grapes at 22.5° or 23° Brix at the most, and you were supposed to feel Zinfandel going down over your tongue. It wasn't sweet, and it wasn't too harsh, but it was right there, you see. This is exactly what the UC Davis people have said, who have come over to see my vineyard. They told me that today's Zinfandel producers have lost the Zinfandel flavor.

" Zinfandel producers have lost the Zinfandel flavor in the last 40 years. They are making Zinfandel too sweet. You were supposed to feel Zinfandel going down over your tongue."

George Zeni

"Nowadays, these younger winemakers, and Kendall-Jackson, too, want the grapes to be 24° or 25° sugar, or even higher. But you get raisins at that sugar content, and the birds get more, so we get way less tonnage. They *must* have a water fairy come in, when they have that many raisins. But many younger winemakers think that Zinfandel made from grapes picked this ripe is the way Zinfandel is supposed to taste. Actually, it is not. Any old-timer will tell you that. There is nothing wrong with the wine. It is just too sweet to be Zinfandel. You should feel it going over your tongue. But everything changes, and that has changed, too."

One thing that hasn't changed, however, is George Zeni's dedication to growing his grapes with as little intervention as possible. "There's no secret," he said. "I just grow them the way the Old Man [his father] and all the old Italian growers did — without water. If you want quality, you have to dry farm. It's as simple as that. Other than that, I just disc 'em, sulfur 'em up, prune 'em back good, and otherwise leave them the hell alone."

The grapes crush into inky-black velvety wine overflowing with black fruit, spices, and earthy chocolate notes that is acknowledged by producers, consumers, and critics alike as some of the finest Zinfandel made. "Grapes have been good to the Zeni family. I must be doing something right," said George in conclusion, as we stepped out of the truck and headed toward the kitchen for that savory lunch we left simmering on the stove under Shirley's expert care. I don't think anyone could disagree.

As I headed down the rain-drenched mountain that afternoon, I was filled with admiration for the Zeni family and the busy, successful, and charming little ranch they have on that remote ridge-top high above Anderson Valley. I also kept thinking about George's views on the loss of true Zinfandel flavors, and his appreciation for his famous grapes. Might a George Zeni Zinfandel appear on the market when his contract with Kendall-Jackson is up in 2001? I wouldn't be surprised.

★ ★ ★ ★ ★

On November 17, 1999, George Zeni died peacefully at home with his wife and family by his side. When I talked to Shirley a few weeks later, she described to me George's last days.

"He died in the same room that he was born in. He was proud of this fact, and also that his two sisters, who were also born in this room, were with him when he died. It was a beautiful thing to see. Two days before he died, he called to me," she said. "When I approached him, he said to me, 'Hold my hand; I'm not here.' "

"His hand was ice cold," said Shirley.

The next night, Shirley thought that George, who was in a semi-coma, was in pain, so she called the hospice, who sent a person up. "The woman from hospice said the hearing is always the last of the senses to go," said Shirley. "So I said, 'Let us see if George can hear us.' So the woman said to George, 'George, are you dying?' Just for a moment, George opened his beautiful blue eyes, looked straight at us, and replied, 'How in hell should I know? I've never died before!' "

"Well," said Shirley, "George's son, Raymond, and I started laughing, since that was so typical of George. Those were his last words. What a nice last memory we have of him."

For my part, I shall always remember my last truck ride with George, and treasure his last thoughts to me on what a real Zinfandel should be.

May his soul rest in peace.

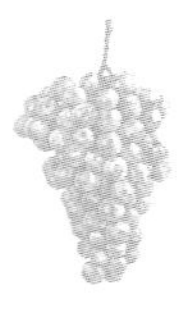

Sonoma County

Valle Rossi Vineyard

Sonoma County is worth a book in itself when it comes to Zinfandel. With over 4,600 acres of Zinfandel vineyards, it is the second largest Zinfandel grapegrowing region in California. Only San Joaquin County is larger. Because of the sheer number of Zinfandel growers and producers in Sonoma County, I have limited my selection to those that I became familiar with as a consequence of my initial research for ***PWV***. My apologies to all the other dedicated growers and producers who contribute to the great bounty of Zinfandel in Sonoma County.

Sonoma County has ten American viticultural areas (AVA): Alexander Valley; Carneros-Sonoma; Chalk Hill; Dry Creek Valley; Green Valley; Knights Valley; Russian River Valley; Sonoma Coast; Sonoma Mountain; and Sonoma Valley. All except Carneros-Sonoma and Sonoma Coast are famous for their Zinfandel. I have included vineyards and producers from several of these AVAs.

My odyssey into Sonoma County begins with my visit to Preston Vineyard and Winery, which was my first visit to the Dry Creek Valley when on assignment for ***PWV*** in 1986.

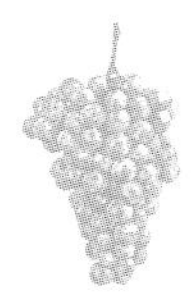

Zinfandel Paradise: Preston Vineyard and Winery

When I arrived in Dry Creek Valley one a mild and misty May 1986 morning in search of Preston Vineyards, I found myself in an incredibly beautiful Zinfandel grapegrowing region. With densely wooded, rugged-looking hillsides rising above rolling vineyard-covered knolls and the valley floor, and the entire scene intermittently veiled in swirling mists, it seemed a place you could visit only in your dreams. Yet here I was, for real, and so were Lou and Susan Preston, together with their viticulturist, John Clendenon, and winemaker Tom Farella, who now has his own Farella-Park label. (No Zin, though.) Kevin Hamel replaced Farella in 1989. Zinfandel is Prestons' original wine; the first vintage in 1975 from old vines was good for 500 cases.

"Zinfandel," said Lou Preston, after a greeting and brief introductions, "never has been out of favor with winemakers or consumers — only with tradespeople."

Preston Dry Creek Zinfandels were the first from that viticultural area that I had tasted. I discovered (never to forget) the almost signature jammy red raspberry fruit. "We like that jammy quality," said Lou back then, "so we go for the higher sugar, which drops the acids, and increases the pH, at least in our vineyards." For Tom Farella, achieving this quality meant, "We have to watch our grapes like a hawk as full ripeness approaches. When the pH of the fruit starts to rise suddenly, the integrity of the fruit is beginning to break down. You need to pick just before that happens. That way, you get the ripe jammy red raspberry character and also a wine that will gain some complexity in the bottle for a few years. But these are not intended to be long-ageing wines."

Although the Prestons liked full ripeness in their Zinfandel, they didn't like the alcohol to be over 14 percent. They had found that using open-top five-ton fermentors enabled excess alcohol to evaporate in the fermentation process. "If we used closed-top fermentors, our Zinfandel would go over 14 percent, given the ripeness of the grapes," said Tom. The wines were finished in 500-gallon oak upright tanks for one year, then in small one-, two-, and three-year-old Kentucky Blue Grass or A&K American oak barrels for an additional year. Total case production of Zinfandel in 1986 was about 4,500 cases.

Since Kevin Hamel came on board, some changes have been made. After a telephone conversation in February 1998 in which he provided a brief overview of these changes, we set a date for my first visit to the winery since he joined the Preston staff. I found him on a lovely early March afternoon standing in the shadow of the oak trees that border the stream along which runs the winery entrance. Tall, fair-haired, relaxed, and trim looking in a red plaid flannel shirt and jeans, he was watching a pair of steelhead trout in this protected tributary stream. With my approach, the steelheads disappeared, so we went into his office for a leisurely chat about Preston Vineyards Zinfandel.

Among the most notable changes since he joined the winery, he said, was the grafting over in 1990 and 1991 of Zinfandel vines planted from budwood selection or on sites unfavorable to them, to the Rhône varieties Syrah, Mourvedre, and Grenache. "We found that some blocks of Zinfandel consistently were disappointing. The color didn't develop; the flavor didn't develop. One block in particular, on a good slope with that gravelly red soil, and budded from some old vine wood from the Mead Ranch (Napa), gave us our worst Zinfandel — poor color, low sugar, a lot of bunch rot — no matter how we nursed it along. Yet right across the avenue was a Syrah block that gave us consistently great Syrah. So we took the hint, and grafted the Zinfandel over to the Syrah. That was a case of just being a site, perhaps with a particular micro-climate, that the Zinfandel didn't like.

"A couple other blocks also have been problematic, so we have either taken them out and replanted to Rhônes, or grafted them. This way, since 1992, only our best Zinfandel blocks remain, which consist of three blocks of vines 80 years or more old and four younger blocks budded from the old vine wood, for a total of 14.5 acres. All are on St. George rootstock. We are also looking to convert a four-acre block currently planted with Cabernet Sauvignon on AxR-1 to Zinfandel, in 1997. Now, we make just one Zinfandel, about 2,000 to 2,500 cases, down from the 4,000 of the late 1980s. It is a blend of Zinfandel planted only to favorable sites and to favorable budwood selection. We gave up some vines, and production, in order to make not only the best Zinfandel possible, but also the best wines overall from this property. This has been the most important evolution in their Zinfandel program for the Prestons, since 1986."

The other major change in Preston's Zinfandel program under Kevin's guidance has been in oak storage. "Storage is now in two-, three-, and four-year-old French oak — no new oak, and no more American oak. I got rid of the American oak the first year I came. But it wasn't for snobbish reasons, or maybe it was, I don't know. I found that new American oak from that period just overpowered the wine. It also lent a hard, tannic character to the wine that I didn't think was appropriate.

"We don't use brand new wood for any of our red wines," Kevin continued. "The small amount of new wood we *do* buy is used to barrel-ferment our two white varieties, which benefit from the structure new wood contributes. These two white wines, Marsanne and Semillon, can, when very ripe, lack acidity and be overly fat. New oak can balance that.

"Our conservatism with respect to new oak is rooted in our all-estate philosophy. We have worked very hard to find varieties which will match our soil and climate — as well as our temperaments. We want to express the character of *this* place. Most of the varieties we make do not need (or will not support) much new wood. This impression was strengthened during a trip my family and I took to southern France in 1993. The wines from that region see very little new wood, and yet they can be profound. Too much new wood also tends to equalize wines. Even good fruit with too much good oak will taste like any other wine with too much good oak.

"New oak can also make the wines less refreshing. It makes them a little bit harder to drink, a little more fatiguing to the palate."

Kevin at the same time complimented the Zinfandel style of Doug Nalle (Nalle Wines) and Grady Wann (Quivira). Both these Zinfandels, he felt, were elegant, fruity wines in which the new French oak was only a part of the total character. Also, he admired Dave Rafanelli's Zinfandel, which was aged in more new French oak for even a longer period. "It has enough stuffing, is concentrated enough, to carry that amount of new wood," he said.

Like many of his fellow winemakers, however, Kevin has brought in a few new American oak barrels to try out on his Zinfandel. "I want to see if the coopering of American oak has really changed as much as people say it has, or whether people have become more accepting of the American oak flavors. It will be for our edification as well as to perhaps add a top note to the Zinfandel. If new oak is used judiciously, I believe it can enhance our Zinfandel by adding another layer of flavor."

With that exception, style and winemaking practices have not changed that much. Perhaps Kevin (who came to Preston after two vintages with Santino/Renwood, in Amador, where he was assistant winemaker to Scott Harvey) relies more on taste than numbers to determine harvest date. "The grapes have to taste ripe for flavor and that jammy quality we've always liked. The numbers are used to back up our taste and visual impressions," he said.

Open-top stainless steel or redwood fermentors are still the choice, and fermentation is still warm (up to 90°+F). Kevin, however, no longer inoculates the wine, depending instead, on the omnipresent indigenous winery yeasts. "I've gone to the lazy way," he laughed.

With these details out of the way, Kevin and I fell into a relaxed conversation about some of the differences he found between Amador and Dry Creek Valley Zinfandels. "In Amador County, the fruit has a peppery, pungent character. On the palate, it has a combination of tannin and acid that gives an impression of an austere wine. So those wines need longer time in the cellar to soften, which I believe is often the case with high altitude wines. Here in Dry Creek Valley, the Zinfandel has more of a floral character. It has a more pronounced berry-like character, which is sometimes high toned like cherry or raspberry, or sometimes in the strawberry/plumy camp. I find the northern Sonoma County wines less tannic, but really no less alcoholic.

"It doesn't seem to me that there is ever a problem getting alcohol in Zinfandel. But the tannin structure is different. For that reason, I used to think the Amador wines could sometimes benefit from fining, but I've never felt a need to fine Zinfandel here. In fact, I would like a little more backbone to them — a little more tannin. But you get what you get. Nor have I filtered. It doesn't seem to be necessary. We used to filter the red wines here, but even those wines at times threw sediment. As long as the wines finish malolactic and alcoholic fermentation, and clarify, I don't see any need to filter."

"What else have you learned about Dry Creek Zinfandel?" I asked.

"These wines — at least our wines — are best when bottled relatively young — with a relatively short barrel time," he replied without hesitation.

"We used to bottle them at 18 to 20 months old. Now, we bottle them at 11 months. You ask yourself, 'What do people like about Zinfandel? What do *I* like about it?' It's the up-front fruit character. It seems to me that you begin to lose that as the wines spend their second year in barrel."

"That's an amazing point," I responded, "because what did people think Zinfandel's great appeal was 10 years ago, for heaven's sake? If it wasn't the fruit then, why is it now? What was it then?"

"That's a good question," said Kevin. "I'm not sure what the answer is. Partly, I think people were following the Cabernet Sauvignon and Bordeaux model, thinking, well, if we want the wine to be taken seriously, then we need to make it along the same lines as we make a Cabernet or Bordeaux. I think we can make a very good wine that way, and it really does depend on what you're after."

This, of course, was a fascinating point, and, I believe, a central one regarding the evolution of Zinfandel as a world class red table wine: that winemakers have stopped trying to treat it like a Cabernet Sauvignon, and have begun to learn its own distinctive character. This point is echoed by Jed Steele in discussing the development of his Zinfandel wines.

"Here at Preston, we emphasize up-front fruit," Kevin continued. "I think it depends upon when you want to drink the wine. If you want to drink the wine young, then you should bottle it young. It doesn't mean the wines won't last. But if you plan on bottling the wines at 20 months old, then you should plan on leaving them in the bottles for a while. I think you get to a point after 16 to 18 months in barrel where you change the nature of the flavors, and flavors that you get are those that need some time in the bottle to develop into an expression of the fruit."

"The opinion I have occasionally read or heard over my 10 years of research," I commented, "has been along the lines of 'Zinfandel is lovely and fruity when released, but in a few years, the fruit will fade, leaving nothing enjoyable.' Specifically, I'm thinking about a column by Rod Smith. 'Why,' he wrote, 'does Zinfandel have this reputation of not being age-worthy, of being all fruit for a few years then doing a quick fade?' [29] The classic comment, though, one Jed Steele told to me, was, 'With all this fruit, it's almost too good to be good!' What do you think? Do young wines have *just* up-front fruit?"

"The 1992 vintage was the first Zinfandel that we bottled young. It was delicious then, and when I tasted it recently [1996], the wine not only has retained its fruit, but also a lot of other interesting things have developed. So I think, yes, these young Zinfandels do have more going for them than just the up-front fruit. Even if they didn't, frankly I'm mystified when I hear people say that Zinfandel has great fruit but nothing else. The question is, 'Why do we drink wine?' Is it not for pleasure? If that great fruit character of Zinfandel tastes so good when it's young, and since most

[29] Rod Smith, *The San Francisco Chronicle*, November 18, 1987

people drink their wines a few weeks after they've purchased them, what's the problem? Is there guilt complex going on here, or what?"

On the subject of ageing, though, Kevin said he hadn't yet had enough time to track his wines on their ageability. The oldest Zinfandel under the new regimen is the 1991 — which was the first made from the vineyards now in production.

In 2001, the Prestons entered their 26th year of estate Zinfandel production. They release just one Zinfandel at a comparatively affordable price for an estate-produced Dry Creek Zinfandel ($19 for the 1999). Affordable, enjoyable, consistently well made from the best fruit their plantings can provide — that's still the Prestons' (and Kevin's) operating principle in making Zinfandel.

"The thing about Zinfandel," said Kevin, "is that it is distinct and original, and so it shouldn't be available to just a few people. Our Zinfandel has always emphasized the ripe fruit of our Dry Creek vineyards, and is made to be enjoyable at release — or put down for a few years. I feel fortunate here in that Lou [Preston] doesn't chase reviews, though we like to get them.

"We've sat down and talked about the development of wine style and the creation of new products. We are all pretty much aware that if you want to get people's attention, there are recipes, which includes new wood, high alcohol, and super ripe fruit. We always come away from these discussions agreeing that we don't want to go in that direction. So we follow our own style, believing that if we are consistent over the years and make balanced wines which are distinctive and reflect this property, we'll make friends."

★ ★ ★ ★ ★

In January 2001, Preston Vineyard and Winery released winemaker Kevin Hamel as part of a downsizing. "We became a small winery overnight," said Lou Preston, when I called him to get the details. "Until Susan and I made this decision, we were making 16,000 cases a year, with capability of going to 25,000 cases. Zinfandel accounted for 3,000 cases. Since we crush everything on premise, our facility was not big enough to accommodate the grapes if they all got ripe at the same time. When that happened, we had problems maintaining wine quality. Now, we will produce just 5,000 cases. Zinfandel will account for 500 to 700 cases a year.

"I felt a need to downsize for two reasons. We have owned our vineyards for nearly 30 years, and I know that only some blocks produce top quality fruit. I know where the good stuff is. Yet we were crushing everything. Also, for some years, most of my time has been spent in travelling and administration. I was getting sick of it and wishing for more of a hand in winemaking. The only way I could do that was to downsize to a winery of about 5,000 cases per year.

"Our focus will be narrower, concentrating on just the best fruit, or the fruit that best suits us stylistically. We will use Zinfandel fruit from only the oldest and best blocks, and sell the remainder of the wine in bulk. We will remain flexible enough to produce an occasional 100 case reserve lot from especially good fruit in exceptional vintages.

"Our other prototypical Dry Creek Valley wine will be Sauvignon Blanc. Zinfandel and Sauvignon Blanc will make up about one-half of our production. Red Rhônes and Barbera will make up the other half."

Lou is resuming his role as winemaker. He will continue producing Zinfandel in the jammy red berry style, but with a little more extraction. Lou's intention is to showcase the characteristics of the Preston vineyards. It will continue to be a style with mid-range alcohol content, and will be soft, fruity, and approachable upon release. "This isn't the style that gets the rave reviews, or commands the highest prices," acknowledged Lou. "Nonetheless, it is the style we like best, and suits our customers best. It is a wonderful wine with food.

"I have talked to many people who have said they wished they could go back to being just a small producer of only the highest quality estate wine, but feel that they cannot. It isn't that hard to do — you just do it — at least when you and your family are the sole owners," said Lou in closing. "I am once again excited about winemaking, and look forward to rebuilding our winery as a small operation."

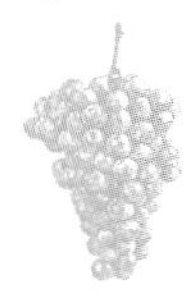

J. Pedroncelli Winery

My second visit to Zinfandel producers while on assignment for *Practical Winery & Vineyard* in 1986 took me on a short drive north on Highway 101 to Canyon Road, west of Geyserville. There, I was to meet the Pedroncellis, who have made a varietally labeled Zinfandel since 1955. Canyon Road is within the Dry Creek Valley viticultural area.

The Pedroncellis' approach to Zinfandel has gone through a few changes over the years.

In the beginning, winemaker John Pedroncelli's main concern was to make a soft, approachable, and affordable Zinfandel that would match well with food. To that end, grapes for his 15,000-case production Sonoma Zinfandel were picked between 22° and 23.5° Brix and fermented cool in 35-ton stainless steel closed-top tanks. They received a low pressure sprinkle-over several times each day, and the skins were taken off before dryness to minimize heavy tannin extraction. The wine was aged in well-seasoned American oak barrels for 15 months or longer to soften tannins and add a little complexity without overwhelming the palate with oak flavors. The Brix at harvest and time in oak barrels depended upon the style of wine being produced. The mature fruit produced a darker, more intensely flavored and full-bodied wine that needed longer time in oak to soften, and would continue to develop complexity for several years in the bottle.

Given the full-flavored fruit character of his grapes that came with the location, soil, and age of his vines, Pedroncelli did not feel that a heavy layer of new oak was necessary to develop Zinfandel that would complement food. This was a typical view of early post-Repeal producers, who liked the flavorful and aromatic components of the wine that reflected the soil and location of the vines. "The early Italian immigrants seemed to know instinctively where to plant Zinfandel for the best wines," he said then. "That is why these old vines produced such great wines." To put his wine in new oak barrels, a practice inspired by the winemaking practices of the Bordeaux and Rhône regions of France, seemed to John a deterrent to creating a fruity, approachable, and, most important, affordable Zinfandel.

John and Jim Pedroncelli

But the Pedroncelli approach to Zinfandel winemaking has changed since then, according to brothers John and Jim, the marketing director. I met with them in January 1997, and these two hospitable gentlemen were happy to talk about the changes and the reasons for them.

"The biggest change has occurred in our barrel program," explained John. "We began using newer barrels around 1989 or 1990. We primarily use American oak, but we turn our barrels over about every three to four years, adding up to 25 percent new oak each year. We built a barrel room to house the 2,000 barrels and we added a tasting room, lined in redwood from those old vats.

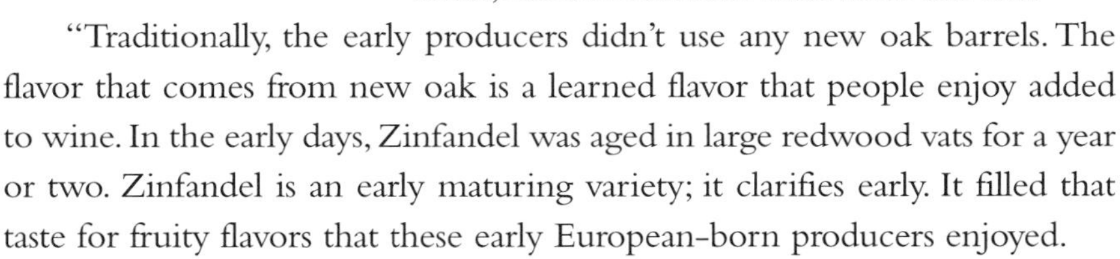

"Traditionally, the early producers didn't use any new oak barrels. The flavor that comes from new oak is a learned flavor that people enjoy added to wine. In the early days, Zinfandel was aged in large redwood vats for a year or two. Zinfandel is an early maturing variety; it clarifies early. It filled that taste for fruity flavors that these early European-born producers enjoyed.

"Our change to newer barrels for our Zinfandel traces back to the wine writers and tasters who used numbers for judging and rating wines. We saw a lot of wines that we knew had a lot of oak getting high marks. We thought, 'What the heck? We've got good grapes.' We're not beyond changing from traditional methods. Through the years, we've always tried to make a better wine, have a better vineyard. We've tried to improve it with whatever new knowledge we acquire — whether that has to do with style or ageing or viticultural practices. In the last seven years [since about 1990], barrel making in this country has changed dramatically. American coopers are learning to air-dry and toast barrels for better balance. Proper toasting breaks down those raw wood tannins.

"We've found that people always say, 'I don't like a lot of oak, I don't like a lot of wood on the wine.' But then, when you have a little tasting," he said, with a wry chuckle while giving particular emphasis to "little," "they always seem to go and select those wines that have the most oak in them. Consumers aren't always sure what the oak flavor is. It just turns out to be a flavor they like."

"Those are the flavors that we like now, too. The fruit is sacrificed slightly, but in the total picture, the flavors of the nicely toasted American oak add to it. It has a softening effect on the tannins, which is important, especially as we get the younger wines [fruit from younger vines], which maintain the fruit to a higher level. But if they're too young, the tannins can be harsh. By softening with the newer oak, you get the balance. Also, our feeling is that the grape should not be the total flavor experience. The thinking is that this other component, if not overdone, can add a desirable dimension. We like that subtle wood background flavor, because it does add another layer. I have come to appreciate our Zins here more than I did 10 to 15 years ago."

"But you have to achieve that balance between oak, fruit, and tannin," Jim emphasized.

Another change in the Pedroncellis' approach to Zinfandel production is to pick the grapes at higher Brix for more intense, riper flavors.

Despite these changes, which have increased production costs, the Pedroncellis, who produce 20,000 cases of Zinfandel annually (80,000–90,000 cases total winery production), still believe that Zinfandel should be affordable. On this subject, they philosophically hold much the same position as they did in 1986.

"Wine should be an everyday beverage, not just for special occasions," said John. "It's a beverage to go with food. In the past, we always made wine to go with food. I can't see any other reason for producing wine if not to drink it with food. Because of the size of our production, the fact that one-third of our fruit comes from our own vineyards, and most of our facility has been in the family for years, we can afford the improvements and still keep our prices in the mid-range. But we're nudging our Zins higher. Our vineyard-designated Pedroni-Bushnell Zinfandel is $13.50, but it's a $20 bottle of wine. If we want it recognized for the quality it is, we have to push our prices a little. However, we're not going to raise the prices by much just to follow a trend."

This marketing pressure to style and price Zinfandel for competitions is a concern of the brothers. "Twenty-five years ago," said John, "a wine was always judged by how it went with food. Now, it's judged against other wines. Those oak flavors are the flavors that stand out. The tasting panels don't sit down and have dinner with a wine to judge it. It's never judged the way it's actually consumed. Yet trophy wines aren't consumed regularly. People talk them up, and maybe dig out one once in a while. There really are not very many Zinfandels available at $20 and up in stores and restaurants; yet these are the wines that usually get the big scores and win the gold medals. They are the very intense, rich, oaky wines whose flavors dominate tastings. And competitive recognition is what the restaurants who carry our wines like to see. It's name recognition that comes with the scores they are after, even though these wines aren't widely available. So it appears we have a contradiction."

Pedroncelli, however, has little to worry about there. Their wines are made to emphasize the fruit, and to be taken home and drunk with dinner the day they are purchased. Their Zinfandels are popular with restaurants and everyday consumers alike — both for their style and their price.

Not to say, though, that some of their wines can't be laid down for a few years. "Zinfandel definitely can age," said John. "But if you start ageing Zins, they tend to lose some of the fruit. The fruit doesn't disappear; but some of its intensity is lost. You get more into a claret style of wine after it ages. The appeal of Zinfandel is its fruit. I'm not a fan of old, old wines. For Zinfandels, give them 10 years, but by then you've lost what you've originally wanted in the bottle — that fruity quality that makes them so attractive."

"Zinfandels traditionally have been attractive earlier on when they still have that freshness," said Jim. "That's one of the reasons why the pioneers here planted Zinfandel. It could be consumed early. Not too many people go to a wine store to buy a bottle of wine to lay away. When our father came here during Prohibition in 1927, Zinfandel was the most widely planted varietal, and it still is. It's the primary variety in Dry Creek, as far as we're concerned. We have more Zinfandel planted than we had a few years ago. We're clearing some new hillsides, not big volume, about 10 more acres — which will bring our total to about 50 acres of Zinfandel."

When I asked John and Jim if there were any other significant changes to their Zinfandel production in the past 10 years, John replied, "Well, the weather has been a lot better the past five years. There hasn't been a weather-affected harvest since 1989. Every fall starting with 1990 has been dry, and a dry harvest is a good harvest."

On that note, John walked me over to the new tasting room, where his son John Jr. poured us a tasting of both the vineyard-designated Pedroni-Bushnell and the Mother Clone bottling. I felt a sense of history standing there in a room lined with redwood from the old vats — vats that held wine when I first visited the winery 10 years earlier. The fact that oak now enclosed the wines during their ageing time, while the redwood enclosed a beautiful space for the visitors, made a striking physical statement about the return of Zinfandel to its revered status.

As for the tasting itself, I found the Pedroni-Bushnell to be a ripe style typical of Dry Creek Valley's older vines, balanced with lush mixed berry fruit, noticeable spiciness, and good finish.

The Mother Clone was medium-bodied, balanced, with lovely delicate red berry fruit, light spicy tones, and a long finish. It was a wine that invited a second glass.

Both wines are available for under $15 in the tasting room.

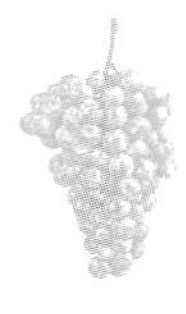

Doug Nalle: The Right Niche

I met Doug Nalle at a Vintners Club tasting in spring of 1988. In fact, I was seated beside him, although I didn't know it until he stood up to take a bow, since his 1986 Zinfandel had just won the tasting. As I recall, I felt more than a little embarrassed, since I had not liked his wine, and in our round-table commentary of the wines before their labels were revealed, I am sure I had contributed some opinionated remarks about his Zinfandel. At that time, despite my awareness of such a temptation, I was still easily seduced by the big, extracted (and often clumsy) Zinfandels. Doug's elegant, balanced Zinfandel with its delicate raspberry fruit aromas and flavors were helpless against the assault the heavier wines had made on my palate.

I was nonetheless able to recover from my embarrassment sufficiently to ask Doug for a chance to visit him at Quivira, where he was winemaker, and learn more about his wines. He graciously extended an invitation, his blue eyes twinkling a little with amusement at my gaffe. A couple of months later, I caught up with him at Quivira, and he gave me a little background on what had attracted him to Zinfandel and led him to develop his style.

In 1984, when Doug established his label, Zinfandel was still rather unpopular, he began. The grapes were mostly going to white Zinfandel or bulk red Zinfandel at bargain basement prices. So growers of the best grapes were looking to sell their grapes to anyone who would compensate them fairly. Doug had been making a non-commercial Zinfandel since 1973 — and he knew it could be an exciting wine. He had made enough vintages to know what fruit he wanted to get, and the style of wine he wanted to make. "High-end balanced Zinfandel was a niche waiting to be filled," said Doug.

In February of 1991, I stopped by Doug's newly built barn-shaped sod-roofed winery on Dry Creek Road to see what was new, now that he had his own facility. Over the next few years, I visited him from time to time, and found, with the help of both barrel and bottle samples, that his style had remained consistent. With an increasingly refined palate, I had begun to appreciate the subtleties of his vinification method. During a winter 1993 visit, Doug explained what had led him to develop and stick with his style.

He had developed his style during the 1970s and early 1980s when he was a cellar worker for various wineries, and also a UC Davis student. He remembers the 1975 vintage, his third as a home winemaker, which fermented out to about 15.6 percent alcohol, and how he and his winemaking buddies thought they had created a truly spectacular Zinfandel. But they had also fermented a batch of pure Petite Sirah, which came in at about 12.8 percent alcohol.

"Well, it was tannic, and a little skinny — at least in California — for a Petite. So we started messing around with blending some of the 12.8

percent Petite with the pure 15.6 percent Zinfandel, and ended up with a pretty good Zinfandel blend at just under 14 percent alcohol. And to my taste, this under-14 percent wine was the best. Then, we aged these wines out. The one at 13.9 percent lasted much longer, was much better balanced, and the much preferred wine to our 'monster' 15.6 percent alcohol pure Zinfandel. That was our first lesson on high alcohol Zinfandels and how they evolved. Of course, it took us five years to find that out.

"But in the meantime, in 1978, just by accident, John Kongsgaard and I got some Zinfandel from Giles Mead on Atlas Peak. The vines were pre-Prohibition, probably late 19th century, and we didn't fully understand what was going on. So we were initially disappointed that the grapes were *only* 23.2° Brix when we picked them, and they *only* sugared up to about 24° in the tank, maybe 24.2°. Yet up until the 1991, that is the best Zinfandel I've ever made — that 1978 Mead Ranch, that was only 13.7 percent or 13.8 percent alcohol. It was a field blend, it had some 'Pets' [Petite Sirah], some Carignane, and other stuff. We made it the way I still make my Zinfandels — in an open-top fermentor and aged in thin stave French barrels. It went through full malolactic fermentation. It was just the most fabulous wine. People loved it when we bottled it; it was delicious when it went into the bottle in 1979, it was delicious in 1980 — and always has been delicious.

"Meanwhile, we're going back and tasting the 1975, waiting for it to keep on getting better, and develop into this fabulous 20-year Zinfandel. But the 1978 is already as good, and staying as good. Then, 10 years later, in 1985, I go back to the 1975. The fruit is gone, the tannin is kind of hanging in there, and the alcohol is still high: the wine is out of balance. The 1978 is just drinking beautifully. As I said earlier, it was purely accidental that we got these Mead Ranch grapes the year we did, and in the condition they came in. It was almost a quirk of fate. The vines were old, the crop was small, and 1978 had no heat bursts. It was an exceptionally even season, somewhat like the great 1990, is how I remember it. We used an open-top fermentor when most producers were still using closed-top tanks. But that vintage taught me one of my most important lessons: it cured me of the belief that the higher the alcohol, and the bigger the tannins, the longer the wine will last. It's just not true! There are many shattered egos along the roadside in earlier California Zinfandel production — among those who thought 'bigger is better.'

"So that is what started me thinking. You have to get the flavor; you can't just go out and pick at 22.5° Brix, so that your alcohols don't go over 14 percent. You really do have to let them hang long enough to get the flavor. How to get power, richness, and finesse without being overripe? This is what got me into hand sorting out all the overripe fruit. And, of course, you've got to have the grapes. Before I established my own label, I was using this approach and style for another winery where I was working. But the grapes were just crummy. All UC Davis clone, cordon-trained, it was table fruit. We were trying to make wine out of Coachella Valley table grapes! I've tasted those wines recently, and they are distinctly inferior — what we used to call 'Cal Zin.' With the same techniques using the best Dry Creek fruit, from properly cropped vines, my wines are showing beautifully."

Nalle buys all his Zinfandel grapes, and knows that great wines begin with great grapes. He devotes as much time and money maintaining consistency in his grape supply as in his vinification. "One needs consistency in grape source to maintain consistency in the product," he said. "There's enough variation among vintages, without jumping from vineyard to vineyard, or changing vinification techniques."

Nalle has been as good as his word. When I sat down with him four years later, in March 1997, I noticed only that the rosemary crop on the roof of his winery was now in full, abundant purple bloom, and that his boyish looks had acquired an attractive maturity. Although a few of his vineyard sources had changed, his winemaking practices had not.

The juice from the crushed grapes is still fermented warm. The cap is irrigated by hand-sprinkling the wine through a hose attached to the bottom of the tank. This procedure is continued until the wine coming from the bottom of the tank no longer feels cold. Since the wine under the cap is always the hottest, and at the bottom of the tank the coldest, when it all feels simply warm, the procedure is complete — at least for a few hours.

"This is working as hard as hand-punching the cap," he pointed out. "This is not a short cut. But instead of breaking up the cap, which releases more of the hard tannin, it just gently moistens the cap while keeping the temperature even throughout the tank." Nalle has never been a fan of punching the cap.

When the wine is dry, it is put into thin stave French oak barrels (20 percent to 25 percent new each year) immediately after pressing, for malolactic fermentation. The wine is fined in barrels, and rough-filtered just prior to bottling, which occurs before the next year's crush. It is held for another seven to eight months before being released in March or April of its second year. Production remains at 2,000 to 2,200 cases.

Appreciation for his stylistically consistent, fruity, somewhat elegant under-14 percent alcohol Zinfandel has been growing. "Every year, our sales to restaurants increase. The sommeliers are tasting our wine, and finding that it will complement their menus. And that makes me happy because I am achieving my goal: I make wine to go with food. That's kind of what we're doing here," he exclaimed, laughing. "Twenty years ago, as I told you, I did make those "bigger is better" kind of wines. But I got cured of that style of wine as a home winemaker. They didn't appeal to my palate and the kinds of food I like — and they didn't keep very well, either. Zinfandel doesn't have to be a big high-alcohol wine to taste good going into the bottle, and to keep well. My Zinfandels taste good at bottling, and they hold up for 10, even 15 years. Best of all, they taste good with food. I think I've proven that."

From the standpoint of economics, he's also proven that he did indeed choose the right niche when he chose to produce a balanced, high end red Zinfandel. The bottle price and consumer base follow when the quality is right. One needs only a discerning palate to appreciate them.

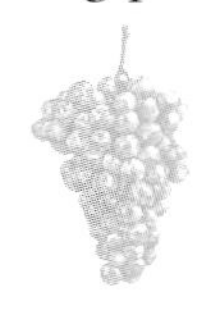

Rafanelli Winery

I met Dave Rafanelli at a Sonoma Wine Library event in February 1991. A short, attractive, dark-haired man with a solid build, he looked like someone who would be more comfortable working in his vineyard that giving a lecture on Zinfandel to the wine library crowd. He nonetheless presented a cheerful disposition and an obvious passion for Zinfandel. A month later, I visited him at his winery. He was on the tractor disking a new vineyard.

A grapegrower at heart, when he saw me arrive, he came to the winery, and invited me on a tour of his new Zinfandel planting on the knoll next to the winery. The vines are spaced at five feet, and were to be head trained. The first yield was expected in four to five years.

"This location is called 'Dry Creek Uplands,'" said Dave as he maneuvered the truck up through the vineyard. "Within this location, there are different kinds of soil. One particular kind is known as 'Dry Creek Conglomerate,' and is usually found near the tops of knolls such as this one. It is a soil type best suited to Zinfandel, and that is why I have planted Zinfandel on the top part of this knoll. You have to choose your soil carefully for Zinfandel. The lower three acres of the knoll, which consist of heavier soil than the Dry Creek Conglomerate, is planted with Cabernet Sauvignon. This expansion is the last. Any more production than this, I would have to expand the winery, and hire help in winery operations. Right now, my wife (Patty), our daughters, and I do all the work, including all aspects of bottling. If the winery gets much bigger, I'd have to increase everything — what's the point?"

After taking me along the crest of the knoll to see the soil and the newly planted rootstock for the Zinfandel, and then down through the new Cabernet planting, he stopped the truck such that we had a beautiful view across the quiet and pastoral late winter Dry Creek Valley. The only sounds coming in through the open windows were a few chirps and squawks of various birds thriving in the balminess of the afternoon. Settling himself comfortably in the truck, Dave began telling me what grapegrowing, winemaking, and Zinfandel mean to him.

"Our customer base has always been Zinfandel," he began, speaking quietly and gazing across the quiet valley that has been his beloved home for so many years. "We are known for our Zinfandel. Where wine is made, who makes it, and where the grapes are grown are among the most important factors to our consumers. The fruit for our Zinfandel wine comes from 26 acres of estate-grown Zinfandel grapes, all planted on Dry Creek Conglomerate soil. We are the owners, and the winemaker has always been a Rafanelli. The wine is still made in our 100-year-old barn that we converted to winery in 1973. It is also a Rafanelli who personally meets the customers at the winery, a family tradition we take pride in.

"The A. Rafanelli winery was established in 1912 in Healdsburg by my grandfather, Albert. He began making Zinfandel that same year. In 1954, my father, Americo, bought this place, which had one Zinfandel vineyard. Soon after, he bought another vineyard, for a total of 26 acres of Zinfandel, all on Dry Creek Conglomerate soil.

"My father established the Rafanelli Winery's reputation by producing the best Zinfandel he could from fruit taken from vines established in proven locations of Dry Creek Valley, and by never forgetting his oldest customers. First, you've got to have the quality in the product. Then, my dad told me, 'You should always treat your oldest customers the best. They are the ones who got you where you are today.' Although I've had to increase my retail prices each year, I've increased them only by about three percent. That way, I keep my oldest customers with me. For every old customer you lose, you need three new ones to make up the difference in lost loyalty."

Dave also described one more piece of advice left to him by his father: 'Run your business in terms of your own costs and lifestyle needs. Don't look to others to determine what you should be doing — or how much to sell your wine for. As long as your wine sells out, you have an income — for whatever.' "My father always told me," he continued, "that if I wanted a big car, a big house, and a flashy lifestyle, I should choose a business that would support it."

Before starting the truck to resume our journey to the winery below, Dave sat in stillness for a few introspective moments. As I sat there with him gazing over the soft-hued valley, I felt a deepening appreciation for his connection to his land and to his Dry Creek Valley.

I returned to Rafanelli Winery in August 1991, to walk with Dave through his beautiful Zinfandel vineyard as the grapes were approaching maturity. During that walk, he explained that he removes the entire second crop each June, and later pulls off all wing clusters. The primary crop is thinned as necessary to provide proper aeration. Yield is kept to 2½ to three tons per acre.

"Growing grapes for premium Zinfandel is more labor intensive and carries greater risk than growing for ordinary table wines — which is not always reflected in the bottle price," said Dave. Now, on our walk, he was showing me the evenly ripening loose clusters of Zinfandel grapes, the results of his labor-intensive earlier work, and explaining why he believed his 1991 vintage was promising to be even better than the great 1990 vintage. Then he stopped to take in the lovely view of Dry Creek Valley, and said, "My life would probably be a lot easier, I'd probably live longer, if I didn't make Zinfandel. I *worry* about it; I lose sleep over it every fall. It's like having a new baby each year."

Was he thinking of getting out of Zinfandel production? I asked.

"No," he replied, with an affectionate laugh. Rather, he has carried on his father's tradition, making only those changes that he felt were necessary for his style of living and winemaking.

Of his 65 to 70 ton yield, Dave uses 50 tons of the best fruit, and sells the remaining at market prices. He uses the money to supplement his estate-grown fruit with 15 tons from a couple of select old Dry Creek vineyards. The juice is fermented with 30 percent whole berries in 2-ton open-top redwood and stainless fermentors; the cap is punched every four hours, even during the night. "You can't neglect the baby in its hours of birth," said Dave.

As I got to know Dave over the years, I became increasingly captivated by his commitment both to Zinfandel and to his father's philosophy. Growing great Zinfandel grapes and producing the best wine possible from them is what makes Dave happy. When I sat down with him again in 1996 for an update on his Zinfandel, he elaborated upon his grapegrowing and winemaking practices, and upon the success he has had by adhering to the lessons his father handed down to him.

"I've been here long enough not to see that the big dollars coming into this valley do not end up in the right places for the right things," he began. "Dollars do not equal success. Never have, never will. Success is determined basically by how dedicated you are to what you are doing, and how much you enjoy it. I am convinced that success in the grapegrowing and winemaking business comes only because you love what you are doing. You are like a little caterpillar inching along taking tiny steps, buying a new piece of equipment when you can afford it, as opposed to buying everything you need in one shopping spree.

"Do you know why this works? Because the producer has earned each dollar spent through his or her own hard work. So there is a lot of thought that goes into each new purchase. And you have also come to realize, by inching along over the years, that there are a lot of variables involved in grapegrowing and winemaking. Quality of product and success is never guaranteed by spending money on the latest and best equipment."

At the same time, Dave acknowledges that each generation brings its own needs to the industry. "The old-timers can say, 'Hey, I'm satisfied with the wine I've always made, and I have a solid customer base. I'm making a living, so why change?' The next generation, though, sees the potential to make the wine even better, and doesn't want to be sitting on the sidelines making what they now see as second-class products. They don't want to be stuck with the reputation of making ordinary wines when they believe they can make top-notch wines. I can sympathize. But how much room in the market is there for top-notch wines? How many people can still afford a Zinfandel with dinner in a restaurant?"

Dave includes himself among those who made changes to make the wine even better when he took over the winemaking in 1986. The sole dramatic change, however, was in converting his storage entirely to French oak, using a mixture of thin-stave Chateau and thicker stave Transport barrels. Each year, he adds 20 percent new oak, leaving 80 percent at two, three, and four years old. "Zinfandel is capable of being a world class wine," explained Dave. "If it is to appeal to Bordeaux and Burgundy consumers, it must have the long finish that the 20 percent to 25 percent new French oak imparts. The best wines of the world have this layer of oak. It's expensive to make Zinfandel this way, but what I feel to be the true quality of Zinfandel can't be brought out any other way."

Dave Rafanelli

The only other change Dave has made to his winemaking practices is the addition in 1995 of a new Delta crusher, must pump, and sorting table. "Because my old Italian crusher came with a pump, and the Delta does not, I had to buy a new pump. Because the top of the crusher is formed differently from the Italian one, I decided to get a sorting table, because the table feeds into the crusher. These pieces of equipment won't change my style; they will just help me make it better.

"The pump certainly will enhance quality because it doesn't break seeds, which the old one did. My old crusher/destemmer did not just crush the berries. It practically macerated the seeds, and ground up the skins. My old pump and crusher were working too hard to get the job done. The result was what I call 'chunky' wines. I like some of that chunkiness, but by the time I retired that old crusher/destemmer, the chunkiness was becoming excessive.

"The sorting table will enhance quality also. It comes with a remote control, which enables us to stop the belt, slow it down, or speed it up. This way you can see every cluster, which is important for Zinfandel. The sorting table has been in use for a long time in Bordeaux. Its advantage is that you can remove the excessively raisined clusters. Keeping just the evenly ripened clusters will give you more fruit character, and keep flavor while lowering the alcohol content. I don't believe that high alcohol content is the trademark of a great, or even good, Zinfandel. Zinfandel wines with over 14 percent alcohol I have found are showy for the first two or three years, and then they turn hot. They won't last 15 years, like the lower alcohol ones do. Our first bottling at this winery (1973-74 non-vintage blend) was under 14 percent alcohol, and was wonderful at 24 years old.

"The lower alcohol comes with the even ripening. That's the secret of great wine — that you get this even ripening from Mother Nature. When you do not, then the sorting table helps you duplicate Mother Nature's best vintages.

"The crusher I can control to handle the berries exactly as I like. I have screwed down the rollers, so that I don't run a lot of whole berries through, like many producers do. It took me a couple of batches of wine to get the hang of it. The result is a little softer wine. The wine still has plenty of backbone because I add in 2 percent to 3 percent Petite Sirah. However, I am able to minimize the extraction of the harsher tannins, so the wine has a little less chunkiness. Now, it goes well with food when it is released, and will also age for several years. My 1995 is the first vintage from my new equipment, and is looking very good [in 1996]," Dave explained.

"I am convinced that the success in the grapegrowing and winemaking business comes only because you love what you are doing."

Dave Rafanelli

Despite these innovations, most of Dave's winemaking practices remain very much rooted in his past. "We still produce 6,200 to 6,300 cases of Zinfandel, all one style, a blend of all the vineyards. I don't want to come out with vineyard designations, because I think it is overdone. The practice of vineyard-designating Zinfandel — 300-400 cases each — is okay, but people should understand that it is just a marketing device. It's a practice that creates a demand by creating scarcity. A vineyard-designated wine is not necessarily a better wine than one that is not vineyard-designated. The same with identifying wines as "old vine." Old Vines is another marketing tool."

Making the best product possible from vineyard to winery, and keeping the style consistent, is the first key to Rafanelli's success. The second key is their attention to customers. Direct sales from the winery and mail order account for up to 80 percent of their business. The wines always sell out within two to three weeks of release. Patty distributes the other 20 percent to restaurants. "Two or three times each week, she loads up 50 cases in the station wagon and personally delivers each customer's allotment," said Dave. "She delivers three or four cases per stop, going down little back stairs and through the kitchens. I don't think anyone else still hand-delivers their wine to restaurants.

"'The niche that I have is being in touch every couple of weeks with the wine buyer, the owner, the chef, and that means a lot,' Patty says. They respect her a lot, too, breaking her back to do this. She doesn't have to, but she enjoys it too much to quit. She prides herself on good restaurant placement and good restaurant relationships. Restaurant people move around, but if you have good relationships with them, you don't lose a customer when someone moves to a different restaurant. The product has to be good, but the people behind the label should be appreciated as well. That's the other half of keeping a good account. So when someone moves on, they will take your wines with them, and in the end, you get a new account, rather than losing one. Still, it's a lot of work. I'm not sure I could do it three or four times a week."

This may seem like a lot of extra, even unnecessary, work to make and successfully market a world class red Zinfandel. Dave and Patty don't think so.

"It's all these little pieces that have made us as successful as we are," said Dave. "As I said, you have to have a good product. But when you add in all the little pieces, that's what makes it work. Some people perhaps envy us our success, but when you tell them the work that goes into it, they back off. These are the pieces most people don't want to put up with. 'I don't want to deliver wine three times a week. I don't have time for that,' are the responses I usually get. Yet it's your business to make time. You have to make the wine, but you also have to service the customers, if you want to be in that niche. Restaurants are personal, and they showcase your wine with food, which is what it is made for.

"What many people do not realize is that marketing is long-term. They develop their strategies only in terms of current trends, which last for one, or maybe two, years — which is sad. Look at the successful people. They have never used short-term marketing tactics. They have used solid, consistent, 'Keep your oldest customers satisfied.' That philosophy is what has built the successful businesses. Yes, I could raise my prices without offending my oldest customers because they know that I have always charged a fair price. In fact, they tell us, 'You should be charging more.' Now I've got a guilt trip, since I could raise my prices. But I also remember another point my father impressed upon me: 'Pigs get fat; hogs get slaughtered.' It's okay to be a bit piggy, but don't get hoggish. Our way, we gain new customers as we go along, but we also keep our oldest ones, because we have never offended them."

Although Dave and Patty sell out 70 percent of their product in nine days through mail order, they have added 1,500 people to their waiting list. "It is nice to have a list of people in reserve," said Dave.

Dave and Patty do not send wine to competitions anymore, because they do not need the publicity, and also because they feel that competitions no longer serve the consumer. "Many producers are cherry-picking their best barrels and entering these lots for the medals," said Dave. "But these are not the wines that will be available to the consumers. Our wines still turn up in competitions, because someone has bought our wine and entered it. Any wine of ours that is entered into a competition is the one available to the consumer."

One last personal touch Dave has added to his operation is the restoration of a couple of 1946 Chevrolet trucks. One is the original that his father bought brand new. "It's an old war truck," he said. "I got to the point where I needed a bigger newer truck, but I didn't want to retire the old Chevy. So I decided to restore it, and then I went looking for another just like it — so I would have two old trucks rather than one big new one. I found my second truck, and restored them both to original condition, including their beautiful original dark green color, with 'Rafanelli, Dry Creek Valley, Sonoma County,' on the doors. I can't tell you how many people stop and take pictures when we are hauling grapes each fall. The trucks seem to suggest the classic wine country as many remember it or have envisioned it. Now, I feel proud when I drive those 50-year-old trucks. They have a lot of history, and when my kids inherit them, they will have inherited a lot of family history."

"You spoke earlier about whether Zinfandel wines age well or not. Should a Zinfandel consumer be able to lay down a Zinfandel for a few years?" I asked, getting back to a subject that I wanted to hear his opinion on. I knew that his Zinfandels had a reputation for ageability.

"A Zinfandel has to hold up for a minimum of five to seven years to be any good," said Dave, unequivocally. "Even my 1989, which was the harvest from hell, held up for five to six years. Yet when I sold it, I was apologizing for it, and advising my customers to drink it within a year or two. When I tried it after four years, I realized it was still gaining complexity and tasting better than either my 1990 or 1991 at the same time.

"An average vintage from this area should hold up for seven or eight years before it starts to decline. With a good vintage, like the 1991, the sky's the limit.

"At the same time, it depends upon what you like. If you like your Zinfandel young, then you will like the higher alcohol, more concentrated wines. If you want to go back and select a vertical of 10 to 15 years, then you should look for a different style, with more consistency. As you wait for grapes to achieve higher sugars, for greater flavor concentration and extraction, the differences among years are magnified tremendously. The grapes are usually over ripe, so the pH and acid can be greatly out of balance; the wines will not hold up. Sometimes you can get that high ripeness and sugar and still be in balance. But it's hit and miss. If you want nice verticals, and all to be sound in your cellar, you had better go for a different style."

"You have spoken highly of your 1990 and 1991 vintages. Do you have any other favorites among the 1990s?" I asked.

"I feel that the 1995, with the long hang time, the color concentration, and more even ripening than I usually get with Zinfandel, should be my best of the 1990 vintages — which have all been good. This one should stand out. For the second time in five years, I'll have a Zinfandel below 14 percent alcohol, because there were so few raisins in the clusters. I have been trying for this for years, but usually get 14.4 percent or 14.5 percent — which is too high for me.

"The 1996, my own gut feeling is that this should be drunk earlier. Look what our temperatures were — 20 days at over 100°F in this area, and I can count the days when we had morning fog in Dry Creek Valley. We had a really hot summer, which showed up in the numbers in winery. We got higher pH and lower acids, both of which mean shorter ageing times. It also meant that we had a very early harvest date — August. Harvest date affects Zinfandel. When you harvest Zinfandel grapes that early, they don't have the hang time, so you are not going to get the color or flavors that come with later harvest dates.

"Maybe there are a few vineyards throughout the state that get the flavor and color and numbers by August. But if you look over the past 15 years, you will see that those vintages where we had to sweat it out, wondering if the grapes were going to get the sugar and flavors before the rains came, were the best."

In 1998, Dave and Patty's oldest daughter, Shelley, became the winemaker for A. Rafanelli, which made Dave a happy man. "She's the fourth generation of Rafanellis making wine under the family name, and that gives me a nice feeling," he said. "She got her degree in agriculture from Cal Poly San Luis Obispo, and then took about eight enology courses at UC Davis. She is much more attentive to details than I ever was, and that is how it should be — each generation bringing something new to the business. Our wines should be even better now."

Gallo of Sonoma

The Ernest and Julio Gallo family produced its first varietally labeled Zinfandel in 1974. In January 1997, I met Caroline Bailey, granddaughter of the late Julio Gallo, at a ZAP general membership lunch in St. Helena. A short conversation about Zinfandel and her family's long heritage with the grape led to an appointment to meet Caroline at Gallo of Sonoma in Dry Creek Valley later in the month. She would take me for a vineyard and winery tour and a tasting of a few of Gallo of Sonoma Zinfandel wines. Gallo of Sonoma is the family's estate- and vineyard-designated label. It was established in 1990, and is Ernest and the late Julio Gallo's final achievement. "My brother and I achieved nearly every goal we set for ourselves. There is one left, however: to create wines that would be recognized as among the world's best," explains Ernest in the Gallo of Sonoma brochure.

Zinfandel, however, was not one of the flagship wines produced by the Gallo of Sonoma facility. The first wines released under this label were two estate-bottled wines — a 1990 Northern Sonoma Cabernet Sauvignon and a 1991 Northern Sonoma Chardonnay. These inaugural wines were released in 1993. In 1994, the winery produced the first of its Sonoma County series, one of which was

Zinfandel. Today there are seven wines: Cabernet Sauvignon, Merlot, Zinfandel, a Russian River-designated Chardonnay, Sangiovese, Barbera, and Pinot Noir. Zinfandel, nonetheless, has been an important grape for the family since it established its operation in the 1930s. I was interested in tasting the Zinfandels produced at the family's Dry Creek Valley facility, and learning a little more about the viticultural and winemaking practices the third generation of Gallos were giving to the historic grape.

At the appointed time, Caroline, a beautiful woman with dark hair and an olive complexion accented with rosy cheeks and lips, met me in her pickup truck at the unmarked gates to the family's Dry Creek vineyards and winery. She was seven months pregnant with her third child. Soon we were climbing up through the picturesque slopes covered with neatly tended vineyards. As we drove, Caroline gave me some background on the vineyard and her grandfather's farming philosophy.

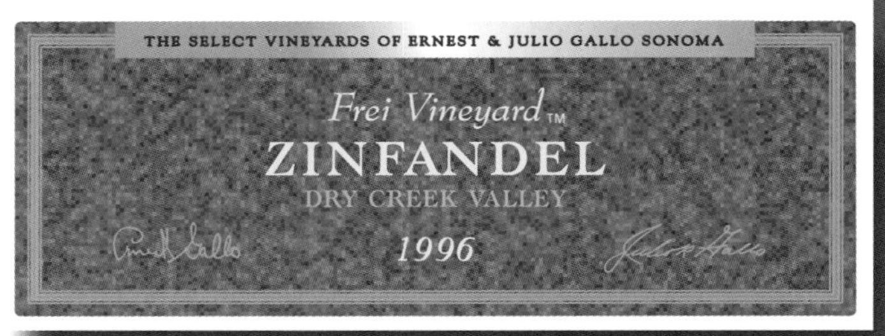

"You will see a lot of open space here," she began, "because my grandfather always believed in a 50-50 policy with the land: 50 percent to be planted, and 50 percent to be left as undeveloped wild and open space." By now, we had reached a ridge overlooking the beautiful Lake Eileen at the base of tree- and shrub-covered hills. "The lake is stocked with bass," said Caroline, "and a great variety of wildlife lives in the woods. My grandfather loved it all."

A little further up, along the edge of a trellised 20-acre Zinfandel vineyard planted in 1990-91, Caroline stopped the truck and pointed out the remnants of an oak tree. "That was a favorite tree of my grandfather, and he insisted that it be left there. A few years ago, it came down in a storm, but we still call this vineyard 'Julio's Tree Vineyard.' The vineyard produces seven to eight tons of fruit per acre, and part of the Sonoma County blend."

At the state-of-the-art winery, Caroline showed me Gallo of Sonoma's barrel cellar (home to 50,000 barrels). "We use barrels from coopers all over the world," she explained. "We match the type of oak, the degree of toast, to the character of the wines we make. We are fortunate in that the land gives us some astonishing fruit to work with."

From the barrel room, we proceeded to a small room where Caroline had set out a tasting table with three Zinfandel wines and a tray of hors d'oeuvres. The room overlooked the facility that takes the grapes from the harvest bins to bottle. "Our investment in equipment that is gentle with the grapes and the wines is giving us excellent results," she pointed out, as we surveyed the vast and well-equipped space below us.

When we sat down to the aromatic set of wines on the table, Caroline explained to me the myriad brands of wines made by her family. "In addition to the Gallo of Sonoma wines," she began, "at this winery we also make Anapamu wines using Monterey and Central Coast grapes, Rancho Zabaco wines using grapes from our Sonoma Country growers, Indigo Hills wines using Mendocino and North Coast grapes, and Marcelina wines using Napa grapes. These are all lovely wines, expressing their own regional character. We reserve the family name for the Sonoma County wines where most of our own grapes are used."

I replied that I had been confused by all the different Gallo brands, so her explanation helped.

To supply the grapes for the Gallo of Sonoma premium wines, the family has acquired eight Sonoma County vineyards located mostly on Dry Creek Valley hillsides, for a total of about 3,000 acres in vines. The grapes are vinifed at the winery, located in the heart of the 2,000-acre Dry Creek Valley property, 700 acres of which are in the Frei Vineyard.

The Single Vineyard series was begun in 1996. It now includes three vineyard-designated Zinfandel wines — Barelli Creek, Chiotti, and Stefani — as well as the estate-bottled Frei Ranch Zinfandel. Caroline had selected three representative Zinfandels: a 1995 Indigo Hills, the family's North Coast brand; a 1995 Gallo of Sonoma, Sonoma County; and a 1994 estate bottled Gallo of Sonoma Frei Ranch Zinfandel. Zinfandel was a favorite wine of Julio Gallo.

First was the 1995 Indigo Hills, a lovely, spicy Zinfandel with lots of lush blackberry fruit character, and a lingering finish, with alcohol content under 14 percent. Next was the Gallo of Sonoma, Sonoma County Zinfandel, a lighter, fruitier wine with a pleasant balance of fruit and spice, and an enjoyable finish. Grapes for this Zinfandel are taken from younger trellised vines yielding between five and eight tons of fruit per acre.

The last wine was from the 1994 Frei Vineyard, situated on a gravelly clay loam hillside near Lytton Springs Road, and is considered by the family to be one of the best situated of their Zinfandel vineyards. It is one of two vineyards the family has owned since the mid-1940s. The old Zinfandel vines have long since been removed. The vineyard was replanted in 1982, and the vines are vertically shoot-positioned and drip irrigated. At 15 percent alcohol, I found the Frei Vineyard Zinfandel a little heavy for my taste. Yet it was a fine example of its style: full-bodied in the mouth, with lush blackberry fruit, a hint of anise, and a dusting of black pepper. Average yield is 3½ tons per acre.

The fruit for all Gallo of Sonoma single-vineyard and estate bottled Zinfandel wines is gently destemmed and crushed — just enough to split the skins of the berries. The wine is moved into 40- to 50-ton stainless steel tanks where it is inoculated with yeast cultures determined through extensive research to be best suited to the fruit. The cap is pumped over several times each day until dryness is reached. From the fermentation tank, the wines are put into a mixture of French and American oak barrels, a small percentage of which are new, and allowed to age for 12 months. Malolactic fermentation is completed in the barrels.

"Some of us think our Frei Ranch Zinfandel is our best," said Caroline, "but since you liked our Indigo Hills, you will probably also like our Barelli Creek, our only single-vineyard Alexander Valley Zinfandel. You will have to come by our table at the ZAP tasting, and try our 1996 barrel sample, which will be our first Barelli Creek release."

Following our tasting, Caroline drove me back to my car in the twilight of the winter afternoon. As in the Rafanelli family, the third generation of Gallos is taking over and is bringing its own style to the family's wines. At the end of the month, I found her at the Gallo table at the ZAP barrel tasting, where I accepted her offer of a taste of the Barelli. It was a Zinfandel in the style I enjoy — a medium-bodied wine with luscious blackberry flavors and delicate spices.

Perhaps Zinfandel does not yet occupy a place in the line up of Gallo of Sonoma's most prestigious products. But among the premium Zinfandels of the region, the four vineyard-designated and estate wines under this label certainly hold their own.

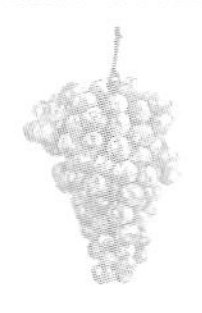

Occidental Vineyard: Legendary Late Harvest

Robert von Weidlich purchased the 43-acre Occidental Vineyard in 1969 from the Morelli family, the original owners. There were five acres of old Zinfandel vines, three acres planted in 1937 and two more in 1947. The property also came with an historic redwood winery, a couple of houses and some other buildings, and a large one-room fully inhabitable tree house circa 1900 that had been anchored to four ancient redwood trees about 20 feet above the ground just in front of the winery.

In 1970, the year following his purchase of the vineyard, Robert planted an additional four acres, which he trellised and cordon-trained. In 1974, he planted another five acres, which he has trained a little taller for easier pruning of the vines and harvesting of the grapes. Today, he has a total of 14 acres of Zinfandel. None of the Zinfandel is irrigated.

The five-acre block planted in 1974, called Robert's Vineyard, was trained to be shoulder-high rather than knee-high. "It was an experiment," Robert explained. "I got the idea from a vineyard manager for Sonoma Vineyards. I wanted to train the vines higher, but didn't want to put any more on trellises. You are asking for trouble when you put Zinfandel on wires. It is too easy to over-crop. The advice I got was to stay with head training, but make the vines a little taller. I wondered if pruning style might affect the character of the grapes. It now seems to me that Robert's Vineyard grapes have acquired the character of the oldest blocks."

Situated on Harrison Grade Road just outside the village of Occidental, Occidental Vineyard is uniquely situated in a frost-free microclimate. Because of its location on the ridge, the cold air drains to the lower elevations, where a vineyard just 800 feet away does need frost protection. Also, the fact that the ocean is just five miles to the west seems to have a moderating influence on the temperatures in Occidental Vineyard. The elevation is noticeable when you exit the lovely narrow and twisting Gratton Road, which you have followed for six miles from Highway 116 towards the village of Occidental, onto Harrison Grade Road. A short climb brings you to the vineyard and a spectacular view across the vines to Mount St. Helena, which rises 3,000 feet above the northern end of Napa Valley.

Robert von Weidlich

I met Robert in 1991 as part of my research into the economics of Zinfandel. Arriving at the vineyard on a sunny winter day, I discovered a short, soft-spoken, and charismatic man who had many business ventures in his lifetime before settling down on Occidental Vineyard. Although his reddish blond hair and beard were showing much gray, his blue eyes flashed clear and bright when he told me the story of the economic windfall he received from his vineyard. Because Occidental Vineyard occupies land that used to be forested with coastal redwood trees, it had an economic advantage for the times. The soil, called Gold Ridge Loam, produces fruit with high acid (13 g/L), which, according to Robert, means that the fruit needs to be 26° Brix at harvest in order to produce balanced and flavorful wines. The ability of the fruit from this vineyard to produce big wines with bottle life of up to 20 years influences the economics, he said, because producers were willing to pay additional money for degrees of Brix above 24°. This set Robert apart from the economic conditions faced by many Zinfandel growers until recently. His good fortune began with his first customer, Ridge Vineyards' Dave Bennion, in 1970.

"The original Occidental Vineyard Zinfandel was exactly what Bennion was looking for to make a late-harvest benchmark Zinfandel," said Robert. Although the going price for Zinfandel grapes then was only $175 per ton, Bennion offered him $650, plus $100 for each degree over 24°, plus $100 for shrinkage. The grapes were harvested at 29°, which gave Weidlich $1,250 per ton. In addition, he paid Robert $100 per ton for delivery. The crop off his five acres totaled 15 tons, which grossed Robert $20,250.

"I was able to pay my $7,000 yearly mortgage plus some my living expenses for two years off that first sale," said Robert, his face crinkling up in a delighted smile. Bennion also bought Occidental Vineyard Zinfandel in 1971, 1972, and 1973. The 1970 and 1971 vintages were vineyard-designated; the 1972 and 1973, North Coast.

The reputation of Occidental Vineyard Zinfandel was firmly established by the Ridge Zinfandels of 1970-73. (Still beautiful wines, said Paul Draper)

Its fruit has never wanted for buyers or a fair price — although Robert never again was offered such a lucrative contract as his first with Bennion. "That 1970 Ridge Zinfandel had an alcohol content of 16 percent. While it isn't a style of wine that many Zinfandel producers make now, people still come out of the woodwork for those few that do turn up," Robert remarked.

In 1987, the Gallo brothers offered Robert $1,000 per ton, when the average price was around $550. Lytton Springs, however, wanted the grapes, so it matched Gallo's price. Robert was pleased, but "I had no intention of selling to Gallo — for any price," he said.

"Why not?" I asked. "Did not Mr. Morelli sell to the Gallo brothers before you bought the vineyard?"

"Well, yes, he did. The Gallos were Italians, and wanted the Zinfandel from this region for their new Hearty Burgundy. Their intention was to make a great wine for a low price — which they did. They had great choice in grapes. But after the first three years, the Old Man became unhappy with how the Gallo brothers were doing business. According to old Mr. Morelli, what the Gallos did was to use the wonderful Russian River Valley fruit for the Hearty Burgundy for only the first three or four years. Then they began to dilute it with lower quality Central Valley grapes. But by then, the customer base was established, and they had also locked up their growers in long contracts — 15 years. I didn't want to get into that kind of a contract for these grapes," said Robert. "Besides, by 1987, there were more and more small premium wineries wanting my Zinfandel for high-end wine. I was just happier selling to them." Of course, Robert acknowledged, it did not hurt his feelings that Lytton Springs was willing to match the Gallo Brothers offer of $1,000 per ton.

Older, dry-farmed hillside vineyards deserve high compensation, Robert believes, because their location and farming practices naturally limit crop size to about three tons per acre of uniformly ripened and well-colored fruit. "The quality is always there."

In the early 1990s, Dan and Dee Wickham, owners of Sea Ranch Winery, purchased Occidental Vineyard Zinfandel until 1995, when they ended their winemaking business.

Since 1995, Eric Ross Wines has been buying all of Occidental Vineyards fruit, most of which is Zinfandel.

Eric Ross Wines

Eric Ross Wines was established in 1994 by Eric Luse and John Ross Storey, photographers for the *San Francisco Chronicle*. Their winemaking endeavor began as members of a home winemaking group headed up by Eric Luse. In 1994, Eric and John decided to go commercial, using grapes from the Porter-Bass Vineyard on Mays Road in the Russian River Valley, which had been their source as home winemakers. For their commercial venture, however, their allotment from Porter-Bass was insufficient. To help them out, vineyard owners Sue and Dirck Bass suggested that they talk to Robert von Weidlich. Since the Wickhams were just getting out of the winemaking business, Robert had grapes to sell to Eric Ross Wines. Eric Ross's 1994 vintage was a blend of grapes from the Porter-Bass and Occidental Vineyards. In 1995, Eric Ross Zinfandel was made from 100 percent Occidental Vineyard grapes. Two years later, Eric Ross Wines was winning critical acclaim. Its 1997 and 1998 Zinfandels placed first and second in Orange County Fair competitions.

"I didn't know about Occidental Vineyards until Sue told me about it," said Eric, who is the winemaker. "But our interest, even as home winemakers, was always in high-end fruit." So when Eric and John met Robert, saw the vineyard, and heard of its history, they knew that they wanted the grapes. "We are happy with it. It is a cool area, and yes, the grapes have high acidity, so they have to be fully ripe to produce a balanced wine. But balanced with about 40 percent new American oak mostly from Demptos, we are able to produce the kind of wine we like," said Eric.

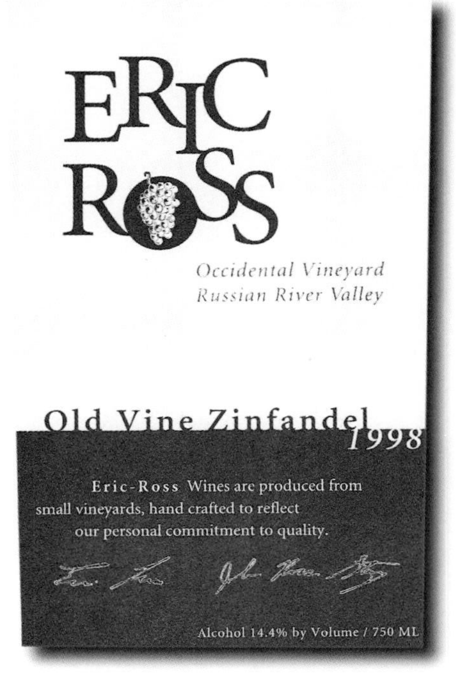

Eric and John's style of wine is one that complements food. "We like balanced wines, not 'monster' wines by any definition of the term," said Eric. "John is a real 'foody.' He has a wonderful palate both for food and wine. He tastes wines for the effects of both fermentation techniques and particular kinds of barrels. He is able to discern combinations of flavors and how winemaking practices achieve them. His palate has altered how we do things at Eric Ross."

Although their Zinfandels are winning awards, "we also have our critics," said Eric. The criticism has to do with the style of wine they are producing from the historic Occidental Vineyard. "The wine definitely retains acidity," he said. While Eric and John pick fully ripe fruit, they do not go for the super ripe fruit that made Occidental Vineyard famous. "People who understand and appreciate what we are trying to do with this vineyard really like our wines." However, he suggested, some people do not like the noticeable acidity without the really ripe fruit flavors to off-set it. Although the alcohol content is usually over 15 percent, the wine does not have any super ripe, jammy flavors.

When I tasted the 1997, I understood what both Eric's supports and detractors were talking about. It is a big, intensely flavored wine, but the flavors are more the big spicy, earthy flavors with undertones of ripe, but not over-ripe, blackberries and black currants. And, yes, it has a noticeable acid content. Beside a more fully extracted Zinfandel made from very ripe fruit, it would likely be overpowered. But paired with food, it was a great complement. To my taste, it would benefit from a couple more years in the bottle. It is a wine that needs a little patience.

So what led Eric and John to establish their label on Zinfandel? "Admittedly, I adore Cabernet Sauvignon. I have always felt it is the king of wines. But our *passion* has always been for Zinfandel," replied Eric. "Cabernet is our basic wine, but Zinfandel goes beyond basic. While it evokes similar body style, we feel that it has more complexity in its wonderful wild berry and spicy character. It is also phenomenal in how many styles of Zinfandel there are. It is really a remarkable grape, when you think about it."

Eric also enjoys the tradition of things, which is partly why he is a photographer and why he photographs the subjects he does: vineyards, winemakers, subjects that have a history. Zinfandel, of course, fits right in. Also in keeping with the partners' appreciation for tradition, Eric Ross Wines are now produced in the historic redwood winery at Occidental Vineyards. Annual production of Zinfandel is 1,200 to 1,400 cases. Total production averages 2,500, which includes 100 cases of 500 ml bottles of Zinfandel port, 450 cases of Merlot from the Occidental Vineyard, and 500 cases Russian River Valley Pinot Noir.

Martinelli Vineyards: Sometimes, It Takes a Jackass!

On a sunny July day in 1996, I met Julie Martinelli at the family's River Road winery and tasting room a few miles west of Santa Rosa. She had invited me to visit their famous Jackass Hill Vineyard, and to meet her 93-year-old grandfather, Leno Martinelli. It was a relatively short drive from the winery to the vineyard on Martinelli Road near Forestville. Leaving her vehicle at the base of the vineyard, she invited me to join her in a walk to the top of the vineyard. With camera in hand, I was soon following the tall, long-legged, and dark-haired Julie up the farm road beside the steep Jackass Hill Vineyard. I had heard much about the century-old vineyard from her cousin Darek Trowbridge, whom I had met the fall before at California State University, Fresno. When we had gained the top of the hill, she described her memories of helping to pick the grapes when she was growing up.

"You had to securely prop your bucket of grapes against a vine if you didn't want it rolling down the hill. Because if it did this," she said, "you had to go down the hill and pick up all the spilled grapes, then drag your bucket back up the incredibly steep hill and finish picking."

It must have been a challenge for the pickers themselves not to take an occasional tumble.

But this steep hill was exactly what her great-grandfather, Giuseppe, was looking for when he arrived in California, Julie said. He and his teenaged bride, Luisa, had brought with them from Italy the notion of planting a specific grape variety on a site ideally-suited to that variety. So after finding a job grafting Zinfandel vines for a local grower, Giuseppe went walking the Green Valley area on Sundays, his day off, looking for the perfect site to plant his own Zinfandel. When he saw Jackass Hill, he knew he had found his spot.

"Jackass Hill has the perfect southeastern exposure, so that the morning sun reaches the vines early in the morning long before it reaches the valley vineyards," Julie explained. "This makes it a perfect warm site in a cool area. The vines are later relieved from the intense afternoon heat by shade from the forested hills to the west. This combination of warmth and coolness gives the grapes time to mature ripe fruit flavors slowly. The steepness of the slope allows the air to circulate, allowing the cold air to drain downwards, and the heat from the bottom to rise, aiding the ripening process and discouraging mildew."

In late 1890s, Giuseppe and Luisa bought the property and set about clearing 12 acres of redwood forest to establish their homestead. In 1899, they planted three acres of Zinfandel on the steeply sloped Jackass Hill, keeping the flatter land for prunes and apples. The rootstock was St. George; the cuttings came from a neighboring vineyard. Jackass Hill Vineyard remains the steepest non-terraced hillside vineyard in Sonoma County. (In 1998, the Martinellis had the hill surveyed, and discovered that the slope was 60 degrees, not the 45 degrees that they previously thought.)

"The day Helen Turley walked into the vineyard was the day my dad went from grapegrower to wine grower."

Julie Martinelli

Following the untimely death of Giuseppe in 1918 at age 56, Giuseppe and Luisa's 13-year-old son Leno, Julie and Darek's grandfather, decided to quit school and take over care of Jackass Hill Vineyard.

After about a half-hour with Julie negotiating the steep vineyard (christened "Jackass Hill" by Leno's older brothers because, "Only a jackass would farm such a steep hillside!"), Julie took me to meet her grandfather. We found him waiting for us in the kitchen with a woman named Mary, who had been his companion for 15 years.

A tall, sharp-eyed, vigorous-looking man now considerably stooped over, Leno welcomed me into the kitchen, where I was offered coffee and wine. I accepted the coffee for starters, and joined Leno and Mary at the well-worn country kitchen, prepared to hear Leno's reminiscences. He began by telling me the story of quitting school at age 13 after his father's death in order to care for the vineyard and help support the family of five.

In 1927, Leno married Alma Bondi, and the couple carried on the work started by Leno's parents. Often, they would pick the entire three-acre vineyard themselves, while their two babies, Joyce and Lee, were set down to nap upon blankets under the vines. Like many children of Zinfandel growers, Lee and Joyce can also rightly lay claim to having been born under a Zinfandel vine.

Leno also described the many struggles he had over the years to make a living and to support his two children, not only through Prohibition but also through the lean years following Repeal when grape prices were down, especially for Zinfandel.

"In the late 1930s, commercial winery prices were $12 per ton, but $35 per ton from home winemakers," recalled Leno. "So I said, To hell with the wineries; I'll sell to the home winemakers. In 1938, I had a new International truck with a flatbed. That year, I loaded the 50-pound wooden boxes of grapes onto the flatbed along with the crusher, and headed into the Italian neighborhoods in San Francisco. Once they saw my truck with the boxes of grapes, they purchased them right then and there. Most of the cellars were under the big city buildings, so we would carry the crusher, on boards, and the boxes of grapes through the narrow passages into the cellars, and set up over the fermentation tank, and crush the grapes on the spot. We emptied the boxes of grapes one at a time into the crusher. Then we would move onto the next customer. It was slow, hard work, but you gotta find a way to make a living." Leno sold his grapes to his home winemaking customers in San Francisco for 30 more years.

By the 1960s, Italian Swiss Colony was matching the price paid by the home winemakers, which had risen to $150 per ton, Leno said. But most wineries were still paying less than $50 per ton.

Despite the hard work and the low prices, Leno didn't consider giving up on his Jackass Hill Zinfandel. "Never!" he exclaimed, when I asked him. "Zinfandel is the best red wine there is." Leno continued caring for Jackass Hill Vineyard until 1993, when he was 89 years old.

Before I left Leno and Mary, I accepted that glass of Zinfandel he had offered me — a 1967 wine made from grapes that didn't get picked until November. The deep burgundy-colored wine that was made the year Julie Martinelli was born still tasted good. It had rich dried fruit and dried spice flavors, and a lingering finish. On the way out, I met Julie's father, Lee, who since 1973 has managed the estate. On the way back to the winery, and later with copies of her newsletters, Julie supplied a few more details of the story of Martinelli Vineyards.

Despite advice to stay out of the grapegrowing business, "because it is hard work and there is little money in it," her father, Lee Martinelli, took over the management of Martinelli Estate in 1973. He immediately began planting additional vineyards in the perfect Green Valley microclimate of the Russian River Valley. Soon considered a premium grape producer in Sonoma County, Lee's fruit was in great demand from many wineries. By 1986, Lee and his wife, Carolyn, decided to do what many growers do: establish their own winery. In their case, however, it was more like re-establishing the Martinelli Vineyards winery, since his great-grandfather Giuseppe had established a winery in the early 1900s that thrived even through Prohibition.

In 1993, Lee and Carolyn were looking for some winemaking help, and through a chance meeting with Helen Turley, whose Marcassin Vineyard is on the same ridge near Cazadero as Lee and Carolyn's Charlie Ranch Chardonnay, hired her as consulting winemaker. Winemaker Steve Ryan was hired at the same time.

Helen's first direction to Lee, who was now in charge of all the vineyards, was to cut the crop level in half. Despite the steep terrain and absence of any irrigation, Jackass Hill Vineyard naturally produces three tons per acre. Helen wanted it to be 1½ tons. "The day Helen walked into the vineyard was the day my dad went from grapegrower to wine grower," Julie said.

It was also the day both Lee and his father, Leno, had to adjust to a revolutionary philosophy of Zinfandel grapegrowing and winemaking. "They had to let go of the old way of farming that saw a big crop as a big check. It was easier for my father," said Julie, "but difficult for him to explain such new practices to my 'Nono' (Italian for grandfather), especially since Nono had just turned Jackass Hill over to his care that same year. To Nono, tossing clusters of grapes on the ground was like tossing money in the dirt. He could only watch in disgust, and mutter some unprintable words," she laughed.

Julie and Leno Martinelli

Helen advocates three fruit thinnings and a leaf removal, explained Julie. The first fruit thinning happens after bloom. The smaller clusters are removed in order to direct the vine's energy towards the strongest clusters. For the second fruit thinning, each vine is pruned to leave one cluster on each short shoot, and two clusters on the long ones, for a total of about three pounds of fruit per vine. The third fruit thinning occurs after verasion, and is done to remove any clusters predominantly pink, and to remove wing clusters from fully colored clusters. Leaf removal is done last in order to allow flecks of sunlight onto the clusters and provide good air circulation. Such practices, explained Julie, discourage Zinfandel's characteristic uneven ripening.

Under Helen's direction, Jackass Hill Vineyard is limited to about four tons from the three-acre vineyard.

Add to this hand labor the general difficulty of cultivating Jackass Hill because of its steepness, and one can see why the price per bottle of wine is as heady as the purple treasure that it contains. The 1998 Jackass Hill sells for $75; the Jackass Vineyard, $50; and the Giuseppe and Luisa, the only Zinfandel available in the tasting room, for $36.

"Because you can disk it only by driving the tractor down hill, it takes twice as long to do as any of our other vineyards," Julie said. "These are definitely labor-intensive practices. But the quality of fruit that we have been getting, and the lovely velvety wines that such grapes produce, make it worth it."

Even Nono Martinelli, who was 95 in 2000, is coming around to this view. "He has tasted the wines we have made from his old vineyard using Helen's practices, and he has seen the prices we are able to get for each bottle. So his initial disgust at seeing beautiful clusters of grapes lying in the dust is somewhat mitigated. One thing you can say for my Nono," said Julie, "is that his daily climb for 71 years up his beloved Jackass Hill Vineyard gave him opportunity to appreciate evolution. He has seen transportation go from horses to cars to planes. And now he has seen Zinfandel go from a home winemaker favorite that was roughly crushed in home cellars to one of the most coveted red wines in the world. After cars, that is probably the biggest change during his lifetime that he has seen."

In 1995, Lee Martinelli increased the family's Zinfandel acreage by planting 10 acres beside the winery on River Road. He used budwood from Jackass Hill Vineyard, and grafted it onto St. George and other rootstocks, depending on the soil. The first vintage, called Giuseppe and Luisa, was harvested in 1997, and is already showing some of the Jackass Hill Vineyard character. Martinelli Vineyards Zinfandel acreage now totals 20. Case production of Zinfandel wine in 1999 was 1,700.

In 1997, winemaker Steve Ryan moved on from Martinelli Vineyards to White Oak in Alexander Valley, and Helen went from consulting on the wines to making them.

Helen Turley

Helen Turley became consulting winemaker for Martinelli Vineyards in 1993 and its winemaker in 1997. She also was the founding winemaker for her brother, Larry, when he established Turley Wine Cellars in Napa Valley that same year. She made Turley Wine Cellars' first three Zinfandels (1993-94-95) from grapes, she said, that had never before been picked at full maturity. Helen also grows grapes and makes wine with her husband, John Wetlaufer, from their own Sonoma coastal ridge vineyard, Marcassin.

On a quiet fall day in 1996, I had lunch with Helen in the Wappo Cafe in Calistoga. Meeting me there was a tall, handsome woman with long silvery-blond hair and a straightforward, frank manner. After shaking hands and introducing ourselves, we sat down at a window table and ordered a 1994 Dry Creek Valley Zinfandel from the wine list. While we were waiting for the wine, Helen told me of tasting the 1967 Jackass Hill Vineyard Zinfandel. "I felt very privileged to be invited to taste it," she said. "It was 25 years old, it was Julie's Martinelli's birth wine, and it was one of the greatest Zinfandels I have ever drunk." That wine, I was to learn later from Julie, was picked late in the season at full ripeness. Not so with the wine that came to our table. Upon our first taste, Helen exclaimed, "This wine isn't ripe; the flavors are green; the grapes were picked too soon!"

The food coming to table and the wine, despite its slightly green flavors, were conducive to discussion of the subject at hand, and Helen was open and forthcoming. She explained what happens in a vineyard like the Moore Vineyard, one of Larry Turley's favorite Zinfandel vineyards in

Napa Valley, when the grapes have developed mature flavors. "Wonderful things happen when a great vineyard gets ripe," she said. "For example, when you let the grapes hang for an extra couple of weeks in the Moore Vineyard, all sorts of exotic, oriental flavors start turning up at 25° and 26° Brix that are not there at lower Brix." Her eyes shone with excitement as she was describing this flavor phenomenon.

She also spoke of the skepticism other Zinfandel producers had shared with her about returning to a fully ripe style. The California wine industry went through that rustic, high alcohol stage of Zinfandel making in the early 1970s, and found that the wines were often out of balance, didn't match well with food, and didn't age well, they told her. "Yet," she said, "the most serious and dedicated of Zinfandel producers of the 1980s still wanted that fully-flavored Zinfandel. So they revisited their approach, both in their vineyards and in their winemaking practices.

"What I've tried to do is to take this revisited approach to its ultimate refinement. I am looking for very ripe flavors, soft tannins, and full body. To get these qualities, you need a great vineyard site, and we spend much time in the vineyard thinning crop at various stages, and removing all raisined clusters or underripe clusters by hand. When the harvest date is selected according to my taste, the grapes are picked and put through a gentle destemmer. Then the wine is cold-soaked for about six days, after which time wild and indigenous yeasts take over, fermenting the wine to dryness in from 12 to 21 days. When the wine is dry, it is pressed and aged in a mixture of new and used French oak. The wine is bottled unfiltered.

"This usually leads to a highly extracted and moderately high- to high-alcohol wine (14 to 16 percent), but one that does not taste hot because it is in balance. Yes, the pH can go as high as 3.9," Helen admitted, but she was not concerned about the effects this pH might have on the wine's ageability. When I asked her how these wines would age, how would they be in five or seven years, she replied, "As far as Turley Wine Cellars Zinfandels that I made, I don't know. Most people drink them within a year or two of purchase, because that is when the rich ripe fruit of this style is at its best. As for the Martinelli Vineyards Jackass Hill Vineyard Zinfandel, I do know that it ages extremely well."

Like many before her, Helen came into winemaking through the back door. Born in Georgia, she attended St. John's College in Annapolis, Maryland, in the mid-1960s, where she studied the classic "great books" curriculum. She also met her husband there. Drinking good wine was part of their lifestyle. In 1974, Helen returned to school to earn a B.S. degree from Cornell's College of Agriculture and Life Sciences. She devised her own program, which was made up of equal parts plant science, soil science, viticulture, entomology, and enology. Upon graduation from Cornell in 1976, Helen came to California and went to work for the Robert Mondavi Winery. After six years of working in the cellars of Mondavi and other Napa Valley wineries such as Chappellet and Stonegate, she became the winemaker at B.R. Cohn's Olive Hill Winery, where she made benchmark Cabernet Sauvignons in 1984 and 1985.

In 1985, her husband founded a tasting group known as the Pinot Project. It is devoted to tasting and learning about Pinot Noir wines from around the world. This ongoing Pinot Noir symposium, said Helen, has greatly influenced her winemaking style. "Much of the California wine industry's focus is on the numbers, and while numbers are useful, they don't tell you the whole story," she said. Her approach has been to taste the grapes, and make only as much wine as she could taste and smell, barrel by barrel. That is about 100 barrels.

In 1990, Helen established her own label using Chardonnay and Pinot Noir grapes. "It was time to make the wines that *I* wanted to make," she explained. For her first release, she managed to scrape together just enough fruit for 300 cases of wine. "Without the reputation of a famous winery behind me, I was a nobody when I tried to buy grapes on my own," she laughed. But when the wine was released in 1992, no one was laughing anymore. Receiving rave reviews from the top wine critics, she became a household word in the wine industry almost overnight.

Helen became interested in Zinfandel in 1993 as winemaker for her brother's start-up operation. By approaching old vine Zinfandel with the same philosophy of wine growing that she applied to her own projects, she won acclaim for Turley Wine Cellars Zinfandel and also for herself. "We took a risk, bottling Zinfandel wine unfiltered that has been made from very old vines," Larry had said. "But Helen told us what to do. We did it, and it worked out just fine."

When I spoke to Helen in 1996, Pinot Noir, Zinfandel, and Syrah were her three favorite red wines. "What is especially appealing about Zinfandel," she said, "is that it is a wine you can grab off the shelf for a lunch like this." When Helen and I parted two hours later outside the cafe, I watched in admiration as she crossed the street and stepped into her big pickup truck. Quite a woman, I thought, as she drove off with a wave of her hand.

Now, as winemaker for Martinelli Vineyards, Helen has full control over one of the great Zinfandel vineyards most suited to her style: the 60-degree sloping Jackass Hill, a vineyard that can be cared for and harvested only by hand. Martinelli Vineyard produces other Zinfandels besides the Jackass Hill, and I am sure that Helen's enthusiastic fans will be glad to know that there are still at least a few Zinfandels on the market that are touched by her special kind of magic.

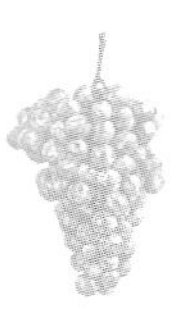

Limerick Lane Vineyards

I met Michael Collins, owner with his brother Tommy, and partner, Ted Markoczy, of Limerick Lane Vineyards and Cellars on the Russian River benchland just south of Healdsburg, at a party in Napa in early October 1990. The host was an English Department colleague who was a mutual friend. The subject of Zinfandel didn't even come up that evening, and if I had not returned next morning to retrieve an article I had left, Michael and I might never have connected. But I did return — with a batch of freshly baked scones — and found Michael the only one up when I arrived. Handsome, urbane, blue-eyed, black-haired, articulate, cultured, I thought he was probably a guest from San Francisco. So you can imagine my surprise when, over breakfast, our host, to help the conversation along, remarked to Michael, "Rhoda is writing a report on Zinfandel for a wine magazine."

Michael's eyes as blue as the morning sky flicked my way, and he remarked, "I have Zinfandel."

I looked at him, incredulous. "You have Zinfandel?" I echoed "What do you mean — you *have* Zinfandel? Where?"

"I have a vineyard in Healdsburg."

"You do! How big is it, how old are the vines?"

"I have nine acres; my brother has 20 across the road. Much of the acreage is over 80 years old, planted in 1910; some we planted in 1980. We have our own label now, since 1988. I have a bottle in the car. I'll get you one." Before I could ask any more questions, he had disappeared out to the street. So much for judging people by appearances.

Before the morning ended, Michael had invited me to Limerick Lane Vineyard (LLV), on Limerick Lane just south of Healdsburg. The following weekend, I found myself walking through the beautifully tended blocks and photographing some of the younger vines whose lush fruit was still hanging, its destiny a Late Harvest Zinfandel (1990) for Davis Bynum Winery.

When I told Michael of my newest Zinfandel question — "Where's the money in Zinfandel?" he offered the following perspective on why growing Zinfandel grapes and producing Zinfandel wine was a viable venture for him and his brother and partner.

"Location, location, location: the three most important factors in real estate are equally important in viticulture," he said. "Our 30 acres of Zinfandel are set on rolling benchland and hillsides in the Russian River Viticultural Area. While almost any red grape varietal grown here will yield superior fruit, owing to the soil, which is clay and rock and is well drained, Zinfandel is especially well suited, both for the quality of fruit and the economics. Zinfandel vines average 85 years in the oldest blocks, are mostly intact, and consistently produce two to three tons per acre of evenly ripened well-colored fruit. I don't know of even one block of Cabernet Sauvignon in Sonoma County that can make these claims 85 years after its planting."

Michael also pointed out that because of the consistent T.A. and pH profile of the vineyard, choosing harvest date by degrees Brix is entirely reliable at Limerick Lane.

"Our pH is incredibly consistent here season to season — 3.3 at harvest," he said. "Most of Limerick Lane's T.A. is made up of tartaric acid, with only a little of it being malic acid. The 3.3 pH before malolactic fermentation, therefore, rises to only 3.37 after. This phenomenon, although rare, is common to great sites the world over, and may be the reason for Limerick Lane Zinfandel being of the consistent quality that it is. That is why we can pick by degrees Brix, usually 24°, because we know what T.A. and pH numbers consistently accompany that Brix reading. Our grapes make winemaking relatively easy because we get the great numbers that only a great site can consistently give you."

Michael has also found that traditional farming methods are well suited to Limerick Lane Vineyard Zinfandel. "The manner in which we raise our Zinfandel is not very different from the viticultural methods used for centuries in southern Europe. Consequently, our production costs are less than those of growers of other varieties such as Cabernet. We forego the costs of trellises at planting, and never have the cost of maintaining them later. We use negligible amounts of fertilizer because we do not want to encourage over-production of fruit or vegetation, which would reduce our grape quality. Except for two or three sulfur dustings per season, we use no insecticides or fungicides. We monitor the crop level carefully, hedge the vines in June, and pull leaves on the vines' north side. That's about it."

Mike Collins

To emphasize the economic viability of growing Zinfandel at Limerick Lane, Michael makes a contrast to a tiny block of Cabernet that was also planted there in 1980. "While it produces fruit of outstanding quality, despite all manner of coaxing, it will not produce even two tons per acre, less than that of our oldest Zinfandel blocks. Probably every variety of grapes will grow fairly well here, but of those that have been tried, Zinfandel is surely the best bet. It can and should be grown without irrigation, since the plant is thrifty with water, and the berries are of fair size. Cabernet, conversely, has small berries, and the vine uses more water since it is more vigorous than the Zinfandel vine.

"Any characteristic of a variety that necessitates additional cultural steps," Michael said, "such as irrigation or trellising, necessarily introduces the chance for error and consequently a grape crop of less than optimum quality. As has been proven by centuries of trial and error on the European continent, what grows most easily in a given location grows best. Location is paramount. Look at Reisling in the Rhine, Syrah in the Rhône, and Zinfandel in California. The specific location of a vineyard, the *terroir,"* emphasized Michael, "is the single most important and basic element necessary to produce really fine wine. Zinfandel is 'site-specific.' That's what makes it so interesting."

Now I understood better why I was so impressed with both Limerick Lane Vineyard's 1988 and 1989 Zinfandel, even though Michael felt that both wines had suffered impositions from the custom winemaking facilities he used for those first two vintages.

My first visit to Limerick Lane ended with a delicious and memorable grilled salmon dinner prepared by Teddy, and served up in Tommy's house — which had been the family home. Tommy, Michael's younger brother, however, was nowhere to be seen; he'd been golfing at Silverado Country Club in Napa Valley. The sweet aromas of the grilled salmon must have reached him, however. About the time Teddy began dishing up the food, Tommy appeared. He had the same black hair and blue eyes as Michael, and was about the same height but with an athletic build. For a moment I thought I was seeing double.

I wasn't, though, and soon we were seated around the large oval table beside the stone fireplace, our dinner accompanied by brimming glasses of Limerick Lane's 1988 Zinfandel. The view out the deck doors looked across the vineyard to the sunset at the end of Dry Creek Valley.

Although a skeptic at first, it was Tommy who designed and built Limerick Lane's own winery beside his house, its cost paid for by income from his grapes, supplemented by his "day job" as a 15-year veteran with the San Francisco Fire Department. It took a little persistence, however, from brother Michael and partner Ted to convince Tommy of his vineyard's potential for not just good but great Zinfandel. Tommy's block was the largest and oldest of the two vineyards that make up Limerick Lane Vineyards.

Nicknamed Inspector Clouseau by Michael and Ted, Tommy was calculator-dependent. Everything for "Clouseau," they said, depended upon the numbers in his calculator, including tons of grapes per acre. The thought of dropping a few tons of fruit on the ground in order to improve quality caused Tommy to blanche. Yet Michael and Ted, determined to show Tommy his vineyard's potential for greatness, did just that one August day in 1990 when Tommy was on duty at the San Francisco fire station. They went into his vineyard and dropped almost half the crop in the younger block. When Tommy came home that evening, they gave him a flashlight, and told him to have a walk through his vineyard. Shocked and angry when he saw the beautiful clusters of grapes lying under the vines, he stormed into the house ready to nail the hides of his partners to the walls. But they settled him down with the promise that when the wine was bottled he would be proudly collecting gold medals. So he did. The 1990 Zinfandel was Limerick Lane's first multi-gold medal winner, and it became the inspiration for Tommy to proceed with construction of Limerick Lane Cellars.

The winery, complete with a wine-bottle-shaped swimming pool — Tommy's brainchild for the winery's fire protection — was finished in time for the 1993 crush.

Tommy, however, never tasted the ultimate fruits of his labor. He was shot to death in his home the evening of October 14, 1993, at age 37. The killer was his father, who then fatally turned the gun on himself.

Michael and Tommy's mother had died from leukemia a few years previously, just after her 61st birthday. Their father never recovered from his grief. With subsequent deaths in his family from terrible illnesses, he became increasingly despondent and angry. Unfortunately, he vented a good deal of irrational rage at his two oldest sons, who had tried, unsuccessfully, to have him stay with them following their mother's death. That morning, he had visited his wife's grave in Healdsburg on the 44th anniversary of their wedding day, which somehow fueled his final, terrible rage.

Michael was in the winery at the time of Tommy's murder. He and Ted found the awful scene.

Both were devastated. Michael had lost both his father and his beloved brother; Ted felt as if he had lost a beloved son.

Tommy is buried beside his mother, whom he greatly resembled. Michael's sister claimed the body of their father. Michael's youngest brother, Eddy, who lived with Tommy but was not a partner in the winery, was at work the evening of the murder. He is now married and lives in the area with his wife and a beautiful daughter born in July 1998.

"Tommy knew the quality of our Zinfandel before he died," said Michael on the day of Tommy's funeral. "He had seen the evolution of the wine through the 1992 vintage." A bottle of his 1992 was laid to rest with his body.

Despite this awful tragedy, Michael and Ted were able to carry on, and the winery has flourished. The state-of-the-art passively cooled winery that Tommy had completed before he died gives Michael and Ted complete quality control of their product. Such control has enabled them to shape marketing strategy to complement both the wine's exceptional quality and their economic needs.

Limerick Lane Vineyards stands near the edge of "progress" in the form of encroaching development from Healdsburg, but Michael and Teddy continue to hope that such progress will allow the vineyards to exist.

"Where else could we have a place like this — space, beauty, and an income from the property?" asked Michael. "The vines are old; the wine they produce is among the best. There's a lot of satisfaction in tending these vineyards, and producing something fine from them. While none of us realized just what exceptional fruit this vineyard was capable of producing when we bought it, we feel extraordinarily fortunate to have such a place. It's much more than just a business proposition. One ought not grow grapes just for money."

Having produced an estate Zinfandel since 1988, Michael knows whereof he speaks. Each vintage, that luscious, red berry fruit character that took the San Francisco's Vintners Club by storm in 1992 (it was the 1990 vintage) is recognizable.

"Apart from only the most basic of vineyard care, the vines require little interference," said Michael in 1997. "The fruit is so consistent in the acid content, pH, as well as sugar, that the best thing we can do for our wine is let it alone. The grapes ferment; the wine goes through malolactic; it is aged in a mixture of French and Hungarian oak barrels, some of it new; and then it's bottled. We never have to fine or filter. Year after year.

"While I realize that winemaking has something to do with the product, it is mostly in being scrupulously clean at every stage, and being meticulous when it comes to volatile acidity (V.A.). Wines that need significant help at any stage in the process are vulnerable to things going wrong — and to inconsistency in the vintages."

Among the great *terroir* for Zinfandel vineyards in California, Limerick Lane Vineyards surely holds a place.

By year 2001, the tasting room is to be finished in a style suitable to the fastidious tastes of Michael and Teddy. The last room in the winery to be completed, it had taken eight years to accumulate the finances necessary for the finer details. But at last Limerick Lane Cellars has achieved this success. "Who would have thought in 1990, when we first talked about the 'economics of Zinfandel,' that this would be possible in less than 10 years," commented Michael in a July 1999 conversation, when he was describing how the tasting room would look when it was done.

Who, indeed, from a Zinfandel-only vineyard and winery? It is, among other things, a living testament to the power of the romantic to withstand tragedy, and then to go on creating beauty in tragedy's dark wake.

Gary Farrell Wines

I met Gary Farrell, a dark-haired, soft-spoken, and introspective man, at Davis Bynum Winery early one August morning in 1992. Gary had been winemaker for Davis Bynum Winery, which lies snug and secluded against a tree-covered hillside on Westside Road in the Russian River Valley, since 1978. Better known for his Pinot Noir, he began making wine under his own "Gary Farrell" brand in 1982 — 50 cases of Pinot Noir from the Allen and Rochioli vineyards. Inspired by his experience of working with Collins Vineyard Zinfandel fruit for the Davis Bynum label, he produced his own first Zinfandel (250 cases) in 1985 from this same vineyard. Since then, his total production has slowly but steadily increased to its present level of 10,000 cases. He has increased production only when new and exciting grape sources have become available, not because of marketing demands.

It was Michael Collins of Limerick Lane Vineyards who told me I should call on Gary, "the Prince of Pinot Noir." Not only did Gary use Collins Vineyard Zinfandel grapes for his own and Davis Bynum wines for many years, he was also consulting winemaker for Limerick Lane Cellars from its beginning in 1986 until 1993. "You need to meet him," said Michael. "He's famous for his Pinot Noir now, and he is going to be famous for his Zinfandel."

His prophecy proved true. In 1993, the 1990 Gary Farrell Zinfandel from the Collins Vineyard was awarded "Best of Show" at the Sonoma County Fair. His 1995 Russian River Zinfandel won an unprecedented three "Best of Show" awards during 1997: at the California State Fair, the New World International Wine Competition, and the Sonoma County Fair. He also won "Best of Show" awards in consecutive years (1998 and 1999) at the San Diego National Wine Competition with his 1996 Sonoma County Zinfandel and his 1997 Maple Vineyard Zinfandel, respectively. In addition, the Maple Vineyard won the 1999 Orange County Grand Cru Sweepstakes Award.

Gary Farrell

We had our first conversation about his wines and winemaking philosophy at Davis Bynum Winery while sitting at a picnic table still damp from the morning fog that is part of the region's summer climate.

Gary attributed his success with Zinfandel to his focus on quality, never mind the profit margin. "Zinfandel grapes from the most favorable sources have always had the potential to produce a world class style of red wine," Gary told me. "But because the profit margin historically has been low compared to Cabernet Sauvignon and Pinot Noir, few winemakers in the early 1980s invested time and money in this style of Zinfandel. Zinfandels in the 1970s and early 1980s were more of a business proposition then, and were mostly made for power — high alcohol, heavy tannins — rather than for balance. They rarely saw quality oak-ageing.

"I have always sought to make a balanced Zinfandel with potential for ageing. I do not consider profit when I make wine. If I did, I would not produce Zinfandel, as profit margins are very low at the bottle price one can command. Production costs are only slightly less than for our finest Cabernet Sauvignon or Pinot Noir. The French oak barrels are expensive, and the price per ton of grapes for the finest old vine Zinfandel is increasing. Yet my Zinfandel sells for $14 [1990 vintage] and my Pinot Noir sells for $30. I intend to continue producing Zinfandels because I love the varietal and I have access to some of the finest grape sources. Producing the highest quality wine will always be my primary consideration. If I get a reputation for quality, I believe that the profit will follow."

"What are your standards for quality?"

"Great vineyards — period. We look for vineyards whose grapes reach full maturity while maintaining good acid and pH structure. We like head trained vines, whose growers are committed to quality over maximum tonnage. We do small lot fermentation in open-top fermentors, and punch down by hand. I have also found that ageing in François Freres French oak barrels, which is somewhat untraditional, suits my stylistic preference perfectly. I like full ripeness in the grapes, but correct balance is the key to a great wine."

"Even with the best site, rootstock, budwood selection, and farming practices, is it not still difficult to determine optimum harvest date," I asked, "especially when you are buying from several growers in several *terroirs* and micro-climates?"

"Daily testing for acid, pH, and sugar content is a necessity as grapes approach full maturity," replied Gary. "It's a pretty hectic time as harvest date gets near."

"When we spoke on the phone, you told me that you choose wines that are a challenge to make: Pinot Noir and Zinfandel. But I know there is more to it than that. What first attracted you to Zinfandel?" I asked. "When did you first realize it had world class potential? What early Zinfandels had an influence upon you?"

"My love for the great Zinfandels of the 1980s — Ridge, Rafanelli, Nalle, Bynum from Collins Vineyard, and others like them — prompted me in the direction of Zinfandel production."

By summer of 1999, when I had my final interview with Gary, only a few things had changed.

He still sought out vineyards that produce grapes with full ripeness while maintaining good acid content and low pH — ideally about 3.25; and he still uses small open-top fermentors, hand-punches the cap, and ages the wine in French oak barrels, about 30 percent to 40 percent new each year.

But his Zinfandel grapes are now almost entirely from Dry Creek Valley sources. Overall, his style of Zinfandel has perhaps acquired some of the nuances of his best Pinot Noirs. This may be attributable to his use of many of the same winemaking techniques used for his finest Pinot Noirs. His choice of yeast, fermentation techniques, and barrel selection parallel that of his Pinot Noir wines. Especially, I noted a Pinot-like character to his 1997 Maple Vineyard, which he opened, along with a Bradford Mountain vineyard and a Sonoma County blend. "It has that delicate red raspberry bouquet and flavor, and a zesty spicy quality that reminds me of my favorite style of Pinot Noir," I remarked.

"You are making some of the same comments that *The Wall Street Journal* wrote about my Zinfandels," replied Gary. The Gary Farrell Zinfandels were the highlight of a report on expensive Zinfandels in the January 8, 1999 issue.

Hardly a surprise. Although Gary has enjoyed great Zinfandels from his earliest days as winemaker at Davis Bynum, "Pinot Noir has always been the wine I have been most fascinated with. Seven out of 10 bottles of wine that I purchase are Pinot Noirs," he admitted. "But two out of ten are Zinfandels. It is obviously second to my interest in Pinot Noir, but it is becoming increasingly more fun and interesting, especially because of the character of the old vineyards.

"It is very exciting for me to go out to an old vine Zinfandel vineyard and talk to the people who are caring for it, and hear their philosophies. They are passionate about what they are doing, whereas those growing other varieties may treat grapegrowing as more of a business than a passion. Zinfandel growers get really excited about their vines. They love talking about them and discussing their growing philosophies. Even growers who have endured the hard times — when you could not give Zinfandel grapes away — have always believed in the value and potential of their vineyards. They believed that their vineyard sites and the quality of their fruit was unparalleled, and that eventually others would realize those facts. They are Zinfandel lovers. There is an artistic sensibility involved with both growers and wine-makers that finds its creative outlet primarily in working with Zinfandel. You are far less concerned with the commercial value of the product than you are with the artistic value — although obviously you need both.

"This is especially true with Tom and Tina Maple, owners of one of my best and most recently acquired Dry Creek Valley sources. Zinfandel is what they have always loved; Zinfandel is what they believe has always excelled in Dry Creek Valley, and so they just waited out the market. They knew their Zinfandel vineyard was special, people had acknowledged that, and even though there wasn't a huge demand for it 20 years ago, they stuck with it and continued to plant nothing but Zinfandel. The youngest vines are 10 years old, and the oldest about 90 years old. All the vines, which are entirely on St. George rootstock, are head trained and are primarily dry farmed. The newer sections have been propagated with bud-wood from healthy old vines."

"Do you take just the old vine fruit?" I asked.

"By the year 2000, I will be taking 50 percent of the vineyard," replied Gary. "We are able to select fruit from whichever blocks we like each year, so the percentage of old vine fruit varies from year to year."

"Then there is more to your interest in this vineyard than just the remaining old vine blocks," I remarked.

"Frankly," said Gary, with his customary candidness, "all the talk about old vines is little more than a gimmick that I kick myself for falling into or ever using on my label. There are no set standards for what 'old vines' actually means when used on a wine label. Some wineries use the term if only a percentage of the fruit is from old vines, or perhaps when the vines are only 20 years old. The term 'old vines' does not equate to quality, either. Interestingly, I have made individual small lots of wine from many Maple Vineyard blocks — the 8-year-old, the 12-year-old, and the oldest blocks. For both the 1997 and 1998 vintages, my favorite wine came from the 12-year-old blocks. All the budwood, however, is from the older vines. Maybe the budwood selection is more important to the quality of fruit than is the age of the vines."

"I've been thinking about what you said earlier when you were speaking of the Maple Vineyard," I said. "Do you not think that it is vineyard location as well as the budwood selection that is responsible for the great fruit these vines produce?"

"You've probably hit the nail on the head," replied Gary. "There has been so much emphasis put on both age of vines and clones lately. Yet it is really the site, the climate, and how the vineyard is cared for that is of primary importance. I do not mean to suggest, however, that clones are not important, but site and climate are of primary importance. If you don't have the proper site, the clonal selection isn't going to make much difference. If you have the site, probably a number of clonal selections will do well. Furthermore, when it comes to the quality and style of wine produced from a particular vineyard, the winemaker's role and the decisions he makes will certainly be of great importance.

"If I were going to plant a new vineyard, in the order of importance, I would say that, first, find a great site for the variety (90 percent of success), then choose your rootstock (8 percent), then choose the right clone (2 percent). Remember that viticultural practices will affect all of the above."

"Would it be safe to say, then, that the Maple Vineyard, Brandford Mountain Vineyard, as well as your other sources, produce great grapes because they are on great sites for Zinfandel?" I asked. "Add to that the caretakers' thoughtful viticultural practices, and everything is there for superior fruit."

"I would say so," replied Gary.

Gary's profit margin on his Zinfandel has increased a little, but it is still less than that of his Pinot Noir. Nonetheless, he was in the middle of building his own winery on Westside Road near the Russian River just west of the Wohler Bridge, where he will produce primarily his two favorite wines: Pinot Noir and Zinfandel — about 4,000 cases of each. He will produce smaller lots of other varieties as well, but only as great grape sources become available. His intention was to be in the new winery by summer 2000.

"I will have a spacious facility with expansion possibilities to 25,000 cases. I will continue to work closely with my growers, the fruit will still be fermented in small lots with manual punch-down. It's going to be a high-tech winery, but will still also be a hands-on operation. Absolutely no compromises will be made when it comes to decisions involving quality."

While seven out of 10 bottles of wine that Gary buys may still be Pinot Noir, in his new winery at least, Zinfandel is on now par with Pinot Noir — in every way except price. Gary expects, however, that Zinfandel prices will catch up, as consumers have more experience with the finest wines produced from this varietal.

Seghesio Vineyards and Winery: Where Zinfandel is the Boss Grape

"Zinfandel is a piece of Americana that most people don't know about," said general manager Peter Seghesio Jr. (grandson to founder Edoardo), when I met him upon my first visit to Seghesio Vineyards and Winery one gorgeous July 1996 morning.

I was there on an invitation from Peter's wife, Cathy. "If you are looking for some old vine Zinfandel vineyards for your story," she had said in a phone call, "you must come and see ours."

I was pleased — and just a little surprised — by the phone call, since I had not known that Zinfandel was a particular focus for the Seghesio Winery. A few days later, I set out for Healdsburg, curious, and in anticipation of what awaited me. I arrived shortly after 9:00 a.m. at the historic winery located on a back street. Peter was awaiting me. Within minutes, we were on our way to tour the family's Home Ranch Vineyard near Geyserville in the Alexander Valley, and its other estate Zinfandel vineyards in Alexander and Dry Creek Valleys, including the beautiful San Lorenzo Vineyard. The first vines on the Home Ranch were planted in the 1890s. "Zinfandel is an old farmer's grape," Peter continued, as we headed out on the freeway north towards Geyserville in his "loaded" 4x4 pickup equipped with two-way radio and cellular phone.

Dark-haired, good-looking, articulate, energetic, and polished in his manners and dress, he struck me as anything but an "old farmer" when I had met him in the winery's portable offices that morning. I soon discovered, though, that his old farmer roots go deep.

His father is Eugene "Pete" Seghesio, Edoardo's youngest son. Pete Sr. and his wife, Rachael, still live on the Home Ranch where Peter Jr. was born and reared. Pete Sr. echoed his son's sentiment when I met him at the house that morning, only more bluntly. "It's the boss grape. It always has been, always will be."

Seghesio Vineyards and Winery was known and respected from 1902 to 1985 as a bulk wine producer. Then the bulk wine market crashed, so the family established a label and began bottling its wines.

The wines were well made and of good value. By 1993, production had reached 120,000 cases, primarily of Cabernet Sauvignon and Chardonnay made mostly from purchased grapes. However, times were changing, so 1993 was also the year that saw the family make a crucial and aggressive decision to scale back production to 35,000 cases per year of primarily estate-grown premium Zinfandel, along with a small amount of the Italian varieties. Their goal is to grow to 80,000 cases by year 2002, with all their wines being made from at least 80 percent estate grapes.

It was this decision that had inspired Cathy's phone call to me, and it explained why I had not realized how important Zinfandel was to the Seghesio family.

As Peter Jr. and I were later cruising along Dry Creek Road en route to the family's Dry Creek Valley vineyard, and then to pay a visit to the

Forcini Vineyard, one of a small group of exceptionally well-situated growers they purchase Zinfandel from, Peter explained what caused the family to make such a dramatic shift in focus and wine styles.

"The catalyst was an Internal Revenue Service (IRS) audit begun in 1989," he said. "As the audit came to a climax in 1994, we could see that there was a risk of debt, and that we would have to borrow money to pay it. This was the first debt our family ever had to face, so we had to critically evaluate our company and our direction. We realized that we needed to find a product mix that would pay off the debt and return us to the profitability that the older generation had achieved in its glory days of the 1960s.

"The younger generation family members like myself and my cousin, Ted, our winemaker, were the first among the family to realize that estate grapes are needed to make great wine. We already had 150 acres of well-situated Zinfandel, and the idea of shifting focus to just estate-grown Zinfandel and Italian varieties greatly appealed to us. Also, 40 percent of the family's land was either open space or in varieties such as Carignane, French Colombard, Chenin Blanc, Napa Gamay — varieties that were not ultra-premiums. With that much open land together with acreage dedicated to those four non-ultra premium varieties, we had a great opportunity to return to our roots, to Zinfandel and the northern Italian varieties of Sangiovese and Barbera. We would also make Pinot Noir, because along with Zinfandel, it is Ted's passion.

"At that time, we were making huge quantities of Cabernet Sauvignon and Chardonnay, 125,000 cases annually. But we were purchasing nearly two-thirds of the Cabernet and three-quarters of the Chardonnay. When it came time to think about making a 25-year commitment to the ground that was going to require us to borrow money for the first time in 100 years, we became nervous about Cabernet Sauvignon and Chardonnay. We weren't passionate about these varieties, and didn't want to involve ourselves in a huge planting of varieties we didn't really care about.

"But before we made any decisions, we ran our first 10-year plans, we ran our first financial scenarios, and realized that the best thing we could do financially was to downsize and become a much smaller winery, with 80 percent of our grapes estate-grown. It was the planting needs of those empty acres, together with the need to replace the non-viable varieties, in conjunction with the realization that no grower can be as committed to growing ultra-premium quality fruit as an estate grower is, that led us to do what we have done.

"We always come home to Zinfandel. We have to grow great Zinfandel *and* produce great Zinfandel to be successful. You can't make great wine if you have to buy your grapes. Also, dealing with growers sometimes can be difficult, and I hate to beg!"

It doesn't look like Peter will have to do much begging anymore. Thanks to the good sense his grandparents, father, and uncles demonstrated in buying and planting Zinfandel over the past century, Seghesio in 1996 had nearly 400 acres of land suitable for vineyards, 160 of which is planted with Zinfandel. Another 100 acres was planted with Zinfandel over the next two to three years.

When the replanting is finished and the changes are all in place, 65 percent of the winery's production will be Zinfandel.

When the decision was made to reduce production from 120,000 cases to 35,000, some lessons were to be learned. "At 100,000-plus cases, we thought we were hot stuff. But when we went to just 35,000 cases of quality Zinfandel and a few northern Italian varieties" said Peter, "we found out we had a lot to learn — about both viticultural practices and winemaking." To facilitate achieving the desired improvements, the family hired viticultural consultant Phil Freese.

As Pete explained it, in the vineyards, Phil set about developing each site to its highest potential using simple methods. He began by defining wine styles and then working with the vineyards to achieve the grapes needed for these wines. He changed the structure of canopy and fruit display, changed timing of some operations, changed some pruning to increase shoot density on old vines that had lost cordon positions, and in three vineyards, took chain saws to old vines. In these vineyards, "stacked" cordons of canopy and fruit were greatly out of balance, and the upper cordons were shading lower cordons. Fruit character, wine quality, and fruitfulness were all suffering.

"We had to learn a lot about the importance of leaf removal, positioning the clusters, and other improvements such as water delivery," said Peter. "Our oldest vines, the Home Ranch, had been showing a lot of stress, so now we're babying them along. We installed drip irrigation, to deliver precise amounts of key nutrients and to prevent late season stress. In fact, we are going to install drip irrigation in almost all our vineyards to minimize late season stress. Water delivery is site-specific. With addition of nutrients and our improved viticultural practices, we expect that some of the fruit this year [1996] from Home Ranch Chianti Station Vineyard will be of the quality we need to keep it separate.

"What Phil has been able to offer us is how to use new technology to improve grape quality. What my father and cousin Ed have brought to this restructuring is their years of knowledge of the ground and the sites. Our terraced and closely spaced new planting on Rattlesnake Hill best exemplifies this shared knowledge. Of course, my dad and Ed have used many terms to describe Phil's approach. The only one publishable is 'unorthodox!'" (For an in-depth account of Phil Freese's contributions to the Seghesio family's restructuring, see Freese's report, "From the Vineyard Perspective," ***PWV,*** September/October 1998, Vol XIX, No.3:25, 30-31.)

The family also had a lot to learn about determining grape ripeness and selection of harvest date, said Pete. "It doesn't matter what the numbers and chemistry of the grapes are at harvest; it's how the grapes taste. I learned how to chew and taste not only the grapes but also the seeds. We want brown seeds, and grapes that taste good. We want mature tannins, not green ones."

To be able to harvest at optimum ripeness for best flavors, acidity, and pH, Peter and Ted have found that 26° or 26.5° Brix in the tank after crushing is tops. "Anything higher than 26.5°, either you retain a little residual sugar [r.s.], or you have to start playing God, or find some creative ways for the wine to reach dryness. Also, when the sugar content is over 26.5° Brix, the pH tends to go as high as 4, which means there is greater likelihood of the wine developing volatile acidity, aldehydes, and the spoilage yeast brettanomyces is more likely to thrive. We like the pH to be no higher than 3.5; 3.4 is ideal."

Peter Seghesio, Jr. and Ted Seghesio

Apart from using an active yeast developed in France and capable of fermenting to 17 percent alcohol, Ted and Pete prefer not resorting to tricks to get the wine to go dry, so they can leave it unfined and unfiltered. The yeast Ted uses is known as L2226. It is a sugar- and alcohol-tolerant vineyard isolate from *Côtes du Rhône* for red wines.

"It is difficult to harvest your Zinfandel fruit with ideal numbers because of Zinfandel's characteristic uneven ripening," Pete continued. "This creates a condition we call the 'soak-up' factor, meaning that the grapes will soak out to a higher Brix in the fermentor than what your berry sample indicated. As the raisined berries soak out in the tank, they release their sugar. Interestingly, if the fruit is picked at 22° Brix, there is very little soak-up, because few berries are raisined at that level of ripeness. But by 22.2° Brix, you get noticeable soak-up.

"I think one of the reasons we are seeing more and more higher alcohol Zinfandel wines on the market carrying a touch of residual sugar is that the producers are missing the window — especially producers who purchase their grapes. It's really hard to track ripeness in your own estate vineyard, let alone have to run all over several counties to track ripeness. My job this fall is going to be to help Ted nail the harvest window. Give me a call after harvest," he said, "and I'll tell you how we did."

"I will do that," I promised. (See below for results.)

Also part of the family's winemaking evolution was the major renovation of the original 1895 winery and other facilities. Twenty-six of the original 32 open-top concrete fermentors constructed in 1939 were replaced with 24 small stainless steel tanks. Fourteen have heating and cooling jackets, and all are either open-top or have removable lids, to allow for traditional hand punch-down of the cap during fermentation. Five more eight-ton open-top tanks were added in 1998.

Sixty percent of Seghesio's 40,000-case production is now made from estate-grown grapes; the goal is to reach 90 percent. Production will be limited, for the foreseeable future, to what the family's vineyards can produce, supplemented only by those few growers of extremely well favored old vineyards with whom the family has developed an enduring relationship.

Estate Zinfandel vineyards currently consist of both old plantings as well as newer ones. There are three primary old vine vineyards:

- Home Ranch, Alexander Valley, just north of Geyserville, which is the Seghesio family's original vineyard. Purchased in 1895 by Edoardo and Angela Seghesio, eight acres were planted with Zinfandel that year and another eight acres in 1905 — all on St. George rootstock. The Home Ranch also includes the 40-year-old, 12-acre block east of Highway 101 and directly across from the original Home Ranch. Budded onto low vigor rootstock and head trained, this vineyard, according to Peter, is perhaps the best located of all the family's Zinfandel vineyards. There is also a younger block of Zinfandel on the Home Ranch that is used for the Sonoma blend. A new planting has been established on top of Rattlesnake Hill above the original old vineyard. New ground is also being prepared for additional Zinfandel and Sangiovese vines.
- San Lorenzo (seven acres) was planted in 1893 by the family of Peter's mother, Rachel Ann (Passalacqua) Seghesio, who owns the vineyard today. It is located in a beautiful, secluded little valley in the hills east and north of Healdsburg.
- Frank's Vineyard, Cloverdale, which was purchased in 1933 by Edoardo. Eleven acres of Zinfandel were planted in 1936.

The family's goal, said Peter, is to produce three Zinfandels from the old plantings: San Lorenzo, Home Ranch, and Old Vines. In 1995, they were able to release an Old Vines Zinfandel and their first San Lorenzo. The fruit from Home Ranch, which includes the 1896 vineyards beside Peter Sr.'s and Rachael's home, and a 40-year-old, 12-acre planting across the freeway propagated with cuttings from the original Home Ranch, would find its way into a Home Ranch bottling for a 1996 vintage release. Until then, the fruit formed a solid base, with that of Frank's vineyard and the purchased fruit from a few select vineyards — such as the Forcini — for the Old Vines Zinfandel. Some Home Ranch fruit will continue to be used for the Old Vines blend.

In addition to their specially designated releases, Seghesio's other mainstay Zinfandel is its 30,000-case production of Sonoma Zinfandel. It is made from 60 percent estate fruit primarily from the family's 35-year-old, 50-acre, Dry Creek Valley vineyard, together with fruit from Alexander Valley. Some Home Ranch fruit also goes into the Sonoma Zinfandel. Age of the vines delivering fruit to this blend ranges from 35 years (Dry Creek Valley) to 110 years (Home Ranch).

While Peter was explaining all this to me, we had arrived at the Seghesio Estate Dry Creek Vineyard. As we strolled a few yards down one of the trellised rows, Peter explained how the quality of the fruit has been dramatically improved with new viticultural practices. He showed me the canopy management and leaf removal practices. "While the fruit will never achieve the quality of the fruit from the old vine vineyards, primarily because of its location on the valley floor, it is the perfect fruit to form the base of our medium-bodied, approachable Sonoma County release," he remarked.

Of the Sonoma Zinfandel, Peter raised the rhetorical question: "Who else produces this much quality *estate* Zinfandel at under $15 a bottle? This is a really good value Zinfandel."

From the Seghesio Dry Creek vineyard, we went up the road a few miles further to the Forcini Vineyard. "This is possibly one of the best located vineyards in Dry Creek Valley," commented Pete. "We are fortunate to get the fruit from the seven-acre old vine block."

By the time we had met the Forcini family, and had looked over the beautiful vineyard and the surrounding mountains of Dry Creek Valley, it was nearing the noon hour. "How about some lunch?" asked Peter, as we pulled up in front of the legendary Dry Creek Valley General Store.

"Love some," I replied. So we went into the historic store, and ordered a couple of its huge sandwiches to carry back to the winery to accompany a tasting of the current Zinfandels.

At the winery, we sat down in a small conference room where the 1994 Old Vine and the Sonoma Zinfandels awaited us. "Rocket juice," remarked Peter as I sampled the two luscious, spicy, blackberry-currant wines with my turkey breast and sprouts sandwich on whole wheat bread.

"Rocket juice, indeed!" I corroborated. What a combination!

As we finished our lunches, Peter handed me a "100 years of Zinfandel" T-shirt, and the remnants of the two bottles of wine. I held up the shirt, and couldn't help remarking, "It must be pretty wonderful to be celebrating 100 years of Zinfandel."

"Yes," he replied," his eyes glowing with pride and happiness. "It's an incredible gift to be a third generation member of a Zinfandel-growing family celebrating '100 Years on the Vine' in 1995."

In mid-October 1996, I fulfilled my promise to Peter, and called him. "Well?" I asked, "Did you nail the 1996 vintage, and how does it compare to your 1995 vintage?"

"Yes," he replied. "We nailed it. And we feel our 1996 vintage is definitely going to be better than our 1995 because the wine came in right at 25° after soak-up. That's our ideal ripeness for a fully extracted Zinfandel in the claret style with great ageability. As I told you, my job this past fall was to help Ted by tracking Zinfandel ripening curves. I devoted myself to this job, and we nailed it. I am discovering that it takes that kind of commitment.

"I also found that it seems to be easier to track the ripening of older vines on great sites, because they are really reaching for those nutrients deep down, and so they produce a small crop whose overall chemistry is more naturally balanced. Yet the fruit from our younger vineyards is almost better than the fruit from the old vines. We average about four tons per acre. The fruit is at the same level, with uniform exposure, and it achieves maturity and ripeness at 24° Brix. The fruit is uniformly beautiful. This ultimately is what we are going to need, if we want to continue making 'rocket juice!'"

As I described above, the younger vineyards were propagated from clean field selection budwood grafted onto lower vigor rootstock (101-14 and 420) in seven-foot tractor rows with four-foot spacing between vines.

"Zinfandel is the boss grape. It always has been, always will be."

Pete Seghesio, Sr.

In early October 1998, I made a second visit to the Seghesio Family Vineyards and Winery to hang out again with Peter for the day, shoot some harvest images, and also to see the results in the winery of the innovations and renovations. The October weather was holding beautifully, after the cold, late spring, warm summer, and cooler-than-usual September. Despite the smaller crop and plentiful evidence of botrytis (and wet bunch rot), the sound fruit had intense rich flavors and was achieving respectable, if not great, levels of sugar content.

"It has been a challenging year," began Pete, "because of the amount of dehydration and a slight botrytis effect inside the clusters. Nonetheless, we are having good morphological ripeness, great seed color, and good flavors — possibly even better than the 1997 — and we are getting good color extraction. In our old vine lots — the vineyards we use for Old Vine, Home Ranch, and San Lorenzo, we are even getting good sugars. All are 24.5° to 25.5° Brix. In our Dry Creek vineyard, and the younger Home Ranch, we aren't going to get the sugars. The younger Home Ranch is being picked today, with a cluster sample showing 23.5° Brix. Dry Creek is still at between 22° and 22.5° Brix. We aren't going to have the alcohol in this blend, because we aren't going to get the sugars. The sugars have not moved in 10 days."

The grapes for the Old Vines blend, the San Lorenzo, and Home Ranch were already in fermentors.

"We have micro-sized our processes," commented Ted, the winemaker, when I entered the winery that morning to survey the renovations. He had just stepped off a ladder with a sample of the San Lorenzo Zinfandel taken from one of the gleaming new eight-ton tanks. Tall, athletic-looking (as a college student, he had dreams of becoming a professional baseball player) and with short reddish-sandy-colored hair showing distinguishing traces of silver at the temples, Ted is a quieter and more reserved counterpart to his cousin, Pete. More likely to tolerate me than welcome me into the winery while harvest activities were going on, he was nonetheless gracious when he had a moment to pause between the demands of the crush. "Now, we can process large or small lots (six tons) for maximum quality. We have also added two 17-ton rotary fermentors, primarily to process our Sonoma Zinfandel. They are ideal for intensifying the fruit qualities in a four- or five-day cycle, to make this moderately priced blend more opulent and appealing at release. They are just outside, and will be receiving the grapes coming in right now. Go and have a look."

I did, while Ted took his tank sample to the lab. A little later, Ted offered me a taste of the fermenting San Lorenzo as Pete joined us for lunch. It was obvious that the difficult year had not compromised the quality of the San Lorenzo Zinfandel. The hands-on winery operation also seemed to have complemented the fruit quality, with the result being a richly extracted, intensely flavored wine showing great promise.

Lunch this time consisted of locally made burritos and some Sonoma Zinfandel, which was served on a picnic table behind the tiny laboratory. We were joined by Ted's dog, Bear, who was sure one of the burritos was for him. None were, but his mournful eyes managed to coax us all to share a few tidbits with him. The casual setting provided me an opportunity to ask Ted how his family survived Prohibition.

"It wasn't easy," he replied. "For a time, we shipped grapes east to home winemakers, who liked our dark colored grapes and the deep, dark wine that they crushed into. We also produced some sacramental wine. Then the grape market dried up, we stopped producing the sacramental wines, and the vineyards went to hell. To preserve the redwood tanks, we kept them full of water. When Repeal came along, the winery was ready to resume production."

After lunch, I met Ted's father, Ed, and asked him what he thought of the direction the winery had taken. Commenting on the "innovations" while sorting out leaves from Zinfandel being conveyed to the destemmer/crusher, he responded, "We're back doing what I did when I was 14 years old — punching down in small tanks. In the vineyards, we never dropped a single bunch of grapes. We controlled crop size by pruning. We never left double spurs, and never heard of stringing up Zinfandel on wires! All this talk about the rains this fall, no one here even knows what a wet harvest is if they didn't experience the harvest of 1967 — or was it 1968? We had six inches of rain in September in one day. We harvested the grapes anyway. We had to. The gondolas of grapes were streaming juice and water on the way to the winery. We even found mushrooms on the grape clusters. Now that's a wet harvest!" he emphasized, looking sharply at me. "While it didn't make great wine, it was still wine, and it's better to have wine to sell than no wine. No, as far as I am concerned, this 1998 harvest is a dry harvest!"

As of 1998, 40 acres at the Home Ranch's Rattlesnake Hill and the Sisters were terraced with Zinfandel. Closely spaced and trellised, the vines are budded with four estate clones: Padrone, Home, Frank's, and San Lorenzo. About 300 mother vines have been virus-tested.

Ted continues to work towards developing a consistent style for his wines. For now, he ferments the old vine Zinfandels in small lots, punches down the cap several times daily, and presses the wines when they have achieved dryness, usually in seven to 10 days. He racks the wines into French oak barrels, one-third of which are new, for 10 to14 months. The Sonoma blend is put into American oak, one-third of which is new. The wines are bottled unfined and unfiltered.

Although the Seghesio family has celebrated 100 years of Zinfandel grapegrowing and winemaking, it has never become stuck in a rut. Always ready to change with the changing times, the family members today look as if they are ready for a second hundred years of growing and producing the finest Zinfandel wines possible. May it be so.

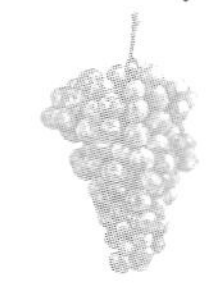

Ravenswood: Quoth the Raven, "No Wimpy Wines Allowed"

I was a few weeks into research for my "The Challenge of Zinfandel" report that spring of 1986 when I got a call from Don Neel telling me to add Ravenswood to my list of producers to interview. So one beautiful June morning, I found myself waiting outside the unmarked, battered door to Ravenswood Winery at its original location on Broadway in the town of Sonoma, behind a furniture factory. There, I was to meet Joel Peterson, its founder and winemaker. From Joel (also a Zin guru to many, only I didn't know that then), I was also to learn about an entirely different approach to making Zinfandel.

It was June 10, 9:30 a.m. I was on sabbatical that year from Napa Valley College, and was living in my new house in Plymouth, at the entrance to the enchanting Shenandoah Valley.

The two-and-a-half-hour early morning drive down to Sonoma was beautiful, and I arrived at Ravenswood Winery right on time. That is, I arrived in the parking lot of the artisan woodworking shop on time, and found the door at the back of the shop that resembled the description I had written down. But no Joel, and no signs of a winery did I notice, not even a Ravenswood sign could I find — just a "No Wimpy Wines Allowed" banner across the top of the door. So I waited — and waited; then went into the woodwork office to ask if Ravenswood was somewhere on the premises. Did anyone know Joel Peterson? Had anyone seen him?

The answers were yes, the winery operated out of the warehouse at the back of the shop, yes, they knew of Joel Peterson, but, no, they hadn't seen him — in fact, no one there claimed to have actually met him. At that moment, I saw a dark gray Peugeot with the "Ravenswd" license plate enter the parking lot. I exited the woodwork office and approached the halted car, whose occupant was a slender Scandinavian-looking man with thinning blond hair, piercing blue-green eyes, and a slightly ragged blond beard and moustache that set off a warm and engaging smile. "Are you Joel Peterson?" I inquired. Yes, he was. "I'm Rhoda Stewart, with *Practical Winery & Vineyard*, for a story on Zinfandel," I said.

"Sorry I'm late. Do you mind going for a ride in a truck? I have to move some cases of wine from our warehouse to our shipper," he announced, more than asked, flashing me that engaging smile.

How many times in the course of my research was I to hear winemakers and growers greet me with those words, "Do you mind going for a ride in a truck?" My answer was consistent: "Not at all!"

Joel Peterson in Cooke Vineyard

So after Joel moved some pallets of wine with a forklift at the back of his winery, I collected my notebook, we climbed into the cab of the old flatbed truck, and rumbled off across the backroads to the warehouse. There, Joel picked up the cased wine to deliver to the shipping company on 8th Street, a few back country blocks farther. The wine was heading east.

Over the roar of the truck and the wind from open windows, Joel told me of his initiation into the world of Zinfandel production. It began with his mentor, Joseph Swan (who died in the winter of 1992), under whom Joel apprenticed in 1976. He told me of his two special Zinfandel vineyards, the Dickerson on Zinfandel Lane in Napa Valley, and the Old Hill, in Sonoma Valley. I scratched a few notes as we bounced along. Before our day was over, he told me how Joe Swan was the first Sonoma producer that he knew of to put Zinfandel in French oak, and how, in Joel's estimation, that single choice did much to establish Zinfandel's worth as a premium wine grape — at least in Sonoma.

"He had a lot to do with the rebirth of Zinfandel in Sonoma. I acquired many of the same prejudices." One of those prejudices was the use of French rather than American oak barrels. "To me, American oak imparts a sourness that I never have liked. French oak gives a soft vanilla character to the wines that's complementary, never harsh or bitter." By 1986, Joel was adding 30 percent new French barrels yearly to his Zinfandel program.

But Joel differed from Swan. He isn't as concerned with alcohol levels going above 14 percent as Swan was — as long as the wines don't have any raisin or prune flavors. His winemaking practices also are designed for maximum extraction of tannins; his wines are intended for ageing rather than for drinking upon release. These practices include warm fermentation, lots of hand-punching of the cap, hard pressing of the wine, and adding back some portion of the very tannic press wine to the free-run wine. (Press wine is the wine that is squeezed off the skins and seeds after the free-run, which is the portion of wine drained out of the fermentor. The press wine is always thinner and contains more harsh tannins than the free-run.)

"Premium Zinfandel has benefited as much as any variety from innovations over the past eight to 10 years in California winemaking practices [since the mid- to late 1970s]," Joel explained. "These innovations include controlled fermentation temperatures, understanding of color and tannin management, improved crushing and pressing equipment, and the use of small oak cooperage. What makes this industry special to me is that I'm making something that takes skill, thoughtfulness, and artistic endeavor. In Bordeaux, winemaking has a centuries' long existence; there's a more strictly codified style. Here, and especially with Zinfandel, there's no codified style. We use a mixture of old and new, of art and science, which tends to make the cult of the winemaker more obvious. When it comes to the production of premium Zinfandel, the winemaker is as important as where the grapes come from."

Joel also believes that Zinfandel has benefited from American wine consumers' support for creativity in wines. "Zinfandel would have had a rough time in Médoc."

Before my day had ended, Joel said that my report would be incomplete if it didn't include Joe Swan. I left with the promise to call Joe, and also to return to Ravenswood in September, when the grapes were rolling in, to see Joel's fermentation operation first hand.

That September, I did indeed return to Ravenswood as the crush was in full swing. The day I stopped by, I found Joel standing on a plank laid across one of the fermentation tanks, punching down the cap. When he came down, he offered me a taste of the fermenting wine from that tank, as well as from a couple of others at different stages of fermentation. Already, Joel was commenting on the future of the vintage. I wondered how he did it, since they all tasted nearly the same to me at that stage on their way to becoming wines. But a bucket in his office contained a harvest sample from the Old Hill Vineyard. As it happened, I had a couple of just-picked clusters from the Monte Rosso ranch, where I had been photographing. The opportunity to taste ripe Zinfandel grapes from two distinctive vineyards proved more informative for me, for in the grapes even I could taste noticeable differences. The clusters and grapes even looked and smelled different.

Over the years following my initial meeting with Joel, I called upon him at the winery many times, sampling his vintages both in bottle and in barrel. There was always something new going on — a new blend or a new vineyard source. Upon two occasions, I traveled with him on his tour of several of the Zinfandel vineyards that were sources for his wines.

In December 1991, Ravenswood moved into the former Haywood Winery on Gehricke Road, Sonoma. When I visited Joel in his new office overlooking one of the barrel rooms, he told me that his view of the economics of Zinfandel had not changed with the move. "Overall return on Zinfandel is still less than on other premium red varieties," he said. "Premium Zinfandel cannot support a large overhead. For our first 15 years, we operated out of the back room of a woodworking factory. It was our highly popular Vintners Blend, whose production reached 20,000 cases there, that facilitated our move here to the Haywood Winery." By 1996, Ravenswood's total annual case production had reached nearly 100,000 cases. Over half of that was Zinfandel, with over 50,000 cases being the Vintners Blend.

In December 1996, I sat down with Joel for a retrospective interview. He had been in his new facility for five years, and I wondered how he felt about his greatly expanded operation.

Retrospective Interview with Joel Peterson, December 1996

When I met Joel on the sunny but cool December afternoon, the raven was still proclaiming "No wimpy wines allowed," but its voice was not so strident. I began our conversation with a request that Joel expand upon an earlier comment that Zinfandel is the Bordeaux wine grape of California.

"The great winegrape-growing regions of the world all have certain things in common," he began. "Bordeaux is a classic example of a great winegrape-growing region, where there is a selected grape for the region from which is consistently produced excellent wine. Yet within that region, there are many sub-regions: Pomerol, Saint Emillion, and Médoc. Each has particular climatic characteristics associated with them that cause the general mix of grapes to be different. So in the Médoc, you're talking primarily Cabernet Sauvignon-based wines. In Saint Emillion, the wines have substantially higher percentage of Cabernet Franc and Merlot, with Cheval Blanc being almost entirely Cabernet Franc. In Pomerol, you have Cabernet Sauvignon/Merlot and Cabernet Sauvignon/Cabernet Franc. The primary grape is Merlot, because the soils are so heavy. The most famous wine of the region is Petrus, which is 99 percent Merlot.

"So you get these twists on grapes within each region, depending on the micro-climate. They are all considered superb wines.

"In California, we have Zinfandel. Zinfandel is pervasive in California, but the original planters saw that in certain regions, Zinfandel needed complementary grapes. In Bordeaux, the primary complementary grapes to Cabernet Sauvignon are Cabernet Franc and Merlot. Those contribute certain desirable qualities to the Cabernet Sauvignon wines — deeper color, rounder structure, spiciness, acidity. The same in some instances is true of Zinfandel. There are some regions where Zinfandel is perfect alone. The grapes have deep color, lots of fruit, pepper, spiciness, and well-balanced acid and a full, round body. Sonoma Valley is a good example of such a region.

"There are regions where Zinfandel needs the support and complement of Petite Sirah (for its peppery, spicy quality), Carignane (also for its spiciness), or Alicante Bouschet (for its blueberry nose and incredibly deep rich color). These are the three primary varieties used with Zinfandel, to augment its naturally occurring character. These grapes were chosen because they are compatible with Zinfandel, just as, for centuries, the main complementary grapes Merlot and Cabernet Franc were chosen in Bordeaux. So primarily for these reasons, I consider Zinfandel the Bordeaux of California."

"If you bounce around from style to style, trying to make what the market seems to be supporting, you will lose your soul as a winemaker, because you will have nothing that is yours."

Joel Peterson

"There has been discussion on whether the finest wines come from the un-augmented variety. Do you prefer Zinfandel without the complement of any other variety?" I asked.

"Yes, I prefer pure Zinfandel in the best instances. I do blend in the complementary varieties if I think that will produce a better wine by doing so."

"Do you still believe that old vineyards, or what you consider old vineyards, are the sources for the best Zinfandel?" I asked.

"For my purposes, when I think of an old vineyard, I generally think of them as over 50 years. There's no doubt that they are the sources for the best Zinfandel wine. But having said that, one of Ravenswood's vineyards, Cooke, is considerably younger. There are a whole series of elements that go into the old vines being the best vines. They are non-irrigated, they are planted in the best locations, they have open canopies, and they can ripen only relatively small crops. Those are the immutable characteristics of old vines. Planted in the right locations, if you try to put a big crop on them one year, they will give you almost no crop the next year. They do not have the vigor of young vines, so you cannot over-crop them. So you have to set a crop level that is best for the vines, and if you are consistent with the crop level, you can get consistently high quality Zinfandel wine.

"You can do the same thing with a young vineyard, but it takes a huge amount of management. Zinfandel by nature is a fairly vigorous vine, depending on the rootstock. Nonetheless, you can develop a vineyard like Cooke, which will give you low tonnage yields of high quality fruit — just as high quality as the fruit from old vines, depending upon your selection of site, soils, and rootstock."

"Are you therefore saying that you could not distinguish between a Zinfandel wine made from an old vine vineyard and one made from a well-managed, well-situated young vine vineyard?" I asked.

"I could not tell the difference," Joel acknowledged. "I could tell the difference between Zinfandel wine made from vines that have been overcropped, or with too much canopy (vegetation), or that have been over-irrigated. These conditions can exist in both old vine and young vine vineyards. Yet with old vines, the potential for consistently high quality fruit is greater because the quality is less dependent upon human intervention. Old vines provide less opportunity for human greed to interfere."

"I like your frankness," I replied, as we both laughed a little at the significance of his remark.

"During the 10 years since I talked to you for my report on Zinfandel for ***PWV,*** what has changed?"

"We make a broader range of Zinfandel wines now," Joel replied. "In 1984, I had just started making Vintners Blend, and was producing only 500 cases. Now, I am producing 50,000 cases. I have broadened my scope of what I do with Zinfandel based upon the market point I am trying to hit. There is a broader-based market for Zinfandel now. In 1980, there was no market for a Vintners Blend, nor was there fruit available, because it was tied up in long-term contracts with big wineries. Since the mid-1980s, some of that fruit has become available, as well as some bulk wine. This enabled me to produce an under-$10 bottle of Zinfandel that drinks very well upon release, and is representative of the variety."

"Have you moved away, then, from making Zinfandel wines strictly with great ageing potential?"

"The average bottle of wine is consumed within two hours of leaving the store shelf," replied Joel. "I do not think that you need to play to that category exclusively. Certainly, if you are making moderately expensive wines, there is a certain crowd that will drink them immediately. Zinfandel usually drinks nicely a few months after being bottled. The vast majority of Zinfandels made today are made with up-front fruit, softness, color, and not much tannin. These wines do not have as much structure as wines meant to be laid down for a few years. They develop some complexity for two or three years, but they are usually best consumed within five to seven years of their vintage date.

"Yet the beauty of Zinfandel is that it has the potential for producing a broad range of styles of Zinfandel wine. It is probably the English who invented the concept that a wine that ages is a superior wine. They bought great quantities of wine, and while they consumed some of it while it was young, they stored much of it, and in fact developed a taste for older wines."

"Do you think that the wine that gains complexity in the bottle over several years is a better wine than the one that does not?"

"No, I do not," replied Joel. "I think that a wine that ages is a more interesting wine, and that such wines will be more pleasurable to drink over a longer period of time. It is also a rarer wine; it's harder to make; and it is difficult to find the vineyard that produces fruit that will make into a long-ageing wine. But wine runs the whole spectrum, and always has, from being a jug-quaffing wine that you get for pennies, to a wine that is exceedingly expensive — several hundred dollars per bottle upon release. Most people who love wine buy in the middle to the upper end of that range."

"Why is it harder to make a wine that ages well?" I asked.

"Because not all wine grapes have the extractable elements necessary for age-worthiness. Grapes with these elements are harder to find, because only a few locations are so exceptionally well suited to producing the finest grapes. Once you do find the grapes, it takes more skill on the part of the winemaker to make a balanced wine that will age."

"Then I am sure you determine the style of Zinfandel wine you will make each season by the character of the grapes that come in. Is that not so?"

"Absolutely," affirmed Joel. "We have a style, or approach, to Zinfandel winemaking at Ravenswood. It's a full-flavored, spicy wine that gives you the fullest expression possible of the nature and character of the vineyard. For our upper-end wines, in our winemaking process we are looking to make wine that tastes like wine. So there is full extraction of tannins, less expression of the fruit, warmer fermentation, and the wine is aged in from 30 percent to 50 percent new French oak for several months, giving it a recognizable oak component. Within our vineyards, we have several that consistently produce balanced, age-worthy wines that gain in complexity for 10 to 15 years.

"Yet within that style, we also have multiple variations. When we make Vintners Blend, which is bottled within the year, our primary objective is to maintain the flavor of fruit, the lightness and brightness that makes that wine so appealing. So we treat that wine more like fresh fruit. It has the elements of winemaking, but they are held back, so the fruit comes through. There is less tannin extraction, more expression of fruit, the wine is fermented at slightly cooler temperatures, and there is less oak component."

"What are your concerns with the alcohol content of your Zinfandel wines, since I assume you do have concerns?"

"Yes, I have concerns," Joel replied quickly. "The object, however, is not the alcohol. When people become obsessive about the alcohol, they miss the essence of winemaking. Winemaking is about ripe fruit, and alcohol is a product of the ripeness of the fruit. In some vintages, you get ripeness at lower sugars, and a wine with 12.5 percent alcohol. In other vintages, ripeness doesn't occur until the grapes have much higher sugars, which converts into much higher alcohol percentages. I harvest grapes for ripeness and ripe flavors. There are many elements that go into the physiological ripeness of fruit. The least important one is sugar content. Of course, you can get too much sugar in excessively hot years. If your alcohol content goes over 16 percent, it hasn't been a particularly good year. That is as bad a vintage as those of excessively cool years, which prevents the sugar from developing."

"The super-ripe style of Zinfandel, then, is not among your range of variations, is it?" I remarked. "Do you not like them, or do you disapprove of that style? They do seem to be capturing a lot of attention, and high scores, among wine writers."

"Yes, they usually do well in tastings," agreed Joel. "They are big wines, they are full-flavored wines, and in many ways, they are interesting and enjoyable wines. In other ways, they are almost undrinkable. In the best examples, the pruniness that comes with the over-ripe character of the fruit is nicely offset with judicious use of new French oak. I can enjoy drinking those wines once in a while. For their style, they are wonderful. Yet I certainly wouldn't want to drink them every day. Nor do I think that people should herald them as the quintessential Zinfandel wine. If all Zinfandel wines were made in that particular style, the Zinfandel market would probably be destroyed. There are far better balanced, far nicer wines out there, that will give the consumer more satisfaction over the long term than those wines.

"Part of the glory of Zinfandel, though, is that it can produce a fair number of exotic styles that are really good. That is part of the appeal of the variety, and what makes it unique."

"Moving along to my next subject, are you still a fierce advocate for the use of French oak rather than American oak for the ageing of Zinfandel?" I asked.

"American oak has gotten better, and it is certainly credible to try it with Zinfandel, and even with Cabernet Sauvignon, because it will give you a distinct character. The best samples of each are still distinguishable to me. Although I do not dislike all Zinfandel aged in American oak barrels, I still rate Zinfandel aged in French oak higher. My tasting notes consistently show this. To my taste, American oak dominates a wine. It is a coarser-grained wood, and the oak character comes out quickly, so you cannot leave your wine in new American oak barrels very long. If you believe that part of the character of Zinfandel wine comes from leaving the wine in barrels for 17 to 24 months, you will have to limit the amount of new oak you use — which is self-defeating — or use a tighter-grained barrel. American oak just doesn't fit my philosophy of winemaking.

"The benefits of oak-ageing wine do not just have to do with the slow oxidation that occurs through the wood. They also have to do with slow integration of the oak tannins and other components in the oak with the wine components at a molecular level. That slow combination that takes place in the barrel is of critical importance in developing fine wine. Without it, you may lose the center of the wine, nuances in the aroma, and much of the lingering finish."

"Occasionally, people will tell me that choosing French oak over American oak is just a marketing decision, and has little to do with the quality of the finished product," I remarked. Before I could pose my question, Joel burst out laughing. When he had recovered sufficiently to reply, he said, still greatly amused: "Of course it is a marketing choice! If you want to sell your wine, you age it in new French oak. The finished wine is better, and people will buy it because they like it better. It makes wines that I like better."

Then Joel qualified his answer a little. "If you have been making wine without ageing it in oak barrels, or only in neutral oak barrels, and you decide, because of customer preferences, to start using some new oak in your ageing program, then it is purely a marketing decision. But if you use new oak barrels because you believe that that is the way to make better and more age-worthy wine (as I do), then it is a stylistic decision based upon producing a certain kind of wine."

"The objection to using new or even one-year-old oak barrels that I hear most often is that oak covers up the beautiful Zinfandel fruit, and that the fruit is what makes it such an appealing wine," I said.

"Zinfandel with just fruit character is an incomplete wine," replied Joel. "It is a lovely wine to drink when young, but it lacks complexity and age-worthiness. The issue of oak is an old one, and is as much an issue of style as anything. It's also an issue of money. It is an expensive proposition not only to invest in the new barrels, but also to hold the wine for two years before you sell it. When a new region is being developed, it isn't as easy to extract capital for the wine production, nor can you sell your wines for as high per bottle price when you are new. Both these factors make it difficult to afford the new oak barrels that I believe are necessary to produce the best product possible.

"So whether or not to use new oak barrels becomes both a style and marketing decision. By necessity, some people may argue that the fruit is enough. Inevitably, however, as they become more profitable almost all wineries in the world will convert their wine ageing program to more new oak. For my part, not using new French oak barrels was never an option. From the first moment I decided to make Zinfandel, I decided I would use French oak. If I were going to make my statement as a winemaker with Zinfandel, it would have to be in the style of the finest wine possible.

"This ultimately takes us back to the question, 'What is wine?' I disagree that it is all about the fruit — a very important component, but just one component. Wine isn't about fruit; wine is about wine. Fruit is one of the components of that wine. Admittedly, with Zinfandel the fruit may be a more important component than with any other variety, because it does have such magnificent fruit. Yet it is important to make it into a wine, a complete wine, and not just a wine with a predominant fruit character. So the object is to develop the most interesting and complex beverage that you can, using the elements that you have to work with."

"On the subject of region, farming practices, age of vines, and winemaking style, how would you rank these in importance to the quality of the finished wine?" I asked.

"Wine isn't about fruit; wine is about wine."

Joel Peterson

"I would say region is the first consideration, then winemaking style, then farming practices, and then age of vines," Joel replied. "Region is a more universal factor than age of vines. Age of vines and their condition of health and balance are dependent upon farming practices. Winemaking style can have an enormous effect on the quality of the finished wine, all else being equal."

"At what age does a properly farmed young vineyard in a well suited region achieve quality of fruit equal to the fruit from a properly farmed vineyard 50 years old in a well suited region"? I then asked.

"All else being equal? At about 10 years," replied Joel. "The key is in farming practices. Young vines require more work to achieve consistent quality, and it is always tempting to try to get a few more tons per acre than is best for the quality — just because the young vines have the vigor to produce more. Most old vines will produce only 3½ tons per acre and stay in balance. Young vines can easily produce six or more tons per acre. With today's prices, dropping three or more tons of fruit per acre on the ground is like throwing away $6,000 per acre. Since the quality of fruit in well suited regions is quite good even at six tons per acre from young vines, that is probably what most growers will try to get. Given the high costs of establishing a new vineyard, few growers can afford to put half their crop on the ground."

As a closing question, I asked Joel what he felt was the most important part of a winemaker's job.

"Making wine," he replied with a good-natured smile.

"Well, then, what is the most important aspect of making wine?" I countered.

"I don't think there is one most important aspect. There are several aspects to making wine. If you fail in any one of them, the quality of the finished product will be diminished. To begin with, one has to understand the fruit, and what ripeness is all about. One has to have a wide range of winetasting experience so one knows the possibilities of what you can make and what you can't make, so you know what tastes good and what does not. One needs a sense of style. If you bounce around from style to style, trying to make what the market seems to be supporting, you will lose your soul as a winemaker, because you will have nothing that is yours.

"Another requirement of a good winemaker is flexibility. You do not want to be so rigid that you do not see the possibility of making something a little bit better. You want to see all the choices in a given set of circumstances for making the best product.

"The last requirement for me personally is to set up a system to keep track of what is happening in the winemaking process now that I do not personally monitor every single barrel of wine. When I started, I was winemaker for a 400-case winery. Now I am winemaker for a 120,000-case winery. This has meant setting up a good system and getting good people to work with me. As a result, I am probably making better wine now than when I was working two jobs and doing all the winemaking myself. I have a vastly improved understanding of winemaking, and have maintained and improved my sources for grapes."

By the end of our interview, I, too, had a vastly improved understanding of Joel and Ravenswood. As I was about to leave, I recalled one long-simmering question. "By the way, how *did* you ever come up with that slogan, 'No Wimpy Wines Allowed'?"

Joel laughed. "That's quite a story. It was about 1982, when white Zinfandel had become such a hot item. It was also the year that my partner, Reed Foster, and I realized that we needed a cash flow product, since our cash flow at the time was negative. We needed a product that we could turn around in a year. So one day, Reed said, 'Let's do white Zinfandel.'

"I replied, 'No way! There will be no wimpy wines at Ravenswood!'"

Joel said that he knew he could come up with a red Zinfandel product that would create a cash flow, which turned out to be Vintners Blend. But before that happened, Reed was in San Francisco selling wine to one of their wine merchants. "We pretty much hand-sold all our wines in those days," said Joel.

During his visit with the wine merchant, Joel told me, the merchant asked Reed, "Well, when is Ravenswood going to come out with a white Zinfandel?"

"That probably is not going to happen," replied Reed. "Our winemaker is so adamantly opposed to white Zinfandel that he has a sign over the door to the winery, 'No Wimpy Wines Allowed!'"

"Well," said Joel. "There was no sign. So when a few weeks later the merchant said he was coming to Sonoma, and wanted to come by the old winery to see the 'No Wimpy Wines Allowed' sign, Reed's son had one made, so that his father would not be seen as one who embellished the truth. After that, the slogan seemed to acquire a life of its own. Soon, Reed had it printed in several languages. T-shirts with different translations appeared; buttons followed. And that's the story of 'No Wimpy Wines.'"

Now we all know why there are no wimpy wines allowed at Ravenswood.

★ ★ ★ ★ ★

In April 2001, Constellation Brands, Inc. and Ravenswood Winery, Inc. entered into a merger agreement under which Constellation will acquire Ravenswood. Ravenswood will be managed by Constellation's fine wine division, Franciscan Estates. Joel Peterson, Winemaker and President of Ravenswood, will become General Manager and Head Winemaker of the Ravenswood Winery with Justin Faggioli as General Manager and Chief Operating Officer. Both will report to Agustin Francisco Huneeus, President of Franciscan Estates. Reed Foster, Chairman and Chief Executive Officer of Ravenswood, will remain a valued part of the management team.

Said Joel Peterson, "Constellation and Franciscan Estates value our hand-crafted approach to winemaking, and have the resources and infrastructure to help Ravenswood expand the number of consumers who can enjoy our wines. I look forward to working with Agustin Francisco Huneeus, and to continuing our strong relationships with our first-rate growers."

Joseph Swan Vineyards: Swan's Song

By the end of summer 1986, I had caught up to the tall, quiet, erect, white-haired Joseph Swan at his home on Laguna Road in the Russian River Valley. He began by describing how he became enamored of Zinfandel. It was by way of a 20-year-old 1937 Fountain Grove — which he felt was the perfect Zinfandel — a model to strive to match: "It was 12.5 percent alcohol, and had the perfect balance of components. The fruit was there, but as a part of the whole effect." I also learned that he had made his first home Zinfandel in 1968, and his first commercial vintage in 1969.

Yes, Joe expressed a distinct preference for French oak as the barrel of choice for Zinfandel ageing. "The best French wines in the world have always been aged in French oak," said Joe. "Since I believe Zinfandel can be a world-class red wine, that is why I, too, use French oak." Joe even went so far as to say that he felt there was "an excess of American oak" used in California winemaking.

Joe also described his Rhône-style approach to crushing and fermenting Zinfandel, and how in the early 1980s his attempt to produce a claret style, 12.5 percent alcohol Zinfandel, after the style of his beloved 1937 Fountain Grove (a more restrained, food-oriented wine) failed with consumers and tasting groups alike. This failure inspired some dislike for such tasting clubs as San Francisco's Vintners Club. "Tasting groups have done more harm than good," said Joe. "They are looking for the most powerful Zinfandel, the one to knock others off the table. They overlook the fact that wine is intended to go with food. Americans aren't European enough in their approach to wines. Europeans never consider wine except as an accompaniment for food."

Of course, what Swan overlooked was the fact that his customers had fallen in love with his big, earthy, full-bodied, fruity wines of the early 1970s. Perhaps he wasn't proud of these early Zinfandels; still, his customers loved them. They never did take to his restrained "food Zinfandels" — no matter how much "finesse" they had. Swan picked grapes for these at a field sample of 21° Brix (meaning he tested his sample in the vineyard) which soaked out to 22.5° in the fermentor. When I finally had the privilege of tasting a 1973 Swan, I could sympathize with his customers. The year was 1988, and the wine was 15 years old. A beautifully balanced, full-bodied, chocolatey, earthy wine with a rich aroma of moist dried cherries and spices, it was the centerpiece of the dinner. In fact, I've forgotten the dinner. The memory of the wine, however, has remained a benchmark for what a fully extracted, full-bodied 15-year old Zinfandel table wine can be.

1999
Frati Ranch
Russian River Valley
Zinfandel
Joseph Swan Vineyards
Produced and Bottled by Joseph Swan Vineyards
Forestville, California, Alcohol 15.1% by Volume

In a recent conversation with Joel Peterson, I asked him what led Joe to abandon his full-flavored, intense, and luscious style of Zinfandel in the early 1980s for a more elegant and restrained style.

"Several reasons," said Joel. "One was that he lost his Dry Creek Valley Zinfandel source about then, and his cooler region replacement vineyard didn't ripen as well. Also, he liked French wines, especially the Rhônes and Bordeaux, so he sought to recreate them in his Zinfandel, because of that early Fountain Grove. But what he failed to consider was that California is not France, and that the Zinfandel is a heat-loving Mediterranean grape, not the cool-climate grape that does well in Bordeaux."

Zinfandel, however, can achieve a desired ripeness in some of California's cooler regions. Joseph Swan was not the only winemaker who liked the wines made from such fruit. His difficulty with his customers and wine tasting groups had more to do with his radical change in style than in the quality of his wines. His 1984, a luscious, full-flavored, deep ruby colored 12.6 percent alcohol wine with the acid/pH numbers for great ageing potential, came close to achieving what he had liked in the early Fountain Grove, and certainly was a wine to be proud of.

Following Joe's death in 1992, his daughter, Lynn, and son-in-law, Rod Berglund, took over Joseph Swan Vineyards. When I once asked Rod about the practical reasons for producing Zinfandel, he replied with a laugh, "No one makes it for practical reasons; we make it because we love it!" Rod's respect for Zinfandel is such that in 1978, when he began making wine (partially at Joe Swan's insistence), Joe asked him what he intended to make. "Cabernet and Chardonnay," Berglund answered.

"What?" exclaimed Joe, "No Zinfandel?"

"No," responded Rod, "*you* make Zinfandel!"

Nonetheless, Rod is today producing Zinfandel in Joe's tradition with fruit from the Stellwegen Vineyard, Sonoma Valley, and a few other select old vineyards under lease to Swan Vineyards.

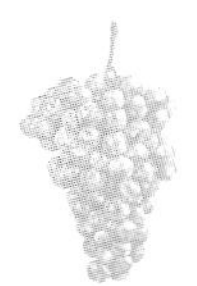

Pagani Vineyard: "Junk Grapes" Reconsidered

In 1984, a few years after I had settled into Napa Valley and before I got hooked on Zinfandel, I set out one early March morning to do a Sonoma County wildflower photography assignment for *Wine Country* magazine. By late afternoon, I was on my homeward journey down Sonoma's beautiful Valley of the Moon. Just south of Kenwood, a brilliantly beautiful head-trained vineyard up to its ancient fingertips in luxuriant golden mustard captured my attention. The vineyard stretched from the road back to the mountains, which the western sun had turned to shades of lavender and indigo blue. Silvery hints of the incoming fog were visible across the tops of the dark-hued mountains. Within seconds of happening upon this view, I had relinquished my space on the road to the car riding my bumper, and had parked on the broad shoulder. Foregoing my tripod, I reached for my camera, and began roaming along the edge of the vineyard, seeking a range of compositions.

One image turned out to be as nearly perfect as I could hope for, and I longed to know who owned the vineyard. It would take me eight years, however — until Veteran's Day, 1992, to find out.

Having that day off from my classes at Napa Valley College, I used the opportunity to arrange for a rendezvous with Paul Draper, winemaker for Ridge Vineyards, at Lytton Springs Winery. I wanted to be shown the Valle Vista Vineyard and the renowned Geyserville Vineyard. I met Paul and his vineyard manager, David Gates, early, and after a few photographs in the November-hued Valle Vista vineyard, we went on down Lytton Springs Road to Geyserville. After a visit with the Trentadues and a look at the vineyard, Paul asked me if I might like to join him and a "new grower we've just started buying from" for lunch. "He manages the Pagani Ranch, a wonderful old Zinfandel vineyard near Kenwood, and we've made arrangements to meet at the Golden Bear restaurant for lunch. We are going to have a barrel sample of the 1991 Zinfandel — our first from that vineyard, and also two samples of Alicante Bouschet — since we had to take the old vine Alicante Bouschet if we wanted the Zinfandel."

I felt a delightful tingle of electricity run up my spine. I was sure that I was at last to meet the owners of my wonderful old mustard-filled vineyard, so I enthusiastically accepted Paul's invitation to join his party for lunch, but said little of my secret thoughts and hopes as to whom this vineyard owner might be.

I had to stop for gas at Kenwood, and when I arrived at the Golden Bear, Paul and David were already seated with the dark-haired, soft-spoken Dino Amantiti, vineyard manager of the Pagani Vineyard and grand-nephew to its owners, Louis and Olive Pagani. After introductions, I explained to Dino just how many years I had been looking forward to this moment, and promised to show him a print of my image as soon as possible.

Then it was on to the barrel samples, and lunch. The 1991 Pagani Vineyard Zinfandel was showing great promise, and I knew I would have to have a case of this flagship vintage when it was released in 1993. (I got my case in fall of 1993, and it turned out to be one of my all-time favorite Zinfandels.)

After lunch, we all followed Dino to the vineyard, where he gave us a description of its layout and showed us a photograph dating to about 1900 of the Pagani Vineyard and the Kunde Vineyard beyond. No question that the Pagani Vineyard is pre-Prohibition and that most of the original vines are still thriving.

Upon parting, Dino invited me to make arrangements to meet his uncle and aunt, who, although healthy and active, were nearing 90 years old. "They can give you some interesting stories about this vineyard and the old winery beside my parents' home that nearly collapsed in the 1906 earthquake," he suggested.

It wasn't until summer of 1996 that I was able to schedule some time to sit with the 93-year-old Louis Pagani and his 88-year-old sister, Olive. The last of seven children, Louis and Olive are proud of their ranch, their long healthy lives working it, their ancient Zinfandel vines, and the richly-flavored wines made from the grapes these vines have been producing for nearly 100 years.

Although they were looking a little frail when they met me at the door of their ranch house at the northern edge of the beautiful Zinfandel, Alicante Bouschet, and Mataro vineyard, both Louis and Olive were nonetheless firm in their handshakes and cordial and warm in their greetings. They then invited me to take a stroll through the cozy kitchen, living room, and hallway, to see the many photographs of their beloved vineyard. I looked forward to a print of the image I'd made joining them. After being asked to admire the view from the living room window across the vineyards to the tiny original winery at its far edge, Louis, Olive, and I sat down at the big, square kitchen table to talk. We were soon joined by Louis's old dog, who stretched himself with a lazy groan beneath us.

Louis began to tell me a little about his life on the 187-acre Pagani Ranch, 55 acres of which is planted with grapevines.

"I never went to college. By the time I was 12 years old, I was driving a four-horse team, and working seven days a week. There was no time for vacations, or even parties. Half the Zinfandel was planted before 1900," he said. "The block west of the railway bed was already planted when my father bought the property in 1884. The rest, my father planted in 1902, the year I was born. That makes the vineyard and me the same age. The Alicante Bouschet was planted in 1918."

During Prohibition, Louis said, the grapes from the family ranch were shipped to East Coast home winemakers. The white grapes brought $35 per ton, the Zinfandel, $50 per ton, and the Alicante Bouschet, $200 per ton. "The Alicante was popular because of its color," explained Louis. "Some people even mixed in a little Alicante with ordinary white wine to give it color, so they could sell it as Burgundy. It didn't make good wine, but it made good average wine. Back then, people weren't so finicky as they are today."

Louis Pagani and Dino Amantiti

Although a Pagani Zinfandel won a gold medal at the 1946 California State Fair, in recent years wine producers have thought of his 32 acres of Zinfandel, 15 acres of Alicante Bouschet, six of Mataro, and another four of mixed white, as "junk grapes." In 1991, Paul Draper was the first winemaker (except for the 1946 Pagani Zinfandel winemaker), to keep the Pagani Zinfandel grapes separate, and to bottle the wine under the Pagani Vineyard designation. With quick sell-out of that 2,700-case production upon its release in fall 1993, followed by the critically acclaimed 1992 vintage released in 1994, Louis has been getting more attention from the press than he knows what to do with.

"I don't like my photograph taken," he said to me when I returned a little later for some photographs beside a Zinfandel vine that he remembers planting. "But I guess I should just enjoy all this attention, now that it's come. I always knew those were good grapes. These vines never have been pushed to carry big crops. Two and a half tons per acre has been its consistent production for as long as I can remember. Draper recognized the quality of the vines, and that they had never been over-cropped. I've never left more than seven or eight spurs per vine, and I always removed the weak shoots. So when Paul came by to see them, he knew the grapes were worth keeping separate. Of course, he picks them riper than we did in 1946. He also knows what to do with the Alicante Bouschet, while all the other 'Johnny-Come-Latelys' didn't know what to do with it. I wouldn't sell the Zinfandel without the buyer also taking the Alicante. All our previous buyers just dumped the grapes into their red wine blend."

"Did you ever consider taking out your Zinfandel, and replanting to the more popular French varieties?" I asked Louis.

"No!" he exclaimed. "Not that there wasn't a lot of pressure to do just that — it might surprise you to know from whom," he commented, looking rather sharply at me. "But I loved these grapes, and if I had taken them out and planted to Cabernet Sauvignon on AxR-1, where would I be now? I'd have nothing. No, those vines have been in the ground for as long as I have been alive. Now, those people who wanted me to take them out have come to their senses, and are really glad I didn't. Now, I get people asking to lease my vineyard — or even buy it, but no way! My contracts are long term, with Ridge taking the most tons. The rest goes to St. Francis, Topolos, and Wellington." (Since 1998, the Pagani Ranch grapes are contracted only to Ridge and St. Francis.)

"I am sure that over the 80 or more years that you have been working this vineyard, you have pretty much gotten to know every vine as if it were a friend. I am sure you spent many hours in this vineyard," I remarked to Louis.

"Yes, we hand-hoed everything to keep the weeds down, we suckered the vines, and all the sulfuring was done with a hand-held sack of sulfur, or, later, with a backpack duster machine. When I sulfured, I would have to be out in the vineyard by 5:30 a.m. and be finished by 8:00 a.m. for one and a half weeks. It certainly wasn't fun. When I finished the sulfuring, there were many other chores to do, since we also kept dairy cattle and pear trees. Eleven-hour days were pretty common.

"Ploughing and disking were done with horses. We were the first to disk in the vineyard and cuttings 55 years ago, using a heavy disk. Today, all the sulfuring is done by helicopter, and we don't keep dairy cattle any longer. We also hire crews to do the pruning. But we still do not have much use for any sprays other than a little Round-Up herbicide."

Dino Amantiti, who is vineyard manager for St. Francis Winery located north of Kenwood, as well as vineyard manager for his great-uncle and aunt Pagani, expanded upon the story of how Paul Draper became the first producer to keep the Pagani Ranch Zinfandel separate.

"Our grapes went to Sebastiani for many years," said Dino. "Before Sebastiani, they went to Martini and Prati in Forestville, who bulked the wine to Paul Masson for 25 years. When the market changed, and the deal with Paul Masson fell through, Sebastiani got them for quite a few years — until they flat out dropped us in 1988, because they didn't want the Alicante Bouschet, Mataro, or Petite Sirah. So I was scrambling for someone to buy the grapes. St. Francis had just started its Zinfandel program with the old vine four-acre Francesco Vineyard, and couldn't handle the 55 acres of grapes I needed a market for. I had to find a home not just for our Zinfandel but also our Alicante, Petite Sirah, Mataro, and mixed whites.

"I came across Ridge, and Paul Draper immediately recognized the quality of the Zinfandel. His keeping the grapes separate, and bottling the wine under the Pagani vineyard designation really helped to give the ranch the recognition it deserved. It took a long time to find someone who was interested in keeping the grapes separate, and working with them. We acknowledge and appreciate that Ridge did that. Like my uncle told you, people used to call his grapes 'junk grapes.' But my uncle knew that it was the Alicante that gave Pagani Zinfandel its deep color and spicy, rich flavors. Paul Draper understood that, too, and is happy to have the Alicante and the Mataro. My aunt and uncle also sell St. Francis about 10 to 12 tons of Alicante. There isn't much Alicante around anymore."

For a few years, Michael Topolos got two to three tons of Pagani Zinfandel and a little Alicante Bouschet. Topolos' last vintage of both the Zinfandel and Alicante Bouschet Reserve was 1997. Allocation of Alicante Bouschet grapes to St. Francis increased to 23 tons in 1998.

Dino admitted to me after my conversation with his uncle that, yes, it was he who had tried to talk his uncle into taking out the old Zinfandel and replanting with Cabernet Sauvignon on wires. "I was young, and thought I knew everything. He of course would have nothing to do with my suggestions, and it caused some hard feelings between us for a few years," recalled Dino. "But I grew up, and today, I am very happy that Uncle Louis stood by his Zinfandel. One of my greatest pleasures, and also of my mother, who helps in the vineyard, is taking care of these magnificent old vines."

On November 21, 2000, Louis Pagani died peacefully in the Santa Rosa Hospital at age 98. According to Dino, Louis collapsed in the kitchen of his home Thursday, November 16, and was rushed to the hospital where he was put into intensive care. His heart just stopped five days later. May God rest his soul.

St. Francis Vineyards

In December 1996, I managed to get ahold of the amiable and philosophic Tom Mackey for an hour's meeting. I was hoping to round out my perspective on St. Francis Vineyards Zinfandel and the Pagani Vineyard. After all, wasn't St. Francis famous for its Chardonnay and Merlot? How did Zinfandel get into the mix? Dino Amantiti joined us for a few minutes in Tom's office at the lovely St. Francis Vineyards.

"I remember drinking Zinfandel since the early 1970s," said Tom, whose appreciation for Zinfandel has gone through something of a rebirth. "Especially the big, rich, extracted wines with alcohol between 17 percent and 18 percent. This was the style of Zinfandel that was getting all the attention, although it wasn't the only style being made. In fact, when I was at California State University, Fresno, one of the classes I gave was on Zinfandel styles. There were pretty much three styles back then. One was a very ripe style with high alcohol made by Ridge, Sutter Home, David Bruce, Mayacamas, and Monteviña, who became known for these wines, and which were perceived by some consumers as oddities. A second was a mid-level claret style with lower alcohol. And there was a Beaujolais, which was a light and fruity Zinfandel made for immediate consumption. From the mid-1970s to early 1980s, those seemed to be the main styles.

"Then by the mid-1980s, almost everyone shifted to what was being called 'food-friendly' Zinfandels. A perception had developed that there was too much alcohol in the big wines to match up with food. The trend for many producers went towards a more restrained, more immediately accessible claret style. Only since about 1990 have producers reverted to the bigger style of the old days. They have learned that you can go for that extraction and that style without reaching those excesses of alcohol and overripe flavors that turned them into more novelty wines. The big ones sold back then, but there weren't many of them.

"Today, producers such as Ridge have learned that you can be a bit more mainstream and still make some of the best fully-extracted Zinfandels. These are very good Zinfandels, but they are not 'off the charts' in extraction and alcohol. And you can make enough so that the Zinfandel-drinking public has access to it. Of course, some producers are still making huge Zinfandels that are bottled with over 17 percent alcohol, and there's always room in the industry for an oddity. But at 10,000 cases, or even 4,000 to 5,000, you don't want to produce an oddity.

"We got into producing Zinfandel almost by accident. We were buying Chardonnay from a vineyard that Dino farms, the Francesco, and when Francesco's white Zinfandel contract to a big Napa Valley producer ended in 1988, we were asked if we wanted the grapes, or should he pull the vines and plant Chardonnay. We thought we should give them a try — at least Dino thought we should, being from four generations of a Zinfandel-growing family. The wine came out better than expected — over 15 percent alcohol. We had rain that year, so we couldn't pick them as soon as we would have liked. Also, I wasn't that familiar with how to select the harvest date for Zinfandel then. Basically, all I knew was that there should be some raisining in the bunches when you picked them. So by chance, I ended up picking the grapes when they were fully ripe, which led to a 15 percent wine. But to tell the truth, I don't think 15 percent alcohol is out of line for Zinfandel.

"Today, I try for the finished wines to have close to 15 percent alcohol. I have found that we can balance it with the other varieties that are in the vineyard mix, and with proper use of wood, it doesn't taste alcoholic. It tastes like a big, rich wine. I'm not shooting for alcohol, though. I'm shooting for the flavors that occur when the grapes get that ripe. When we got rid of that old food-wine thing, we became free to let the grapes get as ripe as they needed to, for the best flavors."

Again, Dino offered his perspective on how St. Francis became a prestigious Zinfandel producer. "I began working for St. Francis Winery in 1989. I was already managing the Francesco Vineyard, owned by Dewey Bargiacchi. The vineyard was made up of Chardonnay, Pinot Noir, and four acres of 70-year-old Zinfandel, which had been going for white

Zinfandel for three years. I felt it was an outrage to sell that beautiful fruit from those old vines for white Zinfandel. So when the contract ended in 1988, I convinced Dewy to let St. Francis try them, and also convinced the St. Francis partners, and Tom here, to make a small trial release of red Zinfandel wine from these old vines. I felt it was important for St. Francis to be the first to use these grapes for red Zinfandel.

"It turned out to be an incredible wine, and from then on, the Francesco Zinfandel fruit has been used by St. Francis in an 'Old Vine' designation. The vines are 70 years old, and I limit their production to three tons per acre. Anything more than that, the vines just don't have the capacity to ripen the grapes. For the four-acre vineyard, we get 12 tons, which gives us about 720 cases. For our 1992 Old Vine Zinfandel, we used 50 percent Francesco and 50 percent Pagani Zinfandel."

"Do you limit your Pagani Vineyard to about the same yield?" I asked.

"No, that vineyard is so old that it self-regulates," responded Dino. "Some blocks yield only about one-half ton per acre, others maybe as much as 2½ tons. I never get more than that. You have to prune the vines to just a few spurs per vine. If you leave too many spurs, the vines will drop leaves prematurely in the early fall, and you won't get ripeness or flavor. Each vine tells you how to prune it so that it won't become stressed. If you stress it, you will kill it. These old 100-year-old vines can't handle stress. I have to work in partnership with that vineyard, and let the vines tell me how much crop they can carry."

"We've been getting Pagani Zinfandel grapes since 1991, the same year Ridge began to take the grapes, but just a small amount," Tom resumed. "Dino asked us if we could take the few acres of the white grapes, since Ridge had dug in its heels against taking the white grapes. We didn't mind taking the white grapes as long as we could have a few tons of the Zinfandel as well. We couldn't take the entire crop because there was too much for our capacity, and we had just begun our Zinfandel program. So we got a few tons — too little to bottle separately. We get about 12 tons now. We have been bottling a Pagani Vineyard Zinfandel since 1994 — which gives us about 800 cases. It still seems like a small amount, almost too little to bottle separately, since it isn't enough to be widely available."

"I wonder if there is not another problem," I remarked. "I agree that these small lots of intensely-flavored Zinfandel are such special wines that it becomes almost unconscionable not to bottle them separately. However, if you serve other red wines along with these dramatic wines at a meal, you have to be sure to serve the other red wines — Pinot Noir, Merlot, Cabernet Sauvignon — first. The Zinfandel will overwhelm the flavors in the other wines if it goes first."

"It's true," said Dino. "Zinfandel is a special variety. It's time it's being recognized, and accorded respect at the table."

"What makes it special to you?" I asked.

"It's the quality of the fruit from these old vines," Dino responded.

"You can't discount the history, either," said Tom. "There's a lot of history involved in these old Zinfandel vineyards. You can trace the whole pre-Prohibition course of Zinfandel by looking at where the fruit from these vines went. Even if people weren't calling it Zinfandel back then, the fruit from these historic vineyards often formed the basis for the best red wines being made then.

"There's a lot of things going for Zinfandel that other varieties in California have yet to achieve," continued Tom. "It's not constrained by the European model, so we're getting to play around a little more with it. Zinfandel is no longer judged in terms of the Bordeaux, the finest of which need to age up to 20 years before drinking. We're pretty much beyond thinking of Zinfandel as an inferior, more or less everyday, grape.

"There are too many good Zinfandels out now, and each has its own type of complexity. Nor is it any longer being judged in terms of its ageability, any more than a Burgundy is. Pinot Noir does not necessarily improve in flavor and complexity in the bottle beyond a few years. Yet does that make it inferior? Of course not! The same can be said of Zinfandel. For my taste, I think putting 10 years of age on a Zinfandel is pushing it. It isn't that it won't still be a good wine at 10 years. But after 10 years, that initial attractive fruitiness that makes it so appealing will have dissipated."

"What have been your best Zinfandel vintages?" I asked.

"The 1989 vintage got rained on, but it came out good nonetheless," observed Tom. "The 1990, I picked too early, so it was a lighter vintage, but still okay. The 1991 was lighter than the 1990 — I again picked too early. So I sold it in bulk because that wasn't the style I was trying to develop. Our 1989 was our first Zinfandel, and it established a benchmark for us. After the slightly lighter 1990 vintage, I didn't want to put our Old Vine Zinfandel label on the 1991 because I didn't want to seem to be going away from that intense and extracted style two years in a row. We came back in 1992 with a big one. Then in 1993 and 1994, we had good vintages, all the way through to 1996."

"Your 1992 vintage was the one that placed second in the Vintners Club taste-off," I remarked. "In fact, it came within a point or two of placing first. But I think one of the tasters was put off by the amount of American oak, and so scored it pretty low — enough to keep you out of first place."

"1992 was the first year we bottled our Old Vines blend with the Pagani," explained Tom. "1989 and 1990 were both strictly Francesco. Our 1992 and 1993 were both a blend of Francesco and Pagani. Since then, we've managed to secure enough additional old vine Zinfandel vineyards to fill out our Old Vine blend — Dino gets the credit for that — and still keep our Pagani separate. Dino located three or four old vineyards whose fruit used to go to white Zinfandel. The growers are interested in getting their fruit into the red Zinfandel program, and so we checked out the vines and tried the wine for a year. We liked it.

"We have been able to expand Old Vine production and keep the Pagani separate, thanks to Dino's efforts at scouting out these fine old vineyards. These vineyards all fulfill exactly our profile of what we want in old-vine Zinfandel vineyards. They are head trained and dry farmed, and the fruit has intensity and richness. The youngest was planted in the 1930s.

"We have also secured an old Alicante Bouschet vineyard up the road just to use in my Zinfandels to bump up the color, and also to balance out the alcohol and sugar. Some of these old vine vineyards are planted mostly in Zinfandel, without a coloring grape. As a result, while we may end up with fully flavored, high-alcohol wine, it can be a lighter-colored wine. We now get 20 tons of old vine Alicante. Those vines are as old as some of the old vine Zinfandel we get."

With the increased allocation in 1998 of Pagani Ranch Alicante Bouschet grapes, and St. Francis' new Wild Oak Winery debut in 1999, Tom made about four barrels of Alicante Bouschet for sale in the tasting room of Wild Oak.

"The Old Vines blend now has 27 vineyards, many of which are just one or two acres. The St. Francis Pagani Vineyard blend Zinfandel now is a blend of mostly Zinfandel from the Pagani Vineyard, a little Alicante Bouschet, and a bit of Petite Sirah."

"Why are more growers interested in getting into the red Zinfandel program?" I asked. "There is still considerable demand for white Zinfandel, and aren't there additional risks in leaving the fruit on the vines longer for red Zinfandel, and more work in limiting the crop? They must really have wanted to see their grapes go into red Zinfandel."

"Oh, sure," replied Tom. "We increase their incentive by paying them double the price per ton over what they were being paid for white Zinfandel. That also gives us the incentive to work with them to take care of the vines so that they will ripen their fruit to a higher sugar content without suffering stress."

"Also," Dino added, "the growers of these fine old vineyards have a lot of pride in their fruit, and are pleased to see their grapes going to a high-profile winery with a good reputation for producing award-winning red Zinfandel."

"Have you ever thought of separating out any other vineyards from your Old Vine blend besides the Pagani, and bottling them as vineyard-designated Zinfandels?"

"I'd like to, but it's as much a marketing decision as a winemaker decision. Believe me, it was pulling teeth just to get the Pagani on the label," replied Tom. "Very small lots create problems for our marketing staff. There is only enough wine from each lot for each market to have only a few bottles. Quite often, our smallest markets don't get any, and they are unhappy about this. Perhaps when we have enough vineyards to keep up our current production of our Old Vine blend *and* keep these two vineyards separate, we will offer them as vineyard-designated lots — perhaps by 1998."

"Those two are nice Zinfandel lots," affirmed Dino.

"I know vineyard-designating their best lots of Zinfandel is one of the things serious Zinfandel producers do," Tom continued. "Kenwood has five or seven, as does Ridge; and Rosenblum has 15 or 20. That is also one of the things that makes Zinfandel distinct. Few other varieties lend themselves as well as Zinfandel to vineyard designation. There are a few, but not nearly so many as with Zinfandel. That seems to be one of the elements of the mystique of Zinfandel — that many vineyards are distinct enough to keep them separate. It has almost become expected of top flight Zinfandel producers that they have more than one Zinfandel."

"How many cases of Zinfandel are you now producing?"

"We made 1,700 in 1989; in 1996, we made about 9,000 cases — 7,500 Old Vine and 800 to 900 Pagani Ranch."

"How does this compare with your other varieties?" I queried. "I imagine it is still a small amount, relatively speaking?"

"Oh, yeah," Tom answered. "For example, we have produced 60,000 cases of Chardonnay. Our winery production is at about 150,000 cases, with plans to expand to about 250,000 to 300,000 cases over the next four to five years (through construction of St. Francis/Wild Oak Winery)."

"What are your winemaking practices for Zinfandel?" I asked.

"We use 10- to 20-ton tanks, and pump-over three times each day," explained Tom. "At the end of fermentation, we sluice out the grapes from tanks, which gives us our last pump-over. The Zinfandel is pressed in a tank press, then put into 100 percent new American oak, where it goes through malolactic fermentation. The wine stays in the barrels for 12 to 15 months, and is racked as necessary.

"I like to pick when a bunch sample shows 23.5° to 24° Brix, so that the wine soaks out to 25° or 25.5° Brix in the tank. This gives me a 14.8 percent to 15.2 percent alcohol in my finished wine. Fortunately, we are not hung up anymore on the Bordeaux style of austere wines. There is a narrow window as to what Cabernet Sauvignon should taste like, and all the variations are slight. Obviously, no one is going to make a 17.5 percent alcohol Cabernet Sauvignon, Merlot, or Pinot Noir. The wines would seem way out of balance, and would not fit into a certain way people think of those varieties. The range of acceptable style is much narrower with the Bordeaux and Burgundy varieties, as well as with the Rhône and Italian varieties. Of course, that means Cabernet Sauvignon and these other varieties are much easier to judge than Zinfandel.

"With Zinfandel, which does not have a strong European counterpart as do the French varieties, you are allowed to be a bit exotic. It's okay for Zinfandel to be luscious and fruity, and over 12.5 percent alcohol. I think the range of acceptability for Zinfandel styles has narrowed down a little in the last six or eight years, but you still can have anything from your Beaujolais-style to your dry port-like style.

"I figure Zinfandel is where we can exaggerate."

Tom Mackey

"Generally speaking, I am looking for clean, simple, fruity aromas from the grapes when they are crushed. Zinfandel grapes do not have a pungent smell. I look for 15 percent to 20 percent raisins, which soak out in tank. Since 1996, I add a little sulfur to tone down any off-yeasts or bacteria that could cause problems later on. Sulfur addition is especially necessary when you let grapes hang out there a little longer for these riper styles. A little fermentation could begin in the clusters, or even a little bunch rot. Last year, we had a stuck fermentation from one of our vineyards. A slightly elevated VA developed, because I didn't sulfur. I hit it with some potent yeast, but I didn't knock down the wild yeasts as much as I would have liked. I decided not to make that mistake again, so this year, I blasted the grapes with some SO_2 at the crusher, then I inoculated next day. I had no problems. The wines all fermented out clean and rich, and they are just finishing up malolactic now [December]."

"What kind of acid/pH numbers are you getting with this sugar content?" I asked.

"At this ripeness, the acid/pH is all over the board," responded Tom. "Acid can range from 6.0 g/L to 8.5 g/L — although not often is it that high; pH ranges from 3.2 to over 4.0. When you're bringing in ripe fruit, the acid tends to be somewhat subdued. Nonetheless, I don't add acid to red wines, even though the pH goes up a bit after malolactic."

"Does the higher pH mean your Zinfandels will have a shorter ageing time in the bottle?"

"Probably a little, but not as you would notice," Tom replied. "I think that after 10 years, Zinfandel takes on claret-like qualities anyway, and so are best consumed before then. You won't find too many Zinfandels over 10 years that have retained the berry character that makes them so attractive in their first few years. That is just the nature of the grape. Of course, if you like that claret character better than the berry fruit character of the younger Zinfandels, then you should age them. My Zinfandels will certainly age for 10 years."

"Do you filter?"

"Usually not. I don't filter Zinfandel at all. I'll rack it a couple of times, and after it has finished malolactic, I'll rack it, sulfur it, then rack it one more time, and put it into barrels — 100 percent new American oak for 12 to 14 months. When I first started, I used a mixture of one- and two-year-old wood. Then I found that with our Zinfandel, and picking it as ripe as we do, it can stand up to 100 percent new wood.

"When I was sitting with others for the *Practical Winery & Vineyard* report (May/June 1997), I discovered most of us preferred American oak to French oak for Zinfandel. There was one Napa Valley producer who is a stickler for French oak. His style is more restrained, more elegant. I can appreciate that style. At the same time, I figure Zinfandel is where we can exaggerate. I don't like to overwhelm the wine with wood, because I think the wood should be just one of many elements in the wine. I don't think 100 percent new American oak overwhelms our style of Zinfandel — because of the rich ripe character of the fruit."

"You're making a pretty dramatic statement by using that much new American oak," I remarked. "I can think of a couple of other producers who use 100 percent new American oak, but not for 12 to 14 months."

"I didn't know he used that much new wood for that long, either," said Dino, looking almost as surprised as I know I felt.

"I prefer that the oak be noticed, although not overwhelming," explained Tom. "I like not only to taste the fruit but also to taste the barrel. The fruit should be tasted first, then the oak. Another thing barrels do besides adding flavor and helping to age the wines is they help to clarify the wine. If a wine isn't what I consider clean, I'll filter. I don't have any religious proscription against filtering. If the wine hasn't fallen bright in the barrel or through subsequent rackings, I'll filter it. So far, I haven't filtered any Zinfandel."

"Do you find that new barrels contribute more to clarification than older barrels?" I asked.

"I think so. New oak has more phenolics that aid in precipitating out colloids and other suspended materials in the wine. With the vineyards we've been able to get, and the intensity of the fruit, I have not seen any problems keeping Zinfandel in 100 percent new American oak for a year or so. The wine has been well accepted by both the critics and the consumers," he added, showing no signs of reconsidering his oak program. "The barrels are mostly A & K Missouri, with medium toast, done in the European style. We are their second largest purchaser of wine barrels. We had about 360 barrels of Zinfandel in 1996, and that is all going into new A & K, for about 10,000 cases."

"Tell me more about the style you have settled upon. You were saying that you don't mind if your wine has over 15 percent alcohol, as long as it has rich, ripe balanced flavor."

"Most people are going for the riper style of Zinfandel," responded Tom. "You go with what you like to do, and also with what sells. With Zinfandel, you have to make something that appeals to consumers, and even though people don't like to admit it, you have to make something that appeals to critics. Most influential critics are going to like a Zinfandel with lots of up-front character, strong regional varietal character, a little bit of noticeable wood. I seem to remember 20 to 25 years ago, even back then, these oddities, as they were sometimes called, seemed to rate the highest. David Bruce's 1970s Zinfandel with 18.2 percent alcohol usually garnered the highest marks. Writers were enamoured with these concentrates, and still are, although not to such a degree. In some ways, things haven't changed that much."

"Don't you think that the wine writers are sometimes as influenced by consumer trends as well as the reverse?" I countered. "It has seemed to me that the enthusiastic, even passionate, response of consumers to the Zinfandels of the 1990s has substantially influenced writers to readjust their perception of Zinfandel. It seems that consumers have had significant influence on the critics to become more receptive to Zinfandel being Zinfandel. Critics have had to become more receptive to Zinfandel's luscious up-front fruitiness and more appreciative of a wider variety of styles and regional character than they were previously known for."

"That's an interesting thought," replied Tom. I waited for a further comment, but since none was forthcoming, I moved to my next question.

"What are your thoughts on the future of Zinfandel?" I asked.

"The trouble with Zinfandel is that, as far as vineyards go, we are not going to plant much more," responded Tom. "We are concentrating on getting grapes that have been going to other producers, often for white Zinfandel. I don't see a lot of new Zinfandel planting going on. There's some, but even so, I believe the supply of fruit from well-favored mature vineyards will always be limited. Of course, none of these old vineyards is immortal. Many of them will die off in the next 10 to 15 years. Will they be replanted? It depends on the economics.

"We try to encourage our growers to replant with Zinfandel, and we do what we can to help them. Of course, as more and more of the vineyards are replanted, the character of the wine could possibly change. Fortunately, there already are a fair number of mid-aged and younger Zinfandel vines that could well mature into something really nice. Nonetheless, the mystique for current Zinfandels is for older vines and small yields, which does not encourage new growers to plant Zinfandel — unless they want to establish something of value for their grandkids. With the cost of land in this region together with the cost of establishing a vineyard, growing Zinfandel at four tons per acre will probably not be enough to break even. With a big investment in land and vines, you have to be able to show a profit in five or six years."

"The Pagani Vineyard," commented Dino, "has been manicured all its life. That's why it is still alive and producing such wonderful fruit. But the tonnage doesn't justify it as a business. My uncle and aunt have kept the vines around basically for their history — and the quality of wine."

"Is it not feasible, then, to grow Zinfandel?" I asked.

"Only if you have the land paid for," said Tom. "If you are paying off land with a Zinfandel vineyard, you have to have a lot of money. Even at

$2,000 per ton, you will be losing money every year. You will need at least three tons per acre to break even. So if you were to buy a vineyard now, unless you have a lot of money to lose, you wouldn't buy an old-vine Zinfandel vineyard."

"Is it feasible to buy land, and plant a new Zinfandel vineyard?" I asked.

"That's a tough call," responded Tom. "You would have to find good soil. I personally might do that, but it is still a tough call. You need to graft your wood to St. George, and you need old budwood. Anything over five tons per acre even from young vines, you won't get the intensity of color to make the best wine. By contrast, if you were to plant Merlot, Cabernet Sauvignon, or Cabernet Franc, with trellises, irrigation, and judicious use of fertilizer, you can get up to nine or 10 tons per acre while maintaining the quality. So it's a tough decision to plant Zinfandel."

"Do you consider yourself a serious Zinfandel producer now, as well as a serious Chardonnay and Merlot producer?" I asked.

"Well, yes! As I said earlier, I have been a fan of Zinfandel since the early 1970s. It was just that my attention had gotten focused on other things. You could say that Zinfandel fell into our lap in 1989, and we decided to go with it. You also have to keep in mind where the trends are going. Obviously, we're in this business to make money. If this had been an old Grenache or Gamay vineyard, I may have thought twice about going into production of those varieties just because there was a fine old vineyard available. Knowing that Zinfandel was on its way back into fashion, I decided to see what we could do with it, as a small trial release. See what kind of demand there was."

"As it turned out, our 1989 was one of the hottest wines we made that year," said Dino. "It blew out of here instantly."

"We are in the Zinfandel business," reiterated Tom. "It started out as a lark in 1989, and now we're seriously into making Zinfandel. Dino, of course, had much to do with it. Coming from a family which has been growing Zinfandel for 100 years, and which still owns one of the finest and largest stands of remaining 95-year-old Zinfandel in Sonoma Valley, gave him an edge. He obviously brought a lot of passion and enthusiasm for the variety. Besides," he added with an appreciative laugh, "he's very persistent. Another 10 years, who knows what the trends will be. I don't think it will have changed that much."

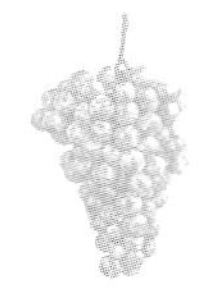

Valle Rossi Vineyard

I met Valle Rossi in February 1997. He was a small-statured man, somewhat frail, but with a wiry build. His step was firm, and his deep-set blue eyes were bright and intense — even piercing — in their steady gaze. He walked with me through a portion of the vineyard, and talked of his life on this beautiful 132-acre ranch located on Lawndale Road, just above the Pagani Ranch in Kenwood. About 30 acres of the ranch are in vineyard, but producing vines amount to only about 10 acres. Lawndale Road, little more than a one-lane road, cuts through the vineyard.

Valle was born in 1910. Louis Pagani remembers riding his horse over to the Rossi ranch when he was 7 years old to see the new baby, who was Valle Rossi. For Valle, the ranch was one of his last remaining sources of joy. His daughter had died from cancer when she was 20, his wife died young, also from cancer. A few years after these terrible losses, his only son suffered severe head injuries in a motorcycle accident. Under Valle's care, he recovered, but was stricken with seizures that became increasingly severe and more frequent. Then, early one morning, he took his own life with a shotgun. After this final tragedy, all that Valle had left was his beautiful Zinfandel Ranch set upon rolling hills overlooking Sonoma Valley, and a few old friends including Michael and Lisa Topolos, and their sons Marcos and Lucas. In fact, the Topoloses, who began buying Valle's grapes in 1985, had become Valle's replacement family, watching out for him, he said, and including him in their family dinners several times a week. They also helped him take care of the vineyard.

The Rossi Ranch has a long history. "My father came from Italy in 1890 when he was 17 to work for his uncle, who was foreman on the Louis P. Martini Monte Rosso vineyard," recalled Valle. "He was given room and board and paid $15 a month. In 1906, he bought this property, pulled out the stumps, and began planting Zinfandel budded onto St. George rootstock. Most of these 25 or 30 acres were planted before Prohibition, all with Zinfandel budded onto St. George rootstock. One small block at the top was planted in 1935, and another four acres over there," he said, pointing and laughing wryly, "we planted in 1965 — on AxR-1. It's dying now, and will have to be pulled out."

Valle's father also had a winery, bond number 209, which operated as the Rossi Ranch Winery until Prohibition put him out of business. "That white barn down there below my house, where your car is parked, was the winery," said Valle. "My father sold wine for 50 cents a gallon to people who came here from New York to buy our wine. Instead of loading wine into cartons, as we do now, he put it into 50-gallon barrels, took it down to Kenwood, and shipped it out on South Pacific Railway. My dad used to put some Alicante Bouschet in with the Zinfandel, which made it a dark, dark red. The people from New York, they liked the wine so much that they always came back. I don't have much Alicante left, but during Prohibition, we had enough to ship back east in boxes. We sold it for a dollar a box — good money them days. Today, just Pagani, me, and Uboldi still have old Alicante vines."

During Prohibition, the Rossis shipped their Zinfandel grapes to San Francisco in boxes loaded into cattle cars for home winemakers. "We got $35 a ton, which was pretty cheap. But we paid our pickers just 25 cents an hour. Today, I pay $6 an hour, but I am getting about $2,000 a ton."

"Did you ever think you would see the day that you would get such a price?" I asked.

Valle's reply was just a shake of his head.

When Prohibition ended, Valle's father considered reopening the winery. "You're a young guy. Help me open up the winery," he had said to Valle. But Valle had a different idea.

"What are we going to do with the wine?" Valle had asked him. "Even at 25 cents a gallon, no one will buy it. If you have two good years in a row, with two good crops, you will have to enlarge the winery. So let's just sell the grapes," Valle had argued. "So we just sold the grapes. We also still had 10,000 gallons of wine stored from pre-Prohibition, so I made a deal with Sebastiani to take the wine in return for a gallon of 190 proof brandy. Sebastiani made brandy from it.

"I was a little guy but I talked a lot, and if it hadn't been for me, my dad wouldn't have gotten anything for the wine. We wanted the brandy for our cherries. Put the brandy in the cherries, and, Oh, Boy! You got nice colored brandy. So Sebastiani just took the wine away, although he had to pump it down the road since my father's little bridge was not strong enough for Sebastiani's big tanker."

Following Prohibition, customers for the Rossi grapes were varied: home winemakers, Sebastiani, and for 30 years Julius Pagani (Louis and Olive's cousin), who owned what is today Kenwood Winery until his death in the 1970s. "Then Mike Lee and his buddies bought it, and named it Kenwood Winery," said Valle. "But when I asked them if they would like my grapes, since the Pagani brothers had been buying them for 30 years, they replied, 'No, we don't want those junkie grapes.' Now, of course, they would die to get some of my grapes," Valle laughed.

"Then we sold to Seghesio for six years, and later to the Gallo brothers, to their Sonoma facility. But after some years, the Gallos got critical and said our grapes had too many raisins, and cut the price per ton in half. So we dropped out of that deal, and began selling to Mike Topolos in 1985.

"Michael does all the pruning, and so far, I have done all the tractor work. But I don't know how much longer I'll be able to keep it up."

As we walked through the vineyard, Valle pointed out the Alicante and Petite Sirah. "My dad liked the field mix, right from the start, not after you make the wine. Sebastiani liked to keep the Alicante and Zinfandel in separate barrels, and mix it later. But my dad liked it all mixed together as he made the wine."

Valle also spoke proudly of his organic farming practices, especially since he began selling to Topolos. "I just use sulfur, no other chemicals," he said. "But I never did use any chemicals. We always hoed around the vines. Today, we use weedeaters."

"That seems like a lot of work, to take a weedeater to every vine," I remarked as I surveyed the 35 acres of vines.

"No, it goes fast with weedeaters. I get three guys out here, and it's done in no time," said Valle. "The grass has to be dry, so you don't get the weedeaters jammed up, yeah."

Our vineyard walk was over, and Valle had work to do.

"What are you going to do for the rest of the day?" I asked him, as we shook hands at parting.

"My paper work. All the stuff about the ranch — organic farming, how much gasoline I use, costs of labor — the government wants to know everything," he replied cheerfully.

Not bad for a man 87 years old.

In February 1999, Valle Rossi died at age 89 after a brief illness. May his soul rest in peace.

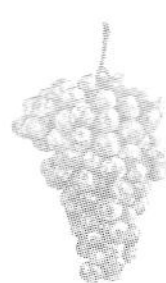

Topolos at Russian River

"For Topolos Winery and our vision, Zinfandel is our grape," began Michael Topolos as we sat in the sunny summerhouse on the upper level of the Topolos winery and restaurant on a beautiful February day in year 2000. Downstairs beside the tasting room, the Topolos's annual Alicante Bouschet party was in full swing. Sounds of talking, laughter, and the catchy rhythmic notes of the jazz trio could be heard.

"It's our grape by default, and we claim it. It is gutsy, just like we are, and so American, and I think that it is marvelous not having to defer to anyone other than ourselves for its nobility. It is a safe harbor, too, because we know that there is not going to be an ocean of Zinfandel coming in from Australian or Chile or South of France," Michael continued.

"When did Zinfandel first catch your attention as a wine grape worthy of serious attention?" I asked, perhaps just a little surprised to hear Michael speak so enthusiastically about Zinfandel. I knew of Topolos's long association with the Rossi Ranch, yet I had no idea that Zinfandel was the winery's primary variety, or that Michael had such passionate thoughts about it. But then Topolos Winery, located in a hollow beside Highway 116 in the Russian River Valley just north of Forestville, is a small family winery, low-key, and just a little mysterious to me.

"I've always liked Louis M. Martini, Pedroncelli, and Sebastiani Zinfandels. Also Fetzer. And Pagani from time to time had made a good one, and Valley of the Moon. Many of these wines in the early days were sold in gallon jugs for $2 or $3. From the beginning of my adult days, I have liked Zinfandel," recalled Mike.

"What was your first Zinfandel?"

"The first Zinfandel that I made was in 1970, as a home winemaker. Friends and I sharecropped the Old Hill Ranch in Glen Ellen. It had 17.2 percent alcohol, and was a magnificent wine, one of the finest I have ever been associated with. I still have one bottle. In 1978, I established my winery and label, and continued to buy the Old Hill Ranch Zinfandel until 1984."

"Valle Rossi told me that you began buying Rossi Ranch grapes in 1985."

"Yes, and I remember that day well. Valle had pulled up to the winery with a truckload of Petite Sirah that Gallo had just refused. Did I want them, he asked. Since I had wanted Valle's grapes for years, I quickly said 'Yes!' Two years later, the Sonoma County Harvest Fair awarded the Topolos Rossi Ranch Petite Sirah a gold medal. Valle and I, dressed in tuxedos, went on the stage to accept the medal and the Grower's Recognition Award — all this for the grapes that Gallo had refused."

"That must have made both you and Valle very happy," I remarked.

"Oh, yes, indeed," replied Mike, a smile illuminating his face as he remembered the gala occasion.

"Why did you give up the Old Hill Ranch?"

"When the Rossi Ranch became available, we had a tough decision to make: to keep the Old Hill Ranch or take over the Rossi Ranch. We weren't large enough at the time to handle both vineyards, which would have been 50 acres total. So we went with the Rossi Ranch, and have not regretted it."

In 1985, the Old Hill Ranch went to Ravenswood, said Michael. Joel Peterson had been making his Ravenswood wines at Topolos under its license between 1979 and 1982, so Joel had first option on the Old Hill, said Michael, which he gladly exercised.

"You go back a long ways with Joel Peterson, as well," I remarked.

"Yes, Joel and I have drunk a few bottles of Zinfandel together," Mike said, a smile playing over his face.

"When you took over the Rossi Ranch, wasn't Aleta Olds buying some of the grapes and helping to care for the vineyard?" I asked Michael. I remembered meeting Aleta, and tasting some of her Las Montañas Zinfandel, in 1988 or 1989. Aleta had formed the Las Montañas label following her divorce from Lore Olds, owner of Sky Vineyards, Napa. In fact, it was from Aleta that I had first heard of the Rossi Ranch, and it was Joel Peterson who first showed me the vineyard, as an extension of a tour of his Cooke and Old Hill vineyards.

"Yes, she was a dear friend of Valle's. He admired her for her work with his grapes, and for the fine person that she is. We did, too. I worked side by side with Aleta for a few years in the vineyard. She was a fascinating woman, and a better worker than many men," recalled Michael. "She continued to get a few tons of Zinfandel even after we took it over, as did a few other producers and home winemakers. Valle had old friendships, which he honored. That is as it should be. We didn't get all the grapes until 1991 or 1992."

There never had been a contract between Michael and Valle, only a handshake, said Michael. With Valle's death, the vineyard, which has fallen to Valle's only relative, a nephew with no grapegrowing experience, is in some danger of becoming just another commodity — an occurrence that Michael had prepared for.

"What I have done to protect my interests is to establish a vineyard on my property on Sonoma Mountain with budwood from the Rossi Ranch, the Pagani Ranch, and my original vineyard that I had established some years ago from budwood taken from the old Harazthy Vineyard. Now I have a 10-acre vineyard that is one-third Rossi Ranch budwood, one-third Pagani Ranch budwood, and one-third Harazthy Vineyard budwood. It's three years old, and will mature into one of the most magnificent Zinfandel vineyards in the world," said Michael confidently.

Mike Topolos and Jac Jacobs

"The vines are grafted to St. George rootstock, and are planted four feet apart in rows 10 feet apart. I farm it organically and bio-dynamically, and, yes, it is drip irrigated now, but it won't be once it is established. It is next door to the Jack London Ranch, has an eastern exposure, and overlooks Rossi and Pagani ranches from 800 to 1,200 feet. It represents the epitome of my lifetime experience with Zinfandel. The wine is a blending of grapes from vines taken from those three ranches. We call it 'Ultimo,' and it is my most expensive Zinfandel. In 1999, we got about three tons; our 2000 vintage should be about 15 tons. We can taste the 1999 later with Jac," he offered. Jac Jacobs is the Topolos winemaker.

"I am so glad to hear that you have preserved some Zinfandel vines from the Rossi Ranch," I remarked.

"I couldn't live with myself if I hadn't kept some connection with that ranch," said Michael. "Valle Rossi had dinner with us most nights, and certainly every Sunday, and I really miss him. We did everything together. We worked together, and did everything socially together, and I was as devastated as he was when his son, Paul, died. He was a wonderful friend, and we spent a lot of time together. He was like a father to me, and a grandfather to my sons."

He fell silent for a moment, giving us both time to remember Valle, and to ponder the impact of his death upon the community.

"So you can see that our association with Sonoma County old vine Zinfandel is a long one," Michael resumed. "If Zinfandel can prevail and excel anywhere in the world, it is in Sonoma. That goes back to my point about Zinfandel being a safe harbor. I've known a lot of varieties to come and go. Assuming that consumers are fickle in their tastes, they may stick with a variety but they will switch brands. It is a challenge to succeed in the wine business. The wine industry is vying for that 11 percent of the population who drink 80 percent of the wine, and we didn't want to establish our presence with Cabernet Sauvignon or Chardonnay. Those are pretty crowded spots. So we concentrated on defining ourselves with Zinfandel, and we've been pretty successful.

"In fact, the popularity that Zinfandel is experiencing now is no surprise to me. I am only surprised that it didn't happen sooner. Zinfandel is mind-boggling. It is versatile; it goes the whole range of wines, from sparkling wine to port, and everything in between. What more could you ask of a wine grape? Of course, we concern ourselves mostly with the production of Zinfandel as table wine. We make eight Zinfandels, depending on our vineyards. We make a fresh, bright Zinfandel, we make some medium-bodied Zinfandels, and we make some multi-faceted complex Bordeaux-style Zinfandels that people have to pay attention to. Four are vineyard-designates.

"With the way we farm, organically and biodynamically, we are able to extract much more essence from the *terroir* than we would otherwise. The vine prevails. It tells us what we have to do; we have to listen to it. That is what makes it so exciting for us."

It's our grape by default, and we claim it. It's gutsy, just like we are, and so American, and I think that it is marvelous not having to defer to anyone other than ourselves for its nobility."

Mike Topolos

Michael's enthusiasm was infectious, but I was curious about one thing.

"Could you explain 'biodynamics'?" I asked.

"Biodynamics was started in the 1920s by Dr. Rudolph Steiner in Austria and Germany. The agricultural community went to him because they were losing viability in their farmlands. He gave eight lectures to help them bring health and balance back into their soils. Part of that discipline is companion planting, composting, and herbal sprays that are put on the soils and plants. Today, we have taken what Steiner put into place — he was a seer like Luther Burbank — and created what we call 'new biodynamics,' which includes companion animals. Cows are a part of both the Pagani and Rossi ranches, and cows are a part of our ranch, too. We have the influence of animal and man in addition to the soil. And we have the birds and the bees. We have orchard bee colonies that we put in each vineyard site. They stir up the air, and land in the flowers. We try to plant a cover crop that flowers at the same time as the vines are flowering so that we create a magnet that brings all the bird and insect habitat in.

"After flowering, we spread a compost, then use a flail mower to cut the biomass so that it lies on top and protects the ground and compost from the sun, and creates diversity that otherwise wouldn't be there. We have the biocomplexity that allows things to vibrate and become alive. Biodynamics works with living energy. It helps us to craft the flavors in our grapes."

My appreciation for this offbeat and low-key Zinfandel grower and producer was increasing by the minute.

"Is Zinfandel, then, your mainstay variety?" I asked.

"Yes," replied Michael. "We produce 10- to 12,000 cases of Zinfandel, out of about 20,000 cases total production. Zinfandel is our grape," he emphasized. "The only wine we offer for sale to the world is Zinfandel. Everything else is just sold from the winery, because we make several little batches of a variety of wines — 400 or 500 cases — such as the Alicante that we are celebrating today. These we sell on-site. In a few years, we will add Sauvignon Blanc and Pinot Noir to our off-site offerings, from our estate vineyard. They will also be certified organic and biodynamic."

Having covered most of the points with Michael that I was interested in, I was ready to join the happy crowd below. I wanted to try some new Alicante Bouschet, a barrel sample of the 1999 Ultimo Zinfandel, and also a few of the award-winning Zinfandels being offered in the tasting room, as well as some of the savory snacks whose aromas were beginning to summon us.

Jac Jacobs, Winemaker

Before the day was over, I also managed to get Jac Jacobs, the amiable and fair-haired winemaker for Topolos since 1992, away from the party for a half-hour, especially to talk about the Rossi Ranch Zinfandel.

"With such great grapes as the Rossi Ranch Zinfandel, we like to extract everything that we can get out of them," began Jac in his quiet and easygoing manner. "We like to have the grapes come in at a field sample of 24.5° Brix in order to have fully mature flavors. Because the vines are spread over four distinct micro-*terroirs*, to maximize fruit quality and reduce uneven ripening we have usually harvested the Zinfandel in four separate pickings. Sometimes we have even picked the other three varieties separately. Sometimes we have gone into the ranch as much as seven times to pick, and we bottle each of these varieties separately. Our pickers, of course, hate it — seven pickings to get three-quarters of per ton per acre of fruit?"

"But the resulting wine quality makes this effort worth it — fully ripe fruit with a minimum of over-ripe or green fruit. We feel that you cannot get top quality wine if you pick for an average of the over-ripe and green fruit. Over-ripe and green fruit together do not make ripe fruit," emphasized Jac. "Doing it our way, we will usually get some 'soak up' from the raisins — as high as 26° or 27° Brix — but we would rather have fully ripe flavors than any green flavors. Rossi Ranch Zinfandel typically has 15 percent alcohol.

"To get these important extractions during fermentation, we want lots of skin contact. We want to extract maximum color, body, flavor, and taste. The way to do that is to ferment over 14 days, which is about the time that the wine goes dry. This way, you get color, body, and flavor, but you also get tannins. Tannins are important to give wine a solid backbone. Less than 10 days on the skins, you will get juice-soluble tannins, which give wine a fresh, luscious, fruity character, but without much backbone. Ten days is not long enough to extract all the tannin or all the color and flavor. From 11 to 14 days on the skins, you get more color and flavor, but you still are getting mostly juice-soluble tannins, which are very simple tannins. They hit your palate, and the wines are perceived as astringent and hard. They will need a couple of years in barrels, and perhaps some egg white fining, to soften them up.

"In order to avoid these harsh, astringent tannins, we go long-term skin contact — a minimum of 21 days, and as long as 50 days," explained Jac. "This gives us alcohol-soluble tannins, which are fat and complex. These fat, complex tannins are too big for the taste buds, so there is no perceived astringency or hardness, which allows the fruit flavors to come through. We now have all the extraction of color, body, and flavor, and the tannins are not overpowering everything.

"The wine is drinkable young because the tannins are soft rather than aggressive; yet the wine will age, because it also has backbone. To me, when you put a bottle of wine on the shelf, the consumer needs to be able to drink it the day he or she buys it, and enjoy it. Whether or not one wants to put it away for a few years should be the consumer's decision. I've had wines off the shelf that are so tannic and hard that I could hardly finish one glass, let alone enjoy it. As far as I am concerned, that is a wasted bottle of wine, and wasted money. It should not have been released.

"With our extended skin contact [maceration], we are able to release the wines when they are two years old. It also cuts down on the barrel time because we don't have to soften the tannins. The barrels become an accent to the wine. We usually bottle between one and 1½ years after harvest, or after eight to 12 months in barrel. Then we keep the wine for up to one year of bottle ageing before we release it."

"Is your Zinfandel 100 percent Zinfandel, or do you sometimes blend in a little Alicante Bouschet or Petite Sirah?"

"Sometimes we blend in a little of the Alicante. It just depends on the vintage. If it takes a little Alicante or Petite Sirah to make the best wine from the vintage, that is what we do. But it is always 100 percent Rossi Ranch," said Jac.

"Do you use much new oak for your Zinfandel?" I asked.

"We have a five-year program — about 20 percent new each year, and 20 percent of one-, two-, three-, and four-year old barrels. For our

Zinfandel, our new barrels are primarily American oak. I find that our old vine Zinfandels are so big, so full-bodied that they can handle the aggressiveness of American oak.

"Also, we use no sulfur on the grapes, and as little as possible during barrel ageing. We had a few wines that did not need sulfur until we bottled them. Sulfur added to the grapes or to the wine early on seems to bring out a bit of harshness. We do check the wines regularly, and top and rack, and if necessary, we do add sulfur. But the less sulfur we use, the better."

"You must have pretty good acid and pH balance in the Rossi grapes," I commented.

"The T.A. usually runs about 6 gm/L. The finished pH is between 3.65 to 3.75. With the tannin backbone, these are good numbers for ageing. These numbers are also the reason why the wine is so drinkable at release. We still have some 1990 and 1991 Rossi Ranch Zinfandels that are holding up beautifully."

"Typically, how many tons of Zinfandel would you get from the Rossi Ranch?" I asked.

"Except for 1999, the Rossi Ranch Vineyard has consistently yielded about 15 tons of fruit, for 900 cases of wine," Jac replied. "We had one high yield of 25 tons, for about 1,500 cases. In 1998, we got 600 cases. Then, in 1999, the fall after Valle died, the yield was only seven tons, or 420 cases. I really do believe that it was because Valle wasn't out there chasing the deer on his all-terrain three-wheeler, or picking off the occasional sucker, or pulling out some of the weeds we hadn't gotten to. It was almost as if the vineyard were in mourning along with us. As for the 2000 yield, I have no idea. We are managing the vineyard on a year-by-year basis until Valle's heirs decide what to do with it. But we still face the same problems that we had last year after Valle died."

At the end of our conversation, Jac rejoined the party, where I later found him serving barrel samples of the 1999 Alicante and also the Zinfandel port. Tucked beneath the barrel was a beaker of the 1999 Ultimo. During a break in the crowd around his station, he grabbed the beaker and poured me a generous tasting. I retreated into the sunny parking area to savor this bit of Zinfandel nectar. Not quite finished with malolactic fermentation, it nonetheless showed its potential to be a fresh-tasting, medium-bodied wine with delicate flavors and aromas of red raspberries, cinnamon, and other light spices. It showed a wonderful combination of the characters of the three vineyards the budwood had been taken from. Definitely a wine to watch.

As for the 1997 Rossi Ranch Zinfandel, I found that it had many of the same qualities that I loved in a 1994 that I had found in my cellar a few weeks earlier. About the 1994, I had written these notes: "1994 Rossi Ranch Zinfandel — dark, dark burgundy, almost black color; aromas of black currants, cinnamon, suggests plum pudding or mince pie. A solid backbone of tannins, with dark fruit flavors making this a truly lovely and distinctive wine. Alcohol, 13 percent." The 1997 had an alcohol content of 15 percent.

"The 1997 is possibly the best Rossi Ranch we made," said Michael as I discussed the wines with him in the tasting room. "It has won several gold medals, and I give the credit to Jac. He outdid himself on this one."

I drove home over Highway 12, which took me past mustard-filled fields, apple orchards, and vineyards under the sunny late afternoon sky, the jazzy beat of the music still in my ears, and my spirit renewed by the simplicity and unpretentiousness of this secluded little Forestville winery.

Napa County

Regusci Vineyard

Zinfandel from Napa Valley?

Between 1885 and Prohibition, Napa Valley was well known for its Zinfandel, usually made in a claret style. "It was the most popular and most widely planted red wine grape here in those early days," said Rick Schuetz, winemaker for the Napa Valley Cooperative from 1979 to 1993. Many of the Cooperative's customers were Italians whose one-, two-, and three-acre Zinfandel vineyards had been planted by their fathers, grandfathers, or great-grandfathers, he said. Rick liked nothing better than to hang out with some of these growers and listen to their stories, and especially drink their homemade Zinfandel. In fact, that is how he got hooked on it. (See Korte Vineyard, below.)

Zinfandel was also a variety that some of Napa Valley's earliest post-Prohibition wineries produced. Yet when I began my research on Zinfandel in 1986, I knew of only a few Zinfandel wines from Napa Valley vineyards made by Napa Valley producers.

Four were estate wineries, and two were remarkable because they made only Zinfandel: Storybook Mountain Vineyards, located on Spring Mountain at the northern end of the valley, and Sky, located high upon the Napa side of the Mayacamas Mountains on the southern end of the valley. The other two estate producers were Clos du Val, in Stags Leap District, for which Zinfandel was one of two flagship wines; and Nichelini, on Lower Chiles Valley Road. Except for Nichelini, all these vineyards were relatively young, planted in the early 1970s. The wines were usually classified as "table wine," and were made in a claret style.

When friends asked me to recommend a Napa Valley Zinfandel made by a Napa Valley producer, I would recommend the above names. I would also perhaps suggest such producers as Ravenswood of Sonoma, who was giving vineyard-designate status to the pre-Prohibition Dickerson Vineyard located on Zinfandel Lane. Also, Ridge Vineyards, Cupertino, was producing a Howell Mountain Zinfandel and a York Creek (Spring Mountain) Zinfandel. And Rosenblum Cellars, located in Alameda, was winning awards and recognition for its Hendry Vineyards Reserve.

Louis M. Martini had been producing Zinfandel for decades, but his vineyards were on Monte Rosso, in Sonoma. Sutter Home, too, was famous for its Amador County Zinfandel wines. I was acquainted also with Burgess Cellars, Cuvaison, Grgich Hills, Caymus, Charles Krug, and Villa Mt. Eden Zinfandels, but most of these Zinfandels were sourced outside Napa Valley.

Many other Napa Valley producers had been making Zinfandel in the years preceding my research. By the time I had gotten interested, however, many of them had given up Zinfandel in favor of Cabernet Sauvignon, Merlot, or Pinot Noir.

Sometimes my friends would accept my recommendation; sometimes they already knew about these producers, but wanted a bigger, more extracted style of Zinfandel. "Napa Valley really is known for its claret style Zinfandel," I would tell them. "While there is some variation among vineyards and winemaker styles, you should look into Sonoma County or Amador County Zinfandels if you are looking for more richly flavored and fully extracted Zinfandels." When I met Cary Gott, founding winemaker for Amador's Monteviña Winery, some years later, he would tell me pretty much the same thing. "You didn't normally see wines like the big rich Amador Zinfandels here in Napa Valley in the 1970s and 1980s. People weren't making heavy, thick Zinfandel wines here then."

That was then. In the early 1990s, several newly established Napa Valley producers making Zinfandel wines from Napa County vineyards with rich, mouth-filling Zinfandel character joined the above named producers. Schuetz-Olds, Robert Biale, Larry Turley, D-Cubed (Duane Dappen), Elyse (Ray Coursen), and Peter Franus had burst upon the scene. When I began to investigate the Zinfandel vineyards of Napa Valley from whose fruit these wines were made, I discovered an amazing treasure-trove of surviving old vineyards — some pre-Prohibition, some post-Prohibition — and also some more recently established vineyards.

Until about 1990, most of the fruit that these produced was sold to the Napa Valley Cooperative, and while some of the best fruit was vinified separately, most of it got tossed in with the rest of their supply. Given the lack of demand for Zinfandel in those years, it is remarkable that so many of these old vineyards survived the fame of Napa Valley as a prime location for the famous French varieties of Cabernet Sauvignon and Merlot. Someone must have loved them greatly to have kept and taken care of them.

I also discovered that many of the established Napa Valley producers had modified their winemaking style to meet the consumers' growing attraction to the riper style of Zinfandel. The claret style was no longer the trademark style of Napa Valley Zinfandel.

Zinfandel in Napa County is found primarily in four viticultural areas: Howell Mountain, with its distinctive black and white cracked peppercorn aromas; Spring Mountain; Mount Veeder; and Napa Valley. There are also a few notable plantings in Chiles Valley (Green and Red; Rustridge; Nichelini), and on Atlas Peak.

Mead Ranch, Atlas Peak: A Piece of Old Napa Valley

It was upon Atlas Peak that I began my sojourn into Napa County, with a visit to the Mead Ranch at the 1,600-foot elevation on Atlas Peak Road. This is a piece of old Napa Valley that I had long heard about from many sources. The quality of Mead Ranch Zinfandel grapes has been recognized for decades both by home winemakers and commercial wine producers. Over the last 19 years, the vineyard has occasionally been given vineyard-designate status. More recently, there is a 1997 Villa Mt. Eden and Conn Creek Mead Ranch Reserve. Also, budwood from the vineyard has propagated many a Zinfandel vineyard throughout Napa and Sonoma counties.

Giles Mead, who was raised on the property some 70-odd years ago, is sole owner of the 1,300-acre ranch, of which 65 acres is vineyard. Twenty-five of those 65 acres are planted with Zinfandel. His daughter, Parry, helps him run the vineyard.

It was an unseasonably cold but clear and beautiful April 1999 morning when, after a five-mile drive up Atlas Peak Road, I turned onto the long lane leading up to the Mead Ranch house and vineyard for my first visit. Upon entering the gate, I found myself flanked by well-cared-for head pruned old Zinfandel vines. This was the vineyard that supplied the grapes that won critical acclaim for Lee Stewart, owner/winemaker of Souverain in 1944. Parry Mead met me in the driveway, and ushered me into the huge and comfortable living room. A sign on the door to the living room proclaimed, "Never mind the dogs; beware of owner." There, Giles and his two Great Dane dogs were enjoying the blazing fire and the view of many birds feeding upon seeds scattered over a huge flat rock just outside the wall-sized picture window. From the dining room window, which formed the end part of the L-shaped room, one had a spectacular view of the southern end of Napa Valley and San Pablo Bay to San Francisco.

I felt that I had indeed taken a step back in time to old Napa Valley.

Giles, a tall and ruggedly handsome man with moderately long gray hair and beard, stood to offer me a robust handshake and welcome. The waist-high dogs joined in with remarkably good manners. They wanted only to be acknowledged with a friendly pat on the head before retiring to their cushions under the window. Perhaps I had better keep my eye on their owner, I was thinking!

However, that thought was fleeting as Giles indicated a big chair for me to be seated in. Soon I was being warmed with a steaming cup of coffee and charmed with the view of the myriad birds feeding on the rock and among the trees. I settled into the roomy chair, and prepared myself to hear the story of Mead Ranch Zinfandel.

Zinfandel was probably first planted on this location about 1900, said Giles. The Mead family bought the property from the silent film star Bert Lytell in 1913, and has owned it ever since. Lytell, said Giles, used to entertain on Saturday nights at the Opera House, and have socialite parties at the ranch.

Parry and Giles Mead

"Can you imagine socialite parties up here in the weeds, in a house that dated to before the turn of the century? There was no electricity, no running water. It wasn't, under the circumstances, what you call a high-toned party for a bunch of important dignitaries, especially since they had to come six miles up from Napa in horse and buggy, or on horseback. But that is what the people liked about it."

Today, the ranch is a break-even operation for Parry and Giles.

"We pay the expenses of the vineyard, which includes a salary for ourselves, with the income from the grapes," began Parry, "but we do not earn much in the way of profit."

"I can add a little to that," added Giles. "We have 1,300 acres, 65 of which are in vineyard, and 30 acres in homestead and roads. The rest is 'forever wild' under a conservation easement with Napa County Land Trust. There will be no more vineyard acreage, no subdivisions, no more home sites of any kind, and no commercial grazing.

"In the 1930s, this was a typical subsistence farm, without enough of anything to be financially viable. There was a little patch of Zinfandel in front that probably dated to 1912 or 1913. There was a patch of pears, a patch of prunes, some sheep so there would be lamb for the table, some cows for milk and cottage cheese. Everybody got up at four in the morning, and went to bed at dark, and no one made a nickel. The economy in Napa Valley in the 1930s was very depressed. All the wineries had closed during Prohibition, and it took time for the industry to recover following Repeal.

"The original vines were spaced six feet by six feet. The land had been cleared with horses, and because some of the rocks were too big to move, the rows weren't all that straight. The vines were crown trained about a foot and a half to two feet above the ground. You had to crawl on your belly like a snake to prune or pick them. But the flavor in the wine was superb. We drank some of what we made here.

"Later, with the help of machinery, the rocks were removed, and vines planted in the spaces. In the later planting, we took out the last of the six-by-six spaced vines, but I kept the budwood for the new plantings. Little by little, we changed over the entire vineyard during and after World War II. That was the end of the old subsistences. We still had grapes here, picked by the neighborhood kids, and hauled in a 1928 Model A truck to the Co-op. We were member number two of the St. Helena Co-op.

"In the early years, most of our grapes were sold through the Co-op. In the wake of the Depression, just after Prohibition was repealed, the going price then was $7 per ton, and all transactions were done on a handshake. The farming community had to pull together then, by being cooperative and completely trustworthy. Yet I can remember riding along with my uncle taking in a load of grapes to a prominent Napa Valley producer at that time, when I was a very small boy, and hearing him being told that his grapes were no longer needed, despite an earlier gentlemen's agreement. He was told he could leave them if he liked, but that there would be no payment. So my uncle drove the truck to the bridge on Yountville Crossroad, and dumped the grapes into the Napa River. [No wonder all the fish are gone! I was thinking.] I've never set foot in that winery since that day. That was an unconscionable way to treat farmers in the wake of the Depression. Fortunately, most people we dealt with honored their handshakes.

"So that is the rough history of the place. There were a few outlying delivery points during Prohibition in San Francisco. The grapes were delivered at two in the morning by backing up to one of those hills to deliver Zinfandel through the window that led to somebody's basement. The same thing up here. I remember my uncles saying that the addresses were always different, but it was always the same crusher. People today remark upon how many wineries there are in Napa Valley — 250 or so. I heard estimates that say there were as many as four thousand wineries in Napa Valley during Prohibition. They were small, and were usually in the basements of Italian households."

"You've had many customers for your Zinfandel over the years, haven't you?" I asked.

"Yes, but we haven't sold to the Co-op for nearly 30 years. I've never had a sales problem," replied Giles.

"What makes this location so well suited to Zinfandel?"

"It's the red soil, the good drainage, and the fact that year-round, we always get temperature-modifying breezes. The breezes usually keep us from getting too hot in the summer and too cold in the winter and spring. I don't have any frost protection up here, and have never really needed it. Maybe once in a while, the leaves get a little frost bite around the edges, but that's about it."

"Is your Zinfandel budded onto St. George rootstock?"

"Yes."

"We have one very small patch on 110R, but that is just to see how Zinfandel gets along with 110R up here," added Parry.

"We have two things working for us as far as Phylloxera goes," said Giles. "One is St. George rootstock, and the other is isolation. We are completely surrounded by brush, and we watch carefully what outside equipment comes into our vineyard. We contract out for picking labor. Our workers drag our bins through the vineyard, then the bins go onto a contract truck for delivery to our customers. That works well. The brush is also host to many good predator insect creatures that are always hungry for something, seeming to keep other diseases out of the vineyard as well — such as the sharpshooter with its hitchhiker, the infectious agent of Pierce's Disease."

"Do you still dry farm your Zinfandel?" I asked.

"We added drip irrigation in 1999," replied Parry.

"The ground water has been falling steadily over the years since the country club at the bottom of the hill began stealing all my water," Giles remarked. "We find water now at a reasonable depth, and we have closed storage capacity for about 60,000 gallons."

"Is that the only reason why you added drip irrigation to your Zinfandel?"

"Crown-pruned Zinfandel is our main reason," said Giles. "The producers love our grapes, and sell the wine they make from them for four times as much as what they sell valley-grown Zinfandel for. But they are reluctant to pay me one plugged nickel more for my mountain-grown, dry-farmed, crown-pruned Zinfandel grapes. So screw it!"

"Even though the quality is better from dry-farmed, mountain-grown grapes, we can't afford it anymore, since we get lower tonnage for high quality fruit, but we haven't been getting comparable prices," added Parry. "We nonetheless won't be adding much water, just enough to up the yield a little, about a half-ton per acre, and to sustain the vines through the growing season in the driest of years. A year ago, we got a little over four tons per acre — which isn't bad for head trained, mountain-grown Zinfandel.

"Our Zinfandel is now all planted at eight-by-eight spacing, and is not trellised. Most of the budwood is taken from the old vines before they were taken out. Some also came from Gallo's Frei Ranch in Sonoma."

"In my lifetime," said Giles, changing the subject a little, "I have seen Zinfandel go from a variety that people looked down their noses at to one which is now considered premium. Unfortunately, that doesn't always mean better prices for the growers. In fact, Zinfandel's improved status as a world class red wine has given rise to a certain kind of boutique Zinfandel winery. Their owners and winemakers have this arrogance about their skill as Zinfandel producers that I can live without quite well! They want to come up here and pick every third bunch of grapes. They seem to think we should kiss their feet just for coming up here to talk to us about taking our grapes. They probably would pay us market price, or higher, but I can't take their arrogance. I usually end up asking them to leave the ranch."

"I've since had a nice conversation with the winemaker for one of these specialty Zinfandel producers," said Parry. "But what he and the owner do not seem to understand is that we've been around Zinfandel a lot longer than either of them, and we have built our reputation over many years on the quality of our Zinfandel. We don't have to sell our grapes to just anybody. We value the relationship we have with the winemaker as much as we value the price paid."

"We don't mind vineyard designation in small letters someplace on the label — sometimes. We're not adamant about that either," added Giles. "A good relationship is more important."

"Doug Nalle has told me how he and John Konnsgaard made a superb Zinfandel from Mead Ranch Zinfandel when they were both home winemakers. Do you remember them?" I asked.

"Sure, I know Judge Konnsgaard," replied Giles. "I had to go to his court once, concerning some family matters. He was sitting there, looking down at me; then he asked me, 'Are you the Mead who sold my son some Zinfandel grapes?' 'Yes, your Honor,' I replied. 'Let's go off the record for a minute,' he said. Then, 'Mr. Mead, did he pay for those Zinfandel grapes?' 'No, your Honor,' I replied. 'I'll take up the matter. Now, back to business.' Judge Konnsgaard was a great guy, absolutely first class," said Giles.

"You said earlier that you are phasing out all your contracts with corporate producers in favor of some local Napa producers. Who are these local producers, and are they paying you closer to market price for your grapes?"

"Hess Collection for now, who has contracted for just the four-acre parcel of the oldest vines out front," replied Parry. "They are quality-oriented, and have always tried to pay reasonable prices for the grapes, and sell their wines for reasonable prices. In year 2000, we will begin selling to Peter Franus. By year 2003, Peter Franus and Hess Collection will be our only customers."

Hess Collection is paying the average market price for the grapes, which has settled out at about $2,000 per ton, Parry assured me.

"What a quantum leap from $7 per ton in post-Repeal years," I remarked.

"Even when I was a teenager, and had my first hands-on experience with the grapes, the price then was only $250 per ton. We paid about $35 an hour to pick the grapes. We now pay as much as $90 an hour for picking. Until very recently, we sold the grapes for $400 to $500 to $600 per ton. When we got our first contract for $700 per ton, we thought we had really moved into the big time. We didn't break $1,000 per ton until about 1990."

The big logs in the fireplace had burned down, the day was brightening a little, and the dogs were getting restless for a walk, as was I. It was time to grab the camera and take a stroll through the vineyards with Parry, Giles, and the two Great Danes. The clouds had become silvery, and the views over the surrounding mountains and across Napa Valley were breathtaking.

"Before we head out, what is it that you like about Zinfandel?" I asked Giles.

"It tastes like real wine, not like grape juice," he replied.

"When did you first taste Zinfandel wine?

"Oh, when I was about two," he replied, his eyes twinkling with merriment.

At the upper end of the vineyard, the view back down to the ranch buildings and over the Napa Valley was still spectacular. I could feel those bay breezes upon my face, and easily understood their mitigating effect upon any extremes of climate the ranch might experience.

Our hike around the vineyards ended, and we returned to the house to warm our freezing hands over the rejuvenated fire — and our bodies with a hearty glass of Zinfandel. (The outside temperature had barely reached a brisk 42° F). After a few desultory words on the subjects of Zinfandel, bobcats, and mountain cats, I was on my way back to the valley floor, a prized and rare bottle of Mead Ranch 1996 home-produced Zinfandel wine under my arm. Not even the hail shower that blasted me on my drive down could shake the warm glow that my long-delayed visit to the renowned Mead Ranch had left me with.

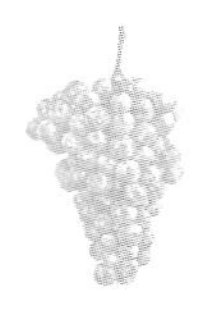

Nichelini Vineyard

Historic Nichelini Vineyard on Lower Chiles Valley Road is almost as attractive to visitors for its rustic outdoor tasting bar as it is for its award-winning Zinfandel. The bar is located at the bottom of a long flight of stairs leading down the hillside from the parking area, which is little more than a wide shoulder of the road running past the historic house. The bar is shaded by towering trees and serenaded by Sage Creek, which runs deep below, always a cool oasis on a hot summer day.

But it is the wines that have kept the family together and the visitors coming back. "I love Zinfandel," said Dick Wainwright, one of the four Anton Nichelini grandchildren who form the present-day partnership. The other partners are Toni Nichelini-Irwin, the marketing director, Joseph Nichelini, the vineyard manager, and Greg Boeger, winemaker, who also owns Boeger Winery in El Dorado.

Nichelini Vineyard Zinfandel has a long history. Swiss-born Anton Nichelini founded the winery with his wife, Caterina, in 1890. The original Zinfandel vineyard was on the steep hillside across from the winery. The last harvest from that vineyard was 1944, after which time it was abandoned. "The terrain was just too steep to work with anything but horses," said Wainwright.

In 1990, five years after the death of the charismatic and popular winemaker, Jim Nichelini, the winery was in danger of being sold, an unacceptable idea to Joe, who lives on the vineyard he owns. In order to save the winery and vineyards and keep it all in the family, he organized his three remaining cousins to form a family consortium. Today, Nichelini Vineyard is Napa's oldest continuously run family winery.

Five acres of the present day vineyard were planted in 1930 with Zinfandel grafted onto St. George rootstock. The budwood most likely came from the original hillside vineyard. In 1968, an additional three to four acres of Zinfandel were planted with budwood from the original vineyard grafted onto St. George rootstock. In 1973, another 35 acres were added. The best fruit from the vineyard is used in Nichelini Zinfandel.

The winery today is a blend of tradition and new technology. The stone tasting room and outdoor bar still invite the visitors to linger over the fragrant Zinfandels and a few other varieties even in the rainy winter. Then, one moves inside to stand at a small bar beside a roaring fire while watching the rain fall through the trees outside the open door. But winemaker Greg has replaced the traditional redwood fermentation tanks with stainless steel, and added new oak barrels to the storage program.

Carol Nichelini, Tony Nichelini-Irwin & Joe Nichelini

"The question we ask ourselves is how much tradition to keep and how much new technology to add," said Greg. "At my own winery in El Dorado County, I am creating a tradition. At Nichelini Winery, however, we never forget that we are the third generation of an historic family, and that our main focus is to maintain connection to the old tradition. We want to keep the winery in trust for many more generations."

With 120 descendents of Anton and Caterina Nichelini, many of them interested in grapegrowing and winemaking, it is likely that Nichelini Winery will continue to be family-run well into the 21st century.

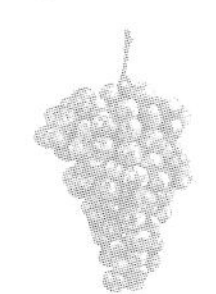

Louis M. Martini Winery: Is Zinfandel Just Another Grape?

Louis M. Martini Winery has made a varietal Zinfandel every year since 1935. In 1977, Louis M. Martini's grandson, Michael Martini, a UC Davis, graduate, became winemaker. I interviewed Michael in summer 1986 for my "Challenge of Zinfandel" report, and toured with him that September the winery's Monte Rosso Vineyards located on Moon Mountain Road in Sonoma Valley. His grandfather had purchased the Monte Rosso Vineyard in 1936.

"What makes Monte Rosso so well suited to Zinfandel?" I asked, as the big pick-up chugged up the steep slopes of the vineyard.

"The vineyard is in the Mayacamas Mountains on the east side of Sonoma Valley above Glen Ellen," said Michael. "The soil is a mixture of red clay/loam and decomposed volcanic shale, and the vineyard is cooled by the breezes that drift over the vineyards from San Pablo Bay. These cooling breezes help the grapes to develop softer unpolymerized tannins that are perceived as bitterness or refined texture, and help a wine to improve in the bottle over several years. It's the polymerized tannins, the big, heavy tannins developed in the grape by high ripeness and excessive heat, that produce the chewy, puckery, astringent quality.

"We've never gone for these big tannins in our wines. That's why I like Monte Rosso grapes. In cool regions like this, the tannins are slow to polymerize. The grapes are picked at a higher Brix than would be possible in warmer regions, where the heat, combined with lower acids and higher pH, bring about earlier polymerization. We are able to get the flavor and body that come with full ripeness, while retaining balance. This means that the wines are soft and fruity at release, but will improve in the bottle for many years, without danger of the tannins outweighing or outliving the fruit. Tannins should never outweigh and outlast the fruit. But it's only the polymerized tannins that you have to worry about. Thus, control of tannins, both viticulturally and during the winemaking process, is important."

Michael and Louis Martini

In 1991, I returned for a conversation about the economics of Zinfandel for my ***PWV*** report on Zinfandel. Where was the money in Zinfandel for Louis M. Martini, I wanted to know? Michael seemed to express wonder that Zinfandel should be worth so much attention.

"Zinfandel? Isn't it just another grape?" he rejoined. Then he qualified his opening remark. "You have to understand, first of all, that winemaking is a business. We have 100 acres of Zinfandel vines in our Monte Rosso Vineyard, and produce nearly 20,000 cases of redwood-tank-aged Zinfandel. We have a customer base for our style and price. Zinfandel is a price-sensitive variety for us. Our niche has always been in the mom and pop stores and the chains. It's the kind of wine those customers take home for dinner, to drink with just about anything they want to serve."

Yet Monte Rosso Vineyard is one of the best Zinfandel vineyards in the state. With the increasing interest in Zinfandel as a premium wine, I wondered if Michael had given any thought to separating out his best lots of Monte Rosso Zinfandel and finishing it in small barrels, as a Reserve wine.

"What you wine writers don't understand is that winemaking is a business," he reiterated. "We have a customer base for our style and price. What do you think would happen to that customer base if I started ageing 20,000 cases (or even 5,000 cases) of my Zin in small barrels? First, I'd have the cost of the small barrels, then the cost of all the cellaring that small barrel production entails. I'd have to pretty much double the price of my Zinfandel to do that. And where am I going to find the customer base for such a radical and expensive change, even for a few thousand cases? We'd lose one-third of our market if we jumped [price] category like that. Besides," he added, "I like the fruit character that you get with the large tanks. Zinfandel doesn't need all that oak."

For Louis M. Martini Winery, Zinfandel has historically been a profitable wine. The family owns its Zinfandel vineyards, and its traditional winemaking style sold well at an affordable price. In fact, I soon found myself seeking out the Martini Zinfandel on restaurant wine lists, since I knew it was one wine I could always count on to be of a consistent style, well suited to a variety of entrees, and, yes, affordable. I also recalled how many Zinfandel producers had cited Louis M. Martini Zinfandel as the wine that inspired them to become Zinfandel producers themselves.

Yet because winemaking is a business, I began to wonder if Michael had considered selling his Monte Rosso grapes to premium Zinfandel producers, and buying lesser quality fruit more in keeping with his style of wine production. Such a move would certainly improve his profit margin, since the Monte Rosso grapes would bring premium prices. "Would your customers notice, if you did," I asked him, "given that they buy your Zinfandel because of its affordable price?"

"I don't know," he replied. "But either way, I'm not ready to do that."

By the 1990s, times had changed for Zinfandel and for the winery. Zinfandel was no longer "just another grape" for anyone. Inspired by the quality of his grapes and the opportunity to make some of the most exciting Zinfandel table wines in the state, Michael was ready to convince his family to limit production of Zinfandel to a reserve style. In 1993, he produced his first ultra-premium Black Label Gnarly Vines Zinfandel from the ancient vines on Monte Rosso — just 250 cases, selling most of the fruit from the oldest and best blocks to such ultra-premium producers as Ravenswood, Biale, and Villa Mount Eden. Each of these producers has given their bottlings a Monte Rosso vineyard designation. Martini uses the fruit from the younger vines, which are now nearly 30 years old, for his 3,000-case second tier Heritage Label Zinfandel.

"So Zinfandel isn't 'just another grape' after all?" I asked him in a July 1997 interview.

"No," replied the burly, six-foot-five, blond-haired and always good-natured Michael with a modest smile, as he proudly poured me a tasting of his 1994 Gnarly Vines Zinfandel. "And you know me well enough to know that it never has been, don't you?"

Yes, I always knew — from the moment in September 1986 when I first went with him to the top of Monte Rosso's Rattlesnake Hill, and we sat looking over the old gnarlies to the peaceful Sonoma Valley below. Fortunately, I had always caught the teasing twinkle in his blue eyes as he tried to convince me that Zinfandel was just another grape. In fact, in 1987 Mike had made an old vine Zinfandel from Monte Rosso, "which was made in the old Italian style, but aged in 500-gallon neutral American oak casks rather than 20,000-gallon redwood tanks. That wine came out spicy and beautiful, with all sorts of interesting components in it," he told me. "But it was still pretty basic winemaking — concrete fermentors, six days on the skins, the way my grandfather used to make it."

"So tell me about your new approach to Zinfandel."

"For our Black Label 'Gnarly Vines Zinfandel,' I use only five tons of fruit from the oldest vines on Rattlesnake Hill, and leave the grapes on the skins for 28 days, and age the wine in 100 percent new oak barrels. Seventy percent are French oak, and 30 percent are American oak."

"For our second tier Heritage label Zinfandel, I leave the grapes on their skins for 14 days before pressing, and the wine is aged in both American oak barrels and uprights. About 30 percent of the oak is new. So I've upped the time on the skins from six days to 14, which gives the wine an extra layer of complexity, use small oak barrels instead of redwood tanks, and bottle the wine unfined and unfiltered, which opens up the mouth by leaving more richness of flavor and body. Our Heritage Zinfandel at $12 is now one of the best Zinfandels in its category," said Mike. "What I did was keep only the best fruit from our younger vines, and upgrade the vinification as I just described, and raise the price a little. Price is part of image, and we decided to make less wine of better quality, and sell it for a higher price. And it has worked. We have a better product, and it is still good value."

"So you are not so opposed to ageing Zinfandel in oak as you stated a few years ago?"

"The best way I can explain what I was saying when we talked then is that you have to get behind what you are doing as a company, whether or not you agree with the policy — especially when you are talking to a writer," said Mike, laughing. He explained that the winery's redwood tank regimen was the style his longtime customers were used to, and could afford. Given that Louis M. Martini produced 20,000 cases annually, this was an important consideration. Storing wines for two to three years in large (20,000-gallon) redwood tanks was the traditional method of ageing large production red wines in California after Repeal until well into the 1970s.

The practice of using small oak cooperage, a certain percentage of it brand new, as part of the ageing program for red wines, came along later, as California's wineries returned to a fine wine focus. (See Appendix I, "Time Out for Quercus.")

"I have personally never liked putting my wines in redwood," Michael continued. "Yes, wines stored in 20,000-gallon redwood tanks do age beautifully. There is low oxidation in large containers, so you maintain high fruit quality, and the wines have a long life in the bottle. My dad always said, and I agreed with him, that for every year you put a wine in a small barrel, you take 10 years off its life in the bottle. Our Zinfandel has always aged well. The 1947 Zinfandel is better than our 1947 Cabernet Sauvignon, and our 1941 Zinfandel is still excellent.

"But redwood strips the wine of some of its complexity, and it contributes a kind of creosote flavor that I came to hate. In fact, anytime I am judging wines today, and I come across a wine with that stripped out creosote flavor, I throw it out immediately. Of course, the consumers back then didn't notice it, because all they see is the finished product, which is a nice drinkable wine. And our wines got out to the consumers, and were consistent in their style, and fairly priced. They have always been a good deal for the style."

"Are you doing anything differently in the vineyard as part of the winery's transition from quantity to quality?" I asked.

"No, we don't need to. The old vineyard is established, and so well suited to its location that the vines pretty much balance themselves. We prune them, crown sucker them, and cultivate them — all the usual things. But we don't remove leaves up there because the vines aren't vigorous on Monte Rosso. They are all open. In fact, those oldest vines, which are 80- to 100-years old or older have been a real lesson to us. Every leaf and every cluster is in the sunshine. It is just the way they have formed themselves. They are like the old Sequoias in Sequoia National Park, which have exactly the amount of wood necessary to grow efficiently. That is how old vines function. Everything extraneous dies.

"On the very young vines (10 years old), we do thin the bunches and remove second and third crop. But we sell the fruit from these young vines, some of it to the same producers who buy the fruit from our old vines. Our plan, however, is to retain more and more of this fruit for our own production, to meet growing demands for our Heritage label, which has taken off like gangbusters. Ultimately, we will sell only to producers who give Monte Rosso vineyard recognition."

It was obvious that far from being "just another grape," Monte Rosso Zinfandel has always been a revered grape for Michael Martini.

Storybook Mountain

Storybook Mountain Vineyards is situated on rolling east-facing hills at the north end of Napa Valley across from Mount St. Helena, which forms a stunning backdrop. Adam and Jacob Grimm originally established the vineyard in the 1880s. Dr. J. (Jerry) Bernard Seps and his wife, Sigrid, bought the property and planted the vineyard in 1976. Jerry and Sigrid named the vineyard "Storybook Mountain" in part to honor the Grimms. Remnants of the early vines can still be found in the forest at the edges of the vineyard. The property came with original wine caves that Jerry and Sigrid have enlarged and improved.

I visited Storybook Mountain Vineyards for the first time in summer of 1996. By way of introduction, Jerry took me on a tour of his beautiful rolling 36 acres of 20-year-old Zinfandel. "I didn't come up here to plant Zinfandel," he began as the truck crept up the steep hillside at the edge of the vineyard. "Our intent was and is to plant the variety that goes best with our soil and location. When I researched the soil (red clay loam), the climate (east facing and cool), and suitable varieties, I always came back to

Zinfandel. Some agricultural advisers thought I should plant Bordeaux varieties, and they likely would have done well here, but the weight of the evidence as well as the advice of people like Andre Tchelistscheff pointed to Zinfandel. We felt that if we made the right match of estate and grape, we would have the opportunity to make great wine."

We were sitting in his truck at the top of the highest slope, with a view down over the entire vineyard towards Mount St. Helena, which was looming strong and clear against the blue sky. It was a magnificent sight.

"Storybook is planted to the smallest berry, smallest cluster clone that UC Davis, developed in its research into a bigger producing clone for the Central Valley's Zinfandel program. We picked the one that least suited its goals," said Jerry, smiling. "Yes, our clone is certified, virus-tested stock; yes, it is propagated on AxR-1 rootstock; and yes, most of it is trellised and cordon trained. However, irrigation and fertilization are closely regulated, canopy management is intense, and crops are kept to a low 2½ to 3 tons per acre."

Jerry Seps

Phylloxera, however, is not a big worry. Jerry does all his own farming, and he harvests the grapes by hand with the help of a family that has worked for him since he established the winery. In its first 24 years, he has seen no symptoms of the root louse.

Harvest takes place over a four-week period in order to achieve the best balance of ripeness, acid, and tannins from all the blocks. "We determine harvest date according to flavor and seed maturation, which we feel is more important than Brix levels," he explained. For his family of pickers, Jerry drops empty plastic tubs beneath the rows to be picked. When the tubs are full, the three pickers leave them beside the rows. Then Jerry drives down the rows with his pick-up truck and loads the full tubs onto the truck bed. From there, he takes the grapes to the winery crush pad. A young assistant hands him the tubs, and Jerry empties them into a small crusher. A positive displacement pump moves the wine to the fermentor.

I watched this operation one lovely October afternoon, and when the last tub was emptied into the crusher, Jerry turned to me with a smile. "You see, that's all there is to it." Then he stepped into the truck, and off he went back to the vineyard for another load.

Picking for fully ripe flavors was not always Jerry's practice. During the 1980s, his preference was for a more elegant, restrained Bordeaux-style of Zinfandel. Jerry describes the style as "having more structure than the norm for Zinfandel, shaped to improve in the bottle after a few years' ageing." Most of the critics and wine store personnel whom I read and talked to in the late 1980s would have agreed with Jerry's description. According to Jerry, his wines of the 1980s won more medals that any other winery, and each vintage sold out. Occasionally, however, I heard wine store personnel comment that the harder, leaner structure of these wines sometimes meant that Storybook Zinfandels took a little longer to move off the shelf than some of the riper styles coming onto the market by the early 1990s.

As I recall, and from notes I made at the time, when I tasted Storybook Mountain Zinfandels of the mid-1980s in tastings that included riper, more extracted styles, Storybook did seem lean and a little hard. However, when I took the wine home to have with dinner, it was inevitably a perfect match-up; and if I left a bottle or two in the cellar for a couple of years, it was better.

Yet times and tastes change. "The 1990s," said Jerry, in explanation of his change in style, "partially reshaped the image of what Zinfandel could and should be. Through changes in viticulture and winery technology, qualities associated with maturing wine could be captured earlier in the life of a vintage, combining accessibility with ageability. The critics on one hand, and increased restaurant use of Zinfandel on the other, put a demand on a combination of intensity with immediate richness. Within the parameters of our estate, we moved with the times."

The Storybook Zinfandels that I have tasted in the 1990s no longer strike me as hard or lean. They are still elegant wines, balanced, but they also have that delicious forward blackberry fruit and subtle spiciness that makes Napa Valley Zinfandels so appealing at release.

Jerry produces two styles: a Napa Valley Zinfandel and a Reserve Zinfandel. Part of the difference is the location in the vineyard that the fruit comes from, along with when the fruit is picked; another part is in cellaring practices.

Storybook Mountain Vineyard is one of two single variety, Zinfandel-only Napa Valley producers. Sky Vineyards is the other one. Jerry's award-winning Zinfandel from this relatively young vineyard has helped to challenge the perception that Zinfandel wines made from the oldest vines are necessarily superior. His wines still win their share of medals, and at least one publication, *The Wine Enthusiast*, declared his 1997 Eastern Exposure as Best Zinfandel of the Year, which greatly pleases Jerry. "Storybook is my life," he said. It shows in the beauty of his vineyards and in the quality of his wines.

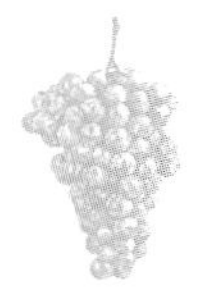

Sky Vineyards

"Zinfandel is precious," declared soft-spoken Lore Olds, owner of Sky Vineyards, which is located near the top of Mount Veeder on the Napa County side. A certain reverence tinged his voice. It was a beautiful July 1999 morning, and we were sitting on the deck of his house looking towards Napa Valley. Lore is devoted to his single variety Zinfandel vineyard, and is enchanted by the essence of pure Zinfandel wine, especially the wine that his mountain vineyard grapes produce.

This was the last of my visits and conversations with Lore about his Zinfandel, which had acquired a devoted set of customers since it first came on the market in the early 1980s. Trying to discover the source of that appeal was quite a challenge. The vineyard is in a remote location, and there is no tasting room or retail outlet on the premises. With little in the way of customer-wooing facilities, how did Sky Vineyard attract its ardent following?

"By making soulful wines that caught the fancy of an *avante garde* group of California foodies and oenophiles who shared my appreciation for pure mountain-grown Zinfandel," answered Lore.

The 12-acre Sky Vineyard is the largest Zinfandel vineyard in the Mount Veeder viticultural area. It is reached by traveling up Cavedale Road out of Sonoma Valley. At the end of the long, steep, and winding road that is badly potholed at the top, the property still has no electricity — and therefore no power lines spoiling the views. It is pretty much a long way from anywhere. Which can be a problem for visitors, since they inevitably underestimate how long it will take them to navigate the mountain roads. They tend to arrive late for their appointed hour. Accepting this phenomenon as a condition of his location, Lore has taken it upon himself to ride his battered dirt bike out to the potholed portion of the road, acting as a herald to dazed visitors. A hatted and hunched figure on his powerful bike, he shouts a greeting — "You're late!" — as the car draws near, then wheels the bike in a tight circle and roars back up the road to the lane to his vineyard. He lets his bewildered visitors keep up the best they can.

Lore Olds

Both bike and car are parked at the side of the vineyard, and Lore, tall, lean, and looking every bit the mountain man that he is, escorts his visitors down the rutted and stone-strewn dirt road to the house and winery a quarter mile below. An adventure always, but worth the effort, for the place is quiet and remote, the air enveloping Sky Vineyard clean and pure. It is a good place to grow Zinfandel grapes and produce wine from them as a complete art form, which is how Lore views his operation. He even creates the labels he puts on his bottles from original block prints. "Sky Vineyard Zinfandel is an expression of both place and self," he said. This is part of what caught the fancy of his earliest customers.

Sky Vineyards' first commercial estate Zinfandel was produced in 1979, but by that time, Lore had been making Zinfandel for nearly 10 years — first as a home winemaker. His first home Zinfandel came from the Old Hill Ranch, which he had pruned for a few seasons before he established Sky Vineyards.

"Zinfandel is a treasure," Lore said. "It is sophisticated and polite and subtle. There are all sorts of interplays going on in the wine that are easy to lose with the addition of other varieties. It is just the way the grape is. Yet it has gotten a reputation for being tough, and that one can make an 'Italian Black' or a 'Rustic Red' from the grapes. It is 'tough,' however, because of the Carignane and Petite Sirah and the Alicante Bouschet that is often added to it. Adding those varieties to Zinfandel can make it rustic and tough.

"Sure, by adding those other varieties, you get that high-toned fruit, which people love. But then you miss out on the essence of Zinfandel, which is easily disturbed. As soon as you add any other variety, even just two or three percent, you change the character of Zinfandel wine. Zinfandel is delicate and subtle. It's easy to lose that precious quality. Sky Vineyards Zinfandel is estate-grown and produced, and is pure Zinfandel. To me, that makes it precious." His voice had the same ring of passion that I had so often heard in the voices of growers whose families had grown Zinfandel for generations.

When I asked Lore what led him to choose Zinfandel as his estate variety, his answer was multi-faceted.

"I grew up in Berkeley, but spent summers working on the family farm in Missouri. As a child growing up in Berkeley, I acquired a passion for following your own path and seeing life with an artistic vision. From my summers on the farm in Missouri, I discovered that I liked working with the earth and the rewards that came from that effort and that place: wonderful food and drink. A family life that centered on the farm seemed right for me.

"It was not until 1971, however, when I got an opportunity to take care of an Oregon vineyard and winery, that I realized that grapegrowing and winemaking would fulfill both my love of working with the earth and my artistic vision. The following year, I founded Sky Vineyards. I chose Zinfandel because I had grown up with the wine, and loved it, and also because it is from California *terroir* that people came to know the Zinfandel grape. Before I planted my own vineyard in 1972, I worked for a couple of years for just about every Italian grower in Sonoma Valley. They all grew Zinfandel, and most of them had vineyards planted before Prohibition. I worked for both Louis Pagani and Val Rossi, and their passion for their old Zinfandel vines must have rubbed off on me. When it came time for me to plant my own vineyard, I knew I wanted to plant Zinfandel, but even though most of the old growers had mixed black Zinfandel vineyards, I knew I wanted Zinfandel only. And I knew I wanted to farm in the old Italian style.

"My last but equally important reason for choosing Zinfandel had to do with viticultural practices. Zinfandel is well suited to head training, rather than growing on trellises. I prune each vine so that it represents a 'city in space.' The spurs are arranged in solar view and at different heights and points of origin. If you look at my vineyard in the moonlight, the vines look like they are dancers, a vineyard full of whirling dervishes, or a Sufi dance of spiritual life — not a techno lineup of wire, metal, and corporate discipline.

"I chose this location because it was already well known for its wine, and I wanted high slopes that faced east. I wanted my vines to get up with the sun (like the chickens), and then to have an exposure that would moderate the hot afternoon sun. This location is on the edge of the ocean, which creates a cooler and more humid climate than you find in the interior valleys. It is on the up-wind side of a large urban area, so the breezes keep the air clean. I can sometimes even smell the ocean during pruning season, although it is 30 miles away. In my vineyard, I get the fascinating flavors and smells of chaparral. I also knew from my Oregon experience that I liked fruit that came from colder winters, later springs, and earlier falls, and the more intense sun that came with the shorter growing season. You get these conditions on an east-facing slope in the north coast mountains of California.

"I also wanted red soil but as a thin topsoil. I wanted to grow red grapes on red soil. I wanted well-fractured subsoil that would allow vine roots to go deep for minerals and moisture. Thin red topsoil and fractured subsoil are usually found on mountain slopes. As an added bonus, this location is also close to my roots.

"My winery is situated in the canyon where cool-to-cold air is constantly draining off the slopes above, thus keeping the wine cool. During each vintage's first winter, the wine is cold, often in the upper 30°F, so it develops slowly. My approach to growing and producing pure Zinfandel yields a medium-alcohol wine that is aged strictly in French oak barrels. The oak becomes an integrated part of the flavor and aroma, which allows the Zinfandel to speak for itself. I have found that by listening to the wine, I am able to produce an elegant wine that is truly a product of this perfect location. It is this quality that my customers have come to love.

"Zinfandel came of age in California, not Europe. California is a special place. The Pacific Coast gives it a distinct climate. Culturally, it's also special because it's such an interesting mixture of old and new. The earliest grapegrowers were mostly Italian immigrants, yet they became fiercely proud to be American and Californian. So the cultural climate is also special and distinct.

"I like to think of Zinfandel as having its own cultural *terroir*, which I describe as 'California heart.' Zinfandel is suited not just to the coastal climate of California but also to its cultural climate inherited from the early Italian grapegrowers. In these coastal mountains, there are not many people. Neighbors are few, and there is lots of space between them. It takes them time to open up both to strangers and to each other. But if you are willing to be patient, and sit on the porch to talk and listen and wait for them to trust you and to open up, you will find them pretty interesting.

"Mountain-grown estate Zinfandel is a bit like that. It opens up slowly, too. If you have the patience to wait for it, you will find that it gets more interesting as it opens up — just like the mountain people. These are all reasons why I chose to establish Sky Vineyards with just Zinfandel. Even as a kid, I drank Zinfandel with my family, who had friends here in Napa Valley. Louis M. Martini Zinfandel was one of their favorite wines."

Lore's Sky Vineyard Zinfandel is indeed a little like him — shy and reserved upon first meeting, although "shy" probably doesn't apply so much to Lore as to his Zinfandel. Because of this character of his wine, he typically holds it for a year in bottle before releasing. Even then, it usually benefits from an additional two or three years in the bottle.

In 1999, Sky Vineyards' 1994 vintage was just approaching its maximum potential. The tannins had softened, the luscious spicy blackberry fruit was exploding in the glass. The wine had transformed from shy and reserved to a bold and confident elegance. Its shy and reserved character makes it a hard sell to the wine writers, although not to his staunch and long-established set of customers, who seem to understand the culture of Sky Vineyards Zinfandel and the man who makes them.

"It's the character of the grapes from this vineyard," Lore explained. "The character depends upon the year. I don't set out deliberately to make a reserved wine."

While he watches the numbers, Lore is more likely to choose his harvest date by how the grapes look, rather than how they taste or what the numbers tell him. "I wait until I see a certain slackness in the skins. Then I know they are at peak ripeness, that dehydration is setting in. It is time to pick. Depending upon the year, the T.A. will approach 1 gram per liter, pH will be 3.2, and sugar content will be between 22.5° and 24° Brix. In cooler years, the sugar content will be lower; in warmer years, it will be higher. In both cases, the flavors will be ripe and mature, but the cooler years will produce a shyer, more reserved wine."

Sales have been so successful that Lore is replanting eight of his 12 acres that were established in 1972 on AxR-1. The entire vineyard is infested with Phylloxera, but the remaining four acres on the best-suited soil are still strong enough to produce a crop for probably another five years.

"These remaining four acres will give me the last vintages from 30-year-old mountain-grown vines," pointed out Lore. "So these next four or so vintages will be small and very special — maybe 700 cases."

Although disappointed that he is not to have a vineyard approaching old vine status, the good news is that he is able to correct the mistakes he made when he put the vineyard in 30 years ago. "I knew much less about planting a vineyard back then," he acknowledged. "So now I have the excitement and joy of doing everything state-of-the-art."

State-of-the-art means developing a farming style that is almost the antithesis of what he learned working in the old Italian-owned vineyards. "As

I found out in the 20 years that I have had my vineyard, the Italian style of farming on the lower elevation vineyards doesn't work so well on my mountain vineyard. The soil down below is much richer than up here, and not so steep. They always grew a large biomass cover crop, then disked it under. I stopped disking up here in 1994, because I found out that disking encourages erosion and loss of soil nutrients. I am sowing a low biomass cover crop that I will just mow. It will be a permanent cover crop, and will add nutrients to the soil, sustain friendly insects, and also help to control erosion."

Lore is also laying a set of drainage pipes throughout the vineyard to carry off excess water from winter rains, and thus control erosion from below the ground surface. These erosion control practices, he believes, will contribute to an overall more natural and sustainable way of farming on the hillsides.

Zinfandel is precious.

Lore Olds

As for his choice in budwood selection, he is using selections from four clones: two are old UC Davis selections, one is Castamagna, and one is an unnamed small-berried selection. For rootstock, he has settled upon 110R. The vines will be head trained, and the plants drip irrigated as necessary for the first two or three years — just until they are established.

His overall wine style won't change much, however. Developed over the years with the help of his former wife, Linn Briner, it always has been a hands-on approach from vineyard to bottle. "Linn didn't have much to do with the vineyard," he said. "I do the work there. What she brought to Sky Vineyards style was meticulousness in the winemaking quality control. A trained winemaker herself, she had a sense of carefulness that I benefited from. I wasn't sloppy, but I didn't focus on all the little details as she did. She liked everything to do with winemaking 'squeaky clean.'"

How nice to hear him give credit to his former wife, I thought.

What Lore hopes to do as his new vineyard develops is to enhance his prevailing style, rather than change it. "Sky Vineyards Zinfandel will always be a farmer's kind of wine, although I may try to develop a slightly more extracted style with these clones and rootstock. So I'm also thinking of getting a new destemmer together with a new pump and press. My old crusher still is good in that it sits on top of the fermentor, and the wine drops directly into the tank. But it requires more work to keep any broken stems out of the mix. My basket press works only as hard as the strength of the kid I hire to do the pressing. The press wine is never bitter and I normally add it to the free run. But when the new planting comes in, it will probably be time to make a change, go a little more high tech. Yet I will continue to look over every bunch of grapes at harvest, turn the wine during fermentation with my hands, and use just the right percentage of new French oak barrels as each vintage needs. I'll design the labels. That won't change."

However, the ground for the vineyard was only then being prepared, Lore reminded me. Until about 2002 or so, Sky Vineyards will produce

Zinfandel from its remaining four acres of 30-year-old vines in its traditional style. This will be classic Sky Vineyards pure mountain Zinfandel, a work of art from vineyard to label.

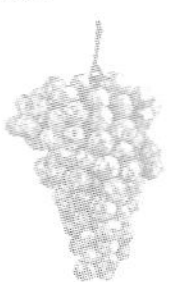

Brandlin Vineyard

"I get goose bumps when I think about Brandlin Vineyard," said Peter Franus as he poured a barrel tasting of his 1996 Zinfandel. It was April 25, 1997. We had met in the tasting room of his winery on Hoffman Lane near Yountville in the Napa Valley. An athletic, fair-haired, and somewhat intense man, he especially glowed when he spoke of his 70- to 80-year-old Brandlin Zinfandel Vineyard located on an east-facing slope on Mount Veeder, well above the morning fog line. Peter has made Zinfandel from there since 1991.

What makes the Brandlin Vineyard special? To answer this question, Peter invited me to return some day for a walking tour of the vineyard. It took me a couple of years to do so, and by then, Cuvaison had purchased the vineyard. Peter retains a long-term contract on the Zinfandel vineyard. I met him there one August 1999 morning.

At the vineyard, the sun was shining brightly, while the valley below was still fog-enshrouded. As we walked into the vineyard, Peter gave me a little background on its history. "When the Brandlins bought this property, it consisted of 600 acres. They bought the entire property for about $6,000. They also owned what is now Mayacamas Vineyard. Over the years, they sold that property, and also sold off bits of the 600-acre ranch. Today, the Brandlin Ranch consists of 170 acres, and is the parcel on which the Zinfandel was planted in the 1930s, all on St. George rootstock. For several decades, the Brandlins sold to Christian Brothers. Then they sold to the Napa Cooperative, Edmunds St. John, Caymus, George Hendry, Kent Rosenblum, and finally, me. And also to home winemakers."

At this point, Chester Brandlin, who with his brother, Richard, inherited the property from their father, joined us. Neither brother had married. "Yes," he corroborated, "we sold to Christian Brothers in the 1940s and 1950s. Grapes weren't worth much then. When World War II started, the going price was $35 per ton. My brother and I did all the picking, and my dad was the boss. You may find this hard to believe, but in some years, I picked 40 tons of grapes all by myself. I still have one old knife I used to use. Since wineries didn't have their own scales then, we went on box average, which was 24 pounds for the grapes we shipped back east. When you learn how to put your grapes in the lug boxes, you get to know how much it takes to make 24 pounds. We shipped grapes back east during Prohibition, and no one ever had to repack our grapes for shipping. For Christian Brothers, the boxes were 50 pounds."

The budwood for the Zinfandel came from some pre-Prohibition vineyards above Lokoya Lodge, long since gone, Chester said. There were five or six Zinfandel vineyards on Mount Veeder in the early 1900s, mostly on St. George rootstock. "Everyone grew Zinfandel then," he said. "The Italians knew what Zinfandel was, and that was what they wanted. Everyone wanted Zinfandel. Unfortunately, my grandfather and father thought the soil was so good that they didn't even need to use the wild root. They were ignorant of the threat of Phylloxera, which did destroy the original vines. But the first vines grew quickly. Within six years, they were full bearing, so we took cuttings from them and planted the rest of the vineyard on St. George.

"This mountain Zinfandel was always good, and we could make five or six kinds of wine from just this vineyard, depending on from what part of the vineyard we took the grapes, and how ripe they were. Of course, that became part of the problem for Zinfandel, which ended up on the skids in the 1970s. But then some smart young winemakers came along who knew more about winemaking than the old-timers did, and began to make a consistent Zinfandel wine. Consumers needed to know what they were buying when they bought a Zinfandel wine, allowing for regional and stylistic differences — which is true of any wine. The variations during the 1970s were too great, so Zinfandel hit skid row, I like to say."

Chester also reminisced about the days when his father made wine at what is today Mayacamas Vineyard, and sold a gallon of Zinfandel for a silver dollar — "a silver dollar a gallon. I can remember people coming in and plunking down their silver dollars. I was a kid then, and I didn't know there was that much money in the world. Those were real silver dollars, too, in those days. A German immigrant named Fischer from Stuttgart built the winery in 1888. Fischer was also a glass engraver, and in 1906, the big earthquake destroyed his business in the Cannery. He could not meet the demands of the Illinois Glass Company, so they foreclosed and took the ranch. My father bought the property in 1922 from an Italian family who had bought it from the Illinois Glass Company. But he had been in the vineyard and winemaking business before he bought Mayacamas."

"Did your father make wine through Prohibition?" I asked.

"Oh, sure, but he never got busted," replied Chester. "He was too smart for them. He was like Snuffy Smith. He always knew when the 'revenoors' were coming around. We had an old hand pump, and with a two-inch line, you could pump thousands of gallons of wine overnight — under woodpiles, in haystacks, anywhere. He continued to make wine after Prohibition, but just for the family's use. He sold most of the grapes to home winemakers both during and after Prohibition — and you can be sure not all of it was for home use. By 1941, he got tired of making wine, and that is when we sold that property."

We retired from our walk in the vineyard to a picnic table under a fig tree near the house. There, we were to taste some 1997 Franus Zinfandel from the Brandlin Vineyard, and look over some old photographs. The

Brandlin Vineyard Zinfandel is always a big, robust, tannic wine with dusky flavors of brambly blackberries, cedar, and a range of spicy flavors. While many people would enjoy this wine in its youth, for my taste, it is a wine to lay down for a few years, until the tannins soften and the flavors mellow and marry to perfection.

Proud of the wine made from his vineyard, Chester's love of Zinfandel has been unwavering throughout the years. "I fought tooth and nail to keep this vineyard in the ground," he said. There had also been a small block of old Mourvedre that he and Richard agreed to take out in 1983. "I would liked to have kept them, too, if we could have," said Chester. "But there wasn't any money in the grapes, and we were getting tired of taking care of grapevines. We kept them as long as we could. But I stood my ground with the Zinfandel vineyard, even though Richard would like to have taken out the Zinfandel as well. To this day, I still think that Zinfandel is the best black grape. Period! I am somewhat like August Sebastiani, who said that he liked Zinfandel so good he could drink it for breakfast. Well, I've never drunk it for breakfast quite yet, but I still think Zinfandel is one great wine — if it is made right."

Peter Franus, Winemaker

Obviously, Chester feels that Peter is making Brandlin Vineyard Zinfandel "right." A few weeks later, I visited Peter at his winery for a barrel tasting of the 1998 Brandlin and the 1999 Planchon Vineyard, Contra Costa, Zinfandels, and to find out about his winemaking practices, especially as applied to Brandlin Vineyard fruit.

"My winemaking style is guided by the desire to make concentrated yet balanced wines," Peter began. "All the great wines I have ever enjoyed have several features in common: richness, complexity, harmony, and an invitation to come back for more. My greatest satisfaction comes when I see a smile and hear the simple comment, 'This is delicious.'

"More often than not, my Zinfandel from Brandlin allows me to achieve my goals. The grapes always have wonderful depth and achieve true ripeness without the overripe or pruny flavors that often accompany Zinfandel. The wines tend to be brooding and slow to evolve and generally age in barrel for 14 to 15 months. I like to use 35 percent to 40 percent new French oak, and to give them several rackings to help them on their way, and to soften their tannins. Over the years, I have gravitated toward the more heavily charred Burgundian coopered barrels, and now use them exclusively for the Brandlin Zinfandel.

"In contrast to Brandlin is the fruit I get from Planchon Vineyard in Contra Costa County. The fruit typically displays a cherry liqueur and plum nose. The resulting wine is forward, lush, and fruity with low tannin.

I keep this wine in mostly American oak, about 20 percent new, for 11 to 12 months because the wine can benefit from some of the grainier tannins found in that type of wood."

Our barrel tasting of these two distinctive wines demonstrated the winemaking practices and the character of each vineyard that Peter was describing. As our tasting was winding down, I had one last question: "What attracted you to Zinfandel in the first place?"

"I can't believe that we never discussed my Zinfandel experiences while I was winemaker at Mount Veeder Winery," exclaimed Peter. "It was the Mount Veeder Estate Zinfandel and circumstances surrounding it that largely launched my Zinfandel career. Mount Veeder Winery produced several Zinfandels over the years, including one in 1973 from Simmons Ranch on Mount Veeder. Simmons is now the property owned by Domaine Chandon. I just had this wine a couple of weeks ago and it is still amazing.

Peter Franus and Chester Brandlin

"Mount Veeder Winery did have an estate Zinfandel from 1977 to 1982. The vineyard was established in 1972 or 1973 with the 'Joe Miami clone,' which is supposed to have come from Monte Rosso. I produced both the 1981 and 1982, and it was these two wonderful wines that showed me how good Zinfandel could be from the area. The winery was sold in 1982, and the former owner convinced the new owner to graft the Zinfandel to Chardonnay because 'Chardonnay was scarce in Napa at that time, and there was no money in Zinfandel.' I argued otherwise, but it didn't matter, although the owners did keep two rows of Zinfandel, which allowed us to produce a barrel a year.

"However, the fact that Mount Veeder Winery was no longer producing a Zinfandel allowed me my opportunity. In 1987 I asked the winery owner if he would mind if I did a small amount of Zinfandel under my own label. He said okay, so I produced my first Franus label Zinfandel from Pickle Canyon Vineyard, owned by John and Renate Wright at the time. I consider it a very good wine, not spectacular, but its longevity has surprised me. I just had a bottle over the holidays, and at 12 years it still offers a lot of pleasure.

"As for what it was about Zinfandel that attracted me to it in the first place," said Peter, getting back to my original question, "I spoke earlier about the satisfaction I feel as winemaker when I hear someone who is tasting my Zinfandel use the word 'delicious.' Zinfandel often evokes that response. The variety in many ways symbolizes what first attracted me to winemaking. Those two estate Mount Veeder wines were truly inspirational. I love Zinfandel for its zesty flavors, unpretentious nature, and the fact that it is so uniquely American. California Zinfandel producers are creating the standard for this variety. They do not emulate anyone else."

Hendry Ranch: "Our Zinfandel is About *Terroir*"

I talked to George Hendry for the first time in 1991 as part of my research into the economics of Zinfandel for a ***PWV*** report. I had opened that interview with, "Where is the money in Zinfandel?"

"Even 10 years ago, my answer to that question would have been 'I don't know,'" replied George, in what I was to discover was his always thoughtful and thorough manner of replying to my probing questions. George is a cyclotron scientist (he designs and builds particle accelerator machines that operate with between 11 million and 50 million volts and are primarily used in nuclear medicine), a meticulous winegrower, and an independent thinker. His scientific background has lent an experimental dimension to the way he approaches grapegrowing and winemaking. George also says he has an intuitive side, which he uses to visualize unconventional solutions. He considers himself extremely fortunate in that he has been able pursue his passion for both physics and for winegrape-growing.

"In the early 1980s, my long-term customer, Christian Brothers, was going out of business, the Robert Mondavi Winery was getting out of Zinfandel, and I had 50 acres of producing Zinfandel that no one was interested in buying the fruit from. Survival was the issue, profitability a distant dream, and Zinfandel as an art form seemed academic: I was selling Zinfandel for white Zinfandel for $240 per ton."

I was surprised to learn that George had had 50 acres of Zinfandel until as recently as 1984, since I knew he had much less than that in 1991 — just eight acres. Most of his vineyard was planted with Chardonnay and Cabernet Sauvignon. What had led him to plant 50 acres of Zinfandel in the first place, and then within a few years, bud most of it over to the other varieties?

His story begins several years earlier.

George is the son of a University of California, Berkeley, professor who moved to the Napa Valley in 1939. In that year, George's parents bought the 135-acre property that they christened Hendry Ranch. It lies on Redwood Road benchlands between Napa and Sonoma, and is characterized by thin stony soils and cooling fog and breezes from San Pablo Bay, which lies eight miles to the south. When George took over management of the ranch in 1963, it still had seven acres of old Zinfandel with a few vines of Carignane and Petite Sirah mixed in.

For several years, George sold the fruit to Christian Brothers for red Zinfandel. Although the old vines, which were planted on St. George rootstock, produced only about 1½ tons of grapes per acre, the price per ton was high enough to pay the taxes and make keeping the old vines an economical endeavor.

In 1973–1975, George made up his mind to do something with all his land. He planted an additional 50 acres of Zinfandel vines on what had been grazing land. George recalled that the conventional wisdom of the time held that Hendry Ranch soil was too poor and that the climate was too cold to produce enough grapes to make a vineyard pay. George's neighbors and friends advised him to graze some cattle, or even better, subdivide, he said.

"I loved the place to much to do that. My family culture was too strong, and my family values are as important to me as the bottom line. After all, my father bought this ranch in order to live in the country, not to live among a bunch of houses. I didn't know much about viticulture back then, but I knew that Zinfandel from old vines, which was growing on St. George roots, was paying its way," said George, resorting to the term typically used by early grapegrowers. "Although St. George was not known for producing a large crop, I believed that it was well adapted to austere sites where water availability is a problem. I resolved to use this rootstock for my new plantings, even though the farm advisers recommended AxR-1. The conventional wisdom may have been appropriate for many growers at that time, but my intuition suggested that the market forces just then starting to emerge would more than justify low-yield, high-quality vineyards. Also, I was familiar with St. George roots, and I was getting enough crop to pay my taxes from the original vines on the ranch. My experience with these vines indicated that new plantings on St. George roots would at least break even in this location."

George Hendry

The new vines were UC Davis Clone #2 Zinfandel, field-budded onto St. George rootstock. In keeping with his independent thinking, George chose to trellis his Zinfandel vines and cordon-train them rather than head-train, as is conventional practice for Zinfandel. He believes that uniform fruit with the right amount of sun exposure is one of the keys to high quality wine, and that in his relatively cool growing area cordon training is the most efficient way to achieve that uniformity. "Clusters can be spaced and the canopy managed for uniform exposure to sunlight," he explained. "You don't want the clusters touching each other, and you want only flecks of sunlight on the fruit — not too much direct exposure, not too little."

He points out, however, that the choice of trellised versus head trained vines is site-dependent, and that he is considering head trained vines for a particularly austere block that is up for redevelopment.

He also believes that uniformity in the fruit begins with uniform vines. Each winter, he examines his vineyard and provides any weak-looking vines with two scoops of fertilizer instead of one. Over the years this has helped promote uniformity on his non-uniform site.

Until the early 1980s, George was able to sell his Zinfandel from his new planting to both Christian Brothers and Robert Mondavi Winery at break-even or better prices.

Then things changed.

Christian Brothers went out of business in 1982, and Mondavi stopped producing a Zinfandel wine. The demand for red Zinfandel was falling off while demand for the new white Zinfandel steadily increased. Because ripeness is not a factor for white Zinfandel, growers could increase production to six or eight or even 10 tons per acre. However, George's Zinfandel couldn't produce enough tonnage to make white Zinfandel profitable. At $240 per ton, he was no longer breaking even. It was time to make some changes.

"In 1984, I had my Zinfandel custom-crushed, and I drained off some of the juice as white Zinfandel, which I sold to a buyer back east. It was the money I received for the white Zinfandel that enabled me to pay my taxes. In 1985, the red portion of the 1984 Zinfandel remained unsold. Fortunately, I was able to sell this wine to Kent Rosenblum. Kent did wonderful things for that wine, and Rosenblum Cellars Hendry Vineyard Zinfandel placed first at a Vintners Club tasting in 1986, and placed 'Best Zinfandel' and 'Best of Show' in the San Francisco fair that year. That was the start of a great relationship that still exists, and also was the first recognition of my particular *terroir* as exceptionally well suited to Zinfandel. It was to provide me with a vision of my vineyard as having premier Zinfandel potential.

"But economics was still a reality. In 1983-84, I budded over 20 acres of Zinfandel to Chardonnay, since there was not much Chardonnay in the valley at that time. I also budded one long row of 183 vines to Cabernet Sauvignon. Contrary to the expectations of some, the grapes got ripe and my friend Phil McGuire made some very good wine from them. This showed me that Cabernet could be viable on my ranch both for its quality and for the economics. In 1988 and 1989, I converted another 22 acres of Zinfandel to Cabernet, leaving me just eight acres of Zinfandel — which I today call Block 7."

George took out the seven acres of old original Zinfandel in 1982, and replaced them with Clone 4 Chardonnay. "There were spaces in the vineyard, and at barely 1½ tons per acre, the old Zinfandel was just too unprofitable," he explained, a little regretfully.

Although Zinfandel has become his least profitable winegrape to grow, George has not considered budding the remaining eight acres to another variety. Just the opposite: he has increased his Zinfandel acreage, partly in response to Kent Rosenblum's success with Hendry Vineyards Zinfandel.

By 1988, Rosenblum Cellars had established its reputation as one of a small group of boutique wineries devoted to producing top quality Zinfandel wines. Hendry Vineyards Zinfandel had become a successful addition to its Zinfandel offerings. As a way of improving his economics of growing top quality Zinfandel grapes, George had proposed a "joint venture" with Rosenblum, whereby the profits from the sale of the wine are shared by both Hendry and Rosenblum.

Both men have been happy with this arrangement. "Premium winemaking doesn't work just by numbers," explained George. "You have to want to make something better, something that is an art form, and to have the confidence that you can make it happen. You have to be willing to experiment, to make mistakes, and to follow hunches. We have a lot to learn about Zinfandel. The joint venture keeps us both focused on the wine, and it is economically advantageous to us both. It's better for me because I ultimately get a substantially higher return on my grapes; it's better for Kent because he doesn't have to carry the cost of the grapes. It's overall a good deal — it puts the emphasis where it should be: on quality. I focus on the grapes; Kent focuses on the winemaking. We're both committed to producing the finest Zinfandel possible. This arrangement provides money to be invested in both the vineyard and the winery."

The revenue from wine sales is shared in proportion to each partner's respective costs, and has helped Zinfandel to become a more profitable grape variety for George.

But George acknowledged that consumers have played an important part in the economic upswing of Zinfandel. "Consumers have come to appreciate the spicy, berry character of Zinfandel, and how it complements a wide range of foods. They are beginning to appreciate how viticultural practices can make dramatic differences in wines. They are becoming more sophisticated, and are beginning to appreciate the art form that premium winemaking is. This means that they are now willing to pay a little more for that bottle of well-made Zinfandel, because they appreciate the work and thoughtfulness that has gone into it." George also points out that "the astronomical price of some Cabernets has caused some folks to see in Zinfandel an economical alternative."

In 1992, George established his own label, and took on the challenge of producing Zinfandel and a little Cabernet Sauvignon.

In 1995, George added Block 22, planted with UC Davis clone #2, and Block 23 planted with a field selection from the Brandlin Vineyard. Although pleased with the wines produced from his Clone #2 Block 7, George had leased the Brandlin Vineyard for a few years, and had found the Zinfandel produced from that vineyard dramatically different from his Block 7. He became interested in discovering if the Brandlin selection budwood grafted onto St. George rootstock and planted in his own vineyard would produce Zinfandel with the same character. He was also interested in examining differences that might exist between Clone #2 Zinfandel and the Brandlin field selection grown side by side in about the same *terroir*.

Typical of George, who is never quite satisfied with his accomplishments.

At his July 1999 ZAP Days luncheon, George unveiled his side-by-side 1997 vintages of his Block 22 and Block 23 Zinfandels. In 1997, the vineyards were in their third leaf and in their first crop year. The fruit had been harvested the same day, and the wines had been vinified in exactly the same way. I was a guest at the luncheon, and with great anticipation, tasted these two Zinfandels side by side. George was sitting with me, and watching intently for my reaction.

The first one I sampled was from Clone #2. It was a somewhat closed wine with hints of delicate red fruit aromas and flavors that were accented with vanilla oak tones from the French oak barrels. Then I sampled the wine from Block 23. Typical of the Brandlin vineyard, this was a wine loaded with dark berry flavors, and with a certain amount of dark, spicy chocolate and briary earthy aromatics. This wine would definitely benefit from a few years in the cellar. One could not have imagined that two side-by-side vineyards planted exactly the same in every way except for their budwood could have produced two such dramatically different wines. I looked at George in amazement. George echoed my thoughts, but from a grower and winemaker's perspective.

"I was not ready for such a dramatic difference as exists between this first vintage of the Brandlin and UC Davis Clone #2. I could not have imagined it," he said. "Block 22 is very closed. It does not have the aromatics. But Block 23 has this wonderful dry spice character and great depth that I associate with the Brandlin Vineyard. It distinguished itself immediately in the aromatics during fermentation. Until I established Block 23 with budwood taken from the Brandlin Vineyard, I would not have believed that genetics could make so much difference to wine character. I thought more of the distinctive character came from *terroir*. I still believe that *terroir* is the most important factor, but now I realize that genetics can also make a great difference."

"Do you agree that the wine from the Brandlin clone will need a few years in the cellar to achieve its full potential?" I asked. "If so, do you plan on holding it back for a year or two, since we all know that most people will drink it the same day that they buy it?"

"The market is a factor. A Zinfandel as tough as a Cabernet would need ageing for longer than economy would permit. In a way, we are experimenting with our Block 28 — 300 cases. I'm not too sure whether 3000 cases of this wine would sell at a price that justifies the additional year of bottle ageing and the additional new French oak. But 300 cases — maybe. Anyway it is fun and that is what makes it worthwhile. Try to remember that the economy stuff is a way to pay the bills; having fun is what it is all about."

In 1998, George added Block 28, with buds selected from Block 23; in 1999, Block 29 was established with a Mendocino field selection obtained from a Robert Mondavi vineyard in Oakville, CA. Block 24 is Primitivo, a Zinfandel "cousin." By 1999, George had expanded Hendry Vineyards to 115 acres, with over 23 acres again in Zinfandel. Block 7 had been increased by 1½ acres.

The new blocks are all on St. George rootstock. Over the years, George's experience suggests that unlike some other rootstocks, St.

George gradually increases the stress level in the vines without allowing the vines to become *overly* stressed. He believes this is an important factor in wine quality, and for this reason he continues to use St. George rootstock in some of the new vineyard blocks he is developing. The vines are trained to a unilateral cordon with vertical shoot positioning. The vine spacing is two meters by 1½ meters. All are provided drip irrigation.

I revisited George in January 2000, to walk through his new blocks of Zinfandel. He commented on how the two succeeding vintages from Block 22 and Block 23 — the 1998 and 1999 — were responding to the *terroir*.

"I don't really have a preference for one over the other," he began. "They have changed; they have varied from year to year. My focus is not so much on how the blocks differ as on how to manage the wines from this *terroir* — both in the vineyard and in the cellar. To me, *terroir* is not just soil and climate; it is everything that the site brings to the wine. It also includes the flora and fauna associated with the vineyard — things like the native yeasts, and the other organisms that live in the vineyard. All these elements make up *terroir*. The Brandlin Block, 23, seems to be a slightly more prolific selection than Clone #2 Block 22. Also, the Brandlin grapes are a little bigger, and weigh a bit more. Each time we take a grape sample, we pick exactly 200 berries. The Brandlin block always weighs just a bit more than the Clone #2. Each selection is responding differently to this *terroir*."

Some growers believe that *terroir* includes human intervention, the viticultural inputs of the grower. In this sense the grower and his philosophy are an extension of the vineyard. George is comfortable with this concept. For example, he believes that appropriate crop reductions in Zinfandel (and in other varieties) have a profound effect on wine quality. In this sense the vineyard manager may have as much influence on wine quality as a gravel layer six feet underground.

It is at least partly because of George's interest in his *terroir* that he has been building his own winery, scheduled to begin operations in fall 2001. "Winemaking practices of each producer modify the character of the wine," George said. "Hendry Zinfandel wine produced from Block 7 is distinguishable from Rosenblum Cellars Zinfandel produced from Block 7 grapes. Kent does some things that we don't do, and we do some things that Kent does not do. These winemaking practices are reflected in the finished wines."

George believes that gaining more control over the winemaking will not only produce better wine but also a better understanding of the vineyard. One of the things he already does that distinguishes his wines from those of Rosenblum Cellars Hendry Vineyard is to use French oak barrels almost exclusively. In the case of block 7, about 33 percent of the barrels are new. George feels that the less focused flavors of American oak tend to get in the way of the flavors that come from the vineyard, and it is the flavor and structure that come from *terroir* that he is striving to preserve.

"We feel that we have a *terroir* especially well suited to full, soft tannins and to elegant and concentrated fruit, and that is what we want to see in our wines. Our winemaking begins in the vineyard, and whatever else you wish to say about Hendry Zinfandel, it all comes from grapes grown on Hendry Ranch," George said.

George has come a long way from the early 1970s, when he added 50 acres of Zinfandel to the original eight acres, simply because Zinfandel had shown that it could pay its way. Although much of its acreage had to give way to the more profitable varieties of Chardonnay, Cabernet Sauvignon, and Pinot Noir, the remaining Zinfandel is still paying its way at Hendry Ranch. The amount of profit in Zinfandel, in fact, has been steadily increasing. The variety is also providing a challenge to George to improve his understanding of Hendry Ranch *terroir*, and to fine-tune grapegrowing and winemaking techniques to best express that *terroir*. Given that George seems to have the most fun when he is faced with a challenge, this should keep him busy, and having fun, well into the new century.

Aldo Biale Vineyard: Suburban Zinfandel

I shall always remember the day I met Napa's Biale family at its Zinfandel (and Sauvignon Blanc) ranch on El Centro Avenue in Napa. It was March 7, 1992, and I was invited to lunch. When I met the family, I felt as if I had arrived in Northern Italy. Ninety-six-year-old Christina Biale (who celebrated her 100th birthday in fall, 1996) is from Liguria. Her daughter-in-law, Clementina, is from Piedmont. Their villages are only a few kilometers apart. Aldo Biale met Clementina when on a visit with his parents to his mother's home village.

I was meeting the family for the first time, to talk about Zinfandel. Also in the luncheon party were Aldo and Christina's son Robert, partner Dave Pramuk, and winemaker for the newly established estate label, Al Perry.

The view out the windows of Aldo and Clementina's new home looked over billowing mustard-filled Zinfandel and Sauvignon Blanc vineyards, over the tops of the subdivision that had grown up around them. It stretched beyond to both the western and eastern hills of Napa Valley, which were emerald after the winter's above-average rains.

Above all this were iridescent rain clouds that were changing from silvery mauve to black to pure brilliant white. Rumbles and cracks of thunder accompanied the changing light, providing a dramatic background for the delicious pasta and Zinfandel lunch and conversation that floated above the table the entire time.

"We always had wine, never bought it," said Aldo Biale. "Before we had this vineyard, we bought our grapes. Then, we planted in 1936, so we had our own grapes ever since, from about 1938. The vineyard is on St. George rootstock."

The Zinfandel grapes from their vineyard went to Christian Brothers until the early 1950s, when Christian Brothers stopped buying them. For the next few years, it was hard to sell grapes, Aldo recalled. "We sold a year at a time, until 1955, when we started selling to Napa Valley Co-op, which is now Bergfeld 1885 Wine Cellars. And they contracted the grapes to Gallo. In the 1950s and 1960s, half the grape crop of Napa Valley went to Gallo. Prices in the 1950s were $50 per ton, which barely paid for the upkeep of the vineyard. In the 1960s, prices were up to $125 per ton. We could make money at that price; we could make a living from our five or six acres."

Aldo, Christina, Clementina, & Robert Biale

In the 1970s, "Gallo almost didn't want Zinfandel, and many growers began pulling out their Zinfandel vines. People thought I was crazy, because I didn't. But I decided, I'm going to stick with them. I felt it wasn't the right thing to do, pulling them out. You've got to have the love for it, though, for you would never stay with it this long. Not at those prices. But Zinfandel was a good wine, and had been good to us. And it still is."

Early cultivation was by hand. "Now we're modernized," said Aldo. "The only hoeing we do is a few weeds right at the base of the vines. But before, we had to break that ground with a special two-pronged hoe. The only machinery we had then was a disk and a plough. Don't tell me about hard labor!" he said with a laugh.

With such good food and wine, and so many guests, "It's like Christmas," said the diminutive Christina to me, as she sipped her tasty 1991 barrel-sample Biale Zinfandel.

The soft contralto Italian of Clementina was interwoven in the table's discussions as she explained to Christina some of the things we were talking about, especially when we turned to her for her recollections of how the Biales got involved with Zinfandel.

Although we had all greeted each other for the first time at 11:30, we parted friends at 4:00. I walked to my car with the lilting sounds of Christina's Italian-accented English in my ears and the lush flavor of the 1991 vintage on my lips — an experimental lot of only a few hundred cases.

With Zinfandel like that, I definitely was in California!!

Based on the results of their 1991 sample crush, the Biales established their estate label. Starting in 1994, the entire crop from this historic family vineyard was used to produce estate Zinfandel wine under the Biale label. They have also added some purchased grapes (Crane, Monte Rosso, Falleri *et al*).

★ ★ ★ ★ ★

In December 1999, Christina Biale died peacefully in the home of Aldo and Clementina. She was 103 years old. May God rest her soul.

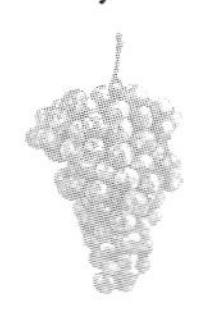

Elyse Wine Cellars

Elyse Zinfandel, established by Ray Coursen and his wife, Nancy, in 1987, caught my attention almost from the day that its first vintage landed on wine store shelves. It was made from grapes grown in the Morisoli Vineyard in Napa Valley, and everyone who had tried it was talking about how good it was. I did not meet Ray, who is also the winemaker, until February 1997. By then, Elyse Wine Cellars was producing three Napa Valley Zinfandels:

- Coeur du Val, which is 81 percent Zinfandel fruit from eight Napa Valley vineyards, 17 percent Petite Sirah, and 2 percent Gamay (600 cases),
- Howell Mountain (Black/Sears) – 82 percent Zinfandel; 4 percent Gamay; 14 percent Petite Sirah (1,300 cases),
- Morisoli – 88 percent Zinfandel;12 percent Petite Sirah, Alicante, Gamay, Grand Noir, Black Malvasia, and Riberia (1,200 cases).

A tall, burly, cordial, and outgoing man with a head of thick, wavy silver hair, Ray's enthusiasm for his wines and winemaking is as imposing as his physical presence. As he set out the wines for us to taste while we talked, he explained his winemaking style, and why none of his "rustic" Zinfandels, as he later described them, were pure Zinfandel.

"I've been through many old Zinfandel vineyards of Napa Valley, and few of them are even close to being 100 percent Zinfandel. These old growers, as I understand it, planted a vineyard for a palate sensation. I have no degree in enology. I have taken a home winemaking class at Napa Valley College, a two-day seminar at UC Davis, and a great one-day class at Napa Wine Lab on bad wine. That was the best class. I worked at Whitehall Lane in the early 1980s with Art Finkelstein, who taught me the art of blending, which I have taken my own way. Winemaking is simplistic. It is a matter of creating enough palate sensations to leave you longing for another taste while your brain is trying to figure out, 'What was that?' To me, that is winemaking.

"We make our Zinfandels all in the same way, yet as you taste these three wines, you will discover that they are all different from each other. We let the differences come from the vineyards."

As for oak barrels, he has some decided preferences."Since 1994, we have been using some wonderful thin staved chateau-style American oak barrels by Seguin Moreau, which I think are perfect for Zinfandel. American oak barrels are much better now, of course — since the early 1990s. They are air dried, and toasted over oak chip fires. Before Seguin Moreau began coopering a thin staved American oak barrel, there were the traditional transport thickness barrels, which had flavors of dill and whisky. The new transport barrels no longer have the flavor of dill, but the whiskey flavor is still there, along with flavors of butterscotch and coconut. These flavors are partly the result of where the trees are grown and also how the barrels are made.

"All these flavors from transport barrels are too strong for Zinfandel, for my taste. I am a fan of berry. That is why I drink Zinfandel. So we try to accentuate the fruit. I like the flavors of American oak that the new thin staved barrels impart, which are flavors of coffee, mocha, and smoked meat rather than butterscotch/-coconut/whisky. I use about 20 percent new barrels, and even such a staunch fan of French oak as Peter Franus admitted that he could have mistaken these barrels for French. So he's starting to see the light," said Ray, laughing.

"Is there that much difference in the flavors between thin staved chateau barrels and the thicker staved transport barrels, even though both are made from American oak and by the same cooper?" I asked

"Oh, yes," Ray replied. "The differences in the flavors are quite noticeable."

Ray also shared some outspoken thoughts on the subject of high-alcohol wines. "I was going through the list of wines at the 1997 ZAP tasting, and noticed how many were 17.1 or 17.4 percent wines. More and more Zinfandels, it seems, are turning up at well over 15 percent. I blame the wine writers, who are pushing both excessive oak and excessive alcohol content. It's too bad. What killed Zinfandel in the 1970s was alcohol and price. And price is going along with these higher alcohol wines today. I admit that the wines are flawlessly made, but I would serve them over ice cream; I would not serve them with the main course. The beauty of Zinfandel as a dry table wine is that it is compatible with food. I can have fish, you can have beef, and the Zinfandel will transcend both courses. Cabernet Sauvignons won't, and Chardonnay is probably the most difficult of all wines to match with food. With this push to higher alcohol Zinfandels and more oak, we are in danger of losing this food compatibility."

"There is a staunch, if small, customer base for these big wines," I remarked. "Some people really do like them, and create menus to complement them."

"Agreed," said Ray. "I am not going to knock the style. But if you put some Zinfandels at under 14 percent on a table with the over-15 percent Zinfandels, the ones that will be left half-full at the end of the dinner will be the big Zinfandels — every time. Yet some producers are being driven by these designer wines or 'furniture wines,' depending on how much oak they have, in order to compete in tastings," he concluded with a hint of displeasure in his voice. I pondered his metaphors, but not his meaning.

"I grew up as a dairy farmer in New Jersey, and, as I like to say, outgrew my need for milk," he continued. "Then I was in the restaurant business for nine years, as bartender, waiter, and finally, manager. Wine is food to me. Although I did not grow up having red wine with my meals, I could give up a lot of things today before I could give up my glass of red wine with my dinner. Because I was in the restaurant business, I consider the food that will accompany my wine when I am making it."

The first Zinfandel that Ray poured was the 1995 Coeur du Val.

"What led you to choose Zinfandel as your primary wine grape?" I asked as I savored the plum- and black-pepper-scented wine.

"My wife is from California, and her father was friends with Dave Bennion, the founder of Ridge Vineyards," he replied. "Her family used to have their family picnics every summer at Ridge. When I met her in Boston, she had some 1970 Ridge Vineyards Occidental Zinfandel that had been sent back to her. Also, my old roommate in Boston had a cousin who was in the wine business out here. So we used to get Zinfandels. I was a fan of Rhône wines. I love Rhône wines, and these Zinfandels were the closest thing I could get to the Rhône wines."

"My other reason for choosing Zinfandel as my wine was simply that we were very poor when we started up. With Zinfandel, we could get our wine on the market in 1½ years, rather than the three years that Cabernet Sauvignon takes. In 1987, I made 280 cases; in 1988, 500 cases. We had to get our wine out to be able to afford the next vintage. We could afford the grapes and the barrels, but we could not afford the packaging for the 1987 vintage. We had to borrow money to get the 1987 bottled, and we sold enough to buy bottles for the 1988, and to buy grapes for our 1989 vintage. We've been trying to get our venture to pay for itself ever since."

"It seems to me that you established your label on Zinfandel about the time many producers were despairing of their Zinfandels, and either budding over their vines, or pulling them out all together," I remarked. "But you seem to have done just fine with your choice."

"We were fortunate in that there has always been a strong customer base for Zinfandel in the East Bay," Ray explained. "They love Zinfandel over there. The North Berkeley Wine Shop and Chez Panisse have done wonderful things for us over the years. That area is probably the premier Zinfandel pocket in California."

"How did you get started as a winemaker? Did you just decide one day to establish your label and go for it?"

"I got started in 1984 as a home winemaker," he began. "My first Zinfandel was a late harvest. In 1985, I had a chance to go through the Morisoli Vineyard, located on the west side of Napa Valley on Neibaum Lane, and pick just Petite Sirah. In 1986, I picked just Morisoli Zinfandel. In 1987, I went commercial with my Elyse label, and began buying most of the fruit from the Morisoli Vineyard."

Before Elyse began buying the Morisoli fruit, the grapes went to the cooperative as "mixed black."

At this point, Ray suggested the second wine. "This is the 1995 Howell Mountain. It is our last crop from the Park-Muscatine, and includes fruit from Black-Sears. The Petite Sirah is from Park-Muscatine, and there is 4 percent Gamay from the Rossi Vineyard near Whitehall Lane."

The wine was scented with aromas of black and white pepper, wild blackberry fruit, and minerals. It was drier, a little more tannic, more angular in taste than the Coeur du Val was. It would need a couple of years in the bottle to reach its peak.

This led me to a favorite question: "How are you settling the issue of making wines that taste good upon release, yet can gain in character in the bottle for a few years?"

"It is a question of balance in the vineyard," replied Ray, after a couple of moments' thought. "We think that we do our fining at the crusher. We do not fine our wines with any agents. We are extremely gentle at the crusher. We separate our rollers to allow more whole berries through, and we ferment all our Zinfandels in open bins, and punch them down by hand. We have not added yeast since 1984. While I do not understand the logic, I think that I am getting a lower conversion rate this way, that is, less alcohol from the sugar than one gets with added yeast.

"We do everything that we can to be gentle. Everything is done by hand, which gives us a cooler, gentler, slower fermentation for richer fruit extraction. Then we press, and we squeeze the skins hard, but with a bladder press. We are not concerned about getting harsh tannins because we have extracted most of the tannins in the fermentation.

"Then we rack the wine twice before putting it into barrels with a 20 percent inoculate for malolactic fermentation to take place in the barrels. We do not take the wine out of the barrel until it is ready for bottling. We like the richer, headier, more exotic berry that comes with the Burgundian-style rather than with the claret style of Zinfandel.

"I also sterile filter, which admission gets me into trouble with my wife. But I would not bottle a wine without sterile filtering. This way, I retain what I call the 'berry-plum' Cabernet character. Without sterile filtering, the organisms that are left in the wine can diminish the plump berry character that we like so much. Our wines do not always finish malolactic fermentation, and they sometimes have a little unfermented sugar. These elements can give wine a Bordeaux/brettanomyces character and aroma, which some people call the Bordeaux *terroir.*

"Whatever beneficial character the organisms can add to a wine, however, they have already contributed during the months that the wine is in barrels. I can accept in Bordeaux wines the barnyard flavors and aromas that come with non-sterile filtering; I just do not like them in Zinfandel. Our 1987 Zinfandels still have a berry character. Perhaps the non-sterile filtered Zinfandel is a fruitier wine for the first six months. But after that, the fruit and varietal character holds up best in the sterile filtered wine. That has been my experience. What makes Zinfandel special is its varietal fruit character."

We were now ready for the Morisoli Zinfandel. "This is my wine," said Ray as he filled our glasses. "I really like this wine. The vineyard is about eight acres. Two acres date to 1915, and six acres were planted in 1986. We get an average of four tons per acre. Eighty-eight percent of the vines are Zinfandel, with the remaining 12 percent made up of Petite Sirah, Alicante Bouschet, Grand Noir, Napa Gamay, Ribiere, and Black Malvasio interplanted throughout the vineyard. That is how we pick it; that is how we make it. I take all the fruit from the old block, and share fruit from the young block with Caymus.

"What killed Zinfandel in the 1970s was the alcohol and price. And price is going along with these higher alcohol wines today. I admit that the wines are flawlessly made, but I would serve them over ice cream; I would not serve them with the main course.

Ray Coursen

"We have to stand by the Black Malvasio with a stick so that the pickers won't eat it all," Ray continued. "It's a heady perfumed grape with aromas of roses and lichee nuts. This is the grape that got me started with the blending. Our 1986 Zinfandel was pure Zinfandel, and I didn't think it was nearly as good as what the old-timers had put together. They put together a complete palate sensation. This wine leaves me longing for more, and leaves my mind wondering, 'Was that rosemary? Was that sage?' It is never the most tannic wine, nor the darkest, but it is always the best food wine. I get carried away talking about this wine," he concluded. "I love the vineyard, and I love the wine. This is the one I drink, although I like all three."

The wine was a luscious dark-colored wine with a cornucopia of wild fresh berries, with a dash of cloves and black pepper.

"The important thing for me is that a wine be seamless, that the flavors go all the way across the palate. Some of your simpler wines have great nose, great entry, but that's all. This one has that continuous, seamless quality," said Ray, still carried away by this wine's magic. "I have learned how to achieve this seamless quality with this vineyard. I strive to get all those palate sensations in the wine. You can even taste these palate sensations in the grapes as they near ripeness."

"Who cares for the vineyard?" I asked. "Do you give any directions as to how you want the vines pruned, or whether to drop crop, or remove shoulder clusters?"

"Gary Morisoli is the owner and manager, and he has a foreman whom he has trained," Ray replied. "Gary has been caring for the vineyard since he was a child, and he knows more about it than I do. The vines are head trained, non-irrigated, and planted seven by seven, which is how I think Zinfandel should be planted. I don't believe in wires for Zinfandel, although I do buy from Black/Sears, which is on wires. And, yes, I may ask him to remove excessively raisined clusters for some vintages. Sometimes, the younger block needs to be crop-thinned."

Nor does Ray believe in modern research attempts to develop a Zinfandel clone with loose clusters and less uneven ripening. "Zinfandel is *made* to have different types of berries on the same cluster. You get a pink berry, a light red berry, a deep red berry, a soft red berry, and a raisin all together, and each one contributes something to the varietal character. We sample by berry, and we read our results instantly, but we pay attention to the results next morning, when the raisins have taken on moisture. We begin our sampling with plastic ziploc bags and end up with cluster samples in a five-gallon bucket. We monitor sugar, acid, and pH, and we like some raisins in the mix, but not too many. Ultimately, sampling by taste is the final test. By November, I don't want to eat another grape."

Given that he buys his grapes, I asked Ray how he kept his growers' loyalty.

"All our contracts are a handshake," Ray continued. "We socialize with our growers, we pay them a fair price, and we pay them on time. We will pay between $1,700 and $1,800 per ton for Zinfandel in 2000," he said. "We always paid a very fair price for our Zinfandels long before Zinfandel became popular. We got Gary Morisoli to drop the Co-op. We began paying $350 per ton in 1988, which was $50 per ton more than he had ever been paid for his grapes. Now, we are paying average price of Napa Valley Cabernet Sauvignon. This means that our price per bottle needs to be about $30. The old formula of the price per ton divided by 100 does not work any more, because the costs of production have gone up disproportionate to the price per ton of grapes. It is more like dividing by 92."

Yet Ray still believes that Zinfandel should be an affordable wine, even as he sees the need for a fair price. "People will pay anything for a fine Pinot Noir or a Cabernet Sauvignon, but get offended by a high price for Zinfandel," he said. " 'Your Zinfandel is getting expensive,' one winemaker told me recently, who was trading some Cabernet for Elyse Zinfandel. 'What are *we* going to drink? This is the wine that *we* drink,' he had said.

They trade me their wine because they want to drink my rustic wine," Ray mused.

"Your wine is rustic?" I echoed. "How can you say that?"

"Because it is just raw berry," Ray replied.

"What else can Zinfandel be?" I asked.

"You can polish it by fining, by using more new oak, especially French oak. I don't fine my Zinfandel, and I leave it in oak for only about 10 months, and use only 20 percent new thin staved barrels. I like to keep that peasant quality. We have developed a following for this style, and I don't even send out our wines for review anymore. The best review that we ever got came from Daniel Jonnes, a master of wine with Montrachet Restaurant in New York. He said, 'Don't worry about the vintage; don't worry about the wine. Just buy it!' That is a good as you can do — be consistent in your style.

"My idea of a significant wine tasting is for a few people to get together for dinner, each person brings a bottle of Zinfandel, and then each person talks about which one he or she likes best with the food," he emphasized.

"After Napa Valley, which region do you like best for Zinfandel?" I asked, wrapping up our conversation.

"I like all styles and regions," Ray said, "although I have my preferences. Dry Creek Valley would be my next choice after Napa Valley."

"What do you think are the defining characteristics of Napa Valley Zinfandel?"

"Napa Zinfandel is much different from Dry Creek or Russian River Valley Zinfandel. The spices are different, and the berry character is different. Quality Napa Zinfandel producers are now catching up or surpassing Sonoma County's Zinfandel," he said. "What we need now is for more people to plant Zinfandel in Napa Valley."

"Isn't the valley too expensive for new plantings of Zinfandel?"

"No, not at all. I chose to become a wine producer to make a living for my family, enjoy what I am doing, and produce a reasonably priced wine. I do not need to drive a new Mercedes to do that. Neither does a grapegrower."

In 1998, Ray began producing Zinfandel from an Amador source.

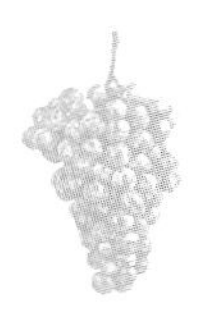

Korte Ranch; Schuetz-Oles

Rick Schuetz came to Napa in 1984 intending to make Cabernet Sauvignon. But then he tasted some Zinfandel made by Italian growers who always made a barrel or two from their old vines for themselves. "That's when I first got interested in making Zinfandel," said Rick, "in 1980 when I tasted the Zinfandel wine these Italian growers were making in their garages. These wines were big, extracted, richly flavored wines.

There were no other Zinfandels like them coming out of Napa Valley."

In 1985, Rick became winemaker for the Napa Valley Cooperative, and got to see many of the grapes coming in from the valley. "Napa Valley growers had been delivering their grapes to the Co-op since the 1930s, when the Co-op was formed. Ten percent of the grapes grown in Napa Valley were still delivered to the Co-op in 1985, and 50 percent of the names on the delivery slips were Italian," said Rick. "Many were delivering Zinfandel from their two- to 10-acre vineyards. The Co-op had fermentors of all sizes — from several thousand gallons to tiny ones of only a few hundred gallons. I tried to keep the grape varieties separate, and keep track of which vineyards were producing exceptional wine. I made many small lots of various varieties — including Zinfandel. It was usually a deal between myself and the grower — grapes for half of the wine."

One notable exception to these tiny Zinfandel vineyards was the 25-acre Korte Ranch, just north of St. Helena. "The Korte Ranch Zinfandel vines were planted in stages, with one-third planted in 1889, another third planted in 1900, and the final third planted about 1910 or 1912," explained Rick. "The entire vineyard was planted on St. George rootstock before Prohibition. The Kortes even had a winery before Prohibition, bonded number 107, which is a pretty low number. The remains of the old winery still stand at the edge of the vineyard."

Russ Oles, who lives beside the Korte Ranch, became vineyard manager of the historic Korte Ranch in 1987, when the previous manager died. The vineyard is situated between the Napa River and Highway 29, just to the north of St. Helena. The soil ranges from an ancient gravelly riverbed to clay/loam. The grapes had been delivered to the Co-op for years, and Russ continued the tradition. In 1990, however, with the renewed interest in Zinfandel wine, Russ decided to make a change. "These grapes are just too good to be used in generic Zinfandel," he told Rick when he delivered the grapes that fall. "I'm going to look for a producer who will pay more for their great quality."

"Well, why don't we buy them, and make the wine ourselves?" responded Rick, who happened to agree wholeheartedly with Russ.

So Schuetz-Oles Zinfandel was founded, with its first Korte Ranch Zinfandel produced in 1991. "I was really glad to see Zinfandel catch on again as a red wine," said Rick. "It surely has saved the surviving old Zinfandel vineyards."

I met Rich and Russ at the vineyard in March 1997. "No vine under 100 years old that produces grapes looks like this," declared the gray-bearded Russ. He was standing beside an ancient vine with twisted trunk and contorted arms, and looking a little like an old Zinfandel vine himself. "These vines, spaced six feet by seven feet, have suffered just about every stress imaginable, yet they are still producing quality grapes.

"I tend every single vine as an individual being. That is why I do not consider myself a farmer of this vineyard, but rather a tender of the vines.

I use a little sulfur, and based on soil analysis may add nitrogen during their dormant season, but I use no chemicals or fertilizer. The soil is intact, not sterile, and I've had no problem with mites."

"Don't you think it's amazing that this historic old vineyard is down here beside the Napa River?" I asked. "Aren't the great old Zinfandel vineyards more likely found on the benchlands or on mountainsides?"

"The soil here is an ancient gravelly river bed," said Russ. "There is lots of water, but because of the gravel bed, there is excellent drainage. In fact, it is the water that has kept these old vines alive all these years. Also, remember that 100 years ago, Zinfandel was the most popular red wine grape to plant. If this was the land you had, then this is where you planted your vines. It turned out to be a terrific matchup."

"It is interesting that in recent years, no one really thinks of Napa Valley as Zinfandel country," I remarked. "But it is obvious that 100 years ago and also after Repeal in 1931, Napa Valley was famous for its Zinfandel."

"Sure, what else was there in those early days? Rick replied. "Certainly not much Cabernet Sauvignon or Chardonnay. There used to be a much greater spectrum of varieties in the Napa Valley, but Zinfandel was the main red grape variety. Now it is mostly Cabernet Sauvignon, Merlot, and Chardonnay. It is only recently that Napa Valley has become famous for its Cabernet and Chardonnay."

"Anyone who thinks that wines should be 10 years old before you drink them must think he is immortal, because you have to cheat death twice! First, you have to believe you will live another 10 years, and second, you have to believe that the wine will be worth waiting for."

Russ Oles

"Given the surge of interest in Cabernet Sauvignon, Merlot, and Chardonnay in the 1970s, don't you think it is remarkable, and wonderful, that this beautiful vineyard survived? Surely there wasn't much money in the grapes," I said.

"Probably not, but there was some, the land was paid for, the second and third generation families didn't have to spend much money on it, the income from the grapes paid for the expense of upkeep and taxes, which was pretty low. There was no compelling reason in the 1940s to the 1970s to take out the vines and go to the expense of replanting something else. Zinfandel had proven itself here. Why change?" explained Rick.

"Who owns the vineyard now?" I asked.

"Hal Pagiendarm, grandson to Mr. Korte," replied Russ. "He and his family come out here on the weekends, and stay in his grandfather's house, which is still pretty much the way it has always been. But he isn't interested in farming the grapes. We have a five-year renewable contract with him for the grapes."

"Besides its age, what makes this vineyard so special? I asked.

"With the variety of soil types and water table levels, each block produces a different flavor spectrum. These differences are perfect to produce an exciting and complex wine, since each block contributes different character to the wines. We have separated the vineyard into blocks according to flavors, and pick them separately, and ferment them separately."

"What winemaking practices and oak storage do you prefer for this vineyard?" I asked Rick.

"We usually pick the Zinfandel between 24° and 25° Brix, ferment the wine in one-ton fermentors, and then put the wine in French and American oak barrels for about 18 months of ageing."

"Do you make Korte Ranch Zinfandel to age, or do you feel that it is best consumed at release, or a few months after?"

On this subject, Russ had a distinct opinion. "Anyone who thinks that wines should be 10 years old before you drink them must think he is immortal, because you have to cheat death twice! First, you have to believe you will live another 10 years, and second, you have to believe that the wine will be worth waiting for. I've had 10-year-old Cabernet Sauvignon, and I say, 'Jesus Christ! You've waited 10 years, and dodged death, just to drink this crap?'"

Rick's opinion on the subject was a little mellower. "Our Korte Ranch Zinfandel is an ager. Our 1991 has yet to reach its peak [in 1997]. But ageability is just part of the equation. Attitudes about ageing wines are something we have in common with wine drinkers throughout the world. Balanced wines from exceptional vineyards can certainly gain complexity in the bottle for a few years. Over several vintages, you start to understand the character of that vineyard, and how wines made from it develop in the bottle. That's an interesting part of the total experience of a great wine. For Russ, the Korte Ranch is a heart-and-soul matter. He's a loyal and gifted vineyard caregiver, who feels blessed to have the opportunity of looking after these wonderful old vines. All that makes up part of the wine drinking experience that comes from the bottle," said Rick with a certain ardor.

"That's right," said Russ. "I don't mess with the vines. You can alter the character of the grapes with water and chemicals. I don't add either."

"Ageing wines is a personal matter," added Rick. "We make our wines to gain complexity in the bottle. If that means that the wine writers don't like them at release, we don't particularly care. Our winemaking style isn't shaped by the writers or the market."

I didn't get the feeling that Rick and Russ had much to worry about there. Just to get a bottle of their Korte Ranch Zinfandel, or any of their other releases, is a piece of luck — since their wines tend to sell out as fast as they are produced. But that is the way it goes with great vineyards like the Korte Ranch.

Turley Wine Cellars

In 1995, Larry Turley released his flagship 1993 Hayne Vineyard Zinfandel with 15.8 percent alcohol content. Some people thought he had resurrected a dinosaur. "Why did Larry Turley do this?" was the question I often heard. "Doesn't he realize that Zinfandel producers experimented with such big, highly extracted Zinfandels 15 years ago, and had come to the conclusion that they were not the direction thoughtful Zinfandel producers should be going in?"

When I entered Turley Wine Cellars' olive tree- and lavender-lined lane just north of St. Helena in early February 1997, this was one of the questions I was hoping to get an answer to in my first conversation with owner Larry.

So my first question to the six-foot-six-inch, fair-haired retired 24-year emergency room physician, was just that. Why is he producing such huge Zinfandels?

"Hey, I'm a big guy, I like robust food and big Zinfandels to go with it. The only way I could get the kind of Zinfandel I liked was to make it myself," he replied.

"But the Hayne Zinfandel isn't the only Zinfandel we make here," said winemaker Ehren Jordan, who joined us in mid-conversation. "The Hayne Vineyard typically achieves the ripe flavors we like at a Brix of 27° or 28°, and is the exception among our vineyards. If you will notice, the other four of our 1993 releases were all *under 14* percent. We don't pick for alcohol content, we pick for ripe flavors. Our style has to do with ripeness, not with alcohol content.

"My take on how we got started in this style is that Larry said, 'I like big ripe, fully extracted flavors in wines. My sister, Helen, is here, so let's examine what perfectly ripe flavors are all about.'"

Larry's sister was the Turley Wine Cellars winemaker from 1993 to 1996. She made Larry's first three vintages (1993-95). Ehren Jordan joined the team in fall 1996, the year Helen left. "Our style has greatly evolved since then," added Ehren.

"Why did you choose Zinfandel for your signature wine?" I asked Larry. "What did you like about it?"

"I began producing Zinfandel under the Frog's Leap Winery label in 1982. My partner, John Williams, and I established the winery in 1981. It was a different style from how we make Zinfandel now," said Larry. "But I was bitten by the Zinfandel bug long before then, in the 1970s, with Zinfandels like the Trentadues. I liked the fruit. The fruit is what makes

Zinfandel so appealing to me. But in the 1970s, the prevailing question was, 'How big can you make a Zinfandel?' It killed the market for a while, because you never knew what you were going to get when you bought a Zinfandel. There was not much in the way of stylistic definition, and in their attempts to make the biggest Zinfandel on the market, people left the grapes on the vines to the point of more raisins than berries. The crushing equipment was not sophisticated, so you got those raisin and prune flavors that people soon got tired of."

"Did you like some of those big, tannic, port-like Zinfandels?"

"Oh, yes, I did. But when I came to make mine, I wanted to eliminate the coarseness and the raisin and prune flavors. I wanted to make a big, balanced, complex Zinfandel with a lot of exciting flavors that was also really smooth. That has been our challenge. I also wanted it to be relatively accessible, since I am not a person who wants to make a wine and have to wait 10 years before I can say, 'Ah, how wonderful! It's finally ready.' I like fruit. When people ask me if my Zinfandels will age for eight or 10 years, I tell them that I don't have a clue.

Ehren Jordan & Larry Turley

"I think our wines are balanced, which is the foundation for long-ageing. Beyond that, I don't know. There seems to be no reason why they shouldn't, but when they are this good now, I am sure I won't wait 10 years to see if they have gotten any better with age. The fruit certainly won't be any better, so what would be the point of ageing them?

"Also, I think the question of evaluating a wine's worth on its ability to age, whether Zinfandel or any other red wine, is no longer the right question to ask of a wine. With better management of vineyards, improved equipment, a little alchemy in the winery, California wines today are all much more approachable at a younger age than previously. Some of those early wines had tannins that required 10 to 15 years to soften up and become palatable. Perhaps the palate of the consumer is also changing. I personally don't care for brown wines and the aged character that accompanies them.

"But I am not saying that people shouldn't like the more tannic wines that require ageing, any more than I would say that people who like their coffee black should put cream in it to soften those tannins in the coffee. I remember when I was in medical school. I was travelling with some Austrian and German students in France. We had stopped for lunch, and the wine they got was a rosé. When they offered me some, I replied, 'No thanks, I do not do rosé.' 'Well, you should try it,' they insisted. 'It's the wine of the region, and goes well with the local fare that we are eating.' So I did try it, and it was fabulous with our lunch. Those people do know what they have been doing for 500 years. So why do we in California keep insisting that there is only one appropriate style of Zinfandel for everything?"

"Are your wines the wines that you drink every day?"

"Absolutely," he replied.

When Larry separated from Frog's Leap Winery, he sold his interest in the name to his partner, and established his smaller operation at his present location. "I have a young family that I want to see more of, and we live here beside the winery."

"How did you learn winemaking?" I asked Larry.

"Fermentation classes in medical school. I learned how to make beer in England, and since my partner, John, was the winemaker here, I got on-the-job training. See one, do one, teach one," he concluded with a degree of irreverence that I found appealing — if unexpected.

Noticing my slightly shocked look, he added, laughing, "That's a joke! Seriously, my sister, Helen, who already had quite a reputation, was available as winemaker. I found the vineyards, so we were off and running. But I am not the winemaker," he added hastily. "Ehren here is my winemaker. We basically work as a team."

"What was Helen's contribution to your winemaking style?"

"The great thing about Helen," replied Ehren, "is her willingness to take chances and make mistakes. She created an atmosphere in which going beyond the conventional limit was okay. Basically, she showed us the door, and encouraged us to step through. 'There's a market for big, soft Zinfandels with fully ripe flavors,' she assured us. So once through the door, we began defining for ourselves where we wanted to go.

"We're still defining our style. We have no one way of doing things. If you taste all the Turley wines, you will see a progression of style, because every year we re-examine what we are doing. We try to learn from our mistakes, and we do make mistakes all the time. We just try not to put them on the market. Sometimes what we thought was a mistake turns into something desirable, and then I go back to my notes to find out what happened — so we can do it again. That is what makes this operation interesting and fun for us. Always, something new is happening — either in the vineyard or in the winemaking. We're comfortable with surprises here. For me, that's one of the things that makes working for Larry a lot of fun."

Ehren had worked with Helen in her Marcassin Vineyard before joining up with Turley Wine Cellars in his first winemaking position.

"Just how do you manage to make these fully ripe wines without coming up with excessively tannic, out-of-balance monsters that nearly destroyed Zinfandel as a red wine in the late 1970s and early 1980s?" I asked Ehren and Larry. "You've said that you object to your Zinfandels being called 'dry port' because that suggests fortifying with high-proof alcohol. How do you avoid the raisins when you leave the clusters on the vines until the grapes reach 27°or 28° degrees Brix?"

"It goes back to the vineyard," said Larry. "If you get a lot of raisins, there are a couple of things going on. Perhaps the canopy is not being managed properly. Or more likely, you waited too long to pick, the TA has gone to hell, and the grapes are drying up from dehydration. You are getting the high sugar content because of dehydration. Those grapes have an entirely different flavor compared to the grapes from a vine that is still alive, not unduly stressed, still making sugar. When the acid content begins to fall, and the pH goes up, then you know that the vine is shutting down. It's time to pick your grapes. From that point on, the only ripening you get is from dehydration."

"Yet Zinfandel characteristically ripens unevenly."

"Again, I emphasize that you have to start in the vineyard. You have to limit crop size to what the vine can ripen before shutting down. We go through all our vineyards at the end of verasion, usually in early August, and drop everything that is pink. Clusters that are pink after verasion will be 2° Brix less than the fully ripe clusters if they make it to the fermentation tank, which is what will give your wine green flavors."

"Given that you purchase all your Zinfandel grapes, what kind of an agreement have you worked out with the growers?" I asked. "Who determines how the vineyards should be pruned, how much crop the vines should carry, and when to pick – decisions such as these?"

"We make those decisions," replied Larry. "The growers we work with respect our winemaking style, and respect our need to determine viticulture practices and harvest dates in order to achieve our stylistic goals. Our finished wines are testament to our ability to make good decisions in the vineyard as well as in the winery."

"Yet even with the most diligent of viticulture practices, don't you always have some uneven ripening within the clusters?"

"Oh, sure, a little," continued Larry. "But the biggest problem is from cluster to cluster. Once you get rid of the 'pinks,' you can monitor the remaining clusters for raisining. When we pick, if there are some excessively raisined clusters, we cut the raisins out on the spot. If we do our work in dropping the pinks at verasion, our clusters will have ripened much more evenly. The destemmer will take out any raisins in the clusters. We don't crush, we just destem, and our destemmer will kick out the raisins. It's amazing to see. It's like watching 17 vestigial virgins in there pulling the berries off one by one," Larry explained, seeming to savor his simile. "The ripe berries fall off, and the raisins stick to the stems. You have to set the machine differently for each vineyard.

"Then we follow up with extended maceration of two to six weeks, and put the wines into the barrels dirty, where they finish fermenting. Since we have abundant whole berries, some unfermented sugar remains in the berries, and is released when we press the cap. This sugar finishes fermenting out for another month in barrels."

"Do your wines ferment dry — no residual sugar?" I asked, somewhat skeptical.

After a moment's hesitation, Larry replied, laughing, "Well, you can tell me when you taste them. I prefer to let my wines speak for themselves."

"That's a deal," I replied.

But I still had other questions. "Do you sterile filter?"

"We don't filter at all — or fine," Larry replied, indicating confidence in the stability of his wines. "Our approach to making wines here is to experiment with ways to extract flavor. Whatever flavors and aromas are in the grapes after destemming we would like to carry over to the bottle. Any steps in the process that can diminish these flavors and aromas we try not to do."

"If you don't filter, what steps do you take to protect the wines in the bottle?" I asked Ehren.

"You have to closely monitor the wine from day one," he replied. "We perform many lab tests, and we top the wine at least every two weeks — which prevents spoilage bacteria from growing. We always make sure that malolactic fermentation is finished before bottling. Also, an alcohol content of 17 percent to 18 percent in itself inhibits spoilage. We also keep the barrel room at a healthy 80 percent humidity with a fogger."

"You really go to a lot of work and expense to make this style of wine," I observed. "You must really like it."

"You have to remember that wine drinking is a purely personal experience," said Ehren.

"It is indeed," agreed Larry. "We had 30 Italian winemakers from Barolo here for lunch recently. I knew I had to provide something non-Italian, so I talked to Michael Chiarello, the chef/owner at Tra Vigne, and he suggested Dungeness crab. 'Well, wait a minute,' I replied, 'It has to go with Zinfandel.'"

"'Then do oven-roasted garlic Dungeness crab,'" he replied.

"I wanted to make a big, balanced, complex Zinfandel with a lot of exciting flavors that was really smooth. I also wanted it to be accessible, since I am not a person who wants to make a wine and have to wait 10 years before I can say, 'Ah, how wonderful! It's finally ready.' I like fruit."

Larry Turley

"We ate for well over three hours, and the crab was a great match with our big ripe Zinfandels. It was a happy group that left here after lunch," said Larry, his blue eyes twinkling with the memory.

"The nice thing about Zinfandel," said Ehren, "is that there are so many styles. It's hard to find one you do not like."

"Yes," I replied. "I know I have yet to find a style I don't like. What is interesting and also puzzling to many Zinfandel producers and consumers alike is that wine critics and tasting panels sometimes hold up your style as the quintessential Zinfandel. Rarely are the many other fine Zinfandels out there scored as highly."

"That is the problem with blind tastings," said Ehren. "The wine with the higher alcohol, if it is balanced, will be viscous and fully flavored, and will carry a perception of sweetness from the high alcohol. If you were to taste our Aida Vineyard Zinfandel, which has about 14 percent alcohol, after tasting our Hayne Vineyard at 17 percent, the Aida will taste simple and dumb. That is why I don't approve of blind tastings. There are many circumstances that can influence how a wine will taste. If people taste 100 wines in each day, the wines are limited in what they can offer you. If they happen to taste a more delicate or subtle wine at the end of the day, most of the subtlety will be missed.

"Yet that is the nature of the tasting business. As a result, our big Zinfandels score well in these tastings. People get really excited about them. In fact, we have had people say to us, 'You make those huge wines so that you can win tastings.' That couldn't be further from the truth. We don't send in our wines for tastings. Our 'sample' budget is non-existent. And we have *never* entered our wines into competitions. If you read about our wines, it is because someone has come out here and tasted them, or has bought them themselves. It really rubs me the wrong way how quickly people want to stereotype us as 'that winery that makes those huge Zinfandels.'

"The point is that we make some balanced but big wines because we like them. Yet they are only a small segment of what we do. Besides, we don't pick our grapes for alcohol content; we pick for ripeness, and that doesn't necessarily occur at a high Brix. Several of our 1996 Zinfandels were at 14 percent alcohol, or maybe 14.2 percent, and we like them as well. It depends on the season as well as the vineyard. It is true that we are usually the last ones to pick in vineyards we share with other producers. What changes in the grapes that have 10 days to two weeks longer hang-time on the vines is mostly in the flavors — not in sugar content. Ripe flavors can and do occur at varying Brix.

"There are some vineyards, though, that always achieve ripe flavors at a high sugar content. The Hayne is one vineyard that typically ripens its Zinfandel fruit to 27° or 28° Brix before the acid content begins to fall."

"True," added Larry. "If we were to pick the Hayne Vineyard at 24° Brix, the fruit would have a higher acid content than any Chardonnay you have ever tasted. When we wait for the grapes to become ripe in that vineyard, we find that the pH is about 3.4. But it depends on the year. In 1996, ripe flavors developed at much lower sugars than in previous years. The pH began to go up at 24° or 24.5° Brix. I have found this phenomenon to be especially common in old vineyards, which typically produce between a ton and 1½ tons per acre. They tend to achieve ripe flavors at higher sugar contents than do young vineyards."

"It definitely depends on the vineyard," emphasized Ehren. "Anyone who might think about copying our style by letting their grapes ripen to 27° or 28° Brix, without taking into consideration the location of their vineyards, the age of their vines, and the characteristics of the ripening curves, will probably be very disappointed with the results. They also do not realize how often we walk our vineyards."

"We spend hundreds of hours in our vineyards every year — both this time of year and after verasion," resumed Larry. "Right now [February], we are pruning. Next to determining harvest date, pruning is the most enjoyable part of winemaking for me. It's a beautiful time to be out in the vineyard. We have enough experience to feel comfortable pruning old vines. Generally, we are halving the number of spurs on the vines in some old vineyards we've taken over. We've noticed that the vines have had a lot of canopy and not much fruit, and a lot of short canes. These old vines cannot carry a lot of crop. So we've reduced the number of spurs in order to create a balanced vine. These old vines cannot both set a large canopy and ripen a respectable crop."

"What is your choice for oak-ageing — French or American barrels?" I asked.

"American and French oak for our new wood — about 20 percent new each year," answered Larry. "We buy the wood, have it air dried, and made into barrels. Some of the barrels are heavy toast, some medium toast, and some have toasted heads — what a great name for a rock group!" he commented, momentarily diverted. "We also sometimes buy one-year-old French oak. Our oak program depends upon the vineyard and the year. It's never the same, year to year. On the average, we leave the wine in barrels for 14 months. But it can vary. You have to spend time in your vineyards to learn their character – and what will best express that character."

"Your Zinfandels are among the most expensive on the market, and also among the least available, since case production per vineyard is small," I observed. "Have you any thoughts about producing a more widely available and more affordable Zinfandel? Do you not have concerns that your consumer base might be too rarified to sustain? Does your style allow for a more affordable wine?"

"We have already addressed that concern," responded Ehren. "Beginning with 1996, we are making an Old Vine Zinfandel, which we will retail for considerably less than our vineyard-designated Zinfandels — in the $20 per bottle range. Our production should be about 1,000 cases. This Zinfandel will be of the same highly extracted, fully ripe style of our vineyard-designated wines, but will be a blend, so a little less costly to produce. In value, we could easily retail it for a higher price, but we do want our wines to be available to those Zinfandel lovers who like our style, but find $40 a bottle too much. Nor do we consider it a lesser wine in quality — just a different style. The 'lesser' wine we bulk out. In fact, we think our Old Vine

Zinfandel might even be the 'sleeper' wine of the vintage — and the tasting panels will probably not even notice it."

Two weeks later, I returned to Turley Wine Cellars for a tasting of the 1994 Hayne (Napa), the 1995 Duarte (Contra Costa), the 1995 Black/Sears Vineyard (Howell Mountain), and the 1995 Grist Vineyard, (Bradford Mountain, Dry Creek Valley, Sonoma). All these wines have an alcohol content of over 15 percent. I did not notice any sweetness in the Duarte, Black/Sears, or Hayne wines. Each was soft and luscious with rich spicy berry fruit flavors. The Hayne had hints of chocolate and espresso coffee, with less forward fruit. The Black/Sears had hints of the characteristic Howell Mountain black pepper. But the first words I wrote down when I tasted the Grist were "sweet black cherries."

"Do you notice any sweetness in any of these?" Ehren asked me.

"Only in the Grist," I replied. "Perhaps as much as one percent?"

"That's probably about right," replied Ehren. "The Grist has 1.7 percent residual sugar. We picked these grapes November 1; the sugar content was 35° Brix. The alcohol is also pretty high, over 17 percent, and basically, the fermentation just stopped. We have indicated on the label with an empty hourglass that this wine falls into the 'Late Harvest' category. The sand in the hourglass has all fallen to the bottom."

"And you are not worried about unwanted developments in the bottle later on?"

"No. We've tested the wine for spoilage organisms, but nothing developed. With such a high alcohol, basically nothing is going to grow, even with the residual sugar."

"What is your annual case production of Zinfandel?"

"Well under 100,000 cases," replied Larry, his irreverent sense of humor again breaking through.

"How about well under 5,000 cases?" I asked, since my question was serious. I wondered how much production Larry and Ehren felt they could sustain while maintaining the consistency of their labor-intensive and vineyard-dependent style.

"It's more likely right around 6,500 cases, depending on the vintage," answered Ehren. "Our total production for the winery is about 7,500 cases. We buy from about 15 growers, and have between 10 and 12 vineyard-designated Zinfandels. Our increased production since last year is made up of the Old Vines line. We could maybe grow to 10,000 cases, if we take time to grow the infrastructure. There is also the problem of finding vineyards that support our style."

Larry Turley was born in Tennessee, but his family moved to Augusta, Georgia, when he was a small child — relatively speaking ("I've *never* been a small child," he commented, in an allusion to his height.) He began college studies in aerospace engineering at Georgia Tech, then moved to New Mexico to study philosophy.

"What brought you on out to California and the wine industry?" I asked.

"My motorcycle," Larry replied. "I got on it one day, and rode west. When I got here, I discovered I liked it very much, and after medical studies in both Europe and then back in the U.S., I returned."

Later that same year, on September 28, I was riding my bike past Bill Moore's "Earthquake Vineyard" on Hagen Road in Napa. It was a lovely, warm and clear Sunday morning. Out in the thick of it were Larry and his picking crew. So I had to stop and find out how it was going.

Larry was standing on the back of the truck examining each tub that was handed up, checking for bunch rot. There was a little rot, both wet and dry, throughout his vineyards, so he had taken it upon himself to hand-sort every bin.

"What does bunch rot look like?" I asked him later, when he had come down to ground level to do his sorting.

"Come here. I'll show you." He bent to the ground and picked up a cluster he had just sorted out. "Smell this. It smells just like vinegar. That's the wet rot. Underneath, you can see the moldy, dried out berries. That's the dry rot." The wet rot did indeed smell like vinegar. Bunch rot was caused by the August 19th rains, which were followed by still, warm days, so that the bunches didn't dry out. Zinfandel is a thin-skinned grape, and with such a rain after verasion, bunch rot is a great danger if the rain is not followed by warm, dry winds.

There wasn't much bunch rot, though, in the Moore Vineyard grapes. "The crop overall is up — about two tons per acre. So I haven't lost much fruit," said Larry. "The Hayne vineyard had even less bunch rot than the Moore.

"This is my last vineyard," he said, "making this year the earliest we've ever finished harvest. Last year, we finished in November; finishing by the end of October is normal."

"What kind of numbers are you getting?" I asked.

"Perfect!" exclaimed Larry. "The Moore grapes are between 26° and 27° Brix, pH is 3.43, and T.A. is 8.5 g/L. Hayne came in a degree or two higher Brix, but with the same great pH and T.A. It's been like that with all our vineyards, including our new Lodi vineyard, the Dogtown, located on the San Joaquin benchlands, near the Amador County border."

"Don't you think the pH and T.A. are pretty amazing, given the sugar content?"

"Yes, indeed," agreed Larry. "But that's what makes these vineyards so special.

★ ★ ★ ★ ★

In June 1999, I had a follow-up visit with Larry and Ehren. By then, their roster of single vineyard Zinfandels had grown considerably. There also had been time to evaluate how the 1993 vintage had held up. "Have you learned anything further about the keeping qualities of your Zinfandels, since your 1993 vintage is now six years old?" I asked.

"They have developed a little aged character, and have changed into another type of wine," replied Ehren. "They have less fruit than when they were released, and more bottle bouquet. But they are still quite lovely."

Turley Wine Cellars had also purchased a vineyard on Howell Mountain. It is right beside their block of the Black/Sears, and they were in the process of planting up to 12 acres of Zinfandel — a bold move given the high costs of establishing a vineyard in Napa County, and the smaller returns available from a Zinfandel vineyard compared to Cabernet Sauvignon or Merlot. The budwood came from Hayne and Moore, and is grafted onto rootstock at a nursery near Modesto. "It will be interesting to compare the fruit in a few years, since the budwood for the Black/Sears also came from Hayne. The Black/Sears was planted in the late 1960s and early 1970s," said Larry.

The first set of vines in Turley Vineyard are spaced three feet by six feet, are vertically trellised, and are budded to a variety of rootstocks, depending on the soils in the vineyard. In 1999-2000, an additional six acres of vines spaced three feet by three feet were planted. Established on a steep hillside, all tillage will be done by hand. "If we had terraced the hillside, we would cause a lot of erosion — something neither us nor the county wants to happen," Larry explained.

The vines will be drip irrigated for the first few years, partly because winds whip through, drying the soil and desiccating the tiny vines.

"As soon as we give them a little water, you can see them revive. Because we farm organically, it is also a way to deliver nutrients," explained Ehren. "With the close spacing, we need this efficiency. Once the vines are established, we expect to dry farm. The little three-foot by six-foot vertically-trellised vineyard here beside the winery is in its third leaf, and is setting a crop of 2½ tons per acre, and we haven't watered it at all this year. As long as you have patience to let the vine establish itself, and to keep its early crops light, it does well without irrigation. It will also live a very long time, since you have given it time to put down deep roots, and become strong. If you want four tons per acre in the third year, you have to beef it up with water and fertilizer. But the vine will probably die in 30 years, and we find that a pretty uninteresting way to farm. Nor do we think the fruit will be as good. So our Howell Mountain Vineyard is another big experiment for us," said Ehren.

It is also part of Turley Wine Cellars' commitment to Zinfandel, a grape both Ehren and Larry clearly love and find exciting to work with both in the vineyard and winery. "We have invested a great deal of time and money into our vineyards and winemaking style. We love Zinfandel, and we like this style," said Larry. "And as long as long we like this style and have fun making it, and as long as we have customers who like it and enjoy drinking it, we will continue to make it. If ever any of this changes, then it will be time to stop."

On May 15, 2000, Larry Turley purchased the Pesenti Vineyards and Winery, Templeton, CA, from the Pesenti and Nerelli families. The winery retains its name of Pesenti Vineyards and Winery, and Frank Nerelli stays on as winemaker. Both Ehren and Larry are excited about the purchase. "The clincher for us," said Ehren, "was that Frank agreed to stay on as winemaker and vineyard manager. When you look at the quality of wines he has been making within the family tradition and with little in the way of budget for innovations, as far as we are concerned, he is a genius winemaker. The only changes we are going to make will be to improve the existing facility. We will install a deer fence around the vineyard, insulate the fermentation and barrel rooms, add cooling systems, rewire the buildings, and give Frank a budget for new oak barrels. Oak pellets in mesh bags have a place in winemaking, but not in the ultra-premium wines the grapes that magnificent vineyard are capable of producing."

"I have taken the winery as far as I can on my own," said Frank when he told me about the deal. "And I'm tired of being stuck in the mud. Most Zinfandel producers were born with their corks. I've had to earn mine. With this partnership, I won't be working harder, just smarter. Pesenti is about to enter the realm of super-premium Zinfandel."

It should be a terrific partnership.

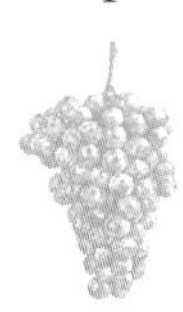

Clos du Val: A Complete Wine is Not a Donut.

"In 1972, no one would want to start a winery in the Napa Valley and not make Zinfandel — red Zinfandel," the Bordeaux-born Bernard Portet, president and winemaker of Clos du Val Wine Company, told me in our December 1996 interview. He was responding to my question as to why a vineyard and winery that was established on the Bordeaux model produced an estate Zinfandel. "At that time," he added, "there was Burgess Cellars, which had been created two or three years earlier, making Zinfandel; there was Robert Mondavi, and there was Charles Krug, all making a Zinfandel."

As Clos du Val's founding president/winemaker, Bernard planted 10 acres of Zinfandel in the winery's newly established Stag's Leap District vineyards next to the historic Grigsby Winery the same year the winery was established. Zinfandel and Cabernet Sauvignon were Clos du Val's flagship wines. "Robert Mondavi and Krug gave up on Zinfandel some years later, but not Clos du Val. We stayed with it," said Bernard. "In fact, we are the only Stag's Leap District estate Zinfandel producer, and one of a few Napa Valley producers, with a continuous 25-year history of making Zinfandel from Napa Valley grapes."

In 1996, Clos du Val still had five of its original 10 acres — the ones that had been planted on St. George rootstock. The others, established on

AxR-1, were taken out in 1994 and replaced, together with "about five more acres, for a total of 15 acres of Zinfandel," said Bernard.

Zinfandel for Bernard "is an unknown variety. I found it mentioned in some old French books," he explained, accounting for his interest in it. "Zinfandel, as it was known in America, was known in Europe then as Hamburg Bleu or Muscat Bleu, and was a variety grown in nurseries as a table grape in the 1890s and early 1900s in the northwest of Europe — Belgium, northwest France, Germany, and also in England. These old books also said that the grape made lousy table wines."

As our conversation progressed, Bernard led the way to the barrel room, where he drew samples of the 1996 estate Zinfandel. It was a lovely, elegant wine brimming with fresh raspberry aromas, some spiciness, and some smoky tones of wild blackberries.

Bernard Portet

"Have you changed your style of making Zinfandel in the 1990s?" I asked, since I had long believed Clos du Val Zinfandels to be less explosive with such wonderful berry characteristics.

"No. When I first started making Zinfandel, I didn't know anything about it, so I made it in the claret style of the Bordeaux. I was not seeking the extraction, but rather was seeking the elegance, the complexity, and the smoky fruit of the blackberries — the wild ones. I started harvesting usually a bit less ripe than most of my colleagues. In those early days, before our vineyard began producing, I got grapes from the Howell Mountain area, so it was a bit more concentrated than here. But never overly alcoholic. We maintained that claret approach from the beginning, and it was a success. So we kept with it."

"What alcohol content do your Zinfandels traditionally have?"

"It's always 13.5 percent to 14.2 percent alcohol. When you harvest Zinfandel, you have to have spiciness. When Zinfandel is ripe, it still has pink berries and raisins, and anything in between. The name of the game is to try to get some raisins, but not much, or else you get too much alcohol. If you harvest too early, you get too many of the pinkish berries. I do not want to make a Beaujolais-style Zinfandel, okay? Yet Zinfandel for me is a very humbling variety. You cannot pick with surety your harvest date. You decide to pick because you think it is the best time, then you get what you get."

"Are you glad you have stayed with it?"

"Yes, because it is a challenge for me. It is a more exciting challenge for me than Pinot Noir, for example."

"Do you find that you have less problem with raisins here in Stag's Leap District than in the Howell Mountain Zinfandel?"

"I think less here," replied Bernard.

At this point in our conversation, Bernard's attention suddenly focused on the wine in his glass.

"The wine is totally changing," he exclaimed in his strongly French-accented English. "The wine is totally coming together. You still have plenty of spritz, because malolactic is just finishing. But what we have today is a huge amount of freshness, which didn't exist three weeks ago. Then, it was hard, with a very clean nose, no tannin. Right now, it is very interesting, because it is no longer so tight, so the tannin is showing now. The wine is breaking in, you know, breaking itself, so that its structure is showing. It is much better now."

His ardent and spirited description of the wine instantly captured my attention, and gave me a new perspective on this gracious and candid yet somewhat reserved native of the Médoc region of Bordeaux. A tall and charming man with curly dark hair showing threads of gray, Bernard's passion and enthusiasm for winemaking may not appear obvious upon a first meeting. Yet these qualities are always there, ready to respond to the slightest nuances of change in the developing wines. It was an exciting and revealing moment.

"What is interesting," Bernard continued, "is that while the vineyard is all trellised, I have used two different styles. The three acres of Vineyard South, which is what we are tasting, is standard California trellis, called 'California Sprawl.' The canes grow up, then fall over each side of the wire. The three acres of Vineyard North are vertically trellised, like Cabernet Sauvignon. What is interesting is that in the beginning, this one, South, was the best at press time. North wasn't so good. Then, two or three weeks ago, North was the better. Now, South is getting better again. It also has a beautiful color."

"Yes, it does," I agreed, then asked, "Since your Zinfandel vines are trellised, does this mean that you drip-irrigate them?"

"No, no water. They are dry farmed," replied Bernard.

We were now at the North vineyard barrels, from which Bernard drew us samples. "This is the same clone, same vineyard, same pruning style," he emphasized, "same everything except for the trellising style. Do you notice any differences from the Vineyard South which we just tasted?"

"The aroma is more delicate and subtle," I replied, "but the flavor is riper, with a chocolatey, earthy richness and a velvety texture. It's a bigger, more intense wine."

"Yes, this one is more complex, more refined," Bernard added. "The one from South is greener."

"It almost reminds me a little of some of the Dry Creek Zinfandels," I replied.

"It's riper than Dry Creek Zinfandels," said Bernard. "At least for me it is. The problem for me is that Dry Creek Zinfandels are among my favorites. Yet this one for me is a perfect Zinfandel. It's more like the

Lytton Springs Zinfandel, which I don't consider as Dry Creek. South Vineyard for me is more like Dry Creek Zinfandels."

"Are these differences primarily due to the vines being vertically trellised rather than being on the umbrella style?" I asked.

"Oh, yeah," he responded, the familiar expression reminding me that Bernard has lived in America for 25 years.

"There isn't an overwhelming oak character to these wines," I observed. "Do you use any new oak for your Zinfandel?"

"Only in 1972 did I use any new oak. After that, the barrels are from one to four years old — and always French. I just don't want the wood to be the backbone to Zinfandel. Wood is just one element of complexity, and it should come together with all the other elements. I do not like the wood to stand out, to be tasted. The use of new oak is evolving as a fashion here, as it has in the Bordeaux over the past 25 years. There, the first growth chateaux always use some new oak. The second growth a bit less, because of cost. And so on down the line."

We were now ready to sample the 1995 estate Zinfandel, which was still in barrel. It was to be bottled in June 1997, and not released until 1998.

"You see, this is very elegant, very well-centered. It is not typical Zinfandel in that it is not overly luscious. Okay? And the color is not that deep, but the balance is very good. The wine is totally together."

"Yes, and it's tasty. Are all your wines made to be laid down for a few years in the bottle?" I asked.

"Yes, which is a bit of a problem in this market where everyone wants a product for immediate consumption."

"It seems that no matter what the style of wine, don't people tend to take it home and drink it that same day anyway?" I remarked.

"Sure, but that's their problem," responded Bernard. "What I am saying is that if you don't know much about Zinfandel, you can drink it tonight. But if you pay $15 or $18 for a bottle of Zinfandel, you should be able to expect something that will have value five or seven years down the road."

"Is that what you think is an optimum time to lay down a bottle of Zinfandel?"

"Yes, and it is up to us to sell the story. You can't expect the consumer to know that without being educated. Our wines are all built for five to 20 years of ageing. A well-made wine is a complete experience. A complete wine is not a donut. It does not have holes. It has a front palate, a middle palate, and a long finish. This complete experience has to be visualized by the winemaker from start to finish.

"If you make a wine to be best in seven years, you cannot expect that wine will be strikingly good if you buy it today and you drink it tonight," he continued. "Sure, you can have it today, but it is foolish to think that you can have the best of both worlds. You see, a wine is like a kid. It takes the first 20 years — at least — to educate a child. But that child gets the most maturity when he or she reaches the age of 40 or 45. That is when a person is most interesting. Same thing with the wines. That is the way I see wine, as a winemaker."

"Is that a particularly French way of seeing a wine?"

"Yes, totally," said Bernard. "It is not American. The concept of delayed gratification is not American."

"It is also British, though, isn't it? In fact, wasn't it the British who discovered, through an interesting series of circumstances, that wine left in good barrels under suitable conditions became a more interesting wine than those that were more immediately bottled and consumed?"

"Yes, it is British. You see, it takes education to produce an elegant wine, just as it takes education to produce an elegant person."

"Does this way of seeing wines affect how your wines sell here in America?"

"Yes, and this is where I am wrong, obviously, yet I am also right. I am wrong in as much as my approach is not in synch with the American market. But I am right in as much as I think that what is most important for you and me is to derive the most pleasure from enjoying that wine with food. It could take time. But sometimes I find that I am totally at odds with today's civilization. Many people think that I am too reserved."

"A complete wine is not a donut. It does not have holes. It has a front palate, a middle palate, and a long finish. This complete experience has to be visualized by the winemaker from start to finish."

Bernard Portet

Though he is obviously a serious and thoughtful winemaker, Bernard Portet has been able to maintain an engaging and unrepentant sense of humor in light of the criticism wine writers too frequently level at him.

"Yet your wines are successful, are they not? Do they not always sell out?"

"Yes, even our Zinfandel, which sells out within nine or 10 months. Of course, we don't make very much of it. That is also the rest of the story. There is no one right approach. The only one who is right is the consumer, and we don't all have the same consumer base."

"Are you suggesting, then, that your consumers buy Clos du Val wines, including Zinfandel, to put down for a few years?"

"Oh yeah. Clos du Val is a layaway type of wine, yes. Of course, I don't have a clue as to what percentage of people come here to buy Zinfandel and put it away for a few years. I do know that people who come to our winery for the most part know that our wines are made to be put away."

"Do you personally like Zinfandel?" I asked Bernard.

"Yes, but I am more of a Cabernet Sauvignon person."

"Do you sell Zinfandel in France?"

"No. They do not like Zinfandel in Bordeaux, although I have a good reputation there. The Bordelais do not like Côte du Rhône, either."

"What do the Bordelais not like about Zinfandel?"

"It's the fresh fruit, and the ultra-generosity of the fruit flavors. That is what the problem is. Much of wine enjoyment comes from an acquired palate. These Zinfandel flavors are not a part of the French wine experience."

To round out my tasting experience with Clos du Val Zinfandels, Bernard led the way back to the tasting room, where he assembled a vertical tasting, beginning with the 1994, and going back through the 1993, 1984, and finishing with the 1979.

"When people buy a bottle of Clos du Val Zinfandel, they know exactly what they are getting, that is for sure," I remarked. "Your style has been consistent for 25 years."

"Yes, they get the claret style, which is the style we've always made."

"And you have no thoughts of changing, or augmenting, your style?"

"No. We try to be consistent with our viticultural area, style, and type of wine. The type of wine comes from a combination of soil, climate, and variety. The style comes from the winemaker. The winemaker at Clos du Val has been the same for some years, so we have consistency both in type and style. Once you change the source of grapes, you change the type of wine. There is no escaping it. Anybody who wants to escape it makes what I call a 'technical wine.' I don't believe in that."

"And yet you've bought in some grapes from the Twin Rivers Vineyard in El Dorado County."

"Yes. The reason we went to Twin Rivers was that I needed more Zinfandel grapes. I love the Zinfandel from the mountains, and we were running short of Zinfandel because we lost half of our vineyard to Phylloxera. I use just a little to augment my production. Sure, I could make all the Twin Rivers claret I wanted, but it would be a different wine.

"In my view, as a winemaker, I see myself as riding a horse cart, but being behind. Okay? The horse pulls the cart. The horse is like the grapes; the wine is the cart. I follow the grapes," Bernard added, closing our conversation with one more of his colorful metaphors.

Within Sight of San Francisco

San Francisco Skyline

Ridge Vineyards: Where the Prince is King

Neither Ridge Vineyards nor winemaker Paul Draper started out to become Zinfandel-famous. Ridge Vineyards was established in 1962 on the merits of the Monte Bello Cabernet Sauvignon that Dave Bennion had made in 1959 as a home winemaker. Paul Draper came on board in 1969 to be the Monte Bello winemaker.

It was early spring of 1986 when I made my long-anticipated first journey to Cupertino, and up Monte Bello Road to find Ridge Vineyards at 2,600 feet above sea level. By then, winemaker Paul Draper had been making Zinfandel for a couple of years longer than even Jed Steele — but not as long as the Pedroncellis. Although Ridge's founding winemaker, Dave Bennion, was still alive then, Paul had been in charge of winemaking operations since 1970. I already had learned from Leon Sobon just how influential Ridge Zinfandels had been on his decision to give up his ceramic engineering career and move to Amador to become a Zinfandel producer. My heart picked up a couple of beats per minute as I entered the gates of the famed ridgetop winery. What would Paul be like in person? How might he feel about sparing a precious hour or two of his time with the novice wine writer that I was then?

Thoroughly a gentleman, as well as poet and philosopher, Paul made every effort to put me at ease. After a cordial greeting, he immediately invited me on a walking tour of the winery. He showed me Ridge's "caves" — that is, the part of the barrel room that was built into the hillside as the winery's original wine cellar. He asked about the caves I had recently written about for ***PWV***.

He then explained how Ridge got into making Zinfandel wine almost by accident a few years before he came on board. In 1964, there was a shortage of Cabernet Sauvignon available in the state, Paul said. Yet the newly re-established Ridge Vineyards needed to grow to pay its way. So Dave Bennion looked to the old Zinfandel vines on the nearby Picchetti Vineyard. He pruned the recently abandoned vines, and what happened next, according to Paul, was simply revolutionary.

Without a second thought, Bennion treated the winery's first Zinfandel as an equal to his premium Cabernet Sauvignon. That is, he held the fermenting juice on its skins for 12 to 15 days (long maceration); he took the new wine through full secondary (malolactic) fermentation; and, perhaps most revolutionary of all, he cellared this first Zinfandel entirely in small used oak barrels — exactly the same treatment accorded his superb Monte Bello Cabernet Sauvignon.

At that time, according to Paul, few producers were cellaring even their Cabernets in small oak barrels. More often than not, he said, it was aged in large oak casks for 18 to 24 months. The "lesser" (that is to say, the non-French) varietal, Zinfandel was traditionally aged in 20,000-gallon redwood tanks.

Using small barrels for the flavors and character that they could add to red wines was a revolutionary concept in California winemaking. The oxidation that occurred as part of the ageing process was the key. Bennion's choice of wood was American oak; later on, he added a small percentage of new wood each year. "Made in this way," recalled Paul, "those Pichetti Zinfandel grapes produced one hell of a wine."

By the time I met Paul, he was an enthusiastic Zinfandel winemaker who liked nothing better than to tell his favorite story about placing some Ridge Vineyards Zinfandel in a blind Cabernet Sauvignon tasting for some folks in New York. It was 1985. At his request, three Ridge Geyserville Zinfandels — a 1973, 1974, and 1975 — were placed in a double blind tasting of 10- to-12-year-old California dry red table wines for the "California First Crew" club in New York. When the blinds came off the bottles, only two non-Ridge Cabernet Sauvignons placed ahead of the Zinfandels — out of 15 wines. The fact that the members of this club had previously sworn to Draper that a Zinfandel could *never* compete with California Cabernets drew a wicked little smile from Paul as he told me this story.

The story, as it turned out, also revealed what Paul liked, and didn't like, in Zinfandel wines back then. He liked vineyards whose mature fruit had both fully ripe flavor and reasonable sugar — so that the tank sample would be a minimum of 24.5° Brix. He preferred vines 40 years old and older for consistent vintages of a rich claret-style Zinfandel. "You cannot produce wines as consistently fine from 10-year-old vines as you can from fully mature vines," he said.

These preferences contributed to Paul's decision to give up fruit from two old Amador County vineyards — the Eschen and Esola. After working diligently for over 10 years with these vineyards, making two single vineyard Amador Zinfandels each year from 1974 to 1984, he came to believe that only in rare years did they produce Zinfandel as complex and long ageing as those he produced from his best Sonoma vineyards. The August and September temperatures up there were, he believed, too consistently warm and did not drop sufficiently overnight to develop the necessary balance of acid, pH, and sugar. "Their overripe style made them very appealing when quite young, and when their intense fruit could carry the alcohol content," he explained. But after10 years, he said, his experience was that most of the fruit had fallen out.

Paul Draper

Although in Paul's view, this meant that Amador was a less desirable region for Zinfandel, fans of Amador Zinfandel wouldn't have them any other way. That the wines should taste very ripe and distinctly Amador Zinfandel was part of their great attraction.

However, Paul's central point about producing consistently well made, balanced Zinfandel was that you had to know your vineyards. "It is the difference between wines made by nature and wines made by man," he emphasized. "Even in areas with ideal climate and mature vines, you have to watch your grapes like a hawk. I prefer not to add water [to the wine, to compensate for over-ripeness and high alcohol] nor to blend in over-ripe fruit to compensate for picking too early. You can achieve the best flavors only when you pick at the best Brix. You can do that only when you can get to know your vineyards and when your vineyards are in regions where potential for over-ripeness is less severe. Wines made from such well suited vineyards are wines made by nature, with no need of 'adjustment' by the winemaker," he said unequivocally. "Only in cooler years and with wines like the 1977 Esola did we see the rich claret style in Amador. Most often, the wines were 'late picked.'"

I visited Ridge Vineyards again in November 1996. Paul had invited me to join the staff for Thanksgiving dinner, and I had accepted with alacrity. It was a sumptuous feast set out in the lower winery with views out the windows over the mist-filled canyon. I was privileged to sit with Paul and David Gates, Ridge's vineyard manager. President Wilma Sturrock was seated nearby. Our table was littered with Ridge Zinfandels of several vintages and vineyards. The dinner recalled to my mind some of the harvest dinners and family feasts on my home farm in Saskatchewan. Of course, there was no wine on *those* dinner tables! It also recalled to my mind Paul's description of his first Thanksgiving dinner in wine country.

He had been invited to the Dry Creek Valley home of a college roommate, he said. The weather was warm and calm, the sky was purest blue, and the vineyards and various trees were resplendent in their fall colors of reds and yellows. "The family lived in a modest country house, too small for the four generations of family that had gathered. So they had set out one long trestle table that began on the front porch and ended on the back porch," Paul said. "As I sat amidst this happy family eating the food of the land and drinking the wine that they had made from their own vines, I knew that I wanted to be a part of this lifestyle."

Now he was, and hosting a staff Thanksgiving dinner at a winery that he had helped to build. Could Paradise be much better than this?

Following dinner, Paul invited me to his office in the upper winery for an update on his views on Zinfandel, and innovations at the winery.

When we were seated in his modest office, Paul began by stating that he no longer felt that Zinfandel needed to age into a claret-like wine in 10 years to be considered world class. He admitted to enjoying Zinfandel four or five times more often than Cabernet, although more often as a young wine — with between two and seven years in the bottle. "What I have come to feel," he said, "is that they are two quite different expressions of great wine. The bottom line for me is that fine Zinfandel is the equal of fine Cabernet Sauvignon in quality, just as fine Burgundy is the equal of fine Bordeaux. They are two different wines and long live the difference. Both are great in their finest expressions."

"Wine is of the earth; it's a connection we need, that we seek out as our lives become more cut off from the natural world. It is part of what's behind the interest in wine that separates it from other alcoholic beverages. Great vineyards are a reflection of that piece of earth the vines grow in and of the sun and rain that fall upon them."

Paul Draper

His focus on the vineyards, however, had not changed, only intensified. "Wine is of the earth; it's a connection we need, that we seek out as our lives become more cut off from the natural world. It is part of what's behind the interest in wine that separates it from other alcoholic beverages. Great vineyards are a reflection of that piece of earth the vines grow in and of the sun and rain that fall upon them. We want consistent style. Having seven great vintages in a row — 1990 to 1996, has spoiled us. We would like to maintain that consistency. In the eight years that David Gates has been with us, we are getting closer. We've learned how to care better for our vineyards. You need two things for consistent vintages: good weather and a properly managed vineyard. David has done much to develop consistency in our Lytton Springs and Geyserville vineyards by opening the canopies and dropping huge amounts of crop."

In 1991, Paul also established a new Zinfandel block in Ridge's Geyserville Vineyard, to investigate the differences among three field selections planted side by side on the same rootstock. His selections came from the DuPratt, the Picchetti, and the old Trentadue "Heart's Desire" Vineyard.

"We wanted to learn the effect, if any, of soil and climate on field selections. We chose 110R rootstock, planted it in 1991, and field-budded the selections in 1992," Paul said. By 1996, according to Paul, *terroir* seemed to be winning out over clonal selections. Wine made from each of the clonal expressions shared the elegant Geyserville character, though each is distinct.

Paul also had this to say about Zinfandel: "I know of no other table wine that is so purely delicious. Zinfandel has given me more sensuous pleasure than any other wine. Yes, it is a heavier style of table wine, meaning that at its best, it usually has an alcohol content of between 14 percent and 14.9 percent alcohol, which is substantial. Zinfandel is a rich, fruity, spicy wine. It can at times be a side dish to the main course. So if your preference is for a lighter style of table wine, you may find Zinfandel a little hard to take."

He also had backed away from the style of the monster Occidental Vineyard Zinfandels of the early 1970s in the late picked, or even late harvest, style of above-15 percent alcohol wines. His preference had turned toward the fully ripe but under-15 percent alcohol wines with good ageing potential that would complement food. Although some of those big Zinfandels were famous back in the early 1970s, the Geyserville and Lytton Springs of those years averaged 14 percent alcohol. "I believe that wine will become a part of our American culture only if it becomes part of our principal daily meal. It was perhaps inevitable that it was our 1992 Late Picked Pagani Vineyard Zinfandel that the *Wine Spectator* chose to list among the 10 best wines of the world. It was very appealing as a young wine, but less typical of the style we would like to be known for. Few people drink those high-alcohol wines every day."

Before I left, Paul invited me to taste the 1995 Geyserville that was still in the tank. We walked into the cool fermentation room with its long rows of steel tanks of various sizes, and he drew me a glass of the fragrant wine. It was a memorable experience, to be standing in that renowned winery in the clouds on Thanksgiving Friday, tasting the newborn Geyserville wine with Paul.

As we enjoyed the wine, Paul explained the importance of tasting wines as they develop. "We have numerous serious blind tastings at various stages. We keep the lots separate, and taste them frequently. One of the reasons Helen Turley is so good," he commented, "is that she actually smells and tastes her wines, barrel by barrel. She doesn't just swirl and spit."

From the tanks, we moved to the barrels, where Paul explained his preference for American oak barrels for his Zinfandel ageing program.

"Zinfandel achieved world class status as a premium American red wine. It seems only fitting that it be aged in American oak, since some of the best oak is grown in America." Ridge's practice was to age all its red wines in American oak, including its Monte Bello Cabernet Sauvignon. From his first use of new American oak in 1970, Draper validated his choice by buying a few barrels yearly of what he thought to be the finest French oak, for taste comparison. Without exception, he remains satisfied that Ridge's finest Monte Bello Cabernets and old vine Zinfandels are best when aged in air dried American oak. I could only imagine what the wine we tasted would be like after a few months in oak barrels.

Paul also explained the tests they had done comparing such practices as pumping the wine from fermentation tank to press versus shoveling it into the presses. The shovel won decidedly. "Gentle handling at every stage makes all the difference in wine quality," Paul emphasized. New equipment and design of the facilities were all done with the belief that meticulous attention to detail and to gentle handling would improve quality and consistency in the wines.

As I made my way down Monte Bello Road in the early fall darkness, with the city lights of the peninsula twinkling below me, I thought of the words of Donn Riesen, marketing director for Ridge Vineyards. Donn has frequently praised Zinfandel as "the prince who will never be king. Zinfandel is a luscious wine one can enjoy while waiting for one's Cabernet Sauvignons to come around," he has said,

At Ridge Vineyards today, however, there is little doubt that the prince is on equal footing with the reigning king.

Average case production of Zinfandel since the 1995 vintage is 43,000. By vineyard: 10,979 Geyserville; 11,496 Lytton Springs; 3,674 Pagani; 2,820 Paso Robles; 8,860 Sonoma Station.

Speaking of Ridge's nearly 30 years of producing several thousand cases of Geyserville and Lytton Springs Zinfandel, Donn has also remarked, "There is no other premium Zinfandel producer in the world that releases this much stylistically consistent high-end Zinfandel from each single vineyard."

Doesn't that make Zinfandel the King of the Ridge?

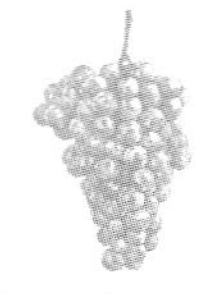

Rosenblum Cellars: "Dr. Zin"

What would lead a talented and successful Minnesota-born doctor of veterinary medicine to seek a second career in winemaking after less than 10 years practicing as a veterinarian? Kent Rosenblum's animal patients and their loyal owners are probably wondering the same thing, and are holding their collective breaths against the day when Kent's love of winemaking will win out completely over his love of caring for animals. Both Provident Veterinary Clinic and Rosenblum Cellars are located in Alameda. Why did he establish Rosenblum Cellars in 1978 after five years as a home winemaker? And why Zinfandel? These were the first questions I asked Kent in the course of my early research into Zinfandel during the 1980s.

In answer to my first question, Kent had said that he became a winemaker for its creative opportunities and for the love of wine.

In answer to my second question, Kent had replied, "I like Zinfandel."

He made his first home wine in 1973. When he was ready to open Rosenblum Cellars in 1977, he felt that the market for premium Zinfandel was wide open. "There were many fine Cabernet Sauvignons available in the market, but there were not many really fine Zinfandel wines available," he said. "While most of the best Cabernet Sauvignon vineyards were taken, there were still many fine old Zinfandel vineyards available. I have been able to get some of the finest Zinfandel grapes in California. While my Cabernet Sauvignons and other red wines sell, they do not fly out the door like my Zinfandels."

Before he settled on his style and launched Rosenblum Cellars, Kent traveled to the winegrowing regions of France, Italy, and Germany. "People in these regions have made wine in the same way for centuries because it works," he said. What he discovered there reinforced his belief that hand-punching and extended maceration were the best methods for making the style of wines that he enjoyed. "Whenever we came across a guy standing on a tank hand-punching the wine, we found a wine that we liked. The wines were wonderfully flavorful and soft."

When he set up his own operation with tiny tanks made to fit in the basement of his house, just to be sure, the first year he tried a submerged cap, a pump-over, and hand-punched Zinfandel. "The hand-punched wine to my taste was much better," he said.

In 1978, he moved out of his basement – first to a facility in Oakland, then to Emeryville in 1982, and finally back to Alameda in 1987. It took the winery a little time to become financially self-supporting. Zinfandel, although popular with his customers, did not earn a big profit. For the first six years after going commercial, Kent and his partners did all the work themselves at the winery in exchange for some of the wine. Only in 1984 did the winery show enough profit for Kent to hire salaried staff.

It took a little longer, until the mid-1990s, to be free of economic restraints in winemaking decisions. The area of greatest expense, after the cost of grapes, is barrels, and Kent for many years solved the problem by buying newly shaved oak barrels rather than new barrels.

"'Did we want to buy 100 shaved oak barrels, or 10 new barrels?' was the question we had to ask ourselves then," said Kent without apology. "At that time, it was not a choice, given the break-even returns on our Zinfandel. Although we did get some bugs from time to time (bacterial contamination that you wouldn't otherwise get in your wines), we mostly got good results with shaved barrels. I would still recommend high quality shaved barrels to someone without a lot of dollars to spend," Kent said.

Even when he was under economic constraints, Kent's European-influenced style was attracting an increasing throng of enthusiastic fans, and also winning critical accolades. "The hand-punching and extended maceration always result in wines that are fruity, soft, and tasty when they are released. In fact, when our customers try our Zinfandels from the barrels, they often exclaim, 'Bottle that right now, and I'll take it,' " he said.

This raised a question on the subject of ageing Zinfandel. "Making a Zinfandel wine that will age magnificently should not be our first premise," Kent said. "Our first premise should be to make a wine that smells and tastes great from the day that it is released, and for up to five more years. Some Zinfandels will smell and taste great in 10 years, even 15, some as long as 20, but that should not be our first goal."

Kent Rosenblum

"Do you really believe that your Hendry Reserve or Maggie's Reserve smell and taste their best when they are released?" I asked. My experience with these wines had been that they definitely improved in the bottle for a few years.

"Typically they do," replied Kent. "Are they better in a year? Probably. Will they be still better in 10, 15, or 20 years? Depending on the vineyard and vintage, some will continue to improve for up to 20 years. The Samsel is one of them. But is that my goal — to make a 20-year Zinfandel? No. In my opinion, Zinfandels should be immensely drinkable when they are released. That is when their incredible fruit is most appealing. Of course, they are also wonderful when they are a little older, if you like to cellar them for a few years."

"Have you always felt this way about Zinfandel?" I asked.

"Yes, I especially like them from the barrel," he replied enthusiastically. "The best red wines in general — and any winemaker anywhere in the world will agree — will taste absolutely stunning right at the press, and they will taste and smell absolutely stunning all the way through the process until they are bottled. These are the wines that will still be absolutely stunning in 20 years. This has been my experience as a winemaker. Any of our wines that have been magnificent at the press have aged beautifully. This was my experience with the European wines," he said.

By 1992, both his financial returns on his Zinfandels and his collection of medals had increased substantially. "While we're not wearing out the tires on our vehicles carrying the cash to the bank, we're not having to mortgage the store, either," he had said then. Kent's Zinfandels have been a testament to his dedication to quality, good value, and understanding of the variety, economics notwithstanding. However, his wines were less expensive then.

In April 2000, I met Kent at the winery for the last of many interviews for this book and other reports on Zinfandel. At this date, he had long been recognized as one of the most highly regarded and eclectic Zinfandel producers in California. The first order of business, however, was a lunch of burritos and salsa on the deck in front of the winery, where we could enjoy the sun and a view over Alameda's estuary to San Francisco, which included both the Bay and Golden Gate bridges.

He opened the conversation by acknowledging that winemaking had become a refuge from the stress that he experienced as a veterinary doctor. "Until I got so involved with the winery, I never realized just how stressful the clinic is. You get 15 or 20 animals coming in during each day, and for each one, you have just a few minutes to examine, diagnose, and prescribe treatment, and make the animal better. That creates stress. Physically, you have to get the work done — dentistry, blood work, surgeries — you do it all. I've done that for 30 years. Winemaking is much more creative, outgoing, social. Look, we're spending a pleasant afternoon talking about wine, aren't we? And no stress."

Indeed, stress is absent at Rosenblum Cellars. Whatever one may think of Kent's Zinfandels, or even his down home, Minnesota-country sense of humor (for which he is noted by associates almost as much as he is for his wines), one cannot fault his warm and generous hospitality. That is always the first order of business with Kent, as important a part of his operation as is making the finest wines possible. In fact, for Kent, the two are inseparable, which accounts for much of the appeal of Rosenblum Cellars.

His animal patients, however, can breathe easy. Kent intends to continue as a partner in Providence Veterinary Clinic for a few more years, for reasons as much non-economic as economic. "I have a responsibility to my partners and to my patients," he explained. "If you have a business that is running at a quality level, if you just leave, that quality drops. You want to leave with a level of expertise and quality intact. I would not want to leave until we have the necessary new partners in place to maintain that quality. That takes a little time."

"What have been the most significant changes in the 23 years since you opened the winery?" I asked.

"We have made some changes in terms of philosophy, how we do things," Kent replied after a few moments' thought. "We have evolved in that it took us nearly 10 years to discover Contra Costa County Zinfandel vineyards. Until then, we thought that Napa and Sonoma counties were the center of the world. It took us even longer, until 1990, to discover Paso Robles vineyards. That came about because we were running out of old Zinfandel vineyards up here. When I met Richard Sauret and saw the vineyard, I liked what I saw even though the vineyard was not terribly old — about 20 years then, but it was head trained and non-irrigated. We signed a contract, and have been getting Sauret Vineyard grapes ever since. We are still working together to refine viticulture practices."

Kent has established 10-year contracts with the few vineyards that he now feels best serve his style and goals, to give him consistency of grape sources. "We want to have about six or eight really great Zinfandel vineyards that we can grow with, and that our sales staff can count on. We have the old vine history; we have the old clone history. Once you have that as your foundation, you can build. We are still exploring clones, *terroir*, and regions, as potential both for purchasing grapes and also as potential for buying land and planting grapes. Our 10-year contracts form the basis of our wine production. These are the vineyards we want to support, so that they can support us. We are helping the growers to plant new vines with old clones, and to replace missing vines. We can do this only with the vineyards that are economically supportive of these efforts."

The Zinfandel vineyards that Kent has 10-year contracts with as of year 2000 are the following:

- in Contra Costa County, Dwight Meadows' "Carla's Vineyard" (labeled San Francisco Bay), and the John Continente Vineyard;
- in Mendocino County's Redwood Valley, the Richard and Annette Rhoads Vineyard, which produces Annette's Reserve;
- in Sonoma County, the Florence's Rockpile Road Vineyard, the Samsel's "Maggie's Reserve" Vineyard, the Cullinane Vineyard, the St. Peter's Church Vineyard, and Harris-Kratka Vineyard;
- in Napa County, the George Hendry vineyard, and the Lyons Vineyard;
- in Paso Robles, the Richard Sauret Vineyard.

At this point in our conversation, we had moved inside for a barrel tasting of several of Kent's 1998 and 1999 vintages. As we moved from barrel to barrel, some new, some older, I found things to like in each of them.

"This is lovely," I exclaimed, as we sampled "Carla's Vineyard" Zinfandel.

"Oh, this is really wonderful," I exclaimed, as we sampled St. Peter's Church Zinfandel.

"Wow, this is great," when we got to Eagle Point.

By the time we had gone though most of the 1999 vintages, I had run out of new exclamations. They were all pretty wonderful, with soft, ripe, luscious fruit and intriguing spices, which is typical of Rosenblum Cellars Zinfandels. Besides, the 1999 vintage is proving to be as great as, if not better than, the fabulous 1990 vintage.

Keeping track of the seasonal care of all these vineyards — especially their ripening curves as harvest dates near — would seem to be a daunting job in itself. Since the mid- to late 1990s, producers have been greatly emphasizing the importance of knowing what is happening in the vineyard. Rosenblum Cellars is located across from the Alameda Naval Station.

When Kent founded his winery in 1977, he was making two Zinfandels. In 1999, he crushed Zinfandel grapes from 35 vineyards located as far north as Redwood Valley in Mendocino County South to Paso Robles on the Central Coast. From these grapes, he will release 16 Zinfandel wines.

For Kent, checking vineyards in August and September to determine harvest dates definitely is not a stroll out the door and down a lane to see how the grapes are doing. On two occasions I rode along with him to check vineyards in Contra Costa County and in Sonoma and Napa valleys. It seemed to me that none of the vineyards we visited were entirely in the condition he would have liked: too many weeds, too much sulfur, over-ripe grapes. Yet in all cases, the wines that came from these vineyards were luscious and beautifully balanced. How he managed to determine a reasonable window of ripeness and deal with other adverse conditions for so many vineyards was a question that I had been pondering for some time.

During an interlude in our conversation, I asked Kent, "What have you learned about how to keep track of the ripening curves and other conditions in so many vineyards and in so many locations?"

"The best red wines in general will taste absolutely stunning right at the press, and they will taste and smell absolutely stunning all the way through the process until they are bottled."

Kent Rosenblum

"We are a little bit blessed in that all the regions and all the vineyards do not ripen at the same time," Kent began. "By mid-August, I know that I should go to Contra Costa to see what's happening. It's a long drive to Paso Robles, so I am not going down there until Richard Sauret calls to say that the grapes are at 22° Brix, usually early September. Within a week or so, I will go down to taste the grapes and check their sugar content with a refractometer. I will also bring back a five-gallon bucket sample to crush and evaluate. That is the most accurate way to determine the numbers," Kent explained.

"I usually try to get to the vineyards for the first visit, to see how things are coming along. Then, I send out the guys to check on the grapes for the second and third samples. They are pretty good about picking accurate samples.

"Generally speaking, though," Kent continued, "I would rather err on the side of over-ripeness than under-ripeness. If the grapes hang an extra day or so, or even a week, that's usually not a problem for Zinfandel. It is easier to blend down over-ripe grapes than try to compensate for under-ripe flavors. With over-ripe grapes, you have the flavor and sugar. You never get the flavor from under-ripe grapes. Sometimes when Sonoma ripens before Contra Costa, the logistics are such that the grapes sometimes come in with higher sugar content than I would ideally like, but I don't mind. I can deal with it. What I find nearly impossible to work with are grapes that barely ferment out from 22°. I've rarely, if ever, made a good Zinfandel wine out of grapes that come in at 22° Brix.

"With over-ripe, however, you are running on the edge the whole time. You can get stuck fermentations. To compensate for this, we use some high-powered yeast cultures such as 'fermachamp' and 'Jackass Hill' isolates that Scott Laboratory has developed. They ferment well up to about 18 percent alcohol. Identifying our best vineyards, working closely with the growers, and making them our top priority also has improved our results," he added.

Kent's cellar crew also had their opinions about how Kent managed to stay on top of the vineyards and the wines made from them, while fulfilling his obligations at Providence Clinic. "It's called talent," said one of them. "Kent is one of the most talented people I know, when it comes to winemaking."

"We don't think that we have a handle on everything," Kent countered. "But we do feel that we have a good vehicle for producing fruity wines with soft tannins that taste and smell good at release. This is the style we like best. Our customers seem to like them too, since we always sell out our vintages."

The other main change at Rosenblum Cellars has been in its barrel program. Since 1997, Kent's success with Zinfandel has improved to the point where economics are far less of a factor in his barrel selection. "With our focus on just a few of our best non-irrigated older hillside and benchland vineyards, we have developed a riper and more extracted style that benefits from more new French-coopered American oak. This is a more costly style to produce, because crop levels are strictly limited, and we use more new wood. But it is the style that our customers like, and are willing to support. So we now buy the barrels we want, which is between 20 percent and 60 percent new American oak, and 40 percent to 80 percent one-, two-, and three-year-old barrels.

"We choose the cooper to suit the character of the wines, and according to how we like the wines to taste. New American oak barrels impart aromatics and help to stabilize the wine," he continued. "From the one-year-old oak, we get some mellow components that we like. We also find that there is significantly less evaporation from the new barrels. So the economic factor is still there, but it is not the main factor in choosing them," explained Kent, with well-deserved pride in the winery's achievement.

"Besides expanding our horizon to Zinfandel vineyards beyond Napa and Sonoma, our winemaking practices are in a constant state of experimentation. We have always just lightly crushed and destemmed the berries with about 10 percent to 15 percent whole clusters. I have always let the grapes soak for a couple of days before fermentation begins. During fermentation, we hand-punch the wine in small bins, which allows us better tannin management, and we allow extended maceration. These practices give us soft tannins, which are important to producing a wine that is good to drink at release. We have adjusted these practices according to our improved understanding of our vineyards."

His goals today are simple, said Kent. "We want to lessen any confusion that people may feel about our Zinfandels, and we want to make the best Zinfandels that we can regardless of the vineyard and the quantity." To this end, Kent limits production of his Cuvee to about 20,000 cases. "Any more and I could not maintain the quality, and I just do not like making lesser quality wine, even if it would probably sell," he explained.

"What is the most important part of your job as a winemaker?" I asked.

In reply, Kent picked up the glass that held the current barrel sample, and took a drink. As he set the glass down, he looked at me and said, "What I just did."

"You mean, tasting the wine?"

"You bet. Wine changes, sometimes weekly. If I came down here and tasted the wine every three months, it wouldn't work. As wine changes, it needs attention — racking, aeration, a different kind of oak. Every Monday morning, my cellar crew gets presented with 'Kent's short list' of emergencies, which is about two pages long," he said, laughing.

"Are your consumers getting a better bottle of wine now, for the higher prices? What does a consumer get in your over $20-bottles of wine compared to your under-$20 bottles?" I asked. "For example, what does a Samsel 'Maggie's Reserve' offer that your Cuvee does not? Are your wines still good value?"

"In some respects, they are getting the results of our ability, which comes from some years of experience, to get the best fruit. The wine that is made from the best fruit has a lush concentration and it has the benefits of the best cellaring that excellent fruit deserves. So it is partly the fruit and partly the winemaking. We also pick the best vineyards carefully, selecting distinctive blocks for a total of six or eight tons, and crushing the fruit separately. With less distinctive vineyards, we pick all 50 tons at the same time, and crush it as a unit. With a vineyard like the Samsel, which needs to develop a sugar content of 24.5° or 25° Brix, have a balanced acid and pH, we may pick the vineyard seven times for eight tons. That labor adds cost, but the fruit and resulting wine make it worth it. Lesser vineyards are not so labor-intensive. The fruit does not benefit from the extra labor, nor does it merit extra attention in the winery. The wines we make from them are therefore less costly. So, yes, I think our wines are still good value."

In year 2000, Kent's style is not greatly different from what he set out to develop – just better. The market is willing to pay for a better-made Zinfandel. Although costs have increased in every aspect of grape-growing and winemaking, according to Kent, the increased cost of the finished wine comes mainly from two sources: higher prices for the best grapes, and new oak barrels. However, consumers are increasingly appreciative of the luscious fruity character of Zinfandel at its best, and sales seem to indicate that despite higher prices, they still consider the wines a good value.

In 1999, in addition to its 20,000 cases of Cuvee, Rosenblum Cellars produced 32,000 cases of premium and ultra-premium Zinfandel.

On closing, I asked Kent if he attributed the success of his Zinfandel wines to anything besides his great vineyards, the soft, luscious, approachable style of the wines, and their good value. "Probably my willingness to blend, but more especially, I have a great story — 'Crazy Alameda veterinary doctor becomes Dr. Zin,'" he replied, speaking seriously but smiling broadly. "Don't you think that makes a great story?"

"Definitely — on both accounts," I replied, with an answering smile.

I also wanted to know, for the record, one more thing. Now that the winery had achieved a level of quality that he had been striving for, might he be thinking of acquiring new partners in order to extricate himself from the wine business and move on to another challenge, just as he was in the process of doing with his veterinary practice? Kent is not only a talented and skilled veterinary doctor and winemaker, he is also a triathlete who usually wins the triathlons that he competes in for his age group.

"Oh, no!" he exclaimed. "This is a life-long venture. You don't leave what you love!" Economics notwithstanding, it could only have happened with Zinfandel.

Part 111

CONCLUSION

APPENDICES

BIBLIOGRAPHY

INDEX

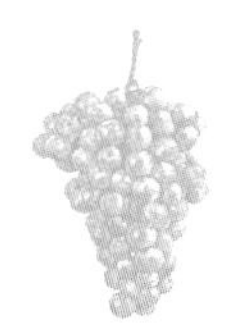

Conclusion

Having concluded my 14-year odyssey through Zinfandel country, I feel exhilarated by the deep and enduring passion the growers and producers show for their beloved Zinfandel. Because of their passionate and resolute belief in the worth of this grape, Zinfandel is at last irrevocably recognized as one of the best red wine grapes in the world. The fragrant, fruity, soft, balanced, and truly luscious wines produced from Zinfandel grapes grown in all the regions best suited to the variety are captivating red wine lovers worldwide. Zinfandel as dry table wine is one of the most appealing and compatible food wines made.

I also feel just a little sad. As a result of Zinfandel coming of age as a world class red table wine, the old style of Zinfandel is all but lost to memory and taste. Only the historic Galleano Winery in Cucamonga Valley continues to make a traditional redwood tank-fermented and aged Zinfandel. Bottled in four-liter jugs, it sells for under $10 in the tasting room, and is still the wine that both Don Galleano and his growers such as Paul Hofer put on their tables for family and friends.

The Zinfandel wines of the 1990s have necessarily become more expensive. The growers are now getting a price per ton that encourages them to keep their vines in the ground, and even to plant new vines. The costs of producing a fine Zinfandel wine have increased. Of course, in comparison to the prices of other world class red table wines, even the most expensive red Zinfandel is still good value. Nonetheless, this has left many working-class consumers who, for decades, could count on finding a thick, robust old vine Zinfandel on the shelf at an affordable price asking, "What are *we* to drink now?" It is the same question posed by winemakers throughout the industry in search of a tasty but inexpensive red table wine for themselves and their staff.

Fortunately, however, producers from every region continue to make affordable (under $12 a bottle) red Zinfandel wines. The quantities range from the 200,000 case production of barrel-aged Mondavi-Woodbridge California Zinfandel to 20,000 cases or less of Rosenblum Cellars Cuvée. No doubt these wines have lost some of the rough peasant robustness of the early Zinfandels, but they also are better complements to the style of food being prepared today. So do not overlook these Zinfandels, including those produced by Sutter Home and Canandaigua wine brands, such as Vendange, Talus, and Heritage, in your search for a tasty red wine to accompany your daily dinners. After all, wine is made to complement food, and even Ernest Gallo unabashedly admitted to *Wine Spectator* that his family put aside a $450 Pétrus for Gallo Hearty Burgundy one Christmas Eve in the mid-1980s.[30]

In closing, I hope that after finishing this book, you, the readers, will continue this Zinfandel odyssey in your own way. Explore for yourselves all these fascinating and beautiful regions. Journey to northern Baja and discover the exotic Valle de Guadalupe and Rancho Escondido and the Zinfandels produced from these vineyards. Continue northward to Temecula Valley and to Riverside County's historic Cucamonga Valley where 600 acres of pre-Prohibition Zinfandel vines and Joseph Filippi and Galleano Wineries still thrive. Travel over to the Central Coast and linger among the many producers and vineyards in this quiet pastoral region of San Luis Obispo County just inland from the Pacific Ocean. Then, continue northward, but before you cross the Golden Gate Bridge, take time to journey up to Ridge Vineyards, for a special Zinfandel experience high above the Bay and within sight of the City. From there, cross the Golden Gate Bridge, and enter the North Coast region, where myriad vineyards, viticultural areas, and Zinfandel producers await you in the counties of Sonoma, Napa, Mendocino, and Lake. The sheer variety of style and regional character in these wines will surely dazzle your palate.

And there is more. On your way east to Contra Costa County, follow directions to the Alameda tunnel leading to Rosenblum Cellars, where a warm and friendly welcome, and another beautiful view of the City, await you. Here, you will be treated to a fine selection of Zinfandels, including those made from Contra Costa County vineyards. Of course, you have already sampled several Contra Costa Zinfandels at Cline Cellars at the south end of Sonoma County. Continue east through Oakley in Contra Costa County and on to the Lodi region to seek out its half-dozen exciting producers. Then enter the Sierra Foothills for a memorable finale within sight of the snow-covered peaks of the Sierra among the wineries of Amador, El Dorado, Nevada, and Calaveras counties.

Or make up your own itinerary on how best to traverse these 1,500 miles long by 150 miles wide of Zinfandel Country. The point is, there is a great adventure awaiting you. Enjoy the journey.

[30] Shanken, 25.

Appendices

Appendix A. A Perspective on Quercus

When I met Paul Draper in spring 1986, I knew that some producers dedicated to making Zinfandel as a fine red table wine were fierce in their belief that you should put such fine wine only in French oak, some of it new. To hear Paul express his long-held preference for American oak therefore registered a discordant note. I knew Ridge's early Zinfandel wines were regarded as benchmarks by many consumers and critics alike. They were even revered as model Zinfandels for many newcomers such as Leon Sobon. Yet I was also hearing that only "lesser" wines were aged in American oak — if they were even put in small barrels at all. Anyone who revered their red wines, I was told by such esteemed producers as Jed Steele, Joseph Swan, and Joel Peterson, put them only in French oak for ageing.

I kept hearing that their reasons for choosing the more expensive French oak had to do with the fact that American oak barrels back then were mainly Kentucky Blue Grass whiskey barrels made from staves that had been kiln-dried, steam-bent, and charred over gas fires. And that you could always taste that charring and those old whiskey flavors in the wines — until the barrels were really "well-tempered," that is, several years old.

Many who claimed to have been among the first to treat Zinfandel as a world class wine by putting it in French oak from day one attempted to explain Ridge's success with American oak by saying, "Well, American oak is much better made now." Then I reminded them that Ridge had *always* used American oak for both its Zinfandels and its expensive Monte Bello Cabernet Sauvignons. I pointed out that, according to Paul, some of these earliest Monte Bellos (such as the 1971, 1972, and 1974, as well as the Geyserville and Lytton Springs Zinfandels of the same years) have held up beautifully for 20 years and longer. Then they become silent.

After learning from John Pedroncelli and Michael Martini that large redwood tanks, not oak barrels, were the customary vessels for ageing red wines following Repeal, I knew I had to investigate the development of the practice of using small oak cooperage for fine red wine production in California. Since Paul was the earliest producer to use small cooperage among those I interviewed, and was certainly one of the earliest overall in California's return to fine wine production, I took my question back to him for elaboration. What I wanted to know was why Paul believed in American oak, and got such good results with it, when all around him his respected Zinfandel colleagues were expressing disdain for American oak.

Like all good storytellers, Paul went back to the beginning — a beginning that I recognized from my literary study of Chaucer and other medieval writers

(1300 –1450). The following are excerpts and paraphrases from two letters Paul wrote me on this question in December 1996 and February 1997.

Historically (that is, back in the Middle Ages), barrels were for transport of heavy products, both liquid and solid. "You rolled them out of your shop (or cellar) up a couple of boards onto a horse cart or wagon, and took them into town or perhaps to a port if you were shipping further. They were rolled up the gangplank onto a barge or ship and then set up on their heads for stability during the journey. . . . Each region in Europe back when they were all separate political units . . . developed its own size and shape of barrel for shipping: Sherry butts; Port pipes; Bordeaux barrels; and Burgundy barrels. . . . Wine was sold and shipped young in the very early times because it tended to spoil. One of the many stories about how small barrel ageing, as opposed to just transporting, began goes something like this," wrote Paul:

"Several hundred years ago when Bordeaux wine was principally sold to England (as was still true until recent years as the U.S. market grew), there was an interruption in trade due to one of the armed conflicts between England and France. The producers in Bordeaux had already racked their wines out of the fermentors and into barrel and sent it to the docks in Bordeaux to be shipped to England. The war began and shipping was held up. The wine sat in barrels in the cool warehouses at the docks for something like two years — until peace was declared and the wine could be shipped. When it arrived in England, the merchants tasted the 'aged' wine and declared it the best they had ever bought, and told the producers to do the same in the future, and they would pay them premium prices for it. So for the *very finest wines*, barrels moved from being simply shipping containers to being ageing containers as well. This practice was limited to the very finest and most expensive wines...."

In California after Repeal, as exemplified by Pedroncelli and Martini, virtually all producers aged their red wines in large redwood tanks. Sometimes, in the best wineries, oak ovals or large oak tanks were also used. (See discussion on Preston Vineyards and Winery.) Virtually no one aged in small barrels – and certainly not exclusively in small barrels. Of course, if you were small and trying to produce the highest quality, Draper pointed out, you would keep your very best wine separate, and there might only be enough to fill a few barrels (rather than a large cask or tank). Martin Ray, said Draper, would be a good example in the late 1940s and 1950s of a small producer using small barrels as his principal ageing containers. Martin Ray Vineyards, Palo Alto, was founded in 1946.

Dave Bennion, Draper continued, visited Martin Ray, and like him was fully aware of the tradition of using small barrels in ageing fine wine. They both understood that barrel ageing had been done with the very finest wine in Europe for hundreds of years, and it had become accepted practice. While there was nothing revolutionary about it *per se*, it *was* revolutionary in California in the 1940s, 1950s, and 1960s. It was part of the rebirth of fine winemaking in the state. *"It was what you did if you intended to try to make truly fine wine,"* Draper emphasized.

As for Bennion's and Draper's choice of American oak, in the beginning Bennion used both American and French oak barrels, all so "well-tempered" no one could have told the difference by tasting the wines. In 1970, Draper, who joined Ridge in 1969 to make Monte Bello Cabernet, moved to buying new air-dried American barrels, and combining them with the old French and old American barrels. Although the new barrels were originally intended just for the Cabernet, Ridge soon began using a small percentage of new oak with the Zinfandel as well. As the old barrels were retired, the oak program became 100 percent American oak.

However, it has been only recently, since about the late 1980s, that American coopers have begun routinely air-drying their oak for two or more years, fire-bending it, and toasting it over oak chip fires. I was curious, therefore, about where Draper got air dried and toasted American oak in 1970.

Well, leave it to Paul Draper to know that the European coopers' centuries-long practice of air-drying oak (as opposed to hot, fast kiln drying), was perhaps the most important step to be taken in making barrels suitable for fine wine ageing. So he took it upon himself to travel to Arkansas to meet with the cooperage company who made his first American oak barrels. There, he personally selected his own air dried staves from those stacked in ricks at the cooperage. There were always small supplies of air dried staves that had been held longer than the six months necessary before kiln drying. Draper's first order was for seven-year old staves. He also insisted on moderating the gas-fire toasting, rejecting anything that looked like char, which under his directions, there was little of, he told me.

With insistence on air-drying staves, and moderate toasting over gas fires, it was possible to obtain American oak barrels suitable to the ageing of fine red wines even in the 1970s, said Draper. However, few (if any other) winemakers in the 1970s and early 1980s insisted on their American oak barrels being made exclusively from air dried staves. Obviously, therefore, a great many American oak barrels coopered primarily for whiskey ageing got converted to red wine ageing as California producers developed a fine wine focus. While the producers perhaps didn't know the reasons why, they did know wines aged in them didn't taste as good as wine aged in French oak barrels.

Since about the late 1980s, most American coopers have adopted the European approach of air-drying the staves, heating the staves over wood fires in order to bend them, and then toasting them over small oak chip fires. French coopers are now manufacturing the barrels in America from American oak, sometimes even taking the wood back to France. A symposium on oak cooperage held in San Francisco in June 1993 revealed that many American oak barrels are as finely made now as French oak barrels.

Does this mean that the controversy over which kind of oak barrels to use for ageing fine Zinfandel has ended? Only in some winemakers' dreams! The controversy continues. Equally controversial is what percentage of the barrels should be brand new, and what percentage of the barrels should be used. That's not the end of it either, because there's little agreement as to how long the wine should be left in the barrels — whether the barrels are new or used.

But what I have discovered is that the controversy, while making for good cellar talk in the wine industry, will never be resolved, because the answer really does come down to how the various ageing materials suit each vineyard and each winemaker's style. The best matchup can be French oak, some of it new, or none of it newer than one year old; it can be American oak, some of it new, or none of it new. Or it can be a combination of both American and French, some or none new. The vineyard, the vintage, and the winemaker's style preference are the keys.

Today, overall wine quality is improving in California, and few would disagree that part of this trend to quality is in the use of small barrels for ageing red wines. The question of whether French or American oak is best, however, is far from settled. The only commonality among producers now – whether large and small – is that all use small barrels of some kind. Producers such as Mondavi/Woodbridge make 150,000 cases annually of barrel-aged Zinfandel alone. Their *small* barrel room, as Brad Alderson calls it, holds 25,000 barrels.

Fetzer and Sebastiani also have several thousand barrels for their Zinfandel wines. Even Cucamonga Valley producer Don Galleano, who has a huge customer base for his traditional redwood tank-aged Zinfandel, has bought in a few dozen small barrels for his "Legendary Pioneer Zinfandel."

So the importance of small oak barrels to world class Zinfandel production has been definitely established. The rest is a matter of taste.

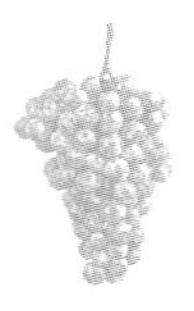

Appendix B: Mayacamas, the ATF, and Late Harvest Zinfandel

Shortly after my initial visit to Ridge Vineyards in spring 1986, I made my way to the top of Lokoya Road, in Napa's Mayacamas Mountains, to find Bob Travers and his Mayacamas Vineyards. I wanted to hear his story of how he got the Bureau of Alcohol, Tobacco, and Firearms (ATF) to approve his 17 percent alcohol, late-picked dry Zinfandel as a table wine. This was necessary for him, said Travers, because Zinfandel had low priority at Mayacamas, so more often than not, the Zinfandel came in over-ripe. Yet Travers felt that his 17 percent alcohol Zinfandels should be included in the table wine category, since they had fermented dry, and were not fortified.

"At that time (the late 1960s)," said Travers, "to be classified as a 'table wine,' wine had to be under 14.1 percent alcohol. Wines 14.1 percent and over were no longer table wines, according to ATF. And the tax category quadrupled, although it was still not a huge increase. So not only did you have to pay four times the alcohol tax, you were supposed to fortify these dry wines with 100-proof alcohol, and label them as dessert wines.

"The first time I applied (it was for my 1968 Napa Valley Late Harvest), ATF told me to fortify it and label it either Sherry or Port. Well, I didn't want to do either, so I resubmitted my application. This went on for the two or so years that the wine was ageing. Then about the time I needed to bottle it, Julius Jacobs from The Wine Institute was going to Washington, and said he had a contact, and would see what he could do. Shortly after that, ATF called to say it was okay *just this once* to sell the 17.5 percent wine as Zinfandel table wine, with the alcohol percent stated.

"So that was the first time a wine over 14.1 percent was identified by its varietal name, and classified as a table wine. That is, I could call it Zinfandel, not Sherry or Port. However, I didn't want to confuse my customers unnecessarily, so along with stating the alcohol percent on the label, I also named it 'Late Harvest Zinfandel.' I was the first to use that term.

"Of course, there was no way ATF could limit its permission to 'just this once.' The cat was out of the bag, so to speak, and the next year, Ridge released an over-17 percent alcohol 1966 vintage called 'Zinfandel Essence.' In 1997, however, Bennion went with my 'Late Harvest' term."

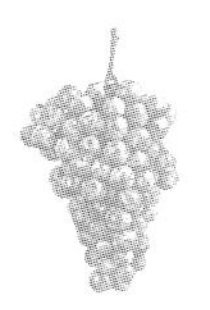

Appendix C: Zinfandel in Australia

In September 1999, John Hewett, an international wine merchant in Perth, Western Australia, called to ask for some slides of Zinfandel for a master class he was presenting in October. It seemed that there was increasing interest in Zinfandel down under. I sent him a selection, and asked him for an account of Zinfandel growing and production in his country. In June 2000, he sent me the following report of Zinfandel's Australian history:

Although small plantings of Zinfandel are thought to have taken place in the period 1920-30, the first commercial Zinfandel vineyard was established in 1967 at the Sandalford Vineyard in Swan Valley near Perth in Western Australia. A two-acre planting, the budwood selection came from UC Davis, which it got in 1963 from the Lodi area. This "Lodi clone" has become the major clone for other plantings in Australia.

Despite some initial enthusiasm for the variety, the early plantings did not meet with success. The vines were overcropped and the clusters developed bunch rot. As a result, all the initial plantings were taken out or budded over with more manageable varieties.

Zinfandel was not abandoned, however. In 1972, Cape Mentelle Vineyard in the extreme southwestern part of western Australia planted a Zinfandel vineyard with the Lodi clone. It now produces a benchmark Zinfandel for the country in a style similar to its California contemporaries. This is now the country's oldest commercial vineyard.

In 1983, two more selections from UC Davis found their way into some small plantings, and in 2000, plantings from a Sonoma County selection are being established.

As of June 2000, about 40 Australian growers have Zinfandel vineyards, which range in size from one acre to 32 acres, and which are spread among six states. Total Zinfandel acreage is just over 280. Some of the largest plantings are around Griffith in New South Wales. These plantings are irrigated to encourage high yields for bulk red wine production. Most of the other growers are directed towards the production of quality table wine, the most notable example of which is the Cape Mentelle.

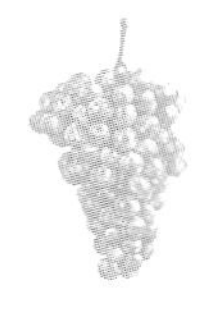

Bibliography

Berger, Dan. "California's Lost Wine Country." *Los Angeles Times.* May 19, 1994, 10.

Bioletti, Frederic T. "The Zinfandel." *California's Most Important Juice Grape Varieties.* Ed. E.M. Sheehan. San Francisco: California Grape Grower. Oct. 1, 1924. 16-18

Costa, Eric. *A History of Winegrape-growing in Amador County.* Jackson, CA: Cenetto Publication, 1994

Draper, Paul. "Zinfandel." *The University of California/Sotheby Book of California Wine.* Ed: Doris Muscatine, Maynard Amerine, and Bob Thompson. Berkeley: University of California Press. 1984. 223-234.

Freese, Phil. "From the Vineyard Perspective." *Practical Winery & Vineyard* September/October 1998. Vol. XIX, No. 3. 25, 30-31

Hussman, George. *Grape Culture and Wine Making in California.* San Francisco: Payot, Upham, & Co. 1888.

Laube, James. "Zinfandel's New Look," *Wine Spectator,* Vol. XVIII, No. 12, Oct. 15, 1992, 25–28.

Lawrence, D.H. "Grapes." *The Complete Poems of D.H Lawrence.* Eds. Vivian de Sola Pinta and F. Warren Roberts. New York: Viking Press. 1964, 1971.

Mendocino Winegrowers Alliance. Press Release. Ukiah, California: November 21, 1997.

Pinney, Thomas. *A History of Wine in America. From Beginnings to Prohibition.* Berkeley: University of California Press, 1989.

Robards, Terry. "Zinfandel: The Mystery Solved." *The Wine Enthusiast.* August 1996. Vol. 9, No. 7. 44-48.

Shanken, Marvin R. "Gallo's Dramatic Shift to Fine Varieties." *Wine Spectator.* Sept. 15, 1991. Vol. XVI, No. 10, 20–29.

Smith, Rod. *The San Francisco Chronicle,* Food, 4. November 18, 1987.

Steele, Jed. "Coastal Ridge Zinfandel." *Ridge Review.* Vol. V, No. 1. 1985, 7-9.

Stewart, Rhoda. "The Challenge of Zinfandel, Part I." *Practical Winery.* May/June 1987. Vol. VIII, No. 1. 51-60

__________. "The Challenge of Zinfandel, Part II." *Practical Winery & Vineyard.* July/August 1987. Vol. VIII, No. 2. 20-26.

__________. "Zinfandel — The Affordable Luxury, Part I." *Practical Winery & Vineyard.* September/October 1993. Vol. XIV, No. 3. 12-17.

__________. "Zinfandel — The Affordable Luxury, Part II." *Practical Winery & Vineyard.* November/December 1993. Vol. XIV, No. 4. 15-20.

Sullivan, Charles. *Napa Wine, A History from Mission Days to Present.* San Francisco: The Wine Appreciation Guild, 1994.

__________. "Zinfandel: A True Vinifera." *The Vinifera Wine Growers Journal.* Summer 1982. Vol. 19, No. 2, 71-86.

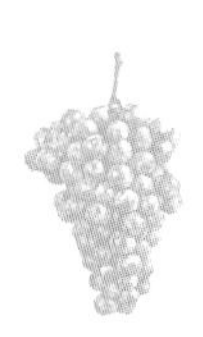

Index

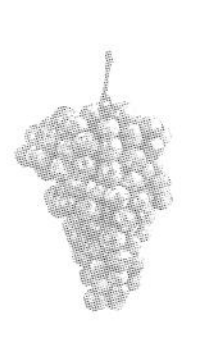